For my Mother and Father

Conversion is like stepping across the chimney piece out of a Looking-Glass world, where everything is an absurd caricature, into the real world God made; and then begins the delicious process of exploring it limitlessly.

EVELYN WAUGH

LITERARY CONVERTS

LITERARY CONVERTS

SPIRITUAL INSPIRATION IN
AN AGE OF UNBELIEF

JOSEPH PEARCE

HarperCollins*Publishers*

HarperCollins*Religious*
Part of HarperCollins*Publishers*
77–85 Fulham Palace Road, London W6 8JB
www.christian-publishing.com

First published in Great Britain in 1999 by HarperCollins*Religious*

© 1999 Joseph Pearce

1 2 3 4 5 6 7 8 9 10

Joseph Pearce asserts the moral right to be identified as the author of this work

A catalogue record for this book is available from the British Library

ISBN 0 00 628111 7

Printed and bound in Great Britain by
Creative Print and Design (Wales), Ebbw Vale

CONTENTS

ACKNOWLEDGEMENTS

I have been most fortunate to receive invaluable assistance from a whole host of people, including friends, relatives and associates of those writers who form the basis of this study. Those who have rendered assistance include, in no particular order of priority: Brocard Sewell, O. Carm., Aidan Mackey, Christina Scott, Sister Juliana Dawson, Christopher Derrick, Stratford Caldecott, Walter Hooper, Leslie von Goetz, Mrs Graham Greene, Professor Norman Sherry, Dr Barbara Reynolds, Patrick Heron, David Gill, Father Charles Smith, Julia Ross Williamson, George Sassoon, Rupert Hart-Davis, Barbara Wood, George Sayer, Gregory Wolfe, Iain T. Benson, Richard Ingrams, Lady Hedwig Williams, the Rt Rev. Cormac Murphy O'Connor and John Seymour. I must record a special debt of gratitude to Owen Barfield and Douglas Hyde, both of whom offered me their time and assistance in spite of ailing health. Sadly, they both passed away before this volume could be completed.

I am grateful to A. P. Watt Ltd for granting permission on behalf of the Royal Literary Fund to publish extracts from several poems by G. K. Chesterton, and for permission, on behalf of The Trustees of the Maurice Baring Will Trust, for permission to include several extracts from Baring's verse. I am indebted to George Sassoon for permission to quote from his father's poems, and to the Peters, Fraser & Dunlop Group Ltd for permission to include extracts from the poetry of Hilaire Belloc.

James Catford and Elspeth Taylor have continued to display the utmost faith in my work, for which I am deeply grateful, and I must acknowledge the efforts of Kathy Dyke and the others at HarperCollins who work tirelessly to bring my efforts to fruition.

I cannot conclude without mentioning Sarah Hollinsworth and Alfred Simmonds, both of whom have continued to offer both practical and moral support.

PREFACE

In 1905, the young G. K. Chesterton published *Heretics*, a volume of essays in which he precociously criticized many of his contemporaries, including, most notably, both Shaw and Wells. One critic responded to *Heretics* by stating that Chesterton should not have condemned other people's 'heresies' until he had stated his own 'orthodoxy'. Chesterton accepted the criticism and rose to the challenge. In 1908 his *Orthodoxy* was published. Its central premise was that the most profound mysteries of life and human existence were best explained in the light of the Apostles' Creed.

Chesterton's 'coming out' as a Christian had a profound effect, similar in its influence to Newman's equally candid confession of orthodoxy more than fifty years earlier. In many ways it heralded a Christian literary revival which, throughout the twentieth century, represented an evocative artistic and intellectual response to the prevailing agnosticism of the age. Dr Barbara Reynolds, the Dante scholar and friend and biographer of Dorothy L. Sayers, described this literary revival as 'a network of minds energizing each other'. Besides Chesterton, its leading protagonists included T. S. Eliot, C. S. Lewis, Siegfried Sassoon, J. R. R. Tolkien, Hilaire Belloc, Charles Williams, R. H. Benson, Ronald Knox, Edith Sitwell, Roy Campbell, Maurice Baring, Evelyn Waugh, Graham Greene, Muriel Spark, Dorothy L. Sayers, Alfred Noyes, Compton Mackenzie, David Jones, Christopher Dawson, Malcolm Muggeridge, R. S. Thomas and George Mackay Brown. Its influence spread beyond the sphere of literature. Alec Guinness, Ernest Milton and Robert Speaight were among the thespians whose lives were interwoven with those of their Christian literary contemporaries.

The publication in 1891 of the Papal social encyclical *Rerum Novarum* had a profound influence on Belloc and, through him, on Chesterton. This ensured that the Christian literary revival had a political dimension. Belloc and Chesterton countered the socialism of Shaw and Wells with the social teaching of the Church, which they called 'distributism'. Eric Gill sought to put the distributism espoused by Belloc and Chesterton into practice, and E. F. Schumacher popularized distributism in the late 1970s with his hugely influential *Small is Beautiful*. In much the same way that Shaw's mixture of Nietzschean philosophy and Marxist socialism had coloured and characterized his literary works, the mixture of Christian theology and the 'small is beautiful' teaching of the Church would colour and characterize much of the literature of the Christian literary revival.

Taken as a whole, this network of minds represented a potent Christian response to the age of unbelief. It produced some of the century's great literary masterpieces and stands as a lasting testament to the creative power of faith. The story of how these giants of literature exerted a profound influence on each other and on the age in which they lived represents more than merely a study of one important aspect of twentieth-century literature. It is an adventure story in which belief and unbelief clash in creative collision.

CHAPTER ONE

WILDE THROUGH THE LOOKING-GLASS

Three weeks into the new century, on 22 January 1901, Queen Victoria died at Osborne House. She had reigned for more than sixty years. As the nation mourned the passing of an era many felt a portentous element in the solemnity of the occasion. The young G. K. Chesterton, still unknown to the reading public, wept when he heard the news of her death. Writing to his fiancée on the day of the Queen's funeral, he declared that 'this is a great and serious hour and it is felt so completely by all England'.[1]

However, the Victorian twilight marked a beginning as well as an end. The dawn of the Edwardian era coincided with the opening of a new century and heralded the birth of a new generation of future writers. The new arrivals included C. S. Lewis, Evelyn Waugh, Malcolm Muggeridge and Graham Greene, to name but a few. The first year of the century quite literally heralded a new arrival for the proud parents of the future writer and historian Hugh Ross Williamson, born on New Year's Day 1901. At three weeks old they carried him into the market square of Romsey in Hampshire, where his father was the Congregational minister, so that he could at least hear, even if he could not comprehend, the proclamation of the Queen's death.[2]

The world inherited by this new generation had been coloured by scepticism and religious doubt. Christopher Dawson described the late Victorian era as 'a low water mark in the Christian world – the age of Combes and Signor Nathan and Giolitti: an age of anti-clericalism and materialism and Fabian socialism, without any great movement on the Catholic side to compensate'.[3] Although such a view ignores the profound influence of the Oxford Movement, the conversions of Newman and Manning, and the aesthetic reaction to materialism epitomized by the Pre-Raphaelites, it is none the less substantially true. Fabian socialism exerted a colossal influence on the early years of the century. Muggeridge wrote of the intellectual atmosphere of his Fabian-dominated childhood as one where the Christian religion was in abeyance, 'replaced by the religion of progress, whereby men of good will are preparing to take over ... No God, they consider, is needed any longer. He must be considered dead, or at any rate, as in retirement.'[4]

In 1903, the year of Muggeridge's birth, Bernard Shaw, the champion of Fabian optimism, had published his play, *Man and Superman*. A witty attack on traditional attitudes towards courtship, marriage and the relations between the sexes, it echoed in its title the elitist philosophy of Nietzsche. Nietzsche had died in 1900, after twelve years of insanity, the most outspoken philosophical foe of Christianity to emerge in the late nineteenth century. Convinced that Christianity was bankrupt, he proclaimed Schopenhauer's 'will to power' and emphasized that only the strong ought to survive. He maintained that Christian charity only served to perpetuate the survival of the weak and the mediocre. His major work, *Also sprach Zarathustra*, developed the idea of the superman or overman (the Ubermensch) who would overcome human weakness and vanquish the meek. In his *Jenseits von Gut und Böse* (*Beyond Good and Evil*) he claimed that morality should be based on the axiom that 'nothing is true; everything is allowed' and he continued his war on the weak by maintaining that the suffering of slaves is insignificant because 'almost everything we call higher culture is based upon the spiritualizing and intensifying of cruelty'.

It is not surprising that many have seen Nietzsche's philosophy as a prerequisite for the rise of Nazism. Cardinal Mindszenty, for instance, said of Hitler and the Third Reich that 'the precursor of this terrible kingdom was Nietzsche, who proclaimed that "God is dead" and that we must all pass beyond the antiquated concepts of good and evil. What a splendid life they led, these human beings who had dispensed with God!'[5]

The Nazis, however, were by no means the only human beings to dispense with God since, at the turn of the century, the intellectual ascendancy had been agnostic for some time. Evelyn Waugh, through the medium of his character Charles Ryder in *Brideshead Revisited*, explained the agnostic indifference which permeated the culture of his childhood:

> I had no religion ... The view implicit in my education was that the basic narrative of Christianity had long been exposed as a myth, and that opinion was now divided as to whether its ethical teaching was of present value, a division in which the main weight went against it; religion was a hobby which some people professed and others did not ... No one had ever suggested to me that these quaint observances expressed a coherent philosophic system and intransigent historical claims; nor, had they done so, would I have been much interested.[6]

Even in Christian circles the evolutionary philosophy of perpetual human progress held sway. Arnold Lunn remembered that his father, at one time a Methodist minister and a missionary in India, 'retained his gallant belief in the greatest of all Victorian myths, the belief in inevitable progress. It was impossible to convince him that there is no predestined bias towards improvement, that progress is varied by regress and that civilizations are born and grow to maturity only to decay and die.'[7]

Perhaps the most famous exponent of this evolutionary optimism was H. G. Wells, who had risen to fame during the last decade of the nineteenth century as the author of science fantasies such as *The Time Machine* and *The War of the Worlds*. Wells's *The Outline of History*, published in 1920, presented the definitive historical exposition of the progressive creed. Alongside Shaw's championing of the more humane elements of Nietzsche, Wells's trumpeting of a brave new world dominated by science seemed to capture the mood of the age. Together they appeared to be presenting a coherent, if not always a united voice: a dawn chorus of optimism to ring in the new century.

In the 1890s, the decadents, led by the indefatigable Oscar Wilde, had provided a counterpoise to Wells and Shaw. Wilde's calculated and measured air of worldly cynicism had come to epitomize the 'naughty nineties'. When he died of syphilis at the end of 1900, his death throes coinciding with those of the old century, the circumstances of his death provided the most bizarre finale to the Victorian age and set an unlikely example to future generations of writers who were to take the same step during the new century. Astonishingly, Wilde, on his deathbed, had been received into the Catholic Church.

A less likely convert can scarcely be imagined. Yet Wilde, the self-proclaimed arch-sinner and archetypal cynic, had an affection for Catholicism which stretched back to his childhood. Three weeks before his death he had told a *Daily Chronicle* correspondent that 'much of my moral obliquity is due to the fact that my father would not allow me to become a Catholic. The artistic side of the Church and the fragrance of its teaching would have cured my degeneracies. I intend to be received before long.'[8] As a young man he had reached the point of conversion when, in April 1878, he had approached Father Sebastian Bowden at the Brompton Oratory. The day after their confidential meeting, Father Bowden wrote to Wilde, stating that it had been God's grace which had made him 'freely and entirely lay open to me your life's history and your soul's state'. The letter continued:

Let me then repeat to you as solemnly as I can what I said yesterday, you have like everyone else an evil nature and this in your case has

become more corrupt by bad influences mental and moral, and by positive sin; hence you speak as a dreamer and sceptic with no faith in
anything and no purpose in life. On the other hand God in His mercy
has not let you remain contented in this state. He has proved to you the
hollowness of this world ... and has removed thereby a great obstacle
to your conversion; He allows you to feel the sting of conscience and
the yearnings for a holy pure and earnest life. It depends therefore on
your own free will which life you lead. As God calls you, He is bound,
remember, to give you the means to obey the call.

Do so promptly and cheerfully and difficulties disappear and with
your conversion your true happiness would begin. As a Catholic you
would find yourself a new man in the order of nature as of grace ...

I trust then you will come on Thursday and have another talk;
you may be quite sure I shall urge you to do nothing but what your
conscience dictates. In the meantime pray hard and talk little.[9]

The priest's advice was not heeded. Father Bowden told André Raffalovich,
himself a convert, that Wilde had failed to materialize on the Thursday but
instead had sent a large package to the Oratory which contained a bunch of
lilies, presumably by way of an apology. From then on, Wilde's way of life
appeared diametrically opposed to that urged upon him by the priest. He talked
hard and prayed little, made affectation an art form and forgot completely the
importance of being earnest. Perhaps what he said later of Dorian Gray was also
true of himself:

> It was rumoured of him that he was about to join the Roman Catholic
> communion; and certainly the Roman ritual had a great attraction for
> him ... But he never fell into the error of arresting his intellectual devel-
> opment by any formal acceptance of creed or system, or of mistaking,
> for a house in which to live, an inn that is but suitable for the sojourn of
> a night in which there are no stars and the moon is in travail ... no
> theory of life seemed to him to be of any importance compared with
> life itself.[10]

One of the most important influences upon Wilde's descent into decadence was
the French novelist Joris-Karl Huysmans, whose *A Rebours* was hailed as
the ultimate guide to a libertine lifestyle. The book's hero, Des Esseintes, an
intellectual dandy dedicated to the pursuit of pleasure, became a role model for a
new generation of aspiring rebels. Following its publication Whistler rushed to

congratulate Huysmans on his 'marvellous book', Paul Valéry acclaimed it as his 'Bible and bedside book' and Paul Bourget, a close friend at the time of both Huysmans and Wilde, professed himself a great admirer. Yet there were few greater admirers of *A Rebours* than Wilde himself. In an interview with the *Morning Post*, he stated that 'this last book of Huysmans is one of the best I have ever seen',[11] and its influence on Wilde's later character can be gauged by his characterization of Dorian Gray. When Gray reads a book resembling Huysmans's novel, 'the hero, the wonderful young Parisian ... became to him a kind of pre-figuring type of himself. And indeed, the whole book seemed to him to contain the story of his own life, written before he had lived it.'[12] In Wilde's view, Huysmans's hero in *A Rebours* 'spent his life trying to ... sum up, as it were, in himself, the various modes through which the world-spirit had ever passed, loving for their mere artificiality those renunciations that men have unwisely called virtue, as much as those natural rebellions that men still call sin'.[13] According to André Raffalovich, Wilde had been particularly fascinated by the part of *A Rebours* in which the book's hero recalls a sexual exploit which, being homosexual, was different from all others he had experienced.

It is clear that Huysmans's effect upon Wilde was both profound and profane. The result was a complete moral role reversal. Virtues were now artificial while sin was a natural rebellion. Wrong was right and right was wrong. In short, *A Rebours* 'was a poisonous book' from which Wilde had drunk with gusto. The poison also worked its spell upon the book's author because Huysmans spent the following years dabbling with diabolism, culminating in his novel, *La Bas*, in which he is both morbidly fascinated with, and revolted by, Satanic mysticism.

The year after the publication of *La Bas* in 1891, Huysmans professed his reconciliation with the Roman Catholic Church in his autobiography, *En Route*. This dramatic return to Christianity appears to have affected Wilde also. When, in 1898, Maurice Maeterlinck informed Wilde that Huysmans had entered a monastery, Wilde responded approvingly that 'it must be delightful to see God through stained glass windows. I may even go to a monastery myself.'[14]

However, there appeared little sign of Wilde showing any real inclination to join the Church himself until the final months of his life. Shortly after his release from prison, having completed the two years' hard labour imposed upon him in the wake of his ill-advised and abortive libel action against the Marquess of Queensberry, he had stated that 'the Catholic Church is for saints and sinners alone. For respectable people the Anglican Church will do.' This statement, a perfect example of Wilde's epigrammatic wit, was hardly a confession of faith. Meanwhile, he replied to his friend Robert Ross's fervent declaration that

Catholicism was true with the candid contradiction, 'No, Robbie, it isn't true.'[15] On another occasion, when he had asked Ross whether he could see a priest, his friend, convinced that his intentions were not serious, had refused. Thereafter Wilde dubbed him 'the cherub with the flaming sword, forbidding my entrance into Eden'.[16]

Ironically, it was Robert Ross who made the decision to call a priest to Wilde's bedside as he lay dying. At first he had hesitated, unsure of Wilde's wishes. Long before, Wilde had said that 'Catholicism is the only religion to die in' and his confession of regret, three weeks before his death, that he had not been permitted to become a Catholic as a child must have helped convince Ross of the dying man's desire. Ross was aware that Wilde had 'kneeled like a Roman' to a priest in Notre-Dame in Paris and had displayed similar humility to a priest in Naples. In addition, Wilde had been moved by a recent visit to Rome in which he had been blessed by the Pope. Finally, on 29 November 1900, the day before his friend's death, Ross made up his mind to get a priest to his bedside. He rushed to the Passionist Fathers and brought back Father Cuthbert Dunne. Ross asked Wilde, who was unable to speak, if he wished to see Dunne and Wilde lifted his hand in assent. Father Dunne asked Wilde if he wished to be received into the Church and he once more held up his hand. He was then given conditional baptism, after which Father Dunne absolved and anointed him. The following afternoon he died.

In death Wilde had finally fulfilled the prophetic lines of his verse, 'Rome Unvisited':

And here I set my face towards home,
For all my pilgrimage is done,
Although, methinks, yon blood-red sun
Marshals the way to holy Rome.

An even more bizarre eleventh-hour change of heart came in the person of the Marquess of Queensberry, Wilde's old adversary. Queensberry, a committed agnostic, had particularly requested in his will that 'no Christian mummeries or tomfooleries be performed over my grave but that I be buried as a Secularist and an Agnostic'. It was surprising, therefore, that before his death on 31 January 1900, Queensberry was said to have renounced his agnostic views, professed his love for Christ 'to whom I have confessed all my sins', and received conditional absolution by a Catholic priest.[17] In the wake of the bitterness of the libel action in which Wilde and the Marquess of Queensberry had been embroiled only five years earlier, their posthumous reconciliation in the same communion is stranger than fiction. One can imagine Wilde smiling at the thought that fate had brought together such unlikely bedfellows.

And so the fading embers of the nineteenth century included the deaths of both Nietzsche and Wilde, each of whom, in his own way, epitomized the spirit of the age that was passing away.

There was, however, one other member of Wilde's circle, largely overlooked and overshadowed by his contemporaries, who was himself a convert to Catholicism and whose life and literary output would stretch far into the new century. John Gray emerged on the literary scene in the late 1880s, penning a fairy tale in the manner of Wilde, entitled 'The Great Worm', for the first issue of the *Dial*. Wilde sought out his new imitator and admirer and he and Gray soon became close friends. A measure of their affection and intimacy can be gleaned from the fact that Wilde named Dorian Gray, the hero of his novel, after his new friend. Gray was suitably flattered and thereafter in his letters to Wilde signed himself 'Dorian'. Their relationship drifted some time around 1892 and soon afterwards Gray was received into the Catholic Church. He became a seminarian in Rome and was ordained in 1901. Although he is now largely forgotten, his biographer, Father Brocard Sewell, describes him as 'an admirable poet, and much else'.[18] From 1905 he was parish priest of Morningside in Edinburgh but this seemed not to interfere with his literary output. He only published in small, limited editions but his work 'was admired by John Masefield, Edmund Blunden and other good judges'.[19] Probably his best known work, the short novel, *Park: A Fantastic Story*, was printed and published by Eric Gill and René Hague in 1932. He died in 1934.

According to Father Sewell, Gray 'was quite free from any Chestertonian influence! He did not much admire G.K.C. or Belloc. He rather liked H. G. Wells.'[20] It is not surprising that Father Sewell should conclude his statement that Gray was free of Chesterton's influence with an exclamation mark. Gray's path to Catholicism, via Wilde and Wells, was an unusual one. A far more common path to Rome, trodden by many in the century about to commence, was one influenced in part at least by the writings of Chesterton and Belloc. As the Victorian twilight made way for the Edwardian dawn, Chesterton and Belloc were about to achieve both fame and notoriety as the champions of 'orthodoxy' in the face of the 'heretics'.

NOTES

1. Maisie Ward, *Gilbert Keith Chesterton*, London, 1944, p. 127.
2. *Smith's Trade News*, 2 September 1972.
3. Maisie Ward, *Insurrection versus Resurrection*, London, 1937, p. 45.
4. Malcolm Muggeridge, *Conversion: A Spiritual Journey*, London, 1988, p. 25.
5. Cardinal Mindszenty, *Memoirs*, London, 1974, p. 289.
6. Evelyn Waugh, *Brideshead Revisited*, London, 1949, p. 69.
7. Arnold Lunn, *Come What May: An Autobiography*, London, 1940, p. 12.
8. Richard Ellmann, *Oscar Wilde*, London, 1987, p. 548.
9. ibid., p. 90.
10. ibid., p. 91.
11. ibid., p. 237.
12. ibid., p. 238.
13. ibid., p. 238.
14. ibid., p. 531.
15. ibid., p. 548.
16. ibid., pp. 548–9.
17. ibid., p. 542.
18. Father Brocard Sewell, letter to the author, September 1996.
19. ibid.
20. ibid.

CHAPTER TWO

BELLOC, BARING AND CHESTERTON

When Sir James Gunn exhibited his famous painting, 'The Conversation Piece', depicting G. K. Chesterton, Hilaire Belloc and Maurice Baring assembled round a table, Chesterton, with characteristic humour, labelled the three figures 'Baring, over-bearing and past-bearing'. Yet Gunn's group portrait, which is now in the National Portrait Gallery, represented much more than a mere assemblage of friends. The three literary figures were considered by the reading public to be inseparable in many respects. They shared not only a common friendship, but a common philosophy and a common faith. If not as indivisible as the Holy Trinity they were at least as indomitable as the Three Musketeers! In the case of the Belloc-Baring-Chesterton chimera, the battle-cry of all for one and one for all is not inappropriate.

However, it would be true to say that Baring is the least known of the trio and that he is often overlooked. He was overlooked by Bernard Shaw when the latter compared Chesterton and Belloc to two halves of a 'very amusing pantomime elephant' known as the Chesterbelloc. For Shaw, writing his lampoon of the Chesterbelloc in 1908, the personae of G. K. Chesterton and Hilaire Belloc had merged to become nothing more than mouthpieces of a monster larger than both of them.

How then did the inseparable friendships of Belloc, Baring and Chesterton begin, and to what extent were the eventual conversions of both Chesterton and Baring influenced by their relationship with Belloc, a militant cradle Catholic who had never seriously doubted the religion of his childhood?

Chesterton and Belloc first met in 1900, probably at the instigation of Lucian Oldershaw, Chesterton's old schoolfriend. The importance of this meeting, and the impact it made on the young and still unknown Chesterton, is summed up in Oldershaw's own view of the occasion: 'I lost Gilbert first when I introduced him to Belloc, next when he married Frances, and finally when he joined the Catholic Church ... I rejoiced, though perhaps with a maternal sadness, at all these fulfilments.'[1]

At the time of the first meeting Belloc was already an established writer, whereas Chesterton had had only the odd article or poem published and was yet to see his first book in print. It was unsurprising, therefore, that the inexperienced Chesterton should have found himself somewhat in awe of the more experienced writer. This is borne out by a letter to Frances, Chesterton's fiancée, dated April 1900, in which he glows with admiration for Belloc:

> ... a moment after there was a movement and we were conscious of a young man rising and saying three words quietly: yet we felt somehow it was a cavalry charge ...
>
> You hate political speeches: therefore you would not have hated Belloc's. The moment he began to speak one felt lifted out of the stuffy fumes of forty-times repeated arguments into really thoughtful and noble and original reflections on history and character.[2]

It is clear from the tone of this letter that Belloc had conquered and that Chesterton had fallen under his influence. Belloc's speech had touched upon a wide variety of subjects, including the English aristocracy, the Puritan Revolution and the Catholic Church. These 'thoughtful and noble and original reflections' caused Chesterton to look at both history and theology in a new light. He wrote of his first meeting with Belloc that 'he talked into the night, and left behind in it a glowing track of good things ... What he brought into our dream was his Roman appetite for reality and for reason in action, and when he came to the door there entered with him the smell of danger.'[3]

In his *Autobiography*, Chesterton's account of the first meeting illustrates the extent to which his developing intellect was ripe for Belloc's bombastic brand of polemics: 'As Belloc went on talking, he every now and then volleyed out very provocative parentheses on the subject of religion ... All this amused me very much, but I was already conscious of a curious undercurrent of sympathy with him, which many of those who were equally amused did not feel ...'[4]

By the end of the year their relationship had flourished sufficiently that Chesterton felt able to accompany Belloc to midnight Mass on Christmas Eve. This was almost certainly the first time that he had been present at a Catholic Mass.

By the beginning of 1901 Chesterton was attracting widespread attention as a writer in his own right. His first two collections of verse had been published and he was gaining a reputation as a journalist with both the *Speaker* and the *Daily News*. His growing fame was alluded to in a letter to Frances, dated 8 February 1901:

Another rather funny thing is the way in which my name is being spread about ...

Belloc, by the way, has revealed another side of his extraordinary mind. He seems to have taken our marriage much to heart, for he talks to me, no longer about French Jacobins and Mediaeval Saints, but entirely about the cheapest flats and furniture, on which, as on the others, he is a mine of information, assuring me paternally that 'it's the carpet that does you.' I should think this fatherly tone would amuse you.[5]

If the fatherly tone adopted by Belloc was indicative of the paternalism of a master–disciple relationship, such a tone would soften in the years ahead as the two halves of the Chesterbelloc matured into a relationship of equality. Later, as Chesterton's grasp of the Christian faith grew, Belloc became increasingly dependent on his friend's fortitude.

Baring's relationship with Belloc predated that of Chesterton by almost three years. On 31 May 1897 Baring described his first impressions of Belloc: 'a brilliant orator and conversationalist ... who lives by his wits'.[6] Yet at their first meeting, in the presence of Basil Blackwood, Belloc had told the young Maurice Baring that he 'would most certainly go to hell', after which Baring understandably thought it unlikely that they would ever be friends. None the less, he still concluded from 'the first moment I saw him that he was a remarkable man'.[7] The earliest extant letter sent by Belloc to Baring, on 5 July 1897, was written in verse.[8] Its tone is both affable and convivial, indicating a warming of their relationship during subsequent meetings in June. These meetings were in Oxford where Belloc, having been refused a Fellowship at All Souls, was earning a living by coaching undergraduates.

Over the following months and years their friendship matured so that, by the time Chesterton was first beguiled by Belloc early in 1900, Baring already knew him well enough to form a more objective judgement of the Frenchman's personality. Writing to a friend from Paris on 7 February 1900, Baring described the time he had spent with Belloc in the French capital soon after the latter's study of Danton had been published:

We went to the Louvre and the Concert Rouge, and to vespers at St. Sulpice and to Benediction at Notre Dame and then for a long, long drive on the top of an omnibus during which Hilaire pointed out to me Danton's house, and Danton's prison, and Danton's cafe and Danton's *kegelbahn* and Danton's tobacconist. I daresay he didn't know anything about it: but I have the faith that swallows archaeologists.[9]

Two days later he wrote to another friend, stating that he liked Belloc immensely 'and think him full of brilliances and delightful to be with' but 'very un-French when seen in France. In fact his gallicanism is an untrained pose. His Catholicism is a political opinion: he is really brutally agnostic. His gallicanism too is a political opinion; it is Anti-Daily Mailism.'[10]

Many years later, after a further quarter of a century of friendship, Baring's view had moderated. Writing to Ethel Smyth on 29 August 1925, he displayed a depth of understanding of Belloc's abilities which were quite lost on many of his contemporaries:

> At first sight he seems to you entirely wrong-headed; at second sight and after due reflection, you think he is impossibly wrong headed with patches and flashes of sense, and what a pity! ... and then after years, ten years, fifteen years, it suddenly dawns on you sometime, not that he has always been right but that he has sometimes been right about the very points where you thought him most wrong and most wrong-headed – points now admitted by universal consent.[11]

Although the final sub-clause suffers from a surfeit of presumption or wishful thinking, the exposition of Belloc's multifarious talents is, on the whole, very perceptive.

At the outset of their relationship, however, Baring had no such wisdom of hindsight to draw from. He was pleased, and no doubt flattered, to find that his new friend approved of a number of sonnets he had written, one of which Belloc had copied out and hung up in his room. Belloc also approved of the draft of some parodies written in French of some French authors. These Belloc translated into English before getting his pupils to translate them back into French. The admiration was mutual, Baring being much enamoured with many of Belloc's early verses and sonnets. Although he lamented that these had not 'excited a ripple of attention at the time', he gained solace from the fact that some of Belloc's early poems had lived, 'and are now found in many anthologies, whereas the verse which at this time was received with a clamour of applause is nearly all of it not only dead, but buried and completely forgotten'.[12]

Belloc, of course, excelled in polemic as well as poetry, and Baring remembered 'wonderful supper-parties' in King Edward Street where Belloc sounded forth on 'the Jewish Peril, the Catholic Church, the *Chanson de Roland*, Ronsard, and the Pyrenees with indescribable gusto and vehemence'.[13] Baring certainly sympathized with Belloc's praise for France and French literature, dedicating a sonnet to Belloc which he offered:

> To you who heard the blast of Roland's horn,
> And saw Iseult set sail for Brittany.[14]

One wonders whether this was the sonnet which Belloc had copied out and hung up in his room.

Baring was less convinced by Belloc's vociferous and vehement championing of the Catholic Church. During the autumn of 1899, he was 'extremely surprised and disconcerted' when Reggie Balfour paid him a visit in Paris and 'suddenly said that he felt a strong desire to become a Catholic'.[15] Until that moment, he had only known two converts – his sister Elizabeth, who had married the Catholic Earl of Kenmare, and an undergraduate who had explained his motive merely as a need to have all or nothing. Upon hearing Balfour's desire he was 'amazed' and sought to discourage him from taking such a drastic step. He argued that the Christian religion 'was not so very old, and so small a strip in the illimitable series of the creeds of mankind … I begged him to wait.'[16]

Even at this stage, however, Baring understood the logic of the Catholic position, telling Reggie Balfour: 'My trouble is I cannot believe in the first proposition, the source of all dogma. If I could do that, if I could tell the first lie, I quite see that all the rest would follow.'[17]

In spite of his unbelief he accompanied Balfour to a Low Mass at Notre-Dame des Victoires. He had never attended a Low Mass before and he was pleasantly surprised:

> It impressed me greatly. I had imagined Catholic services were always long, complicated, and overlaid with ritual. A Low Mass, I found, was short, extremely simple, and somehow or other made me think of the catacombs and the meetings of the Early Christians. One felt one was looking on at something extremely ancient. The behaviour of the congregation, and the expression on their faces impressed me too. To them it was evidently real.[18]

There was a potent postscript to this episode which perhaps had as much to do with Baring's eventual conversion as anything Belloc may have discussed with him. When Reggie Balfour returned to London he sent Baring an epitaph, translated from the Latin into French:

> Ci-gît Robert Pechom, anglais, catholique, qui après la rupture de l'Angleterre avec l'église, a quitté l'Angleterre ne pouvant y vivre sans la foi et qui, venu a Rome y est mort ne pouvant y vivre sans patrie.[19]

[Here lies Robert Peckham, Englishman and Catholic, who, after England's break with the Church, left England not being able to live without the Faith and who, coming to Rome, died not being able to live without his country.]

The epitaph is to be found in the Church of San Gregorio in Rome, and its underlying tragedy produced a marked and lasting effect on Baring's whole view of the Reformation. He always possessed a melancholy nature and such imagery provided the inspiration for many of his novels. More specifically, the epitaph itself provided the starting point for his writing of the historical novel, *Robert Peckham*, thirty years later.

It is worth noting that Baring, by the beginning of 1902, was to be as emotionally affected by the Catholic High Mass, however 'long, complicated, and overlaid with ritual' it may be, as he had been by the Low Mass at Notre-Dame des Victoires. In February 1902 he was in Rome when Pope Leo the Thirteenth celebrated his jubilee. He went to High Mass at St. Peter's and witnessed the Pope being carried in on his chair, blessing the crowd:

> I had a place under the dome. At the elevation of the Host the Papal Guard went down on one knee, and their halberds struck the marble floor with one sharp, thunderous rap, and presently the silver trumpets rang out in the dome. At that moment I looked up and my eye caught the inscription, written in large letters all round it: *Tu es Petrus*, and I reflected the prophecy had certainly received a most substantial and concrete fulfilment ... the solemnity and the majesty of the spectacle were indescribable, especially as the pallor of the Pope's face seemed transparent, as if the veil of flesh between himself and the other world had been refined and attenuated to the utmost and to an almost unearthly limit.[20]

Emotionally, Baring now felt a deep attraction to Catholicism but intellectually he was still unable to believe. At the beginning of January 1900 he wrote to Ethel Smyth: 'I wish we were all born Roman Catholics. I believe in their spirit and refuse to acknowledge their Exclusive Supremacy of their Church.'[21]

Later the same year, when Baring was cycling in the countryside with Smyth, she said to him that she believed he would some day become a Catholic. At the time he had treated her prediction with incredulity, believing that 'nothing was more impossible'. Later, after her prophecy had been realized he told her it was an example of her 'miraculous intuition'.[22]

Several months later still, Baring wrote to another friend, George Grahame, stating that 'for me there are only two alternatives: agnosticism (practically atheism), or R. C.s.'[23] He wrote again a few days later, espousing his own personal theory on the whole issue. This time, he seems to have arrived at intellectual as well as emotional assent:

> ... no one who has ever punched Roman Catholicism and who is religious and believes in Christianity has ever not embraced it at once. Newman arrived at the conclusion purely *a priori*. He had a spirit of hate for Catholics and had never been inside a Catholic church ... Most people don't punch it at all and say, 'Oh priests and idolatry': *but* however bad priests are doesn't affect the question of, 'Is the Roman Church the Catholic and Apostolic Church of the Creed or is the Anglican?' And I think emphatically the Roman is and the Anglican is not ...[24]

In December 1900 he finally arrived at a position where his intellect conformed with his emotions, his head with his heart. He wrote to Hubert Cornish describing how he had changed during the previous twelve months. Previously, he had been quite unable to perform the 'acrobatic feat', the leap of faith required even to begin to contemplate conversion: 'But now I start from the other side. I believe in Christianity, I believe in the redemption.'[25]

Ironically, for one so different from Oscar Wilde in every way imaginable, Baring was also influenced by the return of J. K. Huysmans to the Church: 'If you read *En Route* by Huysmans, his fight at the end with his reason is word for word what I have twice experienced detail for detail.'[26]

For Baring, although the fight with reason was all but over, it would take him the rest of the decade to make the decisive step into the Church. In the intervening period he battled not so much with great philosophical questions as with petty prejudices. In 1906 he told Belloc that he despised Vatican politics and the effect of the Church upon the body politic in Italy and France; he disliked the English Catholics in Rome; and he had doubts about Catholic education.[27] Three years later he buried such doubts and embraced the faith. In the meantime, he could say with Huysmans that he was *en route*.

NOTES

1. Maisie Ward, *Gilbert Keith Chesterton*, pp. 211–12.
2. Maisie Ward, *Return To Chesterton*, London, 1952, p. 52.
3. Maisie Ward, *Gilbert Keith Chesterton*, p. 113.
4. G. K. Chesterton, *Autobiography*, London, 1936, pp. 116–18.
5. Maisie Ward, *Gilbert Keith Chesterton*, pp. 124–5.
6. *The Chesterton Review*, Vol. XIX, No. 1, p. 67.
7. Maurice Baring, *The Puppet Show of Memory*, London, 1930, pp. 222–3.
8. Robert Speaight (ed.), *Letters from Hilaire Belloc*, London, 1958, pp. 1–2.
9. *The Chesterton Review*, Vol. XIX, No. 1, p. 66.
10. ibid., pp. 66–7.
11. ibid., p. 70.
12. Maurice Baring, *The Puppet Show of Memory*, p. 223.
13. ibid., p. 223.
14. Maurice Baring, *Collected Poems*, London, 1925, p. 22.
15. Maurice Baring, *The Puppet Show of Memory*, p. 258.
16. ibid., p. 259.
17. ibid., p. 259.
18. ibid., p. 259.
19. ibid., p. 260.
20. ibid., p. 305.
21. Ethel Smyth, *Maurice Baring*, London, 1938, p. 185.
22. ibid., p. 14.
23. *The Chesterton Review*, Vol. XIX, No. 1, p. 86.
24. ibid., p. 86.
25. Emma Letley, *Maurice Baring: A Citizen of Europe*, London, 1991, p. 142.
26. ibid., p. 142.
27. *The Chesterton Review*, Vol. XIX, No. 1, p. 87.

CHAPTER THREE

THE ARCHBISHOP'S SON

When E. W. Benson became Archbishop of Canterbury in 1882 he had reached, for a zealous churchman and staunch upholder of the establishment principle, the pinnacle of earthly achievement. As head of the Church of England he could not have known, at his death in 1896, that he was also head of one of the most remarkable British literary families of the following century. His eldest son, A. C. Benson, master of Magdalene College, Cambridge, became a prominent biographer, diarist and literary critic. He wrote acclaimed studies of Rossetti, Fitzgerald, Pater, Tennyson and Ruskin, as well as a biography of his father. The middle son, E. F. Benson, wrote prolifically, his output including autobiographical sketches of Edwardian and Georgian society and light novels with a scholarly or historical background. Perhaps he is best known to posterity for his satirical Mapp and Lucia novels which have been successfully adapted for television. The youngest son, R. H. Benson, seemed destined to follow in his father's footsteps, taking Holy Orders in the Church of England. Yet his unexpected conversion to Roman Catholicism in 1903, and his subsequent ordination, caused a sensation. He too was to follow a literary career, writing fifteen highly successful novels before his untimely death at the early age of forty-three in 1914.

The circumstances leading up to Robert Hugh Benson's conversion are described in detail in his autobiographical *Confessions of a Convert*, published in 1913. Born in 1871, he had taken Anglican orders in 1894, largely to please his father. When his father died, Benson read the Litany at the funeral in Canterbury Cathedral. (His father had died at prayer in Hawarden church during a visit to his friend, Mr Gladstone, the former Prime Minister.)

Benson's own ecclesiastical career had commenced with his appointment to the Eton mission in Hackney Wick, before being appointed curate at Kemsing in Kent in 1896. The following year, in search of a monastic ideal, he joined the Community of the Resurrection at Mirfield. It was here that he began to have doubts about the doctrine, discipline and nature of the Church of England. The expression of such doubts had not gone unnoticed and he was greatly surprised when, prior to his profession at Mirfield in July 1901, Dr Gore, the founder of the Community who was about to be appointed Bishop of Worcester, had asked him whether there was any danger of his lapsing to Rome. At the time he had no hesitation in answering in the negative and he recorded that he was able to make his profession 'without alarm', describing the occasion as 'an extraordinarily happy day'.[1] His mother was present in the tiny ante-chapel to witness the proceedings: 'I was formally installed; my hand was kissed by the brethren; I pronounced my vows and received Communion as a seal and pledge of stability. In the afternoon I drove out with my mother in a kind of ecstasy of contentment.'[2]

The contentment was not destined to last very long and the following summer he confessed to his mother that he had experienced 'Roman difficulties, but that they were gone again'.[3] They returned soon after. At a Mission to St Patrick's in Birmingham he had given out the hymn, 'Faith of our Fathers', with the appended remark: 'By those fathers I do not mean Cranmer, Ridley, Latimer and that kind of person.'[4] In a retreat in November 1902 he had preached in such a way that one of those present had remarked that it 'might have been preached by a Catholic priest'.[5] During this particular retreat, Benson had urged upon his listeners the Spiritual Exercises of St Ignatius Loyola, founder of the Jesuits, explaining that 'it is extremely good not to neglect the intellect'.[6]

In a letter dealing with the form of meditation he had recommended in this retreat, Benson gave a profound insight into his own personality:

> As regards depression ... I meant that the cause of depression is subjectivity, *always*. The Eternal Facts of Religion remain exactly the same, always. Therefore in depression the escape lies in dwelling upon the external truths that are true anyhow; and not in self-examination, and attempts at 'acts' of the soul that one is incapable of making at such a time.
>
> ... I would say that 'subjective prayer' and self-reproach, and dwelling on one's temporal and spiritual difficulties, is not good at such times; but that objective prayer, e.g. intercessions, adoration, and thanksgiving for the Mysteries of Grace, is the right treatment for one's soul. And of course the same applies to scruples of every kind.[7]

Deeply concerned at his recurrent doubts over the doctrine and catholicity of the Anglican church, Benson confessed his difficulties to both his mother and his Superior at Mirfield. In a spirit of obedience he 'carried out their recommendations to the letter', reading all the books he was given on the Anglican side and consulting all the living authorities which were proposed to him. Still unconvinced, he had, by October 1902, 'reached such a pitch of distress' that he requested permission from his Superior to write to a distinguished Catholic priest outlining his difficulties. Permission was granted but the reply he received only served to throw him into even greater confusion. The priest replied that he did not feel able to recommend Benson's reception into the Church because he had serious doubts himself about the doctrine of Papal Infallibility and concluded that Benson had better remain where he was. Temporarily the unexpected nature of this reply 'quieted and reassured' him:

> The very fact that I had written to a priest and received an answer of discouragement seemed to me then ... an evident sign of where my duty lay. It seemed to show too that even within the Roman Church wide divergences of opinion prevailed, and that there was not there that Unity for which I had looked. The ultimate history of the priest in question, his excommunication, and his death outside the Church showed, of course, that such is not the case, and that men are not allowed to represent the Church who misrepresent, even in good faith, her teaching.[8]

Benson does not name the priest in question but, bearing in mind his own attraction at the time to Jesuit spirituality and his reference to the priest's subsequent excommunication and death, it seems likely that he had corresponded with Father George Tyrrell, whose theological modernism led to his expulsion from the Jesuits in 1906 and his excommunication. He died in 1909.

After Benson was received into the Church, Father Tyrrell (assuming it was he) wrote to ask how he had managed to surmount the difficulty he had indicated. Benson replied that he 'could not be deterred by such elaborate distinctions from uniting myself to what I was convinced was the divinely appointed centre of Unity and that I had simply accepted the Decree in the sense in which the Church herself had uttered and accepted it'.[9]

In the midst of these difficulties Benson was busy writing *The Light Invisible*, destined to be the first of his novels. The book had been inspired initially by some stories of his eldest brother's and centred on a man whom he called a 'Catholic priest'. Nowhere in the book is it made clear whether the priest in question belongs to the Roman or the Anglican communion, itself an indication of Benson's confused position at the time. Later, when asked to which communion he had intended his hero to belong, he answered that he had intended him 'to be neither in particular':

my difficulties were once more recurring, so I tried not to indicate by the slightest hint the communion to which my hero belonged ... I did not have that supreme confidence in the Church of England which would naturally have made me content to call him an Anglican and have done with it.[10]

The greatest single influence upon the writing of *The Light Invisible* was probably Joseph Shorthouse's spiritual romance, *John Inglesant*. Published in 1881, this novel was read with 'absolute passion' by the youthful Benson who declared that it had helped to develop and direct his sense of worship: 'I read it again and again ... It seemed that I had found at last the secret of those vague religious ceremonies to which I had always conformed with uninterested equanimity.'[11] Coincidentally, Shorthouse died in 1903, the year in which *The Light Invisible* was published.

Another factor in Benson's sudden desire to write spiritual romances was his growing interest in mysticism: 'I put away from me the contemplation of cold-cut dogma and endeavoured to clothe it with the warm realities of spiritual experience; and in the book itself I attempted to embody dogma rather than to express it explicitly.'[12]

A year after the book was published Benson wrote from Rome, where he was studying for the priesthood, in reply to an Anglican who was intrigued to know whether the stories in *The Light Invisible* were true:

> I had a large number of stories of things of that kind that were literally 'true,' and was proposing to make a book of them. I happened to mention it to a clergyman whose judgment I trusted, and he was so emphatic one had no right to make these things public that I gave up the idea ... some *elements* in many of them are actually true. Personally I hold strongly that 'spiritual fiction' is like any other 'fiction': it is bound to contain things that either have happened, or might happen at any time. What I tried to do was to take things that I knew to be true, and represent them in a way that everybody could understand.[13]

The Light Invisible was the only one of Benson's books to be published while he was still an Anglican and he commented in 1912 how its subsequent popularity appeared to be determined by the religious denomination of those who read it. He considered it 'rather significant' that it still sold well amongst Anglicans whereas Catholics appeared to appreciate the book to 'a very much lesser degree': 'most Catholics, and myself amongst them, think that *Richard Raynal, Solitary* is very much better written and very much more religious.'[14]

With the judgement of hindsight, Benson even went so far as to claim that he had come to dislike *The Light Invisible* 'quite intensely ... from the spiritual point of view'.[15] He had written it 'in moods of great feverishness and in what I now recognise as a very subtle state of sentimentality'. Since, at the time, he was 'striving to reassure myself of the truths of religion', he had assumed 'a positive and assertive tone that was largely insincere'. Further, it was 'rather a mischievous book ... since it implies that what I then strove to believe was [that] spiritual intuition ... must be an integral element in religious experience'. This spiritual intuition was, he claimed, 'nothing but imagination'. He believed that such an intuitive – and therefore subjectivist – mode of spiritual belief was inferior and less reliable than 'the simple faith of a soul that receives divine truth from a divine authority'.

> The Catholic atmosphere is, on the other hand, something quite apart from all this. For Catholics it is almost a matter of indifference as to whether or no the soul realizes, in such a manner as to be able to visualize, the facts of revelation and the principles of the spiritual world: the point is that the Will should adhere and the Reason assent. But for Anglicans, whose theology is fundamentally unreasonable, and amongst whom Authority is, really, non-existent, it becomes natural to place the centre of gravity rather in the Emotions, and to 'mistake ... the imagination for the soul.' The Reason, for them, must be continually suppressed even in its own legitimate sphere; the Will must be largely self-centred.[16]

In placing the emphasis on Reason and Will, the objectively apprehensible aspects of spirituality, as opposed to the Emotions, which can only be experienced subjectively, Benson was echoing the chain of thought he had adopted at the retreat in November 1902. There he had contrasted the subjective cause of an emotion, specifically depression, with the objective nature of truth, the 'Eternal Facts of Religion' which always remain the same. In this, he was in fundamental agreement with Chesterton and Belloc, both of whom emphasized the primacy of Reason in the apprehension of spiritual truth.

In 1903, however, Benson had not yet achieved this cohesive position. His 'Roman difficulties' were the cause of both rational and emotional turmoil from which there appeared no escape. It was then that two books helped him see the road ahead more clearly. The first was Newman's *Development of Christian Doctrine* and the other was Mallock's *Doctrine and Doctrinal Disruption*. These books, wrote Benson, helped to break down both 'the definite difficulties that stood between me and Rome', and also 'the last remnants of theory that held me to the Church of England'.[17] In particular, Newman's book had 'like a magician, waved away the last floating mists and let me see the City of God in her strength and beauty'.[18]

Last but not least, or, as Benson put it, 'finally and supremely', it was the reading of the Scriptures that satisfied him 'as to the positive claims of Rome'.[19]

After he confessed to his mother in the summer of 1903 the position in which he found himself, she anxiously urged him to consult three 'eminent members of the Church of England – a well known parish clergyman, an eminent dignitary, and a no less eminent layman'.[20] To their credit none of these stalwarts of Anglicanism sought to reproach him with disloyalty to his father's memory: 'They understood, as all with chivalrous instincts must have understood, that such an argument as that was wholly unworthy.'[21] None the less, all three sought to dissuade him from taking the final, decisive step to Rome. The 'eminent dignitary' asked him whether there were any devotions in the Catholic Church to which he felt a repugnance and he replied that he felt uneasy at the popular devotions to the Blessed Virgin. The dignitary responded with incredulity that Benson could seriously contemplate submitting to a communion in which he would be compelled to use methods of worship of which he disapproved. The response backfired because, as already noted, Benson mistrusted any appeal to Emotion over Reason. He endeavoured in vain to explain that his decision to become a Catholic had nothing to do with any like or dislike of customs, but was linked to a solid belief that the Catholic Church was the Church of God. If, therefore, his opinions on minor details differed from those of the Church it was the worse for him and his duty was to correct such notions as soon as possible. He intended, he stressed, to 'go to Rome not as a critic or a teacher, but as a child and a learner'.[22] His reply met with contempt: 'I think he thought this an immoral point of view. Religion seemed to him to be a matter more or less of individual choice and tastes.'[23]

'This interview,' Benson wrote,

> afforded me one more illustration of the conviction which I had formed to the effect that as a Teaching Body ... the Church of England was hopeless. Here was one of her chief rulers assuming, almost as an axiom, that I must accept only those dogmas that individually happened to recommend themselves to my reason or my temperament.[24]

Towards the end of July he received an ultimatum from Mirfield, 'perfectly kind and perfectly firm', that he must either return to the annual assembling of the community or consider himself no longer a member. The Brother who was given the task of writing the ultimatum had been a fellow probationer of Benson's and they had been on 'terms of great intimacy'. According to Benson, the Brother in question had been obviously in distress while writing the ultimatum. Benson's reply, 'written in equal distress', informed him that he could not, in conscience, return.

At about the same time he received an embittered letter from 'a dignitary of the Church of England, the occupant of an historic see and an old friend of my family'.[25] The correspondent, having failed to convince Benson of the error of his position,

> prophesied that one of three things would happen to me: either (which he hoped) I should return quickly to the Church of England with my sanity regained, or (which he feared) I should lose my Christian belief altogether, or (which he seemed to fear still more, and in which he was perfectly right) I should become an obstinate, hardened Romanist. It appeared to him impossible that faith and open-mindedness should survive conversion.[26]

In turmoil at the distress he was evidently causing, he sought solace in a long cycle ride across Sussex. He called first at the Carthusian monastery at Parkminster where he had arranged to meet one of the Fathers, himself a convert clergyman. He was received 'very courteously' but the visit depressed him still further, his host failing to understand that he sought nothing 'but to be taught; that I was not coming as a critic, but as a child'.[27] Travelling on in despair he stayed a Sunday in lodgings at Chichester, where, in a little church opposite the Cathedral, he made his last Anglican confession. Telling the clergyman plainly that he was now practically certain that he would become a Roman Catholic, Benson received no advice beyond the earnest counsel that he 'cheer up'. With the hollow message ringing in his ears, he received Anglican communion for the last time at the Cathedral. On the Monday he cycled to Lewes, thence to Rye, where he supped in the George Inn. On the following day, with the sun blazing, he returned home via Mayfield, 'looking with a kind of gnawing envy at the convent walls as I passed them, and staying for a few minutes in a beautiful little dark Catholic Church that I ran across unexpectedly in a valley'.[28]

The contrary and conflicting thoughts and emotions which beset him during this lonely cycle tour across Sussex were described in his *Confessions of a Convert*. He was troubled by his mother's anxiety and by her desire that he should allow 'every possible opportunity for a change of mind'. This was coupled by his own troubled state of mind 'which, though intellectually convinced, was still in an extraordinary condition'. He felt as though his mind was trapped in

a huge, soulless, spiritual wilderness, in which, as clear as a view before rain, towered up the City of God. It was there before me, as vivid and overwhelming as a revelation, and I stood there and eyed it, watching for the least wavering if it were a mirage, or the least hint of evil if it were of the devil's building.[29]

Paradoxically, the depths of his emotions did not include an emotional attraction towards the thing to which he felt drawn intellectually:

I knew perfectly well that it was human as well as divine, that crimes had been committed within its walls; that the ways and customs and language of its citizens would be other than those of the dear homely town which I had left; that I should find hardness there, unfamiliar manners, even suspicion and blame.

But for all that it was divine …[30]

This emotional cocktail of apathy and antipathy reacted against the conclusions of the intellect so that Benson 'had no energy, no sense of welcome or exultation … I was deadly sick and tired of the whole thing.'[31]

It was at this time, possibly on the lone cycle tour itself, that he wrote a poem which unravels the conundrum of his condition in the summer of 1903 better than all his subsequent prose efforts:

I cannot soar and sing my Lord and love;
    No eagle's wings have I,
No power to rise and greet my King above,
    No heart to fly.
Creative Lord Incarnate, let me lean
    My heavy self on Thee;
Nor let my utter weakness come between
    Thy strength and me.

I cannot trace Thy Providence and place,
    Nor dimly comprehend
What in Thyself Thou art, and what is man,
    And what the end.

Here in this wilderness I cannot find
    The path the Wise Men trod;
Grant me to rest on Thee, Incarnate Mind
    And Word of God.

I cannot love, my heart is turned within
    And locked within; (Ah me!
How shivering in self-love I sit) for sin
    Has lost the key.
Ah! Sacred Heart of Jesus, Flame divine,
    Ardent with great desire,
My hope is set upon that love of Thine,
    Deep Well of Fire.

I cannot live alone another hour;
    Jesu, be Thou my Life!
I have not power to strive; be Thou my Power
    In every strife!
I can do nothing – hope, nor love, nor fear,
    But only fail and fall.
Be Thou my soul and self, O Jesu dear,
    My God and all![32]

Although the whole world seemed to be 'poised in a kind of paralysis', he applied the principles he had espoused at the retreat the previous November and subjugated his emotions. Remembering that 'the cause of depression is subjectivity, *always*', he turned to the 'Eternal Facts of Religion' knowing that the escape from depression 'lies in dwelling upon the external truths that are true anyhow; and *not* in self-examination'. In so doing, he overcame the inertia which had seemingly held him paralysed and was spurred on to action. At the beginning of September, with his mother's knowledge, he wrote to one of the handful of Catholics he actually knew, an old friend who had converted previously and who had been ordained as a priest. The friend was now contemplating entering the Dominican Order and so recommended Benson to Father Reginald Buckler, OP, then living at Woodchester in Gloucestershire. Two or three days later Benson received notice that he was expected at the Priory, and on Monday, 7 September, in lay clothes, he set out on his last journey as an Anglican.

His thoughts during the long train journey to Stroud were conveyed in cold poetic prose:

I do not suppose that anyone ever entered the City of God with less emotion than mine. It seemed to me that I was utterly without feeling; I had neither joy nor sorrow, nor dread nor excitement. There was the Truth, as aloof as an ice peak, and I had to embrace it ... I was as one coming out of the glare of artificial light, out of warmth and brightness and friendliness, into a pale daylight of cold and dreary certainty.[33]

Even after his arrival at the Priory his spirits barely lifted. He attended Mass each morning, other Offices 'now and then' and was always at Compline. The only part of each day's routine which inspired anything approaching enthusiasm was the Dominican ceremony of the *Salve Regina* which follows Compline. This Benson described as 'exquisite'. He also showed a mild, detached interest in 'the resemblance of the Dominican to the Sarum rite in various points'.[34] Throughout the entire process of his reception this lacklustre spirit remained, mitigated only by 'an absolute certainty that I was doing God's will and was entering the doors of His Church'.[35]

Immediately upon his arrival at Woodchester he wrote to his mother and explained that he would not be baptized, even conditionally, owing to the absolute certainty that his Anglican baptism had been valid in form and intention. As he had been baptized by his father, and given the Archbishop's knowledge of liturgy and his constant practice, such a decision was hardly surprising. None the less, his mother, who replied on 10 September, was relieved at the news. Her letter displayed a deep love for her son and a benign resignation in the face of the unthinkable becoming the inevitable:

My Dearest, – Your letter this morning is a wonderful comfort, and you can understand how hungry and thirsty we are for every smallest detail ... I am deeply thankful as to your not being re-baptized ... It all sounds very straight and simple – which is just what one wants – and it is good that there is no pressing and urging – only putting things before you to see exactly what it means and whether you can accept all. You will let me know *at once*, I know, when you are actually received, or if you can, *before*, so that my heart – our hearts – may be specially with you ...[36]

On the following day she wrote again, presumably in reply to a letter from Benson giving details of the exact time of his reception which would be on that very day, 11 September:

... I am not sorry there are no delays – I am so glad there is no re-baptism ... do come back soon.

I told the household today, that they might know the exact time.

And at 5 o'clock today how specially we shall be with you, my Dearest.[37]

Thus it was that Benson went through the final formalities of conversion. Father Reginald Buckler took him into the Chapter House and there, kneeling down by the Prior's seat, he made his first confession together with acts of faith, hope, charity and contrition. After receiving absolution he went through into the church to make an act of thanksgiving. On the following morning he received his first Holy Communion from the hands of the Prior. Reporting the news to his mother, he wrote simply that 'it has happened'.

She replied at once:

My Dearest Son, – I have your note to say 'it has happened' ... you are now where your heart feels you can be truly loyal, where it finds its home, where you deeply feel God has led you. We trust you to Him in utter love and boundless hope ... Only *let us in*, always, wherever you rightly can – be as you have always been ...[38]

On the same day, 12 September, Lucy Tait, an old friend of the family, also wrote to him: 'It has been such a comfort that all these last weeks we have been all so knit together. It seems as if the inner bond had got so much closer as the outer one has – what shall I say – changed?'[39]

Not everyone was as charitable or as understanding in their response to the news. The press made much of the story that the son of the former Archbishop of Canterbury had become a Catholic, and the revelation rocked the Anglican establishment in a way reminiscent of the days of the Oxford Movement and the conversion of Newman.

Benson's mother informed him that 'Letters are showering in ... how superficial some are, and how Extraordinarily people are ready to think you have overlooked some momentous fact lying close at hand, and that they will kindly draw attention to it.'[40]

In the days immediately after the news had broken Benson lost count of the number of letters he received. There were 'at least two heavy posts every day', and he was disappointed to find that very few of these were from Catholics. Far from exhibiting a sense of triumphalism at what could be construed as a monumental coup for the Church, the response from Catholics was one of indifference, at least if the size of the mail to Benson was an accurate guide. The vast majority of the letters received were from Anglicans – from clergy, men, women, and even children. They offered the new convert anything but comfort: 'most ... regarded me either as a deliberate traitor (but of these there were very few) or as an infatuated fool, or as an impatient, headstrong, ungrateful bigot.'[41]

Benson methodically set about replying to all of them. A 'sincere woman' who besought him to remember a sermon he had preached upon the Prodigal Son, and who beseeched him to 'make haste to come back to the Father's house', was told that this was exactly what he had done. Another letter caused Benson 'considerable pain as well as astonishment'. It was from a middle-aged woman whom he had thought sincerely a friend, 'the wife of an eminent dignitary in the Church of England'. The letter, which was 'short, bitter, and fierce', reproached him for the dishonour he had done to his father's name and memory. Benson, clearly hurt that anyone could make such an accusation, concluded that the letter must have been written in 'a mood of blind anger'. He sought solace in the face of such attacks from the more charitable response of an Anglican Bishop who told his mother, 'Remember that he has followed his conscience after all, and what else could his father wish for him than that?'[42]

One letter, at least, offered a glimmer of consolation. An Anglican clergyman wrote enthusiastically, congratulating him on having been fortunate enough to have found his way into 'the City of Peace'. Eight years later, according to Benson, this unnamed clergyman was himself received into the Church.

However, the shattering impact which Benson's conversion had on many of those who had come to know and respect him is best summed up in the words of an Anglo-Catholic friend, to whom he had acted as spiritual director:

> Father Benson was going to become a Roman Catholic! Then, if he was not a Catholic now in the Church of England, what was he? What was I?
>   ... It is no exaggeration to say that the very foundations of Faith and all the realities of the Spiritual Life rocked and trembled from the violence of this utterly unexpected shock ... It was extraordinarily difficult to know why one whom we looked upon as a pillar of 'English' Catholicism should have found it necessary for his salvation to submit to the Church of Rome.[43]

After the initial shock had subsided the above writer and many others sought to discover why their mentor had felt compelled to take this 'tremendous step'. The result was that 'so many of us were led to study the question under his direction, after he entered the Church, and finally became Catholic ourselves'.

NOTES

1. Robert Hugh Benson, *Confessions of a Convert*, Sevenoaks, 1991 edn., p. 52.
2. ibid., p. 52.
3. ibid., p. 63.
4. C. C. Martindale, *The Life of Monsignor Robert Hugh Benson, Vol. One*, London 1916, p. 165.
5. Robert Hugh Benson, *Spiritual Letters*, London 1915, p. 2.
6. ibid., p. 2.
7. ibid., p. 3.
8. Robert Hugh Benson, *Confessions of a Convert*, p. 65.
9. ibid., p. 64.
10. ibid., pp. 59–60.
11. ibid., p. 20.
12. ibid., p. 60.
13. Robert Hugh Benson, *Spiritual Letters*, pp. 55–6.
14. Robert Hugh Benson, *Confessions of a Convert*, pp. 60–1.
15. ibid., p. 61.
16. ibid., pp. 61–2.
17. ibid., pp. 76–7.
18. ibid., p. 78.
19. ibid., p. 78.
20. ibid., p. 87.
21. ibid., p. 87.
22. ibid., p. 88.
23. ibid., p. 88.
24. ibid., pp. 88–9.
25. ibid., p. 90.
26. ibid., pp. 90–1.
27. ibid., p. 91.
28. ibid., p. 92.
29. ibid., p. 92.
30. ibid., pp. 92–3.
31. ibid., p. 93.
32. Robert Hugh Benson, *Poems*, London 1915, pp. 27–8.
33. Robert Hugh Benson, *Confessions of a Convert*, p. 95.
34. ibid., pp. 96–7.
35. ibid., p. 97.
36. C. C. Martindale, *The Life of Monsignor Robert Hugh Benson, Vol. One*, pp. 251–2.
37. ibid., p. 252.
38. ibid., p. 253.
39. ibid., p. 253.
40. ibid., p. 253.
41. Robert Hugh Benson, *Confessions of a Convert*, pp. 100–1.
42. ibid., pp. 101–2.
43. Robert Hugh Benson, *Spiritual Letters*, pp. 17–18.

CHAPTER FOUR

THE BISHOP'S SON

In the autumn of 1903, with news of Benson's conversion still ringing in the ears of the ecclesiastical authorities, Edmund Arbuthnott Knox, the Suffragan Bishop of Coventry, was translated to the See of Manchester. On Christmas Day 1903, his son, Ronald Arbuthnott Knox, read Benson's *The Light Invisible*. It was to make a lasting impression and, though Benson never became aware of the fact, his writing of this book was to have a pivotal influence upon the boy's future.

In fact, the life of Knox was destined to parallel that of Benson in many crucial respects. Knox, son of the Bishop of Manchester, received his boyhood education at Eton, where Benson, son of the Archbishop of Canterbury, had been educated nearly two decades earlier. Both passed through High Anglicanism, experienced 'Roman difficulties' and entered the Catholic Church in controversial circumstances. Both were youngest brothers in remarkable literary families.

Knox had been induced to read *The Light Invisible* as a result of an argument in which, for the first time, he had been confronted with the usual contentions in favour of Catholic doctrines and practices such as the Real Presence and the Sacrificial nature of the Mass. Knox had 'attempted to controvert them with all the uninstructed zeal of a combative nature'.[1] His interest aroused in such matters, and aware of the controversial nature of Benson's conversion from Anglicanism to Catholicism, he began to read *The Light Invisible* in a spirit of youthful curiosity. He would never be quite the same again: '... that Christmas Day was a turning point. It was the setting of the book – the little chapel in which the priest celebrated, the terms in which he alluded to the Mother of God, the description of confessions heard in an old parish church – that riveted me even more than the psychological interest.'[2] Henceforward, Catholicism, which he had previously considered 'wicked', had now become attractive in its own right. According to Evelyn Waugh, Knox's reading of Benson's first novel was so important that 'Ronald himself designates Christmas Day, 1903, as the birth of his Catholicism'.[3]

Another important step in the embryonic development of Knox's spirituality, and a further parallel between his life and that of Benson, was the reading of Joseph Shorthouse's *John Inglesant*. Knox, like Benson, read Shorthouse's religious romance as an impressionable youth and expressed an admiration for it. Like Benson, he later moderated his views but it is clear that it had still influenced him strongly.

Although Waugh described Christmas Day 1903 as the birth of Knox's Catholicism it is only true in a retrospective sense. Many years were to elapse before he finally joined the Catholic Church. Yet, from the time of his reading of *The Light Invisible*, Knox considered himself changed fundamentally. He saw that particular Christmas as his 'conversion' and, thereafter, he became a weekly Anglican communicant.[4] From this time onwards he also claimed that 'the atmosphere of Catholicism' had started to dominate his imagination and that the history of the Oxford Movement had awakened his latent enthusiasm for lost causes. The result was that, some time in 1904, Knox became an ardent ritualist. He read a book of 'a severely didactic character' called *The Ritual Reason Why*, in which there were 'elaborate explanations of the mystical meaning symbolised by amices, incense, the sign of the Cross'.[5] Later, he came to consider such caricatured excesses as 'disgustingly ritualistic' and a 'new freemasonry', but at the time he 'revelled in them' so that 'every symbol was sacred'. Thus, he observed, 'long before I had ever seen a ritualistic service I became a Ritualist'.[6]

Coupled with, and related to, his new interest in ritualism and the Oxford Movement was a new-found interest in Gothic architecture and Pre-Raphaelite art: 'the spirit of revival in Holman Hunt and Rossetti accommodated itself to the spirit of revival in Pusey and Neale; the two movements were curiously grafted together in my mind.'[7]

Knox's wholehearted plunge into the world of Anglo-Catholicism during 1904 appears to have met with no real opposition at home. This is surprising since his High Church stance differed markedly from his father's own position as a champion of the Evangelical wing of the church. Knox wrote that his views were known at home, 'and doubtless regretted', but 'never led to the smallest discontinuance of kindness on one side nor ... of respect on the other – certainly not of affection on either'.[8] In deference to his father, Knox never attended services in Manchester of a kind he knew the Bishop would disapprove, yet one is still surprised that there were no visible signs of friction in the Knox household. Evelyn Waugh believes this is indicative of the fact 'that the Bishop had not appreciated the force of Ronald's tendencies or exerted himself fully to deflect them'.[9]

Not that Knox would have been easily deflected. He was an extremely intelligent, gifted and well-read young man, whose views were not held from a position of ignorance. Waugh himself described Knox's Etonian career in terms of the utmost respect: 'While still at Eton he had written a book of light verses in English, Latin and Greek and he is still remembered there as the cleverest boy who ever passed through that school ...'[10] Especially gifted individuals often display signs of precociousness and this was evident in a religious sonnet written by the sixteen-year-old Knox in 1904:

> I have an errand on a stony way,
> That rises darkly to the mountain height,
> And, from that zenith, stretching thro' the night
> Sinks to the valleys of eternal day.
> And yet I weary not; for God, my Stay
> Hath ever set before my straining sight
> Some earthly beacon, whose celestial light
> Tempts the numb-hearted traveller to delay.
> And here I meet old friends, whom I have tried
> Beneath the shadow of the chastening Sword,
> And quaff sweet draughts of Memory; or abide
> By the great gulf of Silence overawed,
> And worship, falling on my knees beside
> The everlighted beacons of the Lord.[11]

If R. H. Benson's first novel had excited the precocious Knox at the end of 1903, it was G. K. Chesterton's first novel, *The Napoleon of Notting Hill*, which aroused his passions when it was published in March 1904. Knox described himself at the time he read the book as 'a schoolboy just beginning to think'. It had a profound influence and many years later he was still puzzling over its underlying message:

> Which is right – the cynic who sees everything as amusing, or the fanatic who has no sense of humour at all? The answer to that is, that the two men are in reality only two lobes of one brain; it is only when the world goes wrong that the pure precipitation of cynic or of fanatic is formed; the normal man, living in normal surroundings, is a blend of both.[12]

From this moment on, Knox was addicted to the writing of Chesterton, so that Chesterton's paradoxes soon became the 'platitudes of my thought'. In his autobiography, Knox gives Chesterton the principal credit for shaping his religious views: 'In regard to orthodoxy, my views when I left Eton were orthodox above the average; my oracle was G. K. Chesterton – he is so still.'[13]

Meanwhile, Benson, Knox's other mentor, was also reading Chesterton. Writing to his brother, A. C. Benson, from Rome on 9 May 1904, where he was studying for the priesthood and where he was ordained later that year, he compared Chesterton's biography of G. F. Watts with his brother's study of Tennyson: 'I read Chesterton's *Watts* about the same time [as your *Tennyson*], and I liked it rather – at least parts of it were excellent, but there was a trifle too much Chesterton ... His book made me feel that he was painfully clever – while yours made me feel I was.'[14]

Perhaps Chesterton would have accepted these criticisms, both heartily and wholeheartedly. He had mixed feelings about his earliest published efforts and considered *The Napoleon of Notting Hill* to be his first book of any merit.

Like Knox, Chesterton had become an Anglo-Catholic and his next important book, *Heretics*, published on 6 June 1905, was influential on the intellectual development of Knox and many others of his generation. One of the most poignant points made in *Heretics* concerned the relative merits of Ibsen and Dante:

> If we compare, let us say, the morality of the *Divine Comedy* with the morality of Ibsen's *Ghosts*, we shall see all that modern ethics have really done ... Dante describes three moral instruments – Heaven, Purgatory, and Hell, the vision of perfection, the vision of improvement, and the vision of failure. Ibsen has only one – Hell.[15]

One can imagine the young Ronald Knox devouring these essays and digesting them into the 'platitudes' of his thought; and one can only guess the delight and excited approval with which he would have greeted Chesterton's defence of ritual in religion:

> The most ferocious opponent of the Christian ceremonials must admit that if Catholicism had not instituted the bread and wine, somebody else would most probably have done so. Any one with a poetical instinct will admit that to the ordinary human instinct bread symbolizes something which cannot very easily be symbolized otherwise; that wine, to the ordinary human instinct, symbolizes something which cannot very easily be symbolized otherwise. But white ties in the evening are ritual, and nothing else but ritual. No one would pretend that white ties in the evening are primary and poetical. Nobody would

maintain that the ordinary human instinct would in any age or country tend to symbolize the idea of evening by a white necktie.[16]

Employing the example of ritually taking off one's hat to a lady, Chesterton asked, 'What can be more solemn and absurd, considered in the abstract, than symbolizing the existence of the other sex by taking off a portion of your clothing and waving it in the air?'[17]

Then comes the *coup de grâce*: 'All men, then, are ritualists, but are either conscious or unconscious ritualists.'[18]

Meanwhile, Ronald Knox, now seventeen years old and already very much a conscious ritualist, was about to take another conscious decision, complying with which influenced the direction of his life immensely. One evening in 1905 he knelt down and solemnly bound himself to a vow of celibacy. Aware that such a pledge could be open to misunderstanding, especially when undertaken by a schoolboy, he was at pains in his autobiographical account of this period to put the decision into context: 'The uppermost thought in my mind was not that of virginity: I was not fleeing from the wickedness of the world I saw round me ...'[19] Rather, it was a response to his sudden awareness that the natural craving for human sympathy and support, and particularly 'that tenderest sympathy and support which a happy marriage would bring', would impede his ability 'to attend upon the Lord'.[20]

Even with the benefit of hindsight, Knox confessed to having 'no notion, humanly speaking, whence these ascetic impulses came. I cannot remember that any of my reading up till then would have suggested them to me – there is little trace in *The Light Invisible* of that atmosphere of mortification which inspires so much of Mgr Benson's later writing.'[21]

None the less, Benson's writing continued to influence Knox during these formative years. Since the publication of *The Light Invisible* in 1903, Benson had published historical novels in both the succeeding years. *By What Authority?* in 1904 and *The King's Achievement* in 1905 were both set in Tudor England. *Richard Raynal: Solitary*, his pastiche account of the life of a fifteenth-century hermit, published in 1906, was to become the author's own favourite. Benson described the book as 'very much better written and very much more religious'[22] than *The Light Invisible* and it certainly contains much of the atmosphere of mortification ascribed to his writings by Knox. There are also echoes of the deep theology he had long preached, both as an Anglican and a Catholic, and hints of his own inner struggle prior to conversion:

… there was the conflict of which I have spoken. There was that in him, which we name the Will, which continued tense and strong, striving against despair. Neither his mind nor his heart could help him in that *Night*; his mind informed him that he had sinned deadly by presumption, his heart found nowhere God to love; and all that, though he told himself that God was lovable, and adorable, and that he could not fall into hell save by his own purpose and intention.

Yet, in spite of all, and when all had failed him, his will strove against despair (which is the antichrist of humility) …[23]

Another of Benson's early novels was inspired in part by a visit to Oxburgh Hall, the home of the Bedingfield family in Norfolk. The Bedingfields are one of the oldest recusant families and the impact of Benson's stay with them is evident from his enthusiastic description:

To Oxburgh. Oh!!!! … a great red house, with a moat, towers, (yard-dog), Cromwell's armour in towers … Portraits beyond belief! … The King's room, a great brick-floor place, high, with fourteenth-century tapestry, a vast bed, worked by Mary Queen of Scots; a haunted room, really, with the portrait of the woman who haunts, an Italian.[24]

The excitement of his stay found expression in the 1906 novel, *The Sentimentalists*, in which Oxburgh Hall appears as the house of the character, Mr Rolls. In this, of course, Benson was preparing the ground for Evelyn Waugh who would use similar enthusiasm for the Catholic aristocracy and their houses as inspiration for *Brideshead Revisited*.

The extent to which Knox was influenced by Benson's fiction is illustrated by the fact that, during a visit to Rome in 1907, he had tried to write a short story himself, 'in the manner of Hugh Benson', based upon the diary of a priest who, attempting to exorcise one of his parishioners, is possessed by a nameless, hideous evil.[25] However, Knox was not particularly impressed when he first met Benson in the flesh at a friend's rooms in Oxford. Benson talked almost entirely about odd cases of nervous disease so that Knox recalled that 'I was impressed by the originality of his conversation, but not by its charm.'[26]

Another acquaintance Knox made at Oxford was that of Arnold Lunn. Again he was unimpressed, considering him 'a sour Dissenter'.[27] This, Lunn remembered, was unjust because he had been brought up as an Anglican and was an agnostic when he and Knox first met. They were exact contemporaries, both being born in 1888, but Knox was a year senior at Balliol. He preceded Lunn as editor of *The Isis*, the undergraduate weekly. As President of the Oxford Union he gave Lunn an official nomination for the Library Committee.

Lunn, like so many of his contemporaries, was somewhat in awe of Knox's brilliance. He recalled that 'Knox's triumphant progress to the presidency was never seriously challenged, for as a wit he was famous even as an undergraduate', and in his autobiography he wrote that Knox 'was outstandingly the most brilliant speaker. His wit always seemed spontaneous, however carefully he had prepared his speeches.'[28] In his Oxford Journal, Lunn had recorded that he 'went as Knox's guest to a paper (read by Knox) at "The Shaftesbury". Brilliant paper.'[29]

However, if Lunn bowed to Knox's brilliance he was far from bowing to his beliefs. He was as unimpressed by Knox's ritualistic Anglo-Catholicism as he had been by his first attendance at a Roman Catholic Mass in August 1907. On that occasion he thought the Mass 'inferior, so far as ritual went, to a military funeral'.[30]

In the years ahead Lunn seemingly moved further and further from Rome in direct proportion as Knox was moving closer. Eventually they crossed swords publicly on the subject of religion before Lunn finally conceded defeat and became a Catholic himself. Neither could have known in their undergraduate days at Oxford that, more than a quarter of a century later, Knox, as a Catholic priest, would receive Arnold Lunn into the Church.

NOTES

1. Ronald Knox, *A Spiritual Aeneid*, London, 1958 edn., p. 31.
2. ibid., p. 32.
3. Evelyn Waugh, *The Life of Ronald Knox*, London, 1962 edn., p. 55.
4. Ronald Knox, *A Spiritual Aeneid*, p. 38.
5. ibid., p. 34.
6. ibid., p. 34.
7. ibid., pp. 35–6.
8. ibid., p. 37.
9. Evelyn Waugh, *The Life of Ronald Knox*, p. 56.
10. Ronald Knox, *A Spiritual Aeneid*, p. v.
11. Evelyn Waugh, *The Life of Ronald Knox*, p. 57.
12. Claude Williamson, OSC (ed.), *Great Catholics*, London, 1938, p. 551.
13. Ronald Knox, *A Spiritual Aeneid*, p. 107.
14. C. C. Martindale, *The Life of Monsignor Robert Hugh Benson, Vol. One*, p. 343.
15. G. K. Chesterton, *Heretics*, London, 1905, pp. 29–30.
16. ibid., p. 248.
17. ibid., p. 249.
18. ibid., p. 250.
19. Ronald Knox, *A Spiritual Aeneid*, p. 43.
20. ibid., pp. 43–4.
21. ibid., p. 44.
22. Robert Hugh Benson, *Confessions of a Convert*, p. 61.
23. Robert Hugh Benson, *Richard Raynal: Solitary*, London, 1927 edn., p. 248.

24. C. C. Martindale, *The Life of Monsignor Robert Hugh Benson, Vol. Two*, London, 1916, p. 43.
25. Penelope Fitzgerald, *The Knox Brothers*, New York, 1977, p. 79.
26. Ronald Knox, *A Spiritual Aeneid*, p. 62.
27. Arnold Lunn, *And Yet So New*, London, 1958, p. 1.
28. Arnold Lunn, *Come What May: An Autobiography*, London, 1940, p. 52.
29. Arnold Lunn, *And Yet So New*, p. 1.
30. Arnold Lunn, *Come What May: An Autobiography*, p. 218.

CHAPTER FIVE

DAWSON AND WATKIN

In later years, Ronald Knox looked back on his days as President of the Oxford Union rather dispassionately, confessing that the 'Union itself is less warm and comforting in retrospect'. Yet he also admitted that 'it leaves indelible memories'.[1] These included Winston Churchill 'pouring out fiery invective against F. E. Smith, with whom he had travelled down in the train', and Hilaire Belloc 'waggling a cigar between his fingers as he demolished the House of Lords'.[2]

Another undergraduate with indelible memories of lively debates in Oxford at this time was Christopher Dawson who came up to Trinity College in 1908. Dawson recalled the imposing figure of Belloc speaking in the Eights Week Debate and Ronald Knox making 'a very brilliant speech in which he proved that the Stuarts were disinterested Socialists'.[3] Like Lunn, Dawson was somewhat in awe of Knox who was part of 'the smart Balliol group' and one of the leaders of 'the fashionable Anglo-Catholic faction in the university and the founder of a group called "The Spikes", so named on account of their High Church views'.[4] Dawson began to hover on the fringes of Knox's Anglo-Catholic circle, never actually affiliating to 'the Spikes' but attending weekday mass at Pusey House. He was a relatively new convert to Anglo-Catholicism who, until recently, had described himself as an agnostic. His revival of faith was due in large part to his friendship with Edward Ingram Watkin, an Anglo-Catholic who was to convert to Roman Catholicism in the year Dawson arrived at Oxford.

Watkin, an undergraduate at New College, had become convinced that Christ had established one Church undivided which the Anglican church did not claim to be. He remained, however, if not reconciled to, at least at peace with the communion in which he had been brought up. Concerning his reception into the Catholic Church he wrote that 'Catholicism has been the fulfilment of all I learned and prized as an Anglican', but that he still owed to the Church of England 'an appreciation of liturgical worship and prayer which has enabled me to find treasures in the Catholic liturgy I might otherwise have failed to discover'.[5]

Watkin became the author of many books in the years ahead, ranging from theology and philosophy to popular histories of the Catholic Church in England and studies of Catholic art and culture. A similar contribution to Catholic thought was made by Dawson, who, partly under Watkin's continuing influence, became a Catholic in 1914. Dawson wrote ground-breaking books, particularly on the philosophy of history, which influenced many of his contemporaries, including T. S. Eliot.

Dawson and Watkin first met at Bletsoe in Bedfordshire in the summer of 1905 where both boys had been sent to a private tutor to continue their studies before going up to Oxford. Dawson's daughter and biographer, Christina Scott, described her father's friendship with Watkin as 'the first and greatest friendship of his life'.[6] According to Watkin, their first meeting was 'hardly auspicious for a future friendship' because it was marked by a violent religious argument. Dawson at that stage was passing through a period of religious scepticism whereas Watkin was already an enthusiastic Anglo-Catholic. The volatile mixture came together in an explosion of polemics, culminating in physical violence when the young Anglo-Catholic brought a garden chair crashing down on to the head of the younger agnostic![7] From such unpromising beginnings the relationship developed.

Watkin arrived at Bletsoe at the age of sixteen after a solitary childhood in Wales and an unconventional education with private tutors at home and abroad. From Bletsoe he went to St Paul's School, where Chesterton had been taught twenty years earlier, taking a classical scholarship to New College, Oxford.

Meanwhile Dawson, whose maternal grandfather, Archdeacon Bevan, was a central figure in *Kilvert's Diary*, had been sent to Winchester where he found the religion 'arid and lifeless' and the long hours of formal instruction 'more ethics than religion'. Thus the most religious of English public schools had succeeded only in turning him away from 'Establishment religion'. Later he described the detrimental effect of his religious education at Winchester: 'The haze of vagueness and uncertainty which hung around the more fundamental articles of Christian dogma ... the one standard of authority in the Protestant religious world, namely the Bible, was being swept away by the tide of the new Biblical criticism.'[8]

Desperately seeking a source of authority, he found none in the Anglican church and still less in the Anglo-Catholic wing of the Church of England which was 'weak in the very point where it claimed to be strongest. It was lacking in authority. It was not the teaching of the official church, but of an enterprising minority which provided its own standards of orthodoxy.'[9]

It was this 'conflict of authorities' as he called it which led to his loss of faith. 'The intellectual current,' he wrote, 'was, in fact, setting away from Christianity, and I felt the first influence of that wave of paganism which has since swept the country.'[10] These words were written in retrospect in 1926 but his journal of 1906 records the same views in a less detached way: 'There appears to me to be no certainty except in my own existence, without which we can conceive nothing.' The following year he wrote: 'At present Christianity merely seems to me a possibility among other possibilities. I have not the slightest conviction.'[11] By the time he went up to Trinity College, Oxford in 1908 the doubts had subsided sufficiently for a return to belief in Christianity, part of the credit for which belonged to the continuing influence of Watkin.

From the very first, the initial conflagration aside, Dawson and Watkin had been brought together by a common interest in books. At Bletsoe Dawson introduced Watkin to Shorthouse's *John Inglesant*, which influenced both of them in much the same way as it had influenced both R. H. Benson and Ronald Knox.

In the early chapters of *John Inglesant* there is a description of the seventeenth-century Anglican community at Little Gidding and the church celebrated in T. S. Eliot's *Four Quartets*. During their last term at Bletsoe, Dawson and Watkin made a cross-country journey to Little Gidding where they were aware of 'a peculiar atmosphere of peace and prayer which invests the church'.[12]

Watkin left Bletsoe in 1906 and Dawson soon after, but the friendship developed at Oxford and continued for the next sixty years. Watkin became godparent to Dawson's daughter Juliana, now a nun of the Assumptionist sisters at Hengrave Hall in Suffolk, who remembers that 'they drifted apart in later years'.[13] His other daughter, Christina Scott, described the nature of their friendship in her biography of her father:

> It was one of those rare friendships between two apparently opposite personalities who feel a close kinship of mind and spirit. With Edward Watkin, who was outgoing and talkative, Christopher's shyness and reserve departed and he found he could talk freely or remain silent if he chose: the affinity of their minds was such that speech could become unnecessary.[14]

For Dawson life in Oxford was 'a social whirl' after the quiet years at Bletsoe. He knew very few Roman Catholics apart from Watkin and did not contemplate conversion for some time. However, like so many of his contemporaries he was a reader of Benson's novels and, during an unhappy stay in Germany, he compared that 'most dreadful' country to 'the state of society in *Lord of the World*', Benson's novel about the apocalypse.[15] His respect for Benson remained and twenty years later he was encouraging his own children to read Benson's books. His daughter recalled that she 'was brought up on the novels of Benson ... They were a little exaggerated perhaps but I enjoyed them very much.'[16]

A visit to Rome with Watkin during the Easter vacation of 1909 came 'as a revelation' to Dawson and opened his eyes 'to a whole new world of religion and culture'.[17] The nineteen-year-old's positive impressions of Rome contrasted starkly with his view of Germany where he complained that 'people get on so very well without religion' and that 'they examine Christianity as if it was a kind of beetle'.[18] Whereas Germany had been 'a most soul-destroying place', Rome had exceeded his expectations and was much less spoilt by modernization than he had feared. He wrote home enthusiastically, describing the baroque churches as 'all gilt and coloured marble'. A later account of his conversion illustrated the importance of this first trip to Rome:

> To me the art of the Counter Reformation was a pure joy and I loved the churches of Bernini and Borromini no less than the ancient basilicas. And this in turn led me to the literature of the Counter Reformation, and I came to know St Theresa and St John of the Cross, compared to whom even the greatest of non-Catholic religious writers seem pale and unreal.[19]

Returning to Oxford he came to know several more Catholics and a few priests, again through his friendship with Watkin. At the Newman Society (the Oxford Catholic society for undergraduates) he heard Wilfrid Ward speak on the circumstances in which Newman wrote the *Apologia pro Vita Sua*. It was about this time that he first became interested in Newman and the Oxford Movement, and Newman's *Apologia* was to be a considerable influence on his own conversion. According to Christina Scott, 'His whole attitude was rather like Newman's. He came to the Faith through history and the study of the Fathers of the Church.'[20]

Throughout his life Dawson remained fascinated by Newman and in one of his last Harvard lectures he described the circumstances leading up to Newman's conversion. Dawson recounted that when Newman finally found himself faced with the decision, he found it 'exceedingly hard to make and it took him four years of agonizing intellectual and moral examination to sever the links that bound him so closely to the Church of England and the University of Oxford'.[21] Dawson found himself in much the same situation and one is struck by the similarity of their respective approaches.

Like Newman, Dawson felt bound to the strong Anglican tradition in his family and, like Newman, he was affected by the knowledge that conversion to

Roman Catholicism would meet with the deep-felt disapproval of those close to him. Dawson knew that his mother, who was the eldest daughter of Archdeacon Bevan of Hay Castle, would strongly oppose his 'going over to Rome'.

A further parallel between the conversions of Newman and Dawson is evident in the length of the delay before the irrevocable step was taken. Dawson had referred to the four years that Newman had taken in his spiritual struggle prior to conversion. Dawson was to take almost as long himself.

He wrote of Newman that 'No convert has ever made a more careful and conscientious approach to Catholicism, testing every step, weighing every alternative and considering every objection.'[22] Dawson adopted the same method, embarking upon an intensive study of the Bible and the Fathers of the Church, particularly Athanasius, Irenaeus, Cyprian and Augustine. 'The Fathers made me a Catholic,' Newman had written in a letter to Pusey. Dawson could have said the same. On another occasion Newman had written that 'To be deep in history is to cease to be a Protestant.' By this he meant, Dawson explained, that the cumulative evidence of the Christian past led him to a full acceptance of the Catholic present: 'There were but two paths – the way of faith and the way of unbelief, and as the latter led through the halfway house of Liberalism to Atheism, the former led through the halfway house of Anglicanism to Catholicism.'[23]

These words, though written of Newman, were a vivid description of Dawson's own feelings as he approached conversion. Ironically, however, it was the writings of a nineteenth-century Protestant theologian which finally convinced Dawson of the truth of Catholicism. Adolf Harnack, in Volume VII of his *History of Dogma*, made it clear that Luther had attacked the whole Catholic ideal of Christian perfection, rupturing the Protestant present from the Christian past. This finally convinced Dawson that only the Roman Catholic Church held the true faith in an unbroken tradition from the Apostles. It was with wry amusement that Dawson expressed his unexpected debt of gratitude to the German Protestant theologian who had unwittingly led him to Rome: 'Harnack, a liberal Protestant, never knew how much he contributed to the process of my conversion to the Catholic Church! He had never heard of me, of course, but I wonder if it ever occurred to him that he might have helped anyone along that particular road.'[24]

Dawson's arrival at an orthodox position through the rejection of another's 'heretical' opinion was similar to G. K. Chesterton's experience at this time. In 1909 Chesterton had become embroiled in a controversy with Robert Dell, a Roman Catholic Modernist who later left the Church to become an outspoken agnostic and revolutionary socialist. In reply to Dell, Chesterton had concluded that he had 'never felt so near to Mr Dell's communion as after I had read his attack on it'.[25]

Two years later Chesterton was destined to nudge Dawson closer to the Catholic Church. In August 1911, when Dawson was in the midst of his spiritual struggle, Chesterton's *Ballad of the White Horse* was published. More than twenty years afterwards Dawson wrote to Chesterton acknowledging the *Ballad*'s influence: 'Years ago, when I was an undergraduate, your *Ballad of the White Horse* first brought the breath of life to this period for me.'[26]

None the less, Chesterton's influence was relatively minor compared with that of Newman on the one hand and his in-depth study of history on the other. The latter led him to become increasingly convinced that the Reformation was rooted in fundamental errors:

> It was a classic example of emptying out the baby with the bath. The reformers revolted against the externalism of medieval religion, and so they abolished the Mass. They protested against the lack of personal holiness, and so they abolished the saints. They attacked the wealth and self-indulgence of the monks and they abolished monasticism and the life of voluntary poverty and asceticism. They had no intention of abandoning the ideal of Christian perfection, but they sought to realise it in Puritanism instead of Monasticism and in pietism instead of mysticism.[27]

Finally it was neither Newman nor the study of history that convinced him of the truth of the Catholic Church but a thorough reading of the Bible. In this, he paralleled the path trod by R. H. Benson:

> It was by the study of St Paul and St John that I first came to understand the fundamental unity of Catholic theology and the Catholic life. I realised that the Incarnation, the sacraments, the external order of the Church and the internal work of sanctifying grace, were all parts of one organic unity, a living tree whose roots are in the Divine nature and whose fruit is the perfection of the saints ... [28]

One other major influence, less profound but equally potent, was his meeting with Valery Mills at a party in Oxford in the summer of 1909. He 'fell immediately and hopelessly in love' with the eighteen-year-old Catholic. Four years later they became engaged and at the beginning of the following year he embraced his fiancée's faith. First, however, he had to face the opposition of his mother, a staunch Protestant who was never reconciled to his change of religion. His conversion also placed a strain on his relationship with his sister, a devout Anglo-Catholic who never understood or accepted his reasons for joining the

Roman Church. Indeed, his reception into the Church 'caused a rift between them so that the close relationship of their early years was never quite restored'.[29]

Christopher Dawson was received into the Church by Father O'Hare, SJ, at St Aloysius in Oxford on the eve of the Feast of the Epiphany, 5 January 1914. Appropriately enough Edward Watkin, his friend and fellow-traveller in faith, stood as his sponsor.

NOTES

1. Ronald Knox, *A Spiritual Aeneid*, p. 52.
2. ibid.
3. Christina Scott, *A Historian and his World: A Life of Christopher Dawson*, London, 1984, p. 39.
4. ibid., pp. 41–2.
5. Matthew Hoehn, OSB (ed.), *Catholic Authors: Contemporary Biographical Sketches, 1930–1947*, Newark, USA, 1948, pp. 775–6.
6. Christina Scott, *A Historian and his World: A Life of Christopher Dawson*, p. 36.
7. ibid., p. 37.
8. ibid., p. 37.
9. ibid., p. 37.
10. ibid., p. 37.
11. ibid., pp. 37–8.
12. ibid., p. 38.
13. Sister Juliana Dawson, interview with the author, Hengrave Hall, Suffolk, 9 December 1996.
14. Christina Scott, *A Historian and his World: A Life of Christopher Dawson*, pp. 38–9.
15. ibid., p. 40.
16. Sister Juliana Dawson, interview with the author.
17. Christina Scott, *A Historian and his World: A Life of Christopher Dawson*, p. 47.
18. ibid., p. 40.
19. ibid., p. 48.
20. Christina Scott, interview with the author, Kensington, 28 December 1996.
21. Christina Scott, *A Historian and his World: A Life of Christopher Dawson*, p. 62.
22. ibid., pp. 62–3.
23. ibid., p. 63.
24. ibid., p. 63.
25. *Church Socialist Quarterly*, July 1909.
26. *The Chesterton Review*, Vol. IX, No. 2, p. 136.
27. Christina Scott, *A Historian and his World: A Life of Christopher Dawson*, p. 64.
28. ibid., p. 64.
29. ibid., p. 65.

CHAPTER SIX

BENSON'S CAMBRIDGE APOSTOLATE

On 1 August 1907 Hilaire Belloc wrote to A. C. Benson expressing great admiration for the latter's brother. Belloc wrote that he had met R. H. Benson once or twice 'and liked him enormously'. In the same letter he also confessed a great sympathy for Benson's historical novels: 'It is quite on the cards that he will be the man to write some day a book to give us some sort of idea what happened in England between 1520 and 1560.'[1]

Belloc, increasingly frustrated at the Protestant bias of the Whig historians, soon started to study the period himself. In later life he published studies of key sixteenth- and seventeenth-century figures such as Wolsey, Cromwell, James I, Charles II and Cranmer. His *How The Reformation Happened*, published in 1928, was an endeavour to put the whole period into context.

Benson, however, was diverging. Although he was to write two more historical novels, *Come Rack! Come Rope!* and *Oddsfish*, the majority of his future fiction dealt with contemporary dilemmas or, as in the case of his most recent book, *Lord of the World*, published in 1907, with apocalyptic visions of the future foreshadowing Huxley's *Brave New World* and Orwell's *Nineteen Eighty-Four*.

Furthermore, Benson was more than simply a novelist. He had been ordained in 1904 and, upon his return from Rome that same year, had returned to Cambridge where he had been an undergraduate. Shane Leslie, who came to know Benson well during his years at Cambridge, wrote of his return with a sense of whimsical irony:

> Among the few though pathetic references to Robert Hugh Benson in the well-stored biography of his father, the Archbishop of Canterbury, is an account of his once walking with a friend from Cambridge to Lambeth in the course of a single day. The return journey, back from Lambeth to Cambridge, via Rome, proved a longer and a lonelier progress.[2]

Such an anecdotal aside provides yet another unexpected link with Belloc, since Belloc was himself to claim the record, as an undergraduate at Oxford, for walking from Oxford to London in only eleven and a half hours. Furthermore, Benson's marathon cycle tour around Sussex prior to his conversion invites comparison with Belloc's walk across Sussex in 1902, which was to inspire his writing of *The Four Men*.

In 1905 Benson offered himself to the Rector of Cambridge in the capacity of a new curate. He was accepted. His duties did not rest easily on his shoulders because, after Rome, he felt stifled by the new environment. 'He had become convinced,' wrote Shane Leslie, 'of the irreligious and materialistic atmosphere of Cambridge, which, he used to complain, weighed upon him like lead, and he had made up his mind to lift his thin but denunciatory voice at the gates of that mathematical city ... Nevertheless, he did stout battle against her fogs while he was there.'[3]

One of these fogs was the cult of spiritualism which was all the rage at the time in Cambridge as elsewhere. On one occasion panic-stricken youths, having seen an apparition, supplied Benson with the material he would develop in his novel, *The Necromancers*. Benson perceived the dangers of spiritualism and once wrote that 'To go to *seances* with good intentions is like holding a smoking concert in a powder-magazine on behalf of an orphan asylum.'[4]

These words would have struck a chord with G. K. Chesterton, whose wife at this time had started to dabble with spiritualism in the wake of her brother's suicide. His disapproval found expression in his writing of 'The Crystal'. Its sentiments reflect those of Benson exactly:

> You whom the pinewoods robed in sun and shade
>   You who were sceptred with the thistle's bloom,
> God's thunder! What have you to do with these
>   The lying crystal and the darkened room?[5]

The synthesis of outlook in the published works of Chesterton and Benson was illustrated by the Jesuit, C. C. Martindale, Benson's biographer. Martindale, who had converted on 8 May 1897 and who had been sent by the Jesuits to Oxford in 1901, wrote that Benson's *Papers of a Pariah* were 'noticeable' for their 'Chestertonian quality': 'Mr G. K. Chesterton is never tired of telling us that we do not see what we look at – the one undiscovered planet is our Earth ... And Benson read much of Mr Chesterton, and liked him in a qualified way.'[6]

More surprisingly, perhaps, Martindale sees a 'disconcerting affinity' between Benson's *Papers of a Pariah* and Wilde's *De Profundis*:

Benson had, and Wilde was resolving, so he thought, to get, that direct eye for colour, line, and texture that the Greeks possessed ... in his direct extraction of natural emotion from simple and beautiful elements, like fire and wax, as in his description of the Easter ceremonies, [Benson] reaches, sometimes, an almost word-for-word identity with Wilde.[7]

Evidence of Chesterton's influence on Benson is provided by the very high opinion with which Benson admired Chesterton's *Heretics*. 'Have you read,' he enquired of a correspondent in 1905, 'a book by G. K. Chesterton called *Heretics*? If not, do see what you think of it. It seems to me that the spirit underneath it is splendid. He is not a Catholic, but he has the spirit ... I have not been so much moved for a long time ... He is a real mystic of an odd kind.'[8]

Further affinities with Chesterton were displayed on 22 March 1907 when Benson replied to an enquirer who had said that she had got 'half way from Agnosticism to Catholicism and could get no further'. She stated that Benson's Lenten sermons had convinced her that he knew all about that 'borderland' in which she and so many others found themselves imprisoned. Her principal difficulty arose from the Catholic claim that the Church's dogmas were true historically as well as spiritually so that, for Catholics, the Ascension was as 'true' as the Armada. This she simply could not believe and neither did she believe it mattered, because only mystical language was intelligible in religion. Benson's reply showed the same firm grasp of the Aristotelianism underpinning much of Thomism which Chesterton was to display to great effect in his writing of *St Thomas Aquinas* many years later.

> Your main difficulty seems to me to lie along the old eternal difficulty of the relation between matter and spirit, the inner and the outer, Ideas and History. Now of course I agree frankly that the Spirit, the inner, and the Idea are primary. So I need not say anything about that. But the next fact is that this Inner Side, does as a matter of fact, express itself in outer ways. 'God is a Spirit,' but 'The Word was made flesh.' Further, it is quite evident that the outer is always inadequate to the inner. But, though it is inadequate to Spirit, this does not mean that it is necessarily inadequate to our conceptions of Spirit, nor that its analogies are not 'true.'
>
> What therefore Catholics believe with regard to such things is (a) the spiritual principle, (b) that the spiritual principle did, as a matter of fact, express itself in (material) terms. And the more one contemplates

the Gospels, the more it becomes evident that no other religion in the world links together in so amazing a way the deepest thoughts we can receive from God and outward events as their expression.[9]

As well as indicating his firm grasp of the philosophical foundations of Catholic Christianity, the letter to an earnest enquirer indicates Benson's vocation as patient teacher to would-be converts. This side of his personality was described at length by Shane Leslie, in his essay on Benson's 'Cambridge Apostolate'. Leslie wrote, 'No one individual ever covered a more meteoric and ecstatic career in so short a time. He was there four years only. And now he has become a legend among some who were old when he came up. But for many whom he first met as undergraduates, he remains always the symbol of their spiritual youth and his.'[10]

In his autobiographical *The End of a Chapter*, Shane Leslie returned to his memories of Benson at Cambridge, describing him as 'a flower among controversial thorns'.

> It seemed strange for the son of an Archbishop of Canterbury to become a Catholic priest. Yet never was chrysalis hatched with such jubilant celerity as when the Benjamin of Lambeth Palace became a freelance in the service of the Vatican. As a curate in Cambridge he uttered an ascetic note in the home of 'muscular Christianity.' Yet he exactly appreciated the mixture of fear and fun which goes to the making of true religion. With fecundive fervour he poured forth a series of novels which may be described as the Epistles of Hugh the Preacher to the Anglicans – to the Conventionalists – to the Sensualists, etc.[11]

Leslie remembered Benson 'sitting in the firelight of my room at King's, unravelling a weird story about demoniacal substitution, his eyeballs staring into the flame, and his nervous fingers twitching to baptise the next undergraduate he could thrill or mystify into the fold of Rome'.[12]

Leslie also drew an amusing and perceptive parallel between Benson and Winston Churchill:

> His career was that of an ecclesiastical Winston Churchill, with whom he offered a parallel even to the stutter in his speech. Yet both could command the irritated attention of elder men when they spoke. In each case a father's son made a famous father memorable for his son. It was Archbishop Benson who gave Anglicans their watchword in resisting

'The Italian Mission,' and Randolph Churchill who taught the Tories to chime: 'Ulster will fight and Ulster will be right.' It was a curious *denouement* to hear the sons of both reversing the wisdom of their fathers. Winston preached Home Rule in Belfast, and Hugh Benson upheld the Pope in Cambridge – instances, both, of the old Greek word *peripateia*, which may be translated, the somersault divine![13]

Events in Shane Leslie's own life paralleled the lives of both Benson and Churchill in several curious ways. Leslie became a convert himself in 1908, one of those undergraduates who were thrilled and mystified into the Roman fold by Benson. He was born John Randolph Leslie in 1885, the eldest son of Colonel Sir John Leslie, second baronet, of Glaslough, County Monaghan. After his conversion he changed his name to 'Shane', an Irish form of John, in recognition of his other conversion: to Irish Nationalism. In 1910 he stood as a Nationalist for Derry, breaking with the family tradition of Unionism as he had earlier broken with the family's Anglicanism.

At King's College Leslie fell under the influence of Benson and 'Mugger' Barnes, both of whom were fervent converts and, like Leslie himself, Etonians. Writing of his own conversion, Leslie remarked that 'My strongest feeling then and today is an acute desire to die in the Catholic fold, and to be laid in an anonymous but consecrated monastery corner.'[14]

In later years he became known as a versatile man of letters, writing poetry, novels, biographies, travelogues, historical studies and Catholic apologetics. He became the most prominent of Robert Hugh Benson's converts during the days that Leslie himself called Benson's 'Cambridge Apostolate'.

NOTES

1. C. C. Martindale, *The Life of Robert Hugh Benson, Vol. Two*, p. 45.
2. Shane Leslie, 'The Cambridge Apostolate' in *Memorials of Robert Hugh Benson*, London, 1915, p. 47.
3. ibid., p. 53.
4. ibid., p. 66.
5. Joseph Pearce, *Wisdom and Innocence: A Life of G. K. Chesterton*, London, 1996, p. 104.
6. C. C. Martindale, *The Life of Robert Hugh Benson, Vol. Two*, p. 90.
7. ibid., pp. 90–1.
8. ibid., p. 90.
9. ibid., pp. 258–9.
10. Shane Leslie, 'The Cambridge Apostolate', p. 69.
11. Shane Leslie, *The End of a Chapter*, London, 1917, p. 67.
12. ibid., pp. 66–7.
13. ibid., p. 68.
14. Matthew Hoehn, OSB (ed.), *Catholic Authors: Contemporary Biographical Sketches, 1930–1947*, Newark, USA, 1948, p. 428.

CHAPTER SEVEN

THE ATTRACTION OF ORTHODOXY

In 1908 Chesterton produced one of his most influential books. *Orthodoxy*, published on 25 September, was written in response to a reviewer of his earlier book, *Heretics*, who had complained that Chesterton had condemned the theology and philosophy of others without clearly stating his own. 'With all the solemnity of youth,' Chesterton wrote, 'I accepted this as a challenge; and wrote an outline of my own reasons for believing that the Christian theory, as summarised in the Apostles' Creed, would be found to be a better criticism of life than any of those that I had criticised.'[1]

Orthodoxy was Chesterton's first explicitly Christian title and his biographer Maisie Ward considered it so important that 'more must be said of it than his other published works'.[2] Her father, Wilfrid Ward, whose talk at Oxford had done so much to stimulate Christopher Dawson's interest in Newman, proclaimed it as a major milestone in the development of Christian thought. In an article on *Orthodoxy* and its author in the *Dublin Review*, Ward wrote:

> I class his thought – though not his manner – with that of such men as Burke, Butler and Coleridge ...
>
> The spectacle of this intensely active and earnest modern intellect ... reminds us how much that is indispensable in the inheritance of Christendom our own age has ceased adequately to realise and is in danger of lightly abandoning.[3]

The strength of Chesterton's *Orthodoxy*, and the key to its success, was the way the author made the subject attractive to his readers. Dorothy L. Sayers was a fifteen-year-old schoolgirl when she first read the book and was inspired and excited by Chesterton's image of the Church as a heavenly chariot 'thundering through the ages, the dull heresies sprawling and prostrate, the wild truth reeling but erect'.[4] This invigorating vision rekindled her faith at a time when adolescent doubt and growing disillusionment with the low-church puritanism to which she was accustomed was threatening to extinguish it. 'In the book called *Orthodoxy*,' she wrote, 'there were glimpses of this other Christianity, which was beautiful and adventurous and queerly full of honour.'[5] She told a friend in later years that, but for Chesterton's vision of Orthodoxy, she might in her school-days have abandoned Christianity altogether.[6] In 1952 she put the matter more eloquently: 'To the young people of my generation G. K. C. was a kind of Christian liberator. Like a beneficent bomb, he blew out of the Church a quantity of stained glass of a very poor period, and let in gusts of fresh air in which the dead leaves of doctrine danced with all the energy and indecorum of Our Lady's Tumbler.'[7]

A few years later Arnold Lunn made the same point. The modern world, he wrote in 1956, was in danger of overlooking the debt so many people owed to Chesterton, 'of forgetting the impact which his books made on the minds of the young men who were infected by the fallacy of Victorian rationalism'.[8]

Another writer who was affected profoundly by *Orthodoxy* was Theodore Maynard who had first read the book as a nineteen-year-old: 'It still seems to me a most extraordinary work and it sank deeply into my mind ... Chesterton did not himself enter the Church until thirteen years later ... long before that he had made a Catholic of me.'[9]

Theodore Maynard was a minor literary light, never destined to gain the international reputation of either Chesterton or Dorothy L. Sayers, although he enjoyed a period of renown as both poet and biographer stretching from the beginning of the First World War until the end of the Second. Throughout his literary career he continually acknowledged 'the great influence of G. K. Chesterton upon his thought and writings and to a lesser extent that of Hilaire Belloc'.[10] Other minor literary figures gathering round the flame of orthodoxy around this time included Ernest Messenger, received in 1908, who gave up his career as a Fleet Street journalist under T. P. O'Connor to study for the priesthood before becoming a writer of popular theology and a translator of philosophical works from the French; Naomi Jacob, who converted the previous year as an eighteen-year-old, and who was destined to become one of the most prolific and popular of novelists, writing light fiction chiefly concerned with the delineation of character; and Lewis Watt, received in 1906 and later becoming a Jesuit, the author of several books on Catholic social teaching.

It is not clear whether Chesterton's *Orthodoxy* had any direct influence on Maurice Baring's imminent conversion but considering his admiration for Chesterton's earlier works, and his growing fondness for the author, it would be surprising if Baring had not read *Orthodoxy* in the months immediately preceding his reception into the Church on 1 February 1909.

Although Baring had written to Vernon Lee from St Petersburg in January 1906 asking whether Lee had read Chesterton's books, *The Napoleon of Notting Hill* and *Heretics*, and stating that 'I like his *ideas*',[11] it seems that Chesterton and Baring did not become good friends until as late as 1907. Considering that they had both been friends of Belloc since the turn of the century, this is surprising. As late as March 1908 Baring was writing to Chesterton from Moscow requesting a greater intimacy in their relationship:

> Dear Gilbert may I leave out the Chesterton?
> (Prince, may I call you by your Christian name?)
> (Your surname is so solemn & so long:–
> Prince may I call you by your Christian name?)
> I hope to be back in London this week.
> (Prince, let us meet & swallow wine & beer.)
> I hope to see you very soon on my return.
> (Prince, there is no one like you in the East.)
> I hope you & I & Hilaire may meet.[12]

The slow development of their relationship had a lot to do with Baring's long absences from England in places as diverse as Paris, Copenhagen, Rome, Moscow and Manchuria, but, once formed, their friendship grew stronger as the years passed. Eventually Frances Chesterton was to say that 'of all her husband's friends' there was none he loved better than Maurice Baring.

Baring was received into the Catholic Church at Brompton Oratory by Father Sebastian Bowden, the same priest whom Oscar Wilde had approached over thirty years earlier. The event was recorded in Baring's autobiography, *The Puppet Show of Memory*, with the simple statement that it was 'the only action in my life which I am quite certain I have never regretted'.[13] Apart from the candour of this solitary statement the event is passed over without further comment.

Such uncharacteristic reticence is surprising from an author who later fearlessly used the medium of his fiction as a means of expressing his faith. However, the feelings he felt unable or unwilling to express in prose he expressed admirably in verse, particularly in his sonnet sequence 'Vita Nuova'. Divided into a chronological trinity, the first sonnet deals with the initial approach to conversion: 'I found the clue I sought not, in the night, While wandering in a pathless maze of gloom ...'

The second sonnet describes the act of conversion itself:

One day I heard a whisper: 'Wherefore wait?
Why linger in a separated porch?
Why nurse the flicker of a severed torch?
The fire is there, ablaze beyond the gate.

Why tremble, foolish soul? Why hesitate?
However faint the knock, it will be heard.'
I knocked, and swiftly came the answering word,
Which bade me enter to my own estate.

I found myself in a familiar place;
And there my broken soul began to mend;
I knew the smile of every long-lost face –

They whom I had forgot remembered me;
I knelt, I knew – it was too bright to see –
The welcome of a King who was my friend.[14]

The final sonnet deals with hopes of eternity beyond the grave where 'That tranquil harbour shines and waits ...'[15]

Endeavouring to explain his reasons for conversion he wrote that 'directly I came to the conclusion *inside* that life was for me divine, and that I had inside me an immortal thing in touch with an Eternal Spirit, there was no other course open to me than to become a Catholic'.[16] He explained to Ethel Smyth, a close friend and confidante, that his faith was a fusion of want and need: 'I feel that human life which is almost intolerable as it is, would be to me quite intolerable without this which is to me no narcotic but food, air, drink.'[17] It is not surprising, therefore, that Smyth should describe Baring's conversion as 'the crucial action of his life' and that when she had been informed of the event she 'had the feeling that the missing piece of a complicated puzzle, or rather the only key wherewith a given iron safe could be unlocked, had at last been found'.[18]

A similar view was held by the French writer Raymond Las Vergnas. In his critical study of Chesterton, Belloc and Baring, translated into English by Father Martindale, Las Vergnas wrote that Baring's Christian faith was the 'powerful unifying force' responsible for 'harmonising the complex tendencies' in his artistic temperament.[19]

News of Baring's conversion was greeted with jubilation by Hilaire Belloc who had observed his friend's slow but steady progress over more than a decade.

Three years earlier, on 19 April 1906, Belloc had written a rhyming letter to Baring offering encouragement as his friend fumbled his way faithwards:

> My ardent love
> Accompanies your soul and on the whole
> I doubt if all the saints could roll your soul
> One tittle faster to the Faith than He
> Who made your soul is rolling it. H.B.[20]

Emma Letley, Baring's biographer, gave her study the title *Maurice Baring: A Citizen of Europe* and it is not difficult to see why. Baring travelled widely throughout Europe as diplomat, journalist and man of leisure. He knew Latin, Greek, French, German, Italian and Russian and he was widely read in the literatures of all these languages. He was the quintessential European. With this in mind, Belloc's words in *An Open Letter on the Decay of Faith*, published in 1906, must have struck Baring with a particular resonance:

> I desire you to remember that we are Europe; we are a great people. The faith is not an accident among us, nor an imposition, nor a garment; it is bone of our bone and flesh of our flesh: it is a philosophy made by and making ourselves. We have adorned, explained, enlarged it; we have given it visible form. This is the service we Europeans have done to God. In return He has made us Christians.[21]

Following Baring's conversion, Belloc wrote a celebratory letter to Charlotte Balfour, who had been received into the Church herself in 1904: 'They are coming in like a gathering army from all manner of directions, all manner of men each bringing some new force: that of Maurice is his amazing accuracy of mind which proceeds from his great virtue of truth.'[22]

Belloc's profound gratitude at the gathering army of converts belonged, at least in part, to the work of his friend G. K. Chesterton. More than any writer in the first decade of the century Chesterton had taken on the secularists, doing battle with 'heretics' such as Shaw and Wells with a good-natured joviality which was infectious. Chesterton's Christianity was catching and through his piercing paradoxes and quixotic enthusiasm many were beginning to discover the attraction of orthodoxy.

NOTES

1. G. K. Chesterton, *Autobiography*, London, 1936, p. 177.

2. Maisie Ward, *Gilbert Keith Chesterton*, p. 181.

3. Maisie Ward, *Resurrection versus Insurrection*, London, 1937, p. 206.

4. G. K. Chesterton, *Orthodoxy*, London, 1908, p. 169.

5. Barbara Reynolds, *Dorothy L. Sayers: Her Life and Soul*, London, 1993, p. 57.

6. ibid., p. 74.

7. Dorothy L. Sayers, Preface to Chesterton's play, *The Surprise*, London, 1952, p. 5.

8. Arnold Lunn, *Now I See*, London, 1956, p. 51.

9. John A. O'Brien (ed.), *The Road To Damascus*, London, 1949, p. 114.

10. ibid., p. 105.

11. *The Chesterton Review*, Vol. XIX, No. 1, February 1988, p. 2.

12. Emma Letley, *Maurice Baring: A Citizen of Europe*, p. 140.

13. Maurice Baring, *The Puppet Show of Memory*, London, 1922, pp. 395–6.

14. Maurice Baring, *Collected Poems*, London, 1925, pp. 65–6.

15. ibid., p. 67.

16. Emma Letley, *Maurice Baring: A Citizen of Europe*, p. 144.

17. ibid., p. 144.

18. Ethel Smyth, *Maurice Baring*, London, 1938, pp. 39–40.

19. Raymond Las Vergnas, *Chesterton, Belloc, Baring*, London, 1938, p. 95.

20. Robert Speaight (ed.), *Letters from Hilaire Belloc*, London, 1958, p. 7.

21. Karl G. Schmude, *Hilaire Belloc: His Life and Legacy*, Melbourne, Australia, 1978, p. 5.

22. Robert Speaight, *The Life of Hilaire Belloc*, London, 1957, p. 245.

CHAPTER EIGHT

RELIGION AND POLITICS

It is a modern maxim that religion and politics should be avoided in polite society. Such a view would not have been shared in Edwardian and Georgian England where battle was often joined on both subjects. In the years preceding the outbreak of the First World War attendance at public debates was a favourite pastime and two of the most popular speakers at these debates were George Bernard Shaw and G. K. Chesterton.

Hugh Lunn, the brother of Arnold Lunn and the author in later years of biographies, essays, anthologies and travel books under the name of Hugh Kingsmill, wrote in an article for *Hearth and Home* on 17 October 1912 of Shaw's and Chesterton's fashionable ascendancy in intellectual circles at this time:

> At Oxford, the Chestertonian and the Shavian are well-known types: the Shavian enthroned above human emotion is clever, but a prig; the Chestertonian, less brilliant, is more likeable. He doesn't care for advanced ideas, but he would like to combine wit and probity. So he welcomes a writer who defends old modes of thought with humour, and attacks modern thinkers on the ground that they are antiquated bores in disguise.[1]

Hugh Lunn's description, though amusing, betrays his own bias towards Shaw. Dorothy L. Sayers, on the other hand, was at Oxford at the time and found herself solidly in the Chestertonian camp. She had seen both Chesterton and Shaw give lectures at Oxford, being impressed with Chesterton, who was 'much sounder' than she had expected, but not with Shaw who was 'not particularly original'.[2]

As for Shaw and Chesterton themselves, they had carried on a running battle for several years. In 1908 Shaw had invented the 'Chesterbelloc' suggesting that Belloc and Chesterton were seen so synonymously that they produced a 'quadrupedal illusion … a very amusing pantomime elephant'.[3] Chesterton had responded the following year with his biography of Shaw and his novel *The Ball and the Cross*, a celebration of the type of argument in which he and Shaw were engaged.

In *The Ball and the Cross* the two adversaries were a Roman Catholic and a militant atheist, whereas Chesterton was an Anglo-Catholic at the time and Shaw was a paradoxical mixture of Nietzschean and philanthropist. None the less, the point of the novel was that the pursuit of argument in the service of truth was honourable in itself and preferable to the indifference of secularism. It was better to have beliefs, even the wrong beliefs, than to have no beliefs at all. *The Ball and the Cross* was first and foremost a parable on the relationship between Chesterton and Shaw. The two enemies in the novel are also the two heroes.

Although Shaw and Chesterton seldom agreed and were continually arguing they never quarrelled. Intellectual enemies in a war of words, the beauty of their relationship resided in a genuine 'love for thine enemy'. Owen Barfield, the writer best remembered perhaps as a friend of C. S. Lewis and Tolkien, witnessed Shaw and Chesterton, the loving enemies, during a debate in a London theatre. In between parrying blows thrown by the other, Barfield remembered, 'they rather ragged it because each of them was trying to pretend that the other was hogging the limelight'.[4] The war between them was a civil war with the emphasis always on the adjective.

If Hugh Lunn had taken the side of Shaw in the Chestershavian civil war his brother found himself in the opposing camp. Arnold Lunn recorded in his autobiography that he had read the works of Chesterton and Belloc during his undergraduate days at Oxford 'and their influence was one of the principal factors in my conversion'.[5] It will be remembered that Lunn had also written of the impact which Chesterton's books had 'made on the minds of the young men who were infected by the fallacy of Victorian rationalism'.[6]

Lunn had first discovered the writing of Hilaire Belloc in 1910 while recovering from serious injuries incurred in a climbing accident in Wales the previous year. Wandering into Blackwell's bookshop in Oxford he had picked up a volume of Belloc's verse, was fascinated by what he read and bought the book. The same evening, while dining at the Clarendon, he and a friend took it in turns to read and declaim Belloc's poems. They were particularly taken by Belloc's 'Lines to a Don', a verse of invective levelled at the

Remote and ineffectual Don
That dared attack my Chesterton.

Lunn remembered that 'the effect of poetry and port was exhilarating' so that he felt an inebriated impulse 'that the poem should be recited without further delay to a don in my own college, Balliol, who had spoken disparagingly of Chesterton and who might, for all I knew, be the don who had provoked Belloc'.[7] Returning to Balliol he serenaded the don under his windows with Belloc's lines:

> Don to thine own damnation quoted,
> Perplexed to find thy trivial name
> Reared in my verse to lasting shame.
> Don dreadful, rasping Don and wearing,
> Repulsive Don – Don past all bearing.
> Don of the cold and doubtful breath,
> Don despicable, Don of death;
> Don nasty, skimpy, silent, level;
> Don evil; Don that serves the devil ...
> Believe me I shall soon return.
> My fires are banked, but still they burn
> To write some more about the Don
> That dared attack my Chesterton.

Unfortunately for the young undergraduate the don in question, far from being 'remote and ineffectual', was very much on the spot. Severely chastised, Lunn wrote to Belloc the following day to describe the effect of his poetry. Belloc replied from King's Land on 12 December: 'This is as it should be and warms my heart! Verse is intended to produce that sort of effect.'[8]

His appetite whetted for books Bellocian, Lunn began to read them avidly. One in particular made a permanent impression:

> I had read and been fascinated by *The Path to Rome*, which remains to this day my favourite book. I reread it every year; Belloc's aggressive Catholicism in this, as in his other books, alternately irritated and attracted me ... As an agnostic with an Anglican background I had always assumed that the Catholics appealed from reason to faith, and it was Belloc's emphasis on reason which encouraged me to investigate the case for the Church, if only to discover whether Belloc's insistence on reason was a private whimsy of his own or orthodox Catholicism.[9]

Belloc remained a dominant influence on Lunn over the following twenty years. When Belloc became embroiled in his notorious controversy with H. G. Wells over the latter's *Outline of History*, Lunn recalled that 'all my sympathies were with Belloc, though I was still an agnostic'. 'Even then I knew that Wells, with his "Existence impresses me as a perpetual dawn", had far less claim to be considered a prophet than Belloc, who replied that Wells's "dawn" was nothing more than the 'shoddy remnant of the Christian hope'.[10] Belloc's bellicosity was so persuasive that Lunn was to admit that the 'great blasts' which Belloc 'blew on his Catholic trumpet had an erosive influence on the walls of my Protestant Jericho'.[11]

When Lunn became a Catholic he always emphasized the role of reason as the sound basis of Catholicism but there was from the beginning another fundamental factor in his initial attraction to the Faith. Paradoxically this was a primeval urge, a reason beyond reason. As a young agnostic first reading Belloc's *The Path to Rome* he had been particularly struck by a passage in which the author described how Catholicism transcends differences of race, nation and class so that 'once all we Europeans understood each other'. Lunn remembered that 'this particular passage struck a responsive chord'.

> Belloc had expressed something which I too had felt. In the Catholic valleys of the Alps I felt at home. The Angelus bell, and the little mountain shrines, and the rude statue of some local saint on a mountain church, spoke to me in a language which was not mine, but which in some dim fashion I felt had once been mine ... I was one of many who first discovered in Belloc's writings that sense of a European unity created by the Faith and destroyed by schism.[12]

Another of the many was, of course, G. K. Chesterton who had made the same discovery in Belloc over a decade earlier. In 1911 Chesterton penned perhaps his best poem, 'Lepanto', in honour of John of Austria who had defeated a Moslem fleet threatening a Europe already being destroyed by schism:

> The North is full of tangled things and texts and aching eyes
> And dead is all the innocence of anger and surprise,
> And Christian killeth Christian in a narrow dusty room,
> And Christian dreadeth Christ that hath a newer face of doom,
> And Christian hateth Mary that God kissed in Galilee,
> But Don John of Austria is riding to the sea.

Not surprisingly, this ballad in praise of the Europe of the Faith won an enthusiastic admirer in Belloc. In his essay *On the Place of Gilbert Keith Chesterton in*

English Letters, he wrote: 'The whole of that poem 'Lepanto' is not only the summit of Chesterton's achievement in verse but the summit of high rhetorical verse in all our generation.'[13]

Belloc's championing of 'Lepanto' was remembered by the poet Alfred Noyes:

> Belloc asked me if I did not think it one of the finest of contemporary poems, and before I could express my cordial agreement, he added, 'Oh, but of course you wouldn't. All poets are jealous.' My only possible reply was, 'In that case I'm not a poet,' after which he became quite charming and conciliatory ...[14]

If Belloc and Chesterton were vocal champions of the Church Militant in matters of religion, they were both becoming increasingly militant in matters of politics. In the summer of 1911 Belloc had launched the first number of the *Eye Witness*, a hard-hitting radical weekly. His partner in this enterprise was Cecil Chesterton, Gilbert's brother. The following June, the magazine was renamed the *New Witness* and Cecil Chesterton took over from Belloc as editor. In October 1912 Belloc published *The Servile State*, a definitive critique of modern industrial society, its evils and its origins. Previously Belloc and Cecil Chesterton had collaborated on a book entitled *The Party System*, which they had written 'to support the tendency ... to expose and ridicule as it deserves, to destroy and supplant the system under which Parliament, the governing institution of this country, has been rendered null'.[15]

The extent to which the campaigning of his brother and Belloc was influencing G. K. Chesterton can be gauged from the articles he wrote for the *Daily News* at this time. In particular, his essay entitled 'The Voter and the Two Voices' reflected the central tenet of *The Party System* very closely:

> The real danger of the two parties is that they unduly limit the outlook of the ordinary citizen. They make him barren instead of creative, because he is never allowed to do anything except prefer one existing policy to another. We have not got real Democracy when the decision depends upon the people. We shall have real Democracy when the problem depends upon the people. The ordinary man will decide not only how he will vote, but what he is going to vote about.[16]

Chesterton concluded the article with a scenario which might have proved the inspiration for a typically Chestertonian novel but instead came to fruition many years later in the nightmare visions of Huxley and Orwell:

The democracy has a right to answer questions, but it has no right to ask them. It is still the political aristocracy that asks the questions. And we shall not be unreasonably cynical if we suppose that the political aristocracy will always be rather careful what questions it asks ... the powerful class will choose two courses of action, both of them safe for itself, and then give the democracy the gratification of taking one course or the other.[17]

Belloc's disillusionment with the party system was the result of first-hand experience. In his days as President of the Oxford Union, almost twenty years earlier, he had caused controversy with his outspoken attacks on the House of Lords. These attacks continued during the period when Ronald Knox was President of the Union. One recalls Knox's image of Belloc 'waggling a cigar between his fingers as he demolished the House of Lords'.[18] However, his disillusionment with the party system really began after he had taken the battle not to the Lords but to the Commons.

In 1906 Belloc stood for the Liberals at South Salford in the General Election. It was a marginal constituency which ensured that the campaign would be highly competitive and hard-fought. Belloc's Conservative opponents were quick to capitalize on their adversary's religion and nationality and adopted the campaign slogan: 'Don't vote for a Frenchman and a Catholic.' Belloc responded in characteristic fashion. At his first public meeting he rose and addressed the packed audience:

> Gentlemen, I am a Catholic. As far as possible, I go to Mass every day. This [taking a rosary out of his pocket] is a rosary. As far as possible, I kneel down and tell these beads every day. If you reject me on account of my religion, I shall thank God that He has spared me the indignity of being your representative.[19]

There was a hush of astonishment, followed by a thunderclap of applause. He was elected.

Such candour did not fit comfortably in the relative strait-jacket imposed upon backbenchers in the House of Commons. Belloc became increasingly frustrated and wrote later that 'No private member has any power whatsoever. Legislation is arranged between important financial interests and the front benches.'[20] On 19 February 1908, convinced of corruption in the highest echelons of power, he moved in the House of Commons 'that the secret party funds be publicly audited'.[21] This and other maverick actions left him increasingly isolated and his Commons career came to an abrupt end with the dissolution of Parliament at the end of 1909.

Loosed from party political constraints Belloc began to formulate an alternative to capitalism and socialism. During his parliamentary days he had written an article entitled simply 'The Alternative' in which he had argued that a society built on the ownership of widely distributed private property would offer a solution to the ills of capitalism preferable to the nationalization proposed by the socialists:

> The whole contention of the future in Europe lies between these two theories. On the one hand you have the Socialist theory, the one remedy and the only remedy seriously discussed in the industrial societies which have ultimately grown out of the religious schism of the sixteenth century ... On the other hand, you have the Catholic societies whose ultimate appetite is for a state of highly divided property, working in a complex and probably, at last, in a co-operative manner ...[22]

It was no mere coincidence that Belloc had linked the political question with the religious. He saw religion and politics as inextricably linked. Modern industrial capitalism had developed, he believed, out of the breaking up and pillaging of Catholic civilization during the Reformation. In fact, Belloc's 'alternative' was essentially only a reiteration of the official social teaching of the Church as laid down by Pope Leo XIII in his encyclical, *Rerum Novarum*. This important papal document, published in 1891, laid the foundations of Catholic social teaching for the following century. Its core thesis, that individual human dignity must take precedence over *laissez faire* market principles and that the ownership of private property was desirable and should be enjoyed by as many of the population as possible, was upheld in subsequent encyclicals by Pope Pius XI in 1931 and Pope John Paul II in 1991.

Belloc was aware of the Pope's teaching and it formed the starting point for his own writing on the subject. In 1908 he had written *An Examination of Socialism* for the Catholic Truth Society and the following year he published *The Church and Socialism*.

One of Belloc's earliest converts to this 'alternative' was Cecil Chesterton. As late as 1908 Cecil considered himself a socialist and on 18 November of that year he had shared a platform at a public debate at the Surrey Masonic Hall in Camberwell with Belloc, his brother and Bernard Shaw. G. K. Chesterton and Hilaire Belloc had argued against socialism while Shaw and Cecil Chesterton had argued for it. Soon Cecil defected to become Belloc's most vocal advocate.

In 1911 Belloc had taken part in a public debate with Ramsay MacDonald, the transcript of which was published the same year as *Socialism and the Servile State*. From this, Belloc distilled the line of argument which came together the following year as *The Servile State*. This book, along with his launching of the *Eye Witness* with Cecil Chesterton, became the focal point for many who were seeking alternatives to socialism. In particular, Belloc's brand of politics found a ready-made disciple in the form of a young and versatile craftsman living in the village of Ditchling in Sussex.

Eric Gill had moved to Ditchling in 1907 in order to make a clean break from an extra-marital affair and to leave behind the Fabianism and Nietzscheanism with which he was becoming disillusioned. In his own words, 'It was an escape.'[23]

It was also a beginning. Gill was seeking a simplified life where he could practise his craft away from the industrialism of the cities. With the new way of life came a new way of seeing things. Gill turned away from Nietzsche and Wells, both of whom had been major influences in his days as a Fabian socialist, and towards Chesterton and Belloc who seemed to be offering an alternative to the mechanized madness and materialism he had rejected. According to Cecil Gill, Eric's brother, in his unpublished *Autobiography*, Belloc 'contributed much to Eric's social formation with his *Servile State*'.[24]

Gill's interest in Belloc's politics led him to question Belloc's religion. Were politics and religion inextricably linked as Belloc believed? If so, and if Belloc's politics were correct, did this imply that his religion, too, was correct? Gill set about the problem with the same patient method and commitment which he exhibited in his stone carving:

> Religion was the first necessity, and that meant the rule of God. If then there be a God, the whole world must be ruled in his name. If there be a religion it must be a world religion, a catholicism. In so far as my religion were true it must be catholic. In so far as the Catholic religion were catholic it must be true! The Catholic Church professed to rule the whole world in the name of God – so far as I could see or imagine, it was the only institution that professed to do so ... Of course if the Catholic Church were simply an arrogant upstart institution, with no roots and no history and, more important to the innocent person, no fruits by which you might know her – no good fruits, nourishing and delectable – then there would obviously be no point in considering her. But this was clearly not so; there was fruit in plenty, and, in my mind very good fruit, even though they seemed to be fruits of the past.[25]

Further religious ruminations followed, displaying with complete clarity the enormous influence of Belloc's *The Servile State* on Gill's final approach to the Church:

> I could not but believe that the way of life and work represented by the remains of medieval Europe was mainly a product of the influence of the Catholic Church, and I could not but believe that that way of life and work was not only Christian but normal and human. The way of life and work in the world of modern Europe was obviously neither human nor normal nor Christian, therefore it could not be said that modern Europe was a product either of Christianity or catholicism. Moreover the modern way had only come into existence subsequently to the decay or defeat of the power of the church to influence men's minds, and the modern way flourished in inverse proportion to the degree of catholic influence. The typically capitalist and industrialised countries were the typically non-catholic ones.[26]

Gill later came to realize that he had 'exaggerated the conscious opposition of catholics to the modern world', lamenting that 'most of them are as enthusiastic about the triumphs of industrialism and the British Empire and money as anyone else'.[27]

It is clear that Chesterton was also an influence on Gill's progress towards Christianity. At the beginning of 1912 he went to Caxton Hall in London to listen to a discussion between Chesterton and Bishop Gore on Christian Social Obligations. Later in the year when he set himself a stern course of reading, Chesterton's *Orthodoxy* was top of the list. Many years later, when Gill wrote his *Autobiography*, *Orthodoxy* was the only book of all those he had read at the time which still stuck in his mind. He recalled how much he had disliked Chesterton during his Fabian days and how arguing with Chesterton 'seemed like beating the air': 'I was quite out of tune with him. But as the years passed I got past that and came to revere and love him, as a writer and as a holy man, beyond all his contemporaries.'[28]

The other major influences during Gill's final approach to conversion were the Meynells – Alice, Wilfrid and Everard – with whom he had become acquainted through his work on the altar tomb for the poet, Francis Thompson.

Gill and his wife were received into the Church on 22 February 1913, his thirty-first birthday. Curiously, the Anglican monks at Caldey Island who owned the monastery at Capel-y-ffin where Gill and his family were to set up home in 1924, submitted to Rome on the very same day. Gill's biographer,

Robert Speaight, who himself followed Gill into the Church many years later, wrote of the way the Church authorities were quick to utilize their new recruit: 'Very soon Eric was invited to submit designs for the Stations of the Cross in Westminster Cathedral. On August 16 he met the architect to the cathedral, John Marshall, and immediately set to work on preliminary drawings.'[29]

Following his religious conversion he set about organizing a major conversion in the social structure of the small community of craftsmen who had gathered at Ditchling under his guidance. This was the beginning of the second phase of the Ditchling community described by Gill in a kind of manifesto:

> In 1913 a Catholic family bought a house and two acres of land at the south end of Ditchling Common ... Their object was to own home and land and to produce for their own consumption such food as could be produced at home, e.g. milk, butter, pigs, poultry and eggs, and to make such things as could be made at home, e.g. bread, clothes, etc.[30]

Gill hoped and believed that such a way of life would offer a practical alternative to capitalist industrialism which, he observed, 'makes good mechanics, good machine-minders, but men and women who in every other respect are morons, cretins'.[31]

This was another intricate interweaving of the religious and the political. In raising the banner of self-sufficiency as an alternative to the servile state, Gill was establishing a neo-monastic model for the laity. Ridiculed by some, idolized and idealized by others, the Ditchling community developed into an alternative society in microcosm.

One notable practitioner of this alternative lifestyle who had a profound influence on Gill and the community at Ditchling was the indomitable figure of Father Vincent McNabb. A Dominican who was parish priest of Holy Cross, Leicester, Father McNabb was drawn to Belloc's banner in 1911 and made his first contribution to the *Eye Witness* in August of that year. Like Belloc, he was imbued with the social principles of the Church as expounded in *Rerum Novarum* but, unlike Belloc, he took the Pope's teaching to a fundamentalist extreme, proclaiming that all industrialism was morally evil. A devout advocate of the simple life, he walked everywhere whenever possible, spurning modern forms of transport. He wore homespun robes and even refused to use a typewriter on the grounds that it was machinery. Although the monk went beyond the more pragmatic approach of Belloc and the Chesterton brothers he earned their respect and friendship through the almost fanatical way he practised what he preached.

A larger than life character, Father McNabb was considered by Chesterton the holiest man he knew who was 'walking on a crystal floor over my head',[32] and who was 'spiritually the greatest man in England at the present time'.[33] In an introduction to Father McNabb's *Francis Thompson and Other Essays* Chesterton wrote the following tribute: 'he is one of the few great men I have met in my life ... he is great in many ways – mentally and morally and mystically and practically ... nobody who ever met or saw or heard of Father McNabb has ever forgotten him.'[34]

But Father McNabb also owed a debt to Chesterton. Like Gill and so many others he had been greatly affected by Chesterton's *Orthodoxy*, so much so that one of Father McNabb's students when he was Prior of Hawkesyard bemoaned the fact that 'he tended to ruin his own graceful and accomplished style of speaking and writing, by imitating the paradoxes of Chesterton'.[35]

Gill had first met Father McNabb in June 1914 at the home of André Raffalovich, the convert acquaintance of Oscar Wilde, who was living in Edinburgh, not far from the church where John Gray, fellow convert and fellow acquaintance of Wilde, was parish priest. The meeting was momentous, Gill falling immediately under McNabb's influence.

'Father Vincent McNabb,' Gill wrote in his *Autobiography*, 'was ... a philosopher, a theologian and a man of heroic virtue, a man, moreover, so very much our teacher and leader in our views on social reform and industrial-capitalism, on life and work, on poverty and holiness, that it was natural that we should consult with him on the matters which were concerning us.'[36]

Meanwhile Father McNabb saw in Gill and the Ditchling community great possibilities for the regeneration of Catholic life in England. He looked upon Ditchling as the blueprint for the founding of other self-sufficient Catholic communities all over the country. 'You ask "Is Ditchling practicable?",' he once wrote. 'In the Irish fashion I answer by a further question "Is anything else practicable?"'[37]

With Gill and Ditchling as his inspiration Father McNabb launched a one-man crusade to persuade people to return to the land. Bernard Wall, editor of *The Colosseum*, gave a vivid description of how McNabb preached religion and politics to crowds in Hyde Park, informing them that 'their life was mad, they must set themselves free, leave London and return to nature'. Should any inquisitive heckler desire to know how they were expected to do this, he merely replied, 'On foot'. Wall also recalled how Father McNabb had personally revived the ancient practice of kissing the foot of a host who entertained him: 'I remember the blush on Ronnie Knox's face when the black and white figure threw himself onto the floor at his feet after lunch.'[38]

In spite of such eccentric behaviour, or perhaps because of it, Wall claimed that McNabb's holiness would have been recognized from China to Peru. The same perplexing and paradoxical quality was recognized by Christopher Derrick when he descibed Father McNabb as 'that marvellous saint and lunatic'.[39] Whether or not McNabb would have accepted this back-handed compliment he would doubtless have gained solace from the knowledge that the same description is often applied to St Francis of Assisi. Indeed, Father McNabb was like St Francis in so far as he acted as a beacon bringing others to Christianity. These included Christopher Derrick's own father, Thomas Derrick, who was received into the Church by Father McNabb in 1922.

Like Gill, Thomas Derrick took the political path to Rome, via the Fabians and the early influence of H. G. Wells. Coming from a Quaker background he arrived in London as an idealistic art student and Fabian socialist. He attended public debates between various supporters of Wells, Shaw, Chesterton and Belloc. 'To his fury,' Christopher Derrick recalls, 'he found himself increasingly convinced that Belloc and Chesterton were talking more sense. He became a Catholic under Chesterton's personal influence.'[40]

A parallel path was followed by Gill's friend Hilary Pepler, another key figure in the Ditchling community. Pepler, a Quaker, had visited Father McNabb at Hawkesyard Priory in March 1917 and found himself profoundly moved by the Dominican way of life. He was received into the Church the same year. His son, Conrad, became a Dominican monk and showed in his short study of Dorothy Day, herself a convert, how she and her colleague Peter Maurin had been deeply influenced by Father McNabb in their founding of the Catholic Worker Movement in the United States.[41]

One other notable political convert should be mentioned. During 1912 Cecil Chesterton exposed insider trading in Marconi shares in the pages of the *New Witness*, having recently taken over the editorship of the magazine from Hilaire Belloc. The affair, which became known as the Marconi Scandal, took on a potentially explosive nature because of the involvement of senior government officials including Lloyd George, who was Chancellor of the Exchequer, and Rufus Isaacs, the Attorney General. At the centre of the allegations was Godfrey Isaacs, the managing director of the Marconi Company and brother of the Attorney General, who responded by suing Cecil for criminal libel. In the middle of the trial, which commenced at the Central Criminal Court on 27 May 1913, Cecil sought out the same Father Bowden who had received Maurice Baring into the Church four years earlier. On 7 June he was received himself at Corpus Christi, Maiden Lane.

There was a rather bizarre postscript to this episode that bears a remarkable similarity to the earlier conversions of Wilde and the Marquess of Queensberry.

Some years later, Godfrey Isaacs, who eventually won the libel case, was also received into the Catholic Church. Chesterton referred to this strange twist of the tale in his *Autobiography*:

> many years after my brother received the Last Sacraments and died in a hospital in France, his old enemy, Godfrey Isaacs, died very shortly after being converted to the same universal Catholic Church. No one would have rejoiced more than my brother; or with less bitterness or with more simplicity. It is the only reconciliation; and it can reconcile anybody. *Requiescant in pace*.[42]

The blend of religion and politics championed by Belloc, by both the Chesterton brothers, and by Father McNabb, Eric Gill and an increasing number of others, eventually became known as distributism. In the following decade the Distributist League was formed and, initially at least, it enjoyed considerable success. In his book *The Outline of Sanity* Chesterton represented the moderate voice of the new movement calling for a tax system and other incentives which would favour small businesses instead of Big Business. Although he also favoured a general return to a simpler and more natural way of life, he avoided the fundamentalist extremes of either Gill or McNabb.

Belloc, meanwhile, continued to fire distributist broadsides in the direction of capitalism and socialism alike. In 1920 he wrote *The Catholic Church and the Principle of Private Property*, which was followed in 1922 by *Catholic Social Reform versus Socialism*. By the time he wrote *An Essay on the Restoration of Property* in 1936 the Distributist League was already in decline, squeezed out of existence by the demagogic dead-ends of fascism and communism.

Perhaps the Distributist League's finest hour came in late October 1927 when Belloc chaired a public debate between Chesterton and Shaw at the Kingsway Hall in London. Organized by the League, the debate was broadcast live by the fledgling BBC. Shaw and Chesterton discussed the theme 'Do We Agree?', and, needless to say, they didn't. Shaw still argued for socialism, Chesterton for distributism. There was something stale about the deadlock until Belloc stole the show with his summing up:

> In a very few years from now this debate will be antiquated. I will now recite you a poem:

Our civilisation
Is built upon coal.
Let us chaunt in rotation
Our civilisation
That lump of damnation
Without any soul,
Our civilisation
Is built upon coal.

In a very few years
It will float upon oil.
Then give three hearty cheers,
In a very few years
We shall mop up our tears
And have done with our toil.
In a very few years
It will float upon oil.

In I do not know how many years – five, ten, twenty – this debate will
be as antiquated as crinolines are ... The industrial civilisation, which,
thank God, oppresses only the small part of the world in which we are
most inextricably bound up, will break down and therefore end its
monstrous wickedness ... Or it will break down and lead to nothing
but a desert. Or it will lead the mass of men to become contented
slaves, with a few rich men controlling them. Take your choice.[43]

It was this prophetic quality in Belloc that elicited the admiration and respect of
George Orwell. 'Many earlier writers have foreseen the emergence of a new kind
of society,' Orwell wrote:

neither capitalist nor Socialist, and probably based upon Slavery ... A
good example is Hilaire Belloc's book, *The Servile State* ... it does fore-
tell with remarkable insight the kind of things that have been happening from about 1930 onwards. Chesterton, in a less methodical way,
predicted the disappearance of democracy and private property, and
the rise of a slave society which might be called either capitalist or
Communist.[44]

Orwell, of course, would eventually write a best-selling novel about a slave society which could be either capitalist or communist. Yet his own views always remained something of a mystery. Even during the thirties when he was temporarily influenced by the Trotskyists he still maintained an enigmatic independence, declaring to a friend that 'what England needed was to follow the kind of policies in Chesterton's *G. K.'s Weekly*'.[45]

Whether or not Orwell was right, England never wanted what Chesterton and Belloc believed it needed.

NOTES

1. *Hearth and Home*, 17 October 1912.
2. James Brabazon, *Dorothy L. Sayers: A Biography*, London, 1981, p. 51.
3. *New Age*, 15 February 1908.
4. Owen Barfield, interview with the author, Forest Row, 31 December 1996.
5. Arnold Lunn, *Come What May: An Autobiography*, p. 75.
6. Arnold Lunn, *Now I See*, London, 1956, p. 51.
7. Arnold Lunn, *And Yet So New*, London, 1958, p. 60.
8. ibid., p. 61.
9. ibid., pp. 61–2.
10. ibid., p. 68.
11. ibid., p. 68.
12. ibid., pp. 72–3.
13. Hilaire Belloc, *On the Place of Gilbert Keith Chesterton in English Letters*, London, 1940, p. 78.
14. Alfred Noyes, *Two Worlds for Memory*, London, 1953, p. 224.
15. Michael Ffinch, *G. K. Chesterton: A Biography*, London, 1988, p. 193.
16. *Daily News*, 16 July 1910.
17. ibid.
18. Ronald Knox, *A Spiritual Aeneid*, p. 52.
19. Robert Speaight, *The Life of Hilaire Belloc*, London, 1957, p. 204.
20. Hilaire Belloc, *Audit the Party Funds*, Aylesford Press, Upton, Wirral, Cheshire, 1992, p. 13.
21. ibid., p. 13.
22. Hilaire Belloc, *The Alternative*, London, undated pamphlet, pp. 14–15.
23. Eric Gill, *Autobiography*, London, 1940, p. 272.
24. Cecil Gill, *Autobiography*, unpublished, p. 343.
25. Eric Gill, *Autobiography*, pp. 168–9.
26. ibid., p. 169.
27. ibid., p. 169.
28. ibid., p. 190.
29. Robert Speaight, *The Life of Eric Gill*, London, 1966, p. 70.
30. Fiona MacCarthy, *Eric Gill*, London, 1992, p. 116.
31. A. N. Wilson, *Hilaire Belloc*, London, 1986, p. 293.
32. Maisie Ward, *Return to Chesterton*, London, 1952, p. 206.
33. Ferdinand Valentine, OP, *Father Vincent McNabb*, London, 1955, p. 184.
34. ibid., p. 200.
35. ibid., p. 129.
36. Eric Gill, *Autobiography*, p. 207.
37. Fiona MacCarthy, *Eric Gill*, p. 134.
38. ibid., p. 142.
39. Michael H. Macdonald and Andrew A. Tadie (eds.), *The Riddle of Joy*, London, 1989, p. 4.
40. Christopher Derrick, interview with the author, September 1996.

41. Conrad Pepler, OP, *Dorothy Day and the Catholic Worker Movement*, London, 1986, p. 7.
42. G. K. Chesterton, *Autobiography*, p. 208.
43. 'Do We Agree?', London, 1928, pp. 45–7.
44. Ian Boyd, *The Novels of G. K. Chesterton*, London, 1975, pp. 204–5.
45. Bernard Crick, *George Orwell: A Life*, London, 1992, p. 270.

CHAPTER NINE

KNOX AND BENSON

In the summer of 1909 Ronald Knox had criticized his friend Maurice Hugessen, later to die tragically at the Somme shortly after his reception into the Catholic Church, for his use of the rosary. By the following summer Knox was using the rosary himself. When he went to Mirfield he was told that he was the first person to say his beads in their chapel since Hugh Benson had left them. The link with Benson was portentous in many respects because their paths, already remarkably similar, would continue to run parallel in the following years.

Knox's change of attitude concerning the role of the Blessed Virgin was triggered by a sermon preached at St James's in Plymouth by Maurice Child. Roused to speculation, Knox began to question Catholic doctrines such as the Immaculate Conception and the Assumption in a more positive light. This in turn led the young ritualist closer to Rome. On the eve of his ordination to the Anglican diaconate in the Cathedral at Oxford in 1911, he wrote of his reservations to a friend: 'I can't feel that the Church of England is an ultimate solution: in 50 years or a hundred I believe we Romanizers will either have got the Church or been turned out of it.'[1]

Knox had certainly become a 'Romanizer' by this time and in a sermon preached the following year he bemoaned the separation of the Anglican church from Rome, its 'mother':

> Sorrowing she calls us like that Mother of old, who sought her Son and could not find him, as he sat refuting the doctors in the Temple ... England will once again become the dowry of Mary, and the Church of England will once again be builded on the rock she was hewn from, and find a place, although it be a place of penitence and tears, in the eternal purposes of God.[2]

Knox spent the greater part of the long vacation in 1912 at the monastery on Caldey Island following, as far as a visitor could, the monastic rule. This was his fifth visit to the Anglican monks on Caldey with whom he felt a great affinity. The following year it would not be possible to return, the monks having submitted to Rome in the interim. Meanwhile Knox, who had been ordained to the Anglican priesthood on 24 September 1912 at St Giles's Church in Reading, was clearly desirous that the Church of England as a whole should follow the monks' example. In August 1913, at St James's in Plymouth, he had preached plaintively of the schism that separated Canterbury from Rome:

> It is not for us, the glamour of the Seven Hills, and the consciousness of membership, living and actual, in the Church of the Ages ... And yet, even now, we are not left without hope ... Mary ... has not forgotten her children just because they have run away from their schoolmaster, and unlearnt their lessons, and are trying to find their way home again, humbled and terrified in the darkness.[3]

This feeling of alienation was expressed in a short story Knox wrote at the time. Like his earlier effort at fiction it was written in the style of R. H. Benson and recounts a young man's visit to a ruined church on the Côte d'Azur which is haunted by the ghosts of dead peasants who were attending Mass there when an earthquake swept them away. Trapped in the church, alone in the darkness, the young man struggles with his sense of isolation: 'In an agony of loneliness he stretched out his arms as if to fling them round some warm protecting body, and when they closed upon air he shook with sobbing. His whole body shook with the unquenchable thirst for human contact.'[4]

Knox was influenced by Benson in more than merely his literary style. Like Benson, he sought the objectivity of doctrinal orthodoxy as opposed to the subjective speculations of Modernist theology; and, like Benson, he was more than ready to involve himself in controversy to further the cause of the one against the other. By 1911 his close association with Anglican theologians of different schools had convinced him that the main danger to the Church of England arose not from Protestantism but from Modernism. He perceived that the new generation of Anglican theologians were drifting into a fog of scepticism. Knox knew many of these personally, liked them and revelled in their idiosyncrasies. Drawing on his knowledge of their follies and foibles he published a celebrated lampoon in *The Oxford Magazine* in Michaelmas Term 1912. *Absolute and Abitofhell* was a poem in the manner of Dryden which summarized the weakness of his Anglican contemporaries with superlative wit:

> When suave politeness, temp'ring bigot Zeal,
> Corrected *I believe* to *One does feel* ...

It was an immediate success. *The Oxford Magazine* sold out and was reprinted. Knox's victims greeted the poem good-naturedly. Dr William Temple, who became Archbishop of Canterbury thirty years later, and who was caricatured in the poem under the name of 'Og', sent Knox a postcard inscribed, 'Ta for puff, Og.'[5]

The lighthearted literary tone of *Absolute and Abitofhell* gave way to more serious controversial debate with Knox's next book, *Some Loose Stones*, written in reply to a volume of Modernist speculations entitled *Foundations*. Published in 1913, this was Knox's first serious work and it sold remarkably well for a book of its kind, some four thousand copies. It sought systematically to dissect and refute the inconsistencies of the authors of *Foundations*, asserting that 'the speculations of critics are *hypotheses*, based on *a posteriori* evidence, and, as such, in their very nature uncertain'.[6] *Some Loose Stones* was received everywhere with respect and in many quarters with enthusiasm. It established Knox's reputation as an academic theologian and champion of orthodoxy whose career, it was generally believed, would influence the future of the Church of England.

R. H. Benson had said substantially the same thing as Knox in an essay on the future of Catholicism published three years earlier:

> The modern thinkers take their rise, practically, from the religious upheaval of the sixteenth century ... little by little there came into existence the view that 'true religion' was that system of belief which each individual thought out for himself; and, since these individuals were not found to agree together, 'Truth' finally became more and more subjective; until there was established the most characteristically modern form of thought – namely that Truth was not absolute at all, and that what was true and imperative for one was not true and imperative for another.[7]

To illustrate his belief in the ultimate insanity of subjectivism Benson quoted Chesterton that 'the man who believes in himself most consistently, to the exclusion of cold facts, must be sought in a lunatic asylum'.[8]

For Benson this subjectivism was an anarchy of antitheses, a *reductio ad absurdum* to which the objective authority of the Church was the only solution: 'To the Catholic it appears ... certain that the crumbling of all systematic authority down to that of the individual ... is the death sentence of every attempt to find religious Truth outside that infallible authority to whose charge, he believes, truth has been committed.'[9] In the same article, in typically triumphalist style, Benson listed a string of eminent intellectual converts:

> When men in France like Brunetière, Coppée, Huysmans, Rette, and Paul Bourget, come forward from agnosticism or infidelity; when Pasteur, perhaps the most widely known scientist of his day, declares that his researches have left him with the faith of the Breton peasant ... when, in Great Britain, an Irish Protestant professor of biology, a professor of Greek at Glasgow, and perhaps the greatest judge on the bench, in the very height of maturity and of their reputation, deliberately make their submission to Rome ... surely it is a very strange moment at which to assume that the religion of the future is to be some kind of ethical Pantheism![10]

Such triumphalism, always an integral part of Benson's writing, made him unpopular in some circles. Even among Catholics his energetic proselytizing and uncompromising zeal led to criticism. The Catholic publisher and biographer Maisie Ward spoke for many when she criticized this aspect of Benson's work: 'Most "cradle Catholics" and many converts dislike those jibes at Anglicans ... Moreover, along with the jibes at Anglicanism were attacks upon Catholic complacency.'[11]

Examples of both these alleged faults could be found in Benson's *Confessions of a Convert*, published in 1913. In the preface to the first edition, Benson compared his own view of conversion with that of Cardinal Newman before him:

> Cardinal Newman compares, somewhere, the sensations of a convert from Anglicanism to those of a man in a fairy story, who, after wandering all night in a city of enchantment, turns after sunrise to look back upon it, and finds to his astonishment that the buildings are no longer there; they have gone up like wraiths and mists under the light of the risen day.
>
> So the present writer has found. He no longer, as in the first months of his conversion, is capable of comparing the two systems of belief together, since that which he has left appears to him no longer a coherent system at all.[12]

In similar vein, towards the end of the book, Benson asserted 'that to return from the Catholic Church to the Anglican would be the exchange of certitude for doubt, of faith for agnosticism, of substance for shadow, of brilliant light for sombre gloom, of historical, worldwide fact for unhistorical, provincial theory'. This is strong language but surely not a jibe. At worst it displays a tactless candour. At best it is a forceful and sincere statement of the facts of his position. 'I do not know how to express myself more mildly than that,' Benson continued, 'though even this, no doubt, will appear a monstrous extravagance, at the least, to the sincere and whole-hearted members of the Anglican communion.'[13]

Benson certainly suffered from the 'excess of zeal' so often attributed to Catholic converts, a zeal which often expresses itself with indiscretion and impetuosity, and this was at the root of the criticisms levelled against him. One is tempted to reiterate Knox's lines in Benson's defence, 'When suave politeness, temp'ring bigot Zeal, Corrected *I believe* to *One does feel ...*'

However, if Benson irritated many people he delighted many others. His books were best-sellers and his public preaching attracted sell-out crowds. Brian Masters, author of a biographical study of the three Benson brothers, described him as 'a preacher with fire in his voice': 'Whenever Monsignor Hugh Benson was due to preach one could be sure the hall, no matter how big, would be sold out months in advance ... Hugh gave a *performance* in the pulpit as certainly as Sarah Bernhardt gave on stage.'[14]

Not everyone was impressed. The novelist Robert Hichens was 'utterly amazed' by the sight of Benson preaching but found his performance unconvincing. Hichens's description of Benson's style of oratory illustrates that Benson was as capable of polarizing opinion from the pulpit as he was in the pages of his books:

> In the pulpit he was startlingly sensational. His changes of voice were so abrupt as to be almost alarming. But even more surprising were his movements of body. Sometimes he would suddenly lower his voice and simultaneously shrink down in the pulpit until only his head and face were visible to the congregation. Then he would raise his voice almost to a shriek and, like a figure in a Punch and Judy show, dart up diagonally and lean over the pulpit edge until one almost feared that he would tumble out of it and land sprawling among his fascinated, yet apprehensive hearers below. I have in my time heard a good many preachers ... but Father Benson surpassed them all in exaggerated emotionalism of manner and voice ... he almost stupefied me on that occasion.[15]

Again, these criticisms may not be wholly justified. His stutter, so evident and prominent in his everyday speech, disappeared completely when he preached in public, suggesting an unaffected forgetfulness rather than a coldly calculated delivery. Perhaps his exaggerated movements in the pulpit were not so much the product of affectation as the result of genuine emotion. E. F. Benson, who was entirely out of sympathy with the contents of his brother's sermons and irritated by his monumental certainty, recognized none the less that they were delivered in a 'flawless, flame-like' manner with 'tumultuous eloquence'.[16]

At Easter 1913 Benson preached a series of sermons in Rome which were later published as *The Paradoxes of Catholicism*. In February 1914 he spoke at Cathedral Hall, Westminster on the modern English novel, in June he was at Caxton Hall preaching on modern miracles and the following month he spoke to the Catholic Stage Society on the theme of the Church and the stage. The last of these was particularly close to his heart because Benson had long been a keen theatre-goer. He was particularly fascinated by Chesterton's *Magic*, which was being staged on both sides of the Atlantic in 1914, and during a visit to America he was regularly behind the scenes at rehearsals of the play.

Benson appeared to be at the very height of his power and influence. None could have foreseen that, before the year ended, his life also would come to an abrupt and unexpected end at the premature age of forty-three. The cause of death was pneumonia.

He received the last sacraments on Saturday, 17 October and made his profession of faith in a strong voice. Viaticum was given to him on the following morning and such was his composure that he made the responses himself and even corrected the priest when he made a slip in the prayer *Misereatur*. His strength over the weekend was deceptive and the following day, feeling that he was dying, he asked the priest whether his brother was near at hand. 'Yes,' he was told, 'he is in the house.' 'Thank God,' he answered.

While waiting for his brother's arrival at his bedside he made the responses as the priest read the prayers for the dying. His final moments are best described in the words of his brother, A. C. Benson:

When I entered Hugh fixed his eyes on me with a strange smile, with something triumphant in it, and said in a clear natural voice, 'Arthur, this is the end!' I knelt down near the bed. He looked at me, and I knew in a way that we understood each other well, that he wanted no word or demonstration, but was just glad that I was with him. The prayers began again. Hugh crossed himself faintly once or twice, made a response or two ... Suddenly he said to the nurse: 'Nurse, is it any good my resisting death – making an effort?' The nurse said: 'No, Monsignor; just be as quiet as you can.' He closed his eyes at this, and his breath came quicker ... Once or twice he drew up his hands as though trying to draw breath, and sighed a little; but there was no struggle or apparent pain. He spoke once more and said: 'Jesus, Mary, and Joseph, I give you my heart and my soul.' The nurse had her hand upon his pulse, and presently laid his hand down, saying: 'It is all over.' He looked very pale and boyish then, with wide open eyes and parted lips. I kissed his hand which was warm and firm, and went out with Canon Sharrock, who said to me: 'It was wonderful! I have seen many people die, but no one ever so easily and quickly!'[17]

There was a strange sequel to Benson's death reminiscent of one of his novels. On the morning of his death, Dr Mostyn, the Bishop of Menevia, who was at Caldey Island on retreat, said to a fellow guest: 'I had an extraordinary dream last night: or rather, early this morning. I dreamed that Benson was dead, and that he had died suddenly. I remember thinking: "What a good thing that he had just been making his retreat here!"' The other guest, who unlike the Bishop knew of Benson's illness, was startled. On the following day, while making the crossing from Caldey to Tenby, the Bishop repeated his experience to his two fellow passengers. Reaching the mainland he bought a newspaper and was astonished to read that Benson had died on the very morning he had experienced the dream. Perhaps it was merely coincidental but Benson would have thought otherwise. It is strange too that the Bishop was sleeping in the very bed in which Benson had slept during his retreat at Caldey, and perhaps portentous that Benson and the Bishop were linked spiritually and sacramentally, the latter having confirmed the former many years earlier.

Assuming that the newspaper the Bishop bought on his arrival at Tenby on Tuesday, 20 October was *The Times*, he would have read the following tribute:

> Well known as a preacher, he had a yet larger following as a novelist. His first book, *The Light Invisible* was recognised at once by good judges as remarkable for a peculiar charm of mind and manner ... Considering the number of novels that he wrote, the wonder is that they should be as good as they are ... Undoubtedly he had great gifts ...

A little over a week later, on 31 October 1914, Shane Leslie, most notable of the many 'Bensonian' converts, wrote a tribute in the *Tablet*: 'We cannot imagine he was not glad and interested at the prospect of death, though he may have suffered a slight regret (shared by all his readers) that it was not granted to him to describe the supreme experience which biology calls death, but theology speaks of only in terms of life.'

Benson, although unable to communicate his thoughts on death after the event, wrote about it before with characteristic candour. On the final page of his *Confessions of a Convert* he wrote that 'the very River of Death itself is no more than a dwindled stream, bridged and protected on every side; the shadow of death is little more than twilight for those who look on it in the light of the Lamb'.[18]

The shadow of death loomed large over Europe at this time, the First World War having been declared two months earlier, but it was the shadow of Benson's death which loomed large in the life of Ronald Knox during that October. In *A Spiritual Aeneid*, Knox's own 'Confessions of a Convert', he recalled how the deaths of Benson, Pope Pius X and his friend Father Maturin, who was lost in the sinking of the *Lusitania*, had combined to affect him deeply:

> Three deaths of Catholics during these first few months of the war made an especial impression on me. The late Holy Father was the subject of a bitter attack in one of the Anglican Church newspapers, an attack which maddened me, as I am glad to say it disgusted most people … Monsignor Benson I had only met once, but I never felt towards him that irritation which his name aroused among my friends, and I always looked on him as the guide who had led me to Catholic truth – I did not know then that he used to pray for my conversion …
>
> Father Maturin's death was more personal to me, as well as more impressive from the horror of its circumstances. It was easy to conjure up the picture of him, as he moved fearlessly to and fro in those last moments on the *Lusitania*.[19]

Father Maturin, who had been chaplain at Oxford at the time of his death, was only one of an increasing number of Catholic friends with whom Knox had made acquaintance during 1914. It was during this year that he first met Father Martindale, the convert Jesuit who had been ordained three years earlier and who would soon embark upon the writing of the definitive two-volume biography of Benson.

It was also during 1914 that Knox became embroiled in controversy over what became known as the Kikuyu incident. This was a scandal caused by the sweeping aside of doctrinal differences between the Anglican church and the nonconformists in Africa. It proved decisive to some hesitating members of the Anglo-Catholic party within the Church of England who, in the language of the set, 'poped'. Knox, one of the most prominent members of the party, did not feel at the time that such a drastic step was necessary, but the Kikuyu incident did provoke him to write what Evelyn Waugh described as 'one of his most accomplished essays'.[20] *Reunion All Round* was a pasquinade in the manner of Swift which satirized Modernism in much the same way that *Absolute and Abitofhell* had done two years earlier. It was attacked in the ecclesiastical press, *Cambridge Christian Life* dismissing it as 'a foolish, flippant skit', but the secular press was more discerning, the *Spectator* praising the manner in which 'the turn of Swift's sentences is admirably caught'.[21] Mixed reviews aside, *Reunion All Round* enjoyed a wider popularity than his previous books. It was read aloud to the Prime Minister, Herbert Asquith, as he basked on the river-bank at Sutton Courtenay; it was received with approval by many Anglican bishops; and Knox was amused to hear that it was read in refectory at the English College in Rome, under the impression that the author was a Catholic, and 'caused great doubts of my salvation when it proved that I was not'.[22] Above all, Knox seemed delighted that Chesterton had reviewed the book with enthusiasm: 'It won, in cold print, the commendation of my earliest master and model, G. K. Chesterton.'[23]

Unknown to Knox, *Reunion All Round* was destined to make a lasting impression on the young Evelyn Waugh. Waugh was only eleven when the book was published but he remembered his father's delight when it first appeared. Writing to Knox many years later, Waugh recalled that his father had read the book aloud to him and that he was 'dazzled as I have been ever since ... Since then every word you have written and spoken has been pure light to me.'[24]

Waugh, of course, was too young to see active service in the war whereas Knox's generation were being sucked into the maelstrom. At the outbreak of hostilities, Knox's circle of friends had ignored his advice that they should stay and take their degrees instead of rushing into uniforms. They had signed up to a man, leaving him alone and lonely. 'Oxford is quite indescribable,' Knox wrote to his father after he had returned to an almost empty University in the Michaelmas term of 1914, 'a cloud of depression hangs over it which it would take several Zeppelin bombs to pierce.'[25] Finding the deserted colleges unbearable he went to teach classics, without pay, at Shrewsbury.

One of Knox's closest friends, Guy Lawrence, was at Belton Camp with the 7th Battalion of the South Staffordshire Regiment. 'Yes, I think Gi is happy,' Knox had written to another friend, 'with fifty people to run errands for him he's happy, and they're happy, so what's the odds? But oh, my dear, the thought of his going out to the front.'[26]

It was the thought of going out to the front which led many of his friends to question their religious position. With the prospect of death looming, Guy Lawrence turned to Knox for spiritual direction. Having reached a point of extreme Anglo-Catholicism, could he be content with it? If he was about to die, he wanted to die in absolute certainty. Should he 'pope' now before it was too late? The line of questioning shook Knox's own already shaky position to its foundations. For once, he did not know what advice to offer. If his friend came back alive in a year's time it was possible that he might have 'poped' himself.

With these questions spinning endlessly round in his head Knox attended the first Anglican mass said by his brother Wilfred, now an ordained priest, in May 1915. Knox had travelled from Shrewsbury to London to share in his brother's joy but found the celebration sullied by doubt:

> It should have been an occasion of the most complete happiness to see him now ... in the same church, at the same altar, where I had stood three years before in his presence. And then, suddenly, I saw the other side of the picture.
>
> If this doubt, the shadow of a scruple which had grown in my mind, were justifiable – only suppose it were justifiable, then neither he nor I was a priest ... the accessories to the service – the bright vestments, the fresh flowers, the mysterious candlelight, were all settings to a sham jewel; we had been trapped, deceived, betrayed, into thinking it was all worth while.[27]

His convictions were to take a further buffeting two days after his brother's first mass with news that Guy Lawrence had been received into the Catholic Church by the Jesuits at Farm Street. Lawrence wrote on 28 May: 'You told me to act on my own judgement, and I've done so. My mind was made up for me this morning. God made it clear to me and I went straight to Farm Street, asked for Father St John and explained all to him ... I know I am happy and I only long for you to be happy with me.'[28]

The news of Lawrence's conversion sent shock-waves through the circle of Knox's friends. One wrote to ask what could be done if Lawrence and others 'think they ought to Pope? We can't stop them ... Oh Lord, what a mess.'[29] 'At present,' Knox confessed to another friend, 'I'm like a top that's got outside its grooves and is spinning about all over the place.'[30]

'Poping', to employ the parlance of the day, was becoming ever more popular. The novelist Compton Mackenzie had done so in 1914 as had the future novelists Julian Green and Owen Francis Dudley in the following year. Dudley's conversion is of particular interest because of the curious similarities between his own life and those of Benson and Knox. Born in 1882, he had studied for the Anglican ministry and was ordained in 1911, the same year as Knox. Received into the Catholic Church in 1915 he followed in Benson's footsteps in studying for the priesthood at the English College in Rome. After his ordination in September 1917 by Cardinal Bourne at Westminster Cathedral, he became a chaplain in the army, saw service on the French and Italian fronts and was wounded. Further parallels with Benson and Knox would come with his adoption of a literary career. His trilogy, *Will Men Be Like Gods?*, *Shadows on the Earth*, and *The Masterful Monk*, was a success on both sides of the Atlantic, and was serialized, translated into various languages and transcribed in Braille. One other intriguing parallel is the way that Dudley concluded his own description of his conversion in identical terms to those employed by Benson on the final page of his *Confessions of a Convert*: 'And I have found the kingdom of Heaven on earth. The city of God. That city that "hath no need of the sun, nor of the moon to shine in it; for the glory of God hath enlightened it, and the Lamb is the lamp thereof."'[31]

In 1915 Knox was still groping his way uncertainly in the same direction, his mind filled with contortions and contradictions. Distraught at the lengthening list of his friends who had already been killed in the war, he fought an intense inner struggle with himself. As well as the deeper theological issues, he considered the practical implications of conversion. He wrote a list of the more mundane reasons for and against his conversion to Rome, some of which were not so much a leap from the sublime to the ridiculous as a descent from the profound to the profane. He thought that conversion would make him more popular in the long run but that, in the meantime, he would lose all the popularity he enjoyed already. He would be rid of the Prayer Book but would miss the Authorized Version. He would be able to get an altar whenever he wanted one, even abroad, but would be unable to say mass in old parish churches, like All Saints in York. His fellow priests would be celibate like himself but would be much more vulgar. It would distress his convert friends like Guy Lawrence if he didn't convert but would distress his father and many others if he did. The list was headed '*Diabolus loquitur*' and was intended to isolate those selfish and frivolous elements that were unworthy of consideration in the making of any final decision.

Meanwhile his doubts persisted. 'I never celebrate without wondering whether anything's happening,' he confessed to a friend, 'and I don't think I could hear a confession now. Perhaps it's just a sort of brain-storm and will wear off.' Four days later he wrote again:

> I can't entertain the slightest doubt as to whether the Roman view of us, as a whole, may not be the right one, without feeling the same doubt about every detail of devotion and practice. I have to set my teeth in order to consecrate, and make my thanksgiving after communion or

confession with a mental reservation – simply because I see so clearly that *if* the Roman view should be the right one, our orders and still more our jurisdiction become matters of such uncertainty that the probabilities of there being anything in them are hardly worth considering.[32]

As well as writing to his Anglican friends, Knox was beginning to confide in the few Catholic acquaintances he had. After his friend Charles Lister had been killed he had written to Lister's sister, Lady Lovat, whom he had not met since her conversion and marriage, explaining his doubts and difficulties. These were also hinted at in letters to both the Abbot of Caldey and F. F. Urquhart, a fellow of Balliol; but it was a chance encounter with Father Martindale that was to make the most lasting impression.

Knox came across Father Martindale at Lord Halifax's house at Hickleton in Yorkshire where Martindale was carrying out research for his forthcoming biography of Benson. Knox had always felt a close affinity with Benson, but he also felt an increasing affinity with Martindale. Indeed, they had much in common. Both had been raised by elderly relatives, both showed remarkable promise at their respective public schools and both won every conceivable academic prize. Martindale had converted in 1897 while still a boy at Harrow and had been sent by the Jesuits to Oxford in 1901. He had been ordained a Catholic priest in 1911, the same year that Knox had been ordained an Anglican. But there was one very obvious difference – one was in communion with Rome and the other was not.

Knox decided to grab the unexpected opportunity to discuss his doubts with the Jesuit and both later recalled their memories of the dialogue which ensued. In *A Spiritual Aeneid*, Knox described Martindale as 'one of the very few Catholic priests I knew, one for whose powers I had already the utmost respect'. Meeting Martindale in such surprising circumstances 'seemed too good to be a coincidence', so he set about trying to explain his feelings as best he could. Detailing his doubts and difficulties as an Anglican he wondered whether the state of mind in which he found himself made it right to shut his eyes and 'take a plunge' into the Roman Catholic Church. To his great surprise Martindale told him that he couldn't be received in such circumstances. On the contrary, before he could take the plunge he must not shut his eyes but open them: 'the point of departure must come, as it comes between sleep and wakefulness when you find yourself ready to get up'.[33]

Martindale's memories of the same meeting, recounted to Evelyn Waugh forty-three years after the event, are somewhat different:

He came and said: 'Will you receive me into the Church?' I said: 'Why?' He said: 'Because I don't believe the Church of England has a leg to stand on.' I said: 'But that's only a negative consideration. Why do you think that the RC Church has legs?' ... he seemed quite aghast, and ended by agreeing that he must produce something more positive before he could be received.[34]

In his biography of Knox, Evelyn Waugh wrote that 'The shock of that meeting, whatever precisely was said, was one of the determining processes of Ronald's development.'[35]

Waugh's words are borne out by Knox's own account, given in an introduction to an Oxford Conference in 1936, of his stay at Hickleton and the impact that Martindale made on him:

I still remember going down to dinner dressed up in a cassock and ferraiuolo and heaven knows what (I used to like dressing up in those days) ... I was introduced to the other guest who was staying there, a very thin clergyman with a face that looked like an extremely animated skull; not dressed in a cassock at all, but in a rather seedy frock-coat which didn't fit him too well; and I think I knew in that moment that this was the real thing ...[36]

Martindale's brusqueness masked his ardent desire that Knox should convert. Thereafter Knox was always in his prayers and, by way of adding further spiritual muscle to his own efforts, he secured the regular prayers of a Convent of Poor Clares.

At the same time that Knox was thinking about conversion many of his friends were actually doing it. E. R. Hicks, formerly of Corpus Christi and a friend of long standing, had written from Gallipoli telling him that he was contemplating submission to Rome. Knox believed that the piety of the Irish troops to which Hicks had found himself attached was an important factor in bringing him to the point of conversion. In his letter Hicks had sought spiritual direction to help him come to a decision but Knox had replied that he was no longer in a position to offer advice on such matters. Several weeks later, Hicks wrote from Egypt announcing his reception into the Church. Another friend, Charles Scott-Moncrieff, later to achieve fame as the translator of Proust, Stendhal and Pirandello, had also sought Knox's final advice before being received in France.

Knox recalled that he was, by autumn 1915, 'deep enough in my doubts to be envious of them'.[37] None the less, he still felt unable to follow their example and instead sought the advice of Rev. H. F. B. Mackay, vicar of All Saints, Margaret Street. He was confident of a sympathetic hearing from Rev. Mackay because the latter's curate, Wilfrid Moor, had recently 'poped' and was soon to go on to Rome to study for the priesthood. Mackay's advice was psychological and practical. The war, he said, had put everybody's nerves on edge and Knox's difficulties were probably nothing more than a case of 'war-nerves'. If he waited until the war was over his difficulties would disappear. Knox consulted his brother and found that he also was inclined to believe in the 'war-nerves' theory. Temporarily reassured he decided to do nothing drastic for the time being. His friends might be 'poping' left, right and centre but he, at least for the time being, would stay exactly where he was.

However, to paraphrase Chesterton, if a thing is left alone it does not remain the same but becomes open to a torrent of change. Knox spent the whole of 1916 entrenched at Shrewsbury, teaching classics and determined to bide his time, only to find that everything he read led him closer to Rome. There appeared no escape. He read round the subject of the Papacy and the Reformation with the deliberate intention of getting an understanding of views other than his own. It was almost as if he was willing himself to be converted from the idea of conversion. Among the books he read were Creighton's *History of the Papacy* (in six volumes), Gardiner's *Lollardy and the Reformation* (in four very large volumes), three or four volumes of Milman's *History of Latin Christianity*, Ward's *Life of Newman*, Pater on the Renaissance, A. L. Smith on Church and State in the Middle Ages, Sir James Stephen on the Portroyalists, a volume of Acton's lectures, Church's *History of the Oxford Movement*, Balleine's *History of the Evangelical Party* and Newman (as an Anglican) on the Arians. There was little time for light reading but he did read Martindale's new biography of Benson and reread Belloc's *Path to Rome* twice. The latter book had long been a favourite. He set it as a holiday task to his class and while at home had set himself the task of indexing it under more than three hundred heads.

Try as he might the Roman difficulties were not about to disappear and by Christmas 1916 he felt the urge for conversion more pressingly than ever. His father, sensing that his son was on the verge of taking the unthinkable step, made one last effort to dissuade him. 'I do hope,' he wrote early in the new year, 'as far as I can read my heart, that it is not through mere selfishness that I fight against your submission to Rome. Let me try to put down some of the considerations which weigh with me.'[38]

Unwittingly, many of the points which the Bishop felt worthy of consideration were the very arguments against conversion which his son had itemized as *Diabolus loquitur* and had already answered with *Vade retro me, Satana*.

In many other closely reasoned pages the Bishop had set out his view of the Church and the religious life. This approach was equally doomed to failure because his son's view was so opposed to his own. There was nothing by now that Knox had not read and studied concerning the pros and cons of Anglicanism.

In July, all other approaches and reproaches having failed, the Bishop went one step too far, stooping to emotional blackmail. He accused his son of seeking 'calm' at the expense of others, and of himself in particular, who would be obliged to resign his see if his son left the Church of England.

'I don't think it's quite fair to say I am asking for calm,' his son remonstrated in reply,

> certainly not for *exterior calm* – I mean the absence of conflict with the world, with sin, with doubt, even with temptations against faith. And the only interior calm I hope for is the consciousness of serving God as he wants to be served, of taking my part in his work ... But as for you, Paw, I really don't think my decision ought to affect you in that way ... whatever your personal feelings, I don't see that your official position is compromised ... I don't think anyone will expect you to resign or have a right to be surprised if you don't.[39]

It will always remain a matter of conjecture whether the Bishop's gambit was anything other than a last desperate bluff to influence his son. In the event, he did not carry out his threat to resign but remained in his see for a further four years of unimpaired activity after his son's conversion. 'Whatever his private sorrows,' wrote Evelyn Waugh, 'his public prestige and success were totally unaffected by Ronald's change of communion.'[40]

Knox's final weeks as an Anglican are recounted in *A Spiritual Aeneid*. After celebrating his last Anglican mass on the Sunday in the Octave of the Assumption he returned to Manchester and the following weekend communicated in his father's private chapel. The next Sunday he went to St Barnabas', Pimlico, where he made his last Anglican act of public worship. On 8 September he took the train, destined for Farnborough Abbey where he was received into the Church two weeks later. Knox recalled the coincidence that R. H. Benson had made his own final journey as an Anglican to Woodchester on 7 September fourteen years earlier. Fittingly, the two episcopal sons had finally found themselves in the same home, their parallel lives having converged in conversion.

In the last few days before his reception on 22 September Knox read several Catholic novels. The one he enjoyed most was Benson's *Come Rack! Come*

Rope! It seemed symbolically apt: 'Hugh Benson, who had set my feet on the way towards the Church, watched over my footsteps to the last.'[41]

NOTES

1. Evelyn Waugh, *Ronald Knox*, p. 92.
2. ibid., pp. 92–3.
3. ibid., p. 93.
4. Penelope Fitzgerald, *The Knox Brothers*, New York, 1977, p. 121.
5. Evelyn Waugh, *Ronald Knox*, p. 96.
6. ibid., p. 96.
7. Raphael H. Gross (ed.), *A Century of the Catholic Essay*, Philadelphia, 1946, pp. 325–6.
8. ibid., p. 329.
9. ibid., p. 327.
10. ibid., pp. 327–8.
11. Maisie Ward, *Insurrection versus Resurrection*, London, 1937, p. 153.
12. R. H. Benson, *Confessions of a Convert*, preface.
13. ibid., p. 106.
14. Brian Masters, *The Bensons*, London, 1993, p. 206.
15. ibid., pp. 206–7.
16. ibid., p. 207.
17. C. C. Martindale, SJ, *The Life of Monsignor Robert Hugh Benson, Volume Two*, pp. 432–3.
18. R. H. Benson, *Confessions of a Convert*, p. 120.
19. Ronald Knox, *A Spiritual Aeneid*, pp. 161–2.
20. Evelyn Waugh, *Ronald Knox*, p. 100.
21. Ronald Knox, *A Spiritual Aeneid*, p. 148.
22. ibid., p. 148.
23. ibid., p. 149.
24. Mark Amory (ed.), *The Letters of Evelyn Waugh*, London, 1995, p. 342.
25. Penelope Fitzgerald, *The Knox Brothers*, pp. 128–9.
26. ibid., p. 129.
27. Ronald Knox, *A Spiritual Aeneid*, pp. 173–4.
28. Evelyn Waugh, *Ronald Knox*, p. 118.
29. ibid., p. 119.
30. Penelope Fitzgerald, *The Knox Brothers*, p. 131.
31. John A. O'Brien (ed.), *The Road to Damascus*, London, 1949, pp. 162–3.
32. Evelyn Waugh, *Ronald Knox*, p. 124.
33. Ronald Knox, *A Spiritual Aeneid*, pp. 177–8.
34. Evelyn Waugh, *Ronald Knox*, p. 125.
35. ibid., pp. 125–6.
36. Philip Caraman, SJ, *C. C. Martindale: A Biography*, London, 1967, pp. 124–5.
37. Ronald Knox, *A Spiritual Aeneid*, p. 184.
38. Evelyn Waugh, *Ronald Knox*, p. 130.
39. ibid., pp. 131–2.
40. ibid., p. 132.
41. Ronald Knox, *A Spiritual Aeneid*, p. 215.

CHAPTER TEN

KNOX AND CHESTERTON

Following his reception Knox began the emotionally arduous task of informing his Anglican friends. He wrote dutifully to the Bishop of Oxford, to Lord Halifax and to the President of Trinity. He had expected his conversion to lead to some breaches of friendship but was pleasantly surprised to discover that everyone was uniformly kind, attributing the highest motives to his decision.

The Bishop of Oxford, Charles Gore, with whom Knox had always been on affectionate terms, replied, 'I commend you to God and the power of His Grace and the guidance of His Spirit ... I hope we shall be together again at last, if not on earth, then in paradise.'[1] His brother Wilfred wrote:

> Of course it won't make any difference: why should it? After all our views are far closer than they were when we were at Oxford, when I never believed in anything, and it never made any difference there ... I can say how sorry I am, but it certainly won't make any difference as far as I'm concerned.[2]

Guy Lawrence, the friend whose conversion two years earlier had so shaken Knox, wrote joyfully now that they were reunited: 'I am so glad ... Now you and I are in the same boat, Ron; before we were hailing each other vaguely across a wintry sort of sea. You must be quick and become a priest.'[3]

The letter which Knox had found hardest to write was the one to his father. The Bishop's reply still retained traces of truculence but the subject had been worn thin between them during the preceding year and the underlying tone was tempered with resignation:

> First I must acknowledge gratefully the affectionate spirit in which your letter was written, and express my satisfaction that you will not be required to repudiate your baptism.

Next I will say what I said to both the Clergy from this diocese who went over, that when the time came for their return they might be sure of a most hearty welcome ... I need not say what your return would be to me though I am conscious that my hopes of it must reckon with difficulties almost insurmountable ...[4]

One notable difference between the conversion of Knox and that of Benson was the number of letters of congratulation from Catholics which Knox received. Benson had been surprised at how few Catholics had written to welcome him into the fold whereas Knox was inundated. The main reason for this seems to be the huge number of converts to the Church in the intervening years. Since Benson's conversion in 1903 there had been a steady increase in the annual number of receptions into the Church and the majority of letters to Knox were from recent converts. One of these was Lady Lovat who had been received in 1910 and whose congratulatory letter included a warning of the cultural adjustments Knox would be required to make: 'I think the first year (or six months) after being received are v. difficult – I fluctuated between feeling utterly isolated – or being one of a rather – unsympathetic and *very* dense crowd.'[5]

Lady Lovat became a good friend and Knox soon fell into the habit of spending his summer vacations as the guest of the Lovats at Beaufort Castle in Scotland. It was during these visits that he came to know two other converts whom Lady Lovat had also befriended, Maurice Baring and Compton Mackenzie.

Baring and Knox had much in common. Both Etonians, though not contemporaries since Baring was fourteen years the senior, and both keen classicists, Knox had delighted Baring by translating a line of Rossetti's, 'You could not tell the starlings from the leaves' into Greek and Latin on the spot. At other times they spoke Umble, a language of Baring's invention, in which Dickens's *Old Curiosity Shop* translated as Dumble's Umble Cumble Shumble. 'By far the greatest scholar in this language,' wrote Mumble Bumble to E. V. Lucas, 'is Ronald Knox.'[6]

Although Knox came to share many of Lady Lovat's friends he was far from sharing her sense of utter isolation in the first months after conversion. He felt instead a sense of liberation. He told a friend that during his early days as a Catholic he received the 'consolations' he needed and often ran to church in his impatience to begin his prayers. He looked forward to his meditations as periods of pure joy and his radiant devotion made a lasting impression on those who knew him at the time. Dr Flynn, later Bishop of Lancaster, remembered Knox's first months as a Catholic:

My most outstanding memory of him is his absorption in prayer before the Blessed Sacrament. That made so profound an impression on me that one day, years after, preaching in the North on the Love of God as an act of the will, which would not involve the emotions, I said: 'Don't tell me that this is all the love of God means. I have *seen* people in love with God.'[7]

On 26 November 1917, at the suggestion of Cardinal Bourne, Knox moved to Brompton Oratory. The Cardinal believed that life at the Oratory would allow him to share in the life of a Catholic community and this he did dutifully and contentedly, hearing Mass and Benediction daily, sharing in the community's recreation, and retiring to bed at ten. There was never any question of his entering the Oratorian noviciate but he received much from the thirteen months he stayed, looking back on his days there with a fond gratitude for the happiness, peace and prayer they offered.

It was during his stay at the Oratory that Belloc had 'blown in' on him, as Knox reported to his sister, and exuberantly congratulated him on his conversion. Although he and Belloc had often met at Oxford and had debated together at the Union, Knox's reception into the Church brought them closer together. By 1921 their friendship had matured sufficiently for Knox to be a Christmas guest at King's Land, Belloc's home in Sussex. Their friendship was further bonded by their mutual companionship with Maurice Baring. It was also through Baring that Knox came to know Chesterton.

Chesterton, who had done so much to influence the growing army of converts to Catholicism, Knox and Baring included, was now out on a limb. As a non-Catholic defender of Catholicism he found his own position not so much a paradox as a parody of the orthodoxy he championed. Was the hammer of the 'heretics' not a heretic himself? The question was worrying him sufficiently during the summer of 1920 to elicit the confession to Maurice Baring that he found his position as an Anglican awkward and increasingly incongruous:

before my present crisis, I had promised somebody to take part in what I took to be a small debate on labour. Too late, by my own carelessness, I found to my horror it had swelled into a huge Anglo-Catholic Congress at the Albert Hall ... my experience was curious and suggestive, though tragic; for I felt it like a farewell. There was no doubt about the enthusiasm of those thousands of Anglo-Catholics. But there was also no doubt, unless I am much mistaken, that many of them besides myself would be Roman Catholics rather than accept things they are quite likely to be asked to accept – for instance, by the Lambeth Conference … I am concerned most, however, about … Frances, to whom I owe much of my own faith, and to whom therefore (as far as I can see my way) I also owe every decent chance for the controversial defence of her faith. If her side can convince me, they have a right to do; if not, I shall go hot and strong to convince her.[8]

Continuing to agonize over the nature of his faith, Chesterton wrote another letter to Baring in which he seemed to have reached conclusions which edged him still closer to Rome:

I want to consider my position about the biggest thing of all whether I am to be inside or outside it. I used to think one could be an Anglo-Catholic and really inside it; but if that was (to use an excellent phrase of your own) only a Porch, I do not think I want a Porch, and certainly not a Porch standing some way from the building.[9]

Chesterton was destined to stand shivering in the Porch for a further two years before finally entering the Church. The reason for the delay, as the earlier letter to Baring had intimated, was the opposition of his wife. Indeed, Father O'Connor, an old friend who had known Chesterton for nearly twenty years, despaired of his ever entering the Church without his wife's blessing. O'Connor complained to Josephine Ward that 'he will need Frances to take him to church, to find his place in the prayer-book, to examine his conscience for him when he goes to Confession'.[10]

It was true that most people were surprised that Chesterton had not followed Baring, Knox and his brother Cecil into the Church. Ever since the publication of *Orthodoxy* in 1908 he had been seen by the reading public as a staunch Catholic. His conversion, it was thought, was a mere formality. It was not a question of whether Chesterton would become a Catholic but when. In 1912 Wilfrid Ward had written confidently to Lord Hugh Cecil predicting that Chesterton 'is pretty sure to become a Catholic'.[11] In the event ten more years elapsed before Chesterton fulfilled his prediction and Ward, who died in 1916, did not live to see it.

In another undated letter to Baring, Chesterton again displayed the caginess and caution caused by worries over his wife's position:

For deeper reasons than I could ever explain, my mind has to turn especially on the thought of my wife, whose life has been in many ways a very heroic tragedy; and to whom I am so much in debt of honour that I cannot bear to leave her, even psychologically, if it be possible by tact and sympathy to take her with me. We have had a very difficult time lately; but the other day she rather abruptly faced the thing herself in a new way, and spoke as if she knew where we would both end. But she asked for a little time; as a great friend of hers is also (with the approval of the priest with whom she consulted) delaying for the moment till she is more certain.[12]

On Christmas Day 1921, while Knox was staying with Belloc, Chesterton again wrote to Baring, this time asking whether his friend could suggest a priest with whom he could discuss the possibilities of conversion. Although Chesterton knew several Catholic priests and was sure 'they would consider principles and not friendship', he did not want to 'burden their friendship till I know it is necessary'. Any priest suggested by Baring could 'be a friend of yours, and even know what has passed between us so far. But I don't particularly want him to be a friend of mine.'[13] Baring suggested Ronald Knox who had been ordained in 1919.

Henceforth Knox would play an important part in Chesterton's final approach to the Church. It was a peculiar arrangement because Knox had idolized Chesterton since his days as a schoolboy at Eton. In an unlikely role reversal the pupil had become teacher.

The correspondence between Knox and Chesterton which began very early in 1922 was interrupted by the death of Chesterton's father and by the Chestertons' moving house from Overroads to Top Meadow in Beaconsfield. Knox was informed that 'my normal chaos is increased by moving into a new house, which is still like a wastepaper basket'.[14] Undeterred by the delays Knox persisted and endeavoured to arrange a visit to Beaconsfield. Chesterton's reply still centred on concerns about his wife:

In our conversation my wife was all that I hope you will some day know her to be; she is incapable of wanting me to do anything but what I think right; and admits the same possibility for herself: but it is much more of a wrench for her, for she has been able to practise her religion in complete good faith: which my own doubts have prevented me from doing.[15]

A further delay was caused by Chesterton's departure for Holland where he was to give a series of lectures. Before leaving Chesterton had promised faithfully that he would write to Knox 'more fully about the business of instruction when I return'.[16]

In another remarkably frank letter to Knox, Chesterton discussed both the practicalities of instruction and the psychological factors underpinning his desire for it:

> I cannot tell you how much I was pleased and honoured even by the suggestion that you might possibly deal with the instruction yourself; it is something I should value more vividly and personally than I can possibly express ...
>
> ... I am in a state now when I feel a monstrous charlatan, as if I wore a mask and were stuffed with cushions, whenever I see anything about the public G. K. C.; it hurts me; for though the views I express are real, the image is horribly unreal compared with the real person who needs help just now ... I am concerned about what has become of a little boy whose father showed him a toy theatre, and a schoolboy whom nobody had ever heard of, with his brooding on doubts and dirt and day-dreams ... and all the morbid life of the lonely mind of a living person with whom I have lived. It is that story, that so often came near to ending badly, that I want to end well.[17]

By July, following further discussions with Frances, Chesterton appeared to bow to his wife's desire that Father O'Connor and not Father Knox should be called to oversee the process towards conversion. It seemed that Frances was working on the principle that the priest you know is better than the priest you don't, Father O'Connor having been a close friend of both Chestertons for nearly twenty years. Chesterton wrote as tactfully as possible to Knox explaining the change of plan:

> I have managed to have another talk with my wife, after which I have written to our old friend Father O'Connor and asked him to come here, as he probably can, from what I hear ... Frances is just at the point where Rome acts both as the positive and the negative magnet; a touch would turn her either way; almost (against her will) to hatred, but with the right touch to a faith far beyond my reach. I know Father O'Connor's would be the touch that does not startle, because she knows him and is fond of him; and the only thing she asked of me was to send for him.[18]

Knox appeared unperturbed by being passed over for Father O'Connor and, far from taking the matter personally, wrote to Chesterton on 17 July expressing delight at the decision: 'I'm awfully glad to hear that you've sent for Father O'Connor and that you think he's likely to be available.'[19]

After years of procrastination Chesterton's final approach to the Church proceeded at an accelerated pace. Father O'Connor came to stay at Top Meadow on 26 July and Chesterton was received into the Church four days later. Perhaps this is not so surprising because once the ball started rolling it didn't have far to go. Chesterton had been defending Catholic orthodoxy for nearly twenty years and knew the tenets of the faith better than most cradle Catholics. No instruction was needed, merely assent. All that remained in the final days before his reception was a sense of apprehension at the enormity of the step he was about to take: 'I had no doubts or difficulties just before. I had only fears, fears of something that had the finality and simplicity of suicide.'[20]

For Chesterton his reception into the Church, so slow in coming, was as liberating as Knox's had been five years earlier. As with Maurice Baring before him the occasion inspired a sonnet of thanksgiving:

> The sages have a hundred maps to give
> That trace their crawling cosmos like a tree,
> They rattle reason out through many a sieve
> That stores the sand and lets the gold go free:
> And all these things are less than dust to me
> Because my name is Lazarus and I live.[21]

As with Knox, Chesterton had the unpleasant task of informing a disapproving parent of the step he had taken. 'I write this,' he informed his mother,

> to tell you something before I write about it to anyone else; something about which we shall probably be in the position of the two bosom friends at Oxford, who 'never differed except in opinion' ... I have come to the same conclusion that Cecil did ... and I am now a Catholic in the same sense as he, having long claimed the name in its Anglo-Catholic sense ... I have thought about you, and all that I owe to you and my father, not only in the way of affection, but of the ideals of honour and freedom and charity and all good things you always taught me: and I am not conscious of the smallest break in those ideals; but only of a new and necessary way of fighting for them ... I have thought this thing out for myself and not in a hurry of feeling.[22]

A far easier letter to write was the one he sent to Maurice Baring, in which he referred to his reception as 'this wonderful business, in which you have helped me so much more than anyone else'.[23] Baring, joyful that his friend's 'ship had finally arrived at its port', replied with a candour which would have been unthinkable before his conversion:

> Nothing for years had given me so much joy. I have hardly ever entered a church without putting up a candle to Our Lady or to St Joseph or St Anthony for you. And both this year and last year in Lent I made a Novena for you. I know of many other people, better people far than I, who did the same. Many Masses were said for you and prayers all over England and Scotland in centres of Holiness ...
>
> Well, all I have to say, Gilbert, is what I think I have already said to you, and what I have said not long ago in a printed book. That I was received into the Church on the Eve of Candlemas 1909, and it is perhaps the *only* act in my life which I am quite certain I have never regretted. Every day I live, the Church seems to me more and more wonderful; the Sacraments more and more solemn and sustaining; the voice of the Church, her liturgy, her rules, her discipline, her ritual, her decisions in matters of Faith and Morals more and more excellent and profoundly wise and true and right, and her children stamped with something that those outside Her are without.[24]

Baring concluded the letter with a postscript informing Chesterton that Knox was about to leave for Lourdes with Lady Lovat: 'Needless to say he was overjoyed. So were the Lovats.'[25]

Hilaire Belloc wrote to Chesterton on 1 August, only two days after his friend's reception, with a forthrightness which, as with Baring's letter, would have been inconceivable beforehand:

> The thing I have to say is this (I could not have said it before your step: I can say so now. Before it would have been like a selected pleading). The Catholic Church is the exponent of *Reality*. It is true. Its doctrines in matters large and small are statements of what is. This it is which the ultimate act of the intelligence accepts. This it is which the will deliberately confirms. And that is why Faith through an act of the Will is Moral.[26]

Ironically, Belloc's clinical approach had previously led him to the conclusion that Chesterton would never actually become a Catholic. In a letter to Baring he expressed the belief that, although their mutual friend possessed the Catholic *mood*, he had never believed he would have the *will* to convert:

> People said that he might come in at any time because he showed such a Catholic point of view and so much affection for the Catholic Church. That always seemed to me quite the wrong end of the stick. Acceptation of the Faith is an act, not a mood. Faith is an act of will and as it seemed to me the whole of his mind was occupied in his liking for and attraction towards a certain mood, not at all towards the acceptation of a certain Institution as defined and representing full reality in this world.[27]

Belloc's scepticism concerning the likelihood of Chesterton's conversion meant that he was more surprised than most when news of his friend's reception reached him. On 12 August he wrote to Father O'Connor, 'It is very great news indeed ... I am overwhelmed by it.' On 23 August he again wrote to Father O'Connor: 'I still remain under the *coup* of Gilbert's conversion. I had never thought it possible! The Catholic Church is central, and therefore approached at every conceivable angle!'[28] Two days later, still scarcely able to believe the evidence of his own senses, Belloc wrote to Father O'Connor yet again: 'The more I think on Gilbert the more astonished I become!' Finally, on 9 September, Belloc reported to Father O'Connor that he had visited Chesterton at Top Meadow and had stopped the night: 'He is very happy. In the matter of explanation you are right. But I have no vision.'[29]

Years later Belloc was still struggling to put the significance of Chesterton's conversion into perspective. 'Few of the great conversions in our history,' he wrote in 1940, 'have been so deliberate or so mature. It will be for posterity to judge the magnitude of the event. We are too near to see it in scale.'[30]

Thus did the triumvirate of Belloc, Baring and Chesterton, from its conception at the birth of the century, reach its consummation in the one communion: a triumvirate triumphant. The triumphalism was shared by the Catholic press. The *Tablet*, having checked the authenticity of the news by telegram, published the story in a spirit of jubilation. Letters of congratulation flooded in from all corners of the English-speaking world. To a non-Catholic who responded to his reception into the Church by writing to him on the purpose of ritual, the use of reason and the ideas of Wells, Chesterton replied:

I ought to say first that, saving the grace of God, my own conversion to Catholicism was entirely rational; and certainly not at all ritualistic ... I accepted it because it *did* afford conviction to my analytical mind. But people can see the ritual and are seldom allowed to hear of the philosophy.

About ritual itself I think the truest thing was said by Yeats the poet, certainly not a Catholic or even a Christian; that ceremony goes with innocence. Children are not ashamed of dressing up, nor great poets at great periods, as when Plutarch wore the laurel. Our world does feel something of what Wells says, because our world is as nervous and irritable as Wells himself. But I think the children and the poets are more permanent.[31]

The recipient of this reply followed Chesterton into the Church three years later. Others were less enthusiastic. H. G. Wells, displaying the irritability to which Chesterton had alluded, was not amused: 'I love G.K.C. and hate the catholicism of Belloc and Rome ... If catholicism is still to run about the world giving tongue, it can have no better spokesman than G.K.C. But I begrudge Catholicism G.K.C.!'[32] Another friend who begrudged Catholicism G. K. C. was Bernard Shaw. On first hearing the news Shaw was stung sufficiently to ask sardonically whether Chesterton had been drunk. 'My dear G.K.C.,' he wrote, 'This is going too far.'[33]

When the dust had settled there remained one other solitary figure who still quietly begrudged Catholicism G. K. C. Frances had wept inconsolably on the day of her husband's reception and Father O'Connor, who had earlier despaired of Chesterton ever converting without his wife's approval, had remembered her emotional response: 'Dear Frances – my eyes fill to think of it, was present, in tears which I am sure were not all grieving.'[34] This was wishful thinking on the priest's part. There is little doubt that grief was Frances's overriding response to her husband's conversion. In the practice of their faith, the most important thing in their lives, Frances and Gilbert were now separated.

Belloc observed in a letter to Baring that for a man of Chesterton's 'profoundly affectionate temperament, it must be a terrible strain to have his wife, to whom he is devoted, at his elbow disagreeing with his whole point of view'.[35]

Meanwhile Father Vincent McNabb wrote of the separation in a curiously blinkered fashion in a letter to Father O'Connor, oblivious it seemed to the pain and suffering that Chesterton's conversion had caused his wife:

He has sat on the door-step too long for the patience of his friends who love him; if not for God who loves him more than his friends. As Mrs

Chesterton has not, for the moment, found herself able to go where he has gone his will must have been fast set on the Will of God! ...

We must pray that the pain he is suffering on her account will be to her profit. Ever since I spoke with her and heard from others some of the sad stories of a convert kinsman of hers I have felt sure that her difficulties were psychological rather than logical; and that nothing would be so strong to help her as prayer to God.[36]

It is curious that Father McNabb should overlook the pain that Frances was suffering on her husband's account. Chesterton at least had the consolation of a spiritual homecoming whereas Frances had been left behind feeling both alone and lonely. It was she rather than he who felt the sword piercing to the very division of her soul and spirit.

Regardless of whether Father McNabb was correct in his assertion that Frances's difficulties were psychological rather than logical, it was certainly true that her husband's had not been so much metaphysical as physical. Although he had been convinced of the metaphysical truth of Catholicism for years, and had been responsible for bringing so many others to that truth, becoming a Catholic required a physical act as well as a metaphysical conviction. He relied so heavily on others, and particularly Frances, for all the practical demands of life that acting alone was always a real effort. Hence his obesity; hence his reverence and respect for men of action like his brother and Belloc; hence Belloc's belief that he would never take the practical step of conversion; and hence his complete and utter dependence on Frances to make his practical decisions for him. Seen in this light, his conversion, the only major practical step he had ever taken in the face of his wife's tacit disapproval, assumes something of the quality of heroism. One remembers his anxiety immediately prior to conversion; 'I had only fears, fears of something that had the finality and simplicity of suicide.' He put the matter descriptively and dramatically when he wrote that 'there is in the last second of time or hairbreadth of space, before the iron leaps to the magnet, an abyss full of all the unfathomable forces of the universe. The space between doing and not doing such a thing is so tiny and so vast.'[37] It was one small step for a man but a giant leap for a man like Chesterton.

Certainly, Frances was a very long way from any desire to follow in her husband's footsteps, confessing to Kathleen Chesshire, Chesterton's secretary, that 'there are three things I shall never do: cut off my hair, engage an efficient secretary, or become a Roman Catholic'.[38] It was four years before her commitment to the last of these assertions began to waver. On 20 June 1926 Frances wrote to Father O'Connor expressing her readiness to follow her husband into the Church:

I want now, as soon as I can see a few days clear before me, to place myself under instruction to enter the Church. The whole position is full of difficulties and I pray you Padre to tell me the first step to take. I don't want my instruction to be here. I don't want to be the talk of Beaconsfield and for people to say I've only followed Gilbert. It isn't true and I've had a hard fight not to let my love for him lead me to the truth. I knew you would not accept me for such motives.[39]

Three weeks later, on 12 July, she wrote again to Father O'Connor, stating that she still had a lot to learn and that perhaps, after all, it would be better to 'go quietly to Father Walker', the local parish priest. In a subsequent letter to Father O'Connor, Frances informed him that she had written to Father Walker and 'after having seen him and had a talk I shall know what I ought to do'.[40] Soon she was taking instruction and was received into the Church at Beaconsfield on 1 November, All Saints Day.

Frances achieved her wish that her reception should take place quietly and without fuss because there are no extant eyewitness accounts of the day's events or of the emotional reaction of either her or her husband on the day of their union in the Church. However, Chesterton recorded his own feelings about his wife's conversion in verse:

But not as distance, not as danger,
        Not chance, and hardly even change,
You found, not wholly as a stranger,
        The place too wondrous to be strange.

Great with a memory more than yearning,
        You travelled but you did not roam,
And went not wandering but returning
        As to some first forgotten home.

The mystic city, many-gated,
        Monstrously pillared, was your own;
Herodian stories gave words and waited
        Two thousand years to be your throne.

Strange blossoms burned as rich before you
        As that divine and beautiful blood;
The wild flowers were no wilder for you
        Than bluebells in an English wood.[41]

These words were echoed by Maisie Ward who wrote of Frances that she had 'never known a happier Catholic ... once the shivering on the bank was over and the plunge had been taken. One would say she had been in the Church all her life.'[42] In a strictly practical sense, Frances's conversion meant that she and her husband could practise their faith together and, as with all practicalities, she was far more at ease than her husband. Chesterton recalled how his wife's examination of conscience prior to confession would be thoroughly scrupulous and carried out with the utmost diligence. He, on the other hand, was prone to distraction, his thoughts flying off wildly at a tangent. He would become fascinated by the very nature of sin itself, its history through the ages and the way it was viewed by different cultures. He would dwell speculatively on the theological definition of pride and recall the teaching of the fathers and the doctors of the Church. He would then return to the matter at hand: 'I know Frances is just finding her own sins while I'm lost in all these speculations, and that worries me because I'm far behind.'[43] During Mass, also, Chesterton felt in awe at the way Frances's participation was 'a perfect gesture' compared with what he perceived as his own woeful inadequacy.

For Chesterton, his wife's conversion was nothing less than the final seal and consummation of their sacramental union as husband and wife. After four years in exile she had returned to him. From now on, as Father O'Connor had put it, he could let Frances take him to church, find his place in the prayer-book and examine his conscience for him.

Perhaps the final words should be left to Ronald Knox who, along with Maurice Baring, had played a crucial role in Chesterton's final approach to the Church. Knox wrote of Chesterton's conversion that

> he had found his home. Just as the hero of his own book *Manalive* walked round the world to find, and to have the thrill of finding, the house which belonged to him, so Chesterton probed all the avenues of thought and tasted all the philosophies, to return at last to that institution which had been his spiritual home from the first, the Church of his friend, Father Brown. He would, I think, have done so before, if he had not been anxious to spare the feelings of his wife, the heroine of all his novels ...[44]

NOTES

1. Evelyn Waugh, *Ronald Knox*, pp. 137–8.
2. ibid., p. 138.
3. ibid., p. 138.
4. ibid., p. 137.
5. Penelope Fitzgerald, *The Knox Brothers*, p. 177.
6. ibid., p. 178.
7. Evelyn Waugh, *Ronald Knox*, p. 144.
8. Maisie Ward, *Gilbert Keith Chesterton*, pp. 388–9.
9. ibid., pp. 384–5.
10. ibid., pp. 379–80.
11. Maisie Ward, *Insurrection versus Resurrection*, p. 573.
12. *Tablet*, 26 December 1953.
13. ibid.
14. Undated letter, G. K. Chesterton Library, Westminster College, Oxford.
15. Maisie Ward, *Gilbert Keith Chesterton*, pp. 393–4.
16. ibid., p. 394.
17. Undated letter, G. K. Chesterton Library, Westminster College, Oxford.
18. Maisie Ward, *Gilbert Keith Chesterton*, p. 395.
19. ibid., p. 395.
20. F. J. Sheed, *The Church and I*, London, 1976, p. 103.
21. G. K. Chesterton, *Collected Poems*, London, 1927, p. 387.
22. Maisie Ward, *Gilbert Keith Chesterton*, pp. 396–7.
23. ibid., p. 397.
24. ibid., pp. 404–6.
25. *The Chesterton Review*, Vol. XIX, No. 1, February 1988, p. 11.
26. Robert Speaight, *The Life of Hilaire Belloc*, pp. 374–5.
27. Robert Speaight (ed.), *Letters from Hilaire Belloc*, London, 1958, p. 124.
28. Father John O'Connor, *Father Brown on Chesterton*, London, 1937, p. 141.
29. ibid., p. 142.
30. Hilaire Belloc, *On the Place of Gilbert Keith Chesterton in English Letters*, London, 1940, p. 13.
31. Maisie Ward, *Gilbert Keith Chesterton*, p. 238.
32. John O'Sullivan (ed.), *G. K. Chesterton: A Centenary Appraisal*, London, 1974, p. 136.
33. William B. Furlong, *Shaw and Chesterton: The Metaphysical Jesters*, Pennsylvania State University Press, 1970, p. 129.
34. Father John O'Connor, *Father Brown on Chesterton*, p. 131.
35. Robert Speaight (ed.), *Letters from Hilaire Belloc*, p. 124.
36. Ferdinand Valentine, OP, *Father Vincent McNabb*, London, 1955, p. 268.
37. Maisie Ward, *Gilbert Keith Chesterton*, p. 387.
38. Maisie Ward, *Return to Chesterton*, London, 1952, p. 153.
39. Maisie Ward, *Gilbert Keith Chesterton*, p. 457.
40. ibid., p. 458.
41. Aidan Mackey (ed.), *The Collected Works of G. K. Chesterton*, Volume X, San Francisco, 1994, p. 358.
42. Maisie Ward, *Gilbert Keith Chesterton*, p. 458.
43. Maisie Ward, *Return to Chesterton*, p. 244.
44. D. J. Conlon (ed.), *G. K. Chesterton: A Half Century of Views*, Oxford, 1987, p. 49.

CHAPTER ELEVEN

WAR AND WASTE LAND

The advent, execution and aftermath of the First World War were destined to have a devastating effect on those who lived through it; and, of course, on those who did not. Not only did the war act as executioner of a whole genera-tion; in the course of its four-year duration it often annihilated the spirit even when it failed to annihilate the body. It was the slaughter both of the innocents and of innocence itself.

The bitter-sweet relationship of innocence in the face of slaughter was con-veyed by Maurice Baring in a letter from France to his friend Dame Ethel Smyth on 25 October 1914, at the very dawn of the destruction:

> When the troops arrived, singing 'It's a long, long way to Tipperary' at Mauberge, after forced marches in the dark, it was one of the most tremendous moments I have ever experienced ... they looked so young, so elastic, and so invincibly cheerful, so unmixedly English, so tired and so fresh. And the thought of these men swinging on into horror undreamt of – the whole German Army – came to me like the stab of a sword, and I had to go and hide in a shop for the people not to see the tears rolling down my cheeks ...
>
> I went to Mass this morning and it was nice to think I was listening to the same words said in the same way with the same gestures, that Henry V and his 'contemptible little army' heard before and after Agincourt, and I stood between a man in khaki and a French Poilu and history flashed past like a jewelled dream.[1]

Two years later the jewelled dream had metamorphosed into a cadaverous night-mare as the list of Baring's friends who had fallen victim of the 'horror undreamt of' grew in number. On 20 September 1916 he was again writing to Dame Ethel Smyth from France, this time in sombre mood conveying the news of another friend's death:

Life is a strain now, isn't it? Scaffolding falls about one daily, one's old friends and one's new friends are killed or disappear like flies; the floor of life seems to have gone, and one seems to live in a permanent eclipse and a *seasonless* world – a world with no summer and no winter, only a long, grey, neutral-tinted *Limbo*.

Raymond Asquith is the latest. I was certain he would be killed. I dined with him the night before he went back to his regiment after a spell at G.H.Q. – I felt I would never see him again ...[2]

Raymond Asquith, eldest son of the Prime Minister and distinguished barrister, was also a good friend of both Knox and Belloc.

Knox had already lost several close friends in the months before his conversion but worse was to come in the months following. On 21 November 1917 he heard that Edward Horner, a friend at both Eton and Oxford, had died of his wounds. By now Knox felt he had few friends left to lose but the war still held the most venomous sting in its tail. On 28 August 1918, during the 'last push', Guy Lawrence was killed in the final advance near Arras, only a little way short of the Hindenburg Line. Numbstruck, Knox wrote to his old friend, Francis Urquhart of Balliol: 'There was a time when I used to dread your handwriting, because it might mean fresh bad news. Well, you've got to have it from me this time, if you haven't heard already – yes, the very worst news ... I'm too numbed still to think, far less to write about it.'[3]

Although no letters from Lawrence to Knox are extant after the note of congratulation on Knox's reception into the Church, it is clear that the two friends had regained the old intimacy following their reunion in faith. 'I always felt I was still getting to know him better each time I saw him,' Knox wrote.

After the initial numbness wore off Knox felt that he was left with a scar rather than a wound, a profound sense of what he had lost rather than the loss itself. According to Evelyn Waugh, 'Lawrence's death completed the annihilation of all the human happiness Ronald had found for himself. He was now a stranger in the world, but in his new-found spiritual strength he was able to accept the wreck of his human affections with a submission which surprised himself.'[4]

In another letter to Francis Urquhart he wrote: 'There must be bits of one's heart which can't carry a strong current of emotion and simply fuse (like an electric light). Or there might be a spiritual reason. But the fact is I simply haven't been worried about Guy at all. My thoughts don't travel to him unless I want them to.'[5]

This new-found strength enabled him to offer support to others suffering loss. Five months later he wrote to Lawrence Eyres, a friend from his days as a fellow and lecturer at Trinity College, to condole with him on the death of a deeply loved brother:

> When I heard about Guy Lawrence I was completely numbed to all feeling for three or four days, but expecting all the time that when I became unnumbed I should simply break down. As a matter of fact when the numbed feeling did go off, it was as if I'd had an operation – a sore wound there which I'd never felt as a fresh wound ... I expect God saw I wasn't fit to bear the real smart, being the creature I am ... if you are in that sort of numbed state, don't think it's a loss of faith.[6]

In this letter Knox was displaying a portent of his vocation to the priesthood. Indeed, the letter's recipient was himself received into the Church under Knox's personal guidance in March 1921.

Not everyone was as fortunate in possessing the fortitude of faith capable of making sense of the psychological waste land that was the war's legacy. 'What kind of state of mind are we in?' Knox wrote after another friend, a Magdalen don, had shot himself dead in his rooms: 'What has the war done to us?'[7]

Another victim of the war's dying embers was Cecil Chesterton who died in a field hospital at Wimereux in northern France only days after the Armistice. His last hours were witnessed by his wife:

> I was half across the ward when Cecil's voice rang out clear and strong as on his marriage day.
> 'Kiddy!' he said. 'You've come.'
> He talked and laughed, and declared he felt much better. But he said nothing of the future and asked a little wistfully about Fleet Street and the Cottage, his mother and our friends.
> After a while he grew tired and closed his eyes. One by one the lights went out, till only a glimmer of lampshine remained ...
> 'He's sleeping now,' said a nurse, and asked me to come to another room.
> Before the dawn I was back again. There was a change – for the worse. And when the first pale gleams of lovely sunshine crept through the windows I knew it was the end.
> 'It's goodbye, Kiddy darling,' he said smiling, and clutched my hand ...

Cecil looked up and smiled. Life was all round him and me: only in the brave face that still kept courage was it ebbing little by little, until it passed beyond the last faint breath.

Suddenly the consciousness came down on me that all our hopes and dreams, light-hearted plans, ambitious undertakings had gone. The future – our future – had ended. I should never hear him speak again. I should never feel his touch, or watch the light in his eyes when unexpectedly he saw me.[8]

Cecil Chesterton was buried in a French military cemetery on 6 December 1918. Due to insurmountable obstacles to travel at the war's end, his recently wed and newly widowed bride was the only member of the family present as his body was lowered into one of the hundreds of narrow graves that lined the coastal hillside. His brother was utterly devastated. Eaten by a bitterness fed with despair, G. K. Chesterton allowed emotions akin to hatred to bubble to the surface. Finding it a cruel injustice that Cecil was dead when his persecutors during the trial at the end of the Marconi Scandal were still alive, he wrote a spiteful open letter to Rufus Isaacs: 'It would be irrational to ask you for sympathy but I am sincerely moved to offer it. You are far more unhappy; for your brother is still alive.'[9] Such an outburst was so out of character for the normally affable and affectionate Chesterton that one is forced to repeat Knox's plaintive questions: 'What kind of state of mind are we in? What has the war done to us?' One is also reminded of Chesterton's own words when he recalled that both his brother and his old enemy, Godfrey Isaacs, had died as Catholics: 'It is the only reconciliation; and it can reconcile anybody. *Requiescant in pace.*'[10]

There is little doubt that the emotional maelstrom in which Chesterton found himself in the wake of his brother's death also played a significant part in his own conversion four years later. From the time of Cecil's death, Chesterton felt a great responsibility to his brother's memory and a compulsion to carry on with the work his brother had started. This is seen clearly by his promise on 13 December 1918, a week after his brother's funeral, that he would continue with the work that Cecil has 'left for us to do. There are many of us who will abandon many other things, and recognise no greater duty than to do it.'[11] In practical terms this meant taking over the editorship of the *New Witness*, a job he had originally accepted only on a temporary basis while his brother was on active service. He continued as editor, in spite of the great sacrifices it entailed over the years, until his own death. In spiritual terms, one cannot but feel that he saw his own reception into the Church as a reunion with his brother and an act of service to the honour of his memory. Chesterton would have denied the fact and would have pointed as always to the primacy of rational considerations in his decision to convert. Yet, even accepting that reason was the principal factor, one cannot rule out the role of emotional elements exerting an influence both sublime and subliminal. One of these must have been a desire for communion with his brother.

Cecil's death also caused an artistic conversion in Chesterton, particularly in his poetry. Before the horrors of the war were unleashed his poems of battle such as 'Lepanto' and *The Ballad of the White Horse* were characterized by pomp and triumphalism. Ironically, this made them very popular during wartime. The uplifting quality of both ballads served as an antidote to the misery of the trenches. A short note to Chesterton from John Buchan, dated 21 June 1915, stated that 'the other day in the trenches we shouted your "Lepanto"'.[12] Similarly, *The Ballad of the White Horse* was carried by many in the trenches for both comfort and inspiration and a sailor's widow informed Chesterton that 'a copy of *The Ballad of the White Horse* went down into the Humber with the R.38. My husband loved it as his own'.[13] This uplifting quality was employed again during the Second World War when *The Times*, under the heading '*Sursum Corda*', carried a brief statement of the Allied defeat in Crete, followed by the words from *The Ballad of the White Horse* spoken in a vision to King Alfred by the Blessed Virgin:

> I tell you naught for your comfort,
> Yea, naught for your desire,
> Save that the sky grows darker yet
> And the sea rises higher.
>
> Night shall be thrice night over you,
> And heaven an iron cope.
> Do you have joy without a cause,
> Yea, faith without a hope?

The Times returned to the *Ballad* months later when Winston Churchill spoke of 'the end of the beginning', comparing the Prime Minister's words with those of King Alfred at the battle of Ethandune:

> 'The high tide!' King Alfred cried.
> 'The high tide and the turn!'

Although Chesterton would have been delighted to know that his poetry spoke so potently to his fellow countrymen his grief at the end of the war spoke a different language. His 'Elegy in a Country Churchyard' did not convey the peace of Thomas Gray's more famous poem of the same name, not least because the desolate Chesterton felt no peace. But what it lacked in subtlety and finesse it gained in the packing of the punch:

> The men that worked for England
> They have their graves at home:
> And bees and birds of England
> About the cross can roam.
>
> But they that fought for England,
> Following a falling star,
> Alas, alas for England
> They have their graves afar.
>
> And they that rule in England,
> In stately conclave met,
> Alas, alas for England
> They have no graves as yet.

This was a very different Chesterton, a war-scarred Chesterton expressing himself in the language of the new generation of young war poets such as Wilfred Owen and Siegfried Sassoon. The similarities between this grief-stricken and bitter verse and Sassoon's 'Fight to a Finish' or Owen's 'Apologia pro Poemate Meo' are striking. There were obvious differences. Chesterton, middle-aged and obese, never saw action and was unable to express himself in the language of a war-worn veteran. His verse is not inspired by experience gained but by the experience of loss. It was a bitter experience and in this he could share in the bitterness of returning troops.

Not all the troops returned, of course, and neither did all the poets. Wilfred Owen, like Cecil Chesterton, was killed in the last days of the war. Owen died on the morning of 4 November 1918 during an assault on the Oise–Sambre Canal, near Ors. His death was not only a tragic loss to friends and family but a great loss to literature. His poetry, such as 'Dulce et Decorum Est', 'Exposure' and 'Anthem for Doomed Youth' has earned him a permanent place in the first rank of English letters. Yet his talent, so cruelly and prematurely snubbed out, might never have come to light but for his friendship with Siegfried Sassoon, a fellow poet who survived the war and whose subsequent life would be one long and contemplative search for truth, a poet's pilgrimage to Rome.

Sassoon had enjoyed, or rather endured, a controversially meteoric and mixed military career, his war service making him both famous and infamous, hero and villain. In June 1916 he was very much the hero, being awarded the Military Cross for gallantry in battle after he had brought in under heavy fire a wounded lance-corporal who was lying close to the German lines. This and other acts of bravery earned him the nickname of 'Mad Jack'. Robert Graves, a fellow officer in the Royal Welch Fusiliers and later to become a writer of distinction himself, remembered Sassoon calmly reading *The London Mail* shortly before going 'over the top' during the crucial attack at Fricourt. In 1917, after capturing some German trenches in the Hindenburg Line single-handed, he remained in the enemy position reading a volume of poems, oblivious of the danger. As a result of this latest act of cavalier gallantry he was recommended for the Victoria Cross.

Sassoon was wounded during the fighting in the Hindenburg Line and was invalided home. It was then that he began to reflect upon the human butchery he had witnessed, endured and inflicted. From these moments of reflection the hero hatched the villain. The perfect soldier became the pacifist rebel. This change in outlook was described perceptively by Robert Graves in his autobiographical *Goodbye to All That*: 'Siegfried's unconquerable idealism changed direction with his environment. He varied between happy warrior and bitter pacifist.'[14]

The bitter pacifist found himself in an almost hopeless dilemma. To avoid returning to the Front by becoming a desk soldier would be a coward's option; to lay down his arms publicly required courage but would be misunderstood as cowardice by everyone else; to become an instructor training others to take his place seemed the most repulsive option of all. There seemed to be no choice. He would have to return to the bloodbath - but not before he had made a public stand against the continuance of the war. This he did in dramatic circumstances.

In July 1917, he addressed 'A Soldier's Declaration' to his commanding officer and sent a copy to the *Bradford Pioneer*:

> I am making this statement as an act of wilful defiance of military authority, because I believe that the war is being deliberately prolonged by those who have the power to end it. I am a soldier, convinced that I am acting on behalf of soldiers. I believe that this war, upon which I entered as a war of defence and liberation, may now become a war of aggression and conquest. I have seen and endured the sufferings of the troops, and I can no longer be party to prolong these sufferings for ends which I believe to be evil and unjust.[15]

Sassoon was already becoming famous as a poet, having had poems about the war published in the *Cambridge Magazine* and other periodicals since the previous year, but the declaration made him notorious. In a further gesture of defiance he threw the Military Cross into the River Mersey and his notoriety reached new heights when his declaration was read out by Lees Smith, the Liberal MP for Northampton, in the House of Commons. The wording of the declaration was now public knowledge and was quoted in *The Times* on 31 July. The *Times* extract ended with Sassoon's complaint about 'the callous complaisance with which the majority of those at home regard the continuance of the agonies which they do not share and have not sufficient imagination to realise'.

Many expected that Sassoon's open act of rebellion would lead to his court-martial but in the event, in true Orwellian fashion, he was declared mentally overwrought and not responsible for his actions. He was sent to Craiglockhart military hospital in Edinburgh to be treated for psychological shell-shock. It was here that he met and befriended Wilfred Owen, encouraging Owen to write many of his best poems. According to Jon Stallworthy, Owen's biographer, 'meeting Sassoon was the most significant meeting of his life'.[16] If the meeting had not taken place many of the poems which have come to sum up the First World War might never have been written – and one of Britain's most famous war poets would almost certainly have died unknown.

Sassoon came to know a poet of a very different kind in the first months after the war had ended. His meeting with Hilaire Belloc, whether fated or fortuitous, led Sassoon closer to the communion to which Belloc belonged and to which Sassoon himself, after a lifetime's quest, would also submit forty years later. At first sight, at least if their respective approach to poetry is to be taken as a guide, the two men could not have been less alike. Sassoon's lurid descriptions of the 'base details' of war, coupled with the intrepid introspection which saw Golgotha amidst the Hell, contrasts with Belloc's jocular and jaunty ballades in praise of wine, water and song. Furthermore, whereas Sassoon had seen active service during the war Belloc had been safe at home pontificating in sundry magazines and giving the authorities his 'expert' advice on how the war could best be won. The differences appeared insurmountable and a superficial rendering of the facts would lead one inexorably to that conclusion; but the truth, like the men themselves, was deeper.

Their apparent differences masked much that the two men shared, above all a strong spirituality shaped by suffering and the waste of war. Again, although this may be obvious in the case of Sassoon few would have accredited such a diagnosis to Belloc, whose banter and bombast drowned out the silence within him. Yet if the silence could not be heard it was still there, a powerful silence closer to his heart than all the bravado of his rhetoric. Its cause was a sweet and sour cocktail: the grief of bereavement mixed with the love of God.

The death of his wife in 1914 had affected him profoundly, leaving him guilt-ridden and self-reproachful for his inadequacies as a husband and his inability to make amends in her absence. He remained in mourning for the rest of his life, never entering her room, always crossing himself when he passed her door and wearing black broadcloth as a mark of his loss. Perhaps, as with the lifelong mourning of Queen Victoria after the death of Prince Albert, his actions were over-indulgent and disproportionate. They were none the less genuine and it is true to say that the rumbustiousness and revelry with which he is remembered in retrospect is the product of the earlier, happier Belloc. It is no coincidence that his happiest books, such as *The Four Men*, *The Path to Rome* and his cautionary verses, were all written before 1914.

Neither was he to escape the suffering of the war itself. No one was 'safe at home' during the war and Belloc suffered as much as any from the loss of loved ones. Like everyone else he was affected by the deaths of close friends, not least of whom was Cecil Chesterton. Yet it was the death of his son on 26 August 1918 which was the hardest blow of all. Louis Belloc was killed only weeks before his twenty-first birthday during a Royal Flying Corps bombing raid over enemy lines. His body was never found.

It was in the summer of the following year that Sassoon and Belloc first met. Sassoon was staying with the ageing poet Wilfrid Scawen Blunt who suggested his guest call on Belloc, his 'most valued neighbour'. According to Sassoon, Belloc had for many years helped to sustain Blunt with his 'brilliant powers as a talker and the gusto of his human companionship'.[17] It was therefore suggested that Sassoon walk the two miles across the fields to King's Land with the purpose of persuading Belloc to visit Blunt later the same day. It was a scorching summer's day when he arrived at Belloc's home, 'a rambling old farmhouse with a disused windmill standing near to it'. Belloc received him 'with glowing hospitality' and led him into 'a cool, low-windowed living room ... local in character, with its beamed ceiling, open fireplace, and old oak furniture'.[18] Following the consumption of a goblet of Burgundy, Belloc took Sassoon to see the view from the top of his windmill. Pointing out the various landmarks and waxing lyrical on Sussex folklore, Belloc made an indelible impression on his young guest:

> Broad and sturdy in his black clothes, he was eloquent about the Weald and its local customs and traditions. Observing his fine, ruddy, and uncompromising countenance, I was aware that nothing could be more delightfully Bellocian than his eulogizing of the Sussex landscape. But

the Burgundy had made me slightly tipsy, and I suspected that he must be forming an unfavourable opinion of me as a disapproving and unfriendly example of the younger generation.[19]

Far from being disapproving and unfriendly, Sassoon was already a great admirer of Belloc. Twenty-five years later he wrote that his own generation of writers 'would have been thankful to have written a tithe of his resonant prose. And a few years ago he produced a long poem which will outlive most of the verse published by his contemporaries.' He also praised the 'magnificently perfected couplets' in Belloc's poem 'In Praise of Wine', 'which I can never read without emotion'.[20]

Sassoon's first impressions of Belloc were reinforced that evening when Belloc arrived at Blunt's house and accompanied the old man and his young guest to the paddocks to look at some of Blunt's Arab stallions. Sassoon remembered the evening in evocative prose, describing how they sat quietly 'enjoying the vesperal coolness while shadows lengthened and sun rays glorified the tree-tops':

Mr Blunt, tired but reluctant to return to his room, had asked Belloc to sing something. Not having heard of his country songs, I was taken by surprise when, with complete naturalness, he trolled out a ditty in his high tenor voice. It was 'Ha'nacker Mill' that he sang, to a tune of his own, and he made it sound as if the words had come down through long-vanished generations. In fact I assumed it to be an old Sussex ballad, though in print it has more the quality of a modern poem, except, perhaps, in the first verse.

Sally is gone that was so kindly.
Sally is gone from Ha'nacker Hill.
And the briar grows ever since then so blindly
And ever since then the clapper is still,
And the sweeps have fallen from Ha'nacker Mill.[21]

There is something uncannily apocalyptic in this vision of the three men at sunset: the old man reminiscing, the middle-aged man mourning and the young man seeking. Unity in a melancholic trinity.

Belloc's own melancholy was embodied in the song he sang, the depths of which are plumbed further in the two remaining verses that Sassoon chose not to quote:

Ha'nacker Hill is in Desolation:
   Ruin a-top and a field unploughed.
And Spirits that call on a fallen nation
   Spirits that loved her calling aloud:
   Spirits abroad in a windy cloud.

Spirits that call and no one answers;
   Ha'nacker's down and England's done.
Wind and Thistle for pipe and dancers
   And never a ploughman under the Sun.
   Never a ploughman. Never a one.

In this verse Belloc had, perhaps unwittingly, captured the mood of vast sections of post-war England. The land fit for heroes to which the soldiers had hoped to return was nothing but a dream, the reality a nightmare. Pessimism and cynicism reigned in a vacuum, a waste land where 'spirits abroad in a windy cloud' were 'spirits that call and no one answers'. The key to the whole poem was encompassed by the solitary word 'Desolation' which, even where it was not applicable to others, certainly applied to Belloc. In a letter to Professor Edward G. Browne, a Cambridge don, on 28 July 1920 Belloc, referring to the fiftieth birthday which he had just celebrated, wrote: 'I welcome every birthday because I find it an approach to the grave ... whereas few men seek death, all after a certain age desire to be rid of life.'[22]

These were words of desolation, not despair. Belloc was well aware of the difference between the two and the theological and sinful nature of the latter. Life must go on: where possible it should be enjoyed on the babbling surface even when endured in the still depths. The surface was enriched by a wide variety of friends, the company of whom was a constant comfort. He enjoyed the companionship of contemporaries, such as Baring and Chesterton, but also loved the liveliness of the younger generation. Besides making the acquaintance of Sassoon, he also gathered round him other young acolytes such as D. B. Wyndham Lewis and J. B. Morton. Partly due to Belloc's influence both these rising stars of Fleet Street became Catholic converts, Wyndham Lewis in 1921 and Morton the following year. Morton took over Wyndham Lewis's highly popular 'Beachcomber' column in the *Daily Express* in 1924 and Wyndham Lewis later became 'Timothy Shy' in the *News Chronicle*. Together they established a satirical style of journalism which remained popular in spite of attacks from George Orwell and others who accused them of using their columns to write Catholic propaganda. Orwell wrote scathingly that 'From either a literary or a political point of view these two are simply the leavings on Chesterton's plate.'[23] In fact, they were more the leavings on Belloc's plate. Both remained lifelong friends of their mentor, attending his sixtieth and eightieth birthday celebrations.

At the same time that Belloc's bombastic brand of evangelism was bringing young Fleet Street journalists to the Church, he was displaying a much more subtle approach in his efforts to return the eighty-year-old Wilfrid Scawen Blunt to the faith he had rejected.

In 1916 Belloc had introduced Blunt to Father Vincent McNabb, the eccentric apostle of the Ditchling community. Belloc held Father McNabb in high regard and considered the Dominican's panegyric at Cecil Chesterton's requiem Mass the finest piece of sacred oratory he had ever heard. Although Blunt was well aware of Belloc's ulterior motive in introducing him to McNabb, he accepted him into his circle of friends. According to Elizabeth Longford, Blunt's biographer, 'The friendship with Father McNabb was a growing source of light in Blunt's darkness.'[24]

On 22 October 1921 Blunt was so ill that he made what he thought would be his last ever diary entry. It was a cry for spiritual help, a scream in the dark: 'I should like to die worthily but I feel it is beyond my power. I go out into the darkness where no wisdom can avail. I would wish to believe in another life beyond, for my life here has been a happy one. I would wish to believe a good God loves us all.'[25]

Although his health continued to falter he received a stay of execution. Both spiritually and physically he staggered on, recording in his diary on St Patrick's Day 1922 that Belloc had gone to Rome, bringing Blunt's homage to Pope Pius XI: 'How willingly would I believe if only I could but, woe is me, I cannot.'[26]

A week later Belloc returned with a crucifix blessed for Blunt by the Pope. It was a decisive moment. 'It found me,' Blunt recorded, 'in a mood for conversion and an insistence on the necessity for me of a return to the Sacraments before I die.'[27]

Belloc assured him that being already a Catholic and with no quarrel with the Church he was entitled to ask for the sacraments. Blunt was finally convinced by a personal admission by Belloc that he himself often went to the sacraments 'feeling little'. This was a revelation to Blunt, a mystical moment springing from a sceptical statement. Depth in the dryness of dust. Suddenly he perceived that the faltering, flickering candle of the sincere sinner was as much in need of the oxygen of grace as was the flaming faith of the saints. Since Belloc's faith seemed also to be only a flickering candle he was ideally suited to help an old man groping in the dark. One can imagine the bond between the two natural sceptics as they discussed the difficulties of belief. The line of argument taken by Belloc must have been similar to that which he expressed in a letter to Chesterton a few months later:

> I am by all my nature of mind sceptical, by all my nature of body exceedingly sensual. So sensual that the virtues restrictive of sense are but phrases to me. But I accept these phrases as true and act upon them as well as a struggling man can. And as to the doubt of the soul I discover it to be false: a mood: not a conclusion. My conclusion – and that of all men who have ever once *seen* it – is the faith. Corporate, organised, a personality, teaching. A thing, not a theory. It.
>
> To you, who have the blessing of profound religious emotion, this statement may seem too desiccate ... But beyond this there will come in time, if I save my soul, the flesh of these bones – which bones alone I can describe and teach. I know – without feeling (an odd thing in such a connection) the reality of Beatitude: which is the goal of Catholic Living.[28]

These words were written on 1 August 1922, two days after Chesterton's reception into the Church had come as an oasis in Belloc's desert. The other oasis was the sight of Blunt's final return to the faith of his birth. Assured by Belloc that faith was an act of the will subject to the grace of God which did not require any 'feeling', Blunt requested that Father McNabb be sent for. Shane Leslie, in his account of Blunt's reconciliation, vividly imagined the 'great moment' when the sheikh of Sussex and the Irish Dominican met, 'both wearing white robes'.[29]

Having taken his decision, Blunt began at once a brief daily service of prayer, with a small altar on his bed formed by the Pope's crucifix, an Irish snuff-box and St Winifred's well-water. He felt himself again 'a pilgrim to her shrine'. Physically his new-found faith allayed his pain, enabling him to talk again, but spiritually the return of what Blunt called 'the pieties of my youth' led to the pains of repentance. The sins of the past kept returning, 'repented now but unforgotten', and on one occasion his sense of guilt was so overpowering that he wrote to Father McNabb in a panic. The priest's reply, dated 14 August, was reassuring: 'Do not be anxious. You have received all the Sacraments of the Church.'[30]

Blunt died on the morning of 10 September 1922 and was buried beneath the soil of his own grounds. The monument erected over his grave included six lines from his sonnet 'Chanclebury Ring':

Dear checker-work of woods, the Sussex Weald!
If a name thrills me yet of things of earth,
That name is thine. How often have I fled
To thy deep hedgerows and embraced each field,
Each lag, each pasture, – fields which gave me birth
And saw my youth, and which must hold me dead.

The similarities between this and several of Belloc's poems in praise of Sussex are striking. Six Bellocian lines in particular seem an answering call to the six lines on Blunt's tomb:

He does not die that can bequeath
Some influence to the land he knows,
Or dares, persistent, interwreath
Love permanent with the wild hedgerows;
    He does not die, but still remains
    Substantiate with his darling plains.

The fact that Belloc and Blunt were kindred spirits was perceived in poetic prose by Siegfried Sassoon in his memories of his first evening with them:

what returns to me in sunset light is the broad and bulky yet somehow boyish figure of the singer, sitting on a bench close by the old friend whom he was intent on pleasing, and Wilfrid Blunt, listening with half-closed eyes, his face touched to tenderness and regret by the power and pathos of the words. I see them thus together, and so shall always do ...[31]

The bond, of course, went deeper than the soil of Sussex, and Sassoon, a child of Kent, knew that the real core of their being was best expressed in Sassoon's own favourite of all Blunt's verse, a poem which begins:

Love me a little, love me as thou wilt,
Whether a draught it be of passionate wine
Poured with both hands divine,
Or just a cup of water spilt
On dying lips and mine.

Belloc bid Blunt farewell, envious perhaps that his friend no longer felt that 'desire to be rid of life' which ate away at his own being. A thirsty traveller trudging doggedly and dogmatically through a spiritual desert, Belloc carried the burdens of bereavement with a resolute resignation. As he had confessed to Chesterton, grief had drawn the juices from life. In this he was not alone. Grief had drawn the juices from the lives of a whole generation. England after the war was a waste land of hopes and desires. Ironically it would take a young American poet with no war experience to express the collective anguish of the nation.

NOTES

1. Laura Lovat (ed.), *Maurice Baring: A Postscript with Some Letters and Verse*, London, 1947, pp. 57–8.
2. ibid., pp. 58–9.
3. Penelope Fitzgerald, *The Knox Brothers*, p. 151.
4. Evelyn Waugh, *Ronald Knox*, p. 145.
5. ibid., p. 146.
6. ibid., p. 145.
7. Penelope Fitzgerald, *The Knox Brothers*, p. 151.
8. Ada Chesterton, *The Chestertons*, London, 1941, pp. 237–8.
9. Michael Ffinch, *G. K. Chesterton: A Biography*, London, 1988, p. 251.
10. G. K. Chesterton, *Autobiography*, London, 1936, p. 208.
11. *New Witness*, 13 December 1918.
12. Maisie Ward, *Gilbert Keith Chesterton*, p. 317.
13. ibid., p. 245.
14. Stanley Jackson, *The Sassoons*, London, 1968, p. 164.
15. ibid., p. 164.
16. *Sunday Telegraph*, 24 November 1996.
17. Siegfried Sassoon, *Siegfried's Journey, 1916–1920*, London, 1945, p. 155.
18. ibid., p. 156.
19. ibid., p. 157.
20. ibid., p. 157.
21. ibid., p. 158.
22. Unpublished letter in the author's possession.
23. Sonia Orwell and Ian Angus (ed.), *George Orwell: The Collected Essays, Journalism and Letters Vol. III*, London, 1968, p. 175.
24. Elizabeth Longford, *A Pilgrimage of Passion: A Life of Wilfrid Scawen Blunt*, London, 1979, p. 420.
25. ibid., p. 421.
26. ibid., p. 422.
27. ibid., p. 422.
28. Robert Speaight, *The Life of Hilaire Belloc*, pp. 374–5.
29. Elizabeth Longford, *A Pilgrimage of Passion: A Life of Wilfrid Scawen Blunt*, p. 422.
30. ibid., p. 423.
31. Siegfried Sassoon, *Siegfried's Journey*, pp. 158–9.

CHAPTER TWELVE

POETRY IN COMMOTION

On 21 August 1914 an American graduate student arrived in London. He was twenty-six years old and was reading for his doctorate at Harvard University. He had gained from Harvard one of its Sheldon Traveling Fellowships, under the terms of which he would spend a year at Merton College, Oxford advancing his studies in philosophy. All looked set for the beginning of a promising academic career which his family hoped would lead to an eminent professorship in the United States. It was not to be. Instead, Thomas Stearns Eliot was destined to become probably the most influential poet of the century.

Although Eliot did not pursue the career his family had mapped out for him, his studies did not go to waste. The philosophical foundations laid at Harvard would form the foundations of his poetry and the starting point for a life of metaphysical grappling.

At Harvard he had been fortunate to study under such distinguished teachers as George Santayana, but it was the course he took in French literary criticism under Irving Babbitt which had the most lasting impact. Eliot later criticized Babbitt for not being a believer and for the inadequacy of his humanism, but he owed his tutor a considerable debt. Babbitt had introduced him to many of the classics and had alerted him to the dangers of modern secularism. Most importantly, Babbitt had suggested that the Catholic Church might be the only institution left in the West that could be counted on to preserve the traditions and treasures of the past. If one followed Babbitt's reasoning to its logical conclusion, Eliot remarked, one came to 'a Catholicism of despair'.[1] Babbitt's influence is evident in Eliot's continued interest in the views of Charles Maurras, whose traditionalist and anti-secular views paralleled those of Babbitt in some respects and who, like Babbitt, admired the institutions and traditions of the Church without initially believing in Christianity itself. In the March 1913 edition of the *Nouvelle Revue Française* Eliot saw Maurras described as the embodiment of a traditionalist trinity: 'classique, catholique, monarchique'. It captured his imagination to such an extent that fifteen years later Eliot would describe himself as a classicist, royalist and Anglo-Catholic.

A less controversial influence was that of Dante. As early as 1911 Eliot had begun to carry a copy of *The Divine Comedy* in his pocket as a constant companion. His devotion spilled over in an article on 'Dante as a Spiritual Leader' for the *Athenaeum* on 2 April 1920. He informed a friend, 'I feel that anything I can say about such a subject is trivial. I feel so completely inferior in his presence – there seems really nothing to do but to point to him and be silent.'[2] In *The Sacred Wood*, also published in 1920, Eliot wrote that 'Dante's is the most comprehensive, and the most *ordered* presentation of emotions that has ever been made.'[3]

The Sacred Wood established Eliot's reputation as a literary critic. It seemed to the poet and playwright R. C. Trevelyan 'the wisest and ... the most helpful literary criticism of our time'.[4] Trevelyan's letter of praise gave Eliot 'greater pleasure than the most flattering review' and in his reply he endeavoured to explain his lacklustre attitude to Milton, comparing him unfavourably to Dante: 'Dante seems to me so immeasurably greater in every way, even in control of language, that I am often irritated by Milton's admirers.'[5]

Another crucial influence on Eliot was his arrival in England. His stay, intended as temporary, became permanent. In 1927 he became a naturalized British subject. As early as January 1916 he wrote that he was having 'a wonderful life' in England, acknowledging that it was 'entirely different' from the one he had contemplated two years previously, but that life in Cambridge, Massachusetts 'seems to me a dull nightmare now'.[6] In 1917 his first volume of verse, *Prufrock and Other Observations*, had been published, and this in turn led to his being introduced to many of the new generation of poets.

In December 1917, at a charity poetry reading in aid of the Red Cross held in Lady Sybil Colefax's drawing-room, Eliot first met the three Sitwells: Edith, Sacheverell and Osbert. Others at the reading were Robert Graves, Robert Nichols, Aldous Huxley and Viola Tree. The event was chaired by Sir Edmund Gosse who represented the old guard in the presence of the *avant garde*. Irene Rutherford McLeod read poems by Siegfried Sassoon who had been due to appear but had failed to turn up. It seems that Eliot had a pretty low opinion of most of the other poets. On 31 October he had written: 'I have been invited ... to contribute to a reading of poets, and what a poor lot they are! the only one who has any merit is a youth named Siegfried Sassoon (semitic) and his stuff is better politics than poetry.'[7] The gratuitous reference to Sassoon's ethnic ancestry was indicative of the anti-semitic influence of Maurras and it was odd that Eliot should describe Sassoon as a youth since Eliot was himself two years Sassoon's junior.

Eliot's negative view of his contemporaries did not prevent him fraternizing with the Sitwells, meeting them regularly in London tea-shops during 1918 and 1919. Edith Sitwell in particular held a pivotal position at the very centre of the new poetry, principally due to her editing between 1916 and 1921 of *Wheels*. This was an annual anthology of new poems which were modern in style and challenged traditional poetic form. From the outset Edith Sitwell had employed shock tactics to send tremors through literary conventions, ever since her first published poem, 'Drowned Suns', had appeared in the *Daily Mirror* in 1913. Yet Sitwell's sun, if not drowned, was well and truly eclipsed in 1922 by the publication of Eliot's *The Waste Land*, possibly the most influential and controversial poem written this century. Its appearance was at once a revelation and a revolution, polarizing opinion. A reviewer in the *Manchester Guardian* called it 'a mad medley' and concluded with a sneer of derision: 'one can only say that if Mr Eliot had been pleased to write in demotic English *The Waste Land* might not have been, as it just is to all but anthropologists and *literati*, so much waste paper'.[8] The reviewer for the *Times Literary Supplement* made more of an effort to get to grips with the poet's purpose, though with limited success:

> The poetic personality of Mr Eliot is extremely sophisticated. His emotions hardly ever reach us without traversing a zig-zag of allusion … From the opening part, 'The Burial of the Dead', to the final one we seem to see a world, or a mind, in disaster and mocking its despair. We are aware of the toppling of aspirations, the swift disintegration of accepted stability, the crash of an ideal. Set at a distance by a poetic method which is reticence itself, we can only judge of the strength of the emotion by the visible violence of the reaction …
>
> Mr Eliot, always evasive of the grand manner, has reached a stage at which he can no longer refuse to recognize the limitations of his medium; he is sometimes walking very near the limits of coherency. But it is the finest horses which have the most tender mouths, and some unsympathetic tug has sent Mr Eliot's gift awry. When he recovers control we shall expect his poetry to have gained in variety and strength from this ambitious experiment.[9]

Whether *The Waste Land* was considered waste paper or an ambitious experiment it confounded everyone who read it. It both bemused and beguiled its admirers and irritated and infuriated its detractors. The *avant garde* gazed in awe at its many layers; the old guard claimed that the layers were an illusion and that the Emperor had no clothes. The pessimism of its language and the libertine nature of its form both added to the controversy. The war of the Waste Land was joined.

Many years later, the obituary to Eliot in *The Times* came close to a true perspective of the issues raised by the poem and the nature of the ensuing reaction:

> Its presentation of disillusionment and the disintegration of values, catching the mood of the time, made it the poetic gospel of the postwar intelligentsia; at the time, however, few either of its detractors or its admirers saw through the surface innovations and the language of despair to the deep respect for tradition and the keen moral sense which underlay them.[10]

As is so often the case, such a detached view was not possible in the midst of the fray.

At the time, few critics appeared to understand Eliot's purpose in writing *The Waste Land*. Lack of understanding inevitably led to misunderstanding so that battle lines were drawn according to erroneous preconceptions. On the one side the 'moderns' hailed it as a masterpiece of modern thought which had laid waste traditional values and traditional form. The 'ancients' attacked it as an iconoclastic affront to civilized standards. Both sides had made the grave and fundamental error of mistaking Eliot's pessimism towards the Waste Land of modern life for a cynicism towards tradition. As we have seen from the philosophical foundations of his thought, he was rooted in classical tradition and despised modern secular liberalism. The irony was that he was vilified by the upholders of classical tradition and championed by the doyens of secularism.

The key to understanding *The Waste Land*, overlooked by everyone at the time, was to be found in Eliot's devotion to Dante. Scarcely two years before *The Waste Land* was published, Eliot had written:

> You cannot ... understand the *Inferno* without the *Purgatorio* and the *Paradiso*. 'Dante,' says Landor's Petrarch, 'is the great master of the disgusting.' ... But a disgust like Dante's is no hypertrophy of a single reaction: it is completed and explained only by the last canto of the *Paradiso* ... The contemplation of the horrid or sordid or disgusting, by an artist, is the necessary and negative aspect of the impulse toward the pursuit of beauty.[11]

Eliot perceived that Dante had been grossly misunderstood by the undue emphasis placed upon the 'negative' *Inferno* at the expense of the other two 'positive' books of the *Divine Comedy* and there was something divinely comic in the fact that Eliot himself was to suffer the same fate after the publication of *The Waste Land*. As post-Reformation puritanism had stressed the punishment of Hell in Dante and had ignored the 'papist' parts about Purgatory and Paradise, so post-war cynicism had stressed the negative aspects of Eliot's Waste Land and had ignored the positive conclusion that pointed to a 'resurrection'.

A further irony was the way in which Eliot was hailed as the champion of a modern poetry he obviously despised. In the same essay on Dante he took issue with Paul Valéry's belief that the task of the 'modern poet' was 'to produce in us a *state*'. Eliot countered that 'A state, in itself, is nothing whatever.'[12] Against such subjectivist reductionism, Eliot upheld the 'philosophy of Aristotle strained through the schools', the poetic master of which was Dante:

> Dante, more than any other poet, has succeeded in dealing with his philosophy, not as a theory ... or as his own comment or reflection, but in terms of something *perceived*. When most of our modern poets confine themselves to what they had perceived, they produce for us, usually, only odds and ends of still life and stage properties; but that does not so much imply that the method of Dante is obsolete, as that our vision is perhaps comparatively restricted.[13]

One can only guess at the nature of Eliot's reaction as it became increasingly clear that the success of *The Waste Land* had precious little to do with philosophical perception. Rather, it succeeded only in producing a 'state' in its readers, the very mark of modern poetry he had explicitly rejected. Far from having the ability to plumb the depths of *The Waste Land*, its readers rejoiced in the ephemeral shallows of its form. Its 'jazz' rhythms, its images of urban and suburban life, its fashionable use of anthropological myth, its introduction of quotation and parody, the pseudo-intellectual snob value of its intellectualism, all combined to produce a surrealistic impressionism which was *très chic*. A cult of 'The Waste Landers' developed, particularly among undergraduates and young writers. Cyril Connolly recalled 'The veritable brain-washing, the total preoccupation, the drugged and haunted condition which the new poet produced on some of us'.[14] Overnight, Eliot's classical muse had become 'pop'.

Peer pressure ensured that the moderns fell in behind Eliot. His past involvement with Ezra Pound and Percy Wyndham Lewis, and his friendship with the Sitwells, made him a modern with impeccable credentials. Edith Sitwell herself, although evidently unable to grasp the intricacies of *The Waste Land*, felt dutybound to bubble enthusiastically that 'there are some wonderful lines in it'.[15]

Fortuitously, *Façade*, her own most controversial poem to date, had its first stormy public performance in the same year that *The Waste Land* appeared. The title seemed singularly appropriate in relation to the facile façade displayed in her public support for Eliot.

Another poet who was struggling to come to terms with Eliot in 1922 was Siegfried Sassoon. In his diary on 30 March Sassoon recorded that he had spotted Eliot in the front row of the stalls at a performance of Schubert *lieder* at the Queen's Hall:

> T. S. Eliot was sitting in his pale intellectual aloofness. He always has a chilling effect on me. I found myself, by accident, sitting next to him at the Russian Ballet (*Sacre du Printemps*) last summer, and I felt so antagonistic that I scarcely spoke to him at all. He makes me feel an intellectual hobbledehoy ... But tonight I was impelled by my all-embracing bonhomie to walk across to him during an interval; I touched him on the arm; ... he looked up, and seemed slightly surprised by my hearty handshake.
>
> But I felt that I was failing to thaw his cold-storaged humanity; and I stood in front of him, talking about the concert with clumsy cordiality; utterly incapable of impressing him with even a semblance of analytic ingenuity.[16]

There was more than a semblance of analytic ingenuity when, following a performance of Bach's B Minor Mass at Oxford a few weeks later, Sassoon wrote his 'Sheldonian Soliloquy'. Written in the modern idiom this offered a tantalizing glimpse of an embryonic Christianity which would have a thirty-five-year gestation period. Published in the *Nation* on 27 May it became one of his most popular compositions and helped reinforce his own reputation as a poet of originality. Three days previously his defence of Sitwell's *Façade* had been published in the *Daily Herald* under the provocatively combative title 'Too Fantastic for Fat-Heads'. He recorded in his diary that 'Edith's poetry is original, and beautiful in its modes of fantastic plumage.'[17]

The Fat-Heads in Sassoon's review of *Façade* were the philistines of the old guard who refused to accept the changes in form heralded by the new generation of poets. Curiously he was less outspoken the following month when one of the most prominent members of the old guard attacked Eliot in his presence. The occasion was a dinner appointment with Edmund Gosse who had ridiculed Eliot's Shakespearean criticism. Sassoon, no doubt in deference to his host's feelings, remained silent as Gosse launched a broadside against Eliot. 'I found myself incapable of defending Eliot,' Sassoon confessed. 'And T.S.E. was dismissed as a ninny – a conceited literary humbug. Yet I know quite well that T.S.E. is nothing of the kind.'[18]

Sassoon's failure to stand up and be counted on this occasion was an indication of the ambiguous nature of his own position among the moderns. His own poetic style was more traditional than most of his contemporaries' and he avoided the excesses in experimentation which were becoming fashionable. Furthermore, although peer pressure kept him in the 'poetically correct' camp of the moderns, his sympathies transcended the stereotypes which marked out the adherents to either side. Thus, he recorded his great respect for Gosse: 'He always sends me away with a desire to excel in the honourable craft of literature. He is a faithful servant to the distinctions and amenities of decent writing. He upholds delicacy and precision in the art of letters.'[19]

Although the poetry of the moderns had totally beguiled the majority of undergraduates the young and still unknown C. S. Lewis remained singularly unimpressed, siding with the ancients. As early as 1920 Lewis and a small group of friends had hatched a scheme to bring out an anthology of traditionalist verse to rival Edith Sitwell's *Wheels* anthology. Lewis explained the scheme in a letter to his father:

> It is being got up as a kind of counterblast to the ruling literary fashion here, which consists in the tendencies called 'Vorticist'. Vorticist poems are usually in *vers libre* ... Some of them are clever, the majority merely affected, and a good few – especially among the French ones – indecent: not a sensuous indecency, but one meant to nauseate, the whole genus arising from the 'sick of everything' mood. So some of us others who are not yet sick of everything have decided to bring out a yearly collection of our own things in the hope of persuading the gilded youth that the possibilities of metrical poetry on sane subjects are not yet quite exhausted because the Vorticists are suffering from satiety.[20]

The scheme was abandoned when failure to secure a publisher meant that Lewis and the other contributors would have to finance the project themselves.

According to Walter Hooper, Lewis's biographer, T. S. Eliot 'was, and remained, the incarnation of what he most hated in modern poetry'.[21]

Six years after the original abortive scheme Lewis came up with another idea designed to strike a blow against modern poetry. Beginning on 9 June 1926 there are numerous entries in his diary about his plan to expose Eliot's poetry through his own mock 'Eliotic' verse. Lewis wrote to William Force Stead, enclosing for his criticism a parody of T. S. Eliot which I had just scribbled off: very nonsensical, but with a flavour of dirt all through. My idea is to send it up to his paper in the hope that he will be taken in and publish it: if he falls into the trap I will then consider how best to use the joke for the advancement of literature and the punishment of quackery. If he doesn't I shall have proved that there is something more than I suspected in this kind of stuff.[22]

Eliot was never taken in by any of these 'Eliotic' submissions but Lewis failed to draw the obvious conclusion that 'there is something more than I suspected in this kind of stuff'. Instead he remained obstinately convinced of the intrinsic inferiority of modern poetry, telling Walter Hooper towards the end of his life that 'I never liked Eliot's poetry or his prose but when I met him I loved him.'[23]

It would be many years before Eliot and Lewis finally met and many years also before the world of literature became aware of Lewis's culturally conservative voice. In the meantime his voice was unknown and unheard, a plaintive cry in the wilderness. Instead Eliot and the moderns found a formidable foe in the person of Alfred Noyes, a respected poet of the old guard who was about to throw down the gauntlet in defiance of modern trends.

Noyes had been hailed as a youthful prodigy himself when his first volume of verse, *The Loom of Years*, was published while he was still an undergraduate at Exeter College, Oxford in 1902. His days as an undergraduate were recalled with great respect by Harold Roberts:

I rowed at bow at Oxford and Henley in the Exeter College boat in 1901, in which Alfred Noyes rowed number six ...

... we were directed to come up for a week's extra training before the term began and to be at the boathouse ready to take our seats at three o'clock on a certain Monday afternoon. We were all duly assembled as directed, except our number six, of whom there was no word.

At 3.15 a bedraggled figure in a lounge suit hurried down the towpath to the boathouse, our missing number six, full of apologies ... Just, as he put it, to start his training, he had walked from his home at Aberystwyth, a distance of 140 miles, starting on the Friday morning, sleeping each night in a barn or under a hedge, buying food in the villages as he passed through and in one, a pair of new boots, for his own, completely worn out. On each of the first three days he had covered forty miles and, at 3.15 on the fourth day, he was fifteen minutes late completing the last twenty. We rowed at 3.50.[24]

The phenomenal success of *The Loom of Years* convinced Noyes that his future as a poet was secure and he left Oxford without taking a degree. Other successful collections of verse were published in the following years, all of which were received enthusiastically. In 1903 he reviewed Chesterton's biography of Robert Browning for the *Speaker*, enthusing that 'Mr Chesterton has wrought the old miracle anew, and we have the wild joy of looking upon the world once more for the first time.' In the same review he summarized the highest common factor in all of Chesterton's writing: 'Mr Chesterton's cry throughout is, "I intend to get to God" and that, in brief, is what he wishes the rest of the world to do.'[25] Half a century later, in his autobiography, Noyes remarked that 'I have some pride in the recollection that in the *Speaker* I was one of the first to proclaim the genius of G. K. Chesterton.'[26] Noyes came to know Chesterton personally through their mutual friendship with Wilfrid Meynell and remembered that Chesterton's 'conversation was as gloriously vital as his writing'.[27] In later years Noyes expressed 'a great admiration for some of Chesterton's poems, particularly his 'Lepanto' and also for some of Belloc's verse and prose, including 'that brilliant tour-de-force *Belinda*'.[28]

Noyes's own career had also been something of a tour-de-force. He received many academic honours culminating in his appointment as visiting professor of English literature at Princeton in 1914. This was a position he still held when he wrote the first volume of *The Torchbearers*, arguably his greatest work. Published in 1922, the same year as Eliot's *Waste Land*, Sassoon's 'Sheldonian Soliloquy' and Sitwell's *Façade*, Noyes's panegyric in blank verse to the unsung men of science stood in stark contrast to the new poetry of the *avant garde*. He found himself out of favour and out of fashion, derided as a throwback to an Edwardian age that had been killed off by the war. This general contempt for Noyes was summed up by Owen Barfield, an undergraduate at Oxford who was a good friend of C. S. Lewis. Barfield, however, failed to share his friend's traditionalism and echoed instead the new consensus: 'Alfred Noyes was considered very old fashioned. *We* were the Georgian poets. *He* was very Victorian.'[29] Edith Sitwell set the hostile tone when she described Noyes's poetry as 'cheap linoleum'.[30]

Noyes was not prepared to take such abuse lightly and came out fighting.

The first blows were struck in 1923 at a public debate held at the London School of Economics. Sitwell and Noyes were to discuss 'the comparative value in old poetry and the new' with Edmund Gosse in the chair. Gosse, having been informed before the commencement of the debate that Sitwell was suffering from nerves and was on the point of fainting, asked Noyes not to be too hard on his opponent. 'Do not, I beg of you, use a weaver's beam on the head of poor Edith.'[31] Noyes, for his part, believed that he might become the victim of

Sitwell's vociferous supporters and could 'suddenly be attacked by a furious flock of strangely coloured birds, frantically trying to peck my nose'.[32]

Noyes's quip was an act of sartorial sarcasm aimed at Sitwell's flamboyant taste in clothes. She arrived for the debate dressed in a purple robe and gold laurel wreath which contrasted clashingly with Noyes's sober American-cut suit and horn-rimmed spectacles. The contrast was sublimely appropriate, the dress addressing the issue. Old and new, ancient and modern, fashion and anti-fashion.

The debate began uneasily when Edith asked if her supporters might sit on the platform with her. Noyes agreed, but took advantage of the situation by telling the audience that he wished he could bring his supporters along as well, naming Virgil, Chaucer, Shakespeare, Dante and others. The *coup de théâtre* had the desired effect and Sitwell shamefacedly sat alone on the platform with Noyes and Gosse. First blood to Noyes.

Sitwell then sat and read from a manuscript, ending paradoxically with an oddly traditionalist approach to novelty: 'We are always being called mad. If we are mad ... at least we are mad in company with most of our great predecessors ... Schumann ... Coleridge and Wordsworth were all mad in turn.'[33]

Noyes kept his promise to Gosse that he would not be too hard on his opponent and refrained from a full-frontal attack on the 'new poetry'. Instead he defended traditional forms of verse, declaring with Sainte-Beuve that 'true poetry is a contemporary of all ages'. After the debate Gosse was the model of courtesy. Leading Sitwell away on his arm he remarked reassuringly, and perhaps patronizingly, 'Come along Edith, I have no doubt that in his day Shakespeare was thought mad.'[34]

The following day the press reported that Sitwell, the champion of modernity, spoke without notes, whereas the old-fashioned Alfred Noyes delivered his text from a ponderous manuscript. It was, of course, the other way round. The crassness of the lie, so reminiscent of the press propaganda of the recent war, was an indication of the prevailing bias towards the moderns. Eliot and Sitwell were popularly perceived as marching 'hand in hand ... in the vanguard of progress' whereas the ancients sought to turn back the tide. Tides turn on their own of course but it was true at the time that the waves of sympathy were all flowing with the moderns. It was odd that the paramount paradox was overlooked: Eliot was progressive for his regression into *The Waste Land* whereas Noyes was regressive for hailing *The Torchbearers* of progress. Admittedly much of the argument centred on poetic form as opposed to content but was the loosening of form itself not a regression into formlessness? At what point does free verse become so free that it ceases to be verse? Was poetry 'progressing' towards extinction?

Such questions were central to the furious controversy in the press which followed the debate at the London School of Economics. Rudyard Kipling joined the fray, declaring that a letter he had received from one of Sitwell's supporters was 'one of the most impertinent' he had ever read.[35] Sitwell, ever a seeker of publicity, welcomed the added notoriety which accompanied Kipling's comments. Kipling, after all, was *passé*.

As the Sitwells continued a war of attrition against their enemies many began to feel irritated at the sheer vindictiveness of their attacks. Sassoon deplored a 'silly attack on Alfred Noyes' by Osbert Sitwell in the *Spectator*: 'How drearily O.S. wastes his time and talent with sterile spitefulness directed at authors who don't admire him and his family.'[36]

The following year Noyes went on the offensive, this time in print. His book on *Some Aspects of Modern Poetry* was both a reasoned defence of traditionalism and a forthright attack on modern trends. The war against modern poetry had now taken on the nature of a personal crusade. This left him open to counter-attack and in particular the sort of ridicule and contempt so often levelled against those who stick their necks out on single issues. There is a parallel to be drawn between Noyes's attacks on poetic licence and Mary Whitehouse's later attacks on sexual licence. Both became bywords for stubborn reaction in the face of 'progress'. Soon no self-respecting young poet would dare list Alfred Noyes as an influence.

However, he was not without allies. J. B. Morton was using his 'Beachcomber' column to poke fun at the Sitwells and other *avant garde* poets, and when Noyes published *The Opalescent Parrot* in 1930 Chesterton reviewed the book enthusiastically:

> Some of our latest literary experimentalists in eccentricity and novelty, or at least those who are chiefly praised for eccentricity and novelty, have a peculiar taste in parrots ... In this part of his allegory, I think Mr Noyes is particularly pointed and true ...
>
> Certain things are accepted in a lump by all the Moderns, mainly because they are supposed (often wrongly) to be rejected with horror by all the Ancients. The Muse, that mysterious being the Modern Girl, is supposed to like a list of disconnected things, bobbed hair and cocktails and *Ulysses* and the works of T. S. Eliot. But if a man, daring to exercise his private and personal judgment as well as he could, should come to the conclusion that bobbed hair is nice, cocktails nasty, T. S. Eliot admirable and *Ulysses* a dingy experiment in argot like an artificial poem in thieves' slang, most of the Moderns would not know what to do with him, or where to place him.[37]

Using the example of Edgar Allan Poe, Chesterton went on to illustrate the way in which the moderns hijacked their favourite ancients, bestowing honorary modernity on them. Poe had been 'set apart as a Modern before the Moderns and used almost to illustrate the unreality of the Victorians; probably from some vague (and very much exaggerated) impression that he was wicked. Poe was something much more important than a Modern or a Victorian; he was a poet.'[38]

Noyes wrote that Chesterton was one of the few who 'completely understood my defence of literary traditions, as well as my criticism of them'.[39]

It was significant that Chesterton's defence of Noyes should include a description of Eliot as 'admirable'. It was certainly true that Chesterton had revised his opinion of Eliot by 1930. He had overcome his initial hostility and arrived at the conclusion that Eliot too was 'something much more important than a Modern ... he was a poet'. This was not a view he held at the time of the initial furore in the wake of *The Waste Land*. In 1923 he countered Eliot's rejection of regular rhythms with a spirited defence of the traditions of rhyme, metre and stanzaic form: 'Song is not only a recurrence, it is a return ... It is in this deeper significance of return that we must seek for the peculiar power in the recurrence we call rhyme.'[40]

Neither was Chesterton enamoured with the pessimism rooted in cynicism which he felt Eliot espoused. When Eliot had proclaimed in his poem *The Hollow Men*, published in 1925, that the world would end 'not with a bang but a whimper', Chesterton was stung into a poetic riposte:

Some sneer; some snigger; some simper;
In the youth where we laughed, and sang.
And *they* may end with a whimper
But *we* will end with a bang.[41]

In fact Chesterton had seriously misjudged the poem, overlooking its underlying attack on modern vacuity. Although couched in pessimistic language its shades of gloom belonged to the shadowlands of mysticism, the vale of tears as a veil of tears hiding metaphysical reality.

Meanwhile Eliot was singularly unimpressed by Chesterton. In the early days he had attacked Chesterton with vehemence, comparing him unfavourably with Pound, Joyce and Percy Wyndham Lewis: 'I have seen the forces of death with Mr Chesterton at their head upon a white horse. Mr Pound, Mr Joyce, and Mr Lewis write living English; one does not realize the awfulness of death until one meets with the living language.'[42]

Eliot's attitude mellowed slowly with time but he still wrote scathingly of Chesterton as late as 1927. In a review of Chesterton's biography of Robert Louis Stevenson, Eliot confessed to finding Chesterton's style 'exasperating to the last point of endurance' but this was tempered with praise for the way he had sought 'to expound a Roman Catholic point of view towards *Dr Jekyll and Mr Hyde*'.[43] The root of Eliot's exasperation was his annoyance at Chesterton's inability to recognize kindred spirits among those he thought to be his enemies: 'He seems always to assume that what his reader has previously believed is exactly the opposite of what Mr Chesterton knows to be true.'[44]

Eliot had a point. Chesterton's woeful failure to get to grips with *The Hollow Men*, assuming that he had taken the trouble to read it before passing judgement, illustrated an ignorance based upon impatience. Eliot's poetry was not as it seemed. Beneath the sardonic surface of his verse sprang a hopefulness which was the very reverse of the decadence and despair of which he stood accused by Chesterton and others. Furthermore, Eliot's hopefulness had its source in the same rich soil of Catholic tradition that had nourished Chesterton over the years. The extent to which he had become rooted in this tradition was illustrated clearly in the lectures on metaphysical poetry he delivered at Trinity College, Cambridge in 1926. Take for instance the clarity of his insight into Catholic mysticism:

> I wish to draw as sharply as possible the difference between the mysticism of Richard of St Victor, which is the mysticism also of St Thomas Aquinas and of Dante, and the mysticism of the Spaniards, which ... is the mysticism of Crashaw and the Society of Jesus. The Aristotelian-Victorine-Dantesque mysticism is ontological; the Spanish mysticism is psychological. The first is what I call classical, the second romantic.[45]

In 1929 Eliot wrote to Chesterton in a spirit of reconciliation: 'I should like extremely to come to see you one day ... May I mention that I have much sympathy with your political and social views, as well as (with obvious reservations) your religious views?'[46]

The ice being broken, a cordial relationship built on mutual respect developed. Chesterton became a valued contributor to the *Criterion*, a quarterly review which Eliot edited, and shortly before his death Chesterton had 'greatly wished' to see Eliot's *Murder in the Cathedral* when it was performed at Notting Hill.[47]

The reconciliation with Chesterton followed Eliot's conversion to Christianity in June 1927 and the 'obvious reservations' alluded to in Eliot's letter revolved around Eliot's rejection of the Roman Catholic Church and his decision instead to be received into the Anglo-Catholic wing of the Church of England.

Eliot certainly described himself as a Catholic, and a militantly traditional one at that, but he believed that traditional Catholicism could be practised in the Church of England, or at least in its high church, Anglo-Catholic wing. Surprisingly for one so well versed in theology and philosophy, his decision to become an Anglican was largely taken for cultural and sociological reasons. 'The great majority of English speaking people, or at least the vast majority of persons of British descent ... are outside of the Roman communion,' he said in 1930.

> The Roman Church has lost some organic parts of the body of modern civilisation. It is a recognition of this fact which makes some persons of British extraction hesitate to embrace the Roman communion; and which makes them feel that those of their race who have embraced it have done so only by the surrender of some essential part of their inheritance and by cutting themselves off from their family.[48]

It was more than mere coincidence that he became a naturalized British subject in the same year he became a member of the Church of England. From this time onwards Eliot consciously anglicized himself, attempting a complete metamorphosis from American anglophile to English gentleman, and this in turn required a certain way of seeing things. For example, just as an Englishman's home was his castle so an Englishman's church was the one established by English law. Thus his becoming an Anglican was a necessary part of his becoming an Englishman, part of the psychology of an outsider trying a little too hard to become an insider. The problem was that he had become naturalized without becoming natural. In endeavouring to become English, he became more English than the English themselves and therefore not English at all in any genuine sense. His England was a sanitized, idealized figment of his own imagination, an escape from *The Waste Land*, an English Eden. Eliot, the artificial Englishman, had created an artificial England.

Seen in this light, a quip by Jacques Maritain, the neo-Thomist writer and philosopher, appeared to have more than a grain of truth. Maritain, himself a convert, was asked whether he thought Eliot would ever convert to Roman Catholicism. 'No,' Maritain replied wryly, 'Eliot exhausted his capacity for conversion when he became an Englishman.'[49]

Eliot's anglocentrism was coupled with a contempt for his native land, life in which he had previously described as 'a dull nightmare'. In 1928 he wrote a preface to *This American World*, a book by Edgar Ansel Mowrer which attacked the vulgarity of the United States, painting a picture reminiscent of a waste land full of the hollow men Eliot so despised:

> Our half-educated, self-opinionated citizens can do what they like, read what they like, think as badly as they like, enforce what mental and moral tyranny they like ...
>
> The winning of the West transformed the type of governing class ... Puritanism was useful and survived, while culture was superfluous and perished ... When, after the Civil War, the South ceased to count in anything but statistics and elections, the aristocratic tradition of culture was dead.[50]

It is hard to imagine the impact that Eliot's conversion to Anglo-Catholicism had on the army of moderns who idolized his poetry for its pessimism and its undertones of despair. The extent to which he had been misunderstood by his admirers, and consequently the extent to which his conversion would be misunderstood, can be gauged by the assertion of I. A. Richards, the literary critic, that Eliot in *The Waste Land* had effected 'a complete severance between poetry and *all* beliefs'.[51] This generally accepted assumption was blown asunder by his conversion, news of which was greeted with incredulity. How could the arch-iconoclast have become a Catholic? It made no sense. Yet, when asked what he believed he answered in a direct and straightforward manner that he believed exactly what he was obliged to believe – the Creed, the Invocation of the Blessed Virgin and the Saints, the Sacrament of Penance, and so on. Furthermore he was seen to be practising the faith he proclaimed, going to communion and confession.

It was all too much for Virginia Woolf who greeted the news with horror. 'I have had a most shameful and distressing interview with dear Tom Eliot,' she wrote to a friend on 11 February 1928, 'who may be called dead to us all from this day forward. He has become an Anglo-Catholic believer in God and immortality, and goes to church ... there's something obscene in a living person sitting by the fire and believing in God.'[52]

(One is tempted irresistibly to the Chestertonian retort that it is better than sitting *in* the fire by not believing in God!)

Although Virginia Woolf never took the path towards conversion and was eventually to take her own life in 1940, several of Eliot's other friends did follow the path he had taken, many as unlikely candidates for conversion as he had been. Both Siegfried Sassoon and Edith Sitwell later became Roman Catholics – but not before many more years of trial and error had elapsed.

There was, however, one poet of distinction destined to convert in the same year as Eliot. The reception of Alfred Noyes into the Roman Catholic Church in 1927 was not so surprising. Indeed, he made no secret of the fact that even his conversion was an act of defiance against the moderns:

> In England it gave a new significance to the ruins of Glastonbury and Tintern, a new meaning to Westminster Abbey itself, and even to Christmas, for modern England has forgotten that the Abbey once implied an Abbot, and that Christmas was once the Mass of Christ. It was a renaissance of the mind, in which the literature and philosophy of all the ages acquired a new and vital beauty ...
>
> There is a sun around which the whole universe moves. It does not try to be original, for it is itself the origin. It does not need to be modern, for it is older than time, and new every morning.[53]

So it was that the least fashionable poet in England had reached essentially the same conclusions as the most fashionable – the unity of ancient and modern in something greater than both.

This unsung affinity between Eliot and Noyes is perhaps best illustrated in their shared admiration for Kipling. 'No critic,' Eliot remarked, 'has yet taken the measure of Kipling ... He can only be judged by those who are able to read the whole of his work, and who are capable of entering into his *mystique*, which is something larger than a *mystique* of Empire.'[54]

Noyes, it seemed, was one critic who had been able to enter into Kipling's *mystique*. In a review of *Puck of Pook's Hill*, Noyes saw through the *mystique* of Empire to something beyond:

> Mr Kipling has for the first time dug through the silt of modern imperialism. He has gone back to the old ground-works and seen the inscription upon them ... But let popular imperialists beware of him ... Mystics are always dangerous – to materialists, at any rate; and Mr Kipling has mysticism in his blood and in his bones.[55]

The five years following Eliot's publication of *The Waste Land* were some of the most turbulent in the history of the development of English verse. Yet the divisions in poetic form were as nothing compared with the underlying unity in things essential. In essence, Eliot, Noyes, Sassoon and Sitwell would all be as one, each having 'mysticism in his blood and in his bones'.

In the case of formerly bitter enemies like Sitwell and Noyes one again hears the echo of Chesterton's words, written when the enmity between his brother and Godfrey Isaacs during the Marconi Scandal had found its conclusion with their reconciliation in the Church: 'It is the only reconciliation; and it can reconcile anybody.'

NOTES

1. Lyndall Gordon, *Eliot's Early Years*, Oxford, 1977, p. 22.
2. Valerie Eliot (ed.), *The Letters of T. S. Eliot, Volume One*, London, 1988, pp. 374–5.
3. T. S. Eliot, *The Sacred Wood*, London, 1920 (1960 edn.), p. 168.
4. Valerie Eliot (ed.), *The Letters of T. S. Eliot, Volume One*, p. 426.
5. ibid., p. 426.
6. Tony Sharpe, *T. S. Eliot: A Literary Life*, London, 1991, p. 48.
7. Valerie Eliot (ed.), *The Letters of T. S. Eliot, Volume One*, p. 205.
8. *Manchester Guardian*, 31 October 1923.
9. *Times Literary Supplement*, 20 September 1923.
10. *The Times*, 5 January 1965.
11. T. S. Eliot, *The Sacred Wood*, pp. 168–9.
12. ibid., p. 170.
13. ibid., pp. 170–1.
14. Peter Ackroyd, *T. S. Eliot*, London, 1984, p. 128.
15. Geoffrey Elborn, *Edith Sitwell: A Biography*, London, 1981, p. 44.
16. Rupert Hart-Davis (ed.), *Siegfried Sassoon: Diaries 1920–1922*, London, 1981, pp. 132–3.
17. ibid., p. 155.
18. ibid., p. 165.
19. ibid., p. 165.
20. Walter Hooper, *C. S. Lewis: A Companion and Guide*, London, 1996, p. 170.
21. ibid., p. 171.
22. ibid., pp. 171–2.
23. Walter Hooper, interview with the author, Oxford, 20 August 1996.
24. *The Times*, 8 July 1958.
25. *The Speaker*, 13 June 1903.
26. Alfred Noyes, *Two Worlds for Memory*, London, 1953, p. 17.
27. ibid., p. 29.
28. ibid., p. 224.
29. Owen Barfield, interview with the author, Forest Row, 31 December 1996.
30. Geoffrey Elborn, *Edith Sitwell: A Biography*, p. 147.
31. Alfred Noyes, *Two Worlds for Memory*, p. 168.
32. Geoffrey Elborn, *Edith Sitwell: A Biography*, p. 32.
33. ibid., p. 32.
34. Alfred Noyes, *Two Worlds for Memory*, p. 168.
35. ibid., p. 171.
36. Rupert Hart-Davis (ed.), *Siegfried Sassoon: Diaries 1923–1925*, London, 1985, p. 138.
37. Alfred Noyes, *Two Worlds for Memory*, pp. 174–5.
38. ibid., p. 175.
39. ibid., p. 174.
40. G. K. Chesterton, *Fancies versus Fads*, London, 1923, p. 16.
41. BBC broadcast, 'We Will End with a Bang', from the *Spice of Life* series, 15 March 1936.
42. Bernard Bergonzi, *T. S. Eliot*, London, 1972, p. 39.
43. *Nation and Athenaeum*, 31 December 1927.
44. ibid.

45. T. S. Eliot, *The Varieties of Metaphysical Poetry*, p. 104.

46. Michael Ffinch, *G. K. Chesterton: A Biography*, London, 1988, p. 318.

47. Robert Speaight, *The Property Basket: Recollections of a Divided Life*, London, 1970, p. 177.

48. John D. Margolis, *T. S. Eliot's Intellectual Development 1922–1939*, Chicago, 1972, p. 135.

49. F. J. Sheed, *The Church and I*, London, 1976, p. 89.

50. T. S. Matthews, *Great Tom*, New York, 1974, p. 100.

51. Peter Ackroyd, *T. S. Eliot*, p. 161.

52. Walter Hooper, *C. S. Lewis: A Companion and Guide*, p. 25.

53. Alfred Noyes, *Two Worlds for Memory*, p. 197.

54. Paul Murray, *T. S. Eliot and Mysticism*, London, 1991, p. 182.

55. ibid., p. 182.

CHAPTER THIRTEEN

GRAHAM GREENE: CATHOLIC SCEPTIC

The lives of Graham Greene and Malcolm Muggeridge spanned the twentieth century, beginning in the first years of the first decade and stretching into the first years of the last. Their lives serve almost as parallel parables of the century itself. In an age of disillusionment, cynicism and uncertainty, Greene and Muggeridge reflected this gloomy backdrop. Greene, following his youthful conversion, felt the uncertainty of the age from inside the Church, grappling with disillusionment and looking almost enviously at the shifting uncertainties of secularism outside. Muggeridge, on the other hand, drifted away from Christianity at an early age and savoured the cynicism of the modern world with mixed feelings, looking enviously from outside the Church at the certainties inside.

As schoolboys, however, the travails of later life had yet to take their toll and there is a fragile innocence in their respective descriptions of childhood encounters with G. K. Chesterton. Greene recalled running after Chesterton in his school cap to ask for the famous writer's autograph as Chesterton 'laboured like a Lepanto galleon down Shaftesbury Avenue'.[1] Muggeridge remembered being taken by his father to a dinner at a Soho restaurant at which Chesterton was the guest of honour:

> As far as I was concerned, it was an occasion of inconceivable glory. I observed with fascination the enormous bulk of the guest of honour, his great stomach and plump hands; how his pince-nez on a black ribbon were almost lost in the vast expanse of his face, and how when he delivered himself of what he considered to be a good remark he had a way of blowing into his moustache with a sound like an expiring balloon. His speech, if he made one, was lost on me, but I vividly recall how I persuaded my father to wait outside the restaurant while we watched the great man make his way down the street in a billowing black cloak and old-style bohemian hat with a large brim.[2]

Muggeridge only saw Chesterton in the flesh on one other occasion. This was shortly before the latter's death when Muggeridge observed him 'sitting outside the Ship Hotel at Brighton, and clutching to himself a thriller in a yellow jacket. It, too, like the pince-nez, seemed minute by comparison with his immensity. By that time, the glory of the earlier occasion had departed.'[3] Its departure was due to Muggeridge's adoption in adulthood of a worldly pessimism which found Chesterton's faith unpalatable.

Greene, on the other hand, always retained an affection for Chesterton in spite of their very different approaches to life and literature. In stark contrast to Chesterton's childlike innocence Greene followed a world-weary path, at times reaching the brink of despair. In large part this bleak approach was due to his wretched childhood and particularly to the tortuous time spent at Berkhamsted School where his father was headmaster. His traumatic time as a boarder appears to have affected him deeply and his writing is full of the bitter scars of his schooldays. Barbed references to the wretchedness he felt recur in *England Made Me*, *Brighton Rock*, *The Lawless Roads*, *The Confidential Agent*, *The Ministry of Fear* and *A Sort of Life*.

Norman Sherry, Greene's biographer, stressed the profound influence of these unhappy schooldays, stating that 'several compulsive themes in his novels derive from that experience'.[4] Yet even though Sherry records that Greene's stay at Berkhamsted School was a torment which led to successive suicide attempts, and observes that the pain of Greene's experience was such that he remained unwilling to discuss the period in interviews, he seems to play down its over-riding importance:

> On the face of it, there seems little to justify the emotive language he has used to describe the situation in which he found himself ... he was the Headmaster's son, had moved only a short distance from home at School House to be a boarder ... where his cousins Ben and Tooter were also boarders and his brother Raymond was head boy. Raymond, Ben and Tooter went through the school without being scarred ... Thousands of children ... were born to much greater physical and mental hardships. His advantages in terms of wealth and class were considerable. A decline in his living conditions and a certain amount of ragging and bullying ... seem unimportant.[5]

This view is disputed vehemently by Leslie von Goetz, the daughter of Ben Greene:

My father was one of the cousins and he had to be a boarder in his own home town 'to show support to his uncle' – he was totally wretched in every conceivable way and, probably because of the war, got no sympathy but on the contrary was expected to make dramatic extra sacrifices of anything in short supply like sugar or jam to set an example. One master was so cruel and hateful that it took Ben almost all his life to be able to bear to think of him as he aroused such hatred and fear ... Tooter ... had been there for a year but it had made him so ill that the doctor told his mother that he could not answer for his life if he continued to stay there ...[6]

The measure of Greene's misery can be gauged from his suicidal state and by the fact that he was finally driven in desperation to run away from the horrors of the school. He described the panic in his family after he ran away in his autobiographical *A Sort of Life*: 'my father found the situation beyond him ... My brother suggested psycho-analysis as a possible solution, and my father – an astonishing thing in 1920 – agreed.'[7] He was referred to the analyst Kenneth Richmond and described the six months he spent at Richmond's house in Lancaster Gate as 'perhaps the happiest six months of my life'.[8] No doubt the principal reason for this was the sense of relief following his release from the miseries of Berkhamsted, but he also recalled with fondness 'those breakfasts in bed on a tray neatly laid, brought by a maid in a white starched cap, followed by hours of private study under the trees of Kensington Gardens'.[9] This idyllic daily routine was enhanced in the evenings by the company of authors. Kenneth Richmond was himself an author, 'if only of a book which I found rather dull reading, on educational theory',[10] and he seemed to move in literary circles. Greene remembered the visit of Walter de la Mare, the poet he admired most at the time, who signed his new-bought copy of *The Veil*. Another frequent visitor was Naomi Royde-Smith, literary editor of the *Weekly Westminster Gazette*, who had published Rupert Brooke's early poems. 'She was too kind to me,' Greene recalled, 'so that a year later I began to bombard her with sentimental fantasies in poetic prose (she even published some of them).'[11] Royde-Smith was to play a significant if largely unsung part in the launching of Greene's literary career. She showed an early interest in his work, publishing several of his articles, and Greene remained grateful to her throughout his life. Royde-Smith later became a successful novelist in her own right, her first being published in 1926. In the same year she married the actor Ernest Milton; both were received into the Catholic Church in 1942, and she wrote three explicitly Catholic novels, *For Us in the Dark*, *The Iniquity of Us All* and *Miss Bendix*.

It was also through the *Weekly Westminster Gazette* that Greene first came into contact with Edith Sitwell. He had gone up to Balliol College, Oxford in the autumn term of 1922 and in the following March announced that he had been 'converted to Sitwellianism' and to the cause of the modern poets. He informed his mother that he had read Edith Sitwell's last volume of poetry and was 'absolutely out middle stump'. Filled with enthusiasm he wrote a glowing appraisal of her work and sent it to the *Weekly Westminster Gazette*. On this occasion the editor decided against publication but his essay was forwarded to Sitwell who wrote to Greene in gratitude on 19 June: 'I am not used to people understanding anything whatever about my poetry, excepting perhaps an occasional image, and that only partially, as they do not understand the spiritual impulse behind the image. You have understood it all. Your comprehension appeared to be absolutely complete.'[12] She was also thankful for his defence of her poetry at a time when she believed she had been vulgarly abused in the *Weekly Westminster Gazette*.

Greene was overjoyed to receive such encouragement from his heroine and told his mother that Edith Sitwell's autograph might some day be valuable. He was also hopeful that the good impression he appeared to have made might help him get his poetry published in the next edition of *Wheels*, the anthology which Sitwell edited. The hope was forlorn because no further issues of *Wheels* were published after 1921.

In the February 1924 issue of *Oxford Outlook*, Greene continued his Sitwellian crusade: 'In Miss Edith Sitwell we find the style of the Decadents, broadened in outlook, shorn of its madness, and intensified in emotion and beauty, there is no more room for progress here.' Apart from his obvious devotion to the moderns, Greene exhibited in the same article an interesting reservation about the polarization of poets into either the modernist or the traditionalist camp. Insisting on the right to a true catholicity of taste, he added: 'There is no greater admirer of the Sitwells than myself, but I do not understand why this should prevent my being also an admirer of Mr Drinkwater. Poetry would indeed be dull if all were revolutionaries, none conservatives.' Already Greene was beginning to display that singularity of outlook which would so perplex his readers in later years. By refusing to be bracketed he found himself in agreement with Chesterton's complaint that 'certain things are accepted in a lump by all the Moderns, mainly because they are supposed (often wrongly) to be rejected with horror by all the Ancients'. Greene was not prepared to ditch the favourite poets of his youth, such as de la Mare and Chesterton, simply because he had taken up the cause of the Sitwells. Far from condemning the traditionalists, one senses Greene's irritation at the more extreme forms of poetic experimentation finding expression at the time. In this respect his statement that 'there is no more room for progress here' is revealing. A more reactionary statement, at least if taken literally, could scarcely be imagined. Like Sassoon, Greene sat uncomfortably in the Sitwell camp.

At the end of his freshman year Greene was elected President of the Modern Poetry and Drama Society. As a result he met many of the literary celebrities of the day, informing his mother that he hoped to invite 'Drinkwater and de la Mare down'.

Although his most vociferous praise had been for Edith Sitwell, Greene also fell under the influence of Eliot. His early novels, such as *Stamboul Train* and *Brighton Rock*, would be set in waste lands, peopled with hollow men and haunted with echoes of Eliot's imagery. His second novel, *The Name of Action*, published in 1930, even employed several lines from *The Hollow Men* as the epigraph.

Greene graduated in 1925 and found himself in need of a job. He later wrote that 'no year will seem again quite so ominous as the one when formal education ends and the moment arrives to find employment and bear personal responsibility for the whole future'.[13] Following a couple of unsatisfactory jobs with the British American Tobacco Company and the *Nottingham Journal* he gained employment 'sub-editing and leader writing' for *The Times*. In his resignation letter four years later, he wrote: 'My publisher, Heinemann, has offered me £650 a year for two years in advance of royalties on my next books if I will do nothing else but write.' Although Greene's salary at *The Times* had risen to a not inconsiderable ten guineas a week by 1929, the paper obviously could not match the lucrative publishing contract with Heinemann. None the less, Geoffrey Dawson, the paper's editor, did his best to deter Greene from leaving, assuring him that he would not mind if he continued writing novels in his spare time. Should he leave, Dawson warned him, it would be 'a rash and unfortunate decision'. Greene disagreed: 'There is of course a risk, but as my present book has earned nearly £800 and has only just been published in America, I think that the risk is not too great.'[14] It was a risk that Greene was more than happy to take and, despite Dawson's protestations, he left *The Times* to embark upon a career as a novelist.

The fact that his decision was a wise one is of course borne out by subsequent events but another decision he took during this period would be the cause of controversy throughout the remainder of his literary career. In 1926 he became a Catholic.

Greene had taken this step shortly before he started work at *The Times* and it seems his faith was considered relevant to his employment prospects. When his job application had arrived somebody had scrawled across it the words 'Roman Catholic'. The words were subsequently crossed out.[15]

Whoever crossed out those words at *The Times*, they were unwittingly echoing the belief of many who later suggested that Greene had effectively crossed out the words himself by surrendering to scepticism and abandoning his faith. The suggestion is fundamentally flawed. If anything he surrendered to faith without abandoning his scepticism. Certainly he never abandoned his faith, however sceptically he proclaimed it, still describing himself as a Catholic sixty years later.

Greene's conversion is described in his autobiography, *A Sort of Life*, in which he contrasted his own agnosticism as an undergraduate, when 'to me religion went no deeper than the sentimental hymns in the school chapel', with the fact that his future wife was a Roman Catholic:

> I met the girl I was to marry after finding a note from her at the porter's lodge in Balliol protesting against my inaccuracy in writing, during the course of a film review, of the 'worship' Roman Catholics gave to the Virgin Mary, when I should have used the term 'hyperdulia'. I was interested that anyone took these subtle distinctions of an unbelievable theology seriously, and we became acquainted.[16]

The girl was Vivien Dayrell-Browning, then twenty years old. Five years earlier, as a mere fifteen-year-old, she had had a volume of poems and essays published, entitled *The Little Wings*, which contained an introduction by G. K. Chesterton. 'It may be suggested, perhaps,' Chesterton wrote, 'that a writer whose current works indicate that he is almost in his second childhood may be appropriately associated with a writer who is almost in her first.'[17]

The motive force behind the volume's publication was Vivien's mother, Muriel Dayrell-Browning, whose pride in her daughter's work is evident from the short note at the start of the book: 'All the work of my young daughter contained in this first collection of her verse is original and has been written without aid of any kind.'

The first collection of her verse also proved to be her last and seventy-five years later the author still found memories of the volume embarrassing. She was 'not happy with the volume of poetry to which Chesterton wrote an introduction', it was full of 'idiotic childhood verse' which was 'simply dreadful'.[18] Worst of all was the fact that her mother sent the verses to school with the inevitable result that she was teased terribly.

Soon after *The Little Wings* was published the teenager shocked her family by being received into the Catholic Church: 'I woke up one morning and knew I must be a Catholic. My mother and other members of the family were horrified.

They were low church but my mother had no religion particularly herself.'
Filled with youthful zeal she became a tertiary of St Dominic and came to know
'that saint' Father Bede Jarrett. This led to further objections from her mother
who complained to the Dominicans and told her daughter dismissively that
'your old Pope doesn't want you to waste such time'.[19] The only member of the
family to offer any support was her uncle Robert, himself a convert, who was
'delighted'.

Vivien's new-found faith was given expression in a poem entitled *Lux Mundi*,
published in *Blackfriars* magazine. These lines are from the third stanza:

> Like acolytes the candles stood
> Ranged with their flames of restless gold,
> Above them hung the glimmering Rood,
> Below, the Body and the Blood,
> O Mystery no words have told!
> Nor have men's hearts yet understood –
> (O strange and still Beatitude!)
> The Holy Thing their hearts may hold.

Vivien remembered Chesterton as an influence upon her conversion. She considered him 'a marvellous writer' and 'Lepanto' had particularly captivated her, but
she did not think her future husband was influenced by him to the same extent.
Chesterton's was 'not his style of writing'.[20] Certainly Chesterton's was not the
style in which Greene himself wrote but that does not mean that he did not
appreciate Chesterton. On the contrary, his review of Maisie Ward's biography
of Chesterton illustrates clearly that he very much admired him:

> Time often chooses oddly, or so it seems to us, though it is more
> reasonable to suppose that it is we ourselves who are erratic in our
> judgements. We are already proving our eccentricity in the case of
> Chesterton: a generation that appreciates Joyce finds for some reason
> Chesterton's equally fanatical play on words exhausting ... *Orthodoxy*,
> *The Thing* and *The Everlasting Man* are among the great books of the
> age. Much else, of course, it will be disappointing if time does not
> preserve out of that weight of work: *The Ballad of the White Horse*, the
> satirical poems, such prose fantasies as *The Man Who Was Thursday*
> and *The Napoleon of Notting Hill*, the early critical books on Brown-
> ing and Dickens ...[21]

Of course this review, written in 1944, sheds no direct light on Greene's reading at the time of his conversion and it is possible that he did not become *au fait* with Chesterton's books until after he had become a Catholic. However, considering Greene's early autograph-hunting of Chesterton and his later admiration for his religious books, it would be odd indeed if he had not been aware of *The Everlasting Man*, which was published at around the time he was seeking instruction in the Catholic faith. His wife-to-be has written that 'G.K.C. was an overwhelming influence on me and *The Everlasting Man* one of the very finest convert's aids, a brilliant book.'[22] Is it possible that the book she considered such a fine convert's aid was never mentioned in her correspondence and meetings with her future husband at the very time when Greene was seeking such aid? The fact that Chesterton was both a role model and a topic of conversation between them is illustrated in a letter from Greene to Vivien on 9 August 1925, a month before the publication of *The Everlasting Man*. Seeking Vivien's approval of his plan to leave the British American Tobacco Company in order to follow a career in journalism, he wrote: 'After all (he said with ineffable conceit!) Chesterton and Belloc have been journalists.'[23]

Concerning Greene's conversion, Vivien recalled that 'he was mentally converted; logically, it seemed to him' by a good priest in Nottingham: 'It was all rather private and quiet. I don't think there was any emotion involved.'[24] This was corroborated by Greene himself when he stated in an interview that 'my conversion was not in the least an emotional affair. It was purely intellectual.'[25] Such a view was reinforced by the matter-of-fact and worldly way in which he recounted the steps leading to conversion in his autobiography: 'Now it occurred to me, during the long empty mornings, that if I were to marry a Catholic I ought at least to learn the nature and limits of the beliefs she held. It was only fair, since she knew what I believed – in nothing supernatural. Besides, I thought, it would kill the time.'[26]

He walked to the 'sooty neo-Gothic Cathedral' which 'possessed for me a certain gloomy power because it represented the inconceivable and the incredible' and dropped a note requesting instruction into a wooden box for enquiries. His request was based upon nothing more than morbid curiosity and a desire to please the woman he loved, and had precious little to do with a genuine desire for conversion:

> I had no intention of being received into the Church. For such a thing to happen I would need to be convinced of its truth and that was not even a remote possibility.
>
> The impossibility seemed even more pronounced a week later when I returned to the Cathedral and met Father Trollope. I was to grow

fond of Trollope in the weeks which followed, but at the first sight he was all I detested most in my private image of the Church.[27]

Some weeks into his instruction with Father Trollope, Greene learned that the priest was a convert, the knowledge of which 'came like a warning hand placed on my shoulder', hinting at the dangers involved in going too far with his own search. He came to realize that his first impressions of the priest were erroneous and that he was 'facing the challenge of an inexplicable goodness'.

> I would see Trollope once or twice a week for an hour's instruction, and to my own surprise I came to look forward to these occasions ...
> I had cheated him from the first, not telling him of my motive in receiving instruction or that I was engaged to marry a Roman Catholic. At the beginning I thought that if I disclosed the truth he would consider me too easy game, and later I began to fear that he would distrust the genuineness of my conversion if it so happened that I chose to be received, for after a few weeks of serious argument the 'if' was becoming less and less improbable.[28]

The 'if' revolved primarily on the primary 'if' surrounding God's existence. The centre of the argument was the centre itself or, more precisely, whether there was any centre:

> my primary difficulty was to believe in a God at all ... I didn't disbelieve in Christ – I disbelieved in God. If I were ever to be convinced in even the remote possibility of a supreme, omnipotent and omniscient power I realized that nothing afterwards could seem impossible. It was on the ground of a dogmatic atheism that I fought and fought hard. It was like a fight for personal survival.[29]

In the end the dogmatic atheist was overpowered. Greene's scepticism was subdued though never completely vanquished and it was both apt and prophetic that he should take the name of St Thomas the Doubter at his reception into the Church in February 1926. St Thomas doubted but never deserted Christ and Greene doubted but never deserted the Church.

Having approached the Church as clinically as possible Greene's response immediately after his reception was not as unemotional as he had led his future wife to believe:

I remember very clearly the nature of my emotion as I walked away from the Cathedral: there was no joy in it at all, only a sombre apprehension. I had made the first move with a view to my future marriage, but now the land had given way under my feet and I was afraid of where the tide would take me. Even my marriage seemed uncertain to me now. Suppose I discovered in myself what Father Trollope had once discovered, the desire to be a priest ... Only now after more than forty years I am able to smile at the unreality of my fear and feel at the same time a sad nostalgia for it, since I lost more than I gained when the fear belonged irrevocably to the past.[30]

In this one passage are seen all the hallmarks of Greene's future life and work. No joy, only a sombre apprehension ... uncertainty, unreality and a sad nostalgia.

The Catholic had been born but the sceptic remained, creating a hybrid, a metaphysical mutant as fascinating as Jekyll and Hyde and perhaps as futile. The resulting contortions and contradictions of both his own character and those of his characters give the impression of depth; but the depth was arguably only that of ditch water, perceived as bottomless because the bottom could not be seen. His genius was rooted in the ingenuity with which he muddied the waters.

Perhaps the secret of his enduring popularity lies in his being a doubting Thomas in an age of doubt. As such, his Catholicism becomes an enigma, a conversation piece – even a gimmick. Yet, enigmatic or otherwise, he remained a Catholic, often as a critical supporter from the sidelines, for the rest of his life. However sceptical he was about the Church and its teachings he always remained more sceptical about scepticism, giving God the benefit of the doubt.

NOTES

1. Graham Greene, *A Sort of Life*, London, 1971, p. 59.
2. Malcolm Muggeridge, *The Green Stick*, London, 1972 (1975 edn.), p. 9.
3. ibid., p. 9.
4. Norman Sherry, *The Life of Graham Greene, Volume One, 1914–1939*, London, 1988, p. 65.
5. ibid., pp. 65–6.
6. Leslie von Goetz, letter to the author, dated 5 September 1996.
7. Graham Greene, *A Sort of Life*, London, 1971, p. 95.
8. ibid., p. 96.
9. ibid., p. 96.
10. ibid., p. 97.
11. ibid., p. 97.
12. Norman Sherry, *The Life of Graham Greene, Volume One*, p. 147.
13. Graham Greene, *A Sort of Life*, p. 106.
14. *The Times*, 5 April 1991.
15. ibid.
16. Graham Greene, *A Sort of Life*, p. 161.

17. Vivienne Dayrell, *The Little Wings*, Oxford, 1921, preface.
18. Mrs Graham Greene, interview with the author, Oxford, 20 August 1996.
19. ibid.
20. ibid.
21. Graham Greene, *Collected Essays*, London, 1969, pp. 136–7.
22. Mrs Graham Greene, letter to the author, dated 15 August 1996.
23. Norman Sherry, *The Life of Graham Greene, Volume One*, p. 202.
24. Mrs Graham Greene, interview with the author, Oxford, 20 August 1996.
25. Marie–François Allain, *The Other Man: Conversations with Graham Greene*, London, 1983, p. 154.
26. Graham Greene, *A Sort of Life*, p. 161.
27. ibid., p. 162.
28. ibid., pp. 163–4.
29. ibid., p. 164.
30. ibid., pp. 166–7.

CHAPTER FOURTEEN

WAUGH AND WASTE LAND

In September 1911 the seven-year-old Evelyn Waugh made his first diary entry:

> My name is Evelyn Waugh I go to Heath Mount school I am in the Vth
> Form, Our Form Master is Mr Stebbing.
> We all hate Mr Cooper, our arith master ... Today is Sunday so I am
> not at school. We allways have sausages for breakfast on Sundays I have
> been waching Lucy fry them they do look funny befor their kooked.
> Daddy is a Publisher he goes to Chapman and Hall office it looks a
> offely dull plase. I am just going to Church ... The wind is blowing
> dreadfully I am afraid that when I go up to Church I shall be blown
> away.[1]

'Daddy' was Arthur Waugh, the highly respected publisher and critic, whose
Anglican faith and general outlook were imbued with the complacent post-
Victorian assumption that faith in God and Empire were synonymous. This was
embodied revealingly in his belief that 'with a thorough knowledge of the Bible,
Shakespeare and Wisden you cannot go far wrong'.[2] Similar sentiments underpinned a verse he inscribed in a copy of Mary MacGregor's *The Story of Rome*
which he gave to Evelyn when his son was nine:

> All roads, they tell us lead to Rome;
> Yet, Evelyn, stay awhile at home!
> Or, if the Roman road invites
> To doughty deeds and fearful fights,
> Remember, England still is best –
> Her heart, her soul, her Faith, her Rest![3]

One senses an element of admonition in these lines caused perhaps by Evelyn's
early attraction to Anglo-Catholic ritual.

Evelyn had been introduced to the Anglo-Catholic wing of the Church of England during visits to his aunts at Midsomer Norton in Somerset: 'At Midsomer Norton I made friends with a curate ... who died a Catholic ... He taught me to serve at the altar. I found deep enjoyment in doing so ... I rejoiced in my nearness to the sacred symbols and in the bright early-morning stillness and in a sense of intimacy with what was being enacted.'[4]

His father remarked that his son seemed to spend his entire summer at Midsomer Norton 'serving at the altar, & going to picnics – a weird mixture of faith and frivolity'.[5] The experience left an indelible mark on Evelyn's psyche which would come to maturity many years later in his love for the Latin rite. It also had a more instant effect. 'From now on for a year or more,' Waugh remembered, 'my drawings were no longer of battles but of saints and angels inspired by mediaeval illuminations. I also became intensely curious about church decorations and the degrees of anglicanism ... which they represented.'[6]

During a half-term holiday with his mother in Brighton in 1915, the eleven-year-old Evelyn announced with precocious disapproval his opinion of a church they had attended, 'a horrible low one. I was the only person who crossed myself and bowed to the altar.'[7]

In the night-nursery he made a shrine by his bed on which he arranged brass candlesticks, flower vases and white plaster statues of saints which he had bought from a religious shop recently opened at Golders Green. In front of these he burned little cones of incense on a brass ashtray. His devotions found literary expression in 'a deplorable poem in the metre of *Hiawatha*, named *The World to Come*', which, inspired by Newman's *Dream of Gerontius* with which he had been much impressed, related 'the experiences of the soul immediately after death'.[8]

Here the Devil laid his wager,
And on Job did cast derision.
Hence the cruelties of Nero,
Hence the anguish of the martyrs,
Hence the wailing of the slaughtered
And the shrieking of the murdered.
Here was hatched Our Lord's betrayal,
Here the thirty silver pieces,
Here Christ's Church was first divided
In this house of crime and torture.[9]

Any misgivings Arthur Waugh felt about his son's ritualistic enthusiasm must have been mitigated by the improved behaviour that seemed to accompany it. His sister reported that they were 'all struck by the great improvement in Evelyn. He couldn't be nicer – so pleasant & so ready to do anything we want him to do, & pleased with any little joy we try to arrange. I don't think he is nearly so satirical as he used to be. We are all very happy together.'[10]

Although it seemed that the contentment of his faith had removed the caustic cause of his sharp satirical wit, the disappearance of the latter was but a temporary aberration. In maturity Waugh would have little difficulty combining the two.

In May 1917, at the age of thirteen, Waugh left Heath Mount to begin his career at public school.

Lancing College had been founded in 1848 by Nathaniel Woodard, a high Anglican churchman and subscriber to the Oxford Movement, with the specific intention of providing a sound Church of England education for the professional classes. Architecturally its construction was an audacious and imposing affirmation of the Anglican faith, the grey stone quadrangles and cloisters of the school dwarfed by a vast and magnificent chapel which is exceeded in height only by Westminster Abbey, York Minster and Liverpool Cathedral.

Such an establishment was highly suited to a boy of precociously ritualistic persuasions such as the young Waugh. In his second term, he 'defied convention by kneeling at the *incarnatus* in the creed at Holy Communion' and he often attended chapel twice a day and three times on Sundays, partly to find 'refuge from the surrounding loneliness'.[11] His Anglo-Catholicism also shaped his reading, with the *Divine Comedy*, *The Bible in Art* and *The Child's Book of Saints* all capturing his imagination in the early days at Lancing.

Ironically, however, Lancing College contributed significantly to his loss of faith. Specifically, the theological modernism taught at the school led to a growth in religious scepticism. Waugh remembered the destructive effect of one master in particular. Described by Waugh as 'a fiery young don', Mr Rawlinson was one of the new generation of modernist theologians at Oxford whose liberal speculations had been refuted by Ronald Knox in his controversial book *Some Loose Stones*. Rawlinson arrived at Lancing in 1918 and immediately and unwittingly set about destroying the faith of Waugh and others. Waugh recalled that it was Rawlinson 'whose agnosticism first unsettled my childish faith'.[12] His tutor's agnosticism was contagious and Waugh was soon an agnostic himself. He remembered coming top of Rawlinson's Divinity set and recalled his tutor giving him back a paper in which he had 'proposed something very near agnosticism' with words of warm encouragement: 'No mean theologian, Waugh.'[13]

Very quickly, under Rawlinson's guidance, Waugh graduated from being 'no mean theologian', to a mean theology and thence to no theology at all. In parallel with the modern poets, Rawlinson's theological modernism had commenced with the loosening of form and had regressed into formlessness. Indeed, Knox had asked similar questions of the modernist theologians as Noyes and Chesterton had of the modernist poets: At what point does free theology become so free that it ceases to be theology? Was theology 'progressing' towards extinction?

Rawlinson's 'progressive' theology did not hinder his own progress within the Church of England. He eventually became Bishop of Derby. In the meantime he appears to have left a trail of destruction behind him, at least if the results of his speculations at Lancing are anything to go by. As Waugh observed, 'This learned and devout man inadvertently made me an atheist.'[14]

On 13 June 1921 Waugh wrote in his diary: 'In the last few weeks I have ceased to be a Christian (sensation off!) I have realized that for the last two terms at least I have been an atheist in all except the courage to admit it to myself.'[15]
The atheism was accompanied by a violent reaction against the rites of the church. He described a Confirmation service as 'grotesque': 'I have never noticed how menacing it is before. Some small frightened children taking a lot of oaths they'll never keep with a dressed up coloured thing like a Dulac figure and gloomy, threatening masters and provosts all round.'[16]

The transformation was complete. Waugh, the arch-ritualist in love with the pomp and circumstance of Anglo-Catholicism, had become the anti-clerical cynic sneering at 'grotesque' rites and the 'dressed up coloured thing' who was the Bishop. 'I was losing my taste for everything ecclesiastical,' Waugh recalled:

> I now think it odd that in a place so dominated by religion we should have been given so many hours of instruction in the Greek of the New Testament and the history of the Church of England, and practically none in apologetics ... All the humdrum doubts were raised and left unanswered. We were encouraged to 'think for ourselves' and our thoughts in most cases turned into negations.[17]

Waugh's own negations were confessed to his friend Dudley Carew during a walk over the downs:

> Evelyn has come to the realisation of the minuteness of the world compared with the Universe & the minuteness of his life compared with the World. 'You must keep your nose down in the mud, Carey, once you

look up, or even forward, you're done ... Man is governed entirely by his own self-interest, Carey' ... 'I am convinced there is no ultimate good or evil ... There's a kink in one man's brain which is attracted to what we call good & in another to what we call evil.'[18]

Waugh remained convinced that his drift into dualistic scepticism was due in large part to the amorphous modernism taught at Lancing and the way in which pupils were actively 'encouraged to be unorthodox': 'I think at least half the Upper Sixth in my time were avowed agnostics or atheists. And no antidote was ever offered us. I do not remember ever being urged to read a book of Christian philosophy.'[19] One wonders what Nathaniel Woodard, the school's founder, would have thought of the 'sound Church of England education for the professional classes' being offered by Lancing College in Waugh's time.

The drift into dualism led Waugh to the brink of despair, his diary being 'full of pagan gloom and the consideration of suicide'.[20]

Brief respites from the gloom and despondency were found in literature and the arts. He read the books of Chesterton and admired the verse of Belloc and Wilde; he 'developed an abiding love' for the wood-cuts of Eric Gill although he had 'no interest in his teaching' on either art or religion; he even visited the Ditchling community where the great calligrapher, Edward Johnston 'received me with exquisite charm and demonstrated how to cut a turkey-quill into a chisel-pointed pen and there and then wrote a few words for me on the title-page of his book in what is now called his "foundational" hand'.[21]

Many years later, having developed a sympathy for the teaching of Gill and Johnston which was lacking as a schoolboy, Waugh wrote:

> It has been the irony of Johnston's achievement – just as the Socialist Party which began as a protest against industrialism now finds itself in the thick of it – that his cult of simplicity, which in his own work accentuated the brilliant idiosyncrasy of his craftsmanship, has led to the stark tedium of mechanical repetition ... He was spared the realization of the world of 'plastics' in which the tradition of craftsmanship seems finally to be foundering.[22]

Waugh came up to Oxford in January 1922 and was soon intoxicated by the new world he found there. In fact, he was intoxicated both aesthetically and anaesthetically, excelling in the excesses and the drunken hedonism associated with the Hypocrites' Club, one of the most notorious drinking clubs at the University: 'It was at the university that I took to drink, discovering in a crude way the contrasting pleasures of intoxication and discrimination. Of the two, for many years, I preferred the former.'[23]

Waugh recalled that beer was the staple for undergraduates of average means, although the rich drank 'great quantities of champagne and whisky' and the poor 'were reputed to drink cocoa': 'The average man, of whom I was one, spent £100 a term and went down £300 in debt. Luncheon was served in our rooms with jugs of beer.'[24]

The drunken decadence of the Hypocrites' Club was remembered by Waugh in his autobiography. 'In its brief heyday,' he wrote, 'it was the scene of uninhibited revelry.'[25] To his great surprise he was elected secretary at the general meeting of the Club, all the voters being tipsy, but performed no secretarial duties, his appointment being 'a characteristic fantasy of the place'. His predecessor in the office had left the university suddenly to study black magic and later died in mysterious circumstances in Aleister Crowley's notorious community at Cefalu in Sicily. In spite of its dubious credentials Waugh recalled that the Hypocrites' Club was 'the stamping-ground of half my Oxford Life and the source of friendships still warm today'.[26]

In a rare moment of sobriety Waugh had attended a lecture given by Chesterton to the Newman Society, a group for Catholic undergraduates, where he met Harold Acton, 'one of the most charismatic figures of that Oxford era'.[27] Acton, 'a Catholic but no proselytizer', exerted a telling influence on Waugh who was 'certainly a little dazzled' by Acton's 'manifest superiorities of experience': 'He was always the leader; I, not always, the follower.'[28] In particular, Acton, who was 'vividly alive to every literary and artistic fashion', introduced Waugh to the new poets:

> Harold brought with him the air of the connoisseurs of Florence and the innovators of Paris, of Berenson and of Gertrude Stein, Magnasco and T. S. Eliot; above all of the three Sitwells who were the objects of his admiration and personal affection ... Harold led me far away from Francis Crease to the baroque and the rococo and to the *Waste Land*.[29]

Acton gained notoriety and enhanced his heroic status in Waugh's eyes when he leaned out of his window in Christ Church and with flamboyant bravado recited *The Waste Land* through a megaphone to a League of Nations garden party. He also took Waugh to the first public performance of Edith Sitwell's *Façade* at the Aeolian Hall on 12 June 1923, and afterwards to a party at Osbert Sitwell's house in Carlyle Square where he met Lytton Strachey, Clive Bell, Eugene Goossens and Ada Leverson. In 1925 Acton invited Edith Sitwell and Gertrude Stein to speak at the Newman Society where both were rapturously received.

Waugh's introduction to the heights of literary fashion heightened the alienation he felt towards his parents. His father had dismissed Eliot's work as 'premature decrepitude', Pound's verse as 'wooden prose', and the poetry of the entire modernist movement as 'unmetrical, incoherent banalities'.[30] Father and son were now worlds apart and Waugh wrote to a friend of the 'melancholy mania' with which he was afflicted in the company of his family: 'I hardly know how I shall live through the next ten days until I go up.'[31]

Another friend at Oxford was Christopher Hollis, later to become both a prolific writer and a Member of Parliament, who, like Acton, was destined to play an important part in Waugh's development. Shortly before his death Waugh wrote that 'Christopher Hollis became, and has remained, one of my closest friends' and of Hollis's oratory at the Oxford Union, he recalled that

> his appearance was unstudied, indeed unkempt, his tone of voice harsh;
> he was immensely genial and constantly funny; never a clown as were
> some Union speakers ... His jokes, like Chesterton's, were always
> designed to make a logical point ... At Oxford he had one particular
> audience and could address it in the confidence that every allusion and
> every turn of irony would be recognised.[32]

Like Benson and Knox before him, Hollis was the son of an Anglican bishop – the Rt Rev. George Hollis, Bishop of Taunton. Unlike Benson and Knox, he lost his Christian faith completely and joined Waugh in the ranks of the sceptics. Sooner than most, and certainly sooner than Waugh, he became sceptical about scepticism and began the soul-searching return from the aphelion of doubt to the Christian faith. The faith to which he returned was not that of his father but, as Chesterton would say, the faith of his father's fathers.

Hollis was acutely aware of the similarities between his own path to Rome and that of Knox:

> Thirteen years his junior, I had gone, like him, to preparatory school at
> Summer Fields; like him, from Summer Fields, I had won a scholarship
> at Eton and gone into College there. Like him, from Eton I had gone
> on with another scholarship to Balliol. Like him, I was President of the
> Union at Oxford. Like him, I was the son of an Anglican bishop, and,
> like him, in early youth joined the Catholic Church.[33]

Knox himself remained a giant figure and permanent fixture in Hollis's mind. During his time at Eton he had been aware that Knox's reputation still echoed round the college. Indeed, Hollis claimed in his autobiography that Knox 'might, I imagine, be almost called the greatest schoolboy of all time', remembering that his reputation remained at Eton long after his departure: 'Masters would quote to us from his *Signa Severa*, and his name and his works were familiar to us all.'[34] Hollis was still at Eton when the shock of Knox's conversion shook the school. Many of the masters who had previously reverenced Knox now reviled him and efforts were made to play down the dazzling brilliance of his reputation. Hollis remembered R. H. Malden, who was then his father's successor as Vicar of St Michael's, Headingley, and later became Dean of Wells, preaching in Eton College Chapel in criticism of Knox's conversion and of his *Spiritual Aeneid*.

As an undergraduate at Balliol, Hollis met Knox on a few occasions, usually in F. F. Urquhart's room, but only as one of a crowd, and Knox did not become chaplain to the Catholic students at Oxford until after Hollis had left.

Waugh shared Hollis's admiration for Knox. He remembered his father reading Knox's *Reunion All Round* to him when he was a boy and confessed to Knox years later that he was 'dazzled as I have been ever since ... Since then every word you have written and spoken has been pure light to me.'[35] Waugh was also impressed by Knox's oratory prowess at the Union and considered him the only speaker to have surpassed Hollis in this respect. In 1924 Waugh recounted Knox's appearance at the Union when the question for debate was 'That Civilization has advanced since this Society first met'. Speakers included Gilbert Murray, John Buchan, Douglas Woodruff and Chesterton's old schoolfriend and the author of *Trent's Last Case*, E. C. Bentley, but Waugh reported that it was Knox who stole the show: 'Father Knox showed how from the anthropological considerations of our present ideas about food and drink, the apportionment of work between men and women, burial customs and drama, we were rapidly approaching the civilization of the savage.'[36] Although at the time Waugh was still some way from any serious consideration of Knox's religious position, the extent to which he was moved by the priest's appraisal of modern civilization is evident from the fact that he would soon be in wholehearted agreement with it.

In the meantime Waugh watched Hollis's slow but sure approach to the Catholic Church with intrigued fascination. Unsympathetic to the goal to which his friend's philosophical grappling appeared to be leading he was none the less gripped by the nature of the quest and the questions it raised.

As an undergraduate Hollis was motivated by a political cynicism which found rhetorical expression during a debate at the Union with his proclamation that 'there are three great enemies of freedom – the Conservative party, the Liberal party, and the Socialist party'.[37] This was merely the articulation of Belloc's and Cecil Chesterton's argument in *The Party System* which he had read at Eton:

'At school we had once been set to write a prize essay on the Party System, and one of the books recommended to us was Belloc's and Cecil Chesterton's attack on that system, *The Party System*.'[38]

Having been introduced to the writing of Belloc, Hollis sought out further books by the author. During his last year at school he read two of Belloc's political satires, *Mr Clutterbuck's Election* and *A Change in the Cabinet*. He first learnt that Belloc was a Catholic by reading the caption under a picture of him in the *Illustrated London News* but at the time he had little sympathy for his religion and no real understanding of his political philosophy. He was introduced to the latter by pure chance when asked by Kenneth Lindsay, then President of the Oxford Union, to speak at the Union on a motion in support of the wide distribution of property. Hollis was so pleased at being given the opportunity to make his speaking debut at the Union that he 'would probably have spoken for or against any motion that had been suggested, and a week before the debate I certainly had no very clear views on the distribution of property'.[39] Lindsay suggested he read Belloc's *The Servile State* to get some ideas and Hollis recorded 'how these accidents led me on to Belloc at a time when, agnostic in religion, disillusioned in political liberalism, I was in search of a new faith'.[40]

Since religion and politics were inextricably linked in the writing of Belloc it was natural that Hollis should pass from *The Servile State* to Belloc's defence of the Catholic Church in *Europe and the Faith*. This also appealed to Hollis in the way it challenged 'the prevailing Platonic agnosticism of the Dons'.[41]

Hollis was now hooked on 'the theories of the "Chesterbelloc", to Belloc's theses of the Catholic Church as Europe's creative force and of the coming of the Servile State, to Chesterton's proclamation of "God's scorn for all men governing," to his rhetorical verse and the vision of the Distributist society'.[42]

He was helped in his steady progress towards the faith by his friend and fellow undergraduate, Douglas Woodruff, who was also a close and influential friend of Waugh's. 'Douglas Woodruff,' Hollis wrote,

> was my closest companion at that time ... He led me carefully and tactfully along this road ... I came, as a result of taking the Catholic side in many an undergraduate argument, to believe that there was a Society which took a part in the affairs of this world which was different in kind from any other Society and which it was reasonable to believe to be of divine origin.[43]

Many of these undergraduate arguments were with Waugh who at this time was flaunting a particularly aggressive brand of muscular agnosticism, always eager furiously to debate and if possible destroy the claims of Christianity. Waugh had been the only one of Hollis's friends to actively dissuade him from being received into the Catholic Church. Ultimately the agnostic militant failed in the face of the Church Militant and Hollis was received by Monsignor Barnes in the late summer of 1924.

At around the same time, on 13 September, Waugh's closest friend and companion at Oxford, Alastair Graham, was received into the Church by Father Martindale. Waugh recorded the event in his diary with morose terseness, stating contemptuously that 'Alastair joined the Italian Church.' The following day's entry is in similar tone: 'I went with Alastair to Mass at a church in Hampstead – very ugly.'[44]

Almost exactly a year later another diary entry indicated how his friends' conversions had left Waugh feeling alienated. He recorded that after Hollis and Graham had gone to Mass together they 'began a conversation of incredible inanity which lasted with brief breaks from 6 to 12 and nearly drove me mad ... I did not know Chris had it in him to be such a bore.'[45]

A few months later Waugh sat up until seven o'clock in the morning 'arguing about the Roman Church' with friends.[46] By this time his views were moderating slightly, helped by friends such as Hollis and Graham but also by older influences such as Knox and Chesterton. He had gone to hear Knox preach at Westminster Cathedral[47] and confessed in a letter that in the midst of his antagonistic agnosticism 'Chesterton beckons like a star.'[48]

In particular, Chesterton's *The Everlasting Man*, published in 1925, was to have a major influence. Knox was 'firmly of the opinion that posterity will regard *The Everlasting Man* as the best of his books'[49] and this was a view shared by Waugh: 'In that book all his random thoughts are concentrated and refined; all his aberrations made straight. It is a great, popular book, one of the few really great popular books of the century ... It met a temporary need and survives as a permanent monument.'[50]

On another occasion, many years after its publication, Waugh described *The Everlasting Man* as 'a masterly book, sadly neglected in Europe but honoured in the USA'.[51] The adulation was tempered by an irritation with Chesterton's style, a fact remembered by Douglas Woodruff: 'At one time, he contemplated seeking leave to rewrite G. K. Chesterton's *Everlasting Man*, being greatly influenced by its argument but hating its fireworks style.'[52] Although these comments were all made years later, it is likely that Waugh read *The Everlasting Man* shortly after its initial publication.

If Chesterton was exerting an influence intellectually, other influences, less erudite, were coming into play. Emotionally, aesthetically and psychologically

Waugh was beginning to feel an aversion to the sensuousness and licentiousness of his decadent, drunken lifestyle. In December 1925 this aversion found expression in his disapproval of the behaviour of Olivia Plunket Greene with whom he had become infatuated. The object of his disapproval was the Charleston which Waugh described as 'that disgusting dance of hers', lamenting that she had become literally 'Charleston crazy'.[53] At parties and nightclubs she was miserable and wandered restlessly until she found an empty corner of the room where she could dance it alone and with abandon. Waugh found such exhibitionism both distasteful and disturbing and his disapproval extended to other aspects of her behaviour. Selina Hastings, in her biography of Waugh, describes how Olivia's drinking, manic dancing and increasingly outrageous promiscuity were driving him into a state of jealous fury. Her deportment was deliberately, overtly and provocatively sexual and under the influence of alcohol she indulged in a form of erotic display calculated to attract the attention of every man in the room. At parties she gave herself freely to the embraces of almost any interested male, rolling about uninhibitedly in full view of the other guests. 'Olivia as usual behaved like a whore,' Waugh remarked in his diary, 'and was embraced on a bed by various people.'[54]

No doubt his disapproval was accentuated by jealousy based upon an infatuation which remained unrequited, but the roots went deeper and found expression in the caustic satire of his attacks on the Bright Young People in his early novels. Ironically, the conflict between the luridness of the flesh and the lure of the faith was as much a part of Olivia Plunket Greene's complex character as it was of Waugh's. In 1930, the same year as Waugh, she was received into the Church under the influence of the Spanish mystics, St Teresa of Avila and St John of the Cross, and died in middle age after living a solitary, celibate life.

The conflict between flesh and faith seemed to find natural expression in the poems of T. S. Eliot which Waugh was reading avidly at the beginning of 1926. They were 'marvellously good but very hard to understand. There is a most impressive flavour of the major prophets about them.'[55] Dudley Carew, his old friend from Lancing days, remembered Waugh 'insisting that I buy *The Waste Land*'[56] and it was no mere coincidence that Waugh would later choose a line from *The Waste Land* as the title of his novel *A Handful of Dust*, his own more prosaic attack on the vacuities of modern life.

As with Knox before him, Waugh's approach to the Church was preceded by a love affair with the Pre-Raphaelites. 'I want to write a book about them,' he wrote in his diary:

I can say without affectation that during the last week I have lived with them night and day. Early in the morning with Holman Hunt – the only Pre-Raphaelite – untiring, fearless, conscientious. Later in the day with Millais – never with *him* but with my biography of him – a modish Lytton Strachey biography. How he shines through Holman Hunt's loyal pictures of him. Later, when firelight and rum and loneliness have done their worst, with Rossetti, soaked in chloral.[57]

His studies came to fruition in an essay on the Pre-Raphaelite Brotherhood published in 1926 and in his first book, a biography of Dante Gabriel Rossetti, published two years later.

Waugh's appreciation of the Pre-Raphaelites held the added attraction for him of their being despised by Bloomsbury and wholly out of fashion with the moderns, itself a recommendation as Waugh became progressively more opposed to the more *avant garde* of his contemporaries.

In September 1926, after ten days of drunkenness, Waugh resolved to amend his ways: 'they are to be my last days of this sort of life ... I am resolved to attempt again a life of sobriety, chastity and obedience. On a surer foundation this time I think.'[58] His choice of reading reflected the effort to find a surer foundation and over Christmas 1926 he read William James's classic analysis of the psychology of conversion, *The Varieties of Religious Experience*.

Both the reading and the resolution failed and the contorted contradictions were all expressed in a diary entry on 20 February 1927: 'Next Thursday I am to visit a Father Underhill about being a parson. Last night I was very drunk. How odd these two sentences seem together.'[59] His diary then records that five minutes after the words were written he was sacked on the spot from his teaching post at Aston Clinton in Buckinghamshire. 'Though he told his mother that he was dismissed for drunkenness,' Christopher Hollis recalled, 'the fact, as he confessed to me, was that he was dismissed for trying to seduce the matron.'[60]

With penury in prospect, Waugh was forced to take a job at a down-at-heel academy in Notting Hill which he described in his diary in Dickensian detail: 'The school in Notting Hill is quite awful. All the masters drop their aitches and spit in the fire and scratch their genitals. The boys have close-cropped heads and steel-rimmed spectacles wound about with worsted. They pick their noses and scream at each other in a cockney accent.'[61]

Such were the ignominious circumstances in which Waugh's short and ill-fated teaching career came to an end. Two years later he wrote of his unhappiness as a schoolmaster: 'The early hours, the close association with men equally degraded and lost to hope as yourself, the derision and spite of indefatigable little boys, the gross effrontery of matrons and headmasters' wives, all these and many minor discomforts too numerous to mention are the price you must pay for bare subsistence.'[62]

The price had been too high at one stage and Waugh, driven to despair, actually attempted suicide. Although the episode was tactfully omitted from his otherwise explicit diaries, it was recounted in his autobiographical *A Little Learning*:

> One night ... I went down alone to the beach with my thoughts full of death. I took off my clothes and began swimming out to sea. Did I really intend to drown myself? That certainly was in my mind and I left a note with my clothes, the quotation from Euripides about the sea which washes away all human ill ...
>
> It was a beautiful night of a gibbous moon. I swam slowly out but, long before I reached the point of no return, the Shropshire Lad was disturbed by a smart on the shoulder. I had run into a jelly-fish. A few more strokes, a second more painful sting. The placid waters were full of the creatures.
>
> An omen? A sharp recall to good sense such as Olivia would have administered?
>
> I turned about, swam back through the track of the moon to the sands ... Then I climbed the sharp hill that led to all the years ahead.[63]

The only clue in Waugh's diary of the attempted suicide were the tell-tale lines: 'It looks rather like being the end of the tether. At the moment I can see no sort of comfort anywhere.'[64]

All these emotional upheavals were providing fertile soil from which Waugh's imagination created his first novel. *Decline and Fall* was published in September 1928 to immediate acclaim. Lauded almost unanimously by the critics, with Chesterton a lone dissenting voice, *Decline and Fall* established Waugh's reputation as a new exciting talent. It looked as though the future would now be a happy one but three months before the novel's publication Waugh entered into a hasty and reckless marriage which once more led him to the end of the tether and the edge of despair.

Waugh married Evelyn Gardner on 17 June 1928. Both were twenty-four years old but beyond that they had little in common. His wife, the promiscuous aristocratic daughter of Lady Burghclere, had been briefly engaged in the recent past to three unsuitable men. Waugh was scarcely more suitable, being of modest middle-class background and, the publication of *Decline and Fall* still three months away, appearing to have little money and no prospects. Not surprisingly, Lady Burghclere had opposed the marriage vigorously.

For the first few months after their marriage He-Evelyn and She-Evelyn, as they became known, appeared very happy. She-Evelyn was as excited as her husband by the new celebrity status he had gained in the wake of the success of *Decline and Fall*. 'Our finances have vastly improved,' she wrote, 'at times we are absolutely rolling in money, and at others we have to live on haddock and potatoes, but it is all very amusing.'[65] As the author of a best-seller, her husband was 'now quite a lion and we were asked to meet Max Beerbohm, Hilaire Belloc and Maurice Baring the other night'.[66] Waugh was particularly pleased to meet this particular triumvirate of writers, 'each an idol of mine'.[67]

It was in this spirit of post-marital bliss that Waugh commenced the writing of *Vile Bodies*, his next novel. Bubbling with optimism, he wrote to a friend on 20 July 1929 that he had finished 25,000 words in ten days. 'It is rather like P. G. Wodehouse all about bright young people. I hope it will be finished by the end of the month.'[68] In the event the novel would not be finished for several months because he received a letter before the month's end which shattered his blissful ignorance. His wife sent him a letter confessing that she had fallen in love with his friend John Heygate, a news editor at the BBC.

Stunned by this wholly unexpected news, Waugh rushed back to London where he was confronted by his wife who told him that not only were she and Heygate in love but that they had become lovers. She had gone back to Heygate's flat after a party and stayed the night.

Later that year Bryan Guinness began work on a novel, *Singing Out of Tune*, which was based in part on Waugh's oral account of the breakdown of his marriage. In it the hero receives a letter from his wife, breaking the news of an adulterous relationship. The phrase 'something has happened' stuck in the throat and struck at the heart. 'He pictured her rolling entwined in the greedy arms of the little hunchback. He saw them tugging at each other's clothes, at each other's bodies.'[69]

Waugh was understandably somewhat circumspect in his references to the affair but the fact that his bliss had blistered into bitterness was evident in the letters he wrote after the event. He informed his mother and father of 'the sad and to me radically shocking news that Evelyn has gone to live with a man called Heygate'. Stating that he had filed for divorce, he added: 'I am afraid that this will be a blow to you but I assure you not nearly as severe a blow as it is to me.' As his plans were 'vague about the flat' he found himself temporarily homeless and told his parents he was planning to stay with Bryan and Diana Guinness in Sussex, adding pathetically, 'May I come and live with you sometimes?' As a postscript, he expressed utter bewilderment at the situation he found himself in: 'Evelyn's defection was preceded by no kind of quarrel or estrangement. So far as I knew we were both serenely happy.'[70]

In a letter to Harold Acton, his tone was less restrained:

> Certainly the fact that she should have chosen a ramshackle oaf like Heygate adds a little to my distress ...
>
> Evelyn's family & mine join in asking me to 'forgive' her whatever that may mean.
>
> I am escaping to Ireland for a week's motor racing in the hope of finding an honourable grave ...
>
> I did not know it was possible to be so miserable & live but I am told that this is a common experience.[71]

After being chased by his publisher for the finished manuscript of *Vile Bodies*, Waugh wrote a wretched apology: 'I am afraid my book is not written. When I gave the end of July as a date I had every expectation of delivering the ms. then, but the last weeks have been a nightmare of very terrible suffering which, if I could explain, you would understand ... At present I can do *nothing* of any kind.'[72]

Eventually, in this agonized frame of mind, Waugh retreated to the seclusion of Devon in an effort to finish the novel. Now, however, the words were failing to flow as freely. Writing to his friend Henry Yorke, Waugh complained that writing had been 'infinitely difficult ... It all seems to shrivel up & rot internally.' Waugh then proceeded to express his deep admiration for Diana Guinness who had married earlier in the year: 'She seems to me the one encouraging figure in this generation – particularly now she is pregnant – a great germinating vat of potentiality like the vats I saw at their brewery.' It was as though he needed to identify with, and idolize, an idealized Woman as an antidote to the 'vile bodies' he was writing about. Diana Guinness had become the embodiment of the faithful wife, especially now that she was pregnant, in the face of the philanderer.

Returning to the matter which was rotting internally, he expressed his loathing of Heygate, the 'basement boy': 'My horror and detestation of the basement boy are unqualified. There is practically no part of one that is not injured when a thing like this happens.'[73]

The 'basement boy' made an anonymous appearance in the novel in Waugh's sour reference to 'cocktail parties given in basement flats by spotty announcers from the BBC'. This appears only three pages into chapter seven, the point at which he resumed writing, and the mood thereafter darkens. There is none of the light joviality which invited Waugh's earlier comparison with Wodehouse. Instead it paints a bitter and bleak picture of the waste land of life in the twenties, described by the poet Richard Aldington in his review of the book as 'one of the meanest and most fraudulent decades staining the annals of history'.[74] Waugh's heroine in *Vile Bodies* soon turns to callous infidelity and the endless round of wild parties are dust-storms in a desert, devoid of depth, gatherings of empty, shallow people living empty, shallow lives. Although written in a different medium, comparisons with Eliot's poetry, particularly *The Waste Land* and *The Hollow Men*, are obvious. Waugh, like Eliot, was tired of the vacuity of modern life and craved depth.

The writing of *Vile Bodies* was an act of exorcism and three months later, the pain having subsided, he wrote again to Henry Yorke: 'I have decided that I have gone on for too long in that fog of sentimentality & I am going to stop hiding away from everyone. I was getting into a sort of Charlie Chaplinish Pagliacci attitude to myself as the man with a tragedy in his life and a tender smile for children.'[75]

As the healing process continued, Waugh, needing to fill the abyss of emptiness within, began to search for the depth he desired. In this he was helped by his old friend Olivia Plunket Greene who had been received into the Catholic Church only recently, following in the footsteps of her mother who had taken the same step four years earlier. Gwen Plunket Greene said of her daughter's conversion that she was 'marvellously happy about it, so changed I can't get over it'.[76] Waugh discussed religion regularly with mother and daughter throughout the spring of 1930 and at their suggestion he made an appointment to see Father Martin D'Arcy, the Jesuit, at Farm Street on 8 July. His first impressions were favourable, 'Blue chin and fine, slippery mind',[77] and he visited him on two further occasions the following weekend. In later years he described him as 'a brilliant and holy priest'.[78] Father D'Arcy, along with fellow Jesuit Father Martindale, had a reputation for bringing into the Church an array of prominent members of the higher echelons of society, working on the principle that the bigger the stone, the bigger the ripple. He was immortalized in fiction by Muriel Spark, herself a Catholic convert, when she said of one of her characters in *The Girls of Slender Means* that 'he could never make up his mind between suicide and an equally drastic course of action known as Father D'Arcy'.

Waugh was certainly not suicidal, having put his past well and truly behind him, but he was certainly embroiled in the course of action known as Father D'Arcy. In a television interview thirty years later he said, 'I was under instruction – literally under instruction – for about three months, but of course I'd interested myself in it before, reading books independently and so on.'[79] The course of instruction was later recalled by Father D'Arcy:

Evelyn was never a borrower and had almost too set a mind to accept advice. No one could have made up that mind of his for him no more than anyone could have been co-author of his novels. Gwen and Olivia served like a Greek chorus to sympathise with and echo his *cris de coeur*.

... Evelyn never liked the heart to sidetrack reason or serve as a substitute. On the other hand, the heart's desire, the cry of the innermost self, could ally itself to reason and set him on the quest for a Holy Grail ... It is this special kind of combination of a sick self, bored with and feeding on emptiness, and a hard brain, which prevented him from being taken in by the popular idols ...

... He had come to learn and understand what he believed to be God's revelation, and this made talking with him an interesting discussion based primarily on reason. I have never myself met a convert who so strongly based his assents on truth. It was a special pleasure to make contact with so able a brain ... Hard, clear thinking had with the help of grace given him the answer for which he had been searching, and one can see its effect in his subsequent writings.[80]

In the midst of his instruction Waugh continued to dine with Gwen and Olivia Plunket Greene, discussing religion, and on 9 August 1930 he was visited by two of his friends who had already converted, Christopher Hollis and Douglas Woodruff. He recorded in his diary that 'They are very settled in their minds on all debatable topics. Woodruff slightly more satirical than Hollis, who was shocked by my jokes about the *Universe* or individual Catholics.'[81] Joking aside, Waugh was now convinced of his desire to convert and on 21 August, before leaving for Ireland, he wrote to Father D'Arcy:

As I said when we first met, I realize that the Roman Catholic church is the only genuine form of Christianity. Also that Christianity is the essential and formative constituent of western culture ... But the trouble is that I don't feel Christian in the absolute sense. The question seems to be must I wait until I do feel this ... or can I become a Catholic when I am in such an incomplete state – and so get the benefit of the sacraments and receive faith afterwards?[82]

One can surmise the nature of Father D'Arcy's reply from Waugh's later comment that D'Arcy 'saw it was no good hoping for much & the thing to do was just to get the seed in anyhow & hope some of it would come up'.[83] 'I look back aghast,' Waugh wrote two decades later, 'at the presumption with which I thought myself suitable for reception and with wonder at the trust of the priest who saw the possibility of growth in such a dry soul.'[84]

Soon after his return from Ireland, Waugh broke the news of his intention to his parents. Arthur Waugh recorded in his diary that his wife was 'very, very sad over news of Evelyn's secession to Rome'.[85]

Waugh was received by Father D'Arcy at the Church of the Immaculate Conception in Farm Street on 29 September 1930. According to his own account, the step had been taken 'on firm intellectual conviction but with little emotion'.[86]

One is reminded of Robert Hugh Benson's unemotional reception into the Church a quarter of a century earlier: 'I do not suppose that anyone ever entered the City of God with less emotion than mine ... There was the Truth, as aloof as an ice peak, and I had to embrace it.'[87] In fact, Benson and Waugh shared more than their vastly different temperaments and writing styles might suggest. Both had a deep love for the old Catholic nobility of England, their houses and their traditions, and Waugh's *Brideshead Revisited* was to conjure up the same atmosphere as that which permeated many of Benson's novels. The words Waugh wrote of Benson in an introduction to Benson's novel *Richard Raynal: Solitary* were as applicable to himself:

> Superficially he was an aesthete, but the Catholic church made little aesthetic appeal to him ... What he sought and found in the church was authority and catholicity. A national church, however wide the empire ... could never speak with universal authority and, because it was provincial, it was necessarily narrow, finding room for scandalous doctrinal aberrations but forever incapable of enclosing the vast variety of humanity. Transplanted the Church of England became merely the church of the golf club and the garrison ...[88]

There is no doubt that emotion played its part, in spite of Waugh's apparent lack of it at the time of his reception, and his insistence that his approach to the Church had been predominantly an intellectual exercise. Waugh admitted as much when he confessed that he found life 'unintelligible and unendurable without God'.[89] Intelligibility may indeed be a matter for the intellect but endurance was a matter for the emotions. Endurance of the modern world, caricatured so successfully in his novels, was made easier from the sanctuary of the Church. He had found an island of sanity in a raving world, a light beyond the shadows and depth beyond the shallows, or as he put it himself:

Conversion is like stepping across the chimney piece out of a Looking-Glass world, where everything is an absurd caricature, into the real world God made; and then begins the delicious process of exploring it limitlessly.[90]

NOTES

1. Michael Davie (ed.), *The Diaries of Evelyn Waugh*, London, 1978, p. 5.
2. Selina Hastings, *Evelyn Waugh: A Biography*, London, 1994, p. 38.
3. ibid., p. 30.
4. Evelyn Waugh, *A Little Learning*, London, 1964, pp. 92–3.
5. Selina Hastings, *Evelyn Waugh: A Biography*, p. 39.
6. Evelyn Waugh, *A Little Learning*, p. 93.
7. Selina Hastings, *Evelyn Waugh: A Biography*, p. 40.
8. Evelyn Waugh, *A Little Learning*, p. 93.
9. Selina Hastings, *Evelyn Waugh: A Biography*, p. 40.
10. ibid., p. 39.
11. Jeffrey Heath, *The Picturesque Prison: Evelyn Waugh and His Writing*, London, 1982, p. 31.
12. Michael Davie (ed.), *The Diaries of Evelyn Waugh*, p. 756.
13. ibid., p. 756.
14. Selina Hastings, *Evelyn Waugh: A Biography*, p. 78.
15. Michael Davie (ed.), *The Diaries of Evelyn Waugh*, p. 127.
16. Evelyn Waugh, *A Little Learning*, p. 142.
17. ibid., p. 142.
18. Selina Hastings, *Evelyn Waugh: A Biography*, pp. 78–9.
19. Evelyn Waugh, *A Little Learning*, p. 143.
20. ibid., p. 143.
21. Selina Hastings, *Evelyn Waugh: A Biography*, p. 65.
22. *Spectator*, 24 July 1959.
23. Cyril Ray (ed.), *The Compleat Imbiber – 6: An Entertainment*, London, 1963.
24. ibid.
25. Evelyn Waugh, *A Little Learning*, p. 180.
26. ibid., p. 181.
27. Selina Hastings, *Evelyn Waugh: A Biography*, pp. 92–3.
28. Evelyn Waugh, *A Little Learning*, p. 197.
29. ibid., p. 197.
30. Selina Hastings, *Evelyn Waugh: A Biography*, p. 104.
31. ibid., p. 104.
32. Evelyn Waugh, *A Little Learning*, p. 186.
33. Christopher Hollis, *Along the Road to Frome*, London, 1958, pp. 244–5.
34. ibid., p. 245.
35. Mark Amory (ed.), *The Letters of Evelyn Waugh*, London, 1988, p. 342.
36. *Isis*, 20 February 1924.
37. Christopher Hollis, *Along the Road to Frome*, p. 76.
38. ibid., p. 76.
39. ibid., p. 77.
40. ibid., p. 77.
41. ibid., p. 79.
42. ibid., pp. 80–1.
43. ibid., p. 81.
44. Michael Davie (ed.), *The Diaries of Evelyn Waugh*, p. 178.
45. ibid., p. 223.

46. ibid., p. 237.
47. ibid., p. 167.
48. Jeffrey Heath, *The Picturesque Prison: Evelyn Waugh and His Writing*, p. 32.
49. D. J. Conlon (ed.), *G. K. Chesterton: A Half Century of Views*, Oxford, 1987, p. 49.
50. *National Review*, 22 April 1961.
51. Donat Gallagher (ed.), *The Essays, Articles and Reviews of Evelyn Waugh*, London, 1983, p. 335.
52. David Pryce-Jones (ed.), *Evelyn Waugh and His World*, London, 1973, p. 129.
53. Michael Davie (ed.), *The Diaries of Evelyn Waugh*, p. 238.
54. ibid., p. 234.
55. ibid., p. 242.
56. David Pryce-Jones (ed.), *Evelyn Waugh and His World*, p. 45.
57. Michael Davie (ed.), *The Diaries of Evelyn Waugh*, p. 233.
58. ibid., p. 265.
59. ibid., p. 281.
60. Christopher Hollis, *Oxford in the Twenties*, London, 1976, p. 80.
61. Michael Davie (ed.), *The Diaries of Evelyn Waugh*, p. 282.
62. Selina Hastings, *Evelyn Waugh: A Biography*, p. 149.
63. Evelyn Waugh, *A Little Learning*, pp. 229–30.
64. Michael Davie (ed.), *The Diaries of Evelyn Waugh*, p. 213.
65. Selina Hastings, *Evelyn Waugh: A Biography*, p. 181.
66. ibid., p. 182.
67. *Sunday Times*, 27 May 1956.
68. Mark Amory (ed.), *The Letters of Evelyn Waugh*, p. 36.
69. Selina Hastings, *Evelyn Waugh: A Biography*, p. 193.
70. Mark Amory (ed.), *The Letters of Evelyn Waugh*, p. 38.
71. ibid., pp. 38–9.
72. Selina Hastings, *Evelyn Waugh: A Biography*, p. 195.
73. Mark Amory (ed.), *The Letters of Evelyn Waugh*, pp. 39–40.
74. Selina Hastings, *Evelyn Waugh: A Biography*, p. 205.
75. Mark Amory (ed.), *The Letters of Evelyn Waugh*, p. 41.
76. Selina Hastings, *Evelyn Waugh: A Biography*, pp. 223–4.
77. Michael Davie (ed.), *The Diaries of Evelyn Waugh*, p. 320.
78. John A. O'Brien (ed.), *The Road to Damascus*, London, 1949, p. 15.
79. Jeffrey Heath, *The Picturesque Prison: Evelyn Waugh and His Writing*, p. 33.
80. David Pryce-Jones (ed.), *Evelyn Waugh and His World*, pp. 61–4.
81. Michael Davie (ed.), *The Diaries of Evelyn Waugh*, p. 325.
82. Selina Hastings, *Evelyn Waugh: A Biography*, p. 225.
83. ibid., p. 225.
84. John A. O'Brien (ed.), *The Road to Damascus*, p. 16.
85. Selina Hastings, *Evelyn Waugh: A Biography*, p. 225.
86. John A. O'Brien (ed.), *The Road to Damascus*, p. 15.
87. Robert Hugh Benson, *Confessions of a Convert*, p. 95.
88. Robert Hugh Benson, *Richard Raynal: Solitary*, Chicago, 1956, intro.
89. John A. O'Brien (ed.), *The Road to Damascus*, pp. 14–15.
90. Michael de-la-Noy, *Eddy: The Life of Edward Sackville-West*, London, 1988, pp. 237–8.

CHAPTER FIFTEEN

CONTROVERTING CONVERTS

The news of Waugh's conversion was treated with astonishment by the literary world and the media. On the morning after his reception there was bemused bewilderment in the *Daily Express* that an author notorious for his 'almost passionate adherence to the ultra-modern' could have joined the Catholic Church. In the gossip columns *Vile Bodies* was known simply as 'the ultra-modern novel'. How could the pillar of all things modern have turned to the pillar of all things ancient? Two leaders in the *Express* had already discussed the significance of Waugh's conversion before his own article 'Converted to Rome: Why It has Happened to Me' was published by the paper on 20 October. It was given a full-page spread, boldly headlined. The following day E. Rosslyn Mitchell, a Protestant MP, wrote a reply and the day after, Father Woodlock, a Jesuit, wrote an article entitled 'Is Britain Turning to Rome?' Three days later an entire page was given over to the ensuing letters.

The lucidity of Waugh's article belied any suggestion that he had taken the controversial step from a position of ignorance. After dismissing the suggestion that he had been 'captivated by the ritual' or that he wanted to have his mind made up for him, he commenced an incisive exposition of his reasons for conversion:

It seems to me that in the present phase of European history the essential issue is no longer between Catholicism, on one side, and Protestantism, on the other, but between Christianity and Chaos ...

Today we can see it on all sides as the active negation of all that western culture has stood for. Civilization – and by this I do not mean talking cinemas and tinned food, nor even surgery and hygienic houses, but the whole moral and artistic organization of Europe – has not in itself the power of survival. It came into being through Christianity, and without it has no significance or power to command allegiance. The loss of faith in Christianity and the consequential lack of confidence in moral and social standards have become embodied in the ideal of a materialistic, mechanized state ... It is no longer possible ... to accept the benefits of civilization and at the same time deny the super-natural basis upon which it rests.

Having asserted that 'Christianity is essential to civilization and that it is in greater need of combative strength than it has been for centuries', Waugh argued that 'Christianity exists in its most complete and vital form in the Roman Catholic Church.' He continued by stressing his belief that 'coherent and consis-tent' teaching was 'a necessary sign of completeness and vitality in a religious body'.

If its own mind is not made up, it can hardly hope to withstand dis-order from outside ...
Another essential sign one looks for is competent organization and discipline. Obedience to superiors and the habit of submitting personal idiosyncrasies to the demands of office seem to be sure signs of a real priesthood.

This public confession of faith is peppered with subliminal references to those who had influenced Waugh on his path to Rome. There are echoes of the speech Ronald Knox gave at the Oxford Union warning that the modern world was 'rapidly approaching the civilization of the savage'; there are hints of Belloc's *Europe and the Faith* which had influenced both Waugh and his friend Christo-pher Hollis; there were obvious parallels with Eliot in the rejection of chaos and the desire for order; and there was an aversion to theological modernism reminiscent of Chesterton.

Although none of these writers conformed to a ready-made stereotype it was clear that there was a unity in diversity. Neither was the *Daily Express* the only publication to comment on the fact. On 8 October 1930, the *Bystander* observed of Waugh's conversion that 'the brilliant young author' was 'the latest man of letters to be received into the Catholic Church. Other well-known literary peo-ple who have gone over to Rome include Sheila Kaye-Smith, Compton MacKen-zie, Alfred Noyes, Father Ronald Knox and G. K. Chesterton'. The list was far from exhaustive. By the 1930s the tide of Roman converts had become a torrent and throughout that decade there were some twelve thousand converts a year in England alone.

A similar mood prevailed in the United States. A few weeks after the contro-versy in the *Daily Express*, a debate between Chesterton and the famous Chicago lawyer Clarence Darrow on the question, 'Will the World Return to Religion?'

attracted an audience of four thousand to the Mecca Temple in New York. At the close of the debate a vote was taken. The result was 2,359 for Chesterton's point of view and 1,022 for Darrow's. In Europe there was a major influx of literary converts as impressive as that experienced in England. These included François Mauriac, Léon Bloy, Jacques Maritain, Péguy, Henri Ghéon, Giovanni Papini, Gertrud von le Fort and Sigrid Undset, all of whom were either converts or reverts, Catholics who had lost their faith but had returned to the Church.

Sheila Kaye-Smith had been received the previous year, along with her husband who was the Anglo-Catholic curate of St Stephen's in Kensington. In marked contrast to the sensationalist approach of the *Express* to Waugh's conversion, the news merited only a single paragraph in *The Times* on 23 October 1929. Her conversion, however, was anything but uncontroversial. She was a bestselling novelist on both sides of the Atlantic and the fact that her husband was a Church of England clergyman added to the surprise with which the news was greeted.

Literary converts received into the Church in the same year as Waugh, included Robert Speaight, Brocard Sewell and Edmund Taylor Whittaker. Speaight later achieved fame as a character actor, notably in the roles of St Thomas Becket in Eliot's *Murder in the Cathedral* and of Christ in the BBC radio production of Dorothy L. Sayers's *The Man Born to be King*. He also became both a novelist and a highly respected biographer whose subjects included Hilaire Belloc and Eric Gill. He was received by Father Martin D'Arcy at Farm Street on 31 October 1930, eleven days after Waugh's article was published in the *Express*. Speaight had read the article and mentions it in the account of his own conversion in his autobiography:

> It is recorded of Picasso and Jean Cocteau that, coming out of a church in Rome, one said to the other: 'Nous vivons comme des chiens.' I had no desire to live 'comme des chiens', and I thought it very important to know which Church to enter in order to escape the danger of doing so.
>
> Evelyn Waugh was asking the same questions at the same time, and finding the same answers to them ... He defined the tendencies of his generation in an article for ... the *Daily Express* as a respect for orthodoxy in religious belief and a reaction against sloppy liberalism ... Evelyn had taken the title of his ... novel – *A Handful of Dust* – from *The Waste Land*, and among the cultural influences at work on us Eliot was predominant ... He had set, or confirmed, our steps in the way of orthodoxy and opened our minds to a European tradition where Catholicism had counted for so much.[1]

Brocard Sewell was still a teenager at the time of his reception on 3 September 1930, describing his conversion as 'much influenced by G.K.C. and Belloc'. It was also 'largely a matter of dissatisfaction with the drab public school religion of Weymouth College'.[2] He had fallen under the influence of Chesterton and Belloc as a schoolboy, becoming a regular reader of *G. K.'s Weekly*. In the school library at Weymouth College he had sought out and devoured the novels and essays of both writers and had also read Newman's *Apologia* and Father D'Arcy's *Roman Catholicism*. There followed a brief enthusiasm for Anglo-Catholicism before Sewell became convinced of his desire to become a Roman Catholic. From 1925 onwards, as a mere thirteen-year-old, he began attending Mass at the Catholic church of Our Lady and St Benedict at Birchington-on-Sea in the Isle of Thanet during his school holidays. Both his father and stepmother disapproved of his 'crypto-papist' leanings, and his father refused to grant permission for him to be received into the Church until he was twenty-one, when he would be free to do as he liked. He eventually relented when his son was still only eighteen. Early in 1928 his father, having lost all his capital in a failed business venture, could no longer afford his son's school fees at Weymouth College and Sewell was informed that he would have to leave school that November. 'I was now nearly sixteen,' he wrote in *My Dear Time's Waste*, his first volume of autobiography, 'and I had no clear idea what I would like to do.'

> It was my reading of *G. K.'s Weekly* finally that gave me an idea. Week by week there appeared in that paper an advertisement inserted by a group of craftsmen at Ditchling Common, in Sussex ... A note below the advertisement said that there were vacancies for apprentices in these workshops.
>
> From the context it appeared that the workshops belonged to some kind of fraternity that was putting into practice the ideas of small ownership and responsible craftsmanship that were advocated by the Distributists, and which appealed to me strongly. I felt no leanings towards wood or stone carving, or to weaving, but printing I thought might be interesting. So I sent off a letter of inquiry to Mr Pepler, the proprietor of the St Dominic's Press, to which I received a reply in his beautiful script inviting me to visit him during the summer holidays.[3]

When the holidays came, Sewell took the train from London to Burgess Hill and walked the mile and a half from the station to the community at Ditchling Common. He spent a few days at Hilary Pepler's house, Hopkin's Crank, which had been the home of Eric Gill before Gill and his family had left for Capel-y-ffin four years earlier. They were unfamiliar surroundings for the sixteen-year-old schoolboy – 'I had never stayed with Catholics before and here was not just a Catholic household but a small Catholic hamlet' – but he was delighted with what he saw.[4] Pepler was also pleased with what he saw because he informed Sewell that he hoped he would come to him as an apprentice when he left school that autumn, and that he would write to his father about it. Sewell was to maintain a lifetime's affinity with Pepler and his work at the Saint Dominic's Press, and became co-author of *Saint Dominic's Press: A Bibliography* almost seventy years after this first encounter with it, but he was not destined to become Pepler's apprentice. In the meantime, starry-eyed and with a head full of utopian dreams, he applied for a job in the offices shared by *G. K.'s Weekly* and the Distributist League and was accepted. 'In the office of the Distributist League I acted as George Heseltine's personal assistant ... At the same time I acted as office boy for *G. K.'s Weekly*, running errands and doing odd jobs. Soon I was promoted to doing occasional short book reviews and writing brief comments on current affairs for the "Notes of the Week".'[5]

In this way the sixteen-year-old commenced a writing career which would stretch the remainder of the century. He wrote sympathetic studies of several literary converts, including biographies of Cecil Chesterton, André Raffalovich and John Gray. With the demise of distributism Sewell found his vocation as a religious with the Carmelites.

The conversion of Edmund Taylor Whittaker in June 1930 was very different from those of Waugh, Speaight and Sewell. Whereas they were all young men embarking upon new careers, he was fifty-six years old at the time of his reception and had already enjoyed a notable career in his field. Furthermore, his books were of a very different kind. At the time of his conversion he was Professor of Mathematics at Edinburgh University and many of his books charted the penumbral regions between physics and metaphysics, including *Space and Spirit*, *The Beginning and End of the World*, *The Modern Approach to Descartes' Problem* and *From Euclid to Eddington*. Following his conversion, he had many honours bestowed upon him. In 1931 he was awarded the Sylvester Medal by the Royal Society for his work on both pure and applied mathematics. Four years later Pope Pius XI awarded him the Cross Pro Ecclesia et Pontifice in recognition of his work for the Catholic Students Union and the Graduates Association. He became President of the Newman Association and was knighted in 1945.

Frank Sheed, who had founded the Catholic publishers Sheed & Ward in 1926, dubbed this new wave of converts the 'Catholic Intellectual Revival'. Sheed was himself at the vanguard of this revival and over the years he was responsible for publishing the works of many of the converts who came to

Catholicism in the twenties and thirties. Sheed was not a convert himself but a cradle Catholic, and as such found himself in a small minority within Catholic literary circles. 'Converts,' he wrote, 'can be hardly ten per cent of the Catholic body: that eighty per cent of the first-rate writers should come from this ten per cent seems to argue either a monstrous articulateness in the converts or a monstrous inarticulateness in the born Catholics.'[6] For Sheed the one notable exception to this rule was Hilaire Belloc who was 'that rarity – a Catholic writer of the top rank who had been born and schooled in the Church'.[7] Yet even Belloc, that most zealous defender of Catholicism, appeared to bow to the pre-eminence of converts in the revival of interest in Christianity. In 1929 he wrote to Mrs Reginald Balfour informing her that he was due to read a paper at Oxford on the conversion of England: 'the new Paganism ... unlike the old is a chaos, and may – or rather will – bring collapse. That is our opportunity. But English Catholics – unconsciously and instinctively – shirk it. It is you converts who do all the useful work.'[8]

This theme was taken up several years later when Frank Sheed and Arnold Lunn debated whether converts or born Catholics were of more value to the Church. It was decided that it would be more graceful if Lunn as a convert should state the case for the born Catholics and Sheed as a born Catholic should argue the case for the converts. Sheed remembered that he had 'dwelt especially on what converts had done for the Catholic Intellectual Revival' whereas Lunn 'found it hard to think of anything at all to be said for born Catholics'.[9] Sheed could not remember the year in which this debate had taken place but it must have been after July 1933 because it was not until then that Lunn was actually received into the Church. Before that, for many years, he had been one of the most vociferous opponents of Catholicism, intent on controverting the converts.

Although he had been in awe of Ronald Knox during his days as an undergraduate at Balliol College, Oxford, Lunn had shown no obvious inclination in his youth to follow Knox's road to Rome. Neither had he followed Belloc's path to Rome, although he had admired Belloc's book of that name and much admired his verse. Instead, he appeared to be gripped with a wanderlust which led him in the opposite direction. His first novel, *The Harrovians*, published in 1913, outraged the sentimental but delighted those who acclaimed it as the first realistic account of public school life. It was an immediate best-seller. Six years later, his second novel, *Loose Ends*, announced his arrival as an outspoken opponent of Christianity. Evelyn Waugh remembered the iconoclastic effect that the novel had on his own Anglican faith during his school days at Lancing College:

Another influence was *Loose Ends* by Arnold Lunn. This was read aloud to us by our House-tutor. It recorded, in the form of fiction, the arguments between two schoolboys in which the atheist, as I remember, always made the better case ... Arnold Lunn was himself an atheist at the time of writing and his manner of reasoning was such as to be particularly acceptable to boys of sixteen.[10]

Loose Ends had been written as a riposte to books such as *Some Loose Stones* by Knox and *The Ball and the Cross* by Chesterton, the latter of which had similarly centred on the fictionalized arguments of a Catholic and an atheist. In a more general sense Lunn's book was intended as a counterblast against the rising tide of converts, many of whom were beginning to flex their literary muscle. In 1920 a symposium entitled *God and the Supernatural: A Catholic Statement of the Christian Faith* brought together many of the new generation of Catholic writers, nearly all of whom were converts. Christopher Dawson's contribution, his first published work, was entitled 'The Nature and Destiny of Man'; Father Martindale wrote essays on 'The Supernatural', 'The Sacramental System' and 'Life After Death'; and E. I. Watkin wrote on 'The Problem of Evil' and 'The Church as the Mystical Body of Christ'. These three, all converts, would play a major role in the Catholic revival. Martindale, as a Jesuit priest in Oxford and at Farm Street, presided over the instruction of many notable converts; Dawson had a profound influence on the intellectual development of T. S. Eliot and through him indirectly influenced a whole generation; and Watkin, now sadly neglected, shaped the outlook of many. Frank Sheed wrote of Watkin that 'I had been led to use my mind on the Mystics, partly by Edward Watkin, to whom my indebtedness in every intellectual area is wholly beyond measure.'[11]

By 1920 converts were becoming so commonplace that Martindale adopted an apologetic tone in his introduction to a Catholic Truth Society pamphlet outlining yet another 'Story of an Undergraduate's Conversion': 'It will be felt, I daresay, as a relief that this short essay differs from many others somewhat similar, in that it contains no arguments for or against "conversion" ...'[12]

It was in this atmosphere of a neo-Catholic ascendancy that Lunn took up arms against the Church. In a world increasingly filled with convert crusaders he was resolved to play the infidel and once again it was the figure of Ronald Knox who antagonized him into action. In particular, Lunn had been exasperated by Knox's *A Spiritual Aeneid* which described the latter's conversion in September 1917: 'I remember being particularly irritated by a passage in which this spoiled child of fortune, for as such I regarded him, claimed to have an instinctive sympathy for lost causes, the only evidence for which was a sentimental sympathy with the Stuarts.'[13]

Lunn wrote a scathing attack on *A Spiritual Aeneid* but was unable to find a publisher for the essay as it stood. It was then that he came up with the idea of writing a whole book of essays on converts to Catholicism. Such was the genesis of *Roman Converts*, published in 1924, which contained critical studies of five eminent converts: Newman, Manning, Chesterton, Knox and Tyrrell. Lunn wrote, 'I could not analyse the suasions that induced brilliant men to accept the claims of Rome unless I began by a detailed study of Catholic theology and apologetics. Knox's book provoked me into examining the case for the Church and was thus destined to be the first important influence in directing my steps to the Eternal City.'[14]

Lunn sent a copy of the book to Knox who responded with polite restraint: 'Thank you for the compliment, for it is I suppose a compliment of sorts, like the crocodile pursuing Captain Hook.'[15] Knox's politeness paid dividends because Lunn was 'disarmed by his charming reply ... there must be unsuspected reserves in that strange religion of his, if he could reply with such humour to so hostile a study of himself and his book'.[16]

Another of the 'Roman Converts' to respond in a good-humoured way was G. K. Chesterton who wrote what Lunn described as 'long and friendly review articles' on the book in both *The Illustrated London News* and the *Dublin Review*. The other three converts singled out for attention in *Roman Converts* had all died years before.

Although he did not know it at the time, Lunn's three years of research for *Roman Converts* had led him closer to the thing he had sought to attack:

> Here is a Church committed, so I believed, to fantastic and irrational doctrines and which yet continues to make converts among men distinguished not only for intellectual gifts but also for intellectual integrity. I am glad that in my book *Roman Converts* I had the honesty to confess that I had discovered no solution to this problem. I discovered, of course, that most of the beliefs with which Catholics were credited were not, in fact, held by Catholics.
>
> ... Why is it that so few people pause, as I paused, after asking themselves how Catholics can hold such and such a belief? Why is it that so few people are interested to discover whether in point of fact Catholics do hold the belief in question?[17]

These words were written in 1940, several years after his conversion, and display an objectivity beyond his own capabilities at the time *Roman Converts* was published. None the less, it is true that he approached the problem in a more

methodical and objective manner than any other critic of Catholicism in his generation. Whereas most people were perfectly blissful in their ignorance Lunn
demanded answers and set about asking the questions required to get them. This
led him into disputes with the most surprising people. For example, he criticized
Bernard Shaw's defence of the Inquisition in the play *St Joan*. Certainly *St Joan*,
which had premiered in London in 1923, displayed Shaw's essentially religious
nature and perhaps Lunn, fresh from his writing of *Roman Converts*, had para-
noid visions of Shaw joining their ranks. Shaw, however, had other ideas and
wrote genially and astutely to Lunn's father, Sir Henry Lunn, that 'the Papists
will get your Arnold yet'.[18] Shaw then invited Lunn to his flat so that they could
discuss the matter of the Inquisition.

'Calvin,' Shaw explained during the course of Lunn's visit, 'burnt Servetus,
though I suppose you were brought up to believe that roasting people alive for
their opinions was a monopoly of Papists. I wrote my *St Joan* for people who've
been brought up in that tradition ... I wanted people to realise that the Inquisition didn't have the monopoly of cruelty, torture and so forth.'[19]

Lunn was not as ignorant of history as Shaw supposed but it was interesting
that Shaw should find himself arguing for a fundamental revision of history free
from the bias and distortions of the Whig historians. It was exactly this concern
which had animated Belloc's decision to write a four-volume history of England,
the first volume of which was published in 1925. Shaw and Belloc were friends
but they seldom found themselves in the same rhetorical camp. One wonders
also whether Shaw's vociferous defence of his own position was affected in any
way by knowledge of Lunn's attack on Chesterton in *Roman Converts*. If Shaw
had read Lunn's book, as is likely, it is entirely feasible that he would relish the
opportunity of playing devil's advocate with Lunn as a means of indirectly
defending Chesterton. Shaw was as opposed to Chesterton's conversion as anyone, but his overriding loyalty to a long-standing friendship may still have
prompted the desire to defend him.

Neither was Shaw the only observer to prophesy that 'the Papists will get
your Arnold yet'. Others were also beginning to perceive that perhaps he was
protesting too loudly. '*Roman Converts* had no sooner been published,' Lunn
recalled, 'than my friends began to prophesy my conversion. I was much
annoyed by the forecast, and replied petulantly to my father that I was just as
likely to become a Buddhist as a Catholic.'[20]

For the next few years he endeavoured to let the issue rest and concentrated
instead on his other great passion. From the age of eight he had spent practically
every winter in the Alps, largely due to his father's travel agent's business, and
developed a love for mountain climbing and skiing. In 1912 he edited *Oxford*

Mountaineering Essays and in the same year wrote *The Englishman in the Alps*. Books on *The Alps, Cross Country Skiing, Alpine Skiing* and *Skiing for Beginners* followed before he entered the arena of religious controversy in 1924 with the publication of *Roman Converts*. In the same year, as a pioneer of ski-mountaineering, he made the first ski ascent of the Eiger. In 1927 he wrote *A History of Skiing* and *Switzerland: Its Literary, Historical and Topographical Landmarks*. He was also playing an important part in the development of competitive skiing by initiating a campaign for the international recognition of downhill ski racing, drafting the Downhill/Slalom Racing Rules which were accepted by the Fédération Internationale du Ski in 1930 in Oslo. He is also credited with the invention of the modern slalom and organized the first World Championship in Downhill and Slalom Racing in 1931. Largely due to his efforts downhill ski racing was introduced into the Olympics in 1936 and he was referee for the first slalom to be included in the Winter Olympic games. In later life Lunn was amused to reflect that if he was remembered after death it would not be as a writer but as the inventor of the slalom race.

At the same time that Lunn was grappling with the politics of sport he found himself becoming more interested in the politics of society as a whole:

> I reacted from Radicalism to Conservatism, and I passed on beyond Conservatism to a political creed the very name of which, *Distributism*, is unknown to most Englishmen. During my undergraduate days I had read the works of G. K. Chesterton and Hilaire Belloc ... but it was not until the late twenties that I began to take an interest in their political views.[21]

Writing in 1940, Lunn gave a succinct definition of the creed he now joined Chesterton, Belloc, Gill and others in advocating:

> The Distributist believes in the distribution of property and the means of production. He insists that the love of property, particularly property in land, is a sane and enduring instinct which needs both to be fostered and controlled ... He is opposed to the subordination of the producer to the financier, and of the countryman to the townsman, and he would agree with Burke and Spengler that modern democracy is too often a mask for securing the dominion of the urban proletariat over the peasant. He is convinced that the health of the nation depends very largely on the proportion of men owning their own land or their own small businesses, and he resents the tendency to transform the small owner into the employee of the State or of the chain stores.[22]

Although Lunn now found himself in the same political camp and reciting the same distributist creed as Chesterton and Belloc, he was still some way from being in the same Church and reciting the same religious Creed. It was not until 1929 that the spectre of religion again came to haunt him: 'My deepening distrust of Huxleyism, and of much that paraded itself as modern thought, was reinforced by reading, during 1929, *Science and the Modern World*, by Professor A. N. Whitehead, a distinguished non-Catholic philosopher and mathematician, and a Fellow of the Royal Society.'[23]

Professor Whitehead's book was to have a profound and pivotal influence upon Lunn's subsequent development:

> The Reformation and the scientific movement were two aspects of the historical revolt which was the dominating intellectual movement of the later Renaissance ... It is a great mistake to conceive this historical revolt as an appeal to reason. On the contrary it was through and through an anti-intellectualist movement ... based on a recoil from the inflexible rationality of mediaeval thought ... I do not think that I have even yet brought out the greatest contribution of mediaevalism to the formation of the scientific movement. I mean the inexpugnable belief that every detailed occurrence can be correlated to its antecedents in a perfectly definite manner, exemplifying general principles. Without this belief the incredible labour of scientists would be without hope ...[24]

'Under the influence of this impressive tribute to mediaeval thought,' Lunn wrote in his autobiography, 'I began to read the mediaeval scholastics, and, in particular, the greatest of them, St Thomas Aquinas.'[25]

Aquinas had held centre stage in the philosophy of the Catholic Church for more than six hundred years, but had long been neglected by students of philosophy outside the Church. In the twentieth century, the neo-Thomist revival paralleled the Catholic revival, one feeding off the other, and Lunn was only one of an increasing number of people who were returning to the teachings of the medieval scholastics in general and Aquinas in particular. Neo-Thomism found its greatest champions in France, principally in the persons of Jacques Maritain and Etienne Gilson, but Chesterton's popular biography of Aquinas, published in 1933, brought Thomism to the attention of English speakers throughout the world. The greatest English exponent of Thomism this century was Frederick C. Copleston who had converted to Catholicism in 1925 as an eighteen-year-old. Copleston's interest in philosophy began in 1929, at around the same time as Lunn's, during his final year at St John's College, Oxford, where he took the degrees of BA and MA in *Literae Humaniores*. After a year studying scholastic philosophy at Oscott College, Birmingham, he entered the Jesuit novitiate in September 1930 and was ordained priest in 1937. In 1948 he became a member of the Council and Executive Committee of the Royal Institute of Philosophy. In time he became not only a celebrated philosopher but also something of a celebrity in his own right, broadcasting frequently for the BBC, including discussions on the existence of God with Bertrand Russell and on logical positivism with Professor A. J. Ayer. He is probably best known to posterity as the author of a monumental nine-volume history of philosophy but was also author of the best introduction to Aquinas available in English, published in 1955.

Arnold Lunn was never destined to grasp the intricacies of Thomist thought to the same extent as Copleston. Many years later Barbara Reynolds remembered Dorothy L. Sayers, herself a lover of Aquinas, being rather 'scornful' of one of Lunn's public debates in which Lunn and his opponent discussed transubstantiation with 'neither of them understanding that they were using the word "substance" in the wrong sense'.[26] As an amateur, however, Lunn became a keen student of Thomist philosophy. In his autobiography he wrote that Aquinas 'appealed to me for many reasons': 'Temperamentally I am a sceptic, and am uninterested in creeds which cannot justify themselves at the bar of reason ... personal experience, though convincing for the "experient", has no validity as an argument for those who do not share this experience.'[27]

It was this craving for objectivism in the face of the amorphous subjectivism of modern thought which lay at the heart of his attraction to Thomism:

> I was impressed by the fairness with which St Thomas summarised the principal arguments which tell against his theses. Professor Thomson, F.R.S., somewhere comments on the contrast between the objectivity with which St Thomas states and meets the arguments against the Faith and the evasive conspiracy of silence with which the arguments against evolution are ignored. The contrast between the confident rationalism of St Thomas and the timid emotionalism of our modern prophets was the theme of my book *The Flight from Reason*.[28]

This book, published in 1930, represented the fruit of Lunn's labours into the philosophy of St Thomas and the medieval scholastics. Its title referred to the modern mind's 'flight from reason' but was also his own flight *to* reason, his scrambling on to the rock of scholasticism as an escape from the quicksands of subjectivism:

the suicidal tendencies of modern thought were apparent to competent observers. The principal characteristic of modern philosophy is an implicit premiss which, in effect, denies the validity of all philosophy. If Marx and Freud are to be believed, neither Freud nor Marx should be believed. Marx maintained that the religion, philosophy and art of a given period are the by-products of its economic processes. Scholastic theology is nothing more than the mirror of the feudal system of land tenure. But, if this be true, Marxist Communism is nothing more than the mirror of the *laissez-faire* liberalism and industrialism of Victorian England. It has no objective validity. Freud maintained that the reasons with which a man justifies his beliefs are nothing more than rationalisations invented, *post hoc*, to justify beliefs imposed upon him by his environment and sexual complexes. We can safely ignore the reasoned arguments with which a man defends his belief, for we shall discover all that is worth knowing about those beliefs by psycho-analysing the man in question. If this be true, we shall learn all that is worth knowing about Freudianism by psycho-analysing the Freudian. These modern thinkers are busily engaged in sawing away the branch on which they are sitting.[29]

Predictably Hilaire Belloc was delighted when he read *The Flight from Reason* and wrote telling Lunn that he had bought twelve copies to give away to friends. Lunn recalled that no letter from a reader had ever given him greater pleasure. It was about this time that Douglas Woodruff had asked Belloc whether he thought Lunn would eventually end up within the Church. 'Oh, he'll come in all right,' was Belloc's robust reply.[30]

Another book published in 1930 which delighted both Belloc and Lunn was Knox's *Caliban in Grub Street*. It was in many respects similar to Lunn's in its dissection of the 'flight from reason' of many modern thinkers but was written of course from an orthodox Catholic viewpoint. The idea for the book had been Frank Sheed's who had suggested that Knox reply to the inconsistencies inherent in the theological posturings of many popular writers. As source material for the proposed book, Sheed had handed Knox a collection of newspaper cuttings from the *Daily Express*, the *Daily News*, the *Sunday Chronicle*, the *Daily Telegraph* and the *Sunday Dispatch* in which writers such as Arnold Bennett, Hugh Walpole, John Drinkwater, Conan Doyle and Israel Zangwill sounded forth on subjects as diverse as prayer, belief, life, religion, life after death, the outlook of the churches and hell.

Caliban in Grub Street invited parallels with Lunn's *Roman Converts*, except that whereas Lunn had been intent on controverting the converts Knox was a convert doing the controverting. Another parallel could be drawn between *Caliban in Grub Street* and Chesterton's *Heretics* which had appeared a quarter of a century earlier. Chesterton's 'heretics' had included Kipling, Shaw, Wells and Whistler, whereas Knox's seemed considerably less formidable. According to Evelyn Waugh, Knox's 'fine-trained mind was rather baffled by the naïvety, frivolity, and banality' of the 'highly paid amateurs' whose opinions he was to refute.[31] In many cases his quarry was far too easy:

> Mr Arnold Bennett begins with the confession: 'I do not believe, and never have at any time believed, in the divinity of Christ, the Immaculate Conception, heaven, hell, the immortality of the soul, the divine inspiration of the Bible.' The statement lacks, perhaps, scientific precision. Does Mr Bennett believe in original sin? I imagine not; and if he does not believe in original sin, then he believes in the Immaculate Conception; not merely in the immaculate conception of Our Lady, but in the immaculate conception of everybody else.[32]

It is not difficult to see why Evelyn Waugh came to the opinion that in the writing of *Caliban in Grub Street* Knox had 'dealt with opponents who were mostly unworthy of his attention'.[33] Yet Waugh believed he 'was trying to do more; he sought to identify and examine the ethos which his victims personified ... and his quest led him through a miasma of undefined premises and irrational conclusions, of huge omissions and assumptions, of an almost meaningless vocabulary and fatuous self-complacency'.[34] There was no consistent ethos. Modern thought outside the Catholic Church was entangled in a jungle of jargon devoid of depth or definition.

'The book delighted me,' Lunn wrote of *Caliban in Grub Street* and it was little wonder that he found much in Knox's book which pleased him. It was inspired by the same frustration and exasperation with modern thought that had characterized his own volume. Yet differences remained and Lunn was still unconvinced of the claims of Catholicism. After he had reviewed *Caliban*, early in 1930, Lunn wrote to Knox suggesting a joint book consisting of a correspondence in which he would attack the Catholic claims and Knox would defend them. Knox accepted the challenge and the subsequent exchange of letters appeared in 1932 under the title, *Difficulties*.

The correspondence made intriguing reading. Lunn's letters were comprehensive and forceful, stating his case with great vigour. Knox's were shorter and superficially slighter, transfused with the same spirit of polite restraint displayed in his earlier letter to Lunn after he had been sent a copy of *Roman Converts*.

Opinion was divided as to who had got the better of the struggle. Colonel C. A. de Linde, described by Lunn as 'a sound Protestant, a great friend of mine', believed that the victory was Lunn's. He was frankly puzzled at Lunn's later conversion: 'I cannot understand how you became a Catholic after wiping the floor as you did with Knox.'[35] Neither was opinion divided along sectarian lines. A Catholic, after Lunn's reception into the Church, remarked wryly that 'the only person who thinks that Knox won is Lunn'.[36] As for Lunn himself, he appeared to accept the view of his friend, Viscount Knebworth: '"You scored point after point," he said, "but the odd thing is that you did not make the least impression. There is an odd reserve of strength about Knox's letters which is most impressive."'[37]

Lunn had his own theory concerning Knox's apparent pulling of punches. He suspected that his opponent might have thrown the fight merely to offer him a Pyrrhic victory: 'Knox could, I know, have made his letters superficially more effective to the outside public but for the fact that his object was not a striking dialectic victory which might well have provoked me into trying to improve my weapons of offence, but my conversion.'[38]

In hindsight Lunn recognized that the arguments which did most to hasten his submission to Rome were those in which he felt 'Knox was addressing me and not a crowd of unidentified readers'.[39]

In September 1932, a few months after the publication of *Difficulties*, Knox's *Broadcast Minds* was published. In some respects this was similar to his *Caliban in Grub Street* in so far as it was intended to refute the superficialities and asinine assumptions of modern thought. This time, however, Knox had turned his attention to more challenging prey such as Julian Huxley, H. G. Wells and Bertrand Russell. The purpose of the whole book was summarized by its epigraph, a quote from Russell: 'Our age has been rendered conceited by the multitude of new discoveries and inventions, but in the realm of philosophy it is much less in advance of the past than it imagines itself to be.'

At the same time that Knox was writing *Broadcast Minds*, Lunn was involved in another controversial exchange of correspondence which was published the following year under the title, *Is Christianity True?*. This time Lunn was 'on the side of the angels' while his opponent, the popular philosopher and self-publicist, C. E. M. Joad, argued for atheism. The first letter, dated 18 March 1932, expressed Lunn's acceptance of Joad's challenge:

> I accept your challenge with great pleasure.
> In the first place, though we differ on fundamental issues, we are not personally antipathetic ...

Secondly, you are a good controversialist, with whom it will be a pleasure to cross swords ...

In the third place, I welcome this correspondence because I admire your philosophical writings, which are lucid and well expressed.

In the fourth place, I welcome this correspondence because I do not in the least admire your religious writings, which are confused, badly expressed and plagiaristic. There is evidence of hard thinking in every line that you write on philosophy, but you give your brain a rest when you turn to the uncongenial subject of Christianity. You may console yourself, however, with the reflection that in this respect you are not unique. In your attitude towards Christianity, you are a child of your age, an age which has decided that all standards of sober criticism may be suspended when Christianity is in the dock. H. G. Wells, Huxley and many another modern prophet display in their attitude to the greatest of all problems the same distressing blend of glib assurance and ignorance. In due course I must try to diagnose the malady, but first I must convince you that you yourself are suffering from this modern complaint.[40]

The extent to which Lunn failed to convince Joad of the superiority of his position is clear from a letter written seven months later in which he is reduced to making the same complaints about Joad's 'ignorance' that he had made at the very outset of their correspondence. On 20 October 1932, Lunn had replied to Joad in a typically aggressive manner:

You cover your retreat from the empty tomb by a smoke-screen of sneers at my naïvete, my parochialism, etc, etc. Oddly enough this is precisely the accusation which is levelled by Roman Catholics against the modern intelligentsia ... The main difference between Father Knox and the leaders of the intelligentsia is that Father Knox has carefully studied our modern creeds, whereas the average member of the intelligentsia is completely ignorant of Christianity. Let me remind you once again that my quarrel with you people is not that you refuse to take Christianity seriously, but that nothing will stop you from criticising a creed which you are too idle to study.[41]

C. E. M. Joad was destined for greater things following this early debate with Lunn. In 1936 he published his *Guide to Philosophy* and followed this two years later with a *Guide to the Philosophy of Morals and Politics*. He wrote forty-seven books in all but it was as a member of the BBC Brains Trust that he gained celebrity status and became one of the century's most fashionable atheists. Shortly before his death in 1953 he surprised everybody by becoming a member of the Church of England, describing his change of heart and mind in his last published work, *The Recovery of Belief*.

Lunn's change of heart and mind happened much sooner. On 13 July 1933 he was received into the Church by Father Ronald Knox, less than two years after the last of his letters expressing his 'difficulties' to the priest had been posted. Two years after his reception he employed an unusual analogy as he described his feelings on the day he was received:

> Among the noises of London with which I am most familiar are the grinding of brakes and the critical comments of motorists who have just avoided running over me. My wife never allows me to leave the house without a final exhortation, 'Look both ways.'
>
> The traditional formula was not omitted when I left for Oxford to be received by Father Ronald Knox into the Catholic Church. I was glad to be able to respond with quiet dignity that it was precisely because I had looked both ways that I had found the right road at last.[42]

He wrote in similar vein in his autobiography: 'I entered the Church along the road of controversy and by the gate of reason. I clarified my mind by three controversial books, in the first of which (*Difficulties*, with Father Ronald Knox) I attacked, and in the second and third of which I defended, the Catholic position against Cyril Joad and Professor Haldane.'[43]

It was appropriate that Knox should have been the priest who received Arnold Lunn into the Church. Lunn's love-loathe relationship with Knox had stretched back more than two decades in which Lunn considered Knox truly awful in both senses of the word – on occasions he filled him with awe and at the same time he irritated him immensely. The latter aspect was exorcised by Lunn's conversion and the two erstwhile antagonists became good friends. It was also interesting that Lunn's conversion coincided with Knox's retirement as a Catholic controversialist. Evelyn Waugh, observing that Lunn 'became the most tireless Catholic apologist of his generation' after Knox had received him into the Church, remarked: 'Perhaps Ronald felt that in arming Sir Arnold and putting him in the field, he had fulfilled his own combatant duties.'[44] Elsewhere, Waugh wrote that Knox 'decided that his vocation was not to discomfort the infidel but to work among the clergy and laity of his own Church to fortify and refine their devotion and remind them of their high calling'.[45] Knox confessed as much to Lunn with characteristic wit: 'The Church gets on by hook and by crook, the hook of the fisherman who hopes for a rich haul of converts, and the crook of the shepherd whose chief concern is to safeguard his own flock. I'm more of a crook than a hook.'[46]

Lunn was certainly more of a hook than a crook. As he grew older he appeared ever more untiring and by 1958 had published his fiftieth book. Both as tireless Catholic apologist and prolific author, Lunn invites comparison with Belloc, the other great influence on him in the two decades leading up to his conversion. The two men had much in common, from a love of the outdoor life to a love of continental Europe. Lunn had admired Belloc's books since his youth and Belloc came to admire Lunn's combative brand of apologetics. Most of all they shared the same type of faith, desiccate but deep, and rooted in reason. In 1958 Lunn concluded an essay on his 'Memories of Hilaire Belloc' with a quote from Belloc which illustrated the essential unity of their approach to Christianity:

> If I had continued to trust solely to my emotions and to my feeling I should, perhaps, still disbelieve in immortality, but I can now say with Belloc, '... as to the doubt of the soul I discover it to be false: a mood: not a conclusion. My conclusion – and that of all men who have ever once *seen* it – is the Faith: Corporate, organised, a personality, teaching. A thing, not a theory. It.'[47]

More than twenty years earlier, and scarcely two years after his own reception into the Church, Lunn had chosen another quote from Belloc as the epigraph for his book *Within That City*:

> There is a City full, as are all Cities, of halt and maim, blind and evil and the rest: but it is the City of God ... There are not two such cities on earth. There is One ...
>
> Within that household the human spirit has roof and hearth. Outside it, is the night.

NOTES

1. Robert Speaight, *The Property Basket: Recollections of a Divided Life*, pp. 127–8.
2. Brocard Sewell, O Carm, letter to the author, September 1996.
3. Brocard Sewell, *My Dear Time's Waste*, Saint Albert's Press, Aylesford, Kent, 1966, pp. 23–4.
4. ibid., p. 32.
5. ibid., p. 36.
6. F. J. Sheed, *The Church and I*, London, 1976, p. 97.
7. ibid., p. 110.
8. Robert Speaight (ed.), *Letters from Hilaire Belloc*, p. 206.
9. F. J. Sheed, *The Church and I*, p. 109.
10. Evelyn Waugh, *A Little Learning*, p. 143.
11. F. J. Sheed, *The Church and I*, p. 127.
12. 'W. A. D.', *The Road to Damascus: The Story of an Undergraduate's Conversion*, London, 1920.
13. Arnold Lunn, *And Yet So New*, pp. 2–3.
14. ibid., p. 3.
15. ibid., p. 3.
16. ibid., pp. 3–4.
17. Arnold Lunn, *Come What May: An Autobiography*, pp. 211–12.
18. ibid., p. 227.
19. ibid., pp. 227–8.
20. Matthew Hoehn, OSB (ed.), *Catholic Authors: Contemporary Biographical Sketches 1930–1947*, Newark, N.J., 1948, p. 446.
21. Arnold Lunn, *Come What May: An Autobiography*, p. 75.
22. ibid., p. 76.
23. ibid., p. 200.
24. ibid., p. 200.
25. ibid., p. 201.
26. Dr Barbara Reynolds, interview with the author, Cambridge, 19 September 1996.
27. Arnold Lunn, *Come What May: An Autobiography*, p. 201.
28. ibid., p. 202.
29. ibid., pp. 202–3.
30. Arnold Lunn, *Come What May: An Autobiography*, p. 62.
31. Evelyn Waugh, *Ronald Knox*, p. 202.
32. ibid., p. 202.
33. Ronald Knox, *A Spiritual Aeneid*, introduction to 1958 edn.
34. Evelyn Waugh, *Ronald Knox*, pp. 202–3.
35. Arnold Lunn, *And Yet So New*, p. 5.
36. ibid., p. 5.
37. ibid., p. 5.
38. ibid., p. 5.
39. ibid., p. 6.
40. Arnold Lunn and C. E. M. Joad, *Is Christianity True?*, London, 1933, pp. 3–4.
41. ibid., pp. 326–7.
42. Arnold Lunn, *Within That City*, London, 1936, p. 1.
43. Arnold Lunn, *Come What May: An Autobiography*, pp. 218–19.
44. Evelyn Waugh, *Ronald Knox*, pp. 204–5.
45. Ronald Knox, *A Spiritual Aeneid*, introduction to 1958 edn.
46. Arnold Lunn, *And Yet So New*, p. 13.
47. ibid., p. 82.

CHAPTER SIXTEEN

CHESTERTON AND BARING

As Arnold Lunn, 'the most tireless Catholic apologist of his generation', was making a dramatic entrance at the beginning of the thirties, the most tireless apologist of the previous generation was about to make his final bow. Chesterton had published his biography of St Thomas Aquinas in September 1933, two months after Lunn's reception into the Church. It was his last full-length book, apart from the posthumously published *Autobiography*, and would serve as an appropriate closing chapter to his literary career. Chesterton, like Lunn, had underpinned his faith with a thorough knowledge of scholastic philosophy and it was apt that he should finish his life's work with a study of the saint who, more than any other, had helped him in his diligent search for truth.

Although failing health prevented Chesterton writing further full-length books, he continued writing essays. In September 1935 a collection of these was published by Sheed & Ward under the title, *The Well and the Shallows*. Originally, Chesterton had been tempted to call the book 'Joking Apart': 'It seemed to me a simple and sensible way of saying that the reader of these pages must not look for many jokes, certainly not merely for jokes, because these are controversial essays, covering all subjects on which a controversialist is challenged.'[1]

Most of the controversies covered in *The Well and the Shallows* had been discussed by the author many times before yet he still seemed able to approach them from fresh and entertaining angles. Thus the first sentence in a series of six essays, entitled collectively 'My Six Conversions', commenced with a typical stroke of Chestertonian wit and humour: 'At least six times during the last few years, I have found myself in a situation in which I should certainly have become a Catholic, if I had not been restrained from that rash step by the fortunate accident that I was one already.'[2] There followed fifty pages in which Chesterton expounded his belief in the strength of the Catholic position compared with the relative weakness of other positions, concluding with the literary flourish which had given the collection of essays its title:

I could not abandon the faith, without falling back on something more shallow than the faith. I could not cease to be a Catholic, except by becoming something more narrow than a Catholic. A man must narrow his mind in order to lose the universal philosophy; everything that has happened up to this very day has confirmed this conviction; and whatever happens tomorrow will confirm it anew. We have come out of the shallows and the dry places to the one deep well; and the Truth is at the bottom of it.[3]

Elsewhere, the sceptics who failed to fathom the depths were accused of causing enormous harm: 'the work of the sceptic for the past hundred years has indeed been very like the fruitless fury of some primeval monster; eyeless, mindless, merely destructive and devouring; a giant worm wasting away a world that he could not even see'.[4] Though expressed in more poetic prose this was essentially the same line of argument being put forward by Arnold Lunn. It was the modern world's flight from reason, the antidote to which was the perennial philosophy of the Church:

> There is ... one influence that grows stronger every day, never mentioned in the newspapers, not even intelligible to people in the newspaper frame of mind. It is the return of the Thomist Philosophy; which is the philosophy of common sense, as compared with the paradoxes of Kant and Hegel and the Pragmatists. The Roman religion will be, in the exact sense, the only Rationalist religion ... the return of the Scholastic will simply be the return of the sane man ... to say that there is no pain, or no matter, or no evil, or no difference between man and beast, or indeed between anything and anything else – this is a desperate effort to destroy all experience and sense of reality; and men will weary of it more and more, when it has ceased to be the latest fashion; and will look once more for something that will give form to such a chaos and keep the proportions of the mind of man.[5]

Chesterton had wearied of the chaos of modern thought, even if others had not, and in his final years he began to feel like an exile in an increasingly mad world. During Christmas 1935 he was heard muttering the words *'nobis, post exilium ostende'* from the *Salve Regina*, the words signifying his belief that life on earth was a time of exile and that the fullness of existence was to be found elsewhere. The same view was evident from his love for the Corpus Christi sequence which he had learned by heart during the writing of his biography of St Thomas Aquinas. Time and again, in the company of friends, he would recite the last two stanzas 'thumping his fist on the arm of the chair'.

> Bone pastor, panis vere,
> Jesu nostri miserere;
> Tu nos pasce, nos tuere:
> Tu nos bona fac videre
> In terra viventium.

> Tu, qui cuncta scis et vales,
> Qui nos pascis hic mortales:
> Tuos ibi commensales,
> Coheredes et sodales
> Fac sanctorum civium.

Finishing, he would proclaim, 'What a summary of Heaven: the exact reversal of the slang expression "down among the dead men". There you have it – literally "the land of the living". Yes, my friends, we shall see all good things in the land of the living.'[6]

In patria was another definition of Heaven he often quoted in the final years of his life: 'It tells you everything: "our native land".'[7]

Chesterton began 1936 as he had begun many previous years, embroiled in controversy. This time his opponent was the Cambridge medieval scholar at St John's College, Dr G. G. Coulton, a staunch anti-Catholic who had crossed swords with both Knox and Belloc on other occasions. This time Coulton had chosen Chesterton as his quarry, but Chesterton, uncharacteristically, was not fit for the chase. In increasingly ill health he scarcely had the inclination to put pen to paper and it was left to his secretary to fob his adversary off. On 28 January Coulton replied to her letter, commenting that he was 'very sorry to hear of Mr Chesterton's indisposition'.[8]

However, if Cambridge University had produced a medieval scholar who was hostile to Chesterton, Oxford could boast a scholar who was far more favourably disposed towards him. During the early part of the year Oxford University Press had published *The Allegory of Love: A Study in Medieval Tradition* by a young don named C. S. Lewis. This book, for which Lewis was awarded the Hawthornden Prize, contained a great tribute to Chesterton: 'The *Furioso*, in its own peculiar way, is as great a masterpiece of construction as the *Oedipus Rex* ... There is only one English critic who could do justice to this gallant, satiric, chivalrous, farcical, flamboyant poem: Mr Chesterton should write a book on the Italian epic.'[9]

Chesterton was no more able to fulfil Lewis's desire for a book on medieval romance than he was able to meet Coulton's demands for a battle over medieval Rome. He was finding his weekly journalistic commitments more of a struggle and any remaining energy was expended in the writing of his *Autobiography*. Its completion prompted one friend to remark, '*Nunc dimittis*,' and certainly there was much in the autobiography which sounded ominously as though it was intended as a swan song:

> I am finishing a story; rounding off what has been to me at least a romance, and very much a mystery-story. It is a purely personal narrative that began in the first pages of this book; and I am answering at the end only the questions I asked at the beginning ... This story, therefore, can only end as any detective story should end, with its own particular questions answered and its own primary problem solved ... But for me my end is my beginning ... and this overwhelming conviction that there is one key which can unlock all doors brings back to me my first glimpse of the glorious gift of the senses; and the sensational experience of sensation.[10]

On 15 March Chesterton made his last radio broadcast, apart from a talk to schools on the Middle Ages a week later. His final adult broadcast, portentously entitled 'We will End with a Bang', was a lighthearted response to Eliot's poem *The Hollow Men*. Although Chesterton had been reconciled with Eliot and saw that the refrain applied to the 'Hollow Men' and not to their creator, such defeatism remained anathema to him:

> Forgive me if I say, in my old-world fashion, that I'm damned if I ever felt like that ... I knew that the world was perishable and would end, but I did not think it would end with a whimper, but, if anything, with a trump of doom ... I will even be so indecently frivolous as to burst into song, and say to the young pessimists:
>
> Some sneer; some snigger; some simper;
> In the youth where we laughed, and sang.
> And *they* may end with a whimper
> But *we* will end with a bang.[11]

Such was the emphatic climax to Chesterton's broadcasting career.

Chesterton died soon after ten o'clock on the morning of Sunday, 14 June. Later the same day his wife wrote to Father O'Connor, the old friend who had been the original model and inspiration for Father Brown, his fictional priest-detective, informing him of the news: 'Our beloved Gilbert passed away this morning at 10.15. He was unconscious for some time before but had received the Last Sacraments and Extreme Unction whilst he was still in possession of his understanding.'[12]

Many people observed wryly that there were several coincidences connected with the timing of Chesterton's death. His passing had occurred on the Sunday within the Octave of Corpus Christi, the feast upon which he had been received into the Church fourteen years earlier and to which, through his love for St Thomas Aquinas, he was particularly attached. Father Ignatius Rice also noted with a smile that the Introit for that day's Mass, which was printed on his memorial card, contained a joke about his corpulence: 'The Lord became my protector and He brought me forth into a large place. He saved me because he was well pleased with me. I will love thee O Lord my strength. The Lord is my firmament and my refuge and my deliverer.'[13] To these words on Chesterton's memorial card, his wife had added Walter de la Mare's tribute to her husband:

Knight of the Holy Ghost, he goes his way
Wisdom his motley, Truth his loving jest;
The mills of Satan keep his lance in play,
Pity and innocence his heart at rest.[14]

These lines found a distant echo in a stanza from Chesterton's *Ballad of the White Horse*:

People, if you have any prayers
    Say prayers for me:
And lay me under a Christian stone
In that lost land I call my own,
To wait till the holy horn is blown,
    And all poor men are free.

On the day of his funeral it seemed that many had come to comply with this request because the church in Beaconsfield was filled to overflowing with friends and admirers. They had arrived from all over England, and even from France, Germany and the United States. Hilaire Belloc, Max Beerbohm, Eric Gill, D. B. Wyndham Lewis, Aldous Huxley, Douglas Woodruff, Desmond McCarthy,

E. C. Bentley, Frank Sheed, Maisie Ward, Thomas Derrick, Emile Cammaerts and A. G. Gardiner were among the mourners. Among the clergy in attendance were the Archbishop of Westminster, Dr Hinsley, Monsignor Fulton J. Sheen, of the Catholic University of America, Ronald Knox, Vincent McNabb, C. C. Martindale, Ignatius Rice and Father Josef Stocker from Cologne. The funeral was described by W. R. Titterton, a great friend of Chesterton's who had followed him into the Church in 1931:

> I see the coffin that holds all that is mortal of my captain. I pass with it along the little town's winding ways. It is a roundabout way we go. For the police of the place will have it that Gilbert Chesterton shall make his last earthly journey past the homes of the people who knew him and loved him best. And there they were, crowding the pavements, and all, like us, bereaved. Yet it was almost a gala day. There was no moping, no gush of tears. Nay, there was laughter as one of us recalled him and his heroic jollity to another's ready remembrance.[15]

Not everyone was able to treat the death of a friend so whimsically or philosophically. Hilaire Belloc was found after the funeral weeping tears of disconsolate isolation into a pint of beer outside the Railway Hotel in Beaconsfield, only yards from the makeshift building at the back of the hotel where Chesterton had been received into the Church fourteen years earlier.

Bernard Shaw wrote to Frances Chesterton offering his condolences at her husband's death: 'It seems the most ridiculous thing in the world that I, 18 years older than Gilbert, should be heartlessly surviving him ... The trumpets are sounding for him.'[16]

Dorothy L. Sayers wrote to Frances on 15 June, the day after his death, 'I think, in some ways, G. K.'s books have become more a part of my mental make-up than those of any writer you could name.'[17] Ronald Knox wrote to Frances with what his biographer, Evelyn Waugh, described as 'a touch of hyperbole appropriate to the occasion':

> I'll only hope that you, who know as no one else does what we have lost, will find it easy to imagine as well as believe that he is alive and unchanged. Thank God for that faith; that I have it when so many of my friends lost it was due, I think, under God to him. May he be pardoned all that remains to pardon; I don't think he can be long for Purgatory.[18]

In a lecture given in Scotland some weeks later Knox said: 'To me, Chesterton's philosophy, in the broadest sense of the word, has been part of the air I breathed, ever since the age when a man's ideas begin to disentangle themselves from his education.'[19] Charles Williams exclaimed, on hearing the news of Chesterton's death, that 'the last of my lords is dead', and, in similar vein, Sir Iain Moncreiffe recalled the reaction of his English tutor T. H. White, author of *The Sword in the Stone* and *The Ill-Made Knight*, to the news: 'One morning Tim White came into our beautiful Georgian classroom and announced, "G. K. Chesterton died yesterday. P. G. Wodehouse is now the greatest living master of the English language".'[20]

Arnold Lunn's brother, Hugh Kingsmill, wrote: 'My friend Hesketh Pearson was staying with me when I read of Chesterton's death. I told him of it through the bathroom door, and he sent up a hollow groan which must have echoed that morning all over England.'[21]

Eric Gill wrote to Frances Chesterton on 16 June: 'Nothing I can say can lessen your grief – or ours ... We have lost, in a physical manner, the best man of our time. But I can't stop thinking of the joy in heaven – oh, that we were there. Every time I think of our grief and of yours – it suddenly seems absurd, is blotted out by the knowledge of that joy.'[22]

The *Times* obituary, published the morning after his death, sang his praises with a rumbustiousness worthy of the dead man himself:

> His energy and his versatility were amazing; his exuberant intellect ran riot over letters, art, religion, philosophy, and current affairs ... on all occasions he was sincere, and his hearty optimism was a comfort and a refreshment ... Though he said and wrote a great many extravagant things, he uttered nothing unseemly, and he can have hardly made any enemies. All his life he had a strong touch of true genius in him ... and by his death literature and discussion are made suddenly and most regrettably the poorer.

One of the most poignant tributes was from the pen of T. S. Eliot. In a signed obituary article for the *Tablet* on 20 June, Eliot wrote: 'I never met Gilbert Chesterton ... but his disappearance, from a world such as that we live in, is one of those which give even to us who did not know the man, a sense of personal loss and isolation.'

Although Eliot thought Chesterton's poetry overrated, possessing nothing more than the qualities of 'first-rate journalistic balladry', he had a very high opinion of much of his other work:

He reached a high imaginative level with *The Napoleon of Notting Hill*, and higher with *The Man Who Was Thursday*, romances in which he turned the Stevensonian fantasy to more serious purpose. His book on Dickens seems to me the best essay on that author that has ever been written ... But it is not, I think, for any piece of writing in particular that Chesterton is of importance, but for the place that he occupied, the position that he represented, during the better part of a generation.

On Saturday, 27 June, a requiem Mass was celebrated at Westminster Cathedral with a congregation of 2,000 people, including dignitaries such as the Belgian and Polish Ambassadors and the Irish High Commissioner. Others in attendance included D. B. Wyndham Lewis, Arnold Lunn, Max Beerbohm, J. B. Morton, Hilary Pepler, Walter de la Mare, Eric Gill and Rose Macaulay. Ronald Knox preached the panegyric with an eloquence remembered by Ada Chesterton, the widow of Cecil Chesterton: 'He painted Gilbert's achievements, aspirations, in words as glowing as the dead man himself could have used, and in the triumphant sentences one could hear the leaping of the sword from the scabbard in challenge of justice and oppression.'[23]

The highest honour, however, came in the form of a message from the Pope. Both Frances and Archbishop Hinsley received telegrams from Cardinal Pacelli, later to become Pope himself, for and on behalf of Pope Pius XI. The telegram to Archbishop Hinsley was read to the vast crowd in the cathedral: 'Holy Father deeply grieved death Mr Gilbert Keith Chesterton devoted son Holy Church gifted Defender of the Catholic Faith. His Holiness offers paternal sympathy people of England assures prayers dear departed, bestows Apostolic Benediction.'[24]

Archbishop Hinsley had requested that Monsignor John O'Connor sing the Mass, assisted by Father Ignatius Rice, who had been O'Connor's assistant at Chesterton's reception into the Church. O'Connor described the requiem at Westminster as 'the solemn commemoration of him by and for those who could not be present at Beaconsfield at his burial, myself for instance having been confined to bed all that week'.[25]

Another of Chesterton's closest friends who had been unable to attend either the burial at Beaconsfield or the requiem at Westminster because of illhealth was Maurice Baring. Suffering progressively from Parkinson's disease, Baring scrawled an almost illegible letter to Frances: 'Too paralysed with neuritis and "agitance" to hold pen or pencil. Saw incredible news in *Times*. Then your letter came. All my prayers and thoughts are with you. I'm not allowed to travel except once a week to see doctor, but I'll have a Mass said here.'[26] The following day he wrote again, clearly upset at his inability to attend the funeral: 'There is nothing to be said, is there, except that our loss, and especially yours, is his gain? I wish I could come down tomorrow, but I cannot go even to Mass here on Sundays ... O, Frances, I feel as if a tower of strength had vanished and our crutch in life had broken.'[27]

Tragically, Baring's career also came to an abrupt end in 1936. He was to live for a further nine years, increasingly incapacitated by the progressive nature of his illness, but following the publication of *Have You Anything to Declare?* in the year of Chesterton's death, he wrote no further books. The following year he scrawled these desperate lines of verse:

My body is a broken toy
Which nobody can mend
Unfit for either play or ploy
My body is a broken toy;
But all things end.
The siege of Troy
Came one day to an end.
My body is a broken toy
Which nobody can mend.[28]

Baring's last book, described by Robert Speaight as 'the best bedside book in the English language',[29] was inspired by the author's imagined arrival on the banks of the Styx and his being asked by Charon to declare his literary luggage. As such, *Have You Anything to Declare?* served as a fitting finale to Baring's literary career. Furthermore, his selection, gleaned from the literatures of many of the languages in which he was conversant, displayed an extraordinary catholicity of taste and reminds one of the description of a character in *The Coat Without Seam*, one of his own novels: 'Everything about him ... gave one the impression of centuries and hidden stores of pent-up civilization.' There is a love for Homer and Virgil and a deep devotion to Dante:

Scaling the circles of the *Paradiso*, we are conscious the whole time of an ascent not only in the quality of the substance but in that of the form. It is a long perpetual crescendo, increasing in beauty until the final consummation in the very last line. Somebody once defined an artist ... as a man who knew how to finish things. If this definition is true – and I think it is – then Dante was the greatest artist who ever lived. His final canto is the best, and it depends on and completes the beginning.[30]

Ironically, this book of excerpts from the works of Baring's favourite authors became better known than all his other books, eclipsing his own literary achievement and leaving his novels lurking in the shadows. Yet such neglect does both the man and his work an injustice.

Baring's career as a novelist was relatively short, commencing with the publication of *Passing By* in 1921 when the author was already nearly fifty years old and ending prematurely fifteen years later due to his debilitating illness. In between he wrote several novels of considerable merit. *C*, published in 1924, was highly praised by the French novelist André Maurois who wrote that no book had given him such pleasure since his reading of Tolstoy, Proust and certain novels by E. M. Forster.[31] If anything, Baring enjoyed greater success in France than in England. Ten of his books were translated into French, with one – *Daphne Adeane* – going through twenty-three printings in the edition of the Librairie Stock. Others were translated into Italian, Dutch, Swedish, Hungarian, Czech, Spanish and German. *Cat's Cradle*, published in 1925, was considered by Belloc 'a great masterpiece ... the best story of a woman's life that I know'.[32] Belloc also admired *Robert Peckham*, Baring's historical saga which is so reminiscent of Benson's historical novels. Belloc wrote, 'Where you triumph unusually is in the exact valuation of characters which do not differ in black and white, but in every shade. You do it better in this book, I think, than in any other, even than in *Cat's Cradle* ... It seems to me to have a more permanent quality than any other.'[33]

Not surprisingly, Chesterton shared Belloc's view. Writing to Baring in 1929, shortly after Baring's novel *The Coat Without Seam* had been published, Chesterton announced that he had been 'much uplifted' by his friend's latest book:

> The Protestant English, who prided themselves on their common sense, seem now to be dodging about and snatching at anything except the obvious ... my writing cannot ... be so subtle or delicate as yours. But even I find that if I make the point of a story stick out like a spike, they carefully go and impale themselves on something else. But there are plenty of people who will appreciate anything as good as *The Coat Without Seam*.[34]

Many failed to share Chesterton's and Belloc's enthusiasm. Virginia Woolf attacked what she perceived as Baring's 'superficiality'. Baring found such views frustrating, especially as he believed that failure to understand his work was due itself to superficiality. Both the frustration he felt and the superficiality which caused it were expressed plaintively in *Have You Anything to Declare?*:

It is utterly futile to write about the Christian faith from the outside. A good example of this is the extremely conscientious novel by Mrs Humphry Ward called *Helbeck of Bannisdale*. It is a study of Catholicism from the outside, and the author has taken scrupulous pains to make it accurate, detailed and exhaustive. The only drawback is that, not being able to see the matter from the inside, she misses the whole point.[35]

Sadly neglected and misunderstood in England, Baring gained solace once again from the empathy exhibited by a more discerning readership across the Channel. In particular, he was 'too moved to speak' when, six months before his death, he learned of the deep admiration that François Mauriac had for his novels. Mauriac had told Robert Speaight: 'What I admire most about Baring's work is the sense he gives you of the penetration of grace.'[36]

For the last five years of his life, no longer able to look after himself, Baring was cared for by Laura, Lady Lovat at Beaufort Castle in Scotland. He died on 14 December 1945, his last hours being recorded in Lady Lovat's diary:

> At three o'clock Fr. Geddes read the Prayers for the Dying. I think Maurice heard them.
>
> From three o'clock to eleven o'clock Fr. McGuire, Neill and I never left him. I spoke to him often – if he heard he made no sign.
>
> At a quarter to eleven Fr. McGuire lit the candles on each side of the Crucifix at the foot of his bed, and gave him Final Absolution, and we recited the Litany for the Dying.
>
> At eleven o'clock Maurice died.
>
> Fr. McGuire stood up and said the Magnificat.[37]

His obituary in *The Times* on 17 December acknowledged 'the superb classical foundation of his culture ... the range and sensibility of the reading in the world's greatest literature, classical and modern, from which his original work derived its power'.

Conceding that 'many English readers' saw his novels as 'a form of Roman Catholic propaganda', the *Times* obituary maintained that he was

> above all concerned to express a passionate conviction that belief in God can alone bring storm-tossed humanity into harbour ... Concerning his final position in literature, time may perhaps confirm the judgment of those who see in him one of the subtlest, profoundest, and most original of recent English writers.

Baring's exemplary record with the Royal Flying Corps during the First World War was remembered by Lord Trenchard, Marshal of the RAF, in the following day's edition of *The Times*: 'In the words of a great Frenchman, there never was a staff officer in any country, in any nation, in any century like Major Maurice Baring. He was the most unselfish man I ever met or am likely to meet ... I can pay no higher tribute; words fail me in describing this man.'

None the less, Baring's greatest battle, and the one requiring the highest degree of courage and fortitude, was the one he fought against the pain of Parkinson's disease during the last ten years of his life. His bravery in this battle was described by 'a friend', probably Lady Lovat, in a letter to *The Times* on 19 December:

> it was his faith that inspired the courage which withstood all the suffer-ing and physical humiliation of his last years. Never – even when he grew very weak and his mind sometimes wandered – was he known to utter a word of complaint; and in such fortitude as his there surely is something given that pays the ransom of the world. Life never became a habit with him, it was always a miracle; the inevitable was accepted by his unfailing qualities of gentleness and strength.

Elsewhere Lady Lovat recorded that 'with the maturity of much experience, the virtuosity of genius, the culture of great scholarship and the modesty of the saint, he maintained, until the hour of his death, the mind of a child who walked through life's joys and sorrows with a deep conviction that he was always hold-ing God's hand'.[38]

One is struck in these loving testimonies by the remarkable similarity between the character of Baring and that of his great friend Chesterton. Life never became a habit with either of them, it was always a miracle. Chesterton invoked Baring in the final paragraph of his *Autobiography* when he wrote: 'But for me my end is my beginning, as Maurice Baring quoted of Mary Stuart.' And Baring could say with Chesterton that 'a man does not grow old without being bothered; but I have grown old without being bored'. Both, it seemed, embodied that paradoxical combination of wisdom and innocence which so baffled many of their contemporaries. The two qualities were synthesized in an almost legendary *joie de vivre* for which both men were remembered fondly after their deaths.

Four days after Chesterton's death a correspondent to *The Times* recalled Chesterton's jollity:

I was present at the Oxford Union just after the War when Mr Chesterton was the principal speaker ... When Chesterton finished an undergraduate rose to his feet ... 'I feel myself, sir, most awkwardly placed, between the Devil and the G.K.C.'. Even now after all these years I can hear Chesterton's roar of appreciation, and can see him rocking about, tears of joy streaming down his cheeks.

A week after Baring's death another correspondent to *The Times* recalled Baring's effervescence and 'the depth of the affection he inspired':

Whether he was nursing the sick in a cholera camp in Manchuria or making one of a wild party on his birthday at Brighton, before indulging in a midnight bathe, or intentionally stepping into the sea instead of into the admiral's launch after a luncheon with the commander-in-chief, there was charm and dignity in all he did because of the grace of innocence which never left him.

Many other anecdotes could be cited about Baring's escapades. One of the most memorable was his reciting an Horatian ode, composed by Ronald Knox, while balancing a glass of Burgundy on his bald head during a dinner to celebrate Hilaire Belloc's sixtieth birthday. During the recital he had to brave a barrage of pellets of bread which other guests, including Chesterton, J. B. Morton and D. B. Wyndham Lewis, threw at him in unsuccessful efforts to dislodge the precariously positioned glass.

Beneath this babbling surface there always remained a depth of stillness which strengthened Baring in the painful last years of his life. If, as the correspondent to *The Times* maintained, his sense of fun was rooted in 'the grace of innocence which never left him', it was his abundant wealth of wisdom which sustained him in suffering. Perhaps the key to his strength in the presence of suffering could be found in these words from *Darby and Joan*, his last novel: 'One has to *accept* sorrow for it to be of any healing power, and that is the most difficult thing in the world ... A Priest once said to me, "When you understand what *accepted* sorrow means, you will understand everything. It is the secret of life."'

These words, which for Virginia Woolf and others represented Baring's 'superficiality', were at once both mystical and practical. Baring himself put them into practice, accepting his own sorrows with a contrite and heroic heart.

In 1941 Virginia Woolf took her own life in an act of despair. In the same year Baring answered his earlier complaint that his body was a broken toy which nobody could mend, in a verse which was an act of hope:

My soul is an immortal toy
Which nobody can mar,
An instrument of praise and joy;
My soul is an immortal toy;
Though rusted from the world's alloy
It glitters like a star;
My soul is an immortal toy
Which nobody can mar.[39]

NOTES

1. G. K. Chesterton, *The Well and the Shallows*, London, 1935, p. v.
2. ibid., p. 23.
3. ibid., pp. 71–2.
4. ibid., p. 83.
5. ibid., pp. 193–4.
6. Maisie Ward, *Return to Chesterton*, London, 1952, pp. 266–7.
7. ibid., p. 267.
8. Michael Ffinch, *G. K. Chesterton: A Biography*, London, 1988, p. 342.
9. C. S. Lewis, *The Allegory of Love: A Study in Medieval Tradition*, Oxford, 1936, pp. 302–3.
10. G. K. Chesterton, *Autobiography*, London, 1936, pp. 340–3.
11. BBC broadcast, 'We Will End with a Bang', from the *Spice of Life* series, 15 March 1936.
12. Maisie Ward, *Return to Chesterton*, p. 270.
13. Maisie Ward, *Gilbert Keith Chesterton*, London, 1944, p. 552.
14. ibid., p. 552.
15. Michael Coren, *Gilbert: The Man who was G. K. Chesterton*, London, 1989, pp. 4–5.
16. Michael Holroyd, *Bernard Shaw, Vol. III: The Lure of Fantasy*, London, 1991, p. 327.
17. Barbara Reynolds, *Dorothy L. Sayers: Her Life and Soul*, London, 1993, p. 375.
18. Evelyn Waugh, *Ronald Knox*, pp. 197–8.
19. Fr. Claude Williamson (ed.), *Great Catholics*, London, 1938, p. 548.
20. Barry Phelps, *P. G. Wodehouse: Man and Myth*, London, 1992, p. 200.
21. Maisie Ward, *Gilbert Keith Chesterton*, p. 553.
22. Robert Speaight, *The Life of Eric Gill*, London, 1966, p. 260.
23. Mrs Cecil Chesterton, *The Chestertons*, London, 1941, p. 306.
24. Maisie Ward, *Gilbert Keith Chesterton*, p. 553.
25. Fr. John O'Connor, *Father Brown on Chesterton*, London, 1937, p. 152.
26. Dudley Barker, *G. K. Chesterton: A Biography*, London, 1973, p. 286.
27. ibid., p. 286.
28. Laura Lovat, *Maurice Baring: A Postscript*, London, 1947, p. 15.
29. Robert Speaight, *The Property Basket: Recollections of a Divided Life*, p. 13.
30. Maurice Baring, *Have You Anything to Declare?*, London, 1936, p. 106.
31. Paul Horgan, *Maurice Baring Restored*, New York, 1970, p. 49.
32. Robert Speaight (ed.), *Letters from Hilaire Belloc*, p. 213.
33. ibid., p. 214.
34. Emma Letley, *Maurice Baring: A Citizen of Europe*, London, 1991, p. 217.
35. Maurice Baring, *Have You Anything to Declare?*, p. 147.
36. Laura Lovat, *Maurice Baring: A Postscript*, pp. 4–5.
37. ibid., p. 33.
38. ibid., p. 4.
39. ibid., pp. 15–16.

CHAPTER SEVENTEEN

WAR AND RUMOUR OF WAR

We live in a terrible time, of war and rumour of war ... International idealism in its effort to hold the world together ... is admittedly weakened and often disappointed. I should say simply that it does not go deep enough ... If we really wish to make vivid the horrors of destruction and mere disciplined murder we must see them more simply as attacks on the hearth and the human family; and feel about Hitler as men felt about Herod.[1]

These words were written by G. K. Chesterton in one of his customary Christmas articles at the close of 1935, six months before his death. He was not destined to see the unleashing of the 'horrors of destruction and mere disciplined murder', nor would he live to see the concentration camps and the slaughter of the innocents which really did cast Hitler in the role of Herod. Many of his contemporaries, however, were about to be sucked into the vortex and none more so than the poet Roy Campbell.

Campbell and his wife had moved to Provence largely to escape the decadence of their life in England. Like Waugh and Eliot, the Campbells had reacted against the waste land, feeling an aversion for the 'vile bodies' of high society's party-set which Campbell had satirized in verse in *The Georgiad*. From Provence they moved to Spain, which Campbell loved as 'a country to which I owe everything as having saved my soul'.[2] It was here in 1935 that Roy and Mary Campbell made their final approach to the Catholic Church. 'I don't think that my family and I were converted by any event at any given moment,' Campbell wrote. 'We lived for a time on a small farm in the sierras at Altea where the working people were mostly good Catholics, and there was such a fragrance and freshness in their life, in their bravery, in their reverence, that it took hold of us all imperceptibly.'[3]

The final decision to be received into the Church was taken by Mary Campbell when, shortly after their arrival in Altea, she announced abruptly, 'I'm going to become a Catholic.' Without hesitation Campbell replied, 'Well, kid, if you're going to I will too,' and they presented themselves to the village priest and asked for instruction.[4] Several months later they were received into the Church, and were re-baptized and remarried, most of the village turning out for both the ceremony and the party which followed. Father Gregorio, the village priest, declared that it was the best day of his life and the local peasants wept and embraced the converts. Upon their reception Roy Campbell chose Ignatius Loyola as his saint while Mary chose Mary Magdalene. Both choices seemed appropriate. Ignatius Loyola, the Spanish founder of the Jesuits, had been robustly militant in his life and spirituality and was an obvious role model for Campbell who was soon to fashion himself as a Spanish militant in the forthcoming civil war. Mary Magdalene, the model of the repentant and redeemed 'fallen' woman, struck a resonant chord with Mary Campbell who harboured painful memories of sexual transgressions during the early years of her marriage.

'At last I am in the land of my dreams!' Campbell wrote the next day to a friend. As well as giving details of his religious conversion this letter also displayed a growing political awareness and illustrated the way in which politics and religion were interwoven in his mind:

> I don't know much about communism, but I have seen that many valiant and generous men take up that form of imitation-christianity. But they are not happy.
>
> Yesterday I had the good fortune to be baptised and married in the Catholic Church. I wish you the same luck.[5]

Within two years the Campbells were to know much more about communism as the atrocities of the Spanish Civil War were enacted before their eyes. In the meantime, their new faith signified a new start and Campbell tried hard to control his long-standing drink problem, making several valiant efforts to stop drinking completely. He was certainly happier and wrote contentedly to Percy Wyndham Lewis, 'I seem to be in heaven – with no debts, nothing annoying or troublesome.'[6]

Campbell's 'heaven' was his mother's idea of hell when she arrived to stay for several weeks in May 1935. Accustomed to luxury, she was horrified by her son's spartan lifestyle. The Campbells lived in a bare whitewashed peasant house, complete with outside toilet, set on a few acres of land among scrubby olive trees about a mile out of the village, with orange groves all around. They used a donkey to cart their supplies up the rough track from the village and to fetch water from a nearby spring. Campbell's mother looked on aghast as the donkey was led through the house each evening to its stall at the back. With materialistic maternalism she bought them a new stove, introduced them to some of the American gadgets she had discovered on her travels since her husband died, and bought them new shoes and clothes. However, her efforts to 'civilize' her son were doomed to failure. The simple life in Altea was exactly what he had been looking for, a primitive, pastoral world free from modern conveniences and modern tensions, a peasant panacea. This was reflected in his letters which painted a picture of complete and contented withdrawal from the world: 'Until today I haven't seen a peseta since April 24th: and I had to give the postman a fowl for my last stamp to you. I live entirely on my farm and what it produces ... Beyond my rent I have no other expenses and believe I have at last found the way to deal with the crisis – i.e. by living without any cash at all.'[7]

Writing to Percy Wyndham Lewis, he remarked sardonically that he was breeding 'pigs and donkeys which I hope to sell to the British public as poets'.[8]

Besides renewing contact via post with old friends in England and elsewhere, he began making the acquaintance of fellow foreigners living in the neighbourhood of Altea. These included two Norwegians, Helge Krog and Erling Winsness: 'Helge was a Communist and Erling was a Nazi,' Campbell observed, 'but they were both staunchly united in their hate of Christ and Christianity.'[9] One can imagine the heated discussions which ensued when Campbell met up with these two Scandinavians. Their religious and political arguments must have been a foretaste in microcosm of the struggles about to explode into violence on a worldwide scale. Campbell was beginning to perceive a political dimension to his new-found religious faith:

> From the very beginning my wife and I understood the real issues in Spain. There could be no compromise in this war between the East and the West, between Credulity and Faith, between irresponsible innovation ... and tradition, between the emotions (disguised as Reason) and the intelligence ...
>
> ... now was the time to decide whether ... to remain half-apathetic to the great fight which was obviously approaching – or whether we should step into the front ranks of the Regular Army of Christ. Hitler himself had said, even by then, how much more easy the Protestants were to enslave and bamboozle than the Catholics.[10]

For Campbell the Church had become the Regular Army of Christ and this conviction was behind his decision to fight for Franco's Nationalists when the Spanish Civil War began in 1936. The decision was always easy for him. It was a clear choice between the destructive forces of communism on the one hand, and the traditional Catholic culture he had recently discovered, embraced and loved so dearly on the other. It was a straightforward defence of hearth and home.

Back in England the choice did not appear so cut and dried. In 1936 Nazism was considered a far greater threat than communism and even those who had no time for the communists were worried about Hitler's support for Franco. The *Anschluss*, Hitler's annexation of Austria, had taken place in March and the Nazis were demanding territory in Czechoslovakia. War, it seemed, might engulf far more than Spain and, if it did, Hitler and not Stalin would be Britain's enemy. Yet Catholics throughout the world were horrified by news of atrocities carried out against priests and nuns by the communists and anarchists in Spain. Before the war was over twelve bishops, 4,184 priests, 2,365 monks and about 300 nuns were killed. Churches were burned and George Orwell recorded of Barcelona that 'almost every church had been gutted and its images burned'. Priests had their ears cut off, monks had their eardrums perforated by rosary beads being forced into them and the mother of two Jesuit priests had a rosary forced down her throat. For all Franco's faults, many considered anything preferable to the brutal anti-Catholic atheism of his opponents.

The depth of this conflict of loyalties was felt acutely by Graham Greene, whose view of the war in Spain was affected by far more abstruse considerations than those which had motivated Roy Campbell. Back in 1927, shortly after his conversion, Greene had been horrified by the execution of the priest Padre Pro in Mexico after the anti-clerical revolution in that country. Nine years later Greene copied the following extract of a news report of the Spanish war into his diary:

> Two priests were recently murdered in Durango. In the same town an officer knocked the Vicar of Toniola down with the butt of his pistol and ordered his battalion to shoot him ... In Tacamachaleco soldiers entered the church whilst the congregation was reciting the Rosary. As the officer pulled the priest out of the pulpit, the congregation rushed to his defence; the soldiers fired into the crowd, wounding some fifty people ... In general, the women show greater pluck in resisting the tyranny of the troops.[11]

Although such atrocities still filled him with horror, Greene was now agonizing over his relative attitudes to communism, fascism and Catholicism. He felt that communism was preferable to fascism because it was based to some extent on love. This was a view held by many and even Roy Campbell had referred to communism as an 'imitation Christianity'. Greene, therefore, found himself sympathizing with the communists and anarchists in Spain in spite of their atrocities against the Church. This brought him in line with secular public opinion in England which was concerned mainly with the defeat of Franco's fascists, but found him at loggerheads with most of his co-religionists who saw the civil war as being between Catholic tradition and modern atheism. One can imagine the strong disapproval of most Catholics to Greene's tasteless reaction to a poster in the Catholic newspaper, the *Universe*, which had reported that five bishops had been killed in Spain. 'One feels wrong about the Catholic press trumpeting its martyrdoms,' Greene had responded. 'You don't *complain* about a death of that kind. It should be taken for granted.'[12]

Ironically, Greene's statement was rooted in a deep admiration for the English martyrs executed in the sixteenth and seventeenth centuries. He had a particular attachment to the Jesuit poet and martyr Robert Southwell who was hanged, drawn and quartered at Tyburn in 1595 and had even contemplated writing a biography of him. Evelyn Waugh had recently published a biography of the other famous sixteenth-century Jesuit martyr, Edmund Campion, for which he was awarded the Hawthornden Prize in May 1936. Waugh and Greene, although good friends, disagreed over Spain as they did over most things. Whereas Waugh opposed fascism he none the less echoed the views of the majority of Catholics in seeing the war as a fight between Christianity and atheism. Greene's position was more complex. His left-wing sympathies made it impossible for him to support Franco, especially as the fascists were receiving military assistance from Hitler. Yet the burning of churches and the murder of priests, monks and nuns made it difficult for him to actively support the Republicans. His solution was to support the Catholic Basques who were on the side of the Republicans but were not fighting for a communist or anarchist state. It was a lost cause. The historic Basque city of Guernica was bombed by the Germans every twenty minutes, incendiary bombs were dropped and the fleeing population was machine-gunned by Franco's Nationalists. The Basques were routed and were finally defeated with the fall of Bilbao on 19 June 1937. As well as being a lost cause, it was also an unpopular one. Greene found himself attacked by the left for failing to give unequivocal support to the Republicans, and by Catholics for giving support to the anti-Franco Basques. The only other Catholic writers to come out in support of the Basques were Mauriac and Maritain. Among English Catholic writers, Greene stood alone and isolated.

Arnold Lunn, Alfred Noyes, Ronald Knox, Christopher Hollis and a host of other Catholic writers came out in support of the Nationalists, even though many found the link between Franco and Hitler disquieting. Waugh spoke for many Catholics when, in 1937, he replied to a questionnaire sent to writers in the British Isles asking them to state their attitude towards the war in Spain. In answer to the question, 'Are you for, or against, the legal government and the people of republican Spain? Are you for, or against, Franco and Fascism?', Waugh replied: 'If I were a Spaniard I should be fighting for General Franco. As an Englishman I am not in the predicament of choosing between two evils. I am not a Fascist nor shall I become one unless it were the only alternative to Marxism. It is mischievous to suggest that a choice is imminent.'[13]

One of the most eloquent and impassioned articles was written for the *Catholic Times* by Christopher Dawson:

It is not merely a conflict of brute force, as in the days of the Turkish invasions, it is a battle of will and beliefs, and it is in Spain, which has always been the bulwark of Christian Europe and bore the brunt of the battle with Islam in the past, that the battle with the new enemy of Christendom is being fought out today. It may well be that the issue of the struggle in Spain will decide the fate of Europe.

The victory of Communism in Spain would be a victory for Communism in its most dangerous aspect, for it would not be a victory over capitalism, which is relatively unimportant in Spain, but over Catholicism, which is the very root of the Spanish tradition ...

If Spain could find herself once more, after the dreary century of disunion and weakness – if she could once more take the place to which her history and her genius entitles her – then it will be a victory not only for Spain but for Europe. It will bring back to the European society an essential element without which European civilisation has become one-sided and incomplete.[14]

These lines of Dawson's were an exact reflection of the views of Roy Campbell who had already become embroiled in the grim reality in Spain. His friend, the Carmelite prior at Toledo, had been murdered along with many of the other monks under his charge in spite of Campbell's earlier efforts to hide them in his house. During the siege of Toledo Campbell had saved the Carmelite archives and he and his wife narrowly escaped death themselves, finally escaping from the city in a lorry. He fought for the Nationalists, acting as war correspondent for the *Tablet* while he did so, and was mentioned with honour by General Quiepo de Llano in his despatches of April 1937. Drawing on his experiences of the war Campbell wrote *The Flowering Rifle* which was published in 1939. Speaking of the war and the poem it inspired, he commented: 'To have witnessed and shared in some of this would have enabled a dumb ox to write inspired poetry.'[15]

The same could be said of the poetry which emerged from the First World War twenty years earlier and it was the experience of this earlier conflict that inspired the first book by the Catholic artist David Jones in 1937. Jones's *In Parenthesis* was a highly original and personal account of the author's experience of the First World War in which life in the trenches of Flanders was recalled accurately and with a meticulous eye for detail indicative of his earlier training as an artist. As with all those who survived, the war had left an indelible mark upon Jones's psyche but his account, written 'in parenthesis' many years after the event, possessed a calm coherence and clarity which it was impossible to convey in the poetry written during the war by Sassoon, Owen and others amidst the immediate sense of anger and despair.

Other advantages could be attributed to Jones's delay in writing *In Parenthesis*. The prose poetry was imbued with the 'waste land' imagery of Eliot and the idiosyncratic style of the nineteenth-century Jesuit convert, Gerard Manley Hopkins, whose poems were not published until 1918. Neither of these influences were available to those writing of the war at the time. Furthermore, Jones's life in the years after the war had given him the experience to form his own *Weltanschauung*, the result of his entering the Catholic Church, his friendship with Eric Gill, his life at the Ditchling community and the realization of his powers as an artist. These post-war influences gave Jones's personal memories of the war, recalled in parenthetical hindsight, a unique and potent perspective. Jones's prose poem can only be understood in context by examining his life thus far by way of a short parenthesis.

Jones became a Catholic on 7 September 1921 but the embryonic roots of his faith went back to the trenches of 1917. It was here that he began to discuss religion with Father Daniel Hughes, a Jesuit, the Roman Catholic chaplain attached to his battalion at Ypres. Father Hughes (the Fr. Martin Larkin of *In Parenthesis*) lent Jones a book by St Francis de Sales 'and it was really from then that I began to think of the Catholic Church'.[16]

Another war-time influence on Jones's future conversion was his first sight of Mass near the front line. He had been out hunting firewood between a support trench and the reserve lines when he spotted a farm building, previously damaged by shell fire. Believing it might prove a fruitful place to find dry wood, he made his way to what remained of the building. Finding no door or opening on the side from which he approached he put his eye to a crack in the wall expecting to see 'empty darkness':

But what I saw through the small gap in the wall was not the dim emptiness I had expected but the back of a sacerdos in a gilt-hued *planeta*, two points of flickering candlelight no doubt lent an extra sense of goldness to the vestment and a golden warmth seemed, by the same agency, to lend the white altar cloths and the white linen of the celebrant's alb and amice and maniple ... and kneeling in the hay beneath the improvised *mensa* were a few huddled figures in khaki.[17]

Jones recognized 'a big-bodied Irishman and an Italian naturalized Englishman' amongst the tiny congregation, both of whom were immortalized in *In Parenthesis* as Bomber Mulligan and Runner Meotti. The big Irishman, 'a somewhat fearsome figure, a real pugilist, hard-drinking Goidelic Celt, kneeling there in the smoky candlelight' made a particularly powerful and paradoxical impression: 'I felt immediately that oneness between the Offerant and those toughs that clustered round him in the dim-lit byre – a thing I had never felt remotely as a Protestant at the Office of Holy Communion in spite of the insistence of Protestant theology on the "priesthood of the laity".'[18]

Jones was received into the Church by Father John O'Connor, Chesterton's great friend, and it was Father O'Connor who suggested that he join Eric Gill and the community at Ditchling.

Eric Gill was destined to be a great influence. Gill and his family moved from Ditchling to Capel-y-ffin in 1924 and Jones joined them there the following year. In 1924 Jones had become engaged to Petra Gill, Eric Gill's daughter, and when she broke off the engagement in January 1927 the ensuing psychological trauma triggered Jones's best work. It was no coincidence that he began *In Parenthesis* in 1927, a work which took almost a decade to complete. Before its completion he suffered a major breakdown caused in large part, according to Gill's wife, by the struggles with his art. Mary Gill told Patrick Heron, a young disciple of Gill who described himself at the time as 'a brash young man full of Gill, Chesterton and the rest', that Jones 'got worked up with every new painting, which didn't help his nervous problems'.[19]

Jones's breakdown was at its worst in 1934 and Eric and Mary Gill played an important part in his recovery. Heron remembered the Gills both being 'very fond of David Jones' and recalled that Gill had 'turned down a meeting with Father D'Arcy because he had arranged to meet Jones'.[20]

Cecil Gill, Eric's younger brother, a former Anglican clergyman and missionary who along with his wife had been received into the Catholic Church on 29 September 1934, was also 'very fond' of David Jones and recalled Jones's neurosis in his unpublished autobiography:

David Jones has suffered from either real or imaginary illness all his life, or at least since he left the Army in 1918 it seems, and is a self-acknowledged neurotic. He speaks of this like someone who has a physical infirmity which is accidental, and he regards the neurotic tendency as something he cannot help and had to put up with except for what continual psychiatric support can afford. So having numerous devoted friends, many of them wealthy or influential or both, who love him as much for himself as for his painting and poetry, he 'gets by'...[21]

Another important figure in Jones's recovery was Christopher Dawson, whose books *The Age of the Gods*, *The Rise of the World Religions* and *The Making of Europe* had established his reputation as a leading scholar. Jones had dined with Dawson in Sidmouth at the end of April 1935 while Dawson was in Devon giving a series of lectures at Exeter University on the history of culture. Dawson invited Jones to stay at Hartlington Hall near Skipton, the Dawson family home, and Jones arrived at the beginning of July. His first impressions were very favourable, capturing his imagination and inviting comparisons with his former home with the Gills at Capel-y-ffin. On 2 July he wrote enthusiastically to his friend René Hague:

This is a *simply heavenly place. I do wish you were here.* It's exactly like Capel in many ways – but more prosperous and less instinct with the waste land feeling, but the general formation of river, tree, hill slope, tumbled-stone-wall, sheep-thing – remarkably similar ... This house is solid, comfortable and Victorian and filled tight as tight with books ...[22]

He stayed for a week, renewing his acquaintance with Dawson and also with Father O'Connor who travelled the short distance from his Bradford parish to lunch, sending a fine salmon ahead of him. During his stay Jones painted the landscape from the house, clearly as excited artistically by the wild Yorkshire terrain as he had been by the 'remarkably similar' landscape of the Black Mountains surrounding Capel-y-ffin which he had painted in earlier years. Dawson bought the painting for about £100 and it is now in the possession of one of his daughters who remembered that Jones had painted it from inside the house, studying the view through the bedroom window: 'He always liked painting from inside the house because he hated the cold.'[23]

At the time of Jones's stay at Hartlington Hall he was well on the path to recovery from the previous year's collapse. Dawson, however, was in poor health himself and was plagued by insomnia. As this was one of the symptoms of

Jones's own collapse, he was in a good position to sympathize. In the letter to René Hague he signed off with the observation that he had just heard Dawson put out the light, adding that his host 'never sleeps without Sedormid & Co. and then hardly at all ... *Even* I seem a regular bruiser wid a fine swagger on me and a pipe in the hat of me compared with his health.'[24]

One of the main reasons for Dawson's insomnia was a creative anxiety not dissimilar to that which had caused Jones's breakdown. Whereas Mary Gill had pinpointed Jones's anxiety over his paintings as a cause of his collapse, Dawson had confessed to Jones that he often lay awake all night worrying that 'no one reads my books'.[25]

Christina Scott, Dawson's daughter and biographer, remembered her father's affection for Jones and noted their similar natures. Jones was 'a very good friend' and 'an awfully nice man' who 'had the same approach as my father': 'My father and he had a lot in common: the Welsh side, the mystical side of religion and history.'[26] The influence of Christopher Dawson on the development of Jones's thought bore fruit years later in Jones's other great literary achievement, *The Anathemata*. In the meantime Jones's greatest debt to Dawson was the help he provided on the road to recovery.

In the autumn of 1936 Dawson, increasingly concerned about the delicate nature of his own health, left with his wife for six months in Italy where, through Father Desmond Chute, a friend of both Jones and Eric Gill, he met Ezra Pound who at that time was writing the *Cantos*.

Back in England Jones was putting the finishing touches to *In Parenthesis*. Following its publication one of its most enthusiastic admirers was Evelyn Waugh who reviewed it under the title, 'A Mystic in the Trenches', for *Night and Day* on 1 July 1937:

> It is not easy to describe. It is certainly not a novel, for it lacks the two essentials of story and character; it is not what the publishers take it for, an epic poem, for it presents no complete human destiny. It is a piece of reporting interrupted by choruses ... It is a book about battle rather than war ... it is not the least like any other war book I have ever read ...
>
> The similarity to Mr Eliot's work is everywhere apparent, but it is by allusion rather than imitation ... There are whole passages which, out of the context, one might take for extracts from *The Waste Land* ... But there is an essential difference between *The Waste Land* and *In Parenthesis*. Mr Eliot in his great passage of the unknown intangible companion is writing metaphorically; he is seeking concrete images to

express a psychological state. Mr Jones is describing an objective physical experience – the loss of contact with neighbouring files in a night attack. It is this painter's realism which lifts his work above any of Mr Eliot's followers and, in many places, above Mr Eliot himself. Moreover, he has a painter's *communicativeness* ...

Waugh's poignant perception reached a portentous climax in his conclusion:

It seems to me that Mr Jones sees man in a dual role – as an individual soul, the exiled child of Eve, living, in a parenthesis, a Platonic shadow-life, two-dimensional, the Hollow Man; and man as the heir of his ancestors, the link in the continuous life-chain, the race-unit. Perhaps it is presumptuous to go further and suggest that the final, exquisitely written passages in which the hero abandons his weapons on the field – the ultimate reproach of the heroic age – are meant to show that the race-myth has been sloughed off, leaving only the stark alternatives of Heaven and Hell.

Waugh understood more than he realized; more, perhaps, than Jones realized himself. The conflict between traditional Christian orthodoxy and the new communist and fascist 'heresies' was at the very centre of *In Parenthesis*, as it was at the centre of intellectual thought in the final years of the thirties. Furthermore, the 'heresies' appeared to be emerging triumphant. Many saw the final struggle of history as the fight between Marxism and fascism, while Christianity was seen as a dated and doomed relic of the past. It was the Christ-myth and not the race-myth that had been sloughed off. Old Christian assumptions, 'the stark alternatives of Heaven and Hell', were no longer relevant. The choice was between Marx or Hitler, between red or black, between class-myth or race-myth. For many this choice was alluring, if ultimately illusory.

The frustration of those who refused to be dragooned into either camp was expressed plaintively by Waugh in a letter to the *New Statesman* on 5 March 1938:

There was a time in the early twenties when the word 'Bolshie' was current. It was used indiscriminately of ... anything or anyone of whom the speaker disapproved. The only result was to impede reasonable discussion and clear thought.

I believe we are in danger of a similar, stultifying use of the word 'Fascist'. There was recently a petition sent to English writers ... asking them to subscribe themselves, categorically, as supporters of the Republican Party in Spain, or as 'Fascists'. When rioters are imprisoned it is described as a 'Fascist sentence'; the Means Test is Fascist; colonisation is Fascist; military discipline is Fascist; patriotism is Fascist; Catholicism is Fascist; Buchmanism is Fascist; the ancient Japanese cult of their Emperor is Fascist; the Galla tribes' ancient detestation of theirs is Fascist; fox-hunting is Fascist ... Is it too late to call for order?

This *reductio ad absurdum* of labelling everyone and everything as either 'Bolshie' or 'Fascist', was finding tragi-comic expression in Spain where the communists and anarchists were beginning to turn their guns on each other, each accusing the other of being 'Fascist'. In such circumstances it was certainly 'too late to call for order' because order itself was deemed 'Fascist'.

In his letter to the *New Statesman* Waugh perceived the parasitic nature of both fascism and communism, observing how each feeds off the fear of the other:

It is constantly said by those who observed the growth of Nazism, Fascism and other dictatorial systems (not, perhaps, excluding USSR) that they were engendered and nourished solely by Communism. I do not know how true that is, but I am inclined to believe it when I observe the pitiable stampede of the 'Left-Wing Intellectuals' in our own country ... Those of us who can afford to think without proclaiming ourselves 'intellectuals' do not want or expect a Fascist regime. But there is a highly nervous and highly vocal party who are busy creating a bogy; if they persist in throwing the epithet about it may begin to stick.

The 'Left-Wing Intellectuals' at the *New Statesman* headed Waugh's letter 'Fascist', evidently as a juvenile jibe intended to annoy their hostile correspondent. In doing so they were only reinforcing his point.

Waugh had impeccable anti-Nazi credentials, opposing Hitler's regime from its very inception, and he shared the views of Belloc and Chesterton that a resurgent Prussian militarism, feeding on a tribalistic race-mythology, was as great a threat to Europe as was communism.

Others, however, fell into the trap which Waugh had feared and which he had sought to express in his letter. Believing that 'Bolshevism' was a bigger bogy than the fascists, and believing the platitudinous assumption that one must choose between the two, some were beginning to look to Hitler as a bulwark against communism. At worst, to these 'converts' to fascism, Hitler was the better of two evils; at best he was the saviour of the West from Bolshevism. Although these fascist converts were always a small minority in England, they included some surprising individuals among their number.

Cecil Gill, former Anglican clergyman, former missionary in New Guinea and recent Catholic convert, remembered being raided by the police shortly before the Second World War after information had been received that he and his wife had subversive literature in the house. The literature in question included 'half a dozen quite big volumes of Nazi propaganda, written in English of course, and *Mein Kampf*'.[27] Apart from propaganda received direct from Germany, the police also confiscated a heap of pamphlets which had been given to the Gills by Ben Greene, the cousin of Graham Greene, who was an active British fascist.

David Jones also had a morbid fascination with *Mein Kampf*, Hitler's autobiography, in the months before the war began. In a letter to a friend dated 24 April 1939, Jones wrote:

> I am deeply impressed by it, it is amazingly interesting in all kinds of ways – but pretty terrifying too. God, he's *nearly* right – but this *hate* thing mars his whole thing, I feel. I mean it just misses getting over the frontier into the saint thing ... but, having got so far, the conception of the world in terms of race-struggle (that's what it boils down to) will hardly do ... Anyway, I back him still against all this currish, leftish, money thing ...[28]

It seems that the Jesuits saved Jones from drowning in the dangerous waters into which he had strayed. Eight weeks after this confused letter had been written, Jones went to stay with Father Martin D'Arcy who at the time was Master of Campion Hall, Oxford. D'Arcy's writings and conversation were a great influence on Jones and it appears that the Jesuit had convinced him that Catholicism was incompatible with Nazism. On 23 June he wrote from Campion Hall to the same friend to whom he had conveyed his views on *Mein Kampf*: 'Over all that political stuff, I believe I've altered a bit – I feel less interested in it somehow at the moment. I feel I can't cope with it.'[29]

Jones also discussed the matter with the other great Jesuit of the time, Father Martindale, probably during the same stay at Campion Hall. Jones lent Martindale his annotated copy of *Mein Kampf* and the priest never subsequently returned it. Jones put this down to the fact that Martindale had been caught up in the German invasion of Denmark during the following year and was kept prisoner by the Nazis for most of the rest of the war.

Martindale was not, of course, the only Jesuit in German-occupied territory to suffer persecution and since he was only kept under house arrest he escaped relatively lightly. Others were less fortunate, many priests suffering a similar fate to the Jews.

A portent of the Nazi antipathy towards both the Jesuits and the Jews was provided by an episode in the life of Evelyn Waugh dating back to the early thirties, shortly after Hitler had assumed power. Waugh was present at a fashionable society function in London at which Putzi Hanfstängel, a German who was one of Hitler's intimate circle, was an honoured guest. When all the guests had arrived and settled down, the hostess asked Hanfstängel, a gifted amateur pianist, if he would play for them. He consented and rendered recitals of several major composers before the hostess requested that he sing. According to Christopher Sykes, Waugh's friend and biographer, Hanfstängel sang an anti-clerical and anti-Jewish song, each verse of which ended with the refrain: '*Die Juden und die Jesuiten*'. These words, Sykes recalled, were 'spat out with the venom the song required'. '*Die Juden und die Jesuiten*' was not difficult to interpret and after the first verse of the song, Waugh got up from his chair and ostentatiously escorted his girl, the daughter of the house, from the room. Sykes remembered that 'Evelyn's action made me, who stayed on after to enjoy the party, feel rather a worm, and I did wish afterwards that I had had the guts to follow his example.'[30]

The declaration of war in 1939 effectively destroyed fascism in Britain and, with it, the belief that a choice between communism and fascism was inevitable. Communism remained popular throughout the war years but it remained unpalatable to Christians, many of whom were spurred on to seek alternatives to the disastrous dichotomy between extreme left and right which had led to a second world war.

NOTES

1. Maisie Ward, *Gilbert Keith Chesterton*, p. 540.
2. Matthew Hoehn, OSB (ed.), *Catholic Authors: Contemporary Biographical Sketches 1930–1947*, Newark, NJ, USA, 1948, p. 104.
3. ibid., p. 104.
4. Peter Alexander, *Roy Campbell: A Critical Biography*, Oxford, 1982, p. 150.
5. ibid., p. 156.
6. ibid., p. 150.
7. ibid., p. 151.
8. ibid., p. 154.
9. ibid., p. 151.
10. Roy Campbell, *Light on a Dark Horse: An Autobiography*, London, 1951, p. 317.
11. Norman Sherry, *The Life of Graham Greene, Volume One 1904–1939*, pp. 698–9.
12. ibid., p. 699.
13. Louis Aragon (ed.), *Authors Take Sides on the Spanish War*, London, 1937.
14. Christina Scott, *A Historian and His World: A Life of Christopher Dawson*, London, 1984, p. 128.

15. Matthew Hoehn, OSB (ed.), *Catholic Authors: Contemporary Biographical Sketches 1930–1947*, p. 105.
16. René Hague (ed.), *Dai Greatcoat: A Self-Portrait of David Jones in His Letters*, London, 1980, p. 218.
17. ibid., p. 249.
18. ibid., p. 249.
19. Patrick Heron, interview with the author, Ely, 6 November 1996.
20. ibid.
21. Cecil Gill, unpublished autobiography, pp. 368–9.
22. René Hague (ed.), *Dai Greatcoat: A Self-Portrait of David Jones in His Letters*, p. 72.
23. Christina Scott, interview with the author, Kensington, 28 December 1996.
24. René Hague (ed.), *Dai Greatcoat: A Self-Portrait of David Jones in His Letters*, p. 73.
25. Christina Scott, *A Historian and His World: A Life of Christopher Dawson*, p. 128.
26. Christina Scott, interview with the author, Kensington, 28 December 1996.
27. Cecil Gill, unpublished autobiography, p. 333.
28. René Hague (ed.), *Dai Greatcoat: A Self-Portrait of David Jones in His Letters*, pp. 92–3.
29. ibid., p. 93.
30. Christopher Sykes, *Evelyn Waugh: A Biography*, London, 1975, p. 134.

CHAPTER EIGHTEEN

WAR OF WORDS

In 1938, with the threat of war with Germany darkening the horizon, 19,000 young people joined the National Pilgrimage of Catholic Youth to the shrine of Our Lady of Walsingham in Norfolk. It was an expedition and an exhibition of hope in the face of an increasingly desperate political situation. Organized by H. M. Gillett, a young man who had been received into the Church at Brompton Oratory five years earlier, the pilgrimage symbolized a rejection of, and a positive alternative to, the negations of communism and fascism.

The desire to find positive solutions to the problems of modern society animated many of the leading writers of the day. Dorothy L. Sayers wrote to B. C. Boulter, of the Guild of Catholic Writers, on 1 December 1939: 'I am engaged ... in getting together a group of people, mostly writers, to do books, articles, lectures, etc. about national reconstruction and a creative spirit, not precisely under the Christian banner, but certainly on a basis of Christian feeling.'[1]

Along with the letter she enclosed a 'rough draft of aims and intentions' which detailed a plan to publish a series of books on social reconstruction, collectively entitled *Bridgeheads*. The Statement of Aims of the series stipulated its main purpose to be the preparation of people for the reconstruction of a sound society once peace had been restored: 'We shall try to quicken the creative spirit which enables man to build ... systems in the light of his spiritual, intellectual and social needs. We aim at the Resurrection of Faith, the Revival of Learning and the Re-integration of Society.'[2]

As Sayers was writing this letter she was putting the finishing touches to her book *Begin Here*, which was published the following month:

> The great Economic Obsession, by which (as I maintain) the world is too much governed, dictates that books must be got out in time for the New Year. Consequently, this particular book has had to be written with indecent haste ... I hope, however, that the book does, on the whole, express what I believe to be the truth about our present

troubles, and it will serve its purpose if it suggests to a few readers some creative line of action along which they, as individuals, can think and work towards the restoration of Europe.[3]

Sayers's complaint against the 'great Economic Obsession' was a prevailing feature of the book. Elsewhere she reiterated the point succinctly: '... the great majority of people in Europe accepted - and for that matter still accept – the authority of Economics as absolute, and considered the only "real" history of the universe to be Economic History.'[4]

Far from being indicative of 'progress', Sayers argued that this was a regression towards the primeval soup of primitive necessities. Specifically, she charted the regression in seven distinct phases representing humanity's comprehension, or rather increasing incomprehension, of itself. According to the teaching of Christianity, universally accepted in medieval Europe, man was understood theologically to be a Whole Man, the image of God. This was, and is, the theological man of Christian orthodoxy, Chesterton's 'Everlasting Man'. Then, from the time of the Renaissance, came humanist man – man as a value in himself, apart from God; followed by rational man – man as the embodied Intelligence; then biological man, Homo Sapiens – man as the intelligent animal; sociological man – man as the member of the herd; psychological man – man as the response to environment; and finally, economic man – man as the response to the means of livelihood. The triumph of the till!

Elsewhere in *Begin Here* Sayers described 'Economic Man' as 'our latest, most simplified, least human conception of ourselves – that humourless, passionless, sexless unit in a vast financial system'.[5]

'The most noticeable thing about this gradual development,' Sayers wrote, 'is that the more man knows, scientifically, the less he understands the purpose of existence, and the less is his individual importance in the scheme of things.'[6]

In this way, five hundred years of philosophical philandering had left humanity floundering in a sea of selfish alienation and doubt. It was the modern dilemma, the paradox of progress, that scientific advances seemed to go hand in hand with social disintegration – the result of an increase of knowledge coupled with a lack of understanding and precious little wisdom.

Begin Here ended with an exhortation to action:

If we want our own state to make reforms, we must learn to control the state, lest the state end by controlling us. If we want some hard thinking done, we must think for ourselves, or others will do the thinking. There are only two ways to move the world: the way of the Gospel or the way of the Law, and if we will not have the one we must submit to the other. Somehow we have got to find the integrating principle for our lives, the creative power that sustains our balance in motion, and we have got to do it quickly ... The task is urgent; we must not push it into the future; we must not leave it to others: we must do it ourselves, and we must begin now and here.[7]

The spirit of exhortation continued in 'A Note on Creative Reading', added to *Begin Here* as an appendix:

Do not, I implore you, continue in that indolent and soul-destroying habit of picking up a book 'to distract your mind' ('distract' is the word for it) or 'to knock down time' (there is only too little time already, and it will knock us down soon enough). The only respectable reason for reading a book is that you want to know what is in it.[8]

Sayers then made 'a few suggestions for "black-out" reading ... by modern writers, that illuminate some of the questions we have been discussing'.[9] These included A. N. Whitehead's *Science and the Modern World*, which had influenced Arnold Lunn's conversion ten years earlier, Charles Williams's *He Came Down from Heaven* and Christopher Dawson's *Beyond Politics*, which 'defines with great clarity the Christian view of the right relations between Church and State, and the relation of History to the standards of Eternity'.[10]

No book of T. S. Eliot's was suggested by Sayers for 'black-out' reading but there is no doubt that his play *The Family Reunion* and, more specifically, his book *The Idea of a Christian Society* were major influences on her writing of *Begin Here*.

The Idea of a Christian Society was published in October 1939 and consisted of three lectures, delivered in March of that year at Corpus Christi College, Cambridge. Although the lectures were written and delivered before the war was declared, the coming conflict was clearly in Eliot's mind as he wrote them. In the published volume, dated 6 September, he appended a note stating that the war presented the world with an overriding and inescapable choice between Christianity or paganism, adding: 'We cannot afford to defer our constructive thinking to the conclusion of hostilities.' In the preface to *The Idea of a Christian Society* Eliot, like Sayers, expressed a debt to Dawson's *Beyond Politics*, which had been published at the beginning of the year. Eliot also expressed a debt to the writings of the Rev. V. A. Demant and it was Demant who, in a review of *Beyond Politics*, echoed the praise of both Eliot and Sayers by stating that Dawson's book should be read by all Englishmen with any public influence and particularly by all religious leaders.

In September 1939, Dawson's friend E. I. Watkin's own contribution to the fertile debate at the outbreak of war was published. Like so many of the other writers he was influenced by Dawson, acknowledging in the foreword to *The Catholic Centre* that 'a book which contains so much historical retrospect as the present owes a large debt to Christopher Dawson'. Watkin later stated that the motivation behind the writing of *The Catholic Centre* was 'the passionate realization that the world is now the stage of a conflict between those who genuinely believe in a Divine Creator and those who avowedly or implicitly deify man'.[11]

In the same year, Charles Williams's *The Descent of the Dove: The History of the Holy Spirit in the Church* was published. It was reviewed enthusiastically by Eliot who was particularly pleased that Williams had given St John of the Cross 'his due place'.[12] Eliot was profoundly influenced by the sixteenth-century saint and the monk's mysticism permeated much of the poetry Eliot wrote during the war years. Another poet intent on giving St John of the Cross his due place was Roy Campbell who at around this time commenced the translation of the saint's mystical poems from Spanish. Ten years later Eliot and Campbell collaborated in the final publication of Campbell's translation.

The writer who became the greatest literary popularizer of Christianity during the war years was C. S. Lewis who, for many, seemed in his writing to be brandishing a torch of literary light in a dark and doom-laden world. One of the secrets of Lewis's success was his ability to smuggle theology into his works of fiction, largely undetected, and this was at the core of his children's books in the years after the war. On 9 July 1939, Lewis wrote that 'any amount of theology can now be smuggled into people's minds under the cover of romance without their knowing it'.[13] This idea may have been in his mind during the writing of *Out of the Silent Planet*, his first science fiction novel, which was published in the autumn of 1938. It met with a largely positive response from reviewers and readers alike. Some enjoyed it in spite of its Christian background, some because of it, but most seemed oblivious to its allegorical nature and underlying message. However, those who were affected most profoundly by *Out of the Silent Planet* were those to whom the allegory emerged as a surprising revelation during the reading of the book. Such was its effect on a friend of Dorothy L. Sayers, as Sayers later explained in a letter to Lewis: 'he read *Out of the Silent Planet* with great enjoyment, accepting it quite simply as a space-travel story until quite suddenly near the end ... some phrase clicked in his mind and he exclaimed: "Why, this is a story about Christianity. Maleldil is Christ, and the Eldila are the angels!"'[14]

Another undergraduate reader who experienced the same revelation was Lewis's biographer, Roger Lancelyn Green, who remembered vividly,

> the thrill of excitement ... when Oyarsa was telling Ransom of Thulcandra, the silent planet – 'We think that Maleldil would not give it up utterly to the Bent One, and there are stories among us that He has taken strange counsel and dared terrible things, wrestling with the Bent One in Thulcandra' – and he realised in a blinding flash to what Oyarsa was referring ... it was like stepping into a new dimension ...[15]

Out of the Silent Planet was the first of a trilogy of science fiction stories featuring the character of Ransom as the philologist hero. Ransom was modelled in part on Lewis's friend J. R. R. Tolkien, who wrote to his son Christopher in 1944 of his unwittingly benign influence on Lewis's characterization of Ransom: 'As a philologist I may have some part in him, and recognize some of my opinions and ideas Lewisified in him.'[16] Lewis, in turn, influenced Tolkien's characterization of Treebeard in *The Lord of the Rings*, which Tolkien was writing throughout the war years. Tolkien told Nevill Coghill that he had modelled Treebeard's way of speaking, '*Hrum, Hroom*', on the booming voice of C. S. Lewis.[17] Tolkien also told Lewis's friend and biographer, Walter Hooper, that 'I wrote *The Lord of the Rings* to make Lewis a story out of *The Silmarillion*.' Hooper admitted that Tolkien was 'probably exaggerating lightheartedly', knowing that Lewis 'had a huge appetite for stories', but he did consider Lewis 'a great encourager'.[18]

Lewis and Tolkien had been friends for years and Tolkien, a 'cradle convert' to Catholicism after his mother's reception into the Church in 1900 when he was only eight years old, had been a major influence in Lewis's conversion to Christianity. According to Walter Hooper, 'a realisation of the truth in mythologies triggered Lewis's conversion':

> This came about after a long discussion in 1931 with Tolkien and Hugo Dyson which continued until four o'clock in the morning. At the end of this marathon discussion Lewis believed that myths were real and that facts took the shine off truth, emptying truth of its glory. Thereafter he became an excellent Christian apologist, better than Chesterton because his arguments are so logically structured. He was such a rigorous arguer.[19]

Whether Lewis was a better Christian apologist than Chesterton, it was certainly true that he had been influenced greatly by Chesterton on the path to his own conversion. Indeed, it was love at first sight when Lewis, a nineteen-year-old second lieutenant in the Somerset Light Infantry, first discovered Chesterton's writing while recovering from trench fever in a hospital at Le Tréport:

> It was here that I first read a volume of Chesterton's essays. I had never heard of him and had no idea of what he stood for; nor can I quite understand why he made such an immediate conquest of me. It might have been expected that my pessimism, my atheism, and my hatred of sentiment would have made him to me the least congenial of all authors. It would almost seem that Providence, or some 'second cause' of a very obscure kind, quite over-rules our previous tastes when It decides to bring two minds together ...
>
> In reading Chesterton, as in reading MacDonald, I did not know what I was letting myself in for. A young man who wishes to remain a sound Atheist cannot be too careful of his reading.[20]

Lewis became an avid reader of Chesterton's books but was still unable to accept his Christianity. In Lewis's own words, 'Chesterton had more sense than all the other moderns put together; bating, of course, his Christianity.'[21] Then he read Chesterton's *The Everlasting Man* 'and for the first time saw the whole Christian outline of history set out in a form that seemed to me to make sense'.[22]

At around the time that *The Everlasting Man* was making such an impression on him, Lewis was also falling under the benign influence of Owen Barfield, later described by Lewis as the wisest and best of his unofficial teachers. 'Lewis was very much influenced by Chesterton,' Barfield remembered, 'especially *The Everlasting Man*, but he didn't mention anybody else really. We didn't always talk about philosophy. We used to read together ... we never argued from a doctrinal point of view.'[23]

It was a discussion between Barfield, Lewis and Alan Griffiths, one of Lewis's pupils, which was to prove instrumental in edging Lewis closer to conversion. Barfield and Griffiths were lunching in Lewis's room when Lewis happened to refer to philosophy as 'a subject'. 'It wasn't a *subject* to Plato,' Barfield retorted, 'it was a way.' 'The quiet but fervent agreement of Griffiths, and the quick glance of understanding between these two, revealed to me my own frivolity. Enough had been thought, and said, and felt, and imagined. It was about time that something should be done.'[24]

Even though they unwittingly played such a crucial role in the *coup de grâce* of Lewis's conversion, neither Barfield nor Griffiths were Christians at the time of this providential conversation. By a strange coincidence, however, both Lewis and Griffiths converted to Christianity and received their respective first communions within a day of each other at Christmas 1931, Griffiths as a Catholic on Christmas Eve and Lewis as an Anglican on Christmas Day.

Prior to his conversion to Catholicism Griffiths had passed through a short Anglican phase and was preparing himself for ministry in the Church of England when a reading of Newman's *Essay on the Development of Christian Doctrine* changed his concept of Christianity and the Church:

> I believed that the Church which Christ had founded was a historical reality, that it had a continuous history from the time of the Apostles to the present day. I had thought that this continuity might be found in the Church of England, but now the overwhelming weight of evidence for the continuity of the Roman Church was presented to my mind.[25]

A few months after his reception Griffiths decided to try his vocation as a monk at Prinknash, the Benedictine priory at Winchcombe, and on 20 December 1932 he was clothed as a novice. It was at this point that he changed his name to Bede, after which he was known as Dom Bede Griffiths. He made his solemn vows on 21 December 1936.

From the time of his conversion Griffiths began trying to discuss with Lewis the merits of their respective positions. Lewis, however, was reticent, refusing to discuss the doctrinal differences between Catholicism and Anglicanism. 'The result,' wrote Griffiths, 'was that we agreed not to discuss our differences any more ... there was always a certain reserve therefore afterward in our friendship.'[26]

Though reserved, their friendship remained, as did their respective friendships with Owen Barfield, the only one of the original trio who was still resisting conversion. Sixty years later, Barfield remembered their friendship with nostalgic affection:

> Lewis, Griffiths and I went for long walks together. We talked a good deal about theology ... I was with Griffiths and I told him I was an agnostic and we got talking about being damned and some remark he made elicited the reply from me that 'in that case I suppose that I am damned'. And I'll never forget the calm, collected way he turned round and said 'but of course you are'. This amused Lewis very much of course when I told him afterwards.[27]

Lewis entered the literary fray in 1933 with his first full-length book, *The Pilgrim's Regress*, subtitled 'An Allegorical Apology for Christianity, Reason, and

Romanticism'. The book caused anger and controversy because of its broadsides against both the high Anglicans and the broad Churchmen within the Church of England. To many of those in both camps, Lewis became a new and unwelcome 'enemy within'. His attacks on the broad Church were based on orthodox theological objections to modernism. The broad Church, Lewis believed, suffered from a 'confusion between mere natural goodness and Grace which is non-Christian' and is 'what I most hate and fear in the world'.[28] Meanwhile the high Anglicans he singled out for scorn were 'a set of people who seem to me ... to be trying to make of Christianity itself one more high-brow, Chelsea, bourgeois-baiting fad' and 'T. S. Eliot is the single man who sums up the thing I am fighting against.'[29]

This increasingly awkward positioning of himself on a self-styled 'centre ground' of 'mere Christianity' between the Protestant and pseudo-Catholic wings of the Church of England was to remain the hallmark of his writing and was probably the result of a personal psychological compromise deep in his roots. At least this was the view of Tolkien, who knew Lewis better than most:

> It was not for some time that I realized that there was more in the title *Pilgrim's Regress* than I had understood (or the author either, maybe). Lewis would regress. He would not enter Christianity by a new door, but by the old one; at least in the sense that in taking it up again he would also take up, or reawaken, the prejudices so sedulously planted in boyhood. He would become again a Northern Ireland Protestant.[30]

Elsewhere, Tolkien complained of his friend's anti-Catholic prejudice and the duplicity it caused. If a Lutheran is put in jail, Tolkien observed, Lewis 'is up in arms; but if Catholic priests are slaughtered – he disbelieves it, and I daresay really thinks they asked for it. There is a good deal of Ulster still left in C. S. L., if hidden from himself.'[31] The matter was put poignantly and humorously by Christopher Derrick, a friend and pupil of Lewis and author of *C. S. Lewis and the Church of Rome*: 'If a man is brought up in Belfast in a full Orange Order *Sash My Father Wore* paranoia, and then has his first formation in the great school at Oxford, divine grace has a hell of a nut to crack!'[32]

Walter Hooper conceded that Lewis's Ulster background was 'probably important' as a factor in his attitude to Catholicism but believes other factors also played a part: 'After Lewis started broadcasting for the BBC he became trapped by his own success ... He suddenly became everyman's Christian apologist. Thereafter Mere Christianity became a ring fence and he preferred to stay out of theological dogfights.'[33] This desire to avoid controversy in order to please most of the people most of the time did not please Tolkien who referred to Lewis disparagingly as 'Everyman's Theologian'.[34]

Although the ingrained prejudices of a Belfast upbringing may have contributed to Lewis's ultimate refusal to follow many of his literary contemporaries into the Catholic Church, one suspects that Tolkien overstated the case. Lewis's practice of going to weekly confession, which he commenced at the end of 1940, was hardly the sort of behaviour one would expect from an Ulster Protestant. Furthermore, if Lewis is to be judged by the fruit of his labour there can be little doubt that he brought in a more bountiful harvest of converts to Christianity, both during and after the war, than any other writer of his generation.

Lewis's popularity really took off during 1941 when his booming voice rode the airwaves of the BBC during a series of radio broadcasts. His talks, collectively entitled 'Right and Wrong as a Clue to the Meaning of the Universe', proved so popular that Lewis was asked to give a further series of five talks during January and February 1942, entitled 'What Christians Believe'. In July 1942 the transcripts of both series were published as *Broadcast Talks*.

As well as becoming a radio personality Lewis took up popular journalism. During 1941 he wrote a series of thirty-one *Screwtape Letters* which appeared one at a time in weekly instalments in the *Guardian* between 2 May and 28 November. When these were published in a single volume, dedicated to Tolkien, in February 1942, they became an instant success. Since then *The Screwtape Letters*, consisting of letters from an old devil to a young devil on the art of temptation, has remained one of the most popular, and is arguably the best, of Lewis's books. Certainly, this is the opinion of Walter Hooper: '*The Screwtape Letters* is timeless in its arguments. It fulfills in every sense the idea of a classic. Other recent attempts at similar books by writers in the U.S. have dated immediately.'[35]

One of the greatest admirers of *The Screwtape Letters* was Dorothy L. Sayers who wrote enthusiastically to Lewis, praising him for the book and urging him to contribute a book to the *Bridgeheads* series she was editing. Another of her letters to Lewis even imitated the style of *The Screwtape Letters*, being written from a demon named Sluckdrib, complaining to his superior about the unfortunate effect which certain religious plays are having on atheists. He is, however, gratified by the detrimental effect that writing them has had on the character of the author:

I have already had the honour to report intellectual and spiritual pride, vainglory, self-opinionated dogmatism, irreverence, blasphemous frivolity, frequentation of the company of theatricals, captiousness, impatience of correction, polemical fury, shortness of temper, neglect of domestic affairs, lack of charity, egotism, nostalgia for secular occupations, and a growing tendency to consider the Bible as literature.[36]

Although Sayers had written more than one play, the one she had been alluding to principally in this letter was her radio play, *The Man Born to be King: A Play-Cycle on the Life of our Lord and Saviour Jesus Christ*. This was read over the BBC in twelve instalments between December 1941 and October 1942 with Robert Speaight in the role of Christ. The play was a resounding success but incurred the wrath of the Lord's Day Observance Society and other puritanical bodies who saw it as 'irreverent', 'blasphemous' and 'vulgar'. After it was published as a book in 1943, Lewis read the play and thought it 'excellent, indeed most moving' and considered the objections 'silly'.[37]

Perhaps Sayers had her future critics in mind when she addressed the Public Morality Council at Caxton Hall, Westminster on 23 October 1941. Giving her talk the title of 'The Other Six Deadly Sins' she lamented the sex-obsession of modern life which meant that sin had become synonymous with lust. Vice had come to mean one thing and one thing only and the other six deadly sins were ignored, forgotten, down-graded or even excused as long as the 'sinner' avoided sexual impropriety:

> to the majority of people the word 'immorality' has come to mean one thing and one thing only ... A man may be greedy and selfish; spiteful, cruel, jealous and unjust; violent and brutal; grasping, unscrupulous and a liar; stubborn and arrogant; stupid, morose, and dead to every noble instinct – and still we are ready to say of him that he is not an immoral man. I am reminded of a young man who once said to me with perfect simplicity: 'I did not know there were seven deadly sins: please tell me the names of the other six.'[38]

Sayers was evidently frustrated at this distortion of the true picture, perceiving that the modern world was divided between prurients and prudes, both groups being unhealthily obsessed with sex from opposite sides of the same puritanical coin. It was this solid grounding in orthodox Catholic theology which so attracted Sayers to Dante whom she was to rediscover after reading *The Figure of Beatrice* by Charles Williams in 1943.

Perhaps the most important book by Sayers during the war years was *The Mind of the Maker*, published on 10 July 1941. Its central theme and thesis was summed up succinctly by Sayers's friend and biographer Barbara Reynolds as 'her Trinitarian view of the procedure, the process, the experience of creativity in the artist's mind, in her case the writer's mind. Whatever we do of a creative nature has a Trinitarian structure because we are made in the image of God.'[39]

In *The Mind of the Maker*, Sayers described the creative process as an indivisible trinity: the Idea, the Energy and the Power:

> The Creative Power is the third 'Person' of the writer's trinity. It is not the same thing as the Energy (which for greater clearness I ought perhaps to have called 'the Activity'), though it proceeds from the Idea and the Energy together. It is the thing which flows back to the writer from his own activity and makes him, as it were, the reader of his own book. It is also, of course, the means by which the Activity is communicated to other readers and which produces a corresponding response in them. In fact, from the readers' point of view, it *is* the book. By it, they perceive the book, both as a process in time and as an eternal whole, and react to it dynamically ...
>
> Lastly: 'these three are one, each equally in itself the whole book, whereof none can exist without other.' If you were to ask a writer which is 'the real book' – his Idea of it, his Activity in writing it or its return to himself in Power, he would be at a loss to tell you, because these things are essentially inseparable ... these three are equally and eternally present in his own act of creation, and at every moment of it, whether or not the act ever becomes manifest in the form of a written and printed book. These things are not confined to the material manifestation: they exist in – they *are* – the creative mind itself.[40]

The *Catholic Herald* greeted *The Mind of the Maker* with enthusiasm, stating that 'the doctrine of the Trinity comes to life in a marvellous manner and suddenly becomes of absorbing interest'. The *Times Literary Supplement* hailed 'Miss Sayers's remarkable new volume ... it illuminates the Christian dogmas in a rich and novel way ... her approach to the problem of the Creation is novel, arresting and fundamental', while the *Expository Times* described it as 'one of the most refreshing and stimulating books of recent times'.

Sayers sought to explain her reasons for writing the book in a letter to Ronald Knox on 26 August 1941, stating that she wanted to show 'that the Trinity doctrine did mean something closely related to what one was doing ... I thought the artist's way of making might be useful material for the Trinitarian theologian.' Referring to a good review of the book by a Benedictine monk from Downside, she added: 'The more Catholic and orthodox the critic, the more sympathetic to my curious caperings on theological territory.'[41]

The Mind of the Maker was Sayers's own contribution to the *Bridgeheads* series of which she was the co-editor with Muriel St Clare Byrne. The series represented something of a crusade for Sayers who saw the need to revitalize society so that the world after the war could be better than the world which had preceded it and which had caused it. It was Sayers's own attempt to wage a war of words designed to win the minds of those responsible for shaping the future. The aims of the series were outlined in combative tones at the end of *The Other Six Deadly Sins*, the published transcript of her talk of 23 October 1941:

> As man has achieved more and more mastery in separate spheres of his activity, he has grown less and less capable of relating his achievements to any coherent social purpose or philosophy of life ... If the whole fabric of society is not to collapse into chaos, we must either submit to an artificial uniformity imposed by brute force, or learn to bridge for ourselves these perilous gaps which sunder our behaviour from reality. This series of books is an attempt to establish a few Bridgeheads, by means of which the remakers of civilization may throw forward their pioneering works.[42]

In these superlative efforts to solve society's ills one is reminded of Belloc's herculean efforts on behalf of the David of distributism against the Goliath of greed-based materialism. Surrounded by zealous converts, Sayers and Belloc stood out as examples of Christians who had militantly retained the faith of their childhood, although both owed a debt to Chesterton for strengthening that faith in times of doubt.

By 1942, however, Belloc was a spent force. Grief-stricken at the death of his son the previous year, he suffered a stroke on 30 January from which he never recovered. He lived for a further eleven years but wrote nothing more. In many ways Belloc's decline was a symbol of the decline of the distributist movement he had done more than anyone to promote. The deaths of Eric Gill in 1940 and Father Vincent McNabb in 1943 appeared to represent further nails in distributism's coffin. Yet throughout the war years the distributist spirit was continued in the tireless efforts of Sayers. On St George's Day 1942 she addressed a meeting in Eastbourne on the sanctifying power of work as an act of creation – a theme so resonant and reminiscent of the preaching and practice of McNabb and Gill.

An organization imbued with the same spirit of reconstruction as that which motivated Sayers was the Sword of the Spirit, established by Cardinal Hinsley shortly after the outbreak of war. According to Robert Speaight, who was himself heavily involved in the organization, the Sword of the Spirit was 'launched by Cardinal Hinsley, animated by Manya Harari, put into operation by Barbara Ward, and intellectually nourished by Christopher Dawson'.[43]

Although the Sword of the Spirit was a Roman Catholic initiative, it was scarcely surprising that Anglo-Catholics such as Sayers should have taken an active interest in its work. One of Christopher Dawson's daughters remembered being told 'an amusing story' by her father about how Sayers was present at one of the meetings of the Sword of the Spirit in London: 'There was an air raid and they all dived under the table.'[44]

Dawson had been invited to become Vice-President of the organization by Cardinal Hinsley in 1940, a position he held until 1944, and nowhere have its basic aims been put more explicitly than by Dawson himself. The aim of the movement was, Dawson explained, first and foremost spiritual, 'a return to the foundations on which Western civilisation and our own national life were built and therefore opposed alike to the deliberate apostasy of the totalitarian state and the superficial materialism of our own secularised culture'.[45]

Another exciting development in the war of words was the founding at the beginning of 1942 of the Oxford University Socratic Club, of which C. S. Lewis was president. The idea of the club evolved from a conversation between a Somerville College undergraduate and Stella Aldwinckle, who was spiritual counsellor at the college. The student had complained that there seemed to be no one with whom one could discuss the sort of doubts and difficulties agnostics raised about God. Aldwinckle's response was to put up a notice announcing a meeting in the Junior Common Room to which she invited 'all atheists, agnostics, and those who are disillusioned about religion or think they are'. The meeting, a lively affair with religion coming under attack from all angles, highlighted Oxford's need for an 'open forum for the discussion of the intellectual difficulties connected with religion and with Christianity in particular'.[46]

The Oxford Socratic Club was formed for this purpose and Lewis accepted the presidency with great enthusiasm. It was decided that a paper would be read at each meeting by either a Christian or an unbeliever and this would be followed by a reply by a speaker who held an opposing view, after which the meeting would be thrown open to general discussion. The meetings were to be held every Monday evening during term.

The first meeting, held on 26 January 1942, addressed the question, 'Won't mankind outgrow Christianity in the face of the advance of science and of modern ideologies?' The principal speaker was R. E. Havard, who had been received into the Catholic Church by Ronald Knox soon after taking a first-class degree in Chemistry at Keble College twenty years earlier. The following week Lewis addressed the question, 'Is God a wish fulfilment?' and two weeks later he debated 'scepticism and faith'. The meetings were a huge success with between eighty and one hundred undergraduates present, as well as some senior members of the university. The Oxford Socratic Club soon became the second largest society at the university and attracted some of the best known speakers in the country. On 2 March Charles Williams addressed the question, 'Are there any valid objections to free love?' and, in similar vein on 23 November, the Dominican Gerald Vann, asked, 'Is Christian sexual morality narrow-minded and out of date?' During 1943 Father D'Arcy addressed the Club twice on 'Reason and Faith' and 'Can the existence of God be proved?', and the following year he discussed 'Rational and Irrational'.

However, the most popular speaker during the first years of the Club's existence was C. S. Lewis, his audience relishing the prospect of his countering the opposition 'with logic, quick wit, and his great gift of repartee'.[47] Above all, Lewis was a master of instant riposte as, for example, when his opponent, who was a Relativist, ended his talk with the assertion: 'The world does not exist, England does not exist, Oxford does not exist, and I am confident that *I* do not exist!' Lewis, standing up to reply, remarked, 'How am I to talk to a man who's *not there?*'[48]

Subjects discussed by Lewis during the war years included 'Morals without Faith', 'Science and Miracles' and 'Resurrection'. Most memorable of all was Lewis's debate with C. E. M. Joad of the BBC *Brains Trust*, which attracted 250 people, the largest crowd ever to assemble at the Socratic Club. Speakers after the war included Emile Cammaerts, A. J. Ayer, Arnold Lunn, Hugh Trevor-Roper, F. C. Copleston, Conrad Pepler, J. B. S. Haldane, Douglas Hyde, Gervase Mathew, Iris Murdoch, Christopher Dawson, Konrad Lorenz and Dorothy L. Sayers.

Lewis's popularity at the Socratic Club was only a reflection in microcosm of his enormous popularity beyond the hallowed halls of Oxford. By the summer of 1942 his books had become best-sellers. *The Problem of Pain* was in its eighth impression and *The Screwtape Letters* in its sixth. Two years later Arnold Lunn reported seeing Lewis's books 'prominently displayed' on a railway bookstall in a big industrial town: 'The popularity of his admirable works of Christian apologetics is clear evidence of an increasing demand for undiluted Christianity.'[49] Even Joad, radio celebrity and outspoken opponent of Christianity, was forced to admit of *The Screwtape Letters* that 'Mr Lewis possesses the rare gift of making righteousness readable'.[50] His other rare gift, as displayed in the two series of talks he had given already, was as a broadcaster, a fact recorded in the *Church Times* on 14 August 1942 in a review of his *Broadcast Talks*:

There are broadcasters who feel that it is their function to console. Mr Lewis, who treats belief as a matter of life or death, is not content with proffering consolation. He believes in attack, and bases his argument on the pursuit of truth. 'If you're looking for truth, you may find comfort in the end; if you're looking for comfort you will not get either comfort or truth, only soft soap and wishful thinking, and in the end, despair.'

His addresses are as invigorating as a cold douche. Years of thought lie behind these simple talks. Only thus could the author have put his argument into so palatable, well balanced and popular a form.

This view was shared by programme planners at the BBC who commissioned a third series of broadcasts from Lewis which were transmitted on eight consecutive Sunday afternoons from 20 September to 8 November under the collective title of 'Christian Behaviour'. The series was another resounding success and ensured that *Christian Behaviour*, the collected transcripts of the talks, became a best-seller when it was published the following April. In a review of the book for the *Tablet*, published on 26 June 1943, Robert Speaight wrote:

Mr Lewis is that rare being – a born broadcaster; born to the manner as well as to the matter. He neither buttonholes you nor bombards you; there is no false intimacy and no false eloquence. He approaches you directly, as a rational person only to be persuaded by reason. He is confident and yet humble in his possession and propagation of truth.

In an age when the microphone was becoming more powerful than either pen or sword, Lewis had emerged as a radio star. Inevitably, therefore, he succumbed to the loud and insistent clamour for further broadcasts and wrote one last set of seven talks for the BBC entitled 'Beyond Personality: The Christian View of God'. These were broadcast on consecutive Tuesday evenings from 22 February to 4 April 1944.

Lewis, however, did not confine his talks to radio audiences. As well as his regular commitments to the Socratic Club in Oxford, he accepted speaking engagements in other parts of the country. In March 1943 he addressed a large audience at Southwark Cathedral on 'unchanging faith in a changing world': 'It is just as possible for an unchanging system of faith and morals to coalesce with, or find room for, a changing body of knowledge as it is for the multiplication table to provide the basis for the most abstruse calculations of mathematics.'[51]

Two months later, on 13 May 1943, Lewis received a letter from Dorothy L.

Sayers in which she complained that 'there aren't any up-to-date books about Miracles'. This appeared to have inspired him because he replied on 17 May that he was 'starting a book on Miracles'.[52] Lewis worked on the book for the remainder of the war, delivering the manuscript to his publisher in the spring of 1945. Further delays followed and Lewis's *Miracles*, possibly his most important theological work, was published only in May 1947.

In the meantime, probably even as Sayers was penning her plaintive letter to Lewis, Ronald Knox was writing an 'up-to-date book about Miracles' which was published in September 1943 by the Catholic Truth Society. Although not as comprehensive in its scope as Lewis's book, Knox still made some powerful points. Discussing the alleged credulity of those who believe in miracles, he compared the restrained view of the Church with the dogmatic rejection by materialists of the possibility of miracles. The Church, wrote Knox, never maintains that a miracle is 'theologically certain; we only say that it is, so far, the best account we can give of the facts. We differ from our critics only in this, that we say, "It may be a miracle or it may not," whereas they say, "whatever it is, it certainly is not a miracle".'

Knox, like Lewis, gave highly popular talks on the radio during the war, combining the role of a nationally known radio celebrity with an almost reclusive private life. He spent the war years at the home of Lord and Lady Acton in Aldenham, Shropshire, which had been taken over by a convent school run by sisters of the Assumption evacuated from London. The school comprised fifteen nuns, three lay teachers, a lay matron and fifty-five girls. Initially Knox was apprehensive about this invasion (quite literally) of his privacy and, according to Waugh in his biography of Knox, the girls had been told not to bother 'the Monsignor' who was 'engaged in grave studies'. Soon, wrote Waugh, his relationship with the girls was to prove 'a source of unexpected pleasure':

> None of them had expected to enjoy sermons, still less to laugh during them. He gave them a short instruction after Benediction every Sunday of term when he was at Aldenham, and with his peculiar versatility and felicity he evolved a new, entirely original style, specially designed for his new, unfamiliar audience. As he came to know the girls individually and to enter their lives he adopted their habits of speech and introduced allusions to their routine. These talks were so popular that one girl, who was being taken out for the day by her parents, insisted on returning for Benediction rather than go to the cinema.[53]

Sister Juliana Dawson, a sister of the Assumption and daughter of Christopher Dawson, confirmed Waugh's words, saying that Knox 'was so popular that the girls would ask to come back early on Sundays to listen to him'.[54]

After the war these talks were published as *The Mass in Slow Motion*, *The Creed in Slow Motion* and *The Gospel in Slow Motion*, becoming perhaps the most popular of all his writings.

There is something disarmingly charming about Knox's secret vocation as a teacher to evacuated schoolchildren, a role far removed from his public persona as a radio personality and popular apologist. This life of contrasts was paralleled by Dorothy L. Sayers who also divided her time between public and private vocations. In her case it was the contrast between public controversy and private correspondence. On the one hand, like both Knox and Lewis, she became a radio celebrity, seeing it as a duty during the war to accept as often as possible any invitations to write and speak on matters of national concern. After the enormous success of her radio play *The Man Born to be King*, the public, the press and the religious authorities regarded her as a figure of prominence who was expected to make solemn pronouncements when the occasion called. The Director of Religious Broadcasting at the BBC spoke for many when he wrote: 'We must make you a prophet to this generation and hand you the microphone to use as often as you feel able'.[55] On the other hand, she continued to exert a hidden influence by means of a seemingly inexhaustible exchange of substantial letters. Barbara Reynolds, the editor of Sayers's letters, listed the range of topics which she discussed in her correspondence, including

> the importance of vocation in work (by which she did not mean vocational training), the need for the young to keep in touch with their country's past, the inadequate preaching of Christian doctrine, the position of women, the fallacy of 19th century liberalism, the collapse of materialism, the short sightedness of the theory of 'economic man', the ephemeral nature of many modern scientific concepts, above all, the danger of society's disregard of the human need for creativity.[56]

C. S. Lewis, himself the recipient of many of Sayers's letters, told her jokingly that posterity would see her as one of the century's great letter writers and that people would be surprised to discover that she also wrote detective novels.

Whimsical jesting aside there is no doubt that Sayers was indeed one of the century's great letter writers intent on influencing the 'creative minds' of her day. In one long letter written during the war she concluded with an extensive reading list by means of which her correspondent could delve deeper into the issues under discussion. The list was itself revealing as an indication of those 'creative minds' that had influenced Sayers herself, an example of what Barbara Reynolds called 'this network of minds all reaching out to each other and meshing together'.[57] The list included Lewis's *Broadcast Talks* which Sayers described as 'extremely pungent and witty', and *The Problem of Pain*: 'If anybody was really troubled about human suffering and wanted to know something of Christianity as a living faith, I should be rather inclined to give him this book to start with.' Chesterton's *Orthodoxy* and *The Everlasting Man* were also listed and the comments Sayers appended illustrated the continuing importance of Chesterton to her own position: 'Some people are merely infuriated by Chesterton's "paradoxical" style. But for going down to the centre of things and hitting the nail plumb on the head, it's hard to beat him.'[58]

Between 1939 and 1945 Sayers, along with Lewis, Eliot, Dawson, Knox and a host of other Christian writers, had fought an energetic war of words in an effort to establish 'bridgeheads', by means of which they believed the world could move forward into a constructive future. In the language of the previous world war, they had hoped optimistically for 'a land fit for heroes'. As with the previous war, however, the optimism of war soon gave way to pessimism – the pessimism of Cold War 'peace'. Many of these writers would come to echo the previous generation who had seen destruction give way to decay and the brave new world become a waste land.

NOTES

1. Barbara Reynolds, *Dorothy L. Sayers: Her Life and Soul*, London, 1993, pb edn., pp. 347–8.
2. ibid., p. 348.
3. Dorothy L. Sayers, *Begin Here*, London, 1940, preface.
4. ibid., p. 73.
5. ibid., p. 97.
6. ibid., p. 74.
7. ibid., pp. 151–2.
8. ibid., p. 153.
9. ibid., p. 157.
10. ibid., p. 160.
11. Matthew Hoehn, OSB (ed.), *Catholic Authors: Contemporary Biographical Sketches 1930–1947*, p. 776.
12. Edward Lobb (ed.), *Words in Time: New Essays in Eliot's Four Quartets*, Athlone Press, 1993, p. 61.
13. George Sayer, *Jack: C. S. Lewis and His Times*, London, 1988, pp. 153–4.
14. Roger Lancelyn Green and Walter Hooper, *C. S. Lewis: A Biography*, London, 1987, p. 165.
15. ibid., p. 165.
16. Humphrey Carpenter, *J. R. R. Tolkien: A Biography*, London, 1986, p. 173.
17. ibid., p. 198.
18. Walter Hooper, interview with the author, Oxford, 20 August 1996.
19. ibid.
20. C. S. Lewis, *Surprised by Joy*, London, 1991 edn., pp. 153–4.

21. ibid., p. 171.
22. ibid., p. 178.
23. Owen Barfield, interview with the author, Forest Row, 31 December 1996.
24. C. S. Lewis, *Surprised by Joy*, p. 180.
25. Dom Bede Griffiths, *The Golden String*, London, 1979 edn., p. 120.
26. Walter Hooper, *C. S. Lewis: A Companion and Guide*, London, 1996, p. 671.
27. Owen Barfield, interview with the author.
28. Roger Lancelyn Green and Walter Hooper, *C. S. Lewis: A Biography*, p. 130.
29. ibid., p. 130.
30. Christopher Derrick, *C. S. Lewis and the Church of Rome*, San Francisco, 1981, p. 46.
31. ibid.
32. Christopher Derrick, interview with the author, Wallington, August 1996.
33. Walter Hooper, interview with the author.
34. Humphrey Carpenter, *J. R. R. Tolkien: A Biography*, p. 155.
35. Walter Hooper, interview with the author.
36. Barbara Reynolds, *Dorothy L. Sayers: Her Life and Soul*, p. 410.
37. Walter Hooper (ed.), *They Stand Together: The Letters of C. S. Lewis to Arthur Greeves*, London, 1979, p. 497.
38. Dorothy L. Sayers, *The Other Six Deadly Sins*, London, 1943, p. 3.
39. Barbara Reynolds, interview with the author, Cambridge, 19 September 1996.
40. Dorothy L. Sayers, *The Mind of the Maker*, London, 1941, pp. 30-1.
41. Barbara Reynolds, *Dorothy L. Sayers: Her Life and Soul*, p. 349, pp. 354–5.
42. Dorothy L. Sayers, *The Other Six Deadly Sins*, p. 31.
43. Robert Speaight, *The Property Basket: Recollections of a Divided Life*, p. 218.
44. Sister Juliana Dawson, interview with the author, Hengrave Hall, Suffolk, 9 December 1996.
45. Christina Scott, 'The Vision and Legacy of Christopher Dawson', lecture given at Westminster College, Oxford, 7 September 1995.
46. George Sayer, *Jack: C. S. Lewis and His Times*, p. 172.
47. ibid., p. 172.
48. James T. Como (ed.), *C. S. Lewis at the Breakfast Table*, London, 1980, p. 146.
49. Arnold Lunn, *The Third Day*, Harrison, NY, 1945, introduction.
50. *New Statesman and Nation*, Vol. XXIII (16 May 1942), p. 324.
51. *Church Times*, 19 March 1943.
52. Walter Hooper, *C. S. Lewis: A Companion and Guide*, pp. 343–4.
53. Evelyn Waugh, *Ronald Knox*, pp. 243–4.
54. Sister Juliana Dawson, interview with the author.
55. Barbara Reynolds, article in the *Calcutta Statesman*, 30 August 1996.
56. ibid.
57. Barbara Reynolds, interview with the author.
58. Unpublished letter in the possession of Barbara Reynolds.

CHAPTER NINETEEN

NUCLEAR REACTIONS

On 10 September 1945 Edith Sitwell read an eye-witness description of the immediate effect of the atomic bomb upon Hiroshima. Its effect upon her was chilling. 'That witness,' she wrote, 'saw a totem pole of dust arise to the sun as a witness against the murder of mankind ... A totem pole, the symbol of creation, the symbol of generation. From that moment the poem began'.[1]

The poem was *The Shadow of Cain*, the first of her 'three poems of the Atomic Age', which was about 'the fission of the world into warring particles, destroying and self-destructive. It is about the gradual migration of mankind, after that Second Fall of Man ... into the desert of the Cold, towards the final disaster, the first symbol of which fell on Hiroshima.'[2]

> We did not heed the Cloud in the Heavens shaped like the hand
> Of Man ...
> > the Primal Matter
> Was broken, the womb from which all life began.
> Then to the murdered Sun a totem pole of dust arose
> > in memory of Man.

The poem's imagery was as chilling as its subject. 'The first two pages,' Sitwell explained, 'were partly a physical description of the highest degree of cold, partly a spiritual description of this.'[3] *The Shadow of Cain* had the mark of prophecy, reflecting the fears of many as the world emerged from world war to cold war. *Après le déluge* ... the Cold.

The Shadow of Cain was published on its own in book form in June 1947. In the following month's issue of *Horizon* Kenneth Clark wrote of Sitwell's verse that 'those who care for poetry recognized a true prophetic cry which had not been heard in English poetry since the death of Yeats'.

The horrors of Hiroshima also inspired Siegfried Sassoon, writer of some of the greatest poems of the previous war, to new heights of creativity. In 1945 he wrote 'Litany of the Lost', a verse which echoed the concerns expressed by Sitwell and employed similar resonant religious imagery as a counterpoise to post-war pessimism and alienation:

> In breaking of belief in human good;
> In slavedom of mankind to the machine;
> In havoc of hideous tyranny withstood,
> And terror of atomic doom foreseen;
> *Deliver us from ourselves.*

> Chained to the wheel of progress uncontrolled;
> World masterers with a foolish frightened face;
> Loud speakers, leaderless and sceptic-souled;
> Aeroplane angels, crashed from glory and grace;
> *Deliver us from ourselves.*

> In blood and bone contentiousness of nations,
> And commerce's competitive re-start,
> Armed with our marvellous monkey innovations,
> And unregenerate still in head and heart;
> *Deliver us from ourselves.*

The same concerns were addressed more prosaically, but no less prophetically, by Ronald Knox in his *God and the Atom*, published by Sheed & Ward in November 1945. The opening chapter was headed 'Trauma: Hiroshima':

> At a moment when it seemed as if all our capacity for surprise were already exhausted, one day last August, we opened the paper to find that we were wrong. Something had happened compared with which the General Election, and even Victory Day, would probably seem unimportant in perspective. A Japanese town, rather more populous than Southampton, had suddenly ceased to exist.
>
> We knew that scientists had been busy with the atom; that it had lost the privilege of infinitesimality, and yielded, like everything else, to analysis. But this was only theoretical knowledge, surely? ... And all the time, behind our backs, men of science were working feverishly at unmentionable researches ...[4]

For the book's epigraph Knox had chosen the lines of Wordsworth:

To let a creed, built in the heart of things,
Dissolve before a twinkling atomy!

Evelyn Waugh believed *God and the Atom* was 'a masterpiece of construction and expression which gives no evidence of the speed with which it was written'. Knox, however, was disappointed by its lack of success and Waugh admitted that, in spite of its literary merits, it 'fell quite flat':

> Consciences were dulled by war and minds agitated by the superficial problems of peace ... It appeared out of due time ... more than five years before the public to whom it was addressed, awoke to the fact that they themselves were threatened by the invention they had applauded; ten years before the publicists began to exploit the panic.[5]

Although Waugh shared Knox's disappointment at the lukewarm response to *God and the Atom*, he must have been heartened by the success of *Brideshead Revisited*, his own newly published novel. Written over a year before the bomb was dropped but not published until 1945, Waugh's novel of hope among the ruins of a vanishing civilization was none the less animated by the same post-war pessimism and anxiety which permeated the poetry and prose of Sitwell, Sassoon and Knox. It sold exceedingly well on both sides of the Atlantic. In England, the *Tablet* acclaimed it 'a book for which it is safe to prophesy a lasting place among the major works of fiction'.[6] In America, *Time* described Waugh as a stylist unexcelled among contemporary novelists.

The praise was tempered by a vociferous minority who disliked *Brideshead Revisited* on both political and religious grounds. It was deemed politically incorrect for its nostalgic swan-song of a rapidly vanishing aristocratic way of life and Waugh was vilified for being a reactionary and a snob. In response to the barrage of accusations of snobbery levelled against him, Waugh remained defiant: 'Class consciousness, particularly in England, has been so much inflamed nowadays that to mention a nobleman is like mentioning a prostitute sixty years ago ... I reserve the right to deal with the kind of people I know best.'[7]

In the same article Waugh replied to Edmund Wilson who had criticized the religious dimension in *Brideshead Revisited*: 'He was outraged (quite legitimately by his standards) at finding God introduced into my story. I believe that you can only leave God out by making your characters pure abstractions.' Modern novelists, Waugh continued,

try to represent the whole human mind and soul and yet omit its determining character – that of being God's creature with a defined purpose.
So in my future books there will be two things to make them unpopular: a preoccupation with style and the attempt to represent man more
fully, which to me means only one thing, man in his relation to God.

With the publication of *Brideshead Revisited* Waugh completed the metamorphosis from ultramodern to ultramontane and in so doing passed from fashion to
anti-fashion. The transformation also invited comparisons between the works of
Waugh and those of the disappearing old guard of the Catholic literary revival.
The influence of Chesterton on the writing of *Brideshead Revisited* is patently
obvious. Its central theme of the redemption of lost souls by means of 'the
unseen hook and invisible line ... the twitch upon the thread', was taken from
one of Chesterton's *Father Brown* stories. Waugh told Nancy Mitford that he
was anxious to obtain a copy of the omnibus edition of the *Father Brown* stories
at the time he was putting the finishing touches to *Brideshead*,[8] and a memoran-
dum he wrote for MGM studios when a film version of the novel was being considered illustrated clearly the profundity of Chesterton's influence:

> The Roman Catholic Church has the unique power of keeping remote
> control over human souls which have once been part of her. G. K.
> Chesterton has compared this to the fisherman's line, which allows the
> fish the illusion of free play in the water and yet has him by the hook;
> in his own time the fisherman by a 'twitch upon the thread' draws the
> fish to land.[9]

The Chestertonian metaphor was not lost on Ronald Knox when he first read
the book: 'once you reach the end, needless to say the whole cast – even Beryl –
falls into place and the twitch of the thread happening in the very bowels of
Metroland is inconceivably effective'.[10]

The combination of Catholicism and aristocratic high society in *Brideshead*
also invited obvious comparisons with the novels of Maurice Baring who died in
the year of the novel's publication. Less obvious but equally powerful was the
subliminal influence of Hilaire Belloc who had been one of Waugh's heroes since
his days as a schoolboy at Lancing. Waugh was attracted to Belloc's militantly
aggressive and traditional approach to Catholicism but was equally impressed by
the matter-of-fact, almost humdrum way in which he practised his faith. It was
the simple unaffected faith of cradle Catholics like Belloc, as distinct from the
comparative zeal of converts, which shaped the characterization of the Flytes in

Brideshead. Another Catholic writer who probably influenced the writing of *Brideshead Revisited* was Compton Mackenzie whose evocative description of life at Oxford in *Sinister Street*, a book which Waugh had read and enjoyed at Lancing, found resonant echoes in Waugh's own atmospheric treatment of Oxford undergraduate life.

Amidst the controversy over his religion and politics, Waugh found a surprising ally in the person of George Orwell, whose *Animal Farm* was published at around the same time as *Brideshead Revisited*. On 30 August 1945 Waugh had written to Orwell congratulating him on his 'ingenious and delightful allegory' and Orwell, for his part, had been similarly impressed by Waugh's novel. Although Orwell had flirted with Marxism during the thirties he had become thoroughly disillusioned by the end of the war, a change of heart which proved the inspiration for his two greatest novels. Both *Animal Farm* and *Nineteen Eighty-Four* epitomized post-war pessimism more potently than the work of any other writer. At the time of his death in 1950 Orwell had been planning to write a study of Waugh, using him as an example of the fallacy of the Marxist view that art can only be good if it is progressive.

Although Orwell's nightmare vision in *Nineteen Eighty-Four* has gained pride of place in the plaintive literature of post-war disenchantment, his voice was but one of many raised in protest. One of the most noteworthy novels in similar vein was *That Hideous Strength* by C. S. Lewis, the last of his 'Ransom trilogy' of science fiction novels published in July 1945. Lewis's idea for the N.I.C.E. – the National Institute of Co-ordinated Experiments which appropriates and partially destroys a little university town – had arisen out of the controversy over the founding of an atomic plant near Blewbury fifteen miles from Oxford. The bombing of Hiroshima and Nagasaki within weeks of the novel's publication should have added poignancy to its potency but, in Lewis's own words in a letter to a friend, it was 'unanimously damned by all reviewers'.[11] Undeterred, Lewis continued to consider *That Hideous Strength* his 'favourite' of all his books, though he was quick to differentiate between 'favourite' and 'best'.[12]

His friends appeared divided in their opinions. Dorothy L. Sayers, writing to Lewis on 3 December 1945, expressed her opinion that the book 'is tremendously full of good things'[13] while Tolkien believed it was 'tripish' and spoiled by the influence of Charles Williams. Tolkien's views were particularly interesting. He was in the midst of writing *The Lord of the Rings* at the time and Lewis's ascribing of demoniac powers to the men of science in *That Hideous Strength* bore more than a marked similarity to Tolkien's treatment of the same issues. Lewis's description of *That Hideous Strength* to an American correspondent in

1954 could almost serve equally as a description of *The Lord of the Rings*: 'I think *That Hideous Strength* is about a triple conflict: Grace against Nature and Nature against Anti-Nature (modern industrialism, scientism and totalitarian politics).'[14] This triple conflict between the supernatural, natural and unnatural was arguably the key to both books.

If relatively minor differences of style masked a deeper unity of outlook in Lewis and Tolkien, the same could also be said of Lewis and Eliot. Lewis had never cared for Eliot's poetry or prose, and he despised what he perceived as Eliot's elitism. On the other hand, both were converts to the traditionalist wing of the Anglican church and were equally opposed to theological modernism. It was perhaps not surprising, therefore, that both should share the same pessimism about post-war Europe.

Eliot felt no exhilaration after the surrender of the Japanese in the wake of Hiroshima and refused to participate in the public celebrations on VJ Day. He felt uneasy about the foreign policy of both Britain and the United States, and fearful of the intentions of Russia. In January 1946 he described a public world which was becoming more 'incredible' and a private world which was more 'intolerable'. In spite of the Allied victory, he felt that the world was a less 'moral' place than it had been before the war. He believed that Germany and Japan had brought the sickness which infected civilization to a crisis point but that their collapse had not cured the disease but had left it raging out of control. The relative optimism of the pre-war years, when he had called for the restructuring of society along Christian lines, was replaced by a rearguard action aimed at the very survival of European civilization itself. Before the war ended he had been worried that peace might be associated only with the concept of 'efficiency', and in radio talks in 1946 he spoke of the necessity for maintaining the 'spiritual organization' as well as the 'material organization' of Europe.[15] Failure to do so would lead to 'centuries of barbarism' hastened by the dominance of technology. Furthermore, Eliot was alarmed at the dominance of the United States in post-war Europe and began to feel that he was witnessing the collapse of that culture which, more than thirty years earlier, he had left America to find. To his evident dismay it appeared that the world had rejected tradition for modernity, culture for cash and spiritual comforts for material luxuries.

Ironically, it was this very development that was to be the cause of the greatest number of conversions to Catholicism in the second half of the century as those alienated by the vacuity of consumerism sought sanctuary, sanity and depth in the faith, culture and tradition of the Church.

A celebrated if somewhat controversial conversion took place in St Patrick's Cathedral, New York in February 1946 when Clare Boothe Luce, author, politician and society hostess, was received into the Church by Monsignor Fulton Sheen. She was best known for her successful pre-war Broadway plays, *The Women* and *Kiss the Boys Goodbye*, but had also served as an outspoken Republican member of the House of Representatives between 1942 and 1945. However, the most controversial aspect of her conversion was the fact that she was married to Henry Robinson Luce, the wealthy magazine publisher who had founded *Time*, *Fortune* and *Life*. As Luce was divorced from his previous wife, many believed that Clare Boothe Luce's wealth and social standing 'had entitled her to go on living with a divorced man with the Church's approval ... reinforcing the impression of a double standard for rich and poor'.[16] In fact, the couple had ceased living together connubially several years before her conversion and the physical estrangement had been one of the factors that had led her towards Catholicism. The other factors leading to her conversion were remarkably similar to those affecting other post-war converts. She had long been 'dissatisfied with the answers or the lack of answers to her quest for happiness':

> She saw the vacuity of a system without the Christian ideals. Divorce which had been so much in her background, and the mad race for money and pleasure which characterized the boom, served further to unsettle her mind. The years of depression followed by the war only increased her realization of the nothingness which the various religious or semi-religious groups had to offer to a soul seeking the meaning of life.[17]

At Christmas 1943 her only daughter, Ann Clare, had been killed in a car accident and, from this time on, 'gradually but surely her steps led her to the portals of the Catholic Church'.

A detailed account of her conversion entitled *The Real Reason* began to appear in *McCall's* magazine in February 1947 and in the following year she made a nationwide lecture tour of the United States, speaking on 'Christianity in the Atomic Age'. In November 1948 she dined with Evelyn Waugh who described her as 'exquisitely elegant, clever as a monkey, self centred'.[18] In 1953 she became US ambassador to Italy.

On Easter Sunday 1946, two months after Clare Boothe Luce's conversion, Elizabeth Longford was received into the Church in Oxford. Six years earlier her husband, Lord Longford, had taken the same step, influenced by the patient teaching of Father Martin D'Arcy and the impatient prompting of Evelyn Waugh. On hearing the news of her husband's reception into the Church, Lady Longford had been angry and had reacted to his conversion by becoming vehemently anti-clerical. She referred to his religious books as a 'Chamber of Horrors' and insisted they be relegated to the bottom shelf of a bookcase in the hallway, out of sight and out of mind. Her initial anger mellowed as she came to see what an important part Catholicism played in her husband's life and the tragically early death of her brother in 1941, caused by a brain tumour, led her to thoughts of an after-life. This in turn led her to the 'Chamber of Horrors' and to a sporadic reading of Longford's religious books. She was particularly impressed by the writings of Jacques Maritain.

At the start of 1944 she took her two eldest children, who had been christened in the Anglican church, to the Anglo-Catholic church of St Paul's in south Oxford in preparation for their first communion. An erstwhile agnostic, she accompanied them to church each Sunday. By the autumn she was under instruction and she was received as an Anglican before Christmas. Thereafter, each Sunday as the Longford family set off to church, she felt a great emotional wrench as her husband turned one way to go to the Catholic church and she and the children the other to go to St Paul's. Believing she had chosen a halfway house, and following discussions with her husband on prayer and theology, she received instruction from Father Gervase Mathew to become a Catholic. After her reception, Longford was reported to be overjoyed that the family had become a 'household of faith'.[19]

The following year saw the conversion of Anne Green, best-selling author of *The Selbys* and many other novels, who was received into the Church in July 1947. Her conversion was a belated ratification of the decision by both her father and her brother, the better-known author Julian Green, to join the Catholic Church in 1915. In the same year Elizabeth Sewell, novelist, poet and literary scholar, was received into the Church as a result of her research in French for a Ph.D., 'an odd but good way in which to arrive'.[20]

Another literary scholar received into the Church on 14 June 1947 was George B. Harrison, author of *Elizabethan* and *Jacobean Journals*, *Shakespeare at Work*, *Elizabethan Plays and Players*, *Shakespeare: the Man and His Stage*, *John Bunyan: A Study in Personality* and *The Life and Death of Robert Devereaux, Earl of Essex*. It was during the course of his sixteen years of research for the *Elizabethan Journals* that he became inspired by the English Martyrs:

> it was quite clear that the Jesuit missionaries who came over to England in the 1580's and 1590's were solely concerned with propagating their faith ... such Jesuits as Edmund Campion and Robert Southwell were willing and even eager martyrs. A man who cheerfully sought and faced the rack and the beastly death of a traitor in Elizabethan times had an

extraordinary certainty in something which I could imagine but did not share.[21]

Inspired by the same admiration for Campion and Southwell as that which had influenced Benson, Waugh, Greene and countless others, Professor Harrison found himself increasingly convinced of the rectitude of the Catholic faith. He and his wife approached the Archbishop of Kingston, Ontario who lent them a copy of Ronald Knox's *What Catholics Believe*, telling them to come back again if they were still interested. A fortnight later they commenced instruction.

It would, however, be an over-simplification to suggest that Harrison's Elizabethan research was the only influence upon his subsequent conversion. An interest in philosophy led him to reject the 'leaders of modern thought', most of whom 'conspicuously failed in the practice of their own theories'.

> In the 1920's much was heard of the various guides to happiness put out by Bertrand and Dora Russell, who helped to popularize the notion that happiness consists in freedom from all restraint and that since sex is the greatest of human pleasures, men and women, married or single, should be entirely free to sleep wherever they choose. After a few years it appeared that even the Russell paradise had been invaded by a serpent.[22]

The final straw which broke the back of Harrison's unbelief was the death of two sons on active service in the British army. His eldest son died during the war in July 1942 and his youngest was killed on guard duty in Palestine early in January 1947. For weeks after the second tragedy he and his wife 'moved about in a state of physical numbness and mental pain which was too bitter to share or even to mention'. It was this suffering which made them realize that 'our vague philosophy was useless in times of devastation'.[23]

At the same time as Professor Harrison and his wife were making their final sublimely sorrowful approach to the Church, Evelyn Waugh was involved in an unsubtle attempt to bludgeon his friend John Betjeman out of his Anglo-Catholicism. On 9 January 1947 Waugh informed Betjeman 'that you are being allowed to see a glimpse of the truth broad enough to damn you if you reject it now'.

> I have no patience whatever with the plea of duty to a sinking ship. If your group at Wantage are the Catholic Church they are not sinking. They are one with the angels and saints triumphant. If they are sinking it is because they should never have put to sea ...

You cannot rely on a death bed conversion. Every hour you spend outside the Church is an hour lost ...

... you must give yourself time to take lessons in the rudiments of theology. Don't follow emotions follow reason. The final step must be a step in the dark because you can have no conception of what the Church is like until you see it from inside.[24]

There is no doubting the sincerity and seriousness of Waugh's desire to see his friend 'inside' the Church but the brusqueness was inappropriate. Even allowing for the fact that the apparent rudeness was rooted in a perceived knowledge of the depth of their relationship and in the belief that Betjeman would not take offence, Waugh's tactless tone was ill advised. However, the candour coupled with conviviality and suppressed humour could be almost endearing, imbued with a sweet and sour charm:

Do you feel disposed to come on a house-hunting jaunt in Ireland with me at my expense soon after Easter?

I can't sleep. Can you?

Awful about your obduracy in schism and heresy. Hell hell hell. Eternal damnation.

Love to Penelope.[25]

Waugh was wrong in his belief that Betjeman would not take offence. Shortly after this letter was written he received a letter from Penelope Betjeman informing him of her husband's position: 'He thinks ROMAN Catholicism is a foreign religion which has no right to set up in this country, let alone try to make converts from what he regards as the true catholic church of the country. Your letters have brought it out in a remarkable way'.[26]

Penelope Betjeman's letter also gave an early indication of her own thoughts on the subject and the dilemma she faced, stating that her husband 'says he will leave me at once if I go over'.

On 4 June Waugh replied to her in a spirit of reconciliation: 'I am by nature a bully and a scold and John's pertinacity in error brings out all that is worst in me. I am very sorry. I will lay off him in future.' Inviting Penelope and her husband to come and stay at Piers Court, Waugh promised that, should they come, he would not 'broach theological questions': 'I WILL KEEP SILENCE.' The letter concluded with an abject apology: 'Please tell John I am sincerely sorry for persecuting him and won't again.'[27]

Waugh's reconciliation with John Betjeman was recorded in his diary on 4 August: 'To Farnborough to make my peace with the Betjemans. Successful in this. A drive with John looking at 1860 churches. Penelope seems resolved to enter the Church in the autumn.'[28]

In the event Penelope Betjeman postponed her instruction because of her husband's objections but was finally received into the Church in the following March. Understandably Waugh was delighted at the news and wrote to her on 7 March:

> You are coming into the Church with vastly more knowledge than most converts but what you cannot know until Tuesday is the delight of membership of the Household, of having your chair at the table, a place laid, the bed turned down, of the love and trust, whatever their family bickerings, of all Christendom. It is this family unity which makes the weakest Catholic nearer the angels and saints, than the most earnest outsider.[29]

A very different conversion hit the headlines ten days after Penelope Betjeman's. On 19 March, St Joseph's Day, 1948 the front pages of many national newspapers carried the news that Douglas Hyde, news editor of the *Daily Worker* and one of the country's leading communists, had resigned from both his job and the Communist Party and was becoming a Catholic. Hyde recalled the intense media interest after the news had broken:

> The phone had been ringing unceasingly, journalists and photographers were in and around the house ... The tables had been turned on the news editor with a vengeance for I had to hold a Press conference then and there ...
>
> All that evening the pressmen came, first from the British papers, later from the foreign ones too. I was talking to an American after one o'clock next morning and taking the first of a new flood of phone calls and callers five or six hours later.
>
> For the next few days life was hectic, with broadcasts, newspaper articles, endless interviews. On the Sunday, Palm Sunday, British Movietone News came and filmed us in our home.[30]

Over the following ten days he received more than nine hundred letters from all parts of the world: 'It was clear that I had set in motion something bigger by far than anything I had expected.'

One letter particularly pleased him, from a man 'who had been a communist, had been troubled by the Party's policy and now wrote to say that he had been considering doing what I had done. Now he would follow my example.'[31]

Hyde's slow conversion from communism to Christianity began during the war when he was given an assignment to expose the *Weekly Review* as a fascist journal. The *Weekly Review* was the heir to *G. K.'s Weekly*, which Chesterton had edited until his death, and was a predominantly Catholic journal promoting the cause of distributism. Hyde wrote three articles in which he accused those associated with the paper, including Hilary Pepler and R. D. Jebb, of having fascist links. The articles were later the subject of a libel action which Hyde lost. In the meantime he studied the pages of the *Weekly Review* for evidence of 'fascism' and found to his consternation that he was in sympathy with certain aspects of the paper he was supposed to be condemning.

> I first became aware of this when one day I found in it a quotation from William Morris. For such people to quote my Morris seemed blasphemy.
>
> Then I found that the parts of the paper I had been deliberately missing because, being non-political, they had no bearing on my case, were very much in tune with Morris. It was almost humiliating to discover that these people were medievalists – and so was I.
>
> For years almost my only relaxation had been reading Chaucer and Langland, visiting pre-Reformation churches, listening to plainsong and Gregorian chant or spending hours in the Victoria and Albert Museum studying the craftsmanship of the thirteenth and fourteenth centuries, revealed in gloriously illuminated books and, equally, in perfectly designed things for every-day use.
>
> These were, it seemed, the *Weekly Review*'s interests too ... I resolved the problem by putting the medievalist attraction of the *Weekly Review* into one watertight compartment of my mind and its politics into another.[32]

The compartmentalizing of his political and cultural allegiances led to a psychologically divided existence reminiscent of Jekyll and Hyde. The Marxist Mr Hyde would speak at huge communist rallies: 'To stand on the plinth of Nelson's Column and look down on 50,000 faces, to see the hammer and sickle badge, openly and proudly worn by almost everyone present, to hear great masses of people singing the "International" and "Sovietland", was to be carried away with a terrific emotion.'[33] Meanwhile, his Dr Jekyll *alter ego* was quietly consuming the Christian antidote:

I was coming to look forward to the arrival of my copy of the *Weekly Review* each Thursday morning. I still hated its politics. But I looked forward to H. D. C. Pepler's little Chaucerian rhymes, to the articles impregnated with love of the Middle Ages ...

... I had come now to know that the people behind it were the exact opposites of totalitarians. They were Distributists and I began to find certain aspects of Distributism attractive.[34]

His reading of the *Weekly Review* prompted him to read Chesterton and Belloc, whose books 'had not been among those I had read much in the past'. The only writing by Belloc he possessed was a little pamphlet on St Thomas à Becket which he had taken from the literature rack in a Catholic Church years before when making room for some communist literature he was putting there:

I found it one night and read it for the first time. Its vigorous, polemical style appealed, for it had a certain similarity to that of some of our own Marxist writers.

The fact that it dealt with my beloved Middle Ages heightened its interest, but its religious side did not touch me at all. That was something that died, or should have died, with feudalism – all right in its day but not in ours.[35]

Hyde then went through his library and rediscovered two books by Chesterton, his biography of Charles Dickens and *The Man Who Was Thursday*, 'which I had always loved'. He also recalled reading and admiring Chesterton's *Chaucer*, which he had taken out from the library on the day following Chesterton's death, and remembered how 'it had shed new light on the medieval poet whose works I knew so well'.

Yet reading these books or the *Weekly Review*, late at night after a hectic day in the office, I had almost the same sense of guilt as that experienced by an adolescent indulging in a secret vice.

... As I read the *Weekly Review*, it came, in time, secretly to thrill me to think that Chesterton himself had once edited it. The trouble was that the more I read it, the more I found in it to interest me.

I hated big cities, longed for the sanity of rural life. The impersonal character of the suburb, its piddling values, nauseated me. The soil had a fascination for me that had never died.[36]

Then, months later, while Hyde was reading the *Weekly Review*, a thought struck him 'which was so obvious as to be almost laughably so'.[37] If the unequal distribution of private property led to great injustice it didn't necessarily mean that private property was wrong, as the Marxists claimed, but merely that its unequal distribution was wrong. Such a view was at the heart of the distributist message of the *Weekly Review* but Hyde had hitherto overlooked its ramifications. Now they struck home like a revelation: 'If one of the main starting points of my years in Marxism had depended upon such phoney thought, then what right had I to accept, more or less as gospel-truth, the superstructure ... built upon that foundation?'[38]

Hyde began to read everything by Chesterton and Belloc he could get his hands on and tried to discover more about their distributism and the philosophy behind it. Chesterton's *Orthodoxy* was a particularly potent influence and he passed from that to other Catholic authors. He read the writings of Eric Gill and Ronald Knox's *The Belief of Catholics*.

Previously he had believed that Catholic culture had been outgrown at the time when the new economic system of capitalism had broken the fetters of feudalism, that it could all be explained in terms of economics. Now Marxist orthodoxy had been supplanted by Catholic orthodoxy and he believed that Catholic culture was not outgrown 'but that there had been an attempted murder which had not quite succeeded'.[39]

During his last months as news editor of the *Daily Worker* Hyde was asked to review Avro Manhattan's *The Catholic Church against the Twentieth Century*, along with a pamphlet by the Rev. Stanley Evans. The first was a large book which set out to show that Vatican policies since the First World War proved that the Catholic Church was fascist, and the other attempted to show that the Church was against all 'progress'.

'Once,' Hyde wrote, 'I should have had grand fun with them, using them to smear Catholics and fascists at one and the same time. I tried to do the same now, failed and hated myself for even attempting it.'

> Instead I found myself saying: The Catholic Church against the twentieth century? So what? So am I, if the twentieth century means the crazy world I see about me which has endured two world wars and goodness knows how many revolutions already, and with the war-clouds gathering so soon after the last war.
>
> ... And in any case was it really so certain as we had imagined it to be that the world must inevitably 'progress', that the past was necessarily less good and civilised than the present and still less so than the future?[40]

His position as a leading Communist Party member was becoming increasingly incongruous but he had told no one of his doubts, not even his wife who was also a long-standing party member. Then, after the BBC news had finished one night, his wife suddenly burst out that she was sick of Molotov's negative diplomacy and was 'utterly fed up with Russia's behaviour since the end of the war'. Hyde was shocked and asked whether this was any way for the wife of a leading member of the Communist Party to talk. She remained defiant and followed it up with a wholesale condemnation of all that had been taking place in Eastern Europe since the end of the war, her fears that Russia could cause a third world war, and finished with a broadside on the British Communist Party leaders and a declaration that she was tired of the whole lot of them.

By this time Hyde had recovered from the initial shock at his wife's outburst: 'You talk like the *Universe*,' he scolded half-heartedly. 'What the dickens do you think you're doing? Are you becoming a Catholic or something?'

'I wish I were,' she replied.

Hyde's heart leapt: 'And I wish to God I could do the same.'[41]

For the first time in months they came clean with each other. Hyde told her exactly how far he had travelled. How he believed that the culture of the Middle Ages had not died with feudalism but was still alive in the modern world, 'a living Catholic culture'. How he had become tired of hatred and class war and sought something more positive. How his reading of Chesterton, Belloc and the *Weekly Review* had affected him deeply. How St Thomas Aquinas's five proofs of God seemed unanswerable. His wife then told him how she had wished for some time that their daughter should not grow up in a communist home: 'With the Party's morals being what they were, what would happen to her?'[42]

> Carol had read the Catholic papers which I had been leaving about the house and from them she had got a picture of what a home and family might be like – a picture the exact opposite of that which we had known as communists.
>
> ... We both agreed that all our experience showed that the Marxists were wrong, whether we judged them in the light of our own lives or of the broken homes of the comrades we knew.
>
> But the Catholic Church stood, foursquare, like a rock, utterly uncompromising on this question. How right it was.[43]

Soon after this discussion Hyde saw advertised in his local town hall a meeting organized by the Wimbledon branch of the Sword of the Spirit. He had never been to anything Catholic, had never known any Catholics personally, and had never seen Catholics together at Mass, but found none the less that he wanted to go. Almost shamefacedly, he confessed his desire to his wife who thought it would be a good idea. On the platform at the meeting were Richard Stokes, the Labour MP, Commander Bower, a former Conservative MP, Dr Letitia Fairfield, Robert Speaight and two Jesuit priests. After the meeting Hyde introduced himself to Father Francis Devas, one of the Jesuits, and walked with him to the station.

In the few minutes' walk Hyde confessed his past and the guilt he felt about the trail of misery he had left in his path. Could such a man become a Catholic? Father Devas replied that the Church existed for sinners, a reply which astounded and confounded Hyde because sin had found no place in his communist vocabulary. 'With a twinkle in his eye he told me that if one could not be a good Catholic one could at least be a bad one; that even the bad Catholic had a great deal the communist had not got.'[44]

With these words in his mind Hyde continued his double life; news editor of the *Daily Worker* by day and surreptitious churchgoer by night. He attended Mass for the first time, 'slipping in furtively, sitting at the back and slowly coming to understand what was happening at the altar'.[45] By this time he had read enough Catholic books to know the 'broad significance ... of each move leading up to the Sacrifice', and began to develop a love for the Latin liturgy.

Ironically, it was this new-found love for the Mass which led him to become embroiled in a controversial debate within the Church even before his conversion. Reading the Catholic papers he had learned of a new papal encyclical *Mediator Dei* which dealt, among other things, with the demand in some quarters for an increased use of the vernacular by the Church. Hyde found himself strongly disagreeing with these demands: 'Looking back to the days when all Europe enjoyed a common faith and so possessed a common language, Latin, for its religious and cultural life, I strongly favoured the use of its ancient language by the Church.'[46] Spurred into action, he wrote anonymously to the *Catholic Herald*.

His letter appeared in the issue of 9 January 1948, headed 'From Communism to Catholicism':

At 11.30 p.m. on Christmas Eve I was twiddling the knob of my radio. Unable to get out to Midnight Mass I wanted at least to bring it to my fireside. And as I switched from one European station to the next I tuned in to one Midnight Mass after the other. Belgium, France, Germany, Eire, yes, even behind the Iron Curtain, Prague. It seemed as though the whole of what was once Christendom was celebrating what is potentially the most unifying event in man's history. And the important thing was it was the *same* Mass. I am a newcomer to the Mass but

I was able to recognise its continuity as I went from station to station for it was in one common language.[47]

Hyde's own disillusionment with communism was now complete and his groping his way towards the Church was reaching its final stages. On 16 January he phoned the local Jesuit college to arrange for the baptism of his two children and to discuss instruction for both him and his wife. According to Hyde: 'That telephone conversation meant the end of twenty years of communism.'[48]

The end was also a beginning: 'I could not pick up a copy of the *Daily Worker* – still cannot – without seeing the name of someone I brought into the Party, still working for the Cause ... I took a vow to try and make more converts to the Faith in the next ten years than I had made for communism in the past twenty.'[49]

The vow was fulfilled within three years through the publication of *I Believed*, Hyde's autobiography. Published in 1951, this highly evocative account of his life and conversion was a best-seller and served as a catalyst to the conversion of many who found themselves similarly disillusioned.

Before the publication of *I Believed*, in an article entitled 'From Marx to Christ' published in 1949, Hyde wrote that 'the conquest of Communism will have to be achieved by positive Catholic action, not simply by negative anti-Communism, and least of all by the atom bomb, for Bolshevism thrives on misery and devastation'.[50]

Hyde joined the staff of the *Catholic Herald* and wrote in 1952 of his 'belief in that absolute truth which so many of our generation have rejected or forgotten ... I believe Catholicism has the answer to man's social and political needs.'[51]

There was something prophetically pathetic in these words because Hyde was later to lose his 'belief in that absolute truth', joining the ranks of those who have 'rejected or forgotten'. Furthermore, he ceased to believe that Catholicism had the answers to society's ills. On 13 August 1996 he wrote that

I've not been a practising Catholic for a good many years ... Failure of Vatican II to live up to hopes and legitimate expectations, more particularly after the death of John XXIII, was a contributory factor. More especially my personal, on-the-spot involvement in a profound process of change in Latin America triggered off by Pope John and the way in which Pope John Paul has set about rolling back that process, using methods totally unacceptable to me, led to a situation which I could not possibly justify either to myself or to others.[52]

He died on 19 September 1996, only five weeks after these words were written.

In an ironic twist, Hyde had gone from Marx to Christ and then lapsed into a twilight world of liberation theology between the two. His memorial service included an address by Bruce Kent, 'The People's Anthem' instead of a hymn, a recital of Berthold Brecht's 'To Those Born Later' and concluded with Paul Robeson's recording of 'Joe Hill', the socialist protest song. Hyde's life, it seemed, could be summed up with the poignant ambiguity of the two words which formed the title of the book for which he will be most remembered: 'I Believed'.

A remarkably similar conversion to that of Douglas and Carol Hyde happened almost simultaneously with it on the other side of the Atlantic. In 1948 William and Joy Gresham, both former communists, became Christians, though not Catholics, and recounted their stories in a symposium entitled *These Found the Way*. William Gresham, a gifted novelist whose *Nightmare Alley* was made into a film, had already been married and divorced before he and Joy Davidman met at a Communist Party meeting and were wed in 1942. Joy Davidman had won considerable acclaim for her book of verse *Letter to a Comrade* in 1938 and she published two novels, one before and one after her conversion to Christianity: *Anya* in 1940 and *Weeping Bay* in 1950. Joy Davidman's conversion had been due in part to her admiration for the works of C. S. Lewis. Later, following her divorce from Gresham, she met and married Lewis, the dramatized story of their relationship being documented in the television and film adaptations of the play *Shadowlands*.

The end of the year brought another notable convert who had been affected by the nuclear age in a devastatingly direct way. In December 1948 Group Captain Leonard Cheshire was received into the Catholic Church after reading Vernon Johnson's *One Lord, One Faith*.

Group Captain Cheshire had been one of the most celebrated heroes of the Second World War. An outstanding pilot and leader, he was awarded the DSO in 1940, the DFC in 1941 and the VC in 1944. He completed over a hundred bombing missions, often at low altitude, on heavily defended German targets. In 1945 he was one of the two official British observers of the destruction caused by the atomic bomb on Nagasaki. What he witnessed affected him deeply and changed the course of his life dramatically. With the horrifying vision of Nagasaki impressed indelibly in his memory, he discovered the Christian faith and decided to devote the rest of his life to the care of the sick. The first of his 'Cheshire Homes' for the chronically ill was established at Le Court, a Victorian mansion in Hampshire. By the mid-1950s there were half a dozen further Cheshire Homes and now they are to be found in many countries throughout the world.

Perhaps Leonard Cheshire's compassionate response to the nuclear age was the most outstanding example of good arising out of evil. Others, however, had also responded positively, if not so dramatically. The poetic response of Sitwell and Sassoon to the horrors of Hiroshima marked an important development in the progress of each towards full acceptance of the Christian faith a decade later. Meanwhile other writers, sensing that the nihilism of the nuclear age had put civilization at peril, sought a resurrection of Christian culture as an antidote to modern despair.

NOTES

1. Edith Sitwell, *Taken Care Of: An Autobiography*, London, 1965, p. 154.
2. ibid., p. 153.
3. Victoria Glendinning, *Edith Sitwell: A Unicorn Among Lions*, London, 1981, p. 260.
4. Ronald Knox, *God and the Atom*, London, 1945, p. 9.
5. Evelyn Waugh, *Ronald Knox*, pp. 265–6.
6. John A. O'Brien (ed.), *The Road to Damascus*, London, 1949, p. 11.
7. *Life*, 8 April 1946.
8. Charlotte Mosley (ed.), *The Letters of Nancy Mitford and Evelyn Waugh*, London, 1996, p. 4.
9. Andrew A. Tadie and Michael H. Macdonald (eds.), *Permanent Things*, Grand Rapids, Michigan, 1995, p. 63.
10. Mark Amory (ed.), *The Letters of Evelyn Waugh*, p. 207.
11. W. H. Lewis (ed.), *Letters of C. S. Lewis*, London, revised pb edn., 1988, p. 381.
12. Walter Hooper, interview with the author, Oxford, 20 August 1996.
13. Roger Lancelyn Green and Walter Hooper, *C. S. Lewis: A Biography*, p. 178.
14. ibid., p. 179.
15. Peter Ackroyd, *T. S. Eliot*, London, 1984, pp. 272–3.
16. Wilfrid Sheed, *Clare Boothe Luce*, London, 1982, p. 113.
17. Matthew Hoehn, OSB (ed.), *Catholic Authors: Contemporary Biographical Sketches*, 1948 edn., p. 442.
18. Mark Amory (ed.), *The Letters of Evelyn Waugh*, p. 288.
19. Peter Stanford, *Lord Longford: An Authorised Life*, London, 1994, p. 198.
20. Matthew Hoehn, OSB (ed.), *Catholic Authors: Contemporary Biographical Sketches*, 1952 edn., p. 524.
21. John A. O'Brien (ed.), *The Road to Damascus*, p. 216.
22. ibid., p. 213.
23. ibid., p. 221.
24. Mark Amory (ed.), *The Letters of Evelyn Waugh*, pp. 244–5.
25. ibid., p. 248.
26. ibid., p. 250.
27. ibid., pp. 252–3.
28. ibid., p. 257.
29. ibid., pp. 271–2.
30. Douglas Hyde, *I Believed*, London, 1951, pp. 282–3.
31. ibid., p. 283.
32. ibid., pp. 185–6.
33. ibid., p. 192.
34. ibid., p. 193.
35. ibid., p. 194.
36. ibid., pp. 194–5.
37. ibid., p. 227.

38. ibid., p. 228.
39. ibid., p. 228.
40. ibid., pp. 248–50.
41. ibid., pp. 231–2.
42. ibid., p. 232.
43. ibid., p. 233.
44. ibid., p. 252.
45. ibid., p. 261.
46. ibid., p. 263.
47. ibid., p. 264.
48. ibid., p. 265.
49. ibid., pp. 293–4.
50. John A. O'Brien (ed.), *The Road to Damascus*, p. 186.
51. Matthew Hoehn, OSB (ed.), *Catholic Authors: Contemporary Biographical Sketches*, 1952 edn., p. 260.
52. Douglas Hyde, letter to the author, 13 August 1996.

CHAPTER TWENTY

CULTIVATING CULTURE

On 17 October 1946 an article in *The Listener* claimed that Chesterton was dated. The article infuriated C. S. Lewis who rushed to his mentor's defence in the issue of *Time and Tide* for 9 November. A writer could be dated in a negative sense, Lewis wrote, when he composed poems in the shapes of altars and crosses simply because it was the voguish thing to do; such poetry quickly passed out of fashion. Yet a writer could also be dated in a positive sense when he wrote of 'matters of permanent interest' in the language of his particular age. '*The Prelude* smells of its age. *The Waste Land* has twenties stamped on every line. Even Isaiah will reveal to a careful student that it was not composed at the court of Louis XIV nor in modern Chicago.' Chesterton wrote in the language of his day but he remained as relevant as ever.

Lewis cited the example of *The Ballad of the White Horse* as evidence of the permanent value of Chesterton's work, but perhaps the best illustration of the relevance of Chesterton to the post-war world, which belied any suggestion that what he had to say was 'dated', was the speech he made in the Great Hall of University College, London, on 28 June 1927. Speaking on 'Culture and the Coming Peril', his words had become more relevant than ever by 1946:

> you will hear a vast amount about the danger of Bolshevism. When I talk about the coming peril a very large number of people will probably imagine that I do mean Bolshevism. I quite agree that Bolshevism would be a peril, but I do not think it is coming. I do not think that, especially in England, we have either the virtues or the vices of a revolution. The kind of thing that I want to suggest to you is something that is coming of itself ... I suppose that the very simplest name for it is 'vulgarity' ... I do not know whether it would be safe in such a connection to whisper the word 'America', now by far the wealthiest of States and, in the degraded conditions of our day, therefore the most influential.[1]

Having defined what exactly he meant by 'vulgarity and its war against Culture', he returned to the crux of the matter: 'To put it shortly, the evil I am trying to warn you of is not excessive democracy, it is not excessive ugliness, it is not excessive anarchy. It might be stated thus: It is standardisation by a low standard.'[2] This, he maintained, was 'the chief danger confronting us on the artistic and cultural side and generally on the intellectual side at this moment'. Whereas the 'social remedies' to this danger were political the 'deeper remedies' were theological.

It was this aspect of Chesterton, his defence of culture and civilization in the face of uncultured vulgarity, which lay at the centre of Lewis's admiration for his work. Indeed, the idea that the 'deeper remedies' were theological was at the centre of Lewis's own work. It was also at the centre of Dorothy L. Sayers's writing during the war and was the reason behind Eliot's claim that Chesterton 'leaves behind a permanent claim upon our loyalty, to see that the work that he did in his time is continued in ours'.[3]

In 1944 Sayers had discussed the deeper theological remedies in an address on the Christian aesthetic which found 'its source and sanction in the theological centre'.

'I am to speak to you tonight,' Sayers began, 'about the Arts in this country – their roots in Christianity, their present condition, and the means by which (if we find that they are not flourishing as they should) their mutilated limbs and withering branches may be restored by re-grafting into the main trunk of Christian tradition.'[4] It was the desire to cultivate culture in the post-war desert that inspired Sayers to embark upon her translation of Dante.

Prompted to re-read the *Divine Comedy* after reading Charles Williams's *The Figure of Beatrice*, published in 1943, Sayers removed a copy of the *Inferno* from the shelf during an air-raid in August 1944 and took it to the shelter with her. The next few hours changed the course of her life. Inspired by the depth and permanence of Dante she resolved to work on a new English translation. Soon she was so engrossed in this mammoth project that she wrote to a clergyman who had requested she write one of her Christian plays for his cathedral 'that she really hadn't time because she was translating Dante'. The clergyman replied that 'lots of people translate Dante, you have this unique talent for writing plays of this kind.' Sayers replied that 'many people have translated Dante but who reads their translations?'[5] According to Barbara Reynolds, Sayers 'saw this job of interpreting Dante's view of the world, of human behaviour, of salvation and so on, as ... part of her social concern to educate people's minds in readiness for social reconstruction after the war.'[6]

For Sayers, as for Dante, the possibilities and practicalities of social reconstruction were rooted in theology: 'As an intellectual study it was something that she had read pretty widely ... In her writings on the Christian faith, on social concerns and on human behaviour, she had taken a line which was very similar to the allegory of Dante. And when she came upon Dante she found there, writ large by a master hand, what she herself had been trying to say to people.'[7]

Sayers believed that Dante still spoke with a power capable of changing individuals and therefore society. This appears to be borne out by the profound influence of Dante's *Divine Comedy* on many of the century's converts to Christianity. Eliot, Lewis, Chesterton and Baring all professed a major debt to Dante, who spoke to them across the abyss of six centuries in a language of permanent relevance.

For the next twelve years until her death in 1957 Sayers worked on her translation of Dante with what Barbara Reynolds has called a 'passionate intellect'. At the time of her death she had finished the *Inferno* and *Purgatorio* but her translation of *Paradiso* was still uncompleted. The task of completing the work was left to Reynolds: 'She had done twenty cantos, no commentary, no introduction, but she had tried a few little bits in advance of the remaining thirteen cantos which I worked into my translation. So I did thirteen cantos and the introduction and the notes.'[8]

Speaking nearly forty years after her friend's death, Reynolds finds much to praise in Sayers's translation: 'I think there are parts of her *Purgatorio* especially, some parts of *Inferno*, which are better than anybody's ... She wasn't satisfied with all the *Inferno* but she achieved a greater mastery, greater control of what she was doing. *Purgatorio* has some of the best and most lucid renderings of some of the difficult passages'.[9]

In the four decades since its publication, Sayers's translation has enjoyed considerable popular success and will probably be seen by posterity as her greatest achievement. Her translation of *Inferno*, starkly entitled *Hell*, was so successful upon its initial publication in November 1949 that the whole of the first impression, a total of fifty thousand copies, was sold out within three months. Reynolds believes that ordinary readers have been introduced to Dante in a far more comprehensible way through Sayers's translation: 'She has presented Dante in a clearer way as never before'.[10]

The same desire to cultivate culture through literary translation animated Knox's herculean efforts to translate the Bible from the Vulgate Latin into a 'timeless English'. As with Sayers's translation of Dante, Knox's translation of the Bible was a labour of love which consumed the last years of his life. His translation of the New Testament was finally published in October 1945, six years after it had been begun, with a foreword by Cardinal Griffin: 'Not the least happy circumstance connected with the publication of this translation is that it has received the official recognition of the Hierarchy of England and Wales in the year when we are celebrating the centenary of the reception into the Church of ... John Henry Newman.'[11] Evelyn Waugh observed that Knox's translation soon 'won the hearts and minds of a yearly increasing number of English-speaking Catholics far beyond the dominions of the English and Welsh hierarchy'.[12]

Having completed the New Testament Knox began the even more daunting task of translating the Old Testament from the Latin. Explaining the work he was doing, Knox wrote in the *Universe* that his aim was to 'produce a translation in English (not colloquial but literary English) which is current today, and at the same time to avoid words and turns of phrase which were not equally current in the seventeenth century. The idea is that you want a kind of timeless English.'

His translation of the Old Testament was published on 14 November 1955, ten years after the appearance of his New Testament. A luncheon was given in honour of the occasion at which Cardinal Griffin presided. Knox gave a speech to the two hundred dignitaries, clerical and lay, Catholic and Anglican, in attendance, during which he endeavoured to put his achievement into a wider historical context:

> According to a reviewer in *The Times Literary Supplement*, a translation of the Bible gets dated in fifty years. Will somebody suggest, fifty years hence, 'It is time that the Knox Bible was revised, and brought up to date?' Then, oh, then, gentlemen, I have a charge to leave with you. If any such suggestion is made, then let the youngest person who is present today rise in his bath-chair and cry out, 'No! The whole point and protest of the Knox Bible was that it is a mistake, this continual revising and refurbishing of existing Scripture translations, this continual cutting down of father's pants to fit Willie. To revise the Knox Bible would be a treachery to the memory of its translator. If it is dated, then let it be scrapped; let somebody else sit down and undertake the whole task afresh, in a style of his own, and with a treatment of his own; let him give us, not a pale rehash of the Knox Bible, but a new Bible, and a better!'[13]

In hindsight, these comments appear to lack in humility what they do not lack in humour. Many were less than enthusiastic about his translation. Father Martindale was openly critical and even Waugh, normally Knox's greatest literary ally, had his reservations. Mercifully perhaps, Knox died less than two years after this speech was delivered and did not live to see his version eclipsed by two later translations – the Revised Standard Version and the Jerusalem Bible, translated by the Dominicans straight from the ancient texts. For a short while, however, his Bible enjoyed considerable popularity, his New Testament alone earning the Catholic Hierarchy about fifty thousand pounds in the twelve years following publication.

Writing of Maurice Baring shortly after his death in 1945, Knox could equally have been writing about himself: 'The truth is, I think, that he took an exceptional delight in *translation*; in the delicate shades of difference which manifest themselves when the same idea is perfectly expressed first in one language and then in another.'[14] Baring was conversant in six modern languages, besides Latin and Greek, and, like Sayers and Knox, devoted the last years of his life to translation. However, as he was debilitatingly ill with Parkinson's disease, he was not able to emulate the immensity of their efforts. Instead, his more modest achievement included translations in verse from the German of Goethe and the Russian of Tolstoy, Pushkin and Lermontov. Knox wrote of Baring that his 'nature was one which constantly absorbed, as it constantly exuded, something which (for want of a less abused word) you can only label "culture".'[15] In his rendering into English of these German and Russian classics Baring had bequeathed some of his culture to future generations.

Contemporaneous with these translations by Sayers, Knox and Baring, Roy Campbell was working on his translation of the poems of St John of the Cross from the Spanish, a task he began in 1939 but did not complete until 1950. They were published in June 1951 to immediate critical acclaim. A reviewer in the *Times Literary Supplement* on 15 June considered that 'the translations from St John of the Cross are ... among the most pure and lucid of English mystical poems.' Edwin Muir, writing in the *Observer* on 2 June, called the work 'a triumph', and Kathleen Raine's review in the *New Statesman* on 16 June reflected the positive response of most other reviewers: 'Of all living English poets Roy Campbell is the most masterly in his use of rhyme, and he is able to use metre so as to convey a sense of intense passion.'

The Poems of St John of the Cross quickly outsold any of Campbell's previous works and it earned him the Foyle Prize for Poetry in January of the following year. Campbell claimed that his writing of the book had been inspired directly by the saint himself: 'Were I superstitious I should say that San Juan brought me luck. Not being superstitious, I say that he wrought a miracle.'[16]

Campbell was a larger-than-life character, both in terms of physique and personality, and, in the words of the literary critic Russell Kirk, was 'full of cheerfulness and beer'. Commenting on the war wounds Campbell had suffered in both the Spanish Civil War and in the Ogaden campaign of the King's African Rifles, Kirk observed that 'his back was a mass of scar tissue, and he had a length

of plastic instead of a bone in one leg, but his tremendous body seemed indestructible'.[17] When Evelyn Waugh dined with Campbell in May 1952 he
described him as 'a great boastful simple sweet natured savage', informing
Nancy Mitford that 'I feel quite dizzy from his talking to me'.[18]

Campbell's brash and cavalier Catholicism, overlaid with latin machismo,
stood in stark contrast to the effete faith of Edward Sackville-West who had been
received into the Church in 1949. In an earlier letter to Nancy Mitford, Waugh
had described Sackville-West as 'very elegant, and except for pimples, pretty'.[19]
A blue-blooded aristocrat descended from Thomas, first Earl of Dorset, Lord
High Treasurer and cousin of Queen Elizabeth I, Sackville-West had passed
through a period of decadence influenced by Huysmans in his youth before
becoming an Anglo-Catholic. Reading Newman's *Apologia* as an eighteen-year-
old in March 1920 he found himself attracted to the Catholic Church but did not
succumb to its charms for nearly thirty years. In the meantime he lost his Christian faith completely. Embarking on a literary career, he contributed to the *Spectator* and in 1926 joined the staff of the *New Statesman* as assistant to the literary
editor, Desmond MacCarthy. His first novel, *Piano Quintet*, was published in
1925 and his second, *The Ruin*, in 1926. Three more novels, *Mandrake Over the
Water-Carrier*, *Simpson* and *The Sun in Capricorn* appeared in 1928, 1931 and
1934 respectively. A critical biography of Thomas de Quincey, *A Flame in Sun-
light*, followed in 1936. During the Second World War he was employed in the
Features and Drama section of the BBC, being responsible for the bulk of the
poetry broadcasts. During this period he wrote *The Rescue*, a poetic drama based
on the *Odyssey*, written especially for radio with an elaborate orchestral score by
Benjamin Britten.

Sackville-West's final approach to conversion was helped considerably by Evelyn Waugh and indirectly by Graham Greene. On 19 June 1948 Waugh wrote to
Sackville-West praising him for his review of Greene's *The Heart of the Matter*:

> We agree in thinking the book excellent story-telling. Also in suppos-
> ing that Graham Greene took 'Scobie' for a kind of saint. I have had a
> letter from Greene … saying we entirely misunderstand him in that he
> wished to show nothing but deep spiritual confusion.
>
> But apart from this we disagree very much about the book. In your
> first paragraph you express doubt about the efficacy of repentance and
> that, surely, makes the book, or any Christian book, radically unintelli-
> gable [sic] to you?
>
> Cruelty does not necessarily injure the victim. All the martyrs
> prove this.[20]

Sackville-West replied on 29 June to say that on reflection he agreed with Waugh's remarks about the efficacy of repentance but thought his instancing of the martyrs 'most disingenuous': 'The vast majority of sufferers from cruelty and persecution have not the self-immolating temperament common to all martyrs. Any ordinary person is rendered morally worse, not better, by unkind treatment. However, I realise that, theologically speaking, your position is unassailable.'[21]

The letter continued with a discussion of mortal sin and love, and concluded with Sackville-West distancing himself from the Catholic position:

> If Catholics will write novels drenched in Catholicism (which is of course quite natural) and then *publish* them, they must expect to be read and criticised from a non-Catholic point of view. If they don't like this, they should print privately for fellow Catholics ... *The Heart of the Matter* remains a very moving book, however you understand it. To a naturally religious, but not necessarily Catholic, mind such as mine Scobie appears a kind of saint.[22]

According to Michael de-la-Noy, Sackville-West's biographer, 'Eddy's distancing of himself in this letter from the Catholic point of view, never mind the Catholic Church, was a minor miracle of self-deception; within a year he was receiving instruction'.[23] One wonders, however, to what extent Waugh's reply on 2 July influenced his change of heart:

> Of course you are at the heart of the matter when you ask what right Catholic authors have to try to interest non-Catholic readers in their work. The real answer, which must sound pretentious nonsense to anyone outside the Church, is that the Church is not, except by accident, a little club with its own specialised vocabulary, but the normal state of man from which men have disastrously exiled themselves.[24]

It was while reading George Orwell's newly published novel, *Nineteen Eighty-Four*, some time during the following year, that Sackville-West made the final decision to become a Catholic. Orwell's novel had convinced him the 'the Devil's agents, recently associated with the conquered Nazis, were still very much with us' and that it was 'high time to declare myself – to take the side of Christ against the gospel of materialism'.[25] He contacted the only priest he knew, Father Martin D'Arcy, then attached to the Jesuit church in Farm Street, who suggested he call at the Jesuit parish church in Bournemouth where he commenced instruction. On 5 August 1949 he informed Waugh of developments:

> In view of the letters we exchanged a year ago, it may be of some dim interest to you to know that I am 'receiving instruction' preparatory to being (I hope) received into the Catholic Church. It has taken me just twelve years – a long time – to reach this point, and I am thankful to have got there at last.[26]

Waugh replied the following day:

> How very nice of you to write and tell me your great good news. It is not a matter of 'dim interest' but of intense delight, but not at all of surprise, for it always seems to me the natural and inevitable thing for anyone to become a Catholic and the constant surprise is that everyone does not. Conversion is like stepping across the chimney piece out of a Looking-glass-World, where everything is an absurd caricature, into the real world God made; and then begins the delicious process of exploring it limitlessly.[27]

Sackville-West was received on 17 August by Father Hubert McEvoy. As a gift to celebrate the occasion, Waugh sent him Knox's *The Mass in Slow Motion*. 'Best news of the week Eddy West's reception into the Church,' Waugh wrote in a letter to Nancy Mitford. 'No surprise to me. I knew he was under instruction and I can never understand why everyone is not a Catholic, but I feel deep joy all the same.'[28] If Waugh was not surprised, most of Sackville-West's unsuspecting friends were dumbstruck. Nancy Mitford's own uncomprehending and superficial response was that 'it must be like a lovely new love affair'.[29]

On the same day that Waugh was writing to Nancy Mitford expressing 'deep joy' over the reception into the Church of Edward Sackville-West, he was writing to Thomas Merton, an American Cistercian monk, to 'make one or two technical criticisms' of *The Waters of Siloe*, Merton's latest book:

> I have nothing but admiration for the narrative passages, except that there is no consistency of style. Sometimes you write literary English and sometimes slang.
>
> ... And in the non-narrative passages, do you not think you tend to be diffuse, saying the same thing more than once. I noticed this in *The Seven Storey Mountain* and the fault persists ... It is not art. Your

monastery tailor and boot-maker would not waste material. Words are our materials. Also it encourages vice in readers. They will not trouble to study a sentence for its proper meaning if they have learned to expect much the same thing to be said again later on.[30]

Merton replied: 'Your comments on the structure of *Waters* are true ... In any case I am glad to get such valuable and stimulating direction, and from one so marvellously qualified to give it.'[31]

Waugh edited and wrote a foreword for the British edition of Merton's book which appeared in 1950 as *The Waters of Silence*. Earlier he had edited Merton's *The Seven Storey Mountain*, an autobiographical account of the author's conversion, which became a best-seller on both sides of the Atlantic after its publication in 1949. Waugh described it as 'a book which may well prove to be of permanent interest in the history of religious experience' and Graham Greene considered it 'a rare pleasure to read an autobiography with a pattern and meaning valid for all of us'.

Merton had been received into the Church in 1938 after what Waugh described as 'a disorderly youth' during which he had been much influenced by Waugh's novels and the poetry of Eliot and Gerard Manley Hopkins. The process of transformation from 'disorderly youth' to the contemplative life in a Trappist monastery in Kentucky was documented in *The Seven Storey Mountain*. Merton's British publisher had given Waugh the 'enthralling task of cutting the redundancies and solecisms'[32] out of the American edition with the aim of making it more suitable for the British market. Although Waugh claimed in his foreword to the British edition, which was renamed *Elected Silence*, that 'nothing has been cut out except certain passages which seem to be of purely local interest' and that it had been only 'very slightly abridged in order to adapt it to European tastes', he had in fact cut about one third and had rewritten much of what remained.

The combination of Waugh's stylistic dexterity with Merton's spiritual depth proved a winning formula and *Elected Silence* became almost as popular in England as the unexpurgated version had been in the United States.

The extent to which Waugh admired Merton's book is evident in the foreword he wrote, in which he seems to see in Merton's rejection of modern materialism a model which he hoped the author's fellow countrymen would emulate:

Here in fresh, simple, colloquial American is the record of a soul experiencing, first, disgust with the modern world, then Faith, then a clear vocation to the way in which Faith may be applied to the modern world ... *The Seven Storey Mountain* came as a startling revelation to most non-Catholic Americans who were quite unaware of the existence in their midst of institutions which seemed a denial of the American 'way of life'. The book suddenly made remote people conscious of warmth silently generated in these furnaces of devotion. To one observer at least it seems probable that the USA will shortly be the scene of a great monastic revival. There is an ascetic tradition deep in the American heart which has sometimes taken odd and unlovable forms. Here in the historic Rules of the Church lies its proper fulfilment.

In the natural order the modern world is rapidly being made uninhabitable by the scientists and politicians ... As in the Dark Ages the cloister offers the sanest and most civilized way of life.

And in the supernatural order the times require more than a tepid and dutiful piety. Prayer must become heroic. That is the theme of this book which should take its place among the classic records of spiritual experience.[33]

In between his editing of *The Seven Storey Mountain* in August 1948 and his editing of Merton's second book, *The Waters of Siloe*, a year later, Waugh visited Merton at his Kentucky monastery during a visit to America. During this visit in November 1948 he also met other prominent Catholic converts. He dined with the beautiful, rich and powerful Clare Boothe Luce, eating caviar and 'dover soles flown that day from England' and, at the other end of the spiritual spectrum, he met Dorothy Day, leading member of the Catholic Labour Movement and co-founder of the *Catholic Worker*, describing her as 'an autocratic ascetic saint who wants us all to be poor'.[34]

Waugh returned to the United States at the end of January 1949 for a short lecture tour on the subject of 'Three Vital Writers: Chesterton, Knox and Greene'. His arrival was accompanied by the same blaze of publicity which had accompanied Chesterton's arrival on similar lecture tours two decades earlier. Publicity was aroused further by the controversy over Greene's novel *The Heart of the Matter*, a work which Waugh addressed directly in his talks, and inflamed further still by casual remarks he made during an interview in which he criticized certain aspects of the American 'way of life', saying that 'Americans heat their rooms to 75 degrees, nail down the windows, chew coloured bubble gum, keep their radios on all day and talk too much'.[35] Waugh's words were taken out of context, being intended only as a means of contrasting the artificial life in secular society with the tranquillity of the Trappist monastery in Kentucky. These negative comments overshadowed the positive intention of his visit which was to put America's 'leadership of the "West"' into its spiritual and cultural context:

> The 'West' is incomprehensible unless one understands the CHURCH
> – which is identical everywhere: a single supernatural body. Great
> diversity, however, exists in this essential uniformity ... English
> Catholicism is the natural bridge of understanding between American
> and European Catholicism. The particular character of the CHURCH
> in England can best be illustrated by examining the lives and work of
> three eminent Catholic writers ... Chesterton who came from non-
> conformity and 'Merrie Englandism' ... Knox, the fine flower of auto-
> cratic classical culture, who came by way of High Anglicanism ...
> Greene, the modern par excellence, who came by way of despair and
> doubt ...[36]

Waugh's belief that the 'West' was incomprehensible unless one understood its religious foundations had been central to Eliot's *Notes Towards the Definition of Culture* published the previous year. In fact, Eliot had put the whole issue succinctly in an interview in *John O'London's Weekly* on 19 August 1949. Asked why religion was an inseparable part of his thought, Eliot had replied: 'Why has an elephant four legs? Religion is the most important element in life and it is in the light of religion that one understands anything.'

This pithy riposte could have served as the epigraph for his book on the definition of culture, the core and recurrent feature of which was his assertion that the flowering of culture was dependent upon its religious roots:

> We have already found that the culture of a nation prospers with the
> prosperity of the culture of its several constituents, both geographical
> and social; but that it also needs to be itself a part of a larger culture,
> which requires the ultimate ideal, however unrealisable, of a 'world
> culture' in a sense different from that implicit in the schemes of world-
> federationalists. And without a common faith, all efforts towards
> drawing nations closer together in culture can produce only an illusion
> of unity.[37]

Eliot added as an appendix to his *Notes Towards the Definition of Culture* the translated text of three broadcast talks to Germany which had been published in 1946 under the title of *Die Einheit der Europäischen Kultur*:

The dominant force in creating a common culture between peoples each of which has its distinct culture, is religion ... I am talking about the common tradition of Christianity which has made Europe what it is, and about the common cultural elements which this common Christianity has brought with it ... It is in Christianity that our arts have developed; it is in Christianity that the laws of Europe have – until recently – been rooted. It is against a background of Christianity that all our thought has significance.[38]

Even if an individual European did not believe that the Christian faith was true, Eliot argued, 'what he says, and makes, and does, will all spring out of his heritage of Christian culture and depend upon that culture for its meaning'. Only a Christian culture could have produced a Voltaire or a Nietzsche.

To our Christian heritage we owe many things beside religious faith. Through it we trace the evolution of our arts, through it we have our conception of Roman Law which has done so much to shape the Western World, through it we have our conceptions of private and public morality. And through it we have our common standards of literature, in the literatures of Greece and Rome. The Western world has its unity in this heritage, in Christianity and in the ancient civilisations of Greece, Rome and Israel, from which, owing to two thousand years of Christianity, we trace our descent.[39]

The unity which springs from these common religious roots was very different, Eliot insisted, from the 'unity' sought by the economic determinists:

this unity in the common elements of culture, throughout many centuries, is the true bond between us. No political and economic organisation, however much goodwill it commands, can supply what this culture unity gives. If we dissipate or throw away our common patrimony of culture, then all the organisation and planning of the most ingenious minds will not help us, or bring us closer together.[40]

Far from being a force for unity, Eliot argued that politics and economics divorced from faith and culture were worse than merely futile. They were fatal. This aspect of *Notes Towards the Definition of Culture* was discussed with force and lucidity by Russell Kirk in his study of *Eliot and His Age*:

The spectre of a colossal planned boredom – classless, faithless, frontierless, rootless, deprived of poetry, of historical consciousness, of imagination, and even of emotion; a Waste Land governed, if governable at all, by an 'elite' of dull positivists and behaviorists and technicians, knowing no standards or aspirations but those of their own narrow trade; a world utterly impoverished in spirit, and therefore soon to be impoverished in flesh – this apparition stalks through the calm admonitory pages of *Notes*.[41]

It was the same nightmare vision of a soulless future evoked by Orwell's waste land in *Nineteen Eighty-Four*; the lines whose import Chesterton had for once imperfectly grasped in his parody, the final triumph of the Hollow Men who, knowing the price of everything and the value of nothing, had lost the ability to *feel* or *think* deeply about anything.

This is the way the world ends
This is the way the world ends
This is the way the world ends
Not with a bang but a whimper.

In his ruthlessly reasoned analysis of the dangers threatening European civilization, Eliot seldom allowed the tone of calm admonition to give way to more potent and polemical poetic imagery. The exceptions, however, were memorable as, for instance, when he attacked modern education policies which were 'destroying our ancient edifices to make ready the ground upon which the barbarian nomads of the future will encamp in their mechanized caravans'. Discussing the same issue in more sober fashion he stated that universities were for the cultivation of culture and not for Economic Man to learn the tricks of the trade: 'The universities of Europe ... should not be institutions for the training of an efficient bureaucracy, or for equipping scientists to get the better of foreign scientists; they should stand for the preservation of learning, for the pursuit of truth, and in so far as men are capable of it, the attainment of wisdom.'[42]

Eliot's 'last appeal' in his *Notes Towards the Definition of Culture*

is to the men of letters of Europe, who have a special responsibility for the preservation and transmission of our common culture ... we can at least try to save something of those goods of which we are the common trustees; the legacy of Greece, Rome and Israel, and the legacy of Europe throughout 2,000 years. In a world which has seen such material devastation as ours, these spiritual possessions are also in imminent peril.[43]

It was an appeal which would have met with an enthusiastic response from Sayers, Knox and Campbell, all of whom were making superlative efforts in the post-war years to cultivate the common culture of Christendom.

NOTES

1. G. K. Chesterton, *Culture and the Coming Peril*, London, 1927, pp. 8–9.
2. ibid., p. 16.
3. *Tablet*, 20 June 1936.
4. Dorothy L. Sayers, *Unpopular Opinions*, London, 1946, p. 29.
5. Dr Barbara Reynolds, interview with the author, Cambridge, 19 September 1996.
6. ibid.
7. ibid.
8. ibid.
9. ibid.
10. ibid.
11. Evelyn Waugh, *Ronald Knox*, p. 264.
12. ibid., p. 264.
13. *Tablet*, 19 November 1955.
14. Laura Lovat (ed.), *Maurice Baring: A Postscript*, London, 1947, p. 112.
15. ibid., p. 109.
16. Peter Alexander, *Roy Campbell: A Critical Biography*, Oxford, 1982, p. 221.
17. Russell Kirk, *Eliot and His Age*, New York, 1971, p. 374.
18. Mark Amory (ed.), *The Letters of Evelyn Waugh*, p. 373.
19. ibid., p. 326.
20. Michael de-la-Noy, *Eddy: The Life of Edward Sackville-West*, London, 1988, p. 229.
21. ibid., p. 230.
22. ibid., p. 230.
23. ibid., p. 230.
24. ibid., p. 231.
25. ibid., p. 237.
26. ibid., p. 237.
27. ibid., pp. 237–8.
28. Mark Amory (ed.), *The Letters of Evelyn Waugh*, p. 307.
29. Michael de-la-Noy, *Eddy: The Life of Edward Sackville-West*, p. 238.
30. Mark Amory (ed.), *The Letters of Evelyn Waugh*, p. 308.
31. ibid., p. 309.
32. Michael Davie (ed.), *The Diaries of Evelyn Waugh*, p. 700.
33. Thomas Merton, *Elected Silence*, London, 1949, foreword.
34. Mark Amory (ed.), *The Letters of Evelyn Waugh*, pp. 288–90.
35. *Commonweal*, 11 March 1949.
36. Martin Stannard, *Evelyn Waugh: No Abiding City*, London, 1992, p. 235.
37. T. S. Eliot, *Notes Towards the Definition of Culture*, London, 1962 edn., p. 82.
38. ibid., p. 122.
39. ibid., pp. 122–3.
40. ibid., p. 123.
41. Russell Kirk, *Eliot and His Age*, p. 337.
42. T. S. Eliot, *Notes Towards the Definition of Culture*, p. 123.
43. ibid., pp. 123–4.

CHAPTER TWENTY ONE

A NETWORK OF MINDS

In the Preface to the first edition of his *Notes Towards the Definition of Culture*, written in January 1948, T. S. Eliot expressed 'a particular debt' to Christopher Dawson. The following year, Dawson wrote of Eliot's *Notes* that 'when Mr Eliot comes forward in defence of culture, his first task is to rescue the word from the bad company into which it has fallen, to define its proper limits and to restore its intellectual respectability and integrity'.[1] Dawson concluded his essay on 'T. S. Eliot on the Meaning of Culture' with the ominous observation that the

> planners of modern society ... have come to exercise a more complete control over the thought and life of the whole population than the most autocratic and authoritarian powers of the past ever possessed. In this situation the work of men like Mr T. S. Eliot who are able to meet the planners and sociologists on their own ground without losing sight of the real spiritual issues may be of decisive importance for the future of our culture.[2]

It is clear that Dawson and Eliot were kindred spirits, each respecting and admiring the other's work, but Sister Juliana, Dawson's daughter, recalled that 'they were both very reserved',[3] a fact which impeded the development of their friendship. Although Eliot did pay at least one social visit to the Dawson home at Boar's Hill, Oxford during the war, Christina Scott, Dawson's other daughter, remembered that 'their relationship was more on the intellectual level than the social' adding that 'Eliot admired Dawson's work and once said he was the most important intellectual influence in Britain at the time.'[4]

Eliot's view was corroborated in a survey conducted by the publishers Sheed & Ward in 1947 which showed that Dawson was being recommended to American readers 'more than any other European Catholic author of today'.[5] Earlier, Maisie Ward had written that 'the twofold relationship between religion and civilisation has been worked out more fully by Christopher Dawson than by any other historian of today. He has shown how religion has been in most societies at once the origin of culture and social custom and the dynamic that gives vitality to a society.'[6] This was a recurring theme in Dawson's work and the central theme of the Gifford Lectures which he delivered at Edinburgh University in 1947. When these were published the following year by Sheed & Ward under the title *Religion and Culture*, Dawson received an enthusiastic letter from C. S. Lewis:

> I embarked on it at once and indeed by greedily reading it at lunch and splashing it with gravy have already deprived the copy of some of its freshness. I have now finished it (for the first time). It was exactly what I wanted, going of course, far beyond my knowledge but often linking up with the little I do know – always the most exciting kind of reading, I think. It also was strangely 'corroborating' – I don't know quite how or why. So much for subjective reactions. What makes me feel that it must also be good (*simpliciter* as well as *mihi*) is that on the Humanists, where I am least out of my depth, it seems to me particularly sound. What a lot of error about them is still in circulation![7]

Lewis had been introduced to Dawson by their mutual friend, R. E. Havard, but as with the earlier meeting with Eliot, Dawson's shyness proved an obstacle. 'Dawson was a physically frail, shy, disappointed man,' Havard recalled, 'Lewis did his best to draw Dawson out; but he shrank from our vigorous humour and casual manners … the evening was a frost and it was not repeated.'[8]

Havard also remembered 'another frosty evening' when he and his wife had introduced Lewis to Elizabeth Anscombe, the distinguished philosopher and Roman Catholic, who was then a tutor of philosophy at Somerville College, Oxford, and would later become a highly distinguished Professor of Philosophy at Cambridge. According to Havard, Anscombe 'had perhaps the most acute intelligence of anyone at Oxford', adding that 'she out-argued Lewis'. 'Of course,' Lewis later confessed to Havard, 'she is far more intelligent than either of us.'[9]

Neither was this the only time that Lewis and Anscombe crossed swords. The most famous occasion was at a meeting of the Socratic Club on 2 February 1948 when Anscombe debated with Lewis on the subject of 'Miracles'. This was one of the very rare occasions when Lewis was seen to be defeated in open debate, a fact recounted by Derek Brewer, one of his pupils, who recorded Lewis's reaction in his diary entry two days after the event:

He was obviously deeply disturbed by his encounter last Monday with Miss Anscombe, who had disproved some of the central theory of his philosophy about Christianity. I felt quite painfully for him. Dyson said – very well – that now he had lost everything and was come to the foot of the Cross – spoken with great sympathy.[10]

Brewer recalled that Lewis had described the debate with Anscombe 'with real horror': 'His imagery was all of the fog of war, the retreat of infantry thrown back under heavy attack.'[11]

This defeat of Lewis at the hands of a philosopher and Catholic who appeared to be intellectually his superior, coupled with his deep admiration for the writings of Christopher Dawson, prompts an obvious question: To what extent had Lewis modified his view of the Roman Catholic Church by the end of the 1940s?

Lewis enjoyed the friendship of many Catholics, with Tolkien, Dom Bede Griffiths and R. E. Havard among his closest friends. When Havard introduced Lewis to Ronald Knox they 'both afterward expressed their delight with the other. Each was witty, humorous, very widely read; each had an unobtrusive but profound Christian faith. They had much to say to each other, and it was a pity that Monsignor Knox left Oxford and that they had few further opportunities to meet.'[12] Lewis even went so far as to describe Knox 'as possibly the wittiest man in Europe'.[13]

Lewis also struck up a friendship in the late 1940s with Don Giovanni Calabria, an Italian monk with whom he became engaged in a long correspondence stretching from 1947 until the monk's death in 1954. These letters, written in Latin because it was the only language they shared, serve both as a study in friendship and as an insight into Lewis's enigmatic and singular approach to Christianity. The correspondence had been initiated by Don Calabria who wrote to Lewis on 1 September 1947 concerning a 'great problem':

namely that of the dissenting brethren whose return to the unity of the Body of Christ, which is the Church, is most greatly desired.

... I candidly confess to you that from the first years of my priesthood I have turned my mind with all my strength to this great problem. And so I have begun to propagate the holding of an 'octave of prayers for the unity of the Church' from the 18th to the 25th of January. In one of the houses of our Congregation I have succeeded in obtaining from the diocesan Bishop permission for daylong adoration of the Sacrament, and the offering of public prayers for the sake of unity ...

But you also seem to me to be able to contribute much in the Lord, with your great influence not only in your own most noble country but even in other lands. How and by what means I leave to your prudence.[14]

Lewis replied on 6 September:

Be assured that for me too schism in the Body of Christ is both a source of grief and a matter for prayers, being a most serious stumbling block to those coming in and one which makes even the faithful weaker in repelling the common foe. However, I am a layman, indeed the most lay of laymen, and least skilled in the deeper questions of sacred theology. I have tried to do the only thing that I think myself able to do: that is, to leave completely aside the subtler questions about which the Roman Church and Protestants disagree among themselves – things which are to be treated of by bishops and learned men – and in my own books to expound, rather, those things which still, by God's grace, after so many sins and errors, are shared by us. Nor is this a pointless task; for I find that people are unaware how many matters we even now agree on ...[15]

Surprisingly, one of the 'many matters we even now agree on', in Lewis's view, was the unifying power of Latin: 'If only that plaguey "Renaissance" which the Humanists brought about had not *destroyed* Latin ... we should then still be able to correspond with the whole of Europe'.[16]

Of course, Lewis's belief that there was a 'highest common factor' which united all Christians was both a popular and a populist position. It was, however, not a very easy position to pinpoint. What exactly was the highest common factor?

For Don Calabria the position was absolutely clear. The highest common factor was the deposit of faith entrusted to the Catholic Church and handed down in continuity over two thousand years. His desire for unity was the return of all separated brethren to the one Mystical Body of Christ which was the Catholic Church. Ecumenism was translated as 'you-come-inism'.

As Lewis had no intention of 'coming in', being in Walter Hooper's words 'absolutely loyal to the Church of England',[17] his position was more complex. At a meeting of the Socratic Club in Oxford, Lewis had maintained that 'the core of Christian teaching has for centuries been preserved and handed down by the Church' and, as Hooper observed, 'considering his invariable practice of

receiving Communion on Sundays and major feasts, as well as his practice of frequent confession (generally weekly), I think one must conclude that he most
certainly believed "Institutional Christianity" to be necessary'.[18]

His position was, in fact, strikingly similar to that held by his friend Dorothy
L. Sayers. Barbara Reynolds speaks enthusiastically of Sayers's zealous approach
to promoting Christian unity:

> It is evident that in writing to William Temple and in writing to George
> Bell, who became Bishop of Chichester, she is urging the bringing
> together of what she calls the highest common factor of agreement in
> belief between the Catholics, some of the non-conformists, and the
> Church of England, and instead of saying this is what we disagree on,
> find out what we *agree* on ...[19]

When asked what Sayers considered the highest common factors uniting Christians, Reynolds remarked: 'Trinitarian and Incarnational. Those are the
absolutely indispensable fundamentals ... And the Sacraments, absolutely.'[20]

It was this belief that Sayers shared his fundamental beliefs in 'institutional
Christianity' which prompted Lewis to write to her on 13 July 1948 on the subject of female ordination:

> News has just reached me of a movement ... to demand that women
> should be allowed Priests' Orders. I am guessing that, like me, you dis-
> approve of something which would cut us off so sharply from all the
> rest of Christendom, and which would be the very triumph of what
> they call 'practical' and 'enlightened' principles over the far deeper need
> that the Priest at the Altar must represent the Bridegroom to whom we
> are all, in a sense, feminine. Well, if you do, really I think you will have
> to give tongue.[21]

Sayers's reply was a concoction of contradictions, simultaneously sympathetic
and antipathetic to Lewis's position, which seemed to illustrate the explosive
potential of an issue which was later to cause such turmoil in the Anglican
church:

> Obviously, nothing could be more silly and inexpedient than to erect a
> new and totally unnecessary barrier between us and the rest of Catholic
> Christendom. (It would be rather a link than otherwise with some of
> the Free Churches, as tending to emphasise a ministry of the Gospel

rather than a ministry of Sacraments and as involving a break with Apostolic tradition.)

I fear you would find me rather an uneasy ally. I can never find any logical or strictly theological reason against it. In so far as the Priest represents Christ, it is obviously more dramatically appropriate that a man should be, so to speak, cast for the part. But if I were cornered and asked point-blank whether Christ Himself is the representative of male humanity or all humanity, I should be obliged to answer 'of all humanity'; and to cite the authority of St Augustine for saying that woman is also made in the image of God ...'[22]

On another occasion, when Barbara Reynolds had asked her what she thought about the prospect of female ordination, Sayers had replied: 'Well, considering Our Lord had the wisdom to be born as a man at the time when he was on earth, I think probably the whole thing is left better as it is'.[23] In the course of her editing of Sayers's letters, Reynolds found further examples where she reiterated this view: 'Later I found other letters in which she has said definitely that ... when the churches are now showing signs of wanting to come together, this is something that will so alienate the Roman Catholic Church ... that this is not something that I would want to promote'.[24] This view was also expressed in her letter to Lewis, although it was coupled with an outright refusal to speak out on the issue: 'It would be a pity to fly in the face of all the Apostolic Churches, especially just now when we are at last seeing some prospect of understanding with the Eastern Orthodox, and so on ... The most I can do is to keep silence in any place where the daughters of the Philistines might overhear me.'[25]

For Lewis the silence was deafening, forcing him reluctantly to address the issue himself, and shortly after receiving the rebuff from Sayers he wrote an article entitled 'Priestesses in the Church?'. Unusually his arguments in this article were couched in an almost apologetic tone, due possibly to the fear of being accused of misogyny which was the root of his desire that a woman should have written the article. Perhaps Lewis had Sayers's reply in mind when he stressed that 'no one among those who dislike the proposal is maintaining that women are less capable than men of piety, zeal, learning and whatever else seems necessary for the pastoral office'.[26]

the common sensible reformer is apt to ask why, if women can preach, they cannot do all the rest of a priest's work. This question deepens the discomfort of my side. We begin to feel that what really divides us from our opponents is a difference between the meaning which they and we give to the word 'priest'.[27]

For Lewis the priesthood was not merely another 'job' but a mystical calling, sacramental in nature, which had been pre-ordained as a masculine function as motherhood had been pre-ordained as a feminine function. Motherhood was eternally feminine; priesthood was eternally masculine:

The innovators are really implying that sex is something superficial, irrelevant to the spiritual life. To say that men and women are equally eligible for a certain profession is to say that for the purposes of that profession their sex is irrelevant ... One of the ends for which sex was created was to symbolize to us the hidden things of God. One of the functions of human marriage is to express the nature of the union between Christ and the Church. We have no authority to take the living and seminal figures which God has painted on the canvas of our nature and shift them about as if they were mere geometrical figures.

This is what common sense will call 'mystical'. Exactly. The Church claims to be the bearer of revelation. If that claim is false then we want not to make priestesses but to abolish priests.[28]

The article concluded with the 'shadowland' imagery which was at the heart of so much of Lewis's writing and thought: 'With the Church ... we are dealing with male and female not merely as facts of nature but as the live and awful shadows of realities utterly beyond our control and largely beyond our direct knowledge. Or rather, we are not dealing with them but (as we shall soon learn if we meddle) they are dealing with us.'[29]

If Lewis's objections in principle to the ordination of women were seemingly lost on Dorothy L. Sayers, his practical objections were the same as those that she had readily expressed in her letter to him. Towards the beginning of his article, Lewis had written: 'to cut ourselves off from the Christian past and to widen the divisions between ourselves and other Churches by establishing an order of priestesses in our midst, would be an almost wanton degree of imprudence. And the Church of England herself would be torn in shreds by the operation.'[30]

Walter Hooper described these words as 'extraordinarily prophetic'[31] and it is certainly true that the issue has caused tremendous upheavals in the Anglican church, though whether these are growing pains or death pangs will be left for posterity to reveal.

Posterity, however, will not be able to reveal Lewis's reaction to the ordination of women. Mercifully perhaps, he died thirty years before his fears became reality, leaving the enigmatic loose ends of his position in suspended animation. Inevitably this has fuelled an intriguing though ultimately futile debate concerning where he would stand on such contentious issues 'were he alive today'.

Father Charles Smith, an Anglo-Catholic clergyman in the late 1940s and who became director of the Anglican shrine of Our Lady of Walsingham in the late 1960s before converting to Catholicism and being ordained shortly before his retirement in the 1980s, believed that Lewis was barred by ingrained prejudice from considering conversion himself: 'Lewis had a great influence on the "orthodoxing" of many Anglicans but I never thought that Lewis ever contemplated conversion because there was too much of the Northern Ireland protestatism in him. There was always this anti-Romanism.'[32]

In 1981 the Catholic writer Christopher Derrick, a pupil and friend of Lewis, wrote *C. S. Lewis and the Church of Rome*, a controversial book which analysed Lewis's complicated relationship with Catholicism. Fifteen years later, he was still speculating mischievously on how Lewis would have reacted to the victory of the 'modernists' in the Anglican church:

> There was a rumour that he had Poped or that he was a Jesuit in disguise ... literary men becoming Catholics had been a phenomenon, and Lewis's conversion did seem likely to some but ... I don't think he would have liked to have seen his own infallibility challenged by that of another Pope.
>
> ... it's difficult to imagine what he would make of today's Church of England. The Church of England is such a pathetic ghost nowadays ... You can't agree with it or disagree with it. There's nothing there.[33]

Derrick's cantankerous candour has earned him many critics, even among those who are largely sympathetic with his views. Commenting on *C. S. Lewis and the Church of Rome*, Walter Hooper commented that he found it 'an unpleasant book to read but there were many good points raised', adding that 'Derrick's apologetics sometimes sound bad-tempered'.[34] Like Christopher Derrick, Hooper was a close friend of Lewis and since Lewis's death has been his greatest literary champion. Hooper, however, added fuel to Derrick's speculations by his own conversion to Catholicism in 1988, largely over the issue of female ordination. Hooper had converted to Rome principally over the very issue which had caused his mentor so much distress forty years earlier; and Lewis's stand on the issue continued to cause controversy many years after his death, especially in

America where one of Hooper's lectures on Lewis was broken up on the orders of the local vicar's wife 'because of Lewis's stand on priestesses'.[35] Two other lectures had to be abandoned for the same reason. In contrast, Hooper was invited to Rome in 1984 for a private audience with the present Pope, the letter of invitation stating that 'the Holy Father would appreciate the opportunity to chat with you about C. S. Lewis'.[36] It is of course impossible to know whether Lewis would have found it necessary to take the same step as Walter Hooper in actually joining the Catholic Church 'were he alive today'. What is certain is that he would have found himself in a singularly curious position.

In 1948 these dilemmas facing the Anglican church had not reached their bitter fruition and Lewis and Sayers were able to show a united face on virtually all the other issues of the day. In between her work on the translation of Dante, Sayers continued to correspond with numerous people in her efforts to promote Christian reconstruction. 'Her letters are important,' says Barbara Reynolds. 'She was writing to so many people at the time that it seems to me that she was energising so many people's minds ... that she has left a legacy that we don't know about which is only apparent in the letters ... A network of minds energising each other.'[37]

For his part, Lewis warned that the alternative to Christian reconstruction would be an anti-cultural deconstruction, a demolition of civilization:

> though the 'right to happiness' is chiefly claimed for the sexual impulse, it seems to me impossible that the matter should stay there. The fatal principle, once allowed in that department, must sooner or later seep through our whole lives. We thus advance towards a state of society in which not only each man but every impulse in each man claims *carte blanche*. And then, though our technological skill may help us to survive a little longer, our civilisation will have died at heart, and will – one dare not even add 'unfortunately' – be swept away.[38]

The promotion of the 'right to happiness' in sexual matters as in other areas of life was a major theme in the writings of Bertrand Russell. Russell's *Human Knowledge* was published in 1948, a timely reminder that the network of minds energized by Sayers and Lewis were engaged in mortal conflict with their antimetaphysical counterparts. Both sides were represented in the spring of 1948 as contributors to a BBC series on *The Ideas and Beliefs of the Victorians*. Those who contributed talks for the series were Bertrand Russell, G. M. Trevelyan, Lord David Cecil and Christopher Dawson. Dawson spoke of the beliefs of early Victorian England as 'a strange compound of mutually inconsistent orthodoxies – the bleak rationalism of the Utilitarians and the narrow pietism of the Evangelicals'.[39]

Bertrand Russell crossed swords over the airwaves with another prominent Catholic convert during 1948 when he debated with Father F. C. Copleston on the BBC's Third Programme. 'The Existence of God: A Debate between Bertrand Russell and Father F. C. Copleston, S.J.' confirmed Russell's reputation as an articulate champion of the anti-Christian viewpoint, as well as enhancing the reputation of Copleston as a first-rate philosopher in his own right. The transcript of the debate was published nine years later in Russell's book, *Why I am Not a Christian and Other Essays*.

Christopher Dawson and F. C. Copleston were both key figures in the Catholic intellectual revival who exerted a far greater influence than their present-day reputations would suggest. Even their fields of study were similar, though distinct. Dawson was an authority on the philosophy of history whereas Copleston specialized in the history of philosophy. Copleston's greatest achievement was his monumental nine-part *History of Philosophy*, the first volume *Greece and Rome* appearing in 1946 and the final volume *Maine de Biran to Sartre* appearing in 1975. He was also the author of *Aquinas*, published in 1955, probably the best introduction to Thomist philosophy in the English language.

Even as Copleston was locked in philosophical combat with Bertrand Russell on the BBC, another famous philosopher of the airwaves was undergoing a profound change of outlook which would lead him out of Russell's camp and into Copleston's.

C. E. M. Joad had gained fame as a key figure on the BBC *Brains Trust*. As one of the first generation of 'radio stars' he owed his controversial reputation to a militant agnosticism and regular outspoken attacks on Christianity. As early as 1933 he had been involved in a controversial correspondence with Arnold Lunn, later published as *Is Christianity True?*, in which Lunn, soon to be received into the Catholic Church, had argued to the affirmative, and Joad had argued to the negative, dismissing Christianity as parochial. 'On the general question of parochialism,' Lunn countered, 'has it never occurred to you that ... many moderns who do not accept Christianity are wistfully conscious of the contrast between the coherence of Catholic philosophy and the confusion of all rival creeds?'[40]

To illustrate his point Lunn quoted J. H. Randall, an American critic of Catholicism who had none the less defended Catholic philosophy:

> Compared with it, all the successive philosophies that men have worked out since are mere ephemeral things of a day that have become

for us objects of mere historical interest. It is far superior to the fragmentary, inconsistent, self-contradictory views of modern scientists and philosophers ... In the face of the uncertainty and confusion, muddled thinking and contradictory ideas that abound in modernist circles, its tenets stand out with clarity and precision.[41]

'May I add that I too have been an agnostic,' Lunn continued, 'that I too was once impressed with many of the arguments which you employ, but that I ceased to be impressed by them when I began to study the philosophy and history of Christianity.'[42]

Perhaps Lunn was being more prophetically perceptive than he realized when he referred to Joad's agnosticism as a phase. Joad also passed through agnosticism but in his case the passing would take a lot longer. The first chinks in the armour of his unbelief became visible in 1942 when Joad confessed in a favourable review of Lewis's *The Screwtape Letters* that 'Mr Lewis possesses the rare gift of making righteousness readable.'[43]

Lewis played an important part in Joad's slow transition from agnosticism to Christianity. Lewis's *The Abolition of Man*, published in 1943, was particularly effective. According to Joad, *The Abolition of Man* 'played no small part in preparing my change of view and in precipitating the new outlook which it involved, while it was still, as it were, in solution. A passage in this book puts what I am trying here to express better than I can hope to do.

"For the wise man of old, the cardinal problem had been how to conform the soul to reality and the solution had been knowledge, self-discipline and virtue. For magic and applied science alike the problem is how to subdue reality to the wishes of men: the solution is a technique; and both, in the practice of the technique, are ready to do things hitherto regarded as disgusting and impious ..."[44]

At the same time that the books of Lewis were making such an indelible impression on Joad's questioning mind, the horrors of the Second World War convinced him of the all-pervading nature of evil. In 1943 this fundamental change in outlook led him to a theistic explanation of the universe, a change of heart and mind which he announced to a surprised public in his book, *God and Evil*. It was clear from this book that theism was only the transitory product of a changing mind and that it was unlikely to be the author's final resting place. Nine years later, influenced in the interim by the 'network of minds energising each other', he published *The Recovery of Belief* in which he stated his reasons for accepting the Christian faith.

For all his celebrated status, Joad's exposition of philosophical concepts, both before and after his conversion to Christianity, lacked both the incision and the precision of many of his contemporaries. Yet *The Recovery of Belief* still caused a minor sensation when it was published in 1952 and ensured that Joad, who died shortly afterwards in April of the following year, went out in a blaze of publicity as befitted a master self-publicist.

His obituary in *The Times* on 10 April 1953 emphasized the importance of his 'recovery':

> *The Recovery of Belief* is certainly the most interesting and important of his books. It is marked by a humility which contrasts notably with the intellectual arrogance of his earlier writing. It follows the arguments which led him from agnosticism to Christianity with a fearless honesty, and it equally fearlessly faces and rejects the claims of science as 'a stick to beat religion'. It concerns itself with the fundamental problems of the universe and human nature, about which he had previously been so superficial.

Possibly influenced by the fact that Lewis was an Anglican, Joad spent the last months of his life as a practising member of the Church of England. Like Lewis, however, he managed to raise issues which throw his position as an Anglican into question. Whereas Lewis championed the Catholic concept of priesthood, Joad questioned Anglican opposition to the Catholic dogma of the Assumption:

> At the moment of writing there is a great pother about the announcement of a new dogma by the Roman Catholic Church, the dogma of the physical resurrection and present existence in the body of the Virgin Mary. Clergymen of the Church of England complain of another and, as it seems to them, so gratuitous spoke placed by the Roman Catholics in the wheel of the reunion of the Christian Churches. Nevertheless, they (and I) affirm, in common with all other members of the Anglican Communion, our belief in the Resurrection of the Body. Sunday after Sunday as we do, I (but not they) wonder what all the fuss is about.[45]

NOTES

1. Christopher Dawson, *The Dynamics of World History*, London, 1957, p. 103.
2. ibid., p. 110.
3. Sister Juliana Dawson, interview with the author, Hengrave Hall, Suffolk, 9 December 1996.
4. Christina Scott, letter to the author, 24 February 1997.
5. Matthew Hoehn, OSB (ed.), *Catholic Authors: Contemporary Biographical Sketches 1930–1947*, p. 185.
6. Maisie Ward, *Insurrection versus Resurrection*, p. 358.
7. Christina Scott, *A Historian and His World: A Life of Christopher Dawson*, pp. 158–9.
8. James T. Como (ed.), *C. S. Lewis at the Breakfast Table*, London, 1980, p. 223.
9. ibid., p. 223.
10. ibid., p. 59.
11. ibid., p. 59.
12. ibid., p. 223.
13. ibid., p. 223.
14. C. S. Lewis and Don Giovanni Calabria, *Letters*, London, 1989, p. 29.
15. ibid., p. 31.
16. ibid., p. 35.
17. James T. Como (ed.), *C. S. Lewis at the Breakfast Table*, p. 147.
18. ibid., p. 147.
19. Barbara Reynolds, interview with the author, Cambridge, 19 September 1996.
20. ibid.
21. Barbara Reynolds, *Dorothy L. Sayers: Her Life and Soul*, p. 406.
22. ibid., pp. 406–7.
23. Barbara Reynolds, interview with the author, Cambridge, 19 September 1996.
24. ibid.
25. Barbara Reynolds, *Dorothy L. Sayers: Her Life and Soul*, p. 407.
26. C. S. Lewis, *God in the Dock*, London, 1979, p. 88.
27. ibid., p. 89.
28. ibid., pp. 91–2.
29. ibid., pp. 93–4.
30. ibid., p. 88.
31. James T. Como (ed.), *C. S. Lewis at the Breakfast Table*, p. 147.
33. Father Charles Smith, interview with the author, Oxford, 19 December 1996.
33. Christopher Derrick, interview with the author, Wallington, Surrey, September 1996.
34. Walter Hooper, interview with the author, Oxford, 20 August 1996.
35. Converts' Aid Society, *Annual Report for 1989*, p. 17.
36. ibid., p. 20.
37. Barbara Reynolds, interview with the author, Cambridge, 19 September 1996.
38. C. S. Lewis, *God in the Dock*, p. 108.
39. Christina Scott, *A Historian and His World: A Life of Christopher Dawson*, p. 159.
40. Arnold Lunn and C. E. M. Joad, *Is Christianity True?*, London, 1933, p. 327.
41. ibid., p. 327.
42. ibid., p. 328.
43. *New Statesman and Nation*, Vol. XXIII (16 May 1942), p. 324.
44. C. E. M. Joad, *The Recovery of Belief*, London, 1952, p. 81.
45. ibid., p. 22.

CHAPTER TWENTY TWO

MILITANTS IN PURSUIT OF TRUTH

Cyril Joad died at his Hampstead home on 9 April 1953 at the age of sixty-one. Three months later Hilaire Belloc died shortly before his eighty-third birthday. Had their births coincided as closely as their deaths they would have been sworn enemies for the greater part of their lives: militant agnostic versus militant defender of Catholic dogma. As it was, Belloc's powers were waning even as Joad's were waxing and they never met in intellectual combat. Neither, due to Joad's eleventh-hour conversion, did they meet in the reconciliation of a shared Christian faith.

None the less, the two men had more in common than may seem evident. Apart from a shared militancy in the pursuit of truth they combined the intellectual pursuits of the head with the aesthetic pursuits of the heart with equal vigour. At home with the cut and thrust of intellectual debate, they were equally at home in the peace and tranquillity of the English countryside. Belloc's serenading of his beloved Sussex in poetry, prose and song was almost legendary and Joad's passion for the English countryside, though less well known, was equally intense.

Joad once described England as having the ugliest towns in the world and the most beautiful countryside, a view which echoed Belloc's disdain for towns like Burgess Hill and Haywards Heath which he considered a blot on the Sussex landscape. Joad's horror at the wanton desecration of the countryside was perhaps best summed up in the title of his book, *The Untutored Townsman's Invasion of the Country*. Meanwhile, Belloc had complained bitterly that his Sussex was being overrun by 'Londoners'.

Neither was the similarity superficial or coincidental. It was an expression of something deeper, the parallel existence within the psyche of a love for knowledge and for beauty. Belloc and Joad both displayed to an unusual degree this transcendent synthesis between the head and the heart.

The synthesis is of course present in everybody to some degree, but the relative emphasis between head and heart varies with each individual. This was as true of the Christian *literati* as it was of anyone else. Whereas Lewis, Sayers, Dawson, Copleston and other 'intellectuals' were seeking to win the battle for Christian truth dialectically through a network of minds reaching out, meshing together and energizing each other, others were approaching the same truth from a poetic or artistic viewpoint, feeling attracted to the Church by its beauty more than its depth. This was displayed in a peculiarly obscure way in David Jones's *The Anathemata* which was published in 1952.

Jones admitted that his publishers had been influenced by T. S. Eliot in their decision to publish the poem and that 'they probably would not have taken *The Anathemata* without him'.[1] The link with Eliot is appropriate. Many found *The Anathemata* as baffling as *The Waste Land* and struggled with its meaning in the same way as the previous generation had struggled with Eliot's meaning thirty years earlier. Aware of the danger of being misunderstood, Jones was at pains to explain himself in his Preface to the poem:

> I intend what I have written to be said. While marks of punctuation, breaks of line, lengths of line, grouping of words or sentences and variations of spacing are visual contrivances they have here an aural and oral intention. You can't get the intended meaning unless you hear the sound and you can't get the sound unless you observe the score; and pause-marks on a score are of particular importance. Lastly, it is meant to be said with deliberation ...
>
> ... what I have written will certainly lose half what I intend, indeed, it will fail altogether, unless the advice 'with deliberation' is heeded. Each word is meant to do its own work, but each word cannot do its work unless it is given due attention. It was written to be read in that way.[2]

This passage, and the work it sought to elucidate, displays every facet of Jones's complex character. Highly strung and prone to breakdowns Jones was the opposite of Eliot's despised 'hollow men', spiritual vacuums incapable of feeling. Jones was a man full to bursting with feelings, too full perhaps, feeling too much. Thus the poem's text and context were textural in a tactile sense, a reflection of the fact that Jones was an artist with watercolours and oils as well as with words. Added to this was his insistence that the poem be read aloud, treated as music, so that it could be spoken and heard as well as seen and touched. *The Anathemata* was intended as a sense experience, transcending verse.

Yet this obsession with beauty was not intended to obscure but to reveal his deeper intellectual meaning. On the very page of the Preface where he gave specific instructions as to how the poem should be read there was also an acknowledgement to Christopher Dawson, 'to whose writings and conversation I feel especially indebted'.[3] Specifically the debt was to the depths of Dawson's thought. In the second volume of Gifford Lectures Dawson had stressed the pivotal importance of the Roman liturgy and the ancient veneration of the saints to the continuity of Western civilization and this formed the central theme of *The Anathemata*.

The extent of Dawson's influence on Jones is evident in a letter Jones wrote to his friend Harman Grisewood describing a conversation with Dawson over dinner: 'it's nice to talk to someone whose brain is the right *kind* – that's what one sighs for – the disagreements don't matter – but the *temper* – the *kind* – the *sort* of thing that a chap regards as *significant* – that's what one wants – and that is hard to come by.'[4]

Another surprising influence upon Jones, certainly not apparent in any discernible similarity in style, was that of Hilaire Belloc. Jones had long admired Belloc and had contributed an essay on 'The Myth of Arthur' for a volume entitled *For Belloc* which had been published in Belloc's honour in 1942. As late as 1966 Jones wrote to Harman Grisewood to congratulate him on his reading of a selection of Belloc's verse on the BBC's Third Programme:

> God! he could manage the special sort of biting wit with undertones of deeps possible only to a man who was part of the untranslatable ... *omnibus orthodoxis, atque catholicae et apostolicae fidei cultoribus*, and at the same time was part and parcel of that particular politico-social milieu of the first couple of decades of this century ...'[5]

In the same letter Jones recalled how his friend René Hague used to recite one of Belloc's sonnets to him, and Hague himself, who had known Jones since 1924 through their mutual friendship with Eric Gill, remembered Jones's debt to Belloc:

> Belloc, of course, never wrote with the obliquity with which David approaches his work, but David owes him some considerable debt in the structure of his sentences. There used to be in existence a delightful sketch, symbolic of David's amused pleasure in the man, in which David has drawn Belloc sitting, cigarette in hand, smoke curling upwards, under a large 'No Smoking' notice: Belloc, at the time was taking the chair at a debate in the Essex hall between Chesterton and Shaw.[6]

Jones, it seemed, admired Belloc in much the same way that he admired Dawson, as 'someone whose brain is the right *kind*' and who wrote about 'the *sort* of thing that a chap regards as *significant*'. Yet even allowing for the considerable debt which Hague believed Jones owed to Belloc as regards the structuring of his sentences, they have few similarities with respect to literary style. Jones owed more to the experimentation of Eliot, James Joyce and Gerard Manley Hopkins than to the traditional verse of Belloc; and it is likely that Belloc would have considered Jones's obliqueness an *obscurum per obscurius*.

A man whose work was much closer in style to the more directly confrontational and controversial approach of Belloc was Hugh Ross Williamson. According to Father Charles Smith, who knew Ross Williamson during the late forties when they were both Anglo-Catholic clergymen in London, 'he was one of those people who called a spade a spade, or preferably a bloody shovel, especially when talking about the powers-that-be in the Church of England'.[7] In fact, in the year that Belloc bowed out of the fray, Ross Williamson was involved in the sort of heated controversy which the young Belloc would have relished. The cause of the furore was the play *His Eminence of England* which had been commissioned for the 1953 Canterbury Festival. Ross Williamson was in exalted company in being commissioned to write the play. Previous plays for the Festival had included T. S. Eliot's *Murder in the Cathedral*, Charles Williams's *Thomas Cranmer of Canterbury* and Dorothy L. Sayers's *The Zeal of Thy House*. However, Ross Williamson's contribution caused outrage in some quarters because his subject was the notorious Cardinal Pole. Although Pole qualified technically for treatment at the Festival as a former Archbishop of Canterbury who was buried in the cathedral, his outspoken opposition to the reforms of Henry VIII and his alleged instigation of the persecution of Protestants in the reign of Queen Mary made him an odd choice for veneration at the Church of England's major cultural event. Even Robert Speaight, the Catholic actor who played the part of the Cardinal, considered the choice 'a curious one for an Anglican festival'. Speaight, who had previously played the roles of Thomas à Becket in Eliot's *Murder in the Cathedral* and Christ in Sayers's *The Man Born to be King*, considered Ross Williamson's play 'a quiet, stylish and attractive portrait' of the controversial Cardinal but conceded that 'our audiences were small – undeservedly so, for Norman Marshall had directed the play with exemplary taste and judgement'.[8] The play's failure may have been due to an unofficial boycott by angry Anglicans. Archbishop Fisher was conspicuous by his absence from the performance and it was even rumoured that local tradesmen had been warned not to attend 'on pain of forfeiting their custom in the precincts'.[9]

During the same year Ross Williamson had been on safer and more hallowed ground when he published *The Children's Book of British Saints*. This was a great success and was followed over the next six years by similar children's books of French, Italian, Spanish, German and Patron Saints, collected together in 1960 as *Sixty Saints of Christendom*. He was, however, no stranger to controversy and seemed on occasion even to court the sort of hostile response which his Canterbury play received. In 1939 he had been expelled from the Labour Party after arguing in his book *Who Is For Liberty?* that trade union control of the Labour Party was a major political disaster, suggesting that union control could be broken if socialists gave their political levies to their local constituency parties instead of to their unions. As the Labour Party would take over half a century to reach the same conclusion, Ross Williamson could certainly claim in this instance to be ahead of his time. According to Julia Ross Williamson, the ability to be ahead of his time was the most remarkable aspect of her father's achievement:

> His first book, *The Poetry of T. S. Eliot*, published in 1932, was the first ever written on Eliot. These were the last words of the last chapter: 'It will be found, I dare to prophesy, that T. S. Eliot will be recognised generally as one of the very few great writers of the post-war world.' I think that is typical of my father, he was always ahead of his time ... For example, my father said that the Gunpowder Plot was a put-up job by Cecil, who acted as a sort of *agent provocateur*, to catch the Catholics ... all the time academics like Trevor Roper said 'rubbish, rubbish, rubbish'. Then thirty or forty years later everybody suddenly says 'yes, this is the thing' and now Antonia Fraser is being lauded for just producing *The Gunpowder Plot*. Similarly, my father's claim that Shakespeare was a Catholic in his book *The Day Shakespeare Died*. That got completely panned ... Now I find that there are articles in Catholic magazines saying there is proof that Shakespeare was probably a Catholic.[10]

It could be argued that Julia Ross Williamson's comments are scarcely those of a disinterested observer, but a similar view was expressed by Ian Burford, a correspondent to the *Sunday Times* on 21 June 1992, regarding Ross Williamson's biography of Christopher Marlowe:

> I was very interested to read the review of Charles Nicholl's new book on Christopher Marlowe, *The Reckoning* (June 7).

I was first introduced to this murky world of Elizabethan intrigue by Hugh Ross Williamson's excellent biography, *Kind Kit*, which was published 20 years ago. As no reviewer seems to have mentioned it, I wonder if the author knows of its existence, and that it covers so much of the ground represented as revelation.

Julia Ross Williamson was incensed by the lack of credit given to her father at the time of the publication of Charles Nicholl's book and she also wrote to *The Times*, making the same point as Burford in more forthright terms. Her letter was not published:

My father ... when president of the Marlowe Society in 1972, wrote 'an informal biography' of Marlowe, published by Michael Joseph, sporting the same dust-jacket and coming to the same conclusions about his death ...

Perhaps Charles Nicholl has not come across my father's book ... although I find this surprising, dedicated as it was to the Marlowe Society.[11]

Ross Williamson's revisionist approach to Elizabethan history invites further comparisons with Belloc who had written similar studies with the professed intention of countering and correcting the distortions of the Whig historians. For Belloc such books were part of his Catholic crusade against what he perceived as Protestant propaganda and there is little doubt that Ross Williamson had the same intention. Yet Ross Williamson was a Church of England clergyman at the time he wrote many of his controversial historical studies, a fact which led him increasingly to question the nature of his own position.

Born of Nonconformist parents at the turn of the century, it was intended that Hugh Ross Williamson would follow in the footsteps of both his father and his grandfather and enter the Nonconformist ministry. Instead he showed a singular nonconformity in his approach to Nonconformism and decided instead to pursue a secular career. Between 1925 and 1942 he gained a considerable reputation as editor, playwright, historian, politician and broadcaster. In 1943 he became an Anglican clergyman and during the following decade was well known as an Anglo-Catholic theologian and preacher.

He began, however, as a provincial journalist on the *Yorkshire Post*. During his six years in Leeds he progressed from drama critic to leader-writer and finally to literary editor, before returning south to become editor of *The Bookman*. It was during his time in Yorkshire that he made the acquaintance of Father John

O'Connor, Chesterton's 'Father Brown', who knew many of the century's literary converts: 'I would listen to his wisdom, learn of his beloved Claudel (whom he was translating), look at Eric Gill's Stations of the Cross in his Church of St Cuthbert (which are so much finer than those in Westminster Cathedral) and, because he let me, sometimes try to argue with him.'[12]

Another early influence was T. S. Eliot. In his first book, *The Poetry of T. S. Eliot*, published during his time as editor of *The Bookman*, Williamson wrote:

> Eliot has described his general point of view as 'anglo-catholic in religion', adding that the term does not rest with him to define. His early upbringing and environment were puritan, and for him now the antithesis to 'Catholic' is 'agnostic'. These three clues to his position are supplemented by continual references in his prose and poetry.
>
> It is difficult for a romantic age to appreciate a classicist, for a rebellious age to sympathise with a traditionalist, for a journalistic age to care for literature, it is almost impossible for an irreligious age to understand a man so intensely religious as Eliot.[13]

Ross Williamson's deep-felt sympathy with Eliot's Anglo-Catholic position, implicit in this passage, was stated explicitly elsewhere in the same book: 'Protestantism is a half-way house where one takes refuge because of a disinclination to think the matter out to a conclusion. Only the Catholic and the agnostic dare to reach the end of their journeys.'[14] The extent to which Eliot concurred with this view is evident from a letter he wrote to Ross Williamson on 11 October 1932, shortly after the book was published. After stating that 'I read anything about myself with a childish pleasure', Eliot went on to state that 'you have handled the religious problem with skill and sureness, and I am grateful for that'.[15]

At around the same time, Ross Williamson, in his capacity as editor of *The Bookman*, received a letter from Edith Sitwell which is worth quoting as an amusing example of her acid wit:

> Some time ago, I had occasion to write to the Editor of the *Yorkshire Post*, with reference to someone who was throwing his weight about, a little unwisely, on the subject of my work, and over the initials 'G.G.'. I suggested that he was overrating his size, and that more suitable initials would be A.S.S.
>
> I am delighted to see that the person in question has not only come round to my point of view about himself, but, with becoming modesty, has realised that with the usual reckless generosity of an artist,

even I had suggested a skin that was still too large for him, and he is now content to be that which nature intended him to be, – Geoffrey Grigson.[16]

Ross Williamson was editor of *The Bookman* until 1934, after which he became editor of the *Strand Magazine* before resigning to write as a freelance. More books followed, especially biographical studies of key seventeenth-century figures. *John Hampden* was published in 1933, *King James I* in 1935 and *George Villiers, First Duke of Buckingham* in 1940. In 1941 he wrote a religious tract entitled *AD33* which was described by E. M. Forster in a broadcast talk as 'the most important religious book of 1941'.[17]

After he became an Anglican clergyman he was attached for twelve years to St Cyprian's Regents Park and St Thomas's Regent Street. Over the years he also preached in many other places, including St Paul's Cathedral and Westminster Abbey. The influences which led him from the rejection of Nonconformism to the acceptance of Anglo-Catholicism, a process of conversion which had taken nearly two decades, were manifold. There was the solid theological grounding he had received from his father which had led him out of the 'half-way house' of Protestantism into the murky battlefield where the forces of agnosticism and Catholicism fought for supremacy. There was his intense historical scholarship which led to a deep understanding of the religious issues at the heart of seventeenth-century England. Added to this was the influence of many of his contemporaries. T. S. Eliot had impressed him with his principled Anglo-Catholicism at a time when his own theological position was in a state of flux. Chesterton was also important. 'He was always talking about Chesterton,' his daughter recalled, 'and he thought his *Orthodoxy* was one of the best books he'd read. I would think *Orthodoxy* probably had an important influence on his intellectual and spiritual development.'[18] Her view is borne out by the fact that the title her father chose for his autobiography, *The Walled Garden*, was inspired by a quotation from Chesterton's book.

The novels of R. H. Benson were another influence and they may have prompted Ross Williamson's own interest in English history. In 1959 he wrote an introduction to Benson's *Come Rack! Come Rope!*:

it is impossible not to be moved by the last chapter which, as far as I know, has never been bettered as an account of an Elizabethan martyr's execution …

This achievement is due, I think, to the fact that the book is solidly based on historical truth. The author was at pains to see the men and events of the time as they in fact were, though since his day much has been discovered ...

... The title is taken from a letter of Blessed Edmund Campion's, in which, after torture, he assured his fellow Catholics that he had betrayed 'no things of secret, nor would he, come rack, come rope'. Later writers may have drawn more detailed pictures, but Benson's sketches are true enough ...

So it is that when he comes to his invented personages ... he creates them within the orbit of known truth, leaving us to feel, correctly, that they could have lived and acted as Benson makes them. The whole epoch leaps to life and if any reader should object that this picture of Catholic England under the Elizabethan Terror savours a little of melodrama, there is the author's own unchallengeable answer: 'If the book is too sensational, it is no more sensational than life itself was to Derbyshire folk between 1579 and 1588.'[19]

It certainly appears that Benson's historical fiction influenced Ross Williamson's own literary output because he too was to write several historical novels, 'solidly based on historical truth', which bear all the hallmarks of Benson's earlier efforts in the genre. The first of these was *Captain Thomas Schofield*, published in 1942, which was followed by others including *James by the Grace of God*, based on the life of James II, *The Sisters*, based on the relationship of Mary Tudor and Elizabeth, and *Guy Fawkes*, which complemented his play, *Gunpowder, Treason and Plot* and his non-fictional study, *The Gunpowder Plot*.

Another contemporary influence was Dorothy L. Sayers. According to his daughter, Ross Williamson's *The Story Without an End*, a series of radio plays dramatizing the life of Christ for eleven- to fifteen-year-olds, 'was rather based on Dorothy L. Sayers's *The Man Born to be King*'.[20] He and Sayers corresponded during his days as an Anglican clergyman and a letter from Sayers, dated 21 May 1948, illustrated the meticulously conscientious way that Sayers was embarking upon her study and translation of Dante. Her reply to a query from Ross Williamson about Dante and Arnaut Daniel commenced with the statement that 'my academic conscience says that I ought to set out my argument in full', was followed by eight closely typed pages and concluded with an apology:

It is so easy for somebody like de Rougemont to make a reckless assertion; and away it goes round the world in seven-leagued boots, and one can only plod slowly after it with a lot of heavy, clumping facts and etymologies and dates and references, wearisome to assemble and still more wearisome to read. But if you were misled into writing a footnote on his unverified *ipse dixit*, I'm damned if I'll let you chivalrously withdraw the footnote on the strength of my unsupported denial! I insist on giving you the evidence, and the argument for what it is worth – it's only fair to you.[21]

Ross Williamson was also an avid reader of many other contemporary Christian writers. 'He had lots of Knox's books in his own library,' his daughter remembered. 'He thought Knox was very important.' He also owned Lewis's *The Problem of Pain*, *The Screwtape Letters* and *Surprised by Joy*. 'He thought Lewis was a very fine writer.' He owned David Jones's *In Parenthesis*, bought all of Evelyn Waugh's books and admired the poetry of Sassoon.[22]

Against this literary backdrop Ross Williamson remained a devout Anglo-Catholic priest, seemingly at home in the Anglican communion. Then, in 1955, the crisis over the Church of South India shook his faith in Anglicanism to its very foundations. The 'crisis' has since been buried in the sands of obscurity and has been superseded by subsequent developments so that it is difficult to comprehend the passions it aroused at the time. Essentially it centred on the Church of England's recognition of South Indian Orders as valid. In his autobiography, Ross Williamson explained the position of both himself and many of his Anglo-Catholic colleagues on the issue. Since the Church of South India 'was not a fully Christian Church in any hitherto accepted sense, the inevitable corollary of the decision was that the Orders of the Church of England itself had been declared invalid by its own representatives'.[23] Following the decision, he and many other Anglo-Catholics felt in conscience that there was only one course of action open to them: submission to the Catholic Church. Hugh Ross Williamson and his wife were received into the Church on 15 October 1955 by Father Basil Fitz-Gibbon, SJ, at Farm Street.

At the time of his reception he was chairman of the BBC Brains Trust, on which he had served with Cyril Joad before the latter's death. In those days they had taken contrary positions, Joad as agnostic-turned-theist and Ross Williamson as nonconformist-turned-Anglo-Catholic. Julia Ross Williamson recalls with amusement that her father 'used to go to the BBC every Sunday and come back wearing make-up' and she believed 'he would have been surprised by Joad's conversion to Christianity'.

His position on the Brains Trust was more important than ever following his conversion, his daughter recalled, because it became virtually his only source of income:

we lost the vicarage where we were living, we lost his income, we lost the rent-free accommodation. If it hadn't been for the fact that my mother was working we would have been in severe straits. But he thought at least I still have the Brains Trust money coming in. Very soon after he became a Catholic he was phoned up by Carleton Greene and told that he was no longer needed on the Brains Trust. He couldn't believe it and I remember him sitting in his study looking very dejected for a very long time.[24]

Soon afterwards he received a phone call from Hugh Carleton Greene's wife who told him, off the record, that he had been removed from the Brains Trust because 'you present the wrong image now you are a Catholic': 'My father protested that it was 1955 not 1555 but Mrs Greene said that a trendy Anglican clergyman was fine but that a Catholic convert was not.'[25]

This revelation, though shocking, served only to strengthen Ross Williamson's resolve and six months after his conversion, on Palm Sunday 1956, he looked back not in anger but in gratitude:

I have been a Catholic less than six months and already it is difficult to understand why I did not submit thirty-eight years ago. The slowness with which I saw the truth; the misconceptions, which were only partly the result of my heredity and upbringing, as to what the Christian Faith in fact was; the individualism which persisted in pursuing a course for 'reunion' which I had worked out theoretically without a proper appreciation of the practical difficulties; the laziness in scholarship, which allowed me to accept ... the gross Protestant perversion of facts as 'historical truth' instead of going at the outset to the proper Catholic sources; the comparative triviality of the issue of South India which finally forced a decision in my middle fifties when the major fact of the Reformation had been staring me in the face since my teens – all these, and more, are part of a *mea culpa* which found relief in the formal utterance demanded and made gladly on my reception: 'With a sincere heart and with unfeigned faith, I detest and abjure every error, heresy and sect opposed to the Catholic, Apostolic and Roman Church' ...

No one, I think, has been able to describe a conversion in terms which are objectively appropriate. As in the language of the mystics, analogies which give only a shadow of the substance have to be used. Chesterton, in his sonnet on his conversion, perhaps has suggested the reality of it most vividly when he speaks of the

one moment when I bowed my head
And the whole world turned over and came upright

and how suddenly he found that the old controversies and arguments

are less than dust to me
Because my name is Lazarus and I live.[26]

NOTES

1. William Blisset, *The Long Conversation: A Memoir of David Jones*, Oxford University Press, 1981, p. 101.
2. Harman Grisewood (ed.), *Epoch and Artist: Selected Writings by David Jones*, London, 1959, pp. 130–1.
3. ibid., p. 131.
4. René Hague (ed.), *Dai Greatcoat: A Self-Portrait of David Jones in his Letters*, London, 1980, pp. 119–20.
5. ibid., p. 219.
6. René Hague, *Writers of Wales: David Jones*, University of Wales Press, Cardiff, 1975, p. 42.
7. Father Charles Smith, interview with the author, Oxford, 19 December 1996.
8. Robert Speaight, *The Property Basket: Recollections of A Divided Life*, p. 325.
9. ibid., p. 325.
10. Julia Ross Williamson, interview with the author, Fulham, December 1996.
11. Unpublished letter, courtesy of Julia Ross Williamson.
12. Hugh Ross Williamson, *The Walled Garden*, London, 1956, p. 29.
13. Hugh Ross Williamson, *The Poetry of T. S. Eliot*, London, 1932, p. 151.
14. Hugh Ross Williamson, *The Walled Garden*, p. 45.
15. Letter from T. S. Eliot to Hugh Ross Williamson, 11 October 1932, courtesy of Julia Ross Williamson.
16. Letter from Edith Sitwell to the Editor of *The Bookman*, courtesy of Julia Ross Williamson.
17. Julia Ross Williamson, interview with the author.
18. ibid.
19. Robert Hugh Benson, *Come Rack! Come Rope!*, London, 1959 edn., pp. 5–6.
20. Julia Ross Williamson, interview with the author.
21. Letter from Dorothy L. Sayers to Hugh Ross Williamson, 21 May 1948, courtesy of Julia Ross Williamson.
22. Julia Ross Williamson, interview with the author.
23. Hugh Ross Williamson, *The Walled Garden*, p. 183.
24. Julia Ross Williamson, interview with the author.
25. ibid.
26. Hugh Ross Williamson, *The Walled Garden*, pp. 184–5.

CHAPTER TWENTY THREE

SPARK AND SITWELL

'The reason I became a Roman Catholic was because it explained me,' Muriel Spark told Malcolm Muggeridge during an interview on Muggeridge's television series *Appointment with ...* on 2 June 1961. Twenty years later Muggeridge would himself become a Catholic for similar reasons, coming to the same conclusions as Spark after a lifetime of soul-searching. Spark, however, came to the conclusion much earlier and far younger, being received into the Catholic Church on 1 May 1954 when she was still in her mid-thirties.

'I wasn't able to work and to do any of my writing until I became a Catholic,' she claimed in the same interview. In this she was similar to Graham Greene who also owed his earliest literary inspiration to his religious conversion. Yet Spark's claim is only partially true. Certainly she had been unable to write novels prior to her conversion, and her novels are deeply imbued with her experiences of Catholicism, but she had already gained a reputation as a gifted poet and short-story writer before she accepted the tenets of the Church. Between 1947 and 1949 she was editor of *Poetry Review*. In 1951 she submitted 'The Seraph and the Zambesi' to the *Observer* Christmas story competition. It was awarded first place out of 6700 entries and was published in the *Observer* on 23 December. Her first volume of verse, *The Fanfarlo and Other Verse*, appeared in 1952. It was not until the following year that she took any practical steps in the direction of religion, being baptized as an Anglican by the Rev. Clifford Rhodes, editor of the *Church of England Newspaper*, to which she contributed a study of Proust, 'The Religion of an Agnostic', on 27 November 1953, and a review of T. S. Eliot's play, *The Confidential Clerk*. Spark wrote in her autobiography that she 'tried the Church of England first, as being more "natural" and near to home'[1] but she may have been influenced also by her deep respect for Eliot whose work she idolized. After being confirmed by the Anglo-Catholic Bishop of Kensington, she began to frequent the Gloucester Road church where Eliot was a regular worshipper. Unlike Eliot, however, she didn't feel at home in the Anglo-Catholic 'half-way house' between Anglicanism and Catholicism: 'I felt uneasy. It was historically too new for me to take to.'[2]

Still searching for her final resting place she began to read Newman's *Apologia pro Vita Sua* and found herself, slowly but surely, drawn irresistibly along Newman's path to Rome:

> In 1953 I was absorbed by the theological writings of John Henry Newman through whose influence I finally became a Roman Catholic ... When I am asked about my conversion, why I became a Catholic, I can only say that the answer is both too easy and too difficult. The simple explanation is that I felt the Roman Catholic faith corresponded to what I had always felt and known and believed; there was no blinding revelation in my case. The more difficult explanation would involve the step by step building up of a conviction; as Newman himself pointed out, when asked about his conversion, it was not a thing one could propound 'between the soup and the fish' at a dinner party. 'Let them be to the trouble that I have been to,' said Newman.[3]

Later, when she and Derek Stanford were editing a selection of Cardinal Newman's letters, Father Philip Caraman, a Jesuit at Farm Street and editor of *The Month*, lent her a bundle of Newman's original letters. 'I had them with me all the time I was working on the book,' Spark wrote. 'I found it good to touch the very papers that the sublime Father Newman had touched.'[4]

Cardinal Newman had a similar 'sublime' effect on Graham Greene who always considered Newman's *Apologia* one of his favourite books. Greene appears to have recognized in Spark a kindred spirit and, through Derek Stanford, had sought to befriend her even before he had met her. When Spark fell ill in the early months of 1954, Greene offered to give her a monthly sum of twenty pounds until she was well again: 'He really admired my work and was enthusiastic about helping me. With the cheque he would often send a few bottles of red wine – as I was happy to record when speaking at Graham's memorial service – which took the edge off cold charity.'[5] Such a gesture on Greene's part was not unique. During the war he had sent bottles of whisky to Father Martindale in Denmark to alleviate the priest's predicament when he was under 'house arrest' at the hands of the Germans.[6]

During her illness Spark took refuge at the Carmelite monastery at Aylesford in Kent and then at Allington Castle, near Maidstone, which she described as 'a Carmelite stronghold of tertiary nuns'.[7] During her stay she rented a cottage in the grounds and commenced writing her first novel, *The Comforters*. This was published in February 1957 to generally favourable reviews. Evelyn Waugh gave it a long review in the *Spectator* and praised it in an address to the PEN club. In fact, the novel was remarkably similar to Waugh's new novel, *The Ordeal of Gilbert Pinfold*, which was published in the summer of the same year. 'It so happens that *The Comforters* came to me just as I had finished a story on a similar theme,' Waugh wrote in his review, 'and I was struck by how much more ambitious was Miss Spark's essay and how much better she had accomplished it.'[8]

Waugh remained an admirer of Muriel Spark's fiction and praised her novel *Memento Mori* when it was published in 1959, urging his friends to read it. Further highly successful novels followed, including *The Bachelors* in 1960, *The Prime of Miss Jean Brodie* in 1961 and *The Mandelbaum Gate* in 1965. In 1967 she was made a Dame Commander, Order of the British Empire.

Thirteen years earlier, only a few weeks after Muriel Spark had been received into the Church, the same honour was bestowed on Edith Sitwell when she was also made a Dame Commander, Order of the British Empire in the Queen's Birthday Honours List in June 1954.

For Sitwell, being awarded the OBE was a great relief as well as a great honour. She had always been extremely sensitive to criticism, as the earlier letter to Hugh Ross Williamson when he was editor of *The Bookman* had illustrated, and she was beginning to feel that she was both unappreciated and misunderstood by critics. During the early months of 1954 the *Spectator* had been particularly hostile in its criticism and Sitwell had been as prickly as ever in her response. On 8 March 1954 she wrote plaintively to Kingsley Amis:

> To return, for the last time, to the *Spectator*: the whole affair is too extraordinary for words. Not one of the persons who has had the impertinence to attack me has even a germ of talent for poetry. They simply can't write. And it would never enter the head of a poet of any stature to discuss their verses ... They cannot harm me. All that has happened is that they have made an abjectly ridiculous spectacle of themselves, and are being laughed at, not only all over England, but also in New York.[9]

'Her fierce sensitivity to criticism,' Charles Osborne wrote of Sitwell in the *London Magazine* in December 1962, 'is to be regretted if only because it has encouraged extremes of sycophancy in some and enmity in others, and has in recent years not only obscured her real merits but made any serious discussion of them well-nigh impossible.'[10]

It was this sensitivity which made the OBE all the more important to her. It seemed that it represented not merely an honour but a vindication of her artistic achievement, allowing her to thumb her nose in the face of critical hostility. To

William Plomer, the South African poet, novelist and librettist, she wrote in a spirit of gleeful gloating on 18 June: 'I *am* glad to have been made a Dame, because it has slapped down all the miserable little pipsqueaks in the *New States-man and Nation* and *Spectator*, who have been persecuting me for months'.[11] On the same day that Sitwell was gloating to Plomer, the *Spectator* had responded to her new honour not, as Sitwell herself may have expected, with scornful deri-sion, but with a laudatory tribute by the novelist Compton Mackenzie who had been awarded the OBE himself in 1919 and had been knighted two years previ-ously in 1952:

> Dr Edith Sitwell is the greatest poet that the women of England have yet produced and the Order of the British Empire was beginning to look rather ridiculous on Parnassus without Dr Sitwell as a Dame ... When I shall have the pleasure of addressing her as Dame Edith I shall be addressing, with a prefix hallowed by childhood's fairy dreams, a figure of English history.

Among the many letters of congratulation Sitwell received was one from T. S. Eliot:

> I was very happy to hear yesterday that the Sovereign had recognised the judgment of the world of letters and conferred an honour, which, while it may seem unimportant to yourself, will not only give pleasure to your friends and satisfaction to your admirers but redound to the credit of the source from which it originates.[12]

Of course, as has been seen, the honour *was* important to Sitwell but so was the respect of her literary peers and there was none she esteemed higher than Eliot. As such, Eliot's letter must have given her particular satisfaction. Indeed, when Eliot had been appointed to the Order of Merit in the New Year's Honours List of 1948, the same year in which he was to win the Nobel Prize for Literature, Sitwell had written that she 'had never hoped to see the greatest poet of our time properly honoured and reverenced. Well, I have.'[13]

Eliot's vision of the waste land had affected Sitwell as it had affected almost every other poet of Eliot's generation. Sitwell's own version of *The Waste Land*, *Gold Coast Customs*, published in 1929, expressed a vision of the horror and hollowness of contemporary life which not only echoed Eliot but animated her own slow progress towards religious conversion.

Another major influence on Sitwell's progress towards Christianity was her admiration for Roy Campbell. She looked upon Campbell not only as a friend but as one of the few people who would defend her from her critics. Her favourite story about him, which she told with glee to many of her friends, was recounted by Elizabeth Salter, the Australian novelist and biographer who served as Sitwell's secretary from 1957 until her death in 1964:

'The critic never tired of insulting me,' Sitwell told Salter, 'and Roy decided to teach him a lesson. Roy was very big and enormously strong and he simply knocked him flat. The critic was terrified and crouched where he was on the floor. And Roy said, "If you ever insult Doctor Sitwell (as I then was) again, you know what will be coming to you." And,' she added, 'he never did – until Roy died, and after that it started up again at once.'[14]

This story appeared to have been embellished in the telling and later biographers of Sitwell have even suggested that the story was little more than wishful thinking, a fanciful figment of her fertile imagination. Yet the fact (or fiction) remained and she continued to consider Campbell to be her champion, a chivalrous knight in shining armour protecting her from her enemies. This was expressed by Elizabeth Salter in her memoir of Sitwell, *The Last Years of a Rebel*, published in 1967:

> Roy Campbell represented a great deal to her. Not only was he a poet whom she greatly admired, but he was that rare thing in her life, a champion. Perhaps because she had proved herself to be so formidable, it was not often that she was defended by her admirers and seldom, if ever, defended physically. She had an Elizabethan appreciation of a man who could use his hands as well as his head and she responded to Roy Campbell's championship with an entirely feminine gratitude.[15]

The fact that her knight in shining armour also happened to be a vocal champion of the Church Militant was not lost on Sitwell. When she finally decided to be received into the Catholic Church she wanted Roy and Mary Campbell to stand as her godparents. The fact that the Campbells had returned to live on a smallholding in Portugal and that Roy Campbell's ill-health prevented him from travelling to England for her reception, had left her undaunted in this desire. She wrote to Campbell on 14 July 1955: 'I hope to be received into the Church, as your and Mary's god-daughter, next month. I do not know, yet, who will act for you both. I am being instructed by Father Caraman, whom you know, do you not?'[16]

Sitwell's feelings during her period of instruction were shown in her letters to Father Caraman at the time. On 7 May she wrote:

I believe, and trust with all my heart, that I am on the threshold of a new life. But I shall have to be born again. And I have a whole world to see, as it were for the first time, and to understand as far as my capacities will let me.

Prayer has always been a difficulty for me. By which I mean only that I feel very far away, as if I were speaking into the darkness. But I hope this will be cured. When I *think* of God, I do not feel far away ...

I am at this time reading St Thomas Aquinas, and shall read, daily, in the Missal ...

With my deep gratitude to you for your great kindness to me, and your infinite help ...[17]

The following month, on 3 June, she wrote again:

I cannot express to you my gratitude for having recommended these books to me. The first feeling they give me is one of absolute certainty. They – and especially the wonderful writings of St Thomas Aquinas, and Father D'Arcy's *The Nature of Belief*, make one see doubt – perhaps I am not expressing this properly – as a complete failure of intellect. Then again I see that purely intellectual belief is not enough: one must not only *think* one is believing, but *know* one is believing. There has to be a sixth sense in faith.

How wonderful that passage is in *The Nature of Belief* about 'looking through the appearances at reality. Once this is granted the existence of God must be admitted without more ado ... If there is anything there, then there must be something fully real.' ...

When I was a very small child, I began to see the patterns of the world, the images of wonder. And I asked myself why those patterns should be repeated – the feather and the fern and rose and acorn in the patterns of frost on the window – pattern after pattern repeated again and again. And even then I knew that this was telling us something. I founded my poetry upon it ...[18]

'Mr Sheed's *Theology and Sanctity* is being a great help to me,' she wrote to him in another letter. 'Saint Thomas Aquinas is a wonder of course from every point of view. I do not find Mgr. Knox's book of great help to me for several reasons. One being that I do not like his style of writing.'[19]

The correspondence with Father Caraman seems to belie the belief of many that, in the words of Father Charles Smith, 'Edith Sitwell's conversion was a romantic thing, much more than an intellectual thing'.[20] Rather, it seems that Sitwell saw romance and intellect almost synonymously, the heart and the head as one composite whole. The beauty of knowledge and the knowledge of beauty were not exactly the same, but they were none the less inseparable. Thus her delving into the depths of Christian philosophy was coupled with a confession that it was 'the serenity in the faces of the peasant women praying in the churches in Italy' that had drawn her to the Church.[21] It was this simplicity in complexity which formed the poetic paradox at the heart of Sitwell's conversion.

Commenting on his instruction of Sitwell, Father Caraman wrote: 'She was well-read in the mystic poets, she was eager to enlarge her knowledge of the theological basis of the Faith, and she possessed a natural understanding of the need for the authority of the Church which is so often such a stumbling block to intellectuals.'[22]

Far from being a stumbling block, the authority of the Church appeared to be one of the factors attracting her to Catholicism. When her friend David Horner had become a Catholic over a decade earlier, Sitwell had written to congratulate him: 'I have never understood why people are afraid of constructive rules. Very few people are capable of coming to any great decision, but you have been.' She added that she was sure that such a decision 'gives one an immense feeling of calm and of peace and security, and a great framework on which to build one's day'.[23]

Constructive rules ... peace and security ... a great framework on which to build one's day. These were some of the aspects of Catholicism that Sitwell found so appealing when Horner had become a Catholic in 1944. Although a further eleven years passed before she was able to take the 'great decision' herself, the relief at having finally done so was evident in her words to Father Caraman after their first meeting on 29 April 1955. Their meeting had given her 'a sense of happiness, safety and peace such as I have not had for years ... What a fool I was not to have taken this step years ago.'[24]

On 14 July 1955, the day Sitwell had written to Roy Campbell expressing her desire that he and his wife should become her godparents, Evelyn Waugh was replying to an earlier letter from her in which she had requested that he be her third godparent: 'Welcome. Welcome. Will you be very kind and send me a postcard when the thing is fixed so that Laura and I may make our communions for you? I know of many people who will want to thank God for you and many priests who will want to remember you in their masses. But I presume you don't want the matter spoken of, so shall mention it to no one until you give the word.'[25]

Five days later Waugh wrote to Father Caraman:

Don't please think me impertinent. I am an old friend of Edith's and love her. She is liable to make herself a little conspicuous at times. This morning I have had another letter from her. She says she will be received in London. Am I being over-fastidious in thinking Mount St Mary's much more suitable? What I fear is that the popular papers may take her up as a kind of Garbo-Queen-Christina. I was incomparably less notorious when I was received and I know that I suffered from the publicity which I foolishly allowed then. There are so many malicious people out to make a booby of a Sitwell. It would be tragic if this greatest occasion in her life were in any way sullied. Can you not persuade her to emulate St Helena in this matter?[26]

Waugh had known Edith Sitwell for thirty years and was well aware of her hyper-sensitive nature. His desire to protect her from a hostile secular press is touching, and doubtless Sitwell would have been moved by his concern had Father Caraman made her aware of it. Roy Campbell, it seemed, was not the only one prepared to act as her champion.

Waugh was to find himself a victim of a hostile secular press within a fortnight of writing this letter. On 31 July a 'profile' of him in the *Observer* had ended: 'Embittered romantic, over-deliberate squire and recluse, popular comedian, catholic father of a family, Evelyn Waugh is one of the oddest figures of our time.' In a letter to Nancy Mitford he described the article as 'grossly impertinent'.[27] One suspects, however, that even his friends would have observed with wry amusement and raised eyebrows that the description was pretty accurate! There was something distinctly odd, or at least eccentric, in his choice of attire at Edith Sitwell's reception which took place, in spite of Waugh's protestations, at Farm Street church in Mayfair on 4 August 1955. Alec Guinness remembered that, 'With the exception of Evelyn Waugh, who was to be Edith's godfather, all the other men were dressed as for a funeral. Evelyn wore a loud black and white dog-tooth tweed suit, a red tie, and a boater from which streamed red and blue ribbons.'[28]

Waugh described the day in a detailed entry in his diary:

I took the train at 9 ... From Charing Cross I walked to White's buying a carnation on the way and drank a mug of stout and gin and ginger beer. Then at 11.45 to Farm Street where I met Father D'Arcy and went with him to the church to the Ignatius chapel to await Edith and Father Caraman. A bald shy man introduced himself as the actor Alec Guinness. Presently Edith appeared swathed in black like a sixteenth-century infanta. I was aware of other people kneeling behind but there were no newspaper men or photographers as I had half feared to find. Edith recanted her errors in fine ringing tones and received conditional baptism ...[29]

Sitwell's own feelings on the morning of her reception were conveyed in a letter to Edward Sackville-West who had evidently written to congratulate her on the step she was about to take:

Today is that on which I shall be received into the Church, and I do, in a way, tremble at the thought. Partly because I am in a deep night, in which there is no sound and no light. I might almost be dead – excepting when I pick up and read St Thomas Aquinas, when, for some reason – well, an explainable reason – I become violently alive again. But I have had this happen before I had a poem come to me, so perhaps everything will be all right for me.

And what you say about 'the consolation of no longer being in any doubt about life – what to think or do about it' is deeply and abundantly true. And what you say about God not letting those He has called to Him escape is most wonderful.

You say it took twelve years to bring you to your resolution. It must have taken about the same time to bring me to mine ...[30]

She added a postscript: 'Is Alec Guinness a friend of yours? He is a friend of mine. He, too, is becoming a Catholic.'

On the following day Waugh wrote to Nancy Mitford with the sweet and sour mixture of the sacred and profane, laced with irreverent humour, which make his letters and his books so readable:

Yesterday I went to London to stand godfather to Edith Sitwell who has submitted to the Pope of Rome. She looked fine – like a 16th century infanta and spoke her renunciation of heresy in silver bell like tones. Afterwards a gargantuan feast at her Sesame Club. I have heard gruesome accounts of that place but she gave us a rich blow-out. Very odd company none of whom I had seen before, only one I had heard of – the actor Alec Guinness, very shy and bald. He is turning papist too, so there is something to balance the loss of Miss Clifford who is marrying a man with no legs and two wives. Think of *choosing* to be named Atalanta Fairey! No sense of propriety. Ed Stanley has written a first rate essay on Belloc as preface to the *Cruise of the Nona*. Ann says he is impotent and greatly depressed about it.[31]

The riotous tone of his letter to Mitford was consciously restrained when he wrote to Sitwell four days later:

> I was on the point of writing to you to thank you again for choosing me as sponsor, for your present of your poems and for the delightful luncheon party. I thought your circle of friends round the table remarkably typical of the Church in its variety and goodwill ...
>
> It is 25 years all but a few weeks since Fr D'Arcy received me into the Church. I am aghast now when I think how frivolously I approached (though it seemed grave enough at the time) for every year since has been one of exploration into the mind and heart of the Church. You have come with much deeper insight. Should I as Godfather warn you of probable shocks in the human aspect of Catholicism? Not all priests are as clever and kind as Fr D'Arcy and Fr Caraman ... But I am sure you know the world well enough to expect Catholic bores and prigs and crooks and cads. I always think of myself: 'I know I am awful. But how much more awful I should be without the Faith'. One of the joys of Catholic life is to recognise the little sparks of good everywhere, as well as the fires of the saints ...
>
> I liked Alec Guinness so much and will try to see more of him. I have long admired his art ...
>
> I heard a rousing sermon on Sunday against the dangers of immodest bathing-dresses and thought that you and I were innocent of that offence at least.[32]

Three weeks after her reception, on 25 August, Sitwell wrote to tell Lady Lovat that she was 'still feeling bewildered'. Pressure of work was keeping her from any serious religious reading but she was looking forward to being able 'to read works of doctrine with proper concentration': 'How wonderful the Theological Texts of St Thomas Aquinas, translated by Father Gilbey, are! To read them is like being put into an oxygen tent when one is dying.'[33]

On 4 October Sitwell was confirmed at Farm Street in front of what Waugh described in his diary as 'a large invited congregation, the cream of Catholic London'.[34] However, if Sitwell was able to find solace in the cream of Catholic London, many of her non-Catholic friends appeared bewildered by her conversion. Her brother Osbert was supportive and she even hoped that he would follow her into the Church. Her other brother, Sacheverell, was less sympathetic. 'Where are you refuged, my sister, / Among orisons and litanies?' he wrote in 'Serenade to a Sister':

> The telling of the rosary
> Is but a counting of the petals,
> Is but a rose held in an old and withered hand,
> Not hands as yours,
> Supple and youthful,
> That are the tiger in the tiger-lily.[35]

Strangers, as well as friends and family, were among those who responded to her conversion with hostility. When a carpet dealer from New York wrote reproachfully that she had joined the Church which still bore the bloodstains of the St Bartholomew's Day Massacre, Sitwell sent him a dismissive postcard in reply: 'Don't be silly, Edith Sitwell.'[36] On another occasion she received a 'loathsome, anonymous letter' which 'told me I am hated because I am "vulgar, common" … because I wear "vulgar rings that the lowest barmaid would disdain to wear" (why should barmaids be called low) because I am "a fraud, a fake, a third-rate poetess," because I "read good poetry horribly" … and – of course, because I am a Roman Catholic.'[37]

Despite Evelyn Waugh's efforts, and perhaps inevitably, Sitwell was eventually to be hurt by an unkind reference to her conversion in the press. The offending article appeared in Time and the story surrounding it was recounted amusingly by Alec Guinness in his autobiography:

> The largeness of her capacity to forgive, when truly and deeply hurt, was apparent when Time Magazine printed an article about me which contained the untruthful but not unfunny reference to her. Luckily Time courteously sent me an advance copy, which I received in the morning's post on the day of publication. Horrified at what I read, and alarmed at its possible repercussions, I telephoned Edith immediately asking if I might call on her at the Sesame Club as soon as possible … I found her sitting, alone and forlorn, on a dingy sofa in an ante-room. As I handed her the magazine I assured her that I had never said to anyone that at her reception into the Church she wore white lace and had been carried up the aisle lying on a cushion. She read the article in silence and flushed deeply when she came to the offending passage; then she put it down at her side and said, 'Stay to lunch.'

Guinness refused politely and apologized profusely that his name had been coupled with hers 'in such a ridiculous way':

> she inclined her head graciously and forgivingly. 'Do stay,' she said, 'as I am expecting a very fine Portuguese poet, whom you may have met before.' The words were hardly out of her mouth when a dark haired young man arrived, waving *Time Magazine*. I recognised him immediately as a fellow guest at Edith's reception but he failed to recognise me. 'Edith, my dear,' – and he kissed her hand – 'have you seen *this?*' He thrust *Time* at her. 'Isn't it disgraceful of that actor?' 'I have just read it,' she replied. 'Alec brought me a copy. I don't need to read it again.' The poet went pale and we bowed. He tried to stuff *Time* into his pocket but it wouldn't go; then he concealed it in his jacket, close to his heart. He fell silent. As I kissed her goodbye she whispered, 'Light a candle for me in Farm Street one day.'
>
> Once or twice I have remembered to do so, but I have often remembered her in my haphazard prayers. When I pass the chapel where she was baptised I can still conjure up her tall figure, swathed in black, looking like some strange, eccentric bird and Fr Caraman pouring water over her forehead in the ancient rite. She seemed like an ageing princess come home from exile.[38]

NOTES

1. Muriel Spark, *Curriculum Vitae*, London, 1992, p. 202.
2. ibid., p. 202.
3. ibid., p. 202.
4. ibid., p. 202.
5. ibid., p. 205.
6. Mrs Graham Greene, interview with the author, Oxford, 20 August 1996; Mrs Graham Greene, letter to the author, 30 August 1996.
7. Muriel Spark, *Curriculum Vitae*, p. 205.
8. *Spectator*, 22 February 1957.
9. Richard Greene (ed.), *Selected Letters of Edith Sitwell*, London, 1997, p. 349.
10. Victoria Glendinning, *Edith Sitwell: A Unicorn Among Lions*, London, 1981, p. 310.
11. ibid., p. 311.
12. Geoffrey Elborn, *Edith Sitwell: A Biography*, London, 1981, p. 215.
13. John Lehmann and Derek Parker (ed.), *Edith Sitwell: Selected Letters 1919–1964*, New York, 1970, pp. 155–6.
14. Elizabeth Salter, *The Last Years of a Rebel: A Memoir of Edith Sitwell*, London, 1967, pp. 18–19.
15. ibid., p. 19.
16. John Lehmann and Derek Parker (ed.), *Edith Sitwell: Selected Letters 1919–1964*, p. 201.
17. ibid., pp. 191–2.
18. ibid., pp. 194–5.
19. Victoria Glendinning, *Edith Sitwell: A Unicorn Among Lions*, p. 317.

20. Father Charles Smith, interview with the author, Oxford, 19 December 1996.
21. Victoria Glendinning, *Edith Sitwell: A Unicorn Among Lions*, p. 315.
22. John Pearson, *Façades*, London, 1978, p. 440.
23. Victoria Glendinning, *Edith Sitwell: A Unicorn Among Lions*, p. 314.
24. ibid., p. 315.
25. Mark Amory (ed.), *The Letters of Evelyn Waugh*, p. 445.
26. ibid., pp. 447–8.
27. ibid., p. 450.
28. Alec Guinness, *Blessings in Disguise*, London, 1985, p. 149.
29. Michael Davie (ed.), *The Diaries of Evelyn Waugh*, p. 735.
30. Richard Greene (ed.), *Selected Letters of Edith Sitwell*, pp. 366–7.
31. Mark Amory (ed.), *The Letters of Evelyn Waugh*, p. 450.
32. ibid., pp. 450–1.
33. Victoria Glendinning, *Edith Sitwell: A Unicorn Among Lions*, p. 319.
34. Michael Davie (ed.), *The Diaries of Evelyn Waugh*, p. 745.
35. Victoria Glendinning, *Edith Sitwell: A Unicorn Among Lions*, pp. 316–17.
36. John Pearson, *Façades*, pp. 445–6.
37. Alec Guinness, *Blessings in Disguise*, pp. 152–3.

CHAPTER TWENTY FOUR

ALEC GUINNESS

When Alec Guinness had met Evelyn Waugh for the first time at Edith Sitwell's reception into the Church, he told him that he was on the verge of taking the same step himself. Within months he had done so. The road he followed to his conversion was described in his autobiography, *Blessings in Disguise*. Guinness had lost any residual remnants of childhood Christianity by his mid-teens. 'At the age of sixteen,' he wrote, 'one early summer day, I arose under the hands of the Bishop of Lewes, a confirmed atheist.'[1] For a few months afterwards he continued to go through the motions of a practising Anglican but by the age of seventeen he had gained permission from his headmaster at Roborough School in Eastbourne to attend the local Presbyterian church instead of Anglican services at Holy Trinity:

> Although I was seeking a way out from the Established Religion (unconsciously) during the days I was not fluttering an atheistical or agnostic flag, it would never have crossed my mind even to step inside a Roman Catholic Church ... But one day I did casually visit a high-Anglican church in the town, was amazed by the elaborate decor and, believing I was somehow on spooky Roman property, hastily withdrew.'[2]

This residual anti-Romanism was deeply ingrained from his earliest days and remained long after the residual Anglicanism of his childhood had evaporated.

The depth of anti-Catholic feeling psychologically omnipresent during his schooldays was recalled poignantly in a reminiscence of life at his preparatory school Pembroke Lodge, near Bournemouth: 'there was universal horror when it was rumoured that a sweet woman who taught drawing and botany in the lower house had left to become a nun. There was partial relief when it was learned that she hadn't Poped but had merely joined an Anglican sisterhood.'[3]

Guinness grew into adulthood still carrying the inherited prejudices of his childhood and having little or no contact with Catholicism. A rare exception arose out of his friendship with Ernest Milton, a fellow actor who had been received into the Catholic Church with his wife, the writer Naomi Royde Smith, at Farm Street in 1942. A man of many contradictions, Milton gained much consolation from his faith and he took Guinness to Mass at St Etheldreda's in Holborn on a Sunday morning, during which, according to Guinness, he 'explained what was going on seriously, beautifully, tactfully and with great simplicity'.[4] Guinness remembered that Milton's life 'became accident-prone, embittered and querulous' following his wife's death and that 'he suffered dreadfully from the actor's disease of persecution mania'.[5] The result was that he alienated many people and became alienated himself, eventually ending his days rather pathetically as a resident of Denville Hall, a residential home for retired actors in North London. Largely neglected by the acting fraternity, Ernest Milton died on 24 July 1974. Alec Guinness was among the few who were present at his sparsely attended requiem Mass:

> There was a memorial service for him at the Catholic church in Maiden Lane, not very far from some of the theatres he had graced, at which Albert Finney (always ready with a sympathetic hand for actors in distress) and I read the unintelligible lessons in boring translations. We were, I believe, the only actors present; the very sparse congregation had no idea whose requiem they were attending and made no enquiries. The whole service had an air of indifference, though Albert and I were genuine mourners.[6]

By the time of Milton's death, Guinness had been a Catholic himself for nearly twenty years and Milton, by introducing and explaining the mysteries of the Mass to the younger actor, had played a small but significant part in his conversion.

A larger though unwitting part was played by the Rev. Cyril Tomkinson, Vicar of All Saints, Margaret Street, a church which Guinness described as 'very much the centre of West End Anglo-Catholicism'.[7] Rev. Tomkinson had come to Guinness's dressing room after a performance of *Hamlet* at the Old Vic in 1938. 'I have just come to tell you,' he said reproachfully to the young actor, eyeing him sternly as he did so, 'that you cross yourself incorrectly in the play. You should do it like this – forehead to chest, then left to right.' Two weeks later he returned, saying, 'You are still doing it incorrectly. It offends me. It spoils an otherwise admirable performance. Do please get it right.'[8]

From such an unlikely beginning a friendship developed which would lead in time to a softening of Guinness's attitude to Catholic practices. During the war, Tomkinson presented Guinness with a copy of St Francis de Sales's *Introduction* to the Devout Life and instructed him always to genuflect to the altar explaining that he believed in The Real Presence. At the time, Guinness confessed, 'I didn't know what he was talking about':

> He had a brilliant mind and was a good friend; very perceptive, very snobbish, delighting in the famous, the rich, the beautiful or talented; and very intolerant of bad manners and all solecisms. He was authoritarian and Laudian in ecclesiastical matters but my gratitude to him is enormous, in spite of his foibles, for he opened up for me a new world – the world of Hooker, William Law, Bishop Gore, Archbishop Temple; and the wide world of St Augustine and Newman. He was polite, though distressed, when years later I became a Catholic. 'Oh, dear! They will teach you to think me a heretic,' he said.[9]

Perhaps he would have been even more distressed had he known that he was himself an important influence on Guinness's road to Rome:

> My friendship with Cyril Tomkinson had reduced my anti-clericism considerably but not my anti-Romanism. Then came the film of *Father Brown* ... on location in Burgundy I had a small experience the memory of which always gives me pleasure. Even the fact that, having done insufficient homework and taken instructions in the script for granted, I was incorrectly dressed for a Catholic priest didn't seem to matter.
>
> Night shooting had been arranged to take place in a little hill-top village a few miles from Macon ... A room had been put at my disposal in the little station hotel three kilometres away. By the time dusk fell I was bored and, dressed in priestly black, I climbed the gritty winding road to the village ... then discovering I wouldn't be needed for at least four hours turned back towards the station. By now it was dark. I hadn't gone far when I heard scampering footsteps and a piping voice calling, 'Mon père!' My hand was seized by a boy of seven or eight, who clutched it tightly, swung it up and kept up a non-stop prattle. He was full of excitement, hops, skips and jumps, but never let go of me. I didn't dare to speak in case my excruciating French should scare him. Although I was a total stranger he obviously took me for a priest and so to be trusted. Suddenly with a 'Bonsoir, mon père', and a hurried sideways sort of bow, he disappeared through a hole in a hedge. He had had a happy, reassuring walk home, and I was left with an odd calm sense of elation. Continuing my walk I reflected that a Church which could inspire such confidence in

a child, making its priests, even when unknown, so easily approachable could not be as scheming and creepy as so often made out. I began to shake off my long-taught, long-absorbed prejudices.[10]

This real-life scene set amidst the filmed scenes of *Father Brown* was given added poignancy in Guinness's mind by the fact that his own son Matthew, who was then aged eleven, had been stricken with polio and paralysed from the waist down a few weeks before the filming of *Father Brown* had commenced. The film itself, after its French location, was made at Riverside Studios in Hammersmith and at the end of each day's filming Guinness walked home along the river, heart heavy-laden with worries about his son:

> in my anxiety I formed the habit of dropping in at a rather tawdry little Catholic church which lay on my route home. I didn't go to pray, to plead or to worship – just to sit quietly for ten minutes and gather what peace of spirit I could. There was never anyone else about. After I had done this several times I struck a negative bargain with God. 'Let him recover,' I said, 'and I will never put an obstacle in his way should he ever wish to become a Catholic.' It sounded to me like a supreme sacrifice on my part. About three months later he was able to walk in a stilted way. By Christmas he could play football. And not long afterwards I was taken up on my side of the bargain.[11]

Matthew had been put down to go to Westminster School but when Alec and his wife Merula decided to move out of London it was decided that another public school would be preferable. They discussed the matter with various friends but no suitable school had a vacancy at such short notice. Finally, the film director Peter Glenville, who had been educated at Stoneyhurst and had a high regard for the Jesuits, suggested Beaumont, near Windsor. 'But it is Catholic!' Guinness exclaimed before remembering his promise in the church in Hammersmith.

An interview was arranged with the Rector of the school, the Rev. Sir Lewis Clifford. 'We only have three non-Catholic boys,' he explained, 'and if he comes here I have no doubt that by the time he is sixteen he will wish to conform. They all do. No pressure will be put on him, I assure you, but it is most likely he will express the wish to be received. Would you object?' Guinness hesitated before saying that he would not and the Rector, looking relieved, invited him to see the school play that evening. Guinness declined but asked what the play was. On being told that it was Bernard Shaw's *St Joan*, he expressed surprise that such a play should be thought suitable for a Catholic school, prompting the Rector to continue: 'It's a great play. And if any boy leaves here without good answers for Mr Shaw, well, we will have failed in our job.'[12] Matthew went to Beaumont and, true to the Rector's prediction, announced at the age of fifteen that he was 'going to submit himself to the Holy Roman Catholic and Apostolic Church'.[13]

Before long the father started to think seriously about following in his son's footsteps. He approached the priest of St Lawrence's Catholic church in Petersfield in the summer of 1955 and explained that he was an ex-Anglican who thought he wished instruction. The priest, Father Henry Clarke, was 'kindly, un-pushy and sympathetic' and told the would-be catechumen that he was an ex-Anglican himself. They arranged to meet regularly over the following weeks. Guinness later discovered that Father Clarke had received Group-Captain Leonard Cheshire VC into the Church six years earlier.

Desiring to see the workings of the Church at closer quarters, Guinness arranged to go on retreat to Mount St Bernard Abbey, a Trappist monastery in the Midlands. His stay included some unfortunate encounters with other guests, including one with 'a very serious young man' who 'exuded extreme gloom':

> He stopped me on the stairs. 'You are in films, aren't you?' he asked, almost malevolently. 'Sort of,' I replied. 'I don't go to films,' he hissed. I sensed rising hysteria. Then he screeched, 'And I NEVER will; not until they do away with SEX!' He clattered down the stairs leaving me dumbfounded by his 'holier than thou' thought-for-the-day. I longed for something nasty to happen to him in the woodshed; which was a poor start for a monastic retreat.[14]

If some of his fellow guests left a lot to be desired, Guinness was very impressed by the monks themselves: 'Although the Cistercians of the Strict Observance (they are not keen on being called Trappists, I discovered) keep a formidable silence, except in the case of absolute necessity, a monk was allocated to chat to me whenever I wanted.'[15] The monk in question, Father Robert Hodge, OCSO, had been an Anglican priest at Dartmouth before his own conversion, was in his fifties 'and not in very good health'. He and Guinness were to form a lasting friendship:

> He had great charm and ... gave me a run-down on many of his fellow monks and their past professions ... and asked me what I thought the most difficult part of being a monk might be. 'Other monks,' I replied promptly. He gave me a long quizzical look, of the kind Edith Sitwell was so expert at giving, and said, with some solemnity, 'Yes!' I felt I had gone to the top of the class.[16]

Commenting on the previous professions of other monks, Father Hodge informed Guinness that one had been a Customs official, another had been a major in a Rifle Corps, one was in the Metropolitan Police until the previous year and, pointing to a black monk clipping a hedge, he explained that he 'comes from Abyssinia and is a wonderful farmer. He came here just for a few weeks, oh – twenty years ago. I don't know what we would do without him. *Very* cheerful.'[17]

The most profound impression on Guinness was made by his first attendance at early morning Mass at the Abbey:

> My first morning I was awakened at about 4.30 by a chatty Irish Lay Brother bringing me a cup of strong sweet tea and a chocolate biscuit. He eyed the biscuit enviously, but no doubt offered it up to God. Arriving at the large, draughty, austere, white chapel I was amazed at the sights and sounds that greeted me. The great doors to the East were wide open and the sun, a fiery red ball, was rising over the distant farmland; at each of the dozen or so side-altars a monk, finely vested but wearing heavy farmer's boots to which cow dung still adhered, was saying his private Mass. Voices were low, almost whispers, but each Mass was at a different stage of development, so that the Sanctus would tinkle from one altar to be followed half a minute later by other tinkles from far away. For perhaps five minutes little bells sounded from all over and the sun grew whiter as it steadily rose. There was an awe-inspiring sense of God expanding, as if to fill every corner of the church and the whole world.[18]

Guinness was 'transfixed by the unexpected beauty of it all' and, from that moment, became attached to the monastery, to which he would make subsequent visits:

> The regularity of life at the Abbey, the happy faces that shone through whatever they had suffered, the strong yet delicate singing, the early hours and hard work – for the monks are self-supporting – all made a deep impression on me; the atmosphere was one of prayer without frills; it was easy to imagine oneself at the centre of some spiritual power-house, or at least being privileged to look over the rails, so to speak, at the working of a great turbine.[19]

Certainly life at the Abbey had energized Guinness and he was received into the Church by Father Clarke at St Lawrence's, Petersfield, on 24 March 1956: 'Like countless converts before and after me, I felt I had come home – "and known the place for the first time".'[20] His wife was 'sympathetic and pleased but probably felt a little out of things'.

After the ceremony, a deliberately low-key affair attended by only two or three close friends, Guinness returned to Kettlebrook Meadows, his home on the borders of Hampshire and Sussex. It was 'a beautiful sunny day' and he spent a long time gazing on the line of hills which surrounded the house on three sides; the Hangers to the north-west, Butser Hill to the south and Harting Down in the east.

> Some phrase of Newman, in garbled form, ran in my head – something about the line of the hills being the skirts of the Angels of God … Such was my mood that day and I was more than content: now the trees we planted thirty years ago have grown tall, obscuring much of the view in summer-time. In these latter days, like Roy Campbell, 'I love to see, when leaves depart, the clear anatomy arrive'. The winter hills nourish my faith. There had been no emotional upheaval, no great insight, certainly no proper grasp of theological issues; just a sense of history and the fittingness of things.[21]

During the following year, while Guinness was in Sri Lanka making *The Bridge on the River Kwai*, for which he would receive an Oscar, his wife was received into the Church, only informing him after the event. She joined him in Sri Lanka for a few weeks and they celebrated their first Christmas together as Catholics,

> in a little church, open at the sides to palm trees and the sound of surf breaking on a hot, white, sandy beach, with tropical birds flitting over the heads of the congregation, who squatted on the earth floor in colourful saris in deep devotion. The whole world, however poverty-stricken, seemed a wide-open bright and sunlit place, 'where all contraries are reconciled'.[22]

It was in this spirit of exhilaration that Guinness found himself running up Kingsway in London on another occasion, feeling a sudden compulsion to get to the nearest Catholic church as soon as possible:

> I knelt; caught my breath, and for ten minutes was lost to the world. Coming out into the glare of day, mingling with sensible citizens on their lawful occasions, I wondered what on earth had possessed me and

if I had become momentarily deranged. I decided that I was still fairly sane; that it had just been an unexpected, rather nonsensical gesture of love. My friend, Richard Leech, when I told him about it, was rather distressed, thinking my tiresome convert enthusiasm had gone too far ... There was some reassurance when I discovered that the good, brilliant, acutely sane Ronald Knox had found himself running, on several occasions, to visit the Blessed Sacrament.[23]

The low-key nature of Guinness's reception was indicative of his desire that publicity should be avoided and he was relieved that 'on the whole the press left me well alone'.[24] Yet he was visited by a young reporter from the *Daily Express* who turned up unexpectedly at Kettlebrook Meadows on Good Friday, a few days after his reception, just as he was about to leave for a service:

I welcomed him with a certain amount of dismay, I suspect, but politely. Anyway, I gave him a drink. I was rather amazed to see his article, when it appeared, saying he had found me leaning against a life-size Buddha drinking a tumbler of gin. I *do* possess a carved, wooden, Chinese lamp, which stands about two feet, six inches high (the Buddha must surely have been taller) and I am confident the tumbler of gin was a glass of water. Actors should learn to get used to such things, I know. Only one abusive letter reached me – anonymous of course – and written on the Royal Automobile Club's notepaper. The hundreds of other letters, from people of various persuasions, were pleasing and touching.[25]

The spiritual candour of the chapter in Guinness's autobiography covering his conversion is comparatively rare and much of his other writing is worldly, chatty and gossipy in tone. In this he is similar to Evelyn Waugh. As a result, the writing of both men, though immensely entertaining, is characterized by an obscuring of the depths of belief in the shallows of everyday events – the temporal eclipse of the eternal by life's diversions.

The depth of devotion which underpinned Guinness's faith was perceived by Elizabeth Salter, the Australian novelist who was both secretary and companion to Edith Sitwell from 1957 to 1964. Salter was present when Guinness had arrived at the Sesame Club to apologize to Sitwell for the offensive reference to her conversion which was falsely attributed to him in an article in *Time* magazine:

A quiet man of medium stature, his expression conveyed the melancholy introspection of the contemplative rather than of the actor. He was obviously eager to discuss their religion. In fact, his reason for coming to see her was to apologise for an account of her reception into the Church which had appeared in an American magazine and which had been credited to him – a highly coloured, irreverent description which owed more to imagination than to fact, and from which Sir Alec was anxious to dissociate himself.[26]

Before he left, he discussed his role as the cardinal in *The Prisoner* and Salter gained the impression that

here was an actor who would sink his own personality in a role rather than project his image through it or, as is so often the case, in spite of it … The impression he left was of a man with a vocation and a genius within that vocation, but remaining, because of the depth of his nature, unsatisfied by it.[27]

NOTES

1. Alec Guinness, *Blessings in Disguise*, London, 1985, p. 23.
2. ibid., p. 25.
3. ibid., p. 25.
4. ibid., pp. 178–9.
5. ibid., p. 178.
6. ibid., p. 180.
7. ibid., p. 31.
8. ibid., p. 31.
9. ibid., p. 33.
10. ibid., p. 36.
11. ibid., p. 37.
12. ibid., p. 37.
13. ibid., p. 38.
14. ibid., p. 39.
15. ibid., p. 39.
16. ibid., p. 40.
17. ibid., p. 41.
18. ibid., p. 40.
19. ibid., p. 41.
20. ibid., p. 42.
21. ibid., pp. 42–3.
22. ibid., p. 44.
23. ibid., p. 44.
24. ibid., p. 43.
25. ibid., p. 43.
26. Elizabeth Salter, *The Last Years of a Rebel: A Memoir of Edith Sitwell*, p. 71.
27. ibid., p. 71.

CHAPTER TWENTY FIVE

SASSOON AND KNOX

Elizabeth Salter's impression of 'a man with a vocation and a genius within that vocation, but remaining, because of the depth of his nature, unsatisfied by it', so true of Alec Guinness's vocation as an actor, would have been equally applicable to Siegfried Sassoon's vocation as a poet. After a lifetime of contemplative searching expressed eloquently in his verse, Sassoon, at the time of Guinness's reception into the Church, was on the verge of conversion himself.

It was somewhat ironic that Sassoon should enter the Church so close on the heels of his old friend Edith Sitwell. The two poets had become increasingly estranged during the decades that had elapsed since the halcyon days of their friendship in the years following the First World War. In Sassoon's view, Edith Sitwell's attitude towards him had 'cooled' because the critics had dubbed him 'old-fashioned'.[1] It was therefore with a certain sense of satisfaction that he had read the critical broadside against Sitwell in the *New Statesman* early in 1954, which had so offended Sitwell and had caused her to complain to Kingsley Amis that '*Not one* of the persons who has had the impertinence to attack me has even a germ of talent for poetry.'[2] Sassoon, however, thought the *New Statesman* article 'an amusing and clever summing up of her career as a publicity personality, and her insistence on the role of a Literary Queen':

This reminded me of the factitiousness of contrived reputation, and made me thankful that I have chosen to isolate myself from seeking to be conspicuous. E.S.'s present prestige is upheld by an insecure fabric. Had she remained quiet and unobtrusive ... she would be known and appreciated by her work as a very gifted, fantastical writer ... with a highly sensitive sense of word sounds and effects. But she has assumed the robes of a prophetess and oracle – much influenced by Yeats and Eliot – and her solemnities and apocalypses will, I suspect, be found to be a pretension of powers she doesn't possess.[3]

This was a curious criticism, not least because Sassoon had also cast himself in the role of an oracle. Both he and Sitwell had written doom-laden warnings of humanity's fate in the wake of the dropping of the atomic bombs on Hiroshima and Nagasaki – Sitwell in 'The Shadow of Cain' and Sassoon in 'Litany of the Lost' – and both felt themselves exiles in the atomic age in which they found themselves. In fact, they had much more in common than their estrangement suggested and their enmity would admit. It was the things they held in common which led them individually and independently to the same fundamental conclusions about faith and philosophy.

Another exile in the atomic age was Ronald Knox who had written his prose *God and the Atom* at around the same time that Sassoon and Sitwell were making their similar prophecies poetically. Knox was to become a major influence on Sassoon's final approach to Catholicism, and Sassoon, in turn, became a valued friend of Knox in the last three years of his life. After one of their earliest meetings, 'an enchanting afternoon at Mells in 1955', Sassoon remarked to a friend that 'I adore Ronnie; but somehow he seems, for me, to be behind a plate-glass window. I wouldn't dare to speak of *religion* to him!' 'Of course,' Sassoon confessed in April 1960, three years after his own conversion, 'it was I who was behind the plate-glass.'[4]

It appears that the plate-glass had been removed by July 1956 because Sassoon was one of a few friends from whom Knox sought advice regarding a new work of apologetics on which he was labouring. In June, it seems, Knox was hesitating between two forms of approach, those of plain disquisition and of dialogue, and in July he admitted that he was 'stuck'. He showed the two versions to selected friends, including Frank Sheed, the Catholic publisher and writer, and Dom Sebastian Moore of Downside. He also sought the advice of Sassoon who evidently favoured the direct approach.[5] The fact that Knox valued Sassoon's judgement sufficiently to seek such advice would suggest that the two were now on intimate terms and were able to discuss the finer points of religion. It is reasonable to assume, therefore, that Knox was largely responsible for the ironing out of Sassoon's remaining difficulties. In retrospect, Sassoon confessed a major debt to Knox's spiritual works. 'I like Ronald's conferences to schoolgirls,' he admitted, 'just as much as I like his deeper books. Also of course it's great fun *hearing* him in everything he writes.'[6] On 17 February 1962 he wrote to a friend that he had 'reached the last chapter of *Let Dons Delight*, read for the fifth time since 1938 ... The odd thing is that I enjoyed it so much before 1957, when the discussions about religion meant so little to me.'[7]

Knox's work of apologetics was never completed. He was temporarily diverted from the task by his work on the translation from the French of *The Story of a Soul*, the abridged autobiography of St Thérèse of Lisieux, before being permanently prevented from continuing by ill-health. Although he never finished the book – indeed he hardly even began it – he had written an Invocation which was designed to be its preface. This he had lent to Sassoon in the typescript and Sassoon, considering it to be 'wonderfully fine', made a copy of it. Its concise contents were so important that Sassoon wrote that 'it was the beginning of the immeasurable instruction I have gained from his religious writings'.[8] Moreover, it serves as Knox's last testament and, according to Evelyn Waugh, 'may stand as the epitaph of his life's work'.[9] It is both an indication of Sassoon's state of mind shortly before his conversion, and of Knox's shortly before his death:

> My God, when I dedicate something I have written to any human creature, I am taking away something which does not belong to me, and giving it to one who is not competent to receive it.
>
> What I have written does not belong to me. If I have written the truth, then it is 'God's truth'; it would be true if every human mind denied it, or if there were no human minds in existence to recognise it … If I have written well, that is not because Hobbs, Nobbs, Noakes and Stokes unite in praising it, but because it contains that interior excellence which is some strange refraction of your own perfect beauty; and of that excellence you alone are the judge. If it proves useful to others, that is because you have seen fit to make use of it as a weak tool, to achieve something in them of that supernatural end which is their destiny, and your secret.
>
> Nor is any human creature, in the last resort, competent to receive the poorest of our tributes. When we dedicate a book to any name that is named on earth, we owe it (so we tell ourselves) to the love we bear him, or the admiration he excites in us, or the aid he has given us in the writing of it. But all we can love or admire in him is only some glimpse of your glory that peeps through the ragged garments of humanity; all the contribution he has made is only a part, and a small part, of the sufficiency which is your gift …
>
> Into your hands, then, I remit this book, undedicated … But some of us – and perhaps, at the roots of our being, all of us – cannot forgo that search for truth in which full satisfaction is denied us here. We apprehend that there is no encounter with reality, from without or

from within, that does not echo with your foot-fall. We scrutinize the values, and can give no account of them except as a mask of the divine. Something of all these elusive considerations finds a place in my book. And you, who need nobody's service, can use anybody's. So I would ask that, among all the millions of souls you cherish, some few, upon the occasion of reading it, may learn to understand you a little, and to love you much.[10]

If this Invocation had been 'the beginning of the immeasurable instruction' which Sassoon was to receive from Knox's religious writings it was perhaps appropriate that Knox was the first person Sassoon informed of his decision to take formal instruction to become a Catholic: 'He was the first – he and Katherine Asquith – to whom I told my decision. I have never ceased to be thankful that he had the happiness of knowing about it "in time", and it did give him real happiness.'[11]

The last time Sassoon saw Knox was on 5 July 1957 when he had taken Edmund Blunden to meet him. They talked for three and a half hours. Knox, though gravely ill, spoke to both his visitors 'with full enjoyment of seeing us – and almost made me forget how heartbreaking it was, that farewell'.[12]

Knox died seven weeks later on 24 August. His obituary in *The Times* expressed the belief that 'to men of all creeds and of none, who delight in a personality that combines simple unaffected faith with a brain that could cut like a razor, he was regarded as one of the individually great in his generation'. The same obituary also recorded that 'he moved, throughout his life, in the inner circles of the religious and intellectual elite'. Many of these were to be seen at his requiem Mass at Westminster Cathedral on 29 August where members of both the religious and secular hierarchies brushed shoulders with the *literati*. The newly appointed Prime Minister, Harold Macmillan, was present, having known Knox at both Eton and Oxford, and other mourners included Evelyn Waugh, Lord Longford, Douglas Woodruff, Christopher Hollis, Maisie Ward, Frank Sheed and a host of diplomatic dignitaries. The panegyric was preached by Father Martin D'Arcy, standing in the place where Knox himself had preached the panegyric for Chesterton over twenty years earlier. Father D'Arcy called Knox a defender of English culture and compared him with St Thomas More: 'that English culture, based on the Bible and the humanities which, manifesting itself in St Thomas More, flowed on to define itself again in Ronald Knox ... he did not try to keep up with the latest fashions in philosophy, art, or literature. He used his Dryden-like power of satire to ridicule the pretentious, the mystagogue, and the sophistical.'[13]

'Ronnie Knox entrusted me with his biography,' Evelyn Waugh wrote to Father Hubert van Zeller on 25 September, 'a task for which I have no qualification except love.'[14] There is no doubt that Waugh loved Knox deeply, regardless of whether he was qualified in other respects to be entrusted with his biography, and he had been a great support to him during the final months of his life. Yet opinions vary widely concerning whether his biography of Knox did his friend justice. Reviewing the biography in the *Observer*, Graham Greene wrote of the private life of prayer which presents problems to any biographer of a deeply religious person:

> A priest presents even more difficulties to his biographer than a writer. As with an iceberg, little shows compared with what lies beneath: we have to dive for depth, but if we so dive we have the sense of breaking into a life far more private and exclusive than a bedroom ... His biographer ... must write a life of his hero which excludes the hero's chief activity.
>
> This Mr Waugh does with a sense of style which would have delighted his subject and an exquisite tact which Father Knox had obviously foreseen in asking him to be his biographer.[15]

Christopher Derrick, who met Knox 'quite a number of times but couldn't claim to know him', was also impressed by Waugh's biography:

> he leant over backward and painted, many people thought, too dark a picture, making Knox look more of a neurotic old fuss-pot than he was. But he was a neurotic old fuss-pot ... In the late forties and early fifties a vast crowd would come when he preached at Oxford. He was so popular ... It was all about fashions and styles. The Edwardian dandy. And a priest with literary mannerisms of that kind was then rather enchanting ... To meet the priest who was a cultured gentleman, and a wit, and a scholar, was a glass of wine in a thirsty desert.[16]

This view of both Waugh's biography and Knox's personality was not shared by Siegfried Sassoon. 'I am specially grateful for your commentary on the Ronald biography,' he wrote to a friend shortly after the book was published. 'E. W. does make it clear in the Introduction that he is only offering an *exterior* portrait. As you say, the man and mind and spirit so deeply precious to us are diminished to a character. I dare to say "us" because he has spoken to me with a living voice, through his writings, as no one else has done.' Knox, Sassoon continued, has been near to me every day ... a life line toward illumination in my crepuscular contemplations. And I am only one among thousands. We are told about his virtues and his idiosyncrasies – but where is his creative sanctity revealed in E.W.'s pages? ... In a way he was a dual personality – the early incredibly brilliant and accomplished R. was always there, intermingled with the near-saint and incomparable expositor of alive religion. But in all that he was, he *gave* with both hands – spiritual help, scholarship, entertainment.[17]

If Sassoon had serious misgivings about Waugh's biography of Knox, he appeared to have nothing but praise for Robert Speaight's biography of Belloc which was published in 1957. Sassoon had known Belloc, through their mutual friendship with W. S. Blunt, since the end of the First World War. He had always admired Belloc's poetry, prose and personality but had found his Catholic faith beyond his reach or comprehension. Then he read Speaight's biography and was struck by a letter Belloc had written to Katherine Asquith. This particular letter, he explained to a friend on 29 March 1960, was of crucial importance and was a major milestone on his own personal path to Rome:

'Outcast and unprotected contours of the soul' is not *me*, but beloved *Belloc*. It must have been almost exactly three years ago, when I was in the vortex of struggling toward submission, that I came upon the following passage in Speaight's biography, from a letter to K. Asquith: 'The Faith, the Catholic Church, is discovered, is recognized, triumphantly enters reality like a landfall at sea which first was thought a cloud. The nearer it is seen, the more it is real, the less imaginary: the more direct and external its voice, the more indubitable its representative character, its "persona", its voice. The metaphor is not that men fall in love with it: the metaphor is that they discover home. "This was what I sought. This was my need." It is the very mould of the mind, the matrix to which corresponds in every outline the outcast and unprotected contour of the soul. It is Verlaine's "Oh! Rome – oh! Mere!" And that not only to those who had it in childhood and have returned, but much more – and what a proof! – to those who come upon it from the hills of life and say to themselves, "Here is the town."'

After reading this passage, Sassoon sat all afternoon, gazing out of the window. His mind, a metaphysical reflection of 'a day of wild weather', was 'pervaded by a sort of ghostly climatic disturbance – cloud conflictings and murmurous intimations of spiritual debate'. 'Belloc's magnificent words settled it, once and for all. "That's done it," I said. My whole being was liberated. O that he could have known it, foreknown it when he came here twenty-five years ago.'[18]

In the same letter Sassoon explained that another factor on his road to faith was the experience of visiting churches in Italy while staying with Max Beerbohm. He recalled climbing the steep path behind Beerbohm's house at Rapallo to a hill-top church, and also visiting 'a lovely little old one – S. Pantaleone – on the headland along the Spezzia road - and both produced a wistful awareness of devotion which I longed to share. I *knew* that they were different to Heytesbury church (in which I have never attended a service!)'.[19] One hears echoes of Knox's allusion to 'the Real Absence' in Anglican churches and also of Sitwell's confession that it was 'the serenity in the faces of the peasant women praying in the churches in Italy' that had drawn her to the Church.

One major difference between Sitwell and Sassoon, however, was their respective attitudes to the trappings of secular society. Whereas Sitwell had rejoiced loudly and publicly at her gaining of the OBE in 1954, Sassoon's response to being awarded the Queen's Gold Medal for Poetry on 28 June 1957 was muted. It was left to his admirers, such as the reporter in the following morning's edition of *The Times*, to celebrate on his behalf:

> Announcement from Buckingham Palace yesterday that the Queen's Gold Medal for Poetry has been awarded to Mr Siegfried Sassoon will give general satisfaction to those who, for the past forty years, have followed with attentive interest the humours of his very personal muse ... It would have been easy to find a poet more fashionable than Mr Sassoon – whose concern for fashion is minimal ... What has been sought, however, and found, is a poet whose voice has found its own pitch and its own strength, regardless of the distractions which encroach upon it. *Sequences*, published at the end of last year, shows that the voice has plenty of vigour in it yet.

By the end of June 1957 the vigour of his voice was, Sassoon believed, being put to a higher service than that of Queen and country. It was about this time that he sought instruction to join the Catholic Church. He was received in September 1957, shortly after his seventy-first birthday.

He had intended that his reception be a private affair and was horrified when an unauthorized interview with him appeared in the *Sunday Express*. He wrote to the paper complaining of its invasion of his privacy and when the letter went unpublished he sent a copy of it to *The Times*:

While appreciating its sympathetic treatment of my submission to the Roman Catholic Faith, I am compelled to state that the *Sunday Express*'s interview with me was entirely unauthorised. Everything that I was reported as saying was part of an expostulation against my most sacred intimacies being exhibited as newspaper publicity.[20]

On the morning after *The Times* had published Sassoon's letter, a reply from John Junor, editor of the *Sunday Express*, was published. 'I have no wish further to embarrass Mr Sassoon,' Junor began, before denying that 'the *Sunday Express* either treated him unfairly or quoted him inaccurately. The *Sunday Express* reporter who interviewed Mr Sassoon spent one and a half hours with him. Mr Sassoon was kind enough to entertain him to tea. At no time was he in doubt as to the nature of his visit. The reporter made frequent and open use of his notebook ...'

Three days later, on 5 October, Sassoon's reply was published:

As the editor of the *Sunday Express*, Mr Junor, asserts in his letter today, I 'was at no time in doubt as to the nature of the visit'. His reporter invaded me without warning while sitting in my hay barn. My first – almost frantic – words to him were to the effect that any 'news story' would be an outrage on my most sensitive feelings. Having, seemingly, convinced him of this, I gave him a letter to Mr Junor, begging to be spared all publicity. Thereafter I treated the reporter with too trustful courtesy and confidence.

The idea of my being represented as having given an authorised interview never entered my mind.

Sassoon's 'almost frantic' efforts to avoid his 'most sacred intimacies' being discussed was indicative of his very private nature and his desire to remain as inconspicuous as possible. An illustration of this can be seen in his relationship with his son. When *Memoirs of a Fox-hunting Man*, the first part of Sassoon's semi-fictitious autobiography, *The Complete Memoirs of George Sherston*, was set for GCE in 1954, his son had to answer for his exam the question, 'What sort of man was George Sherston?' He replied: 'As he happens to be my father I prefer to reserve my opinion.'[21] As well as being a highly amusing riposte to his examiners, George Sassoon's reticence appears to be an inherited reflection of his father's own intensely private personality. An example can be seen in George's admission that his father 'never discussed his religious feelings with me'.[22] If Sassoon avoided discussing religion with his own son it is scarcely surprising that he wished to avoid discussing his conversion with journalists.

One result of Sassoon's reticence is a scarcity of written records charting his spiritual and intellectual progress, a dearth of material amongst which any student of his life and work must rummage for precious jewels of enlightenment. Even Rupert Hart-Davis, Sassoon's friend and literary executor, is reduced to a mere generalization when discussing Sassoon's conversion: 'Siegfried Sassoon was unconsciously looking for God all his life, but didn't become religious until very late in life.'[23]

It is as Sassoon would have wished. His testament and his autobiography are to be found in his intensely personal and introspective verse which, from the earliest sonnets of his youth to the religious poetry of his last years, are a sublime reflection of a life's journey in pursuit of truth. These, and not his diaries, his letters or his prose, are the precious jewels of enlightenment that point to the soul within the man. This certainly appears to be Sassoon's own view of the matter because in 1960 he selected thirty of his poems for a volume entitled *The Path to Peace*, which was essentially an autobiography in verse. Even then he appeared to prefer a strictly limited and private audience. The book was published by the Stanbrook Abbey Press in two private editions severely limited by both number and price. The book was handset, and only five hundred, individually numbered copies were printed; twenty copies on Millbourne handmade paper, bound in full vellum, hand-lettered and gilded by Margaret Adams, and the remaining 480 copies on W.S.H. handmade paper, quarter-bound in vellum with hand-lettered initials. For the book's epigraph, Sassoon chose the extract from Belloc's letter to Katherine Asquith which had been so crucial to his own conversion, and he dedicated the volume 'To Mary Immaculate, Mother of God, into whose keeping was given Mother Margaret Mary, Religious of the Assumption'. Sister Juliana Dawson, Christopher Dawson's daughter and herself a religious of the Assumption, remembered that the late Mother Margaret Mary had influenced Sassoon's conversion; Sassoon, it seemed, retained a close involvement with the Assumption sisters. Sister Juliana remembered him 'coming to the convent in Kensington Square to read his poetry'. His niece also became a Catholic and is now Mother Superior of the Assumption sisters.[24]

During his first Lent as a Catholic, Sassoon wrote 'Lenten Illuminations', a candid account of his conversion which invites obvious comparisons with Eliot's 'Ash Wednesday'. Yet his life after his conversion, apart from a few excellent religious poems, was principally characterized by silence. It was as though he was echoing the words of Goethe: 'Once one knows what really matters one tends to stop talking'. The last decade of his life, like the last decades of the rosary he came to love, was a quiet meditation on the glorious mysteries of faith. It was no coincidence that he chose to end his autobiographical *The Path to Peace* with one of those mysteries. 'A Prayer at Pentecost' was a poet's farewell:

> Master musician, I have overheard you,
> Labouring in litanies of heart to word you.
> Be noteless now. Our duologue is done.

> Spirit, who speak'st by silences, remake me:
> To light of unresistant faith awake me,
> That with resolved requiem I be one.

NOTES

1. D. Felicitas Corrigan (ed.), *Siegfried Sassoon: Poet's Pilgrimage*, London, 1973, p. 209.
2. Richard Greene (ed.), *Selected Letters of Edith Sitwell*, p. 349.
3. D. Felicitas Corrigan (ed.), *Siegfried Sassoon: Poet's Pilgrimage*, p. 157.
4. ibid., p. 185.
5. Evelyn Waugh, *Ronald Knox*, p. 284.
6. D. Felicitas Corrigan (ed.), *Siegfried Sassoon: Poet's Pilgrimage*, p. 184.
9. Evelyn Waugh, *Ronald Knox*, p. 292.
10. ibid., pp. 292–3.
11. D. Felicitas Corrigan (ed.), *Siegfried Sassoon: Poet's Pilgrimage*, p. 184.
12. ibid., p. 185.
13. *The Times*, 30 August 1957.
14. Mark Amory (ed.), *The Letters of Evelyn Waugh*, p. 495.
15. *Observer*, 11 October 1959.
16. Christopher Derrick, interview with the author.
17. D. Felicitas Corrigan (ed.), *Siegfried Sassoon: Poet's Pilgrimage*, p. 185.
18. ibid., pp. 181–2.
19. ibid., pp. 182–3.
20. *The Times*, 1 October 1957.
21. D. Felicitas Corrigan (ed.), *Siegfried Sassoon: Poet's Pilgrimage*, p. 183.
22. George Sassoon, letter to the author, dated 22 August 1996.
23. Rupert Hart-Davis, letter to the author, dated 16 July 1996.
24. Sister Juliana Dawson, interview with the author.

CHAPTER TWENTY SIX

CONTRA MUNDUM

I have often asked my poor old self how much I would have been prepared to *give up* by becoming a Catholic. And the answer was always the same. Everything asked of me. How could it be otherwise ... I am, of course, not qualified to comment on the spiritual dangers of being addicted to the arts and enraptured by the sublime and beautiful. But surely the arts, at their highest level, *have* been expressive of God in us. As to renunciation of the world, we have to decide *what* to reject, I suppose. One of my few maxims used to be, 'I believe in life, and will do my little best to prove it!'[1]

These words of Siegfried Sassoon, written on 29 March 1960, could have been written by any of the other literary converts of his generation. Indeed, they offer a key to understanding the motivation behind the conversions of so many. Above all, there was a deep disillusionment with 'the world' and what it had to offer, a longing for depth in a world of shallows, permanence in a world of change, and certainty in a world of doubt. To many of these twentieth-century literary converts an acceptance of God went hand in hand with a rejection of 'the world' and its materialism. The alienation so evident in Sassoon's own poems had been a central theme of many of the writers who eventually found consolation in Christianity, with Eliot's *Waste Land* as the archetype and forerunner of much that followed.

This underlying unity can be seen in the similarities which existed between otherwise disparate individuals, for example men so different in personality as Siegfried Sassoon and Roy Campbell. Sassoon was quiet, reclusive and intensely private; Campbell could be noisy, riotous and notoriously controversial in many of his public pronouncements and actions. Yet both distinguished themselves with acts of bravery in wartime and both will be remembered to posterity for their powerful war poetry. Also, of course, both found their spiritual home in the Catholic Church, although Campbell died a few months before Sassoon was received. Finally, they both shared a deep-felt distrust of the 'progress' being lauded in the wake of the Second World War, a distrust which found expression in ways which reflected their respective personalities. Sassoon's introspection had produced his hauntingly plaintive 'Litany of the Lost' whereas Campbell's bombastic anger had caused outrage during a speech in his native South Africa in 1954 when he referred to Churchill as 'a valiant but superannuated Beefeater' and Roosevelt as 'a tittering zombie'. In the same speech he denounced 'the Yalta boobytrap' and sneered at England for 'hanging around for Marshall Aid, in other words "tips"'. He added to the controversy by attacking the United Nations and praising Franco's Spain. 'The inspiring crash of dropping bricks echoed throughout the Pietermaritzburg City Hall,' the *Natal Witness* reported.[2]

Campbell's undiplomatic choice of words was guaranteed to cause offence in the sensitive days in which world war merged into Cold War, but presented a distorted picture of his own position. Deeply distrustful of America's role in the post-war world, his view was more balanced than the tirade suggests. His support for Franco's Spain was not an indication that he was a 'fascist' in any generally accepted understanding of the word; he had, after all, consistently criticized the Nazi regime and had fought for the allies during the war. For Campbell, Franco was merely the defender of Catholic Spain from communist atheism. It should be remembered that Campbell was a vociferous opponent of apartheid in his native South Africa.

The nature of his fiery politics seemed to form a paradoxical contrast with other aspects of his personality. The hard-drinking, hard-talking side of his character sat uncomfortably beside the poet who had rendered the mystical verse of St John of the Cross so beautifully into English. Similarly, the *wanderlust* which led to an obsessive compulsion to travel as if fleeing from himself, seemed at loggerheads with his desire and need to live on smallholdings among the peasants of Spain and Portugal. Perhaps it was the very clash of these inconsistencies which energized Campbell's creativity.

By 1956 the inconsistencies appeared largely to have reconciled themselves in the tranquillity of age. He and Mary were now living in the small village of Linho in Portugal. Each morning they went to Mass at the nearby convent and each evening they said the rosary together. 'We have to say one fifth for the bolshies' conversion,' he wrote to Edith Sitwell. 'I would sooner be fighting them – but the Holy Father knows best.'[3] The words were rhetorical, designed to play up to Sitwell's view of him as a champion on a charger, but in reality he was no longer able to fight anyone. He was suffering stoically from sciatica so that a walk of more than a hundred yards was a severe struggle. He grew very fat and photographs taken at the end of 1956 show his face puffed and pale. The last-written of his published poems, 'November Nights', possessed a serenity seldom found in his earlier verse, a serenity accentuated by its long lines and gentle, subdued rhythm:

> Now peasants shun the muddy fields, and fisherfolk the shores.
> It is the time the weather finds the wounds of bygone wars,
> And never to a charger did I take as I have done
> To cantering the rocking-chair, my Pegasus, indoors,
> For my olives have been gathered and my grapes are in the tun.

He and Mary spent a quiet religious Christmas in Portugal with their daughters and their two grandchildren. His Christmas letters to old friends conveyed a peacefully resigned and patiently prophetic note. To Daphne Collins, his BBC secretary, with whom he had corresponded since 1950, he wrote, 'I am rather ill; maybe I shall not write to you again, but I send my respectful affection, as from the first day that you so kindly worked with me.'[4]

In January 1957 he finished correcting the proofs of the second volume of his *Collected Poems* but he had no energy left for new work. Even his history of the Spanish Civil War, which he had been writing on and off since 1939 'to correct the Kremlin-crazy liars in England', was quietly shelved and left unfinished. It seemed as though he was ready to sign off and was awaiting the graceful glide towards death. It was not to be.

On 5 April he and Mary set off in their tiny Fiat 600 for Spain, destined for the Holy Week ceremonies in Seville. Mary Campbell noticed that her husband seemed more serious than ever in his devotions throughout the week of processions in Seville and she responded accordingly. They set off home on 23 April and by four in the afternoon had crossed the border and were travelling down the long pine avenues that lined the roads of southern Portugal. Suddenly one of the front tyres burst and the car swerved violently off the road and smashed into a tree. Campbell's neck was broken. He breathed for a little while, sighed twice and then life slipped away. His wife was unconscious, her foot crushed, her arm, ribs, and front teeth broken. She survived and lived for a further twenty-two years, enduring poverty and continuing her ceaseless work for Catholic charitable organizations even though she and her daughter were forced on occasion to live on soup made of fish-heads.

There was something symbolically symmetrical about the violent nature of Campbell's death. Ever a man of action who endured, and even enjoyed, the violent aspects of life, he died, it seemed, as he had lived. Not for him the slow subsidence into sickness and a protracted, deathbed-bound exit. The soldier-poet had died with his boots on. The symbolism was not lost on Edith Sitwell, who had been shocked and horrified when news of Campbell's death had reached her:

> This simple giant, with 'devocioun in his heart', was the true Knight of Our Lady, and if he had to be taken by death, it was suitable that this should have been when he was returning from the celebration of Her Son's Resurrection.
>
> I think, too, that he, who was all energy, all fire, would have hated to die slowly and helplessly, in bed. He died, as he had lived, like a flash of lightning.[5]

One wonders whether Sitwell had also noticed that her champion, the knight in shining armour who had defended her reputation against the attacks of literary dragons, had been killed on the feast of St George.

Writing of Campbell in *The Times* on 1 May, Thomas Moult of the Poetry Society said that

> he will be remembered by friends and enemies alike as the most forth-right and invigorating of all the present-day poets. As a personality he was the most picturesque. He was not only a bullfighter in Spain at one time. He won a silver picador's jacket twice, and a steer-throwing con-test in Provence. His visits to London were frequent. Chelsea, for example, knew this vital, volcanic man of thought and action as vividly as he was known in, say, Madrid.

His requiem was celebrated by Father D'Arcy at Farm Street on 21 May, with Edith Sitwell most prominent among the *literati* in attendance.

It was not until 23 September that Sitwell finally wrote to Mary Campbell:

> My thoughts have been with you *all* this time, in your greatest grief, desolation, and loneliness.
>
> The reason why I have not written before is because ever since the early summer, griefs and disasters have been heaped on my head – to such a degree that I wondered, sometimes, if it was *possible*. The only thing to do, at such a time, is to be *silent* to those who are suffering more deeply than oneself – not to heap one's sorrows and troubles onto their greater ones, which is the height of selfishness. But now I realise that I must be being taught some lesson ...

The *Sunday Times* has promised me that I shall review Roy's poems immediately they come out ...

He is one of the only really great poets of our time, – such fire, such a holy spirit, such ineffable beauty.[6]

From the moment of Campbell's death, Sitwell saw herself as his literary champion, repaying a perceived debt in a quixotic *quid pro quo*. As she believed Campbell had defended her reputation while he was alive, so she would defend his reputation now that he was dead and unable to defend himself. Not only had she elicited the promise from the *Sunday Times* that she be allowed to review his poems, but she began to promote his poetry at every opportunity. In September, during a recital to raise funds for the restoration of Stonor Chapel, where St Edmund Campion had said Mass prior to his arrest, she recited Campbell's translation of 'Upon a Gloomy Night' and his 'Vision of Our Lady over Toledo'. In 1960 she wrote the foreword to the third volume of Campbell's *Collected Poems* in which she repeated her belief that he was 'one of the very few great poets of our time':

His original poems are of great stature, and have a giant's strength and power of movement, without a giant's heaviness ...

The poems have, too, an extraordinary sensuous beauty – a sensuousness that is extremely rare in our time.

Everything, even the humblest flower, is transformed into greatness ...

Campbell had an extraordinary and flawless technique, with every variety, from the superb strength and savagery of *Mazeppa* to the exquisite, cool, vital, dancing sound of *The Palm* ... to the beauty, the ineffable sound, that is like that of water lapping, of the translation from St John of the Cross, *Upon a Gloomy Night*, which is, perhaps, the chief glory of this present book.[7]

Sitwell repeated her adoration of Campbell's poetry in her autobiography, *Taken Care Of*, which was published shortly after her own death in 1964. She also expressed her adoration and admiration for the man behind the poetry. Campbell, she wrote, had 'great stature, build, strength, and vitality' and his eyes had 'the flashing blue of the kingfisher':

One would have noticed him anywhere, towering above the crowd, not only because of his height, and certainly not because of any flaunting characteristics – he was utterly lacking in affectation, in appearance or manner – but because of his extraordinary personality.

He had a great simplicity, and his courtesy and sweetness to his friends could not have been greater. Fantastically brave and chivalrous, he had the simple heart and the faith of a child … He has been accused of being a fascist. He was never a fascist. But, a deeply religious man, he fought against the Reds in Spain. He believed, as I believe, that it is equally infamous to massacre priests, nuns, Jews, peasants, and aristocrats.[8]

Another poet who remained an admirer of Campbell was Edmund Blunden who liked to remember him as a 'literary Sheriff who sometimes came in to clear up the burg'.[9] Blunden, like Campbell, had his literary reputation stigmatized because he backed the 'wrong side' during the Spanish Civil War.

Campbell, however, was always *pro Ecclesia contra mundum* and considered the charge of political incorrectness with contempt. If anything he carried the stigma of the world's scorn as though he had received the stigmata of Christ, brandishing his wounds with honour and, regrettably perhaps, with pride. His attitude, however theologically questionable, was that one should look after the pennies from heaven and let the world go to Hell. It is scarcely surprising then that the world should find itself less than enamoured with Campbell. The conflict was summarized succinctly by David Wright in his early critical study of Campbell, published in 1961. 'It is not easy, so soon after his death,' Wright wrote, 'to assess the work of one so uniquely placed and composed of so many contradictory qualities':

That Campbell was an authentic poet there can be no doubt … As Vernon Watkins has pointed out, 'he maintained a singularly consistent role as inspired campaigner and champion of the under-dog', and, like Dr Johnson, Campbell was in the habit of championing what he considered the real, rather than the obvious or currently fashionable under-dog. Further he affirmed, in his life and in his work, the validity of the poetic vocation, its serious character and its morality of delight … 'There are no substitutes for morality, honour, and loyalty, either in themselves (as we are so painfully learning) or as the substance of poetry.' In this sense Campbell was a Don Quixote whose courage and valour were dedicated to a vanished ethic, and whose values only seem comic or insane in the measure that the world is debased.[10]

Wright's assertion was not strictly true, or at least Campbell would not have thought it so. Campbell did not believe he was dedicated to a vanished ethic in a debased world, but to an inviolable ethic in a world too base to understand the essentials. The ethic was not vanished but merely invisible to a world too blind to see it: 'And the light shineth in darkness; and the darkness comprehended it not.'

This view was at the very core, not only of Campbell's life and work, but also of the lives and works of other Christian writers. It was also at the core of the opposition of many of these writers to the changes, liturgical and otherwise, taking place in the Catholic Church during the fifties and sixties. These changes were perceived, mistakenly perhaps, to be indicative of a 'selling out' of Catholic practices in an ill-conceived effort to come to terms with the modern world. The reforms were seen as nothing but 'standardisation by a low standard', as Chesterton had described the vulgarizing tendency of modern life, a scarring of the Church's beauty with the ugliness of modern trends.

Roy Campbell and Ronald Knox died within months of each other in 1957 and did not see many of the sweeping changes. Knox, however, lived long enough to see the relaxation of the eucharistic fast and what Waugh described as 'the irruption of the laity into the liturgy'. He saw, Waugh continued, 'ecclesiastical architects turn their backs on the Mediterranean and follow the stark, proletarian fashions of the north'.[11] Yet, in spite of his intrinsic traditionalism, Knox endeavoured to overcome any prejudices he had towards the reforms. Some of his later sermons, particularly the Corpus Christi series at Maiden Lane, were conscious rebukes addressed to himself for his sentimental regret at the changing face of the Church.

In spite of such efforts to fall in line, Knox found many of the reforms irksome. He had a love for Latin which stretched back to his Anglican days at Balliol:

> In my first summer I won the Hertford Scholarship, an award made on an examination in Latin only; and my success here … made me think more kindly of the Latin language, hitherto despised in comparison with Greek. The love I afterwards acquired for the Latin tongue as something rich in associations and lying at the roots (I think Hilaire Belloc says) of European culture, must have made it easier for me to fall under the spell of the Latin Mass and the Latin Office, as opposed to English translations and adaptations of them.[12]

It was this love for Latin which led to an unusually caustic response to a request that he perform a baptism in the vernacular: 'The baby doesn't understand English,' he said, 'and the Devil knows Latin.'[13]

If Knox died before witnessing the sweeping extent of the reforms, Waugh was to live long enough to see them in full swing. From the very start he found himself in obstinate opposition. The first intimations of change came during Waugh's retreat at Downside Abbey during Holy Week in 1956. He arrived at Downside on the Wednesday and stayed until after the High Mass of Easter. He recorded in his diary that the triduum was 'rather boring since the new liturgy introduced for the first time this year leaves many hours unemployed'. He attended a series of conferences given by Father Illtyd Trethowan, 'a bright, youngish philosopher', but found himself 'in violent disagreement with almost all he said and resentful of the new liturgy'. The diary entry described in detail the changes to the liturgy with evident disapproval though he still admitted that, 'In spite of all I found the triduum valuable'.[14] Soon his aversion to the new liturgy hardened so much that he felt unable to continue the annual retreat. Six years later he bemoaned what he perceived as the impoverishment of the Holy Week services in an article for the *Spectator*:

> For centuries these had been enriched by devotions which were dear to the laity – the anticipation of the morning office of Tenebrae, the vigil at the Altar of Repose, the Mass of the Presanctified ... Now nothing happens before Thursday evening. All Friday morning is empty. There is an hour or so in church on Friday afternoon. All Saturday is quite blank until late at night. The Easter Mass is sung at midnight to a weary congregation who are constrained to 'renew their baptismal vows' in the vernacular and later repair to bed. The significance of Easter as a feast of dawn is quite lost.[15]

On 3 July 1956 Waugh wrote to Penelope Betjeman, with a whimsical lightheartedness belying the underlying bitterness, urging her to warn her local Catholic Women's League of the 'dreadful influence of French Dominicans'.[16]

Waugh's misgivings about the changes to the liturgy were shared by Christopher Dawson who saw them as evidence that the Church was moving away from the spiritual and intellectual revival into a more materialistic and activist age. In 1956 he wrote to E. I. Watkin of the 'evils' besetting the Church at that time: 'extroversion, legalism, activism and also an excessive concentration of attention on controversial theology and all sorts of stunts like vernacular liturgy etc. Legalism and controversialism are permanent problems, but the rest seem to me either new or far more prominent than in the old days.'[17]

Two years later Dawson was concerned to defend Baroque Catholicism against attacks from within the Catholic Church itself, specifically by Father Louis Bouyer in *Du Protestantism à L'Eglise*: 'He does not realise the great achievement of Baroque Catholicism in mysticism and the interior life. He seems to think that the Church exists for the liturgy rather than vice versa, and personally I would rather see a few St Teresa's or St Philip than a whole tribe of Mass dialogians!'[18]

According to his daughter, Dawson considered these changes as 'largely due to a Puritan movement within the Church'.[19] He loved Baroque spirituality which proclaimed its message through the media of art and music, poetry and mysticism, and had been a major influence on his own conversion half a century earlier. Imagination, he once wrote, was as much a part of the soul as the intellect or the will and he had no sympathy with 'the philistine and patronising' attitude to Baroque Catholicism expressed by certain 'modern' Catholics. These he likened to 'the Victorian protestant of the most narrow and bigoted kind'.[20]

E. I. Watkin, however, took a far more positive view of the changes afoot in the Church. Adopting a position which contradicted many of the views in Dawson's letter to him in 1956, Watkin concluded his study of *Roman Catholicism in England from the Reformation to 1950*, published the following year, with a hymn of praise to the spirit of 'renewal' within the Church:

> Recent years have witnessed a departure from the stereotyped pattern of the Tridentine anti-Protestant Counter-Reformation. New movements are in progress, new experiments being made ... The restoration by St Pius X of frequent, even daily, Communion is being followed by Masses in which the people sing or say their part ... Many forms of Catholic action are giving the laity a share in the apostolate ... The ship of Peter has in short begun her voyage from the Catholicism of the Counter-Reformation to the Catholicism of the future, not a novel religion but a novel presentation, a deeper and wider understanding of the same religion once for all revealed. Tensions indeed are inevitable between the Catholic conservative and the Catholic reformer. But they accompany life and growth and should they threaten unity or question the rule of faith the authority of St Peter's successor will decide differences and settle disputes. Experiment therefore is secured by certainty, speculation by revealed truth, freedom by authority, the future by the past which it continues and carries forward.[21]

One can scarcely imagine a more reasoned exposition of the reformers' case but Watkin's optimism and enthusiasm were not shared by many of his contemporaries. Indeed, this may have been the issue which sullied Watkin's relationship with Dawson. Sister Juliana Dawson, who was Watkin's god-daughter, recalled that Watkin was 'one of my father's best friends' but that 'they drifted apart in later years'.[22] Their friendship was perhaps one of the earliest casualties of the 'inevitable' tensions between the Catholic conservative and the Catholic reformer. Not that Dawson could be described as an unreasonable reactionary. He was in favour of the Second Vatican Council, which was convened in the early sixties, because he believed that 'change was needed', but he believed the Council 'should have kept the form of the Mass'. He also objected to the English in the Mass, complaining to Watkin about the 'poor translation'.[23] Ironically, Dawson had been held in suspicion by conservative Catholics before the war who considered him a theological liberal because of the debt he professed to both Baron von Hugel and Lord Acton.

No such suspicions ever surrounded Evelyn Waugh whose Catholic credentials were conservative *par excellence*. Waugh's hero was 'Pio Nono', Pope Pius IX, the first pope to identify wholeheartedly with ultramontanism. Pius IX had defined the Immaculate Conception in 1854 and ten years later published an encyclical denouncing the principal errors of the age, including the view that the Pope could or should reconcile himself to 'progress', liberalism or modern industrial 'civilization'. He re-established the Catholic hierarchy in England and summoned the First Vatican Council which declared the infallibility of the Pope in questions of faith and morals, and published a constitution deploring contemporary pantheism, materialism and atheism. In its resolute opposition to many aspects of modern life the First Vatican Council had effectively declared war on the secular states of the industrialized world. *Pro Ecclesia contra mundum* appeared to be the battle cry of Pope Pius IX and the Vatican Council he summoned. It was a battle cry with which Waugh felt entirely at home. In contrast, the Second Vatican Council which was opened by Pope John XXIII on 11 October 1962, seemed to Waugh a betrayal of Pio Nono's principles. Far from being a continued defiance by the Church of modern trends the decisions of the Council appeared to Waugh an abject surrender which cast a shadow of desolation over the last years of his life.

Pope John, Evelyn wrote in a letter to his friend Ann Fleming concerning the Second Vatican Council, 'had no idea of the Pandora's box he was opening'.[24] Neither did Waugh have any idea at the outset of the Council's proceedings, writing with an apprehensive but cautious optimism to Nancy Mitford on 27 October 1962 that 'the Council is of the highest importance. As in 1869–70 the

French and Germans are full of mischief but, as then, the truth of God will prevail.'[25]

The following month Waugh wrote an article on the Council for the *Spectator* revealingly entitled 'The Same Again, Please'. Rejecting any increased role of the laity in the liturgy of the Church and defending the position of the ordained priesthood, Waugh wrote:

> ... I know of none whose judgment I would prefer to that of the simplest parish priest. Sharp minds may explore the subtlest verbal problems, but in the long routine of the seminary and the life spent with the Offices of the Church the truth is most likely to emerge ...
>
> Still less did we aspire to usurp his place at the altar. 'The Priesthood of the Laity' is a cant phrase of the decade and abhorrent to those of us who have met it.[26]

Of the Mass itself, Waugh 'wondered how many of us wanted to see any change':

> This was the Mass for whose restoration the Elizabethan martyrs had gone to the scaffold. St Augustine, St Thomas à Becket, St Thomas More, Challoner and Newman would have been perfectly at their ease among us; were, in fact, present there with us ... Their presence would not have been more palpable had we been making the responses aloud in the modern fashion.[27]

This, of course, invites the obvious riposte that their presence is not *less* palpable merely because the responses are made in the vernacular.

Waugh dismissed the liturgical reformers as 'a strange alliance between archaeologists absorbed in their speculations on the rites of the second century, and modernists who wish to give the Church the character of our own deplorable epoch'.[28]

Two days after Waugh's article appeared in the *Spectator* on 23 November 1962, John Heenan, who was then Archbishop of Liverpool, wrote to Waugh from the English College in Rome where he was attending the Council:

> what a pity the voice of the laity was not heard sooner ...
>
> The real difficulty (I think) is that Continentals are twisting themselves inside out to make us look as like as possible to the Protestants. How I wish we could persuade them (a large majority I fear) that to be

at home with our Mass and ceremonies is far more important than being right according to the books of liturgical antiquities.[29]

The original manuscript of Heenan's letter is annotated, 'He went back on all this'. In his recent biography of Waugh, Martin Stannard attributed the annotation to Christopher Sykes who had expressed his own vociferous disapproval of the liturgical reforms in his earlier biography of Waugh. The movement for reform, Sykes wrote, 'was to reduce all Roman Catholic ceremonial to commonplace and to abolish the traditional order of the Mass in favour of a prayer-meeting in which only essential vestiges of the traditional celebration were retained'.[30] Even Waugh never went quite as far as that in his disdain for the changes! Yet Sykes's annotation is none the less true in so far as Heenan's later actions as a liberal-minded defender of post-conciliar developments were at variance with the traditional stance of his letter.

By the early months of the following year Waugh began to fear the full extent of the reforms heralded by the Council. In March he wrote truculently to the *Tablet*: 'Will you promote an appeal to the Holy See for the establishment of a Uniate Latin Church which shall observe all the rites as they existed in the reign of Pius IX?'[31] On 15 March, three days after his letter was published in the *Tablet*, he returned a pamphlet on liturgical reform which Lady Acton had sent him:

Some people, like Penelope Betjeman, like making a row in church and I don't see why they shouldn't; just as the Abyssinians dance and wave rattles. I should feel jolly shy dancing and I feel shy praying out loud. Every parish might have one rowdy Mass a Sunday for those who like it. But there should be silent ones for those who like quiet.

The Uniate Churches are highly relevant. They are allowed to keep their ancient habits of devotion and to have a ritual in languages like Syriac, Byzantine Greek, Ghiz, Slavonic which are much deader than Latin. Why should we not have a Uniate Roman Church and let the Germans have their own knockabout performances? ...

The decision actually taken at the Council, I gather, will be that all the introduction to the Mass will be in vernacular on days of obligation. They also say that we must have the same version as the Americans, heaven help us.[32]

The tract which Lady Acton had sent him was *Liturgy and Doctrine: the Doctrinal Basis of the Liturgical Movement* by Father Charles Davis, editor of *Clergy*

Review and a well-known liberal theologian. The returned copy was heavily annotated with Waugh's 'very cross marginalia': 'Patronising pig! ... I suspect the author of being American ... Rot, ha ha ... old stuff ... Rot ... HERESY ... Ass ...' Amidst the jibes Waugh managed one poignant point, which he scrawled on the title page: '"Active participation" doesn't necessarily mean making a noise. Only God knows who are participating. People can pray loudly like the Pharisee and not be heard.'[33]

On 10 June he was again writing to Lady Acton, this time bemoaning the fact that Douglas Woodruff, an old friend who had been editor of the *Tablet* since 1936, had become sympathetic to certain liberal theologians: 'Woodruff has developed a senile infatuation for a very dangerous clergyman called Küng – not Chinese, central European; a heresiarch who in happier days would be roasted.'[34]

Waugh may still have nurtured hopes that the 'heretics' would be kept at bay when, in 1963, John Heenan became Archbishop of Westminster. Any such hopes were dealt a blow by the conciliatory and conciliar tone of Heenan's Pastoral Letter for Lent 1964, read out at all Masses throughout England and Wales on Quinquagesima Sunday, 9 February 1964:

> Take, for example, changes in Holy Mass. Some of you are quite alarmed. You imagine that everything will be changed and what you have known from childhood will be taken away from you. Some, on the other hand, are all for change and are afraid that too little will be altered.
>
> Both these attitudes are wrong. The Church will, of course, make certain reforms. That is one of the reasons why Councils are held. But nothing will be changed except for the good of souls. With the Pope we bishops are the Teaching Church. We love our Faith and we love our priests and people. We shall see that you are not robbed.[35]

Waugh was not convinced. 'The Vatican Council weighs heavy on my spirits,' he wrote to Lady Diana Cooper. 'I do not believe that there is much immediate prospect of reversing the disagreeable trend in the Church.'[36] On 3 March he wrote to Ann Fleming that he was going to Rome for Easter 'to avoid the horrors of the English liturgy'.[37]

On 7 August 1964, the *Catholic Herald* published a long letter from Waugh in which he attacked 'progressive' trends in the Church:

> you write of 'exploding renewal' and 'manifest dynamism of the Holy Spirit', thus seeming to sympathize with the northern innovators who

wish to change the outward aspect of the Church. I think you injure your cause when week by week you publish (to me) fatuous and outrageous proposals by irresponsible people.

Father John Sheerin is neither fatuous nor outrageous but I find him a little smug. If I read him correctly he is pleading for magnanimity towards defeated opponents. The old (and young) buffers should not be reprobated. They have been imperfectly 'instructed'. The 'progressive' should ask the 'conservative with consummate courtesy' to re-examine his position.

I cannot claim consummate courtesy but may I, with round politeness, suggest that the progressives should re-examine their own? Were *they* perfectly instructed? Did they find the discipline of their seminaries rather irksome? Did they think they were wasting time on the Latin which they found uncongenial? Do they want to marry and beget other little progressives? Do they, like the present Pope, think Italian literature a more enjoyable pursuit than apologetics?

This was Waugh in particularly combative mood, mixing poignantly reasoned argument with viperously venomous invective. Thus his assertion that 'the function of the Church in every age has been conservative – to transmit undiminished and uncontaminated the creed inherited from its predecessors', was followed by a scathing attack on the German reformers: 'It is natural to the Germans to make a row. The torchlit, vociferous assemblies of the Hitler Youth expressed a national passion ... But it is essentially un-English. We seek no "Sieg Heils". We pray in silence. "Participation" in the Mass does not mean hearing our own voices. It means God hearing our voices.'

In the same letter Waugh had written that 'throughout her entire life the Church has been at active war with enemies from without and traitors from within'. To his great distress he now felt that the 'traitors' within the sanctuary of the Church were working to deliver the faithful into the hedonistic and heathen hands of the 'enemies' without. The Church Militant was being betrayed to a modern world seemingly triumphant.

On 6 August, the day before his own letter appeared in the *Catholic Herald*, Waugh read a letter in *The Times* from a correspondent who was distressed by the news that the Catholic Church was officially to adopt English as the language of the Mass. 'This will cause real distress to many people after near 2,000 years of a universal Latin Mass,' the correspondent had written, 'and as the use of the vernacular is to obtain in all countries, we shall be strangers in each other's churches where till now we have been at home, when we go abroad ...

this innovation will split the Roman Catholic Church in England from top to bottom'.

The letter struck a sympathetic chord with Waugh and he sat down immediately to compose a reply which was published in *The Times* two days later. 'Though an imperfect Latinist,' he wrote, he was in 'full sympathy with the regrets expressed' in the earlier letter: 'I think, however, that he exaggerates when he speaks of the proposed innovations as "splitting the Roman Catholic Church from top to bottom". The effect is more likely to be that church-going will become irksome but still a duty we shall perform.'

Such displays of disapproval at the changes in the Church were reinforcing Waugh's public image as an obstinate old reactionary. When his newly published autobiography *A Little Learning* was reviewed in *The Times* on 10 September he was described as an 'enviably articulate Roman Catholic Colonel Blimp'. The description, though amusing and true enough as a caricature, failed to plumb the spiritual depths beneath the indignant surface. These were displayed on 17 September in a letter to Lady Diana Cooper, in which he endeavoured to lift her spirits after receiving a 'sorrowful letter' from her: 'Prayer is not asking but giving ... Have you ever experienced penitence? I doubt it. No wonder you are in the dumps. Do you believe in the Incarnation and Redemption in the full historical sense in which you believe in the battle of El Alamein? That's important. Faith is not a mood.'[38]

On 16 August Waugh sent a copy of his *Catholic Herald* letter to Archbishop Heenan, because he had been 'greatly surprised' by the number of people who had written supportively to him after its publication suggesting he 'do something to lead a party' or that he 'organise a petition to the Archbishop'. Waugh asked the Archbishop 'whether the hierarchy are fully aware of the distress caused ... not so much by the modest and reasonable innovations proposed but by the opening it seems to offer to more radical and distasteful changes'.

> I think I owe it to my very numerous correspondents to put their case to you. A few were priests, mostly laymen and laywomen of middle or old age; about half, I conjecture, converts who ask: 'Why were we led out of the church of our childhood to find the church of our adoption assuming the very forms we disliked?'
>
> Is it too much to ask that all parishes should be ordered to have two Masses, a 'Pop' for the young and a 'Trad' for the old? I think that a vociferous minority has imposed itself on the hierarchy and made them believe that a popular demand existed where there was in fact not even a preference.[39]

Heenan replied on 20 August, stating that he 'had read and enjoyed' Waugh's letter to the *Catholic Herald*:

> The hierarchy is in a difficult position. We have not yet lost the respect of ordinary Catholics but the constant nagging of the intellectuals and their tireless (tiresome?) letters to the Press and articles in the Catholic papers may eventually disturb the ordinary faithful. Most of us would be content to delay changes but the mood of the Council compels us to act ...
>
> But do not despair. The changes are not so great as they are made to appear. Although a date has been set for introducing the new liturgy I shall be surprised if all the bishops will want *all* Masses every day to be in the new rite. We shall try to keep the needs of *all* in mind – Pops, Trads, Rockers, Mods, With-its, and Without-its.[40]

On 25 August Waugh wrote again to the Archbishop saying that 'literally every day I get letters from distressed laymen who think I might speak for them':

> I detect a new kind of anticlericalism. The old anticlericals, by imputing avarice, ambition, immorality etc to the priesthood at least recognised its peculiar and essential character, which made lapses notable. The new anticlericals seem to minimise the sacramental character of the priesthood and to suggest that the laity are their equals.[41]

'Of course you are right,' Heenan replied three days later. 'That is why they are playing up this People of God and Priesthood of the Laity so much. The Mass is no longer the Holy Sacrifice but the Meal at which the priest is the waiter.'[42] After Waugh had dined with the Archbishop, he wrote enthusiastically to Katherine Asquith on 14 September: 'He showed himself as deeply conservative and sympathetic to those of us who are scared of the new movement. He thinks that "the intellectuals" are all against him.'[43] However, if Waugh believed that Archbishop Heenan was about to oppose further reforms he was soon disillusioned. The new liturgy was adopted throughout the country, the vernacular Mass leaving the old Latin in its wake. On 3 January 1965 he wrote again to the Archbishop, this time with an air of exasperated resignation: 'Every attendance at Mass leaves me without comfort or edification. I shall never, pray God, apostatize but church going is now a bitter trial.'[44]

Heenan replied on 17 January, admitting that there were 'so many things' which were 'undesirable', but claiming that 'the *vast* majority (my priests tell me) enjoys the English in the Mass: even many who were opposed before'.[45]

On Maundy Thursday, 15 April, Waugh wrote to Monsignor McReavy who gave 'expert advice to troubled laymen' in the *Clergy Review*, asking what were the minimum legal requirements concerning Mass attendance: 'I do not ask what is best for me; merely what is the least I am obliged to do without grave sin. I find the new liturgy a temptation against Faith, Hope and Charity but I shall never, pray God, apostatize.'[46]

In this frame of mind, Waugh could gain little solace or joy at Easter. His diary entry on Easter Sunday was that of a psychologically battered and broken man:

A year in which the process of transforming the liturgy has followed a planned course. Protests avail nothing ... Cardinal Heenan has been double-faced in the matter. I had dinner with him *à deux* in which he expressed complete sympathy with the conservatives and, as I understood him, promised resistance to the innovations which he is now pressing forward. How does he suppose the cause of participation is furthered by the prohibition of kneeling at the incarnatus in the creed? The Catholic Press has made no opposition. I shall not live to see things righted.[47]

On 24 August Waugh remarked bitterly to Christopher Sykes that 'the hierarchy are like Gadarene swine'.[48] To Nancy Mitford on 23 September, he wrote: 'The buggering up of the Church is a deep sorrow to me and to all I know. We write letters to the paper. A fat lot of good that does.'[49] Father D'Arcy, hearing of Waugh's misery, wrote anxiously in an effort to offer comfort: 'I had not realised the depth of your depression, and wish to heaven that I could be of some help to you'.[50] D'Arcy compared Waugh's position to that of Robert Peckham, a recusant who died in exile after seeking refuge in Rome following the accession of Elizabeth I. Waugh knew the story of Peckham very well and was fond of Maurice Baring's fictionalized biography of him, remarking to Sir Maurice Bowra as recently as November 1963 how much he 'loved Maurice Baring'[51]. Yet he rejected D'Arcy's parallel: 'Peckham had an easy choice of exile. Today there is no refuge.'[52]

On 12 January 1966 Cardinal Heenan kept a new year resolution to write to Waugh, thanking him 'for all that you have done for the Old Faith': 'Recent years have been very trying but reflecting on the Council I am sure that it was a Good Thing. The last session brought sanity to the surface and I expect that before two years have passed we shall begin to reap results.'[53]

Heenan, it seemed, had finally become reconciled to the reforms of the Council. His optimism was not passed on to Waugh who replied two days later: 'It is a joy that you are back amongst us and that the Council is over. I cannot hope that either of us will live to see its multitude of ills put right. The Church has endured and survived many dark periods. It is our misfortune to live in one of them.'[54]

On 20 February the *Sunday Telegraph* reported that Waugh was 'well on the way to recovery after a most distressing year of nervous melancholia' caused by 'his grief at changes in the Roman Catholic liturgy which have stripped the Mass of its traditional Latinity'. In truth, Waugh was very far from recovery. 'I have become very old in the last two years,' he wrote in a letter to Lady Diana Mosley on 9 March. 'Not diseased but enfeebled. There is nowhere I want to go and nothing I want to do and I am conscious of being an utter bore. The Vatican Council has knocked the guts out of me.'[55] Three weeks later he wrote to her again with thoughts of Holy Week and the forthcoming Easter triduum on his mind: 'Easter used to mean so much to me. Before Pope John and his Council – they destroyed the beauty of the liturgy. I have not yet soaked myself in petrol and gone up in flames, but I now cling to the faith doggedly without joy.'[56]

Unable to face the new liturgy, Waugh asked his old friend at Downside, Dom Hubert van Zeller, to celebrate a private Latin Mass for him at Easter. The request was rejected by the Abbot on the grounds that Dom Hubert 'should be with the community at that time'. Waugh then asked Father Philip Caraman to say Mass for him. Caraman had become both friend and confidant during the recent difficult years, staying frequently with Waugh who described him as 'a gentle, uncomplaining visitor'. Being a Jesuit, Caraman required no permission from a higher authority and he consented readily.

On Easter Sunday, 10 April, at ten o'clock in the morning Father Caraman celebrated a Latin Mass at the Catholic chapel in Wiveliscombe, five miles from the Waugh family home. Only a few friends and family were present. As they came out of church, several of those present noticed how cheerful Waugh seemed. Father Caraman remarked how calm and contented he appeared, his depression evaporated, almost as though he had finally come through some dark night of the soul: 'He was benign and at peace, with a kind of tranquillity and serenity that as a priest one often meets in people who are dying.'[57] Waugh collapsed and died an hour or so later.

'I think he had been praying for death for a long time and it could not have happened more beautifully or happily for him,' his wife wrote to Lady Diana Cooper, 'so I can only thank God for his mercy ... But life will never be the same for us without him.'[58]

Margaret, his daughter, also wrote to Lady Diana Cooper, in words more of joy than sorrow:

> Don't be too upset about Papa. I think it was a kind of wonderful miracle. You know how he longed to die and dying as he did on Easter Sunday, when all the liturgy is about death and resurrection, after a Latin Mass and holy communion would be exactly as he wanted. I am sure he prayed for death at Mass. I am very happy for him.[59]

NOTES

1. D. Felicitas Corrigan (ed.), *Siegfried Sassoon: Poet's Pilgrimage*, pp. 182–3.
2. Peter Alexander, *Roy Campbell: A Critical Biography*, p. 232.
3. ibid., p. 239.
4. ibid., pp. 239–40.
5. Edith Sitwell, *Taken Care Of: An Autobiography*, London, 1965, p. 166.
6. John Lehmann and Derek Parker (eds.), *Edith Sitwell: Selected Letters 1919–1964*, pp. 216–17.
7. Roy Campbell, *Collected Poems, Volume 3 (Translations)*, London, 1960, pp. 5–6.
8. Edith Sitwell, *Taken Care Of: An Autobiography*, p. 164.
9. Barry Webb, *Edmund Blunden: A Biography*, London, 1990, p. 302.
10. David Wright, *Roy Campbell*, London, 1961, pp. 42–3.
11. Evelyn Waugh, *Ronald Knox*, p. 94.
12. Ronald Knox, *A Spiritual Aeneid*, p. 53.
13. Evelyn Waugh, *Ronald Knox*, p. 94.
14. Michael Davie (ed.), *The Diaries of Evelyn Waugh*, p. 758.
15. *Spectator*, 23 November 1962.
16. Mark Amory (ed.), *The Letters of Evelyn Waugh*, p. 473.
17. Christina Scott, *A Historian and His World: A Life of Christopher Dawson*, p. 175.
18. ibid., p. 175.
19. ibid., p. 175.
20. ibid., p. 176.
21. E. I. Watkin, *Roman Catholicism in England from the Reformation to 1950*, London, 1957, pp. 229–31.
22. Sister Juliana Dawson, interview with the author.
23. Christina Scott, interview with the author.
24. Selina Hastings, *Evelyn Waugh: A Biography*, p. 617.
25. Mark Amory (ed.), *The Letters of Evelyn Waugh*, p. 595.
26. *Spectator*, 23 November 1962.
27. ibid.
28. ibid.
29. Scott M. P. Reid (ed.), *A Bitter Trial: Evelyn Waugh and John Carmel Heenan on the Liturgical Changes*, Curdridge, Hants, 1996, p. 30.
30. Christopher Sykes, *Evelyn Waugh: A Biography*, p. 382.
31. *Tablet*, 12 March 1963.
32. Mark Amory (ed.), *The Letters of Evelyn Waugh*, pp. 601–2.
33. Selina Hastings, *Evelyn Waugh: A Biography*, p. 619.
34. Mark Amory (ed.), *The Letters of Evelyn Waugh*, p. 608.
35. Scott M. P. Reid (ed.), *A Bitter Trial: Evelyn Waugh and John Carmel Heenan on the Liturgical Changes*, p. 35.
36. Artemis Cooper (ed.), *Mr Wu and Mrs Stitch: The Letters of Evelyn Waugh and Diana Cooper*, London, 1991, p. 311.

37. Mark Amory (ed.), *The Letters of Evelyn Waugh*, p. 618.

38. ibid., p. 624.

39. Scott M. P. Reid (ed.), *A Bitter Trial: Evelyn Waugh and John Carmel Heenan on the Liturgical Changes*, pp. 42–3.

40. ibid., pp. 44–5.

41. ibid., pp. 46–7.

42. ibid., p. 48.

43. Mark Amory (ed.), *The Letters of Evelyn Waugh*, p. 624.

44. Scott M. P. Reid (ed.), *A Bitter Trial: Evelyn Waugh and John Carmel Heenan on the Liturgical Changes*, p. 52.

45. ibid., p. 53.

46. Mark Amory (ed.), *The Letters of Evelyn Waugh*, p. 631.

47. Michael Davie (ed.), *The Diaries of Evelyn Waugh*, p. 793.

48. Selina Hastings, *Evelyn Waugh: A Biography*, p. 620.

49. Mark Amory (ed.), *The Letters of Evelyn Waugh*, p. 633.

50. Selina Hastings, *Evelyn Waugh: A Biography*, p. 623.

51. Mark Amory (ed.), *The Letters of Evelyn Waugh*, p. 615.

52. Selina Hastings, *Evelyn Waugh: A Biography*, p. 623.

53. Scott M. P. Reid (ed.), *A Bitter Trial: Evelyn Waugh and John Carmel Heenan on the Liturgical Changes*, p. 60.

54. ibid., p. 61.

55. Mark Amory (ed.), *The Letters of Evelyn Waugh*, p. 638.

56. ibid., p. 639.

57. Selina Hastings, *Evelyn Waugh: A Biography*, p. 625.

58. Scott M. P. Reid (ed.), *A Bitter Trial: Evelyn Waugh and John Carmel Heenan on the Liturgical Changes*, p. 67.

59. ibid., p. 66.

CHAPTER TWENTY SEVEN

RINGING OUT THE OLD

In a postscript to his biography of Waugh, Christopher Sykes endeavoured to explain the underlying reasons for his friend's obstinate opposition to reform in the Church. 'His dislike of the reform-movement,' Sykes wrote,

> was not merely an expression of his conservatism, nor of aesthetic pref-
> erences. It was based on deeper things. He believed that in its long his-
> tory the Church had developed a liturgy which enabled an ordinary,
> sensual man (as opposed to a saint who is outside generalisation) to
> approach God and be aware of sanctity and the divine. To abolish all
> this for the sake of up-to-dateness seemed to him not only silly but
> dangerous ... he could not bear the thought of modernized liturgy.
> 'Untune that string' he felt, and loss of faith would follow ... Whether
> his fears were justified or not only 'the unerring sentence of time' can
> show.[1]

The unerring sentence has not yet been passed, but it was certainly the case that Waugh was not by any means the only person who held these views. Christo-pher Sykes himself was out of sympathy with the reforms and even Douglas Woodruff, who Waugh had criticized for showing a 'senile infatuation' with Hans Küng, the 'heresiarch who in happier days would be roasted', was deeply suspicious of many of them. This was clear from Woodruff's memoir of Waugh, published in 1973:

> What did overshadow his later years was the Second Vatican Council,
> and still more, all the people who tried to use it to push the Church in
> Protestant or liberal directions which they called, and for that matter
> still call, the spirit of Vatican II ... When I tried in *The Tablet* to bring
> some comfort to the bewildered and unhappy Catholics, particularly
> the elderly and the converts, by reminding them that in every century

some sudden tempest of one kind or another had arisen to toss the bark of Peter, Evelyn pointed out that in Church history the response of the Church to these successive challenges had not been to give way to them, and that as a consequence of the exercise of her authority, most of the challenges had died away so that only scholars know about them.[2]

At the heart of the furious debate surrounding the 'spirit of Vatican II' was the question of whether the 'spirit' at work was the Holy Spirit or merely the spirit of the age. If both 'spirits' were at work the question became one of discernment. Which reforms were the will of God and which merely the will of men following fads? Which were deeply rooted in unchanging fact and which had their shallow roots in changing fashion? Again, the only test can be the 'unerring sentence of time' which will uproot the shallow-rooted and leave the deeper-rooted to flourish in the soil of tradition. Either way, the whole question animated the discussions and debates of those who observed developments during the Council. In 1964 David Jones echoed Evelyn Waugh's fears concerning proposed liturgical reforms. The Church was in danger of 'making the same mistake as those classical dons who used to say that the teaching of the Greek and Latin languages was maintained because it taught men to think clearly, to write clear English, to become competent civil servants or what not'.

> What the dons ought to have said was that the classics were an integral part of our Western heritage and should be fought for on that ground alone. Our Church leaders have even more reason to guard that heritage – for it is saturated with the sacral. It's not a matter of knowledge but of love. It's a terrible thought that the language of the West, of the Western liturgy, and inevitably the Roman chant, might become virtually extinct.
>
> ... At root, I don't believe it's a 'religious' matter at all. I believe it's only part of the Decline of the West. Perhaps I'm talking balls, I don't know. But the *kind* of arguments used I find highly unsatisfactory, and they have just that same tang that distresses me so over the language of my father's *patria*. They prove by statistics that the Welsh language is dying, and that it has no practical value anyhow. Damn such bloody arguments.[3]

At the root of Jones's objections to liturgical reform, apart from the enduring influence of Spengler, was his view that intrinsic value is essentially eternal and thus transcends temporal utilitarian considerations.

Shortly after this letter was written, Jones met Siegfried Sassoon for the first time. It was 'a broiling hot day' in July and they 'had a longish talk'. Jones found Sassoon 'extremely nice, gentle and pleasant, *much* older than I had supposed, and quite different in appearance from what I had imagined'.[4] Jones later recalled in conversation that 'Sassoon in old age had a timeless craggy Jewish face'.[5] Inevitably, they talked about the First World War, in which they had both fought, talking 'about Blunden and Graves and the Welch Fusiliers'. Sassoon told Jones 'that however much he tried he could never get that Ist War business out of his system, which is exactly the case with me. It's a curious thing.' Jones was pleased that Sassoon thought so highly of Edmund Blunden's *Undertones of War*, 'which I've felt to be one of the very best of those various accounts of that infantry war'. Leaving their reminiscences of a war which was already fifty years distant, and endeavouring to talk of more topical issues such as the proceedings of the Vatican Council, Jones 'asked him if he was worried about the fate of the Latin rite, but he didn't seem to be much aware of what was involved – but a jolly nice chap and he *couldn't* have been more friendly and agreeable'.[6]

Sassoon's impressions of their meeting were recorded in a letter to Dame Felicitas Corrigan, dated 5 August 1964: 'David Jones came to lunch ... ultra-sensitive. I talked to him alone for one and a half hours, and worked hard ... Have you tried to read him? Fr Sebastian (Moore) specialised in *The Anathemata* – quite beyond me. *In Parenthesis* is an important war record. But doesn't reach me like *Undertones of War*.'[7]

The most amusing aspect of Jones's description of the meeting was the graphic depiction of two old men struggling with the impediments of age:

> One rather difficult thing is that he is supposed to use false dentures which, very naturally, I think, he hates doing. But the consequence is that he speaks very softly without opening his mouth, and as I am decidedly deaf in one ear, the left ear, I could only make out about half of what he said – got the gist of the rest, but by some considerable concentration, couldn't keep on saying, Would you mind saying that a bit louder.[8]

Sassoon was seventy-seven at the time and Jones a mere sixty-nine. As veterans of the First World War the romantic maxim that 'old soldiers never die' must have seemed more poignant to them with each passing year. They were, however, preparing to 'fade away' and Sassoon had expressed his feelings on the matter in the manner in which he expressed all his deepest feelings. Shortly before his death in 1967 he wrote 'A Prayer in Old Age':

Bring no expectance of a heaven unearned
No hunger for beatitude to be
Until the lesson of my life is learned
Through what Thou didst for me.

Bring no assurance of redeemed rest
No intimation of awarded grace
Only contrition, cleavingly confessed
To Thy forgiving face.

I ask one world of everlasting loss
In all I am, that other world to win.
My nothingness must kneel below The Cross.
There let new life begin.

The sixties saw the passing of many of the literary converts to Christianity who had graced the century with their writings and thought. On 18 March 1963, Father C. C. Martindale died at the age of eighty-three. Martindale had been received into the Church as an eighteen-year-old on 8 May 1897 and had devoted the rest of his life to his priestly vocation. He became, along with Father D'Arcy, the most celebrated of the Jesuits responsible for bringing so many converts, literary and otherwise, into the Church.

C. S. Lewis died on 22 November 1963, his death being largely overshadowed by the assassination of President Kennedy in Dallas and the death of Aldous Huxley in California, both of which occurred on the same day. Conversely, Lewis's funeral on 26 November at Holy Trinity, Headington Quarry, Oxford, overshadowed the requiem Mass for W. R. Titterton, celebrated at the church of St Anselm and St Cecilia in Kingsway, London, on the same day. Titterton, who had reached the ripe old age of eighty-seven at the time of his death, was best known as a journalist, although he also had volumes of verse and prose published. In 1936 he wrote a life of G. K. Chesterton who was the person most responsible for his conversion to Catholicism in 1931. Chesterton and Titterton were on the *Daily News* together and Titterton became Chesterton's assistant on the *New Witness* and later on *G. K.'s Weekly*.

Two days after Lewis's funeral and the requiem for Titterton, Edith Sitwell, herself seventy-six years old, was displaying the caustically sardonic humour which had been the hallmark of her correspondence throughout her life. On 28 November she had a letter published in the *Times Literary Supplement* in response to 'Ugh', a review of various novels by William Burroughs in which the reviewer had compared reading Burroughs to 'wading upstream in the drains of a big city':

> I was delighted to see, in your issue of the 14th instant, the very right-minded review of a novel by a Mr Burroughs (whoever he may be) published by a Mr John Calder (whoever he may be).
>
> The public canonisation of that insignificant, dirty little book *Lady Chatterley's Lover* was a signal to persons who wish to unload the filth in their minds on the British public.
>
> As the author of *Gold Coast Customs* I can scarcely be accused of shirking reality, but I do not wish to spend the rest of my life with my nose nailed to other people's lavatories.
>
> I prefer Chanel Number 5.

Her humour was also expressed brilliantly in a late but undated letter to Sir Maurice Bowra, the conclusion of which would almost serve as an irreverent but risible epitaph:

> I have got a very nice new lunatic – a lady in Dublin. She has written to tell me that all R.C. priests have lots of illegitimate children – usually by their 15-year-old nieces. I am replying that I know they have. My own dear confessor often brings round his happy little brood of ten to have tea with me. Four are by his own niece, but he is sadly forgetful about who are the mothers of the rest. There *were* eleven, but unfortunately he ate one, in a fit of absent-mindedness, one Friday.
>
> Osbert says I must not write this, as it will be published, and people will say (A) that I have no moral sense, (B) that I am flippant; but I reply that it will not be the first, second, or third time that these charges have been brought against me.[9]

Sitwell died on 9 December 1964. Her *Times* obituary described her poetry as being 'essentially of praise and transformation':

> She combined a taste for elaborate and latterly for sweeping technical effects with a basic simplicity of vision: a vision deeply affected in her early poems by childhood memories, and in her later poems by a mixture of deep horror at the violence and cruelty of the world with profound faith in the ultimate goodness of God and holiness of nature ... The total effect of her poetry, like that of her personality, was strange

and formidable, and somehow slightly over life-size ... she retained to the end a sustained elevation and intensity of manner, and a purity of religious vision.[10]

David Blamires, in his critical study of David Jones, wrote that 'Edith Sitwell expresses in much of her later poetry a kind of mystical numinosity, a sense of involvement with the obscure sufferings of the world, and an incantational element that derives ultimately, in the West, from the rites and insights of Catholicism'.[11]

Her requiem was celebrated by Father D'Arcy at Farm Street, with Hugh Ross Williamson, Ernest Milton and Evelyn Waugh among those in attendance. Waugh wrote that he had 'dropped into Edith Sitwell's requiem late and dropped out early. It was sparsely attended.'[12]

Another literary convert who died in 1964 was the novelist Naomi Jacob, who had been received into the Church in 1907 as an eighteen-year-old. Her literary career commenced with the publication of *Jacob Ussher* in 1926, after which she became a prolific writer of light fiction concerned principally with the delineation of character.

On 4 January 1965, only a few weeks after Sitwell's death, T. S. Eliot died at home in London. '*The Waste Land*,' declared his obituary in *The Times* the following morning, 'announced the arrival of a major poet'.

at the time, however, few either of its detractors or its admirers saw through the surface innovations and the language of despair to the deep respect for tradition and the keen moral sense which underlay them ... Eliot's attitude in ecclesiastical affairs was dogmatically, even intransigently, conservative: there was perhaps a certain intolerance here in his zealous but uncompromising defence of tradition ... Of the non-literary influences which most contributed to Eliot's poetic development his religion must be put first ... Eliot's chief literary influences were the French symbolists and, above all, Dante. But, both as poet and critic he drew deep from the whole European tradition which, as editor of the *Criterion*, he had sought to preserve and reinvigorate ...

Although Eliot had become a naturalized British subject in 1928 some of the warmest tributes after his death came from the land of his birth. On the day after his death, American literary figures queued up to pay homage. Tributes were paid by Louis Untermeyer and Robert Lowell, while Allen Tate, poet and professor of English, called Eliot 'the greatest poet in English of the twentieth century, and he had the same relation to this age as Samuel Johnson had to the eighteenth century'.

The poet and critic Robert Penn Warren declared Eliot to be 'a key figure in our century in America and England, the most powerful single influence. This is his age. He gave us the sense of the culture crisis of the western world.'[13]

His memorial service at Westminster Abbey on 4 February was almost a state occasion. It seemed that everybody who was anybody was there: ambassadors, cultural attachés and the cream and the milk of the world's *literati*. The choir sang the anthem 'The Dove descending breaks the air', comprising Part IV of 'Little Gidding', set to music by Stravinsky and dedicated to Eliot, and in the intense stillness Sir Alec Guinness read five passages from Eliot's later works, concluding with the closing lines of 'Little Gidding'.

Edward Sackville-West died on 4 July 1965 at his home in County Tipperary, the day after returning from a holiday in the west of Ireland with Father Christopher Pemberton. Sackville-West and Pemberton had been friends since their days as BBC employees during the war. Pemberton had remained with the BBC until 1958, becoming one of the first four announcers on the Third Programme. He left, as a late vocation, to be ordained a Catholic priest. He and Sackville-West remained friends and it was Pemberton who discovered Sackville-West's body on the morning of 4 July.

Edward was the fifth Baron Sackville and family tradition dictated that the Sackvilles be buried in the crypt at Withyham Church in Sussex. However, Sackville-West had become so devoted to the village of Clogheen, where much to the amazement of the local inhabitants he had attended Mass every day, that he broke with family tradition and made arrangements to be buried there. Prior to his burial he was laid out in his bedroom in the mantle he wore as a Knight of Malta and the entire village processed through to pay their last respects. When the funeral procession arrived at the graveside it was discovered that a neighbour had lined the grave with red roses. The quiet Irish funeral stood in contrast to the requiem Mass celebrated for him by Father Pemberton at Farm Street in Mayfair on 28 July. Evelyn Waugh was present and reported that there was 'a rum mixture of people' in the congregation.[14]

The *Times* obituary to Sackville-West, written anonymously by David Cecil, described him as a dilettante 'in the original and splendid sense of the term: that is to say, as a man who, for pure love of them, devoted himself to the arts – especially literature and music – and whose very contribution to them was tinged with the colour of an odd and vivid individuality'. Cecil mentioned that Sackville-West 'had joined the Roman Catholic Church, of which he became a deeply devout member' and that 'he faced life with courage, with a great power of enjoyment and with spiritual faith'.[15]

Michael de-la-Noy, Sackville-West's biographer, described David Cecil's treatment of the obituary as 'a generous assessment of a schoolboy friend whose path had diverged so considerably from his own'.[16] Yet the warmest tribute to Sackville-West, and perhaps the one the deceased man would have appreciated most, was that written by his Irish neighbours. 'It was,' began the obituary in the Irish *Nationalist*, 'with feelings of deepest regret and a sense of great personal loss that we, in Clogheen, heard on Sunday evening of the sudden death of Lord Sackville.'

> A convert to the Catholic Faith, he was an example to all. On the morning of his death he was unnoticed as he approached the altar rail to receive Holy Communion ...
>
> He came to live amongst us ten years ago and soon we came to accept the quiet, yet intense, Englishman as one of us. To the people this was no nobleman or famous person, just a local who walked up and down our street and popped in and out of the shops, always with a friendly greeting or handshake for those he met ...
>
> May we repeat an old Irish prayer and hope that the green sod of Ireland will lie gently on him as he sleeps in God's peace beneath the Knockmealdowns and that his gentle spirit will always be with us, for truly we believe that this noble Englishman who came to us gave us a fresh appreciation of our faith and country.[17]

With the deaths of Evelyn Waugh eight months later and Siegfried Sassoon on 1 September 1967 it seemed as though the century was ringing out its old guard.

The sixties were a time of great change in many other respects. The 'winds of change' were blowing through the continent of Africa and the other colonial outposts of the European powers. The time of Empire was ending. For most of the surviving literary converts, however, it was the 'winds of change' blowing through the Catholic Church which remained the major concern.

In 1967 Hugh Ross Williamson added to the controversy by criticizing the liturgical reforms in an article for a Catholic newspaper:

> I agree with the words used recently by Mr Christopher Sykes in his broadcast on Evelyn Waugh referring to 'the old rite which he loved and whose abolition by wayward and philistine reform had been a great grief to his last years.' I could think of stronger words than 'wayward and philistine.' But I must not be polemical.[18]

Since his conversion in 1955 Ross Williamson had become one of the foremost literary apologists for the Catholic faith. His autobiography, *The Walled Garden*, published a year after his reception into the Church, charted his progress from Nonconformism via Anglo-Catholicism. His other books included historical novels and reconstructions which concentrated on the turbulent years that followed the English Reformation. These brought to life the characters of James II, Mary Tudor, Elizabeth I, Shakespeare and Guy Fawkes, among others, in the light of research which contradicted the anti-Catholic bias of the accepted history of the period. If such books invited comparisons with Benson, his historical study entitled *The Beginning of the English Reformation*, published in 1957, invited comparisons with Belloc's *How the Reformation Happened*. In 1958 he published *The Challenge of Bernadette* to commemorate the centenary of St Bernadette's visions at Lourdes. In the same year he also wrote a television play on St Bernadette, entitled *Test of Truth*, and *The Mime of Bernadette* which was produced at the Albert Hall. His work on these elicited two letters offering both encouragement and technical advice from the ageing Father Martindale, who wrote that he had 'always been so devoted to St Bernadette personally, as well as the actual contents of the visions'.[19]

In 1961 Ross Williamson wrote a play on St Teresa of Avila with Dame Sybil Thorndike cast in the title role. This was originally staged at the Edinburgh Festival before going on tour. At Liverpool's Royal Court Theatre it was performed to an audience of six hundred nuns and, because they appreciated all the *doubles entendres*, it lasted twenty minutes longer than usual because of the extra applause and laughter. 'Dame Sybil Thorndike played to the most appreciative – and critical – audience of her long career yesterday,' reported the *Daily Mail* on 21 September 1961. 'Applause acclaimed her every exit and frequently interrupted the performance.' The *Daily Mail* reporter wrote that the nuns he spoke to had 'praised the play for its realism, humour, and technical accuracy'.

As well as the six hundred nuns, the full house of 1,600 comprised priests and clergy from many Christian denominations and hundreds of schoolgirls. 'On stage,' the *Daily Mail* report continued, 'Dame Sybil, now in her eightieth year, gave a superb performance of Teresa, the Carmelite who founded a new strict order in sixteenth century Spain against all opposition.' Dame Sybil's reaction was equally enthusiastic: 'For an actor to play to such a perfect audience is sheer joy.'

Ross Williamson, a man of many parts, was also acting in the play he had written, using the pseudonym Ian Rossiter, and wrote to his daughter from his dressing room at Liverpool, enclosing the *Daily Mail* article: 'You ask me about the play. As far as audiences are concerned it's going marvellously: but the notices aren't good, on the whole. I think they're written by people who don't know anything about religion.'[20]

Ian Burford, a family friend who was also acting in the play, had added a postscript to the letter, stating that 'I am determined to make an actor out of him, and to my surprise, I am succeeding!!' Thereafter, Ross Williamson continued to act occasionally and even appeared on television in *Dr Finlay's Casebook*, always under the pseudonym Ian Rossiter.

However, as with Waugh, his opposition to the new liturgy dominated the last years of his life. He had always loved the Canon of the Mass which was the subject of his book *The Great Prayer*, published in the year of his conversion. To one so attached to the old rite acceptance of the new was always going to be difficult. Neither was he impressed by those who argued that the new rite was closer to the Mass of the primitive Church:

> the return to the 'primitive' is based on the curious theory of history, sometimes referred to as 'Hunt the Acorn'. That is to say, when you see a mighty oak you do not joy in its strength and luxuriant development. You start to search for an acorn compatible with that from which it grew and say: 'This is what it *ought* to be like.'[21]

These words were written in 1967, the year in which Cardinal Heenan expressed the doubts of many Catholics about changes in the liturgy during a dramatic intervention at the Synod of Bishops in Rome. Heenan insisted that there was 'more need than ever to stress the Real Presence of our Lord in the Blessed Sacrament' and that no change in the Mass 'should be made which might seem to throw doubt on this doctrine'. On a similar theme he referred to the 'very large number of Sisters and not a few parishes' which dedicated their lives 'to perpetual adoration of the Blessed Sacrament': 'They sometimes feel anxious because of the danger that Exposition of the Blessed Sacrament and, perhaps, Benediction may one day be abolished on the grounds that they were introduced too recently in the history of the Church.'

The Cardinal also addressed the issue of Latin, asking how the Church could be sure of preserving 'the Latin tongue': 'If the Church is to remain truly the Catholic Church it is essential to keep a universal language.'[22]

This was a view held by many. Christopher Dawson had written: 'The existence of a common liturgical language of some kind is a sign of the Church's mission to reverse the curse of Babel and to create a bond of unity between the peoples.'[23]

In an undated letter to Edward Watkin, written in the 1960s, Dawson remarked, 'I hate the changes in the liturgy and even the translations are so bad'[24] and in one of his last letters to Watkin he lamented 'the pro-Lutheran utterances in the Catholic press', failing to comprehend 'how they reconcile this with their liturgical principles'.[25]

The theological liberalism of the Catholic press did not prevent the *Tablet* from publishing a tribute to Dawson on the occasion of his eightieth birthday on 12 October 1969. The tribute was written by Watkin who had known Dawson for sixty-four years. The final paragraphs served not only as a testament of Dawson's achievement but also indicated that Watkin had revised his earlier optimistic approach to the reforms in the Church:

> In too many Catholic quarters ... Dawson and his teaching have been discarded as outdated, without value or even significance for the contemporary Catholic. Some who were foremost in his welcome and in the display of their regard for his work have turned away to a religious and cultural (more truly anticultural and radically irreligious) avantguardism ...
>
> For such men Dawson has not, cannot have, a message. He has not been refuted. He cannot be. For his interpretations are anchored securely to historical fact. He is simply disregarded.
>
> Sooner or later however, sooner I anticipate, if the fabric of our human society survives the perils to which it is exposed, Dawson's illuminating interpretation of history, stated moreover with such literary skill, will find in America, as in England, an audience that can appreciate both.

In May 1970 Dawson suffered a heart attack and soon after contracted pneumonia. Edward Watkin came to visit his oldest friend for the last time and, when he had left, Dawson told his nurse, Sister Mary: 'You know he made me a Catholic.'[26]

On Trinity Sunday he sank into a coma 'from which he never rallied except for one brief and remarkable moment' which Sister Mary recalled:

> All of a sudden he opened his eyes and staring at the painting of the crucifixion, which was on the wall at the foot of his bed, he had a beautiful smile and his eyes were wide open. He then said: 'This is Trinity Sunday. I see it all and it is beautiful.' He then returned to the coma never to regain consciousness.[27]

He died, appropriately enough, on the following day, 25 May, the feast of St Bede, the most 'venerable' of all historians.

His final moments were witnessed by Sister Juliana Dawson, his daughter: 'On his death bed, Father Ryan, a very gentle Irish priest, anointed him. At the very last moment before he died, Father Ryan opened the door and blessed him. It was a beautiful moment.'[28]

David Jones, like Edward Watkin, was 'firmly convinced of the permanent importance as a philosopher and interpreter of history of his dear friend Christopher Dawson'. According to Jones's friend William Blisset, Dawson had 'the same sort of appeal' to Jones as did his metahistorical mentor Oswald Spengler, though Dawson was 'a finer and gentler spirit'. Blisset considered that Jones and Dawson were very close 'in temperament as well as in mind'.[29] They discussed Spengler at length and agreed about his strengths and weaknesses. Jones said of Dawson: 'Other learned men make you feel ignorant, but Dawson made you realize that you knew more than you suspected.'[30]

Jones was also very close 'in temperament as well as in mind' to Dawson over the changes in the liturgy. He was outraged when William Blisset informed him that a priest he knew was prevented from saying Mass in Bayreuth because his German was not good enough and Latin was *verboten*. Jones then told Blisset that an old friend, a retired colonel who had been 'very devout' in the practice of his religion, had specified a Latin requiem in his will but was denied it: 'I can't understand it at all: they'll be pulling down Chartres Cathedral next … One year they abolish the biretta, the next year they abolish the Mass … Surely understanding the Mass is the business of a lifetime.' According to William Blisset, Jones 'spoke with bitterness, out of great suffering'.[31]

Another writer who found herself confounded and confused by the changes in the Church was Antonia White, whose novels included *Frost in May*, *The Lost Traveller* and *Beyond the Glass*. White, like J. R. R. Tolkien, was a 'cradle convert', being received into the Church as a seven-year-old on the Feast of the Immaculate Conception in 1906, following the conversion of both her parents. In early adulthood she lost her faith and became an atheist. She was away from the sacraments for a period of thirteen years. Her return to the faith was recounted in *The Hound and the Falcon: The Story of a Reconversion to the Catholic Faith* which was published in 1965. On 8 September 1969 she recorded in her diary 'the most extraordinary change I have ever known in the Church's ritual':

It would have been unthinkable even a year ago in the Western rite and it was slipped in unobtrusively in the local convent I go to … We now go *up to the altar* for Communion. (In the past, women weren't even allowed in the sanctuary during Mass except nun sacristans and brides at the Nuptial Mass.) We take the Host in our hands (like the Protestants) whereas we were strictly forbidden to *touch* it with our hands ... And then we pick up the Chalice and take a sip. We were never even allowed to *touch* the Chalice, even when empty ... let alone drink from it ...[32]

Perhaps such changes, so surprising in 1969, seem almost trivial today. Yet the sense of shock they caused to many 'old' Catholics is evident in this diary entry. The same entry also recorded 'extraordinary changes' at St Mary's convent in Indiana where the nuns 'wear ordinary dress and even make-up and go in for slimming'. A year later, on 22 December 1970, White appeared to echo the doubts and disapproval of many of her Catholic literary peers:

> In the Mass now there is no space for *silence*. I was struck immensely not just by nostalgia, when I went to that Latin High Mass in September, [but] by how much it had lost in the bald version we have now ... And even the very admirable preoccupation with the injustices of society and the ardent 'revolutionary' priests seem to be putting too much emphasis on what one might call the 'material' side of Catholicism – or perhaps the 'love of one's neighbour' at the expense of the love of God.[33]

Even Graham Greene, normally so sullenly opposed to traditionalist interpretations of Catholicism, was opposed to many of the changes:

> I personally found the liturgical changes irritating because I used to go in London to a small church where Mass was said in Spanish, which I don't speak. Under the old rite one could follow the Latin, because one had the translation in one's missal, so I was irritated in not being able to follow the Mass when it was said in a language I did not know.[34]

Cecil Gill, referring in his unpublished autobiography to a Mass he attended in the United States, had lamented the vulgarization of the Mass: 'the priest and his acolytes arrayed in red and gold-sashed garments lounged around the altar and the sanctuary with slouching irreverence, as though they were determined that no-one should call them "sissies". One sighed for a low Latin Mass instead of this brash-hash version of the Sacred Liturgy.'[35]

Similar disdain was displayed in Robert Speaight's autobiography, *The Property Basket*, published in 1970:

We were concerned to sacralise the world, not to secularise the Church. We may have wished to simplify the altar, in so far as we bothered about such things at all; we had no desire to displace it for a kitchen table. The Latin of the Mass was not only familiar but numinous, and we had no wish to barter it for a vernacular which has justified our worst fears. We did not wish priests to dress like parishioners, any more than we wished judges to dress like jurymen. We were *anti-modernist* and even, except in aesthetics, anti-modernes; radical only in the sense that we wanted to get down to roots, not in the sense that we wanted to pull them up. We were more anxious to preserve the values of an ancient civilisation than to set about the construction of a new one.[36]

Yet, relatively speaking, Speaight was not a reactionary as far as the Second Vatican Council was concerned. Initially at least, he was one of its most enthusiastic supporters, believing that the problem which confronted the Conciliar Fathers was 'to reinterpret, and therefore to safeguard, a number of basic truths in the context of a changing world':

The actual achievement of the Council still seems to me the greatest single event of my lifetime – the most unexpected and the most fertile in promise. My sympathies were wholeheartedly with the progressive majority ...

... Something has happened far beyond the intention of the Conciliar fathers and their attendant *periti* ... The psychology of adherence to Catholicism has subtly changed; authority is flouted; basic doctrines are questioned; and the boundaries of what is understood by the Church are almost indefinitely extended. The vernacular Liturgy, popular and pedestrian, intelligible and depressing, has robbed us of much that was numinous in public worship; there is less emphasis on prayer and penitence; and the personal relationship between God and man ... is neglected in favour of a diffused social concern.[37]

Ultimately Speaight's initial enthusiasm gave way to indignant exasperation: 'What exasperates me in the attitude of many progressives is not their desire to go forward or even to change direction, but their indifference to tradition which is the *terra firma* from which they themselves proceed'.[38]

Alec Guinness was another thespian convert who found his initial enthusiasm for reform tempered by subsequent developments. 'Much water has flown under Tiber's bridges,' Guinness wrote in *Blessings in Disguise*, 'carrying away splendour and mystery from Rome, since the pontificate of Pius XII.'

> The essentials, I know, remain firmly entrenched and I find the post-Conciliar Mass simpler and generally better than the Tridentine; but the banality and vulgarity of the translations which have ousted the sonorous Latin and little Greek are of a supermarket quality which is quite unacceptable. Hand-shaking and embarrassed smiles or smirks have replaced the older courtesies; kneeling is out, queueing is in, and the general tone is rather like a BBC radio broadcast for tiny tots ... The Church has proved she is not moribund. 'All shall be well,' I feel, 'and all manner of things shall be well,' so long as the God who is worshipped is the God of all ages, past and to come, and not the Idol of Modernity, so venerated by some of our bishops, priests and mini-skirted nuns.[39]

Guinness quoted Chesterton as a prelude to this discourse on the reform of the Mass: 'One of Chesterton's most penetrating statements was: "The Church is the one thing that saves a man from the degrading servitude of being a child of his time."'

Paradoxically, the battle to preserve the traditional Latin Mass from the infusion of secular and ecumenical influences became itself a secular and ecumenical issue in 1971 when well-known Catholics joined forces with non-Catholic celebrities and dignitaries in a broad-based appeal to Rome.

On 6 July 1971 *The Times* published the text of an Appeal to Preserve the Mass which was being sent to the Vatican:

> If some senseless decree were to order the total or partial destruction of basilicas or cathedrals, then obviously it would be the educated – whatever their personal beliefs – who would rise up in horror to oppose such a possibility.
>
> Now the fact is that basilicas and cathedrals were built so as to celebrate a rite which, until a few months ago, constituted a living tradition. We are referring to the Roman Catholic Mass. Yet according to the latest information available in Rome, there is a plan to obliterate that Mass by the end of the current year.
>
> We are not at the moment considering the religious or spiritual experience of millions of individuals. The rite in question, in its magnificent Latin text, has also inspired a host of priceless achievements in the

arts – not only mystical works but works by poets, philosophers, musicians, architects, painters and sculptors in all countries and epochs. Thus, it belongs to universal culture as well as to churchmen and formal Christians.

In the materialistic and technocratic civilisation that is increasingly threatening the life of mind and spirit in its original creative expression – the word – it seems particularly inhuman to deprive man of word-forms in one of their most grandiose manifestations.

The signatories of this appeal which is entirely ecumenical and non-political, have been drawn from every branch of modern culture in Europe and elsewhere. They wish to call to the attention of the Holy See the appalling responsibility it would incur in the history of the human spirit were it to refuse to allow the traditional Mass to survive, even though this survival took place side by side with other liturgical forms.

In an ironic role reversal, these plaintive voices seemed to represent a secular David defending sacred tradition against the Goliath-like power of the Catholic hierarchy, who had cast themselves in the role of Philistines.

The Appeal was signed by a host of well-known figures representing a wide spectrum of opinions transcending religious and political divides. These included Harold Acton, Vladimir Ashkenazy, Lennox Berkeley, Maurice Bowra, Agatha Christie, Kenneth Clark, Nevill Coghill, Cyril Connolly, Colin Davis, the Bishop of Exeter, Miles Fitzalan-Howard, Robert Graves, Graham Greene, Joseph Grimond, Harman Grisewood, Rupert Hart-Davis, Barbara Hepworth, Auberon Herbert, David Jones, Osbert Lancaster, F. R. Leavis, Cecil Day Lewis, Compton Mackenzie, Max Mallowan, Yehudi Menuhin, Nancy Mitford, Raymond Mortimer, Malcolm Muggeridge, Iris Murdoch, John Murray, Sean O'Faolain, William Plomer, Kathleen Raine, William Rees-Mogg, Ralph Richardson, the Bishop of Ripon, Rivers Scott, Joan Sutherland, Philip Toynbee, Martin Turnell, Bernard Wall, Patrick Wall and E. I. Watkin.

However, of all the multifarious opponents of liturgical reform, the most vociferous was probably Hugh Ross Williamson. In 1969 he published a pamphlet entitled *The Modern Mass: A Reversion to the Reforms of Cranmer* and the following year he wrote *The Great Betrayal*, an attack on the reforms which had led to the supplanting of the Tridentine Mass. These went beyond mere protest and amounted to a bitter attack on the hierarchy, almost a declaration of war.

At around the time he was writing these provocative pamphlets, the 'war germ' he had contracted as a youth of fifteen, and which had dogged him ever since, finally disabled him to such an extent that he became housebound. He was to spend the last eight years of his life confined to one room in his Bayswater home. 'He had to have a leg amputated,' his daughter explained.

> We lived four floors up with no lift so he stayed in one room for eight years and the priest used to come and say Mass for him, in Latin. He was very upset by the Second Vatican Council. He wrote two or three pamphlets about it. He was one of the founder members of the Latin Mass Society. He wouldn't go to the new Mass and he agreed with Evelyn Waugh who wrote a hilarious letter to *The Times* on the subject. He never went to a modern Mass. He believed that the changes were echoing everything that was done at the Reformation. He, as a Reformation historian, felt very acutely that the Martyrs had died for nothing, and that everything he had written about the Reformation, as indeed had Waugh with his book on Edmund Campion, had been overturned.[40]

Hugh Ross Williamson died on 13 January 1978, shortly after his seventy-seventh birthday. Like Evelyn Waugh, he died under the shadow of reforms he was never able to accept.

NOTES

1. Christopher Sykes, *Evelyn Waugh: A Biography*, pp. 449–50.
2. David Pryce-Jones (ed.), *Evelyn Waugh and His World*, London, 1973, p. 131.
3. René Hague (ed.), *Dai Greatcoat: A Self-Portrait of David Jones in His Letters*, p. 209.
4. ibid., p. 209.
5. William Blisset, *The Long Conversation: A Memoir of David Jones*, Oxford, 1981, p. 110.
6. René Hague (ed.), *Dai Greatcoat: A Self-Portrait of David Jones in His Letters*, p. 209.
7. D. Felicitas Corrigan, *Siegfried Sassoon: Poet's Pilgrimage*, p. 232.
8. René Hague (ed.), *Dai Greatcoat: A Self-Portrait of David Jones in His Letters*, p. 211.
9. John Lehmann and Derek Parker (ed.), *Edith Sitwell: Selected Letters 1919–1964*, p. 253.
10. *The Times*, 10 December 1964.
11. David Blamires, *David Jones: Artist and Writer*, Manchester University Press, 1971, p. 194.
12. Mark Amory (ed.), *The Letters of Evelyn Waugh*, p. 629.
13. *The Times*, 6 January 1965.
14. Mark Amory (ed.), *The Letters of Evelyn Waugh*, p. 632.
15. *The Times*, 6 July 1965.
16. Michael De-la-Noy, *Eddy: The Life of Edward Sackville-West*, London, 1988, p. 312.
17. ibid., pp. 312–13.
18. *The Remnant*, 15 June 1978.
19. Father C. C. Martindale, SJ, letters to Hugh Ross Williamson, courtesy of Julia Ross Williamson.
20. Hugh Ross Williamson, letter to Julia Ross Williamson, courtesy of Julia Ross Williamson.
21. *The Remnant*, 15 June 1978.
22. Scott M. P. Reid, *A Bitter Trial: Evelyn Waugh and John Carmel Heenan on the Liturgical Changes*, pp. 69–70.
23. Christina Scott, *A Historian and His World: A Life of Christopher Dawson*, p. 206.
24. ibid., p. 205.

25. ibid., p. 206.
26. ibid., p. 207.
27. ibid., p. 207.
28. Sister Juliana Dawson, interview with the author.
29. William Blisset, *The Long Conversation: A Memoir of David Jones*, p. 65.
30. ibid., p. 132.
31. ibid., p. 50.
32. Susan Chitty (ed.), *Antonia White: Diaries 1958–1979, Volume II*, London, 1992, p. 206.
33. ibid., p. 221.
34. *Tablet*, 23 September 1989.
35. Cecil Gill, *Autobiography*, unpublished manuscript, p. 441.
36. Robert Speaight, *The Property Basket: Recollections of a Divided Life*, p. 164.
37. ibid., pp. 398–9.
38. ibid., p. 401.
39. Alec Guinness, *Blessings in Disguise*, p. 45.
40. Julia Ross Williamson, interview with the author.

SMALL IS BEAUTIFUL

H ugh Ross Williamson was wedded to controversy. In religion he struggled polemically from Nonconformism to high Anglicanism before reaching his home and final resting place in the Catholic Church. Even then he did not rest in peace, finding himself opposed to the 'home improvements' imposed by the Second Vatican Council. In politics, he remained a devout advocate of social justice but found himself alienated from the policies of all the major parties. Having been expelled from the Labour Party for opposing the power of the unions, he distanced himself from party politics. Yet he always retained firmly held views.

'My father always voted Labour,' recalled Julia Ross Williamson, 'and even stood for the party unsuccessfully on two occasions, but his personal politics were more in line with Chesterton ... distributism. He was in favour of the papal social encyclicals, *Rerum Novarum* particularly. He wanted justice in society but he believed it would never happen because it was a struggle between Mammon and God, and this world is dominated by Mammon. Mammon was a big word for him.'[1]

Chesterton was a major influence on Ross Williamson, both religiously and politically. In religion he considered Chesterton's *Orthodoxy* 'one of the best books he'd read', and his daughter believes that the book 'probably had an important influence on his intellectual and spiritual development'.[2] In politics he echoed Chesterton's advocacy of distributism and shared his admiration for *Rerum Novarum*.

'He was always quoting Chesterton,' his daughter remembers, 'and he had taught me, since I was a little girl, "The Rolling English Road". So, since my father was buried in Kensal Green, I arranged for the lines of Chesterton's poem to be put on his tombstone: "To Paradise by way of Kensal Green – GKC".'[3]

A similar debt to Chesterton was admitted by David Jones in a conversation with his friend William Blisset on 9 September 1972. Blisset had mentioned to Jones that he had recently met Father Ian Boyd, a Basilian interested in Chesterton and distributism who, two years later, was to become editor of the

Chesterton Review. Jones said how much he admired *Orthodoxy* but expressed reservations about other aspects of Chesterton's work. He saw the 'truth of substance through the inadequacy of form in the poems and the fiction' but was sorry that Chesterton wasted so much of his time and talent on weekly journalism. He remembered that T. S. Eliot had once told him that 'Chesterton was like a cabman on a cold night, thumping himself to keep warm'. On distributism, Blisset and Jones appeared to agree that 'the goal but not the way is apparent in the economics and politics of Distributism: between the conception and the act falls the shadow'. Or, to put it more succinctly if less poetically, distributism was fine in principle but was it practicable? By the 1970s, Jones had his doubts: 'It's all very well to live simply and grow things and practise crafts – we had it jolly nice with cows and things in Wales, but what about the hundreds of thousands in Birmingham who can't hope to be self-sufficient in property and craft?'[4]

Although Jones had apparently rejected the distributism he had practised with Eric Gill and others at Ditchling and Capel-y-ffin, his rejection of old ideals was not an acceptance of economic expansionism or modern consumerism. On the contrary, in old age Jones seemed to have accepted the pessimistic determinism of his mentor, Oswald Spengler. Believing, like Spengler, that Western civilization was in terminal decline, he appeared to look upon positive approaches to curing society's ills as merely futile efforts to resuscitate a hopelessly sick patient. With bitter irony he told Blisset that 'old Spengler was an answer to distributist optimism and pious aspiration, to the sort of thing that expressed itself in the sadly ironic title of Michael Roberts's *The Recovery of the West*, which came out at the start of the Second War'.[5]

It is of course impossible to say whether Jones's, and Spengler's, pessimism was justified. Western civilization may be in decline but it is too early to discern whether the decline is terminal or temporary. Perhaps the pessimism is itself the disease which is killing the patient. Which came first – the pessimism or the decline? Did the decline cause the pessimism, or the pessimism cause the decline? Is cynicism the sin which is destroying the soul of civilization?

Such questions were central to the philosophical grappling of Dr E. F. Schumacher, who came to the conclusion that pessimism was self-fulfillingly prophetic. If one believes the worst one will probably get the worst. Negation begets negation. The antidote to such despair, Schumacher believed, was hope. It was in this spirit that he wrote *Small is Beautiful*, a book which not only resuscitated distributism but made it, for a time at least, the most fashionable economic and political creed in the world. The book which would make distributist ideas more influential than ever was being written at the very time that Jones had dismissed distributism as impracticable. Furthermore, Schumacher's trained economic mind had resolved many of the alleged problems so that distributist principles became applicable even to 'the hundreds of thousands in Birmingham who can't hope to be self-sufficient in property or craft'. Schumacher had succeeded where Belloc and Chesterton had failed. He had lifted the shadow which had fallen between the conception and the act.

Schumacher's *Small is Beautiful*, subtitled 'a study of economics as if people mattered', was published in 1973 to immediate acclaim and became an international best-seller. At the time of its publication Schumacher was already well known as an economist, journalist and entrepreneur. He was Economic Adviser to the National Coal Board from 1950 to 1970, and was also the originator of the concept of Intermediate Technology for developing countries. In 1967 he became a trustee of the Scott Bader Commonwealth, a producers' co-operative established in 1959 when the company's owner, Ernest Bader, transferred ownership to his workforce. Bader, a Quaker, believed that establishing co-operative ownership was an expression of Christian social principles in practice. To the surprise of many sceptics, the Scott Bader Commonwealth prospered, becoming a pathfinder in polymer technology and a model of good labour relations at a time of considerable labour unrest throughout the rest of industry. Schumacher also served as President of the Soil Association, Britain's largest organic farming organization.

Born in Bonn on 16 August 1911, Schumacher first came to England in October 1930 as a Rhodes Scholar to study economics at New College, Oxford, where he stayed until September 1932. At the age of twenty-two he went to New York to teach economics at Columbia University. Finding theory without practical experience unsatisfying, he returned to Germany and tried his hand at business, farming and journalism. In 1937, utterly appalled with life in Hitler's Third Reich, he made his final move to England. During the war he returned to the academic life at Oxford and devised a plan for economic reconstruction which influenced John Maynard Keynes in the latter's leading part in the formulation of the Bretton Woods agreement.[6] After the war Schumacher became Economic Adviser to the British Control Commission in Germany from 1946 to 1950, before becoming Economic Adviser to the National Coal Board, a post he held for the next twenty years.

It was clear that Schumacher's credentials as an economist were beyond question, but few realized when *Small is Beautiful* was published that his economic theories were underpinned by solid religious and philosophical foundations, the fruits of a lifetime of searching. In 1971, two years before the publication of *Small is Beautiful*, Schumacher had become a Roman Catholic, the final destination of his philosophical journey.

The journey began shortly after the war with a growing disillusionment with Marxist economic theory. 'During the war he was definitely Marxist,' says his daughter and biographer, Barbara Wood.[7] Then, in the early fifties he visited Burma which 'was really important in beginning the real changes in his economic thinking'.[8] 'I came to Burma a thirsty wanderer and there I found living water,' he wrote.[9] Specifically, his encounter with the Buddhist approach to economic life made him realize that Western economic attitudes were derived from strictly subjective criteria based upon philosophically materialist assumptions. For the first time he began to see beyond established economic theories and to look for viable alternatives. As an economist he developed a meta-economic approach much as Christopher Dawson, as an historian, had developed a meta-historical approach. This fundamental change in outlook was discussed in *Small is Beautiful*. Modern economists, Schumacher wrote, 'normally suffer from a kind of metaphysical blindness, assuming that theirs is a science of absolute and invariable truths, without any presuppositions'.[10] This was not the case: 'economics is a "derived" science which accepts instructions from what I call meta-economics. As the instructions are changed, so changes the contents of economics.'[11]

To illustrate the point, in a chapter entitled 'Buddhist Economics' Schumacher explored the ways in which economic laws and definitions of concepts such as 'economic' and 'uneconomic' change 'when the meta-economic basis of western materialism is abandoned and the teaching of Buddhism is put in its place'. He stipulated that the choice of Buddhism 'is purely incidental; the teachings of Christianity, Islam, or Judaism could have been used just as well as those of any other of the great Eastern traditions'.[12]

Taking the concept of 'labour' or work as an example, he compared the attitude of Western economists to their Buddhist counterparts. Economists in the 'west' considered labour 'as little more than a necessary evil':

> From the point of view of the employer, it is in any case simply an item of cost, to be reduced to a minimum if it cannot be eliminated altogether, say, by automation. From the point of view of the workman, it is a 'disutility'; to work is to make a sacrifice of one's leisure and comfort, and wages are a kind of compensation for the sacrifice.[13]

'From a Buddhist point of view,' Schumacher explained, 'this is standing the truth on its head by considering goods as more important than people and consumption as more important than creative activity. It means shifting the emphasis from the worker to the product of work, that is, from the human to the sub-human, a surrender to the forces of evil.'[14]

The Buddhist view, on the other hand, 'takes the function of work to be at least threefold': 'to give a man a chance to utilise and develop his faculties; to enable him to overcome his egocentredness by joining with other people in a common task; and to bring forth the goods and services needed for a becoming existence.'[15]

From the Buddhist standpoint, Schumacher continued,

> to organise work in such a manner that it becomes meaningless, boring, stultifying, or nerve-racking for the worker would be little short of criminal; it would indicate a greater concern with goods than with people, an evil lack of compassion and a soul-destroying degree of attachment to the most primitive side of this worldly existence.[16]

In England, this view had been advocated already by Chesterton, Belloc, Gill and the other distributists, and also by Dorothy L. Sayers. Yet Schumacher appeared to be unaware of their writings at the time he visited Burma in the early fifties. His introduction to the religious basis of economics was, therefore, a Buddhist not a Christian revelation. Most importantly, however, he had discovered that economics was a derivative of philosophical or religious premises and this led to fundamental changes in outlook. Not only did he begin to see economics in a radically different light, he began to see the crucial importance of philosophy to an understanding both of economics in particular and of life in general.

In spite of the profound effect of Buddhist teaching upon his general outlook, Schumacher's return to England 'was not marked by an intensification of his study of Eastern religions'.[17] Instead he concentrated his efforts on a thorough study of Christian thought, particularly St Thomas Aquinas, and modern writers such as René Guenon and Jacques Maritain. He also began to read the Christian mystics and the lives of the saints.

Although he still did not consider himself a Christian his previously hostile attitude had softened. One result of this was that his wife, who came from a devout Lutheran background, could take their children to church without fear of her husband's objections.

Schumacher first publicly stated his new orientation in a broadcast talk in May 1957 in which he criticized a much-acclaimed book by Charles Frankel, entitled *The Case for Modern Man*. He called his talk 'The Insufficiency of Liberalism' and it was an exposition of what he termed the 'three stages of development'. The first great leap, he said, was made when man moved from stage one of primitive religiosity to stage two of scientific realism. This was the stage modern man tended to be at. Then, he said, some people become dissatisfied with scientific realism, perceiving its deficiencies, and realize that there is something beyond fact and science. Such people progress to a higher plane of development which he called stage three. The problem, he explained, was that stage one and stage three looked exactly the same to those in stage two. Consequently, those in stage three are seen as having had some sort of brainstorm, a relapse into childish nonsense. Only those in stage three, who have been through stage two, can understand the difference between stage one and stage three. This strange blend of mysticism empirically explained in the language of an economist was an early example of the winning formula which was to make *Small is Beautiful* such a huge success.

Schumacher's broadcast provoked a huge response. He was indignant when a correspondent to the *New Statesman and Nation* criticized his talk as typical for a 'Catholic economist'.[18] He did not consider himself a Catholic at this time and resented the fact that anyone should mistake him for one. Yet his reading of Catholic writers was continuing. By the mid-fifties he had developed an interest in Dante and, through Dante, had been introduced to the writing of Dorothy L. Sayers. Schumacher described Sayers as 'one of the finest commentators on Dante as well as on modern society'[19] and quoted at length from her *Introductory Papers on Dante*, which had been published in 1954:

That the *Inferno* is a picture of human society in a state of sin and corruption, everybody will readily agree. And since we are today fairly well convinced that society is in a bad way and not necessarily evolving in the direction of perfectibility, we find it easy enough to recognise the various stages by which the deep of corruption is reached. Futility; lack of a living faith; the drift into loose morality, greedy consumption, financial irresponsibility, and uncontrolled bad temper; a self-opinionated and obstinate individualism; violence, sterility, and lack of reverence for life and property including one's own; the exploitation of sex, the debasing of language by advertisement and propaganda, the commercialising of religion, the pandering to superstition and the conditioning of people's minds by mass-hysteria and 'spell-binding' of all kinds, venality and string-pulling in public affairs, hypocrisy, dishonesty in material things, intellectual dishonesty, the fomenting of discord (class against class, nation against nation) for what one can get out of it, the falsification and destruction of all the means of communication; the exploitation of the lowest and stupidest mass-emotions; treachery even to the fundamentals of kinship, country, the chosen friend, and the sworn allegiance: these are the all-too-recognisable stages that lead to the cold death of society and the extinguishing of all civilised relations.[20]

'What an array of divergent problems!' Schumacher exclaimed after quoting this passage. 'Yet people go on clamouring for "solutions", and become angry when they are told that the restoration of society must come from within and cannot come from without.'[21]

By the end of the fifties he had reached the conclusion that man was *homo viator* – created man with a purpose. It was the failure to recognize this fact which led to society's ills. Once man acknowledged that he was in fact *homo viator*, he would recognize a purpose to life outside himself. Life would be seen as an objectivized existence necessitating a selfless, as opposed to a selfish, appraisal of, and interplay with, reality. And since man was created with a purpose, it was his duty to fulfil the purpose for which he was created. He was individually responsible for his actions.

For Schumacher there were three main culprits who should bear the blame for modern man's refusal to accept or recognize individual responsibility. These were Freud, Marx and Einstein. Dubbing them the 'devilish trio', he considered that they had all been corrosive agents in a world which had lost its way. Freud, through his teaching that perception was subject to the complex interplay of the *ego* and the *id*, both of which in turn were subject to sexually based imperatives, had subjectivized perception, literally rendering it self-centred. This led inevitably to a change of attitude in human relations where self-fulfilment took precedence over the needs of others. Marx, by seeking a scapegoat in the bourgeoisie, had replaced personal responsibility with a hatred for others. If something was wrong with society someone else was to blame. Einstein had undermined belief in absolutes with his insistence on the relativity of everything. The application of 'relativity' in the field of morals led logically to a rejection of all morality except that which was personally convenient.

Schumacher gave a series of lectures at London University in 1959 and 1960 in which he examined the implications for politics, economics and art of the belief that man was *homo viator*. Once one accepted that man was created by God with a designated purpose, politics, economics and art had value only insofar as they were servants helping man reach that higher plane of existence which was his goal. For modern man, ignorant of the purpose for which he was created, the only function of politics, economics and art was to further his greed, his animal lusts and his desire for power.

'It is when we come to politics,' Schumacher insisted, 'that we can no longer postpone or avoid the question regarding man's ultimate aim and purpose.' If one believes in God one will pursue politics 'mindful of the eternal destiny of man and of the truths of the Gospel'. However, if one believes 'that there are no higher obligations', it becomes impossible to resist the appeal of Machiavellianism – 'politics as the art of gaining and maintaining power so that you and your friends can order the world as *they like it*'.

> There is no supportable middle position. Those who want the Good Society, without believing in God, cannot face the temptations of Machiavellianism; they become either disheartened or muddleheaded, fabulating about the goodness of human nature and the vileness of one or another adversary ... Optimistic 'Humanism' by 'concentrating sin on a few people' instead of admitting its universal presence throughout the human race, leads to the utmost cruelty.[22]

Politics dealt with hope, he explained, and since hope had nothing to do with science, politics could not be scientific. Politics, like economics, was derivative of, and subject to, philosophical premises. He believed that this was as true of art as it was of politics and economics. 'High art used unworthily is corruption,' he had said in a talk a year earlier. Using literature as an example, he continued: 'The test is a perfectly simple one: in reading the book, am I merely held in the thraldom of a daydream, or am I obtaining a new insight into the meaning and purpose of man's life on earth?'[23] In applying this test, Schumacher was again echoing Dorothy L. Sayers who had insisted on the need for 'creative reading' at the end of *Begin Here*, her war-time essay. It was scarcely surprising, when such a test was applied, that Schumacher restricted his reading almost exclusively to non-fiction. According to his daughter, he considered most novels 'poison wrapped up in silver paper': 'He didn't like novels where good doesn't triumph. I doubt whether he would have had any time for Graham Greene at all. For him, all art – music, painting, literature – had the purpose of uplifting the soul. When it doesn't it is not fulfilling its function.'[24]

The fact that Schumacher's own reading consisted largely of his continuing studies in Thomism could be gauged from a reference he made in his lecture on Marxism at London University: 'Lenin once said that Marx synthesized German philosophy, French socialism and British classical economics. This is the strength of Marx. In this he has no rival in the nineteenth century, apart from the Thomist synthesis which Leo XIII brought back into the centre of Roman Catholic thought around 1850.'[25]

Apart from the historical inaccuracy (Leo XIII did not become Pope until 1878), this statement is notable for the supreme importance Schumacher placed on the re-emergence of Thomism as a major force in modern philosophy. By 1960 it had certainly emerged as a major force in Schumacher's own philosophy. 'Thomas Aquinas was very important to him,' remembers his daughter. 'He had all his books in his library – in German.'[26] He was also widely read in the works of the neo-Thomists. Jacques Maritain was 'someone he admired', Etienne Gilson was 'another influence' and he had read F. C. Copleston's book on Aquinas which had been published in 1955.

Apart from Thomism, Schumacher admired the works of St Augustine, St Teresa of Avila and St John of the Cross. He was also 'very interested in Russian Orthodox mysticism'.

His daughter remembered that he owned all of Teilhard de Chardin's books but his copy of *The Phenomenon of Man* was peppered with comments in the margins such as 'typical rubbish', 'drivel' and 'nonsense'. 'He disagreed with the concept that humanity was developing towards Christ. He felt very strongly that it was nonsense to suggest that we were more advanced than all the great minds spanning back through the history of the Church.'[27] In this, of course, he was echoing the central theme of Chesterton's *The Everlasting Man* which had helped convince C. S. Lewis 'that the ancients had got every whit as good brains as we had'.[28] Barbara Wood does not recall whether her father had read *The Everlasting Man* but he had 'lots of C. S. Lewis's books. I think he admired him.'[29] Schumacher and Lewis actually met sometime in or around 1960 at dinner in Hall in Worcester College, Oxford. Lewis's friend and biographer George Sayer, who was also present, remembered that 'Schumacher spoke with a strong German accent and had rather crude table manners!'[30]

Schumacher also owned works by E. I. Watkin and some of Ronald Knox's books, including *The Mass in Slow Motion*.

'Another person he admired initially was Thomas Merton,' Barbara Wood remembered, 'but he felt that Merton's later books were disappointing. He said that *The Seven Storey Mountain* was a very dangerous book to read because it was likely to make anyone reading it *want* to become a Catholic. He wouldn't have been a Catholic when he first read *The Seven Storey Mountain*.'[31]

For all his theorizing, Schumacher still practised no faith and it took a major crisis to change things. 'He didn't actually start going to church until after my mother's death in 1960,' Barbara Wood recalls. 'My mother had come from a devout Lutheran background and perhaps he felt that he had a duty to continue taking us to church.'[32]

Throughout the early sixties he was taking his children to a Protestant church on Sundays and reading Catholic theology throughout the rest of the week! 'He read avidly,' says Barbara Wood, 'and it was in the sixties during the Cold War that he began to discover various papal encyclicals. He was introduced to them by Harry Collins, a friend who was also a Catholic. Slowly he came to see that the people he was agreeing with were all Catholics.'[33]

Important to Schumacher's final distillation of the ideas which came to maturity in *Small is Beautiful* were the social encyclicals. On 15 May 1961 Pope John XXIII published *Mater et Magistra* (*Mother and Teacher*), his first social encyclical. In the opening paragraphs the Pope restated the Church's right and duty to teach on matters of justice in society. He then devoted the whole of Part One to emphasizing that he adhered faithfully to the social teaching of his predecessors Leo XIII, Pius XI and Pius XII. Pope John drew attention to the teaching of Pius XI that the wage contract 'should, when possible, be modified somewhat by a clear reference to the right of the wage-earner to a share in the profits, and, indeed, to sharing, as appropriate, in decision-making in his place of work'. Reinforcing his predecessor's teaching, Pope John wrote that 'it is our conviction that the workers should make it their aim to be involved in the organized life of the firm by which they are employed and in which they work.'

These principles animated the efforts of many Catholics working for social justice throughout the sixties. Perhaps the most dramatic fruition of papal teaching was in the Mondragon region of Spain where whole sections of industry became successful producers' co-operatives.

Pope Leo XIII is popularly attributed with laying the foundations of modern Catholic teaching on social issues with his groundbreaking encyclical *Rerum Novarum*, published in 1891. This had become a focal point for social reform throughout the world. In England it had made a deep impression on Hilaire Belloc and formed the basis of his exposition of distributism in the early years of the century. Pope Pius XI had commemorated the fortieth anniversary of the publication of *Rerum Novarum* with the publication of his own social encyclical *Quadragesimo Anno* in 1931. This had stressed the continued relevance of Pope Leo's teaching. The teaching, which was summarized in the documents of the Second Vatican Council, centred on the principle that 'business enterprises' were not primarily units of production but places where 'persons ... associate together, that is, men who are free and autonomous, created in the image of God'. Such a view was music to the ears of Schumacher since it put *homo viator* at the very centre of economic life, 'economics as if people mattered' as he would subtitle *Small is Beautiful*. The practical principle which sprang logically and inevitably from this was that, to employ the modern jargon, economic activity must become 'user friendly'. Wherever possible economics should be carried out on a human scale so that people could express themselves in a natural environment free from the alienation inherent in macro-economic enterprises. Small was beautiful!

In June 1968, while Schumacher was in Tanzania advising the government of Julius Nyerere on how best to apply intermediate technology to his country's developing economy, his second wife approached the local Catholic priest and asked to be instructed in the Catholic faith. According to Barbara Wood, 'Father Scarborough was an old and experienced priest, who received Vreni kindly but not with the open arms she had expected.'[34] Rather than welcoming her immediately into the fold, he suggested she should come to Mass from time to time if she was interested. Consequently, when Schumacher returned from Tanzania he found his wife regularly attending Mass. The next time she went he accompanied her. Although he had lived on a regular diet of Catholic writers, ancient and modern, supplemented by papal encyclicals supplied by his friend, he knew next to nothing about the actual form of worship in the rites of the Church. His experience of Catholicism was all theory and no practice. Observing Mass for the first time, he found himself fascinated by the drama unfolding before him. He was 'struck particularly by the reverence with which the priests handled the chalice and the paten after they had distributed communion, the care with which every vessel was carefully wiped and polished'.[35]

A few weeks later the Catholic Church hit the headlines in controversial circumstances when Pope Paul VI issued his famous encyclical *Humanae Vitae*, in which he reaffirmed the Church's belief in the sanctity of marriage and marital love. The most controversial aspect of the encyclical, and the only aspect the media considered worth mentioning, was the Pope's condemnation of the use of artificial methods of contraception. The late sixties were of course a time of licentiousness masquerading as liberation and *Humanae Vitae* was accused principally of being an attack on liberty. The spirit of the late sixties was dominated by the clichéd 'freedoms' of sex, drugs and rock and roll and the Pope's prohibitions fitted uncomfortably into this fashionable hippy culture. Not for the first time in its history the Church found itself *contra mundum*. Even many Catholics found themselves uneasy at a teaching which seemed so at odds with 'progress'. Graham Greene, during a visit to Paraguay in 1969, defied the Pope by advising a group of schoolgirls 'not to worry about the encyclical, for it would soon be forgotten': 'I tried to reassure them that it had little to do with Faith, and was not – as the Pope himself indicated – an infallible statement.'[36]

Surprisingly perhaps, Schumacher took a very different view from Greene. 'If the Pope had written anything else,' he told Harry Collins, 'I would have lost all faith in the papacy.'[37] Barbara, his daughter, phoned him to ask what he thought of the encyclical and was told that the Pope could have said nothing else. His wife also found comfort in the Pope's pronouncement:

For her, the message it conveyed was an affirmation and support for marriage, for women such as herself who had given themselves entirely to their marriages and who felt acutely the pressure from the world outside that shouted ever louder that homebound, monogamous relationships were oppressive to women and prevented them from 'fulfilling themselves'.[38]

Vreni Schumacher returned to Father Scarborough and requested again that he accept her for a course of instruction in the Catholic faith.

At the same time, but unknown to either her father or her stepmother, Schumacher's daughter Barbara was also 'going through a period of soul-searching'. She had felt a strong attraction to the Catholic Church since her schooldays 'but had always feared to explore'.[39] Then, in the wake of *Humanae Vitae*, she finally decided that she must become a Catholic: 'For me, the encyclical was proof that I could trust the Church, that it wouldn't drift with the whims of society. It wouldn't be a slave to fashion.'[40] When she informed her father of her decision she was surprised at his aggressive and apparently hostile reaction. He bombarded both Barbara and his wife Vreni with a barrage of questions: 'We were both taken by surprise. We knew of his sympathy with the Catholic Church and his devotion to many Catholic writers. Some time later he explained that he had wanted to make sure that we knew what we were doing and had therefore taken up the position of Devil's advocate.'[41]

When his daughter was received into the Church some months later he presented her with a gift of four volumes of *The Sunday Sermons of the Great Fathers*, inscribed with the words: 'To Barbara, with love and good wishes, joy and fullest approval. Papa.'

Schumacher's support and approval of the step that his wife and daughter had taken was so unreserved that it prompted the obvious question: 'If you agree with the teachings of the Church, why don't you become a Catholic too?' When his daughter had asked him this he replied that 'I couldn't do it to my mother'. 'There were all sorts of emotional things holding him back,' his daughter explained. 'His family had all been Lutheran and the divide is quite great.'[42] It is a sobering insight into the divisions caused by the Reformation that Schumacher should consider conversion to Catholicism a more revolutionary step from his Lutheran roots than his earlier involvement with Marxism and Buddhism, both of which had caused his parents anxiety and sorrow.

Soon after Schumacher had given his blessing to the conversions of his wife and daughter, he settled down to work on two separate but related books. One was a kind of spiritual map in which he would draw together all the threads of his own spiritual quest. This he hoped would be of benefit to others who were lost and confused in a world of conflicting goals. He already had a title in mind for this book. It was to be called *A Guide for the Perplexed*.

The second book would be an alternative view of economics which he initially proposed to call *The Homecomers* because he believed it would be advocating a return to traditional sense as opposed to the 'forward stampede' that characterized modern life. The subtitle he chose was less esoteric and more explanatory: 'Economics – as if people mattered'. This would be published as *Small is Beautiful*.

Although he considered the first book the more important, he decided to begin with the other. With calculated realism he thought the book on economics would sell better and he might therefore reach a wider readership with the spiritual book if he had interested people in the economics book first.

Schumacher relied heavily on his past articles and lectures to form the body of the book, adding a little here, updating a little there, and adding linking passages. A few chapters were essentially new but others were from articles he had already published in magazines for which he had been writing regularly. Principal among these were *Manas*, an American publication edited by Henry Geiger, and *Resurgence*, a journal started by John Papworth but taken over by Satish Kumar. *Resurgence* espoused the principles of smallness and decentralization and provided a forum for radical alternative thinkers such as Leopold Kohr, Ivan Illich and John Seymour, leading light in the self-sufficiency movement.

In the spring of 1971, in the midst of his work on *Small is Beautiful*, he finally decided that he must be received into the Catholic Church. During the following months he went every Wednesday morning to receive instruction from Father Scarborough. He appears to have undertaken instruction in a spirit of humility because his wife observed that he never complained 'that he already knew everything after years of study and reading, and it was obvious that his affection and respect for his local parish priest grew with each session'.[43] He was received into the Church by Father Scarborough on 29 September 1971. The only witnesses were his wife, his daughter and his son-in-law, who was also a convert. His daughter remembered that he was very moved as he recited the Creed and took communion. 'He had,' she said, 'at last, come to rest after a long and restless search.'[44] More amusingly, Schumacher himself declared that he had 'made legal a long-standing illicit love affair'.[45]

Some time after his conversion he formed a lasting friendship with Christopher Derrick. 'I often went down to him on the bus,' Derrick remembers, 'and he plied me with whisky … We sat and drank and chattered.' Derrick's reminiscences of these conversations offer a unique insight into Schumacher's long and intellectually arduous path to Rome:

He started out as a fuel economist and became the chief economist of
the National Coal Board. The policy then was, as it still is, to cut down
on the coal industry ... and increase dependence upon oil. That struck
him ... as lunacy because the sources of oil are very much more limited
and crucial amounts, as we know, come from some of the most unstable
parts of the world ... He opposed government policy and maintained
that such a course of action was no way to run a world. In response,
someone said to him 'how should we run the world then?' Good question. So he decided to study that question and with a completely open
mind. He embarked upon an enormous course of reading ... Then
somebody said you should read the social encyclicals of the Popes of
Rome. He replied, 'No, no, I'm sure that the Popes are very holy men
living in their ivory tower in the Vatican but they don't know a thing
about the conduct of practical affairs ... But this friend ... insisted that
he should read the social encyclicals, *Rerum Novarum* and *Quadragesimo Anno* above all ... He did so and was absolutely staggered. He said,
'here were these celibates living in an ivory tower ... why can they talk
a great deal of sense when everyone else talks nonsense' ...[46]

During the course of their conversations Schumacher discussed with Derrick the
twentieth-century writers who had influenced him. 'He mentioned Chesterton,'
Derrick remembered, 'but of course many others including, say, Gandhi, and
Gandhi, like Vincent McNabb, was a fine mixture of the wise sage and the
lunatic ... I think Chesterton was a formative influence on him'.[47]

Both Christopher Derrick and E. F. Schumacher were able to see the debt
they owed to the earlier distributists. 'Distributism is very closely related to
what we now call environmental and ecological questions,' says Derrick. 'I went
in 1972 to Stockholm for the United Nations Conference on the Environment. It
was fascinating to see the number of people – scientists, economists, even politicians – who were starting from very un-Chestertonian premises and reaching
very Chestertonian conclusions.'[48]

Among those giving lectures at the UN Conference in Stockholm was Barbara Ward whose advocacy of distributist solutions to the world's problems
went back to before the war. Like Schumacher, she transcended what Derrick
described as that 'damned-fool dichotomy of left and right, Labour or Tory'[49]
and played a significant and largely unsung part in the rise of the ecological
movement. She may also have played a significant part in Schumacher's conversion because her friendship with him stretched back to the days when he was still
clinging to the last remnants of his Marxism. Certainly Ward, a cradle Catholic,

held the views of distributism long before Schumacher did. It seems likely that he must at least have been intrigued by her views, both religious and economic, in the early days of their friendship – a friendship which was close enough in the post-war years for him to choose to name his daughter after her. 'I am called Barbara after Barbara Ward,' says Barbara Wood. 'She was asked to be my god-mother but she refused because we weren't Catholics. He liked her. He said to me in later years that Barbara never had an original idea in her life but she was marvellous at putting over other people's ideas.'[50]

When Schumacher's *Small is Beautiful* was published in 1973 it seemed to synthesize and epitomize all that Barbara Ward and the other 'experts' had been saying the previous year at the United Nations Conference. The timing of its publication could not have been better. Immediately it seemed to encapsulate the environmental anxieties of a whole generation. 'Saving the World with Small Talk' was the headline of an article on Schumacher by Victoria Brittain in *The Times* on 2 June:

> Schumacher … believes that the Western world's loss of the Classi-cal/Christian ethics has left us impoverished devotees of the religion of economic growth, heading for every conceivable kind of world disaster. His book is a polemic for smallness, and for what he calls meta-economic values, in which people come before profits.

Almost overnight Schumacher became famous throughout the world. Idolized as a guru both by the Californian counter-culture and by a rising generation of eco-warriors, he was simultaneously recognized on the Queen's Honours List, being awarded a CBE in 1974. He spent the last few remaining years of his life basking in the reflected glory of his best-selling book, secure in the knowledge that he had radically changed the outlook of millions of people. By 1977 his views had become so popular that he was invited by President Carter for a half-hour talk in the White House and the President was keen to be photographed holding a copy of *Small is Beautiful*.

Schumacher died on 4 September 1977, at the age of sixty-six. His obituary in *The Times* two days later seemed almost dismissive, referring only briefly to the fact that he was 'an ardent conservationist'. This elicited an irate response from Christopher Derrick which was published on 9 September:

> Dr E. F. Schumacher was a very much more influential man than your brief obituary suggests. His book *Small is Beautiful* was not merely 'published in 1973', it has been translated into fifteen languages and has

received world-wide attention, and is taken very seriously in circles as diverse as those of the White House and the Vatican ...

If he became something of a cult-figure in recent years – notably among young people in America – this was not simply because of his characteristic presence and personal magnetism. Partly at least, it was because he combined scientific thinking at its most rigorous with religious commitment at its most compassionate; it was also because he seemed to have put his finger, with unprecedented accuracy, upon several of the issues concerning 'development' ...

His was a message of extraordinary universality ...

The following day's edition of *The Times* carried a tribute by Barbara Ward, whose book *The Home of Man*, published the previous year and written for the United Nations 1976 Conference in Vancouver on Human Settlements, was a reiteration of the principles Schumacher held so dear. 'Anyone fortunate enough to have known Fritz Schumacher,' she wrote, 'will now be chiefly mourning the loss of a friend who combined a remarkable innovating intelligence and rigour of mind with the greatest gentleness and humour. But what the world has lost is of far greater importance.' Ward recounted Schumacher's achievement, laying special emphasis on his pioneering work in the field of intermediate technology, before concluding with elegaic enthusiasm: 'To very few people, it is given to begin to change, drastically and creatively, the direction of human thought. Dr Schumacher belongs to this intensely creative minority and his death is an incalculable loss to the whole international community.'

On 30 November a requiem Mass was celebrated for Schumacher at Westminster Cathedral. During the service, Jerry Brown, Governor of California and a friend and follower of Schumacher, described him as 'a man of utter simplicity who moved large numbers by the force of his ideas and personality. He challenged the fundamental beliefs of modern society from the context of ancient wisdom.'[51] An address was also given by David Astor, and the High Commissioner for Zambia read a message from President Kaunda. Other dignitaries present included the High Commissioner for Botswana, the US Ambassador and members of both Houses of Parliament.

On the following day *The Times* described Schumacher as a 'pioneer of postcapitalist, post-communist thought' and more than made up for its earlier alleged indifference by devoting its editorial to his memory:

There has never been any shortage of prophets and preachers asserting that mankind is moving in the wrong direction, that the pursuit of wealth does not necessarily bring happiness, that a renewal of moral and spiritual perception is necessary if disaster is to be avoided. From time to time one of these prophets evokes a response which tells as much about the time in which he lives as about the message he brings. Dr Fritz Schumacher ... was such a one.

Amidst the laudatory valedictions his conversion to Roman Catholicism late in life was seemingly lost. Perhaps it was overlooked, forgotten or merely considered irrelevant. It is certain, however, that Schumacher considered his conversion of supreme importance. This can be seen from the fact that he considered his spiritual work, *A Guide for the Perplexed*, to be his most important achievement.

'Pop handed me *A Guide for the Perplexed* on his deathbed, five days before he died,' says his daughter. He told her 'this is what my life has been leading to'. Yet when she began researching her biography of her father a lot of people were 'astounded' when they discovered his conversion. 'They hadn't realized that he had become a Catholic. They thought it was a real let-down, a betrayal'.[52]

For all the songs of praise to Schumacher's achievement many, it seemed, had missed the point.

NOTES

1. Julia Ross Williamson, interview with the author.
2. ibid.
3. ibid.
4. William Blisset, *The Long Conversation: A Memoir of David Jones*, pp. 109–10.
5. ibid., p. 110.
6. Barbara Wood, interview with the author, Kew, 3 January 1997.
7. ibid.
8. ibid.
9. ibid.
10. E. F. Schumacher, *Small is Beautiful*, London, 1973, p. 44.
11. ibid., p. 43.
12. ibid., p. 43.
13. ibid., p. 45.
14. ibid., p. 47.
15. ibid., p. 45.
16. ibid., p. 45.
17. Barbara Wood, *Alias Papa: A Life of Fritz Schumacher*, London, 1984, p. 256.
18. ibid., p. 257.
19. E. F. Schumacher, *A Guide for the Perplexed*, London, 1977, p. 157.
20. Dorothy L. Sayers, *Introductory Papers on Dante*, London, 1954, p. 114.
21. E. F. Schumacher, *A Guide for the Perplexed*, p. 158.
22. Barbara Wood, *Alias Papa: A Life of Fritz Schumacher*, p. 264.
23. ibid., pp. 262–3.
24. Barbara Wood, interview with the author.
25. Barbara Wood, *Alias Papa: A Life of Fritz Schumacher*, p. 264.
26. Barbara Wood, interview with the author.

27. ibid.
28. Roger Lancelyn Green and Walter Hooper, *C. S. Lewis: A Biography*, p. 208.
29. Barbara Wood, interview with the author.
30. George Sayer, letter to the author, 22 January 1997.
31. Barbara Wood, interview with the author.
32. ibid.
33. ibid.
34. Barbara Wood, *Alias Papa: A Life of Fritz Schumacher*, p. 336.
35. ibid., pp. 336–7.
36. Marie-Françoise Allain, *The Other Man: Conversations with Graham Greene*, London, 1983, p. 177.
37. Barbara Wood, *Alias Papa: A Life of Fritz Schumacher*, p. 337.
38. ibid., p. 337.
39. ibid., p. 338.
40. Barbara Wood, interview with the author.
41. Barbara Wood, *Alias Papa: A Life of Fritz Schumacher*, p. 338.
42. Barbara Wood, interview with the author.
43. Barbara Wood, *Alias Papa: A Life of Fritz Schumacher*, p. 349.
44. ibid., p. 350.
45. ibid., p. 350.
46. Christopher Derrick, interview with the author.
47. ibid.
48. ibid.
49. ibid.
50. Barbara Wood, interview with the author.
51. *The Times*, 1 December 1977.
52. Barbara Wood, interview with the author.

CHAPTER TWENTY NINE

MUGGERIDGE: PILGRIMAGE AND PASSION

On 26 September 1971, three days before Schumacher's reception into the Church, around thirty thousand people marched from Trafalgar Square to Hyde Park as part of the national campaign for moral renewal in Britain, known as the Festival of Light. Speakers at the rally in Hyde Park included Mary Whitehouse and Malcolm Muggeridge. Along the route of the march, opponents from the Gay Liberation Front and other militant groups hurled stink bombs and abuse. The demonstration and counter-demonstration were a living symbol of the larger struggle in society between the opponents and the proponents of the permissive society.

The same conflict between supporters of the Festival of Light and its opponents had erupted at a meeting held at Central Hall, Westminster on 9 September. The meeting was attended by four thousand people but was constantly disrupted by activists from the Gay Liberation Front, the Women's Liberation Movement and associated organizations. When a Danish man had got up to testify to the harmful effects of pornography in his country, he was shouted down. Not long into Malcolm Muggeridge's address to the meeting he was forced to stop while a number of women dressed as nuns 'cavorted across the hall' beneath the podium before being ejected. Muggeridge managed to complete some of his address, which began with the assertion that without moral order, a society can have no real order at any level. He went on to condemn the commercialization of sex and violence which had become the most effective way for the entertainment industry and its financial backers, the advertisers, to sell their products. Television, he said, had even sensationalized news-reporting so that it was impossible for the public to get at the real issues. He attacked the abuse of language, asking what words like 'love' and 'freedom' could mean when they were being championed by those who were really addicted to promiscuity and drugs.[1]

Muggeridge, like Schumacher, was a latecomer to Christianity. Schumacher had been sixty when he was received into the Catholic Church and Muggeridge, eight years Schumacher's senior, would be nearly eighty before he finally became a Catholic in 1982. For both of them the journey to faith took a lifetime of searching.

In 1971 Muggeridge was still some way from completing his journey to the gates of the Church and considered himself a non-denominational Christian. 'Even though he was now a Christian,' Gregory Wolfe, his biographer, observed of this period of Muggeridge's life, 'he remained an outsider, standing on the church steps, but refusing to go inside and kneel down with others.'[2]

An insight into Muggeridge's conversion to Christianity had been elucidated, perhaps unwittingly, in a dialogue with his life-long friend Alec Vidler, during a documentary series Muggeridge made on the life of St Paul. The series, *Paul: Envoy Extraordinary*, broadcast in five parts by the BBC in February and March of 1971, included a scene on the road to Damascus where Muggeridge and Vidler discussed the nature of conversion:

> MUGGERIDGE: Conversion is something that you as a priest must have met with often – a person being reborn, becoming a new man. Paul is said to have been blinded by the experience, but he was blind only because afterwards he truly could see whereas before he couldn't.
>
> VIDLER: Paul's conversion does seem to have been sudden, but of course sudden conversions are seldom as sudden as they seem. I remember reading somewhere that our twentieth-century psychologist Jung had remarked that Paul had been a Christian for a long time before his conversion, only unconsciously.
>
> MUGGERIDGE: You mean fighting against something he knew would ultimately captivate and capture him.[3]

Muggeridge had been 'fighting against something he knew would ultimately captivate and capture him' for his entire life. Born on 24 March 1903, Muggeridge's early years were dominated by the socialist ideas he learned from his father who had been a founding member of both the Fabian Society and the Independent Labour Party. He became acquainted at an early age with the authors who had most influenced his father: Thomas Carlyle, John Ruskin, William Morris, Bernard Shaw, Charles Dickens, Walt Whitman, Prince Kropotkin, Edward Bellamy and the husband-and-wife team of Sidney and Beatrice Webb.

In old age Muggeridge remembered with fondness the loving relationship he enjoyed with his father. Writing in the third person, he recalled 'as a child going for walks with his father. There might be rough ground, a heavy climb, marshland, etc., but he did not worry. He had faith in his father; he knew that his purpose was loving not malign, and that he could be counted on to arrive safely back at home, and to deal with any difficulties which might arise.'[4]

Although the young Muggeridge had an innocent faith in his father, faith in God was not part of the education he received, either from his parents or from his school. Scripture played 'a negligible role' in his upbringing. The school he attended fulfilled 'only the minimum requirements of the latest Education Act', and at home the Bible was 'seldom opened, and then usually to check some ironical quote from it'.[5] Against this agnostic backdrop, Muggeridge still found himself inexplicably drawn to the scriptures. He acquired a Bible of his own and read it 'surreptitiously, as it might have been some forbidden book like *Fanny Hill*'. Guilt-ridden, he even put a brown paper cover on it so that nobody would know what book he was reading. He took it to bed with him, marking the passages which particularly moved or impressed him. Years later he came across this Bible among his books and was surprised to find how crumpled and torn it was, and how the 'worst ravages' were in the passages relating to the Passion – 'there, stains that might be from tears'.[6]

In addition to the Bible, Muggeridge found himself strangely moved by the edition of Dante's *Divine Comedy* in his father's library. This fired his fertile imagination, as did the lurid and apocalyptic illustrations by Gustave Doré which complemented the text.

With images from Dante and the Bible grappling for supremacy over the Victorian rationalism inherited from his father, Muggeridge went up to Cambridge in 1920 in a spirit of confusion. Partly under the influence of his new friendship with Alec Vidler, he underwent a religious conversion which, though it did not last, sank deep psychological roots that would bear fruit decades later.

'At Selwyn College,' Muggeridge wrote, the prevailing style was Anglo-Catholic, 'with a propensity to call all clergymen "Father", burn incense, wear birettas and generally emulate the Roman rite.'[7] Of the Anglo-Catholic ordinands he met, Vidler was the one who made the deepest impression on the teenage undergraduate. Vidler was 'in his fourth year and soon to be ordained, good at games, with a First in his Theology Tripos, and altogether an outstanding figure in the college'. To Muggeridge's 'great surprise and delight', they became friends 'despite the gap between them in years, in scholarship, in games and in their standing in the college'.[8]

Through his friendship with Vidler, Muggeridge moved for two terms into Oratory House, the headquarters of the Anglican Order of the Good Shepherd. This, he later recalled, was 'a period of great, and … unusual contentment', the days passing smoothly, 'broken up by the daily offices and certain duties'. These included serving at the morning Eucharist, ringing the Angelus, and working in the garden with Wilfred Knox, brother of Ronald Knox, who Muggeridge described as 'a saintly man'.[9]

His contentment at Oratory House led him to consider whether he had a vocation for the religious life. This he soon rejected as indeed he would soon reject Christianity as a whole. In the interim, however, his short stay in a religious community had left an indelible impression. Then and subsequently, Muggeridge wrote, he found 'that abstemious ways make for happiness, and self-indulgence, especially sexual, for misery and remorse. To put aside worldly ambition, lechery, the ego's clamorous demands, what joy! To succumb, what misery!'[10]

The two terms at Oratory House were to be the calm before the storm. Muggeridge was about to 'succumb' to 'worldly ambition, lechery', and the rest of 'the ego's clamorous demands'.

As the end of his time at Cambridge drew closer, Muggeridge began to sense his faith drifting away. In November 1923 he wrote a long letter to Vidler:

> You're so lucky in a sense because having one great belief in life must be wonderful. I ask myself sometimes if I believe anything and then once again the guts question comes in; because it takes guts to believe – I suppose God willed that … When anything happens you look at it through your belief and are strengthened. I see it naked and shudder …[11]

Seeking a respite from all the questions to which he seemed to have fewer and fewer answers, Muggeridge sought to escape by accepting a teaching post in India. Yet even in India there was no physical escape from metaphysical questions. Soon after his arrival he encountered Mahatma Gandhi whose 'saintly style' of political resistance to British rule he much admired. Writing to Vidler, Muggeridge described Gandhi as 'a great man with a great message. I was thrilled with him. Like all extremists he gives the only practical plan; like all visionaries he talks common sense.'[12] Muggeridge wrote to his father that 'India is a place in which it is impossible to avoid thinking' and his thoughts were seldom far from religion. His first-hand experience of Hinduism, Buddhism and Islam during his time in India never detracted from his deep respect for Christianity. 'I love the paradoxes and inconsistencies of Christianity,' he wrote to his father on 10 October 1926. 'Christianity is to life what Shakespeare is to literature; it envisages the whole. It sees the necessity for man to have spiritual values and it shows him how to get at those through physical sacraments.'[13]

It was during his time in India that Muggeridge's imagination was caught up in the romantic image of St Francis of Assisi as painted by G. K. Chesterton in his biography of the saint, first published in October 1923. Gregory Wolfe maintains that he was 'profoundly influenced by Chesterton's book on St Francis'.[14] Chesterton depicted the saint as a medieval troubador singing courtly love songs to the Blessed Virgin. For Chesterton, St Francis was *le jongleur de Dieu*, a romantic and jovial figure who delighted in playing the fool for Christ. Chesterton described the life of St Francis with a spiritual *joie de vivre* which was infectious. After reading the book, Muggeridge wrote to his father with truly Chestertonian enthusiasm. St Francis was 'a rough and tumble acrobat, horseplay jester for God ... this is the very spirit of Catholicism. We burn incense because it is fun – we wear vestments because they are gaily coloured – we go to the very heart of the common man's common happiness and love, we express it for him in worship.'[15]

Although Muggeridge could revel in the Chestertonian *idea* of the Church, his experience of the Anglican church's practical work in the Indian missions left him disillusioned. He wrote to Vidler that he still loved Christ but was angry at the institutional Church and its fatuous missionaries: 'Wordy or "creedy" religion kills the living beauty of God. Its whole tendency is towards limitation.'[16]

Not long after these words of disillusionment were written, Muggeridge encountered a Roman Catholic bishop on a train. The bishop was travelling to a conference and Muggeridge was transfixed by the spiritual intensity he seemed to possess. They conversed in French, the only language they shared, and the bishop maintained that without faith one must remain earthbound. In that case, Muggeridge replied, he must remain earthbound. Yet even as he spoke, his protestation of agnosticism sounded hollow even in his own ears. Writing to his father about this incident, he compared his own tendency to vanity, to 'put on airs', with the bishop's humility; 'My Bishop had no airs, only *la foi* – and I much prefer that. His attempts to shake hands with the drunk soldier was very beautiful – almost like the washing of the disciples' feet.'[17]

Muggeridge had little difficulty in dismissing this episode from his mind. He remained convinced that institutional Christianity 'kills the living beauty of God', the bishop being merely an exception to the rule.

Returning to England in 1927, Muggeridge became a supply teacher in Birmingham. The job had been found for him by his old friend Alec Vidler, who was now a curate at St Aidan's in Small Heath. Vidler arranged for Muggeridge to stay as a paying guest at St Aidan's rectory, meaning a return to the clerical atmosphere he had shared with Vidler at Cambridge as an undergraduate. Now, however, he had declared his intellectual independence from Christianity and was constructing his own view of religion and politics. Although he still believed that human beings needed to achieve an inward, spiritual harmony, he thought that this could be best achieved through the establishment of a socialist state: 'I am a Socialist because I believe that a gracious environment will help men to be good; and that only collectivism can create this.'[18]

In the summer of 1927, Muggeridge married Kitty Dobbs, a wealthy niece of Sidney and Beatrice Webb, after a lightning romance. 'It somehow became understood that Kitty and I would get married, and quite soon,' Muggeridge wrote in his autobiography. 'I cannot recall ever "proposing" to her – something we both should have regarded as very bourgeois and conventional; terms of abuse in our vocabulary.'[19]

Having 'liberated' himself from the constraints of conventional religion, Muggeridge celebrated his new-found freedom by ensuring that the wedding was devoid of all religious trappings:

> Our union was duly registered at the Birmingham Register Office; a drab little scene in a dreary sort of place ... Kitty's father, and a friend of hers named Elsie, were the only others present, and acted as witnesses. We affected to regard the occasion as of no particular importance; a mere legal formality, like signing a contract for a job or a lease of a house. It was not our intention, we insisted, to put one another under any sort of obligation; we were free to do what we liked, and would only stay together as long as both of us wanted to; not a moment longer.[20]

Thus, the thoroughly modern couple had teamed up in a thoroughly modern marriage, 'a partnership agreement, terminable by either party'.[21]

On 19 January 1931, a little over three years after the marriage, Beatrice Webb described Muggeridge as 'the most intellectually stimulating and pleasant mannered of all my "in-laws" ... Ultra modern in his view of sex, theoretically more than practically I think ... yet I think Malcolm is a mystic and even a puritan in his awareness of loyalties and human relationships.'[22]

In fact, Malcolm and Kitty Muggeridge both put their 'ultra-modern' view of sex into practice. Over the years there were a string of extra-marital affairs, both partners in the agreement paying the price of 'free love' in the pain and suffering they caused each other and their children. Surprisingly perhaps, their marriage survived the abuse so that Muggeridge could write sixty years later of his 'infinite thankfulness to God that in His mercy He should have allowed so fragile a plant in such barren soil to grow into so sturdy, deep-rooted and productive a tree as my marriage to Kitty'.[23]

In hindsight, Muggeridge had nothing but contempt for the selfish pursuit of gratification which led to the succession of infidelities punctuating his married life: 'Of all the different purposes set before mankind, the most disastrous is surely "the Pursuit of Happiness".'[24]

'Happiness,' he wrote, 'is like a young deer, fleet and beautiful. Hunt him, and he becomes a poor frantic quarry; after the kill, a piece of stinking flesh.'[25] In this piece of self-perception one catches a tantalizing glimpse of the way that Muggeridge's sexual infidelities led him, paradoxically and perhaps perversely, to an eventual return to Christianity. In pursuing 'happiness' he found only passing pleasures which turned almost instantly into 'stinking flesh'. In all his philandering the pleasures were accompanied by a sense of guilt and remorse, the living proof of Beatrice Webb's belief that he was 'a mystic and even a puritan in his awareness of loyalties and human relationships'. He proved himself capable of disloyalty but incapable of being happy about it. Self-gratification was no more than a frustrating diversion, a sensual cul de sac. True happiness was to be found elsewhere: 'in forgetfulness, not indulgence, of the self; in escape from carnal appetites, not in their satisfaction.'[26]

It would take Muggeridge the greater part of his life to finally escape the carnal appetites which denied him the happiness he sought.

This emotional struggle was accompanied throughout his life by an intellectual struggle. In the early thirties he embraced communism. Then, after firsthand experience of Stalin's totalitarian excesses in the Soviet Union, he rejected it in disgust. By the end of the Second World War he had become convinced that Western civilization was on the brink of destruction from within, the victim of a suicidal liberal death wish. The conviction that liberalism was destroying civilization became a major factor in his eventual return to Christianity.

Disillusioned with both totalitarianism and liberalism, Muggeridge began to feel ideologically isolated, seeing himself as a lone voice crying in the wilderness. According to his biographer, Gregory Wolfe,

> Muggeridge felt himself to be too much of an outsider to admit to affinities with the major Christian writers and their circles. But the truth is that he did read Eliot, Waugh, Mauriac, and the books of his good friend Graham Greene. He also knew the work of Christopher Dawson. He was close to becoming a Catholic in the 1940s and 1950s, but he drifted away from that.[27]

Even if Muggeridge would not admit his affinities to these Christian writers, others were beginning to see him as a fellow traveller with them. Towards the end of the war, George Orwell had characterized him as a 'neo-reactionary', along with such writers as Evelyn Waugh, Wyndham Lewis, T. S. Eliot, Aldous

Huxley and Graham Greene.[28] This was a curious comparison because Muggeridge, in many ways, had more in common with Orwell in the years immediately after the war than with almost any other writer. Orwell had greatly admired *The Thirties*, Muggeridge's pessimistic view of the decade which culminated in war, and they had become good friends after Orwell introduced himself to Muggeridge in Paris in 1944. Both were originally 'of the left' and both had become increasingly disillusioned and critical. Ultimately, of course, Orwell wrote two novels, *Nineteen Eighty-Four* and *Animal Farm*, which could themselves be bracketed as 'neo-reactionary' and were certainly a disillusioned reaction to socialist utopianism. Where Orwell's critical disillusionment would have led him had death not prematurely intervened it is idle to speculate. Muggeridge, however, was being drawn relentlessly closer to orthodox Christianity.

The process was accelerated in the years after the war by his discovery of *The Cloud of Unknowing*, a classic of Christian mysticism written by a fourteenth-century monk. This had a profound effect, as did his reading of the works of St Augustine. It was in these timeless volumes, rather than in the books of any contemporaries, that Muggeridge made real progress. 'In the end,' says Gregory Wolfe, 'I would have to say that by temperament MM was not well suited to learn from the writers of his own day. He was always a bit too combative and defensive when thinking of his contemporaries.'[29]

It was inevitable that Muggeridge's renewed interest in Christian mysticism should fuel speculation that he was considering conversion to Catholicism. According to Beatrice Webb's diary, he had seriously considered the step as early as 1944. The publication of his novel, *Affairs of the Heart*, in 1949 prompted others to the same conclusion and the following year his friend Auberon Herbert asked him directly if he was considering becoming a Catholic. The answer was negative and he recorded in his diary on 26 June 1950: 'I see the force and importance of the Catholic Church, but I could not, in honesty, accept its dogma.'[30] It would be a further thirty-two years before he finally felt able to do so.

In the meantime, his position seemed increasingly anomalous. Only days after stating that he could not accept the Church's dogma for himself, he was recording in his diary that he desired its acceptance by society as a whole:

Had discussion with Bill Deedes about Liberalism, which was, I said, an attractive doctrine, but which I increasingly abhorred because false. Its great fallacy, I pointed out, was the perfectibility of Man ... My experience has been the exact opposite – namely, that, left to himself, Man was brutish, lustful, idle and murderous, and that the only hope of keeping his vile nature within any sort of bound was to instil in him fear of God or his fellow men. Of these two alternatives, I preferred fear of God ... And, as a matter of fact, more potent and wonderful is fear of being cut off from the light of God's countenance and living in darkness – this fear the only deterrent which is, at once, effective and ennobling.[31]

This was the line of argument adopted by Muggeridge in a much-publicized television debate with Bertrand Russell at the beginning of 1953. In his diary, Muggeridge wrote: 'It seems that in *The Listener* my discussion with Bertrand Russell on television is highly praised. Can't but think of him as vainglorious, ape-like. The true destroyer of Christendom isn't Stalin or Hitler or even the Dean of Canterbury and his like, but Liberalism.'[32]

At the end of that year, Muggeridge spoke at a rally at the Albert Hall, staged by Roman Catholics in protest at persecution of the Church in Poland. Muggeridge was speaking in his capacity as president of the Anglo-Polish Society. 'The conflict, as I see it, is between Christianity and Materialism,' he concluded.[33] Clearly Muggeridge had now taken the side of Christianity without actually becoming a Christian himself. A month later, on 5 January 1954, he wrote revealingly in his diary: 'Bad night full of dark fears. While shaving suddenly thought with infinite longing how, of all things, I'd most love to live a Christian life. This the only wish now I'd ever have. And yet other satisfactions, known to be spurious, still pursued.'[34]

The contradictions continued and Muggeridge wrote in the *St Martin's Review* on 1 January 1957 that 'though the sacramental concept seems to be both comprehensive and admirable, the actual practice of taking the sacraments is meaningless and even distasteful'.[35] On 8 February 1958 he wrote in the *New Statesman*: 'To me the Christian religion is like a hopeless love affair. I carry its image about with me, and look at it from time to time with sick longing.' Four years later the same sick longing persisted: 'The only wish I have left in this life,' he confided in his diary on 18 January 1962, 'is that there should be burnt out of me all egotism, all pride, all lechery, all greed ... I want my being's dwindling flame to burn clearly and steadily, with no smoky spurts, until it flickers out.'[36]

It would be another four years before he finally felt that his 'only wish' had been granted. 'After sixty,' he told Godfrey Winn in an interview in the *Evening News* on 3 December 1965, 'a man must decide either to curb his appetites or surrender to them. I have conquered mine.' Such a statement from an old man who had indulged his 'appetites' in extra-marital affairs whenever the opportunities arose, was bound to prompt both criticism and ridicule. The case against Muggeridge was put by Bernard Levin in a way that would be repeated again and again in the years ahead: 'How sad was that decline, how sad that one of the bravest and most astringent minds of the time should now cower so cravenly in a corner, begging the world to stop trying to inflame his withered desires, lest the attempt prove successful!'[37]

The same point was expressed more lightheartedly in an anonymous poem in *Private Eye*:

> You are old, Father Malcolm, the young man said
> And your hair has become very white
> And yet you incessantly talk about bed
> Do you think at your age it is right?
> In my youth said the sage, as he shook his grey locks
> I behaved just like any young pup
> But now I am old I appear on the box
> And tell others to give it all up.[38]

Added to such ridicule was the fact that Muggeridge's late conversion to asceticism coincided with the hedonistic optimism which surrounded the birth of the permissive society. He had decided to abstain at exactly the time when it had become thoroughly unfashionable to do so. The spirit of the 'swinging sixties' was one of indulgence not abstemiousness and Muggeridge found himself on a collision course with the age in which he lived.

Yet Muggeridge's asceticism was not, as most people believed, merely a relapse in old age into reactionary puritanism; it was, as he noted in his diary, the result of a positive desire: 'Just now I am in love with abstemiousness. One should not give up things because they are pleasant (which is Puritanism) but because, by giving them up, other things are pleasanter.'[39]

The new asceticism led to peace of mind and peace in his marriage. From this time onwards, he and Kitty enjoyed each other as never before and the next twenty-five years became the happiest of their long and turbulent life together. For Muggeridge, the sacrificing of transient sensual pleasures for this greater peace was a small price to pay.

It was scarcely surprising, however, that those with different priorities saw things otherwise. For those who advocated the 'sexual liberation' of the sixties it was easy to cast Muggeridge in the role of a puritanical prude, a killjoy who wished to deny others the sexual promiscuity which he had not denied himself throughout his own life.

Superficially, such a view seems credible. It is only when one sees Muggeridge's attacks on promiscuity as acts of self-perception and self-criticism that

they gain genuine potency. His warnings are those of one who had experienced
the frustrating emptiness of loveless sex and sought to warn others about the
dangers of partaking of its bitter fruit. He is not a prude who frowns upon sex,
but one who believes that sex is too beautiful to be abused. This can be seen in
his criticism of Dr William H. Masters, one of the self-styled 'sexperts' whose
clinical studies had helped promote the cult of sexual freedom:

> It would seem that the cycle is now complete. Sex begins in ecstasy,
> momentarily fusing two separate egos into union with one another and
> with all life; it ends in the total separation of one ego exclusively preoccu-
> pied with its own orgasm. Sex begins as a window on to eternity, and it
> ends in a dark cellar self-enclosed and boarded up with time. Sex begins as
> the sap rising in a tree to make buds and blossoms and leaves and fruit; it
> ends in Dr Masters's movie. Sex begins as a mystery out of which has
> come the art, the poetry, the religion, the delight of successive civilisations;
> it ends in a laboratory. Sex begins in passion which comprehends the con-
> cepts of both suffering and joy; it ends in a trivial dream of pleasure which
> itself soon dissolves into the solitude and despair of self-gratification.[40]

These were not the words of one who prudishly despised sex, but those of one
who saw the sexual act as a gift too precious and too powerful to be used care-
lessly or to have liberties taken with it. Neither did the fact that he had himself
regularly abused the gift detract from the truth of the statement. Since he
believed that extra-marital relationships were illicit, he was a hypocrite when he
indulged in them not when he gave them up. To suggest hypocrisy when Muggeridge condemned acts he no longer performed was akin to calling a former
drug addict a hypocrite for condemning drug abuse.

Early in 1966, shortly after his new asceticism had caused such controversy
and derision in the Press, Muggeridge expressed a desire to become a Christian:
'I should be proud and happy to be able to call myself a Christian; to dare to
measure myself against that sublimely high standard of human values and human
behaviour'.[41] Yet he still found himself in an awkwardly incongruous position: 'I
find myself praising a position I cannot uphold, enchanted by a religion I cannot
believe, putting all my hope in a faith I do not have.'[42]

His progress towards the faith he did not have was tentative and slow, and
was helped by a visit to the Holy Land in the autumn of 1967 where he filmed
a three-part programme for the BBC entitled *A Life of Christ*. Yet it was his
meeting with Mother Teresa during the spring of 1969 which was to have the
profoundest effect on his embryonic Christianity.

Muggeridge had gained permission to make a film about Mother Teresa's Missionaries of Charity and the work they were doing in India. During the five days of filming the daily attendance at Mass became an emotional experience resonant of his past and accentuated by his current quest for faith. Kneeling on the hard straw mat with the Sisters he recalled the liturgical life at the Oratory of the Good Shepherd in Cambridge and remembered his happy years in India. In the small, wizened figure of Mother Teresa he saw an image of the similar figure of Gandhi who had impressed him so deeply thirty years earlier.

There is no doubt that Mother Teresa was a crucial influence upon Muggeridge's subsequent conversion, a fact which he readily confessed: 'Mother Teresa is, in herself, a living conversion; it is impossible to be with her, to listen to her, to observe what she is doing and how she is doing it, without being in some degree converted.'[43]

In 1969, however, Muggeridge was still not ready to convert. Despite Mother Teresa's irresistibility and his growing love for the Church to which she belonged, he could not bring himself to become a Roman Catholic. The reason centred primarily on his dislike of the reforms instigated at the Second Vatican Council. To Muggeridge, the 'spirit of Vatican Two' was merely the surrender by the Church to the secular liberalism that was destroying Christendom. Catholicism, he declared, was rushing to reproduce all the 'follies and fatuities of Protestantism', and he would not climb on board a sinking ship.[44] It was the saintly response of Mother Teresa to such doubts which struck home most forcefully. In a letter to him, she had written: 'Today what is happening on the surface of the Church will pass. For Christ, the Church is the same, today, yesterday and tomorrow.'[45]

Although Muggeridge still felt unable to commit himself to the Church, he began to consider himself a Christian, a fact illustrated in the summer of 1969 by the publication of *Jesus Rediscovered*. This was a collection of his essays on his religious search which, though full of contradictions and inconsistencies, were imbued with sincerity and passion. In this book he acknowledged that his critics had attacked him for being a lecher-turned-puritan, and that he had 'gone soft' and become a bore. These criticisms he could understand. Yet he resolutely rejected the notion that Christian faith 'amounts to a kind of escapism, an evasion of the ardours and responsibilities of reality'.[46] To prove the point, he cited the example of Dietrich Bonhoeffer, who had returned to Germany under the Nazis and who opposed them in word and deed, only to be executed by them weeks before their surrender. He could also, of course, have cited the living example of Mother Teresa.

Muggeridge did not make the superlative sacrifices of either Bonhoeffer or Mother Teresa, but his defence of the Christian position was to bring him into open conflict with a hostile world which found his views unpalatable. In the same summer that *Jesus Rediscovered* was published he had been jeered by angry students at Melbourne University.[47] On 14 January of the previous year he had resigned in dramatic circumstances from his position as Rector of Edinburgh University for refusing to accept or condone student demands for the legalization of LSD and free distribution of the contraceptive pill. In combative mood Muggeridge condemned and derided the vacuity of the students' demands in his resignation speech. He began by comparing the West in the late twentieth century with the final decaying years of the Roman Empire. In both eras men were utterly credulous about the fantasies of materialism, while being sceptical about spiritual truth. He then turned his attention to the controversy at the university:

> The students here in this university ... are the ultimate beneficiaries under our welfare system ... there is practically nothing they could do in a mood of rebelliousness or refusal to accept the ways and values of our run-down, spiritually impoverished way of life for which I shouldn't feel some degree of sympathy or, at any rate, understanding. Yet how infinitely sad; how, in a macabre sort of way, funny, that the form their insubordination takes should be a demand for pot and pills, for the most tenth-rate sort of escapism and self-indulgence ever known! ... The resort of any old, slobbering debauchee anywhere in the world at any time – dope and bed.[48]

Muggeridge's resignation gained a great deal of media attention and elicited further accusations that he had become a crazed puritan. In many respects he must have still felt himself an outsider, out of step with prevailing trends. Against this background of alienated isolation he would have received considerable consolation in the knowledge that his own children had not taken the hedonistic path of so many others. In 1969, Valentine, the last of his three children to get married, was wedded to a Dutchman named Gerrit-Jan Colenbrander. A few years later they became the Dutch co-ordinators of Mother Teresa's Co-Workers, helping to organize supplies, money and volunteers on behalf of the Missionaries of Charity. Muggeridge's eldest son Leonard had earned a degree in theology from the London Bible College and served as a lay preacher for the Plymouth Brethren. His other son John had emigrated to Canada, married a devout Roman Catholic and had become a Catholic himself in 1962.

Feeling that he had wasted away most of his life in 'the expense of spirit in a waste of shame', Muggeridge was determined to spend the few years he had remaining more positively. He was literally making up for lost time. In *Jesus*

Rediscovered he had lamented the wasted years: 'You called me, and I didn't go – those empty years, those empty words, that empty passion!' This became the central theme of his autobiography, collectively titled *Chronicles of Wasted Time*, the first volume of which was published in 1972.

Amidst the memoirs in *Chronicles of Wasted Time* were parenthetical perceptions about the state of modern society such as, for example, a view of the detrimental effect of Freud and Marx which exactly paralleled E. F. Schumacher's view. Freud and Marx, wrote Muggeridge, had 'undermined the whole basis of Western European civilisation as no avowedly insurrectionary movement ever has or could, by promoting the notion of determinism, in the one case in morals, in the other in history, thereby relieving individual men and women of all responsibility for their personal and collective behaviour'.[49]

Another parallel with Schumacher was Muggeridge's defence of Pope Paul VI's encyclical *Humanae Vitae*. Speaking to a conference in San Francisco, Muggeridge explained that he had come to understand sexuality as a sacrament: 'out of the creativity in men, their animal creativity, came the sacrament of love ... which created the Christian notion of family, of the marriage which would last, which would be something stable and wonderful'.[50]

From his defence of *Humanae Vitae* his growing interest in 'life' issues was an obvious and natural development. The Catholic defence of life was the perfect antidote to what Muggeridge called the liberal death wish. He recalled that whenever he heard the phrase 'unwanted child' he remembered the tiny newborn baby that Mother Teresa had found in a dustbin in Calcutta. Holding up the child in the palm of her hands, Mother Teresa had smiled: 'See? There's life in her!'[51]

Although Muggeridge became involved in various Christian missions, Mother Teresa's included, he was particularly drawn to efforts to help the mentally handicapped. One of the charitable organizations working in this field was L'Arche, founded by a French Canadian named Jean Vanier. As with Mother Teresa, Vanier's efforts were motivated by a strong Christian faith, which came across in Muggeridge's documentary film on L'Arche, *An Ark for Our Time*. Vanier's writings as well as his work with L'Arche were an important influence on Muggeridge, and Gregory Wolfe described Vanier as one of 'the most important contemporary Christian writers to him', along with Alexander Solzhenitsyn and Simone Weil.[52]

Muggeridge had long admired Solzhenitsyn and had written in adulation to the Russian novelist when he was expelled from the Soviet Union in February 1974: 'in a dark time in history, you have been for me, as for countless others, a great light. I particularly appreciate, and share, your Christian position, which, you will have noticed in our Western press and media, is rarely mentioned.'

Muggeridge went on to remind Solzhenitsyn that Tolstoy had entertained the notion of seeking refuge in a monastery during his last runaway journey: 'If there was some religious house that you could go to for a time, would this perhaps be a way of finding the seclusion and peace to make your plans and collect your thoughts without the intrusion of press and media scavenger birds?'[53]

Nine years later, in May 1983, when Muggeridge interviewed Solzhenitsyn for the BBC, the Russian author was surprisingly optimistic about the future. 'In a strange way,' Solzhenitsyn said, 'I not only hope, I'm inwardly absolutely convinced that I shall go back ... History is so full of unexpected things.'[54] Two years later Mikhail Gorbachev became head of the Soviet Communist Party and instituted the policy of *glasnost* which precipitated the eventual collapse of communism. Solzhenitsyn returned to Russia in 1994.

In 1975 Muggeridge's *Jesus: The Man Who Lives* was published, which Gregory Wolfe described as 'arguably the book Malcolm was born to write ... a book that deserves to be ranked alongside G. K. Chesterton's *The Everlasting Man* and C. S. Lewis's *Mere Christianity* as a supremely imaginative defence of Christian orthodoxy.'[55] Had Muggeridge been alive to read his biographer's appraisal he would most certainly have been flattered. He had a high opinion of both Chesterton and Lewis and remarked on television in 1975 that *Mere Christianity* had been a major influence on his own conversion to Christianity.[56]

As Muggeridge plodded further into old age he seemed to provoke less hostility and was afforded the veneration or at least the toleration due to one of his years. The tabloid media had even waggishly canonized him as 'St Mugg'.

At the beginning of 1981 his old friend, Lord Longford, noted in his diary that 'Malcolm is having a splendid Indian summer just now'.[57] The words were prophetic because the year would finally see Muggeridge's public image ripen and come of age. Ian Hunter's biography of him had recently been published and an edited version of his diaries, entitled *Like It Was*, reached the shelves a few months later. The year also saw the ultimate retrospective on his life in the form of an eight-week series of television programmes on the BBC. The series was amusingly called *Muggeridge: Ancient and Modern*, after the Anglican hymnal, and each programme comprised the broadcast of one of his documentaries, followed by his current thoughts about his television career.

It was both appropriate and ironic that the ultimate tribute to Muggeridge was in the form of a television series. Appropriate because he was one of the original 'talking heads' in the pioneering days of television in the fifties, and as one of the original 'stars' of the small screen had been responsible for some of the best documentaries of the sixties and seventies; yet also ironic because he had since become one of television's fiercest critics. In the mid-seventies he had disposed of his own television set, telling everyone that he had had his 'aerials removed'. Television, he maintained, was 'the repository of our fraudulence', the camera 'the most sinister of all the inventions of our time'.[58]

Ironies and anomalies aside, the series offered a unique and fascinating retrospective of Muggeridge's life. The first programme, which consisted of Muggeridge's autobiographical documentary *A Socialist Childhood*, allowed the 'modern' Muggeridge to condemn his 'ancient' alter ego who had been responsible for making the documentary fifteen years earlier:

> What a terrible man I was! There's a certain arrogance about myself as narrator – the way I lay down the law. I think it's rather horrible. I'd put it differently now. What is completely lacking is any humility... I'm glad to have an opportunity of repudiating this figure of fifteen years ago, who to me is the most appalling S.O.B. I've seen in a long time.[59]

The extent to which Muggeridge had walked the path of humility since the seventies, so evident in this retrospective appraisal of his former self, was also evident in the epilogue he had written to *Like It Was*, the volume of his diaries published a few months earlier:

> the day-by-day record of a life, mine or anyone else's, becomes, as it were, the scenario for a documentary on our human condition – as Dante saw it, a Divine Comedy; as Bunyan, a Pilgrimage; as Milton, a Paradise Lost; as Shakespeare, a tale told by an idiot, full of sound and fury, signifying nothing; an infinite variety of concepts, but the same essential theme – of mortal men peering into the Cloud of Unknowing that lies between them and their creator, sojourning in an earthly city on their way to a heavenly one where they belong.[60]

He now saw his life, and the life of Everyman, as a sublime Mystery Play involving a fusion of these classic concepts. Life, fully understood and fully lived, was a pilgrimage in a divine comedy in search of a paradise lost.

Meanwhile, as the world paid its tributes to one of the century's celebrated television personalities and journalists, Muggeridge lived a life free from both television and newspapers in the tranquil seclusion of Sussex. On 1 October 1981 he and Kitty had been deeply moved by a visit to their home in Robertsbridge by a woman who had been born with no arms or legs who was standing as a 'right to life' candidate in the forthcoming Croydon by-election.[61] Her visit was still fresh in his mind when Muggeridge was interviewed by Iain T. Benson at Roberts-bridge two days later. From the outset he was keen to compare the Christian defence of life with the modern liberal 'death wish': 'There is ... going on now in the western world what you could call a "humane" holocaust'. Comparing this to Nazi atrocities, he added that it represented 'an act of suicide on the part of the western countries. In their decadence they are committing suicide.'[62]

Benson, who became a close friend of Muggeridge during the last years of his life, considered this interview to have captured him 'at his peak'.[63] It was certainly true that the poignancy of his words belied his seventy-eight years and he remained as controversial as ever: 'One thing is certain, that you cannot have an egalitarian society because men are not equal. Jesus told us men are brothers. He never said men were equal ... but they're brothers which is of course quite different and much more important.'[64]

Asked by Benson what was the most difficult thing he had to face as a Christian, Muggeridge replied: 'The enormous power of fantasy. Man has created in this age a machine of fantasy such as has never existed before. Everywhere you turn this fantasy is presented to you that happiness is to be achieved through carnality, that the fullness of life is found through success.'

Technology had allowed humanity to swap reality for virtual reality with the result that even the most fundamental values had been warped or rejected: 'Never in human history have the unworthwhile things of life been presented so alluringly, through advertising making people want more and more things, and especially the idea that joy and supreme happiness can be achieved through carnality.' He continued with an eloquent, if depressing, prophecy of doom:

> My wife and I are reading through the Old Testament, straight through, which I've never done before. The eternal theme of it is the creating of images and the worshipping of them. Well, in the twentieth century, man's created the most disastrous of all images which is himself and he falls down and worships him ... Even Bunyan's man when he got into Vanity Fair, he stopped his ears and shut his eyes and ran for it. Well, this is Vanity Fair into every single person's sitting room, hours and hours of it, day after day ...[65]

More esoteric, and perhaps more profound, were his thoughts on the meaning of life itself:

Science is imposing upon human beings the idea that life is a process ...
But life is not a process. And if it had been a process you wouldn't have
had things like Chartres Cathedral, and *King Lear* and the *Missa
Solemnis* ... They're the products not of an idea of a process but the
idea of a drama. And God would have spoken to us in quite a different
way than through the drama of the Incarnation, which of course is the
central drama of all.[66]

It seemed that, as life drew to an end, Muggeridge had come to the conclusion
that he had played his part, however badly, in a Mystery Play:

When you get to the end of your life ... you look back ... on the most
disgusting things that you've done, all sorts of really desperate things,
and you think to yourself if only I could manage not to have done that.
Then you think that, wait a minute, supposing I pulled out all those
things, that would not be the life that I've lived ... to complete the
drama ... involves everything that happens to you ... it's how you do
that and what you can feel about it afterwards and how you fit it in to
the totality of your experience, the sense of the whole drama.[67]

Even as he reached eighty years of age the drama of Muggeridge's life was still
incomplete. The final twist in the tale was about to unfold. His Mystery Play
was reaching its climax.

NOTES

1. *The Times*, 10 September 1971.
2. Gregory Wolfe, *Malcolm Muggeridge: A Biography*, London, 1995, p. 366.
3. Malcolm Muggeridge and Alec Vidler, *Paul: Envoy Extraordinary*, New York, 1982, pp. 45–6.
4. Malcolm Muggeridge, *Conversion: A Spiritual Journey*, London, 1988, p. 89.
5. ibid., p. 28.
6. ibid., pp. 28–9.
7. ibid., p. 37.
8. ibid., p. 38.
9. ibid., p. 38.
10. ibid., p. 39.
11. Gregory Wolfe, *Malcolm Muggeridge: A Biography*, p. 41.
12. ibid., p. 51.
13. ibid., p. 56.
14. Gregory Wolfe, letter to the author, 8 October 1996.
15. Gregory Wolfe, *Malcolm Muggeridge: A Biography*, p. 56.
16. ibid., p. 56.
17. ibid., p. 57.
18. ibid., p. 65.
19. Malcolm Muggeridge, *The Green Stick*, London, pb edn., 1975, p. 153.

20. ibid., pp. 153–4.
21. Malcolm Muggeridge, *Conversion: A Spiritual Journey*, p. 55.
22. Richard Ingrams, *Muggeridge: The Biography*, London, 1995, pp. 36–7.
23. Malcolm Muggeridge, *Conversion: A Spiritual Journey*, p. 55.
24. ibid., p. 55.
25. ibid., p. 55.
26. ibid., p. 55.
27. Gregory Wolfe, letter to the author, 8 October 1996.
28. Sonia Orwell and Ian Argus (eds.), *The Collected Essays, Journalism and Letters of George Orwell, Vol III*, New York, 1968, p. 63.
29. Gregory Wolfe, letter to the author, 8 October 1996.
30. Gregory Wolfe, *Malcolm Muggeridge: A Biography*, p. 249.
31. John Bright-Holmes (ed.), *Like It Was: The Diaries of Malcolm Muggeridge*, London, 1981, p. 404.
32. ibid., p. 452.
33. Gregory Wolfe, *Malcolm Muggeridge: A Biography*, p. 284.
34. John Bright-Holmes (ed.), *Like It Was: The Diaries of Malcolm Muggeridge*, p. 457.
35. Richard Ingrams, *Muggeridge: The Biography*, p. 211.
36. Gregory Wolfe, *Malcolm Muggeridge: A Biography*, p. 313.
37. Bernard Levin, *Run It Down the Flagpole: Britain in the Sixties*, New York, 1971, pp. 89–98.
38. Richard Ingrams, *Muggeridge: The Biography*, p. 208.
39. John Bright-Holmes (ed.), *Like It Was: The Diaries of Malcolm Muggeridge*, p. 520.
40. Gregory Wolfe, *Malcolm Muggeridge: A Biography*, pp. 332–3.
41. ibid., p. 341.
42. Ian Hunter, *Malcolm Muggeridge: A Life*, London, 1980, p. 225.
43. Malcolm Muggeridge, *Conversion: A Spiritual Journey*, p. 15.
44. Gregory Wolfe, *Malcolm Muggeridge: A Biography*, pp. 358–9.
45. Richard Ingrams, *Muggeridge: The Biography*, p. 213.
46. Gregory Wolfe, *Malcolm Muggeridge: A Biography*, p. 359.
47. *The Times*, 21 July 1969.
48. Malcolm Muggeridge, *Jesus Rediscovered*, London, 1969, pp. 54–5.
49. Malcolm Muggeridge, *The Green Stick*, p. 144.
50. Gregory Wolfe, *Malcolm Muggeridge: A Biography*, p. 395.
51. ibid., p. 394.
52. Gregory Wolfe, letter to the author, 8 October 1996.
53. Richard Ingrams, *Muggeridge: The Biography*, pp. 239–40.
54. ibid., p. 240.
55. Gregory Wolfe, *Malcolm Muggeridge: A Biography*, p. 382.
56. Walter Hooper, interview with the author, Oxford, 20 August 1996.
57. Lord Longford, *Diary of A Year*, London, 1982, p. 7.
58. Richard Ingrams, *Muggeridge: The Biography*, p. 224.
59. Gregory Wolfe, *Malcolm Muggeridge: A Biography*, p. 403.
60. John Bright-Holmes (ed.), *Like It Was: The Diaries of Malcolm Muggeridge*, p. 542.
61. Unpublished taped interview between Iain T. Benson and Malcolm Muggeridge, Robertsbridge, 3 October 1981.
62. ibid.
63. Iain T. Benson, letter to the the author, 22 August 1996.
64. Unpublished Benson–Muggeridge interview, Robertsbridge, 3 October 1981.
65. ibid.
66. ibid.
67. ibid.

CHAPTER THIRTY

ENDS AND LOOSE ENDS

On 27 November 1982 Malcolm and Kitty Muggeridge were received into the Catholic Church at the Chapel of Our Lady, Help of Christians in the Sussex village of Hurst Green, not far from their home in Robertsbridge. The ceremony was celebrated by the Bishop of Arundel, the Rt Rev. Cormac Murphy-O'Connor, assisted by Father Paul Bidone, a friend of the Muggeridges through his work for the mentally handicapped, and by Father Maxwell, the local parish priest. Their sponsors were their good friends Frank and Elizabeth Longford.

The news of Muggeridge's reception came as a shock to many of his friends. According to Richard Ingrams, 'Muggeridge told no-one about his conversion'[1] and even close members of the family were not informed. His son John was 'not told anything'[2] when he visited his parents three months before the event, and Iain T. Benson, who was visiting Robertsbridge at the same time, recalled that 'I spoke with him expressly about Catholicism ... and was surprised by his responses then and positively astonished at his conversion when it occurred a few months later'.[3] Asked as recently as April 1981 by John Mortimer in a *Sunday Times* interview whether he would have liked to have been a Catholic, he gave no indication that he was moving in that direction and turned the discussion instead to Graham Greene.

Yet if few people knew of the event beforehand, Muggeridge ensured that as many people as possible knew on the morning itself. 'This morning,' reported *The Times*, 'Malcolm and Kitty Muggeridge will be received into the Roman Catholic Church, sponsored by Lord and Lady Longford. Here Muggeridge describes the long process that led to what he regards as an inevitable decision.'

There then followed a long article by Muggeridge entitled 'Why I am becoming a Catholic' in which he confessed that it was 'something I have brooded over for many years; longing to take the step, and yet mysteriously held back'. He expressed his gratitude to Mother Teresa who had urged him to join the Church many years before:

Words cannot convey how beholden I am to her. She has given me a whole new vision of what being a Christian means; of the amazing power of love, and how in one dedicated soul it can burgeon to cover the whole world.

Mother Teresa had told me ... how the Eucharist each morning kept her going; without this, she would falter and lose her way. How, then, could I turn aside from such spiritual nourishment?

Other factors in his final acceptance of the faith included the 'sheer survival' of the Church. For two thousand years, 'despite lapses and confused purposes, every day, perhaps even every hour, someone somewhere will have been handing out the body and blood of Christ in sacramental form'. Furthermore, he seemed to echo countless earlier converts who had seen the Church as the antidote to the evils of modern society. He, like they, was *pro Ecclesia contra mundum*:

St Augustine lived at a time in some ways very like ours, when the great Roman Empire was visibly collapsing, and decadence – what we call permissiveness – was everywhere apparent. When news was brought to him in Carthage that Rome had been sacked by the barbarians, he told his flock to turn away from cities like Rome which men build and men destroy, and concentrate their attention on the City of God, which men did not build and cannot destroy.

In the late twentieth century, as in the last days of the Roman Empire, the decay of civilization was 'due, not as the media and the politicians would have us believe, to economic and political factors, but to an overall moral crisis. The Catholic response to this crisis has always appealed to me.'

Muggeridge then echoed the views he had expressed in the interview with Iain T. Benson a year earlier. Abortion and euthanasia constituted a 'humane' holocaust 'far outdoing Hitler's in the numbers slaughtered'. Modern society had transformed the traditional image of a Christian family 'into one of a factory farm whose only concern is the wellbeing of the livestock and the profitability of the enterprise'.

In his biography of Muggeridge, Richard Ingrams wrote that 'although the announcement in *The Times* came as a surprise, the conversion itself, to anyone who had followed Malcolm's career over the years, came as a logical conclusion'.[4] This is borne out by Muggeridge's own description of his conversion as a 'sense of homecoming, of picking up the threads of a lost life, of responding to a bell that has long been ringing, of finding a place at a table that has long been

left vacant'.[5] To employ his own analogy expressed in the previous year's interview with Benson, his reception into the Church was not only a logical conclusion to a process, but the completion of a drama. Threads had to be picked up,
loose ends tied, the knell of bells answered and the place at table taken. In fact,
according to Muggeridge's own dramatic insight, his submission to the Catholic
Church was not only the completion, but the purpose of the drama. His conversion was the *end* of his life in both senses of the word, metaphysical as well as
physical.

In the physical sense, however, and as much as Muggeridge may have thought
otherwise at the time, his life was not quite at an end. Already well into his eightieth year, he had joked at the start of his article for *The Times* that as an octogenarian he would be 'received into a church shortly before leaving it in a coffin'.
In fact he was to live for a further eight years.

'I have described becoming a Catholic as though it was a solitary experience,'
Muggeridge wrote at the end of his *Times* article. 'Actually, my wife for 54 years
has been at my side all the way. Nor have we needed even to discuss the matter at
issue, but proceeded as one person.'

In fact, as was so often the case throughout their half-century of marriage,
Kitty Muggeridge was the unsung heroine. A literary figure in her own right,
having written several books including a biography of Beatrice Webb, she had
been ready and willing to become a Catholic for some time. If they now 'proceeded as one person' it was merely because she had waited patiently for her
husband to catch up. 'No one who knew Kitty in these years,' wrote Gregory
Wolfe, 'doubted for a moment that though she always went last, she was, in reality, first.'[6]

In the days and weeks following Muggeridge's confession of faith in *The
Times* letters arrived by the sackload at Robertsbridge. Many were from
Catholics who had been praying for his conversion and others were from well-
wishers simply offering support and gratitude. One or two brought particular
joy, such as one from an old woman who had prayed for him at daily Mass for
twenty years, and another from a man who had contemplated suicide but was
comforted by something Muggeridge had written. He was also delighted to
receive a letter from Alec Guinness:

> The news in *The Times* this morning of your reconciliation with the
> Church made my day. Doubtless you will receive hundreds of letters of
> congratulations and perhaps a handful of spiteful ones from fanatics. This
> scribbled note is just to add to the number who rejoice – and there will be
> much rejoicing ... May I wish you and your wife peace and happiness.[7]

By and large Guinness's wish was granted. Malcolm and Kitty Muggeridge spent the following years in the quiet contentment of their own company and that of a small number of friends.

Two of the regular visitors during these final years were Lord and Lady Longford who had visited them 'almost every weekend' since 1950. In *Avowed Intent*, his autobiography, Longford paid a moving tribute to the Muggeridges in the last years of their lives. 'For more than half a century,' Longford wrote, 'I have been a practising Catholic, and I am more grateful than I can say to my family and my Church. I would not, however, describe myself as deeply religious. I would apply such a phrase to Malcolm and Kitty Muggeridge, as they were at the end of their lives. By that time they could fairly have been described as mystics.'[8]

Lady Hedwig Williams remembered accompanying her husband and the Longfords to visit the Muggeridges in the years following their conversion: 'I first knew Muggeridge in '82 when Longford, Muggeridge and my husband discussed a scheme to raise money with and for Father Bidone ... When the four of us were alone, Malcolm talked to my husband, Kitty to me, with, of course, long pauses when Kitty listened to her husband and more and more frequently helped out his memory.'[9]

Another occasional visitor to Robertsbridge throughout the 1980s was the Rt. Rev. Cormac Murphy-O'Connor, the Bishop of Arundel and Brighton, who had been the chief celebrant at the Muggeridges' reception:

Each time I visited them at their home in Robertsbridge, Malcolm and I would talk about mutual acquaintances and events and had many a laugh together. But we always ended with prayer. He and Kitty used to recite Evensong together and I always felt quite humbled and grateful as we joined together in that prayer in the evening.

Malcolm was a remarkable man ...[10]

On 21 March 1983 *The Times* carried a full page profile of Muggeridge to commemorate his eightieth birthday, including an interview between Muggeridge and Alan Watkins and an amended reprint of Muggeridge's introduction to *Tread Softly for you Tread on my Jokes*, published originally in 1966. Four days later, under the heading 'St Mug's Day', the *Times* Diary announced a gathering at the Garrick Club that evening to celebrate Muggeridge's birthday:

A catholic mixture of left and right, sacred and profane, gathers tonight to celebrate the eightieth birthday of Malcolm Muggeridge, the country's only full-time saint. The party has been organised by Richard Ingrams, editor of *Private Eye*, and those who will be feting the sage of Roberts-bridge at the Garrick Club include Alec Vidler, Lord Longford, Wally Fawkes, James Cameron, Hugh Cudlipp, A. J. P. Taylor, Andrew Boyle, William Deedes, Auberon Waugh, John Wells, Christopher Booker, Alan Watkins and our own Frank Johnson. Also on hand will be Father Paul Bidone, the Mug's confessor. Black tie has been decided upon to discourage rowdiness and bread-throwing.

One is reminded of the earlier literary gatherings to celebrate the birthdays of Belloc and Baring, during which 'rowdiness and bread-throwing' were very much the order of the day. In old age, Muggeridge had developed an admiration for Belloc and he was fond of quoting Belloc's remark that 'the Church must be in God's hands because, seeing the people who have run it, it couldn't possibly have gone on existing if there weren't some help from above'.[11] He also contin-ued to admire Chesterton and had grown to admire C. S. Lewis, an admiration expressed in a foreword he wrote in 1983 to Michael D. Aeschliman's *The Resti-tution of Man: C. S. Lewis and The Case Against Scientism*. Lewis's *Screwtape Letters*, Muggeridge wrote, 'is now as established as, say, Swift's *Gulliver's Trav-els* or Orwell's *Animal Farm*, and there must be few English-speaking Christian converts of recent decades who will not acknowledge their obligation to, partic-ularly, his *Mere Christianity*, and quote with approval and zest his words, his ideas, and his fantasies'. In the same foreword, Muggeridge maintained that Lewis saw Chesterton as 'the prototype of the good Christian' in his own time, while Muggeridge himself praised Chesterton as a journalist 'who managed to inject the Holy Ghost, the Comforter, into the outpouring of words requisite in his profession – as it were, a gargoyle writing the script for a steeple'.

Although in *de facto* retirement, Muggeridge continued to speak out on life issues and was one of the main speakers at an anti-abortion rally in Hyde Park on 25 June 1983. Yet his health and memory were fading and as the years passed he spent less and less time away from Robertsbridge. Increasingly, he and Kitty retired and retreated into the mysticism alluded to by Longford. 'I have always felt myself to be a stranger here on earth,' Muggeridge wrote in 1988, 'aware that our home is elsewhere. Now, nearing the end of my pilgrimage, I have found a resting place in the Catholic Church from where I can see the Heavenly Gates built into Jerusalem's Wall more clearly than from anywhere else, albeit if only through a glass darkly.'[12]

At the same time, Longford was 'in awe of Kitty Muggeridge's ability to detach herself from the world and focus her attention on the spiritual':

As the years pass, she thinks less and less of this world and more and more of the world to come ... The supernatural world seems to her more and more the real one. She points to the chairs and sofas in her drawing room and says 'They are losing their texture, they are beginning to become pale reflections of the spiritual reality.'[13]

Yet failing health and increasing mysticism had not impeded their sense of humour. Once, when Muggeridge told his wife that he had 'one of those head-shrinking chappies' coming to lunch, Kitty had responded: 'In that case, we had better have Freud fish and Jung potatoes.'[14] Meanwhile Muggeridge gained much amusement from a framed photograph that hung above the fireplace in the sitting-room. It was a picture of the fire, started by a lightning strike, that burned one of the transepts of York Minster in 1984, just four days after the consecration of the controversial Anglican Bishop of Durham, David Jenkins. Bishop Jenkins had caused outrage both inside and outside the Anglican Church by questioning the literal truth of the Virgin Birth and the Resurrection. Muggeridge would wait for a visiting guest to point out the photograph and then would lean back and laugh: 'The wrath of God, my dear boy, the wrath of God.'[15]

Muggeridge was deeply traditional in the practice of his relatively new-found faith, moved by an intense love for the Blessed Sacrament. The *Catholic Herald* reported on 18 March 1988 that he scorned the use of guitars and what he called 'pop-like hymns'. Instead, he preferred Mass to be celebrated with dignity and those who observed him at Mass, including his son John and daughter-in-law Anne, noticed his intense reverence and devotion throughout the service. When his health failed so that he could no longer get to Mass, the Sacrament would be brought to him at home. Once, a lay minister arrived in blue jeans and a sweater, asked him if he wanted to receive the Sacrament and pulled it out of a container in his hip pocket. Muggeridge grew incensed and threw him out, finding the man's careless and casual attitude to the Eucharist a 'shocking abomination'.[16]

During 1989 Muggeridge's health began to deteriorate rapidly. His mental faculties had been degenerating slowly for some time and at first this was thought to be the onset of Alzheimer's disease. Eventually, it was decided that he had suffered from several episodes of something known as TIA – a 'transient ischemic attack', or minor stroke. Each of these kills off areas of brain cells and can lead to a condition known as 'multi-infarct dementia', which is characterized by progressive memory loss, disintegration of personality and increasing depression.

Muggeridge manifested all these symptoms towards the end of his life, much to the distress of his friends and family. Reporters who visited Robertsbridge hoping for an interview found him incoherent, strangers were turned away angrily and even his own son John was thrown out of the house in a fit of frenzied forgetfulness. In the end almost everyone became a stranger to him and he lost all interest in bathing and shaving. He was about to die an undignified death, a perverse or profound answer to his recent prayer, written and used as the foreword to his *Conversion: A Spiritual Journey*, that God should 'humble my pride'.

Of course, whether one believes the prayer was answered perversely or profoundly – or whether it was answered at all – depends upon one's outlook on life and one's belief in the efficacy of prayer. This whole question was at the very heart of Muggeridge's own quest for an understanding of life. An essential part of his conversion had been a realization that everything had a purpose in life's unfathomable drama, however superficially absurd, unjust or grotesque. In *Conversion* Muggeridge had written that what he had taken to be 'a Theatre of the Absurd' proved 'on closer examination to contain within itself a Theatre of Fearful Symmetry', 'revealing the meaning that lies embedded in meaninglessness, the order underlying confusion, the indestructible love at the heart of the holocaust of hate, the still, small voice of truth that makes itself heard above thunderous falsity.'[17]

Certainly, Muggeridge's undignified exit from the world could be considered 'fearful', with all the nuances that word conveys, and one is reminded of his visit, almost forty years earlier, to Hilaire Belloc who was dying in similar fashion. Muggeridge had travelled down to Belloc's home in the Sussex village of Shipley with Auberon Herbert in early December 1950. He recorded the visit in his diary and it reads, in the light of his own debilitating illness forty years later, almost like a self-portrait:

> Belloc's house fairly roomy, but shabby, rather desolate ... Belloc came shuffling in, walks with great difficulty because he has had a stroke, inconceivably dirty, ... mutters to himself and easily forgets what he said, heavily bearded, fierce-looking and angry ... Not at all a serene man. Although he has written about religion all his life, there seemed to be very little in him ... thought of King Lear.[18]

Another example of what Muggeridge would have called 'fearful symmetry' was the fact that, before his own mental faculties began to desert him, he had devoted so much of his time and effort to the mentally handicapped, through his friendship with Father Bidone and the influence of his mentor Jean Vanier. He had described his 'trepidation' on the day of his and Kitty's reception into the Church when he had discovered that Father Bidone had brought some of the Down's syndrome children from the centre in Hampton Court which he had been responsible for setting up. He was worried that the children would spoil the solemn occasion by 'fidgeting, moving about, emitting strange sounds'. Yet when this actually happened, 'quite unexpectedly and mysteriously', a great satisfaction possessed him, transforming the ceremony into 'an unforgettable spiritual experience'. Afterwards, when he mentioned his feelings to Kitty, he discovered that she had 'precisely the same experience'. Thinking this over afterwards, he came to the conclusion that these Down's syndrome children had 'a special role in the world to make outward and visible the physical and mental distortions which we all have inwardly and invisibly'.[19]

On 27 July 1990, Muggeridge suffered a major stroke and was rushed to the intensive care unit at St Helen's Hospital in Hastings. His son Leonard arrived at the hospital and was able to sleep in a room adjoining his father's. Throughout the night he could hear his father shouting in a loud voice: 'Father, forgive me! Father, forgive me!'[20]

Unexpectedly, Muggeridge made a partial recovery from this stroke and some time later, John, his other son, witnessed an event which seemed to balance the earlier tortured cries for forgiveness. He had watched his father obstinately refuse to take a small pill no larger than a peppercorn in spite of patient appeals by the original nurse, a nursing aide and finally the charge nurse. Soon afterwards the hospital chaplain arrived to give Muggeridge Holy Communion. Having just witnessed the drama of the pill, John Muggeridge thought the chaplain's efforts would also prove in vain. 'But the priest lit a candle, said the usual prayers, gave a piece of the Host first to my mother and me and then to my father, who closed his eyes and consumed it reverently.'[21]

Muggeridge received the last rites and died on the morning of 14 November 1990. The funeral, conducted by Bishop Cormac Murphy-O'Connor, took place five days later at Salehurst Church. Lord Longford gave the address and commenced by quoting the words Cardinal Manning had used at the funeral of Cardinal Newman exactly a hundred years earlier in 1890: 'We have lost our greatest witness for the faith and we are all poorer and lower by the loss.' As one prominent twentieth-century convert speaking of another, it was appropriate that Longford should begin with those words. They had been used by one of the nineteenth century's most prominent converts of that century's most prominent convert of all. It was fitting in another sense because Muggeridge had developed 'a late love for Cardinal Newman'.[22] Concluding his panegyric, Lord Longford said: 'Those of us who have known Malcolm longest will agree that all his life he was conscious of another world and in later years of another presence.'[23]

A requiem Mass was held in Westminster Cathedral on 26 February 1991, the principal celebrant being Cardinal Hume. The panegyric was given by William

Deedes, an old friend of Muggeridge's from his days as a Fleet Street journalist. At the end of his address, Deedes referred to the patronizing tone with which Muggeridge's worldly colleagues had viewed his conversion, gleefully, in some cases, reminding him and the world of his past misdemeanours:

> Reflecting on it, though, I have come to the conclusion that herein perhaps lies Malcolm's most valuable bequest to us. For, it seems to me, we are offered a welcome reminder that Christ came to call not the righteous but sinners to repentance. The life of our friend Malcolm was surely not all that far removed from something at the centre of our beliefs.[24]

Following her husband's death, Kitty went to stay with her son John and daughter-in-law Anne in Canada. In the next few years she suffered some of the same mental clouding that had overtaken her husband – 'as if she had to share everything that Malcolm had experienced, both in sorrow and in joy'.[25] At her death in June 1994, at the age of ninety, she was both conscious and peaceful. Her body was brought back to England to be buried alongside her husband in the churchyard at Whatlington.

One of the most poignant tributes to Muggeridge was made by Paul Johnson, writing in the *Sunday Telegraph*. Muggeridge, wrote Johnson, was

> a representative 20th-century man, born in progress, nourished in modernity, apotheosised on the Box, but in the end finding personal fulfilment only in the simplest form of Christianity, which he believed with all the purity and fervour of a child.
>
> His life and example help to explain why, at the end of the 20th century, religion, far from disappearing, is alive and well and flourishing in the hearts of sophisticated men and women.[26]

Meanwhile, at the conclusion of his biography of Muggeridge, Gregory Wolfe wrote:

> As a twentieth-century Christian apologist, Malcolm Muggeridge stands beside G. K. Chesterton and C. S. Lewis. Malcolm's sensibility – more darkly satirical, more willing to balance doubt with faith, more deeply informed by a huge store of worldly experience – complements the romanticism of Chesterton and Lewis. His life was too unruly and too complicated for him to become the centre of a cult, a fate that has befallen Lewis.[27]

David Gill, Eric Gill's nephew, who worked for many years as a film cameraman, also found that Muggeridge and Chesterton had much in common:

> Often I hold Muggeridge up as rather like Chesterton in the sense that when I was in television, current affairs, working with a lot of hard-boiled journalists who were deeply entrenched in scepticism, and who had no time for humbuggery at all, how they respected Muggeridge and how their respect for him remained intact after his conversion and also how Chesterton would often come up as a pillar of light and enlightenment even though he was a Catholic ... Chesterton was still held up with enormous respect as a consummate craftsman with integrity and intelligence ...[28]

Even if, as Wolfe maintains, Muggeridge's life was 'too unruly and too compli-cated' to be compared too closely with the lives of Lewis or Chesterton, the fact remains that he arrived at the same conclusions and reached the same goal. How-ever entangled Muggeridge's life had been it ended with most of the loose ends neatly tied. As Chesterton put it at the conclusion of his own autobiography, his life story had ended 'as any detective story should end, with its own particular questions answered and its own primary problem solved'.[29]

If this can be said of Muggeridge and Chesterton, it cannot be said so easily of Lewis, whose Christian apologetics seem increasingly at loggerheads with the Anglican church in which he died. The anomalous nature of Lewis's position, so evident in his writings, was accentuated by Walter Hooper's conversion to Catholicism in 1988. Hooper, the most loyal of Lewis's disciples and the most prominent exponent of Lewis's thought in the years since his mentor's death, evidently found Lewis's teaching incompatible with the modernism in the Church of England. Whether Hooper is correct in this assumption there is little doubt that the arguments will continue and the loose ends remain. Shortly before he died, the American political philosopher Russell Kirk added fuel to the controversy by throwing doubt on whether either Lewis or T. S. Eliot could be reconciled with today's Church of England. Kirk, who had known Eliot and had written the authoritative work *Eliot and His Age*, was asked by Iain T. Benson at a conference in Seattle in 1990 whether he believed 'T. S. Eliot and C. S. Lewis would have stayed C. of E. had they been alive today'. Kirk replied that he thought it 'extremely unlikely for both of them but particularly so for Eliot'.[30]

Yet Eliot, Lewis and other traditionalists within the Anglican Church are not the only people placed by posterity in an anomalous position. Graham Greene's uneasy and critical relationship with the Catholic Church, particularly in the years prior to his death in 1991, displayed frayed edges and loose ends that continue to cause controversy and fuel debate. If Muggeridge's life had ended in November 1990 leaving 'its own particular questions answered and its own primary problem solved', Greene's ended five months later leaving many questions unanswered and the primary problem still unsolved.

NOTES

1. Richard Ingrams, letter to the author, January 1997.
2. Iain T. Benson, letter to the author, 22 August 1996.
3. ibid.
4. Richard Ingrams, *Muggeridge: The Biography*, pp. 233–4.
5. *The Times*, 27 November 1982.
6. Gregory Wolfe, *Malcolm Muggeridge: A Biography*, p. 412.
7. Richard Ingrams, *Muggeridge: The Biography*, p. 237.
8. Lord Longford, *Avowed Intent: An Autobiography*, London, 1994, p. 202.
9. Lady Hedwig Williams, letter to the author, 27 July 1996.
10. Rt. Rev. Cormac Murphy-O'Connor, letter to the author, 17 July 1996.
11. Malcolm Muggeridge, *Conversion: A Spiritual Journey*, p. 139.
12. ibid., p. 134.
13. Peter Stanford, *Lord Longford: An Authorised Life*, London, 1994, p. 469.
14. *National Review*, 31 December 1990; *The Times*, 14 June 1994.
15. Gregory Wolfe, *Malcolm Muggeridge: A Biography*, p. 406.
16. ibid., p. 413.
17. Malcolm Muggeridge, *Conversion: A Spiritual Journey*, p. 69.
18. John Bright-Holmes (ed.), *Like It Was: The Diaries of Malcolm Muggeridge*, p. 420.
19. Malcolm Muggeridge, *Conversion: A Spiritual Journey*, p. 11.
20. Gregory Wolfe, *Malcolm Muggeridge: A Biography*, p. 419.
21. ibid., p. 419.
22. Gregory Wolfe, letter to the author, 8 October 1996.
23. Gregory Wolfe, *Malcolm Muggeridge: A Biography*, p. 420.
24. Richard Ingrams, *Muggeridge: The Biography*, p. 246.
25. Gregory Wolfe, *Malcolm Muggeridge: A Biography*, p. 420.
26. *Sunday Telegraph*, 1 October 1995.
27. Gregory Wolfe, *Malcolm Muggeridge: A Biography*, p. 422.
28. David Gill, interview with the author, London, 21 October 1996.
29. G. K. Chesterton, *Autobiography*, London, 1936, p. 342.
30. Iain T. Benson, letter to the author, 22 August 1996.

CHAPTER THIRTY ONE

PAINTING GOD GREENE

Graham Greene was one of a very select few who were informed of Malcolm Muggeridge's conversion prior to the event. Greene's reply, written on 3 November 1982, displayed what Gregory Wolfe described as his 'complex' attitude to the Catholic Church: 'I don't know whether to congratulate you or to commiserate with you on making your decision, but I can sincerely wish you good luck and I can also hope that you will make a better Catholic than I have done'.[1]

In many respects, Muggeridge and Greene epitomized the struggle involved in being a Christian during the twentieth century. Both were born at the century's outset and spent its duration grappling with the claims of eternity in a temporal turmoil of change. Muggeridge spent most of the century searching for the meaning of life and found it eventually, so he believed, in the Catholic Church. Greene spent most of the century as a Catholic, having embraced the faith as a young man in 1926, but was continually and restlessly searching for aspects of the truth outside the Church. Muggeridge put the matter amusingly in his autobiography, comparing himself with Greene: 'I once without thinking said of him that he was a saint trying unsuccessfully to be a sinner, and I a sinner trying equally unsuccessfully to be a saint ... What sort of sinner are you? he asked scornfully, as though I had claimed some quite undeserved achievement or beatitude.'[2]

The inherent tension in Greene's relationship with his adopted faith was the motive force behind the labyrinthine morality plays which were his novels. The same inherent tension was also behind the labyrinthine morality play of his life. His turbulent and torrid love affair with the Church lasted a lifetime and was marked by infidelities which prompted the tacit admission of failure in his letter to Muggeridge.

As early as 1938 the tension had been expressed in his diary: 'And they say that religion is an escape. The man who believes in eternity must often experience an acute nostalgia for atheism to indulge himself with rest. There is the real escape.'[3]

At this time Greene was also beginning to seek an escape from his marriage. Arthur Calder-Marshall, a young writer whose novel *The Changing Scene* had been criticized the previous year by Evelyn Waugh, had befriended Greene and was 'particularly impressed by Vivien's behaviour as the Protective Wife'. Yet he was 'conscious that there was another part of Graham which felt imprisoned by the comfort of the house in Clapham and his protective wife, which yearned for the seedy, the dangerous, the uncomfortable'.[4]

Although Greene was on the verge of betraying his wife and children, there is no doubt that he and Vivien were very much in love during the first ten years of their marriage. This was evident in a letter which Vivien sent to her husband on 27 February 1938: 'I wanted to tell you at once how dear you are and how happy I've been with you for years & years & especially on this trip & the bits of New York … I wish I were back with you on Fifth Avenue in the evening, or with you anywhere at all.'[5] Greene had taken to travel as one of his 'ways of escape' and it was clear from this letter how much his wife missed him during the increasingly long periods which he spent away from home.

Greene's second cousin, Leslie von Goetz, recalls that 'he was besotted with Vivien at first':

> My parents commented on what bad form it was that they sat holding hands on the settee – I think this was quite some time after they'd married because I remember my mother's scorn as she said it was 'ridiculous' when you've been married for years … *I* don't think he treated Vivien well but she is very much her own woman … I only once heard her say anything nasty about Graham's mistresses – something to the effect that he liked them to wear mink coats but not care about them trailing in the dirt![6]

Greene's extra-marital affairs soon formed an intrinsic part of his life, yet it was not until after the end of the war that he finally left his wife for another woman. Returning home to Vivien, he told her that he would be sending someone to pack his books and clothes. 'It was very difficult with the children coming back soon from school,' Vivien remembered. 'We went upstairs into the drawing room and then he left. And I thought, well, I'll probably never see him again and looked out of the window that was facing the street, and he looked back for a minute, didn't wave, but looked back.'[7]

This dramatic moment ingrained itself as indelibly in Greene's memory as it had in his wife's. Eight years later, it re-emerged in his novel *The Quiet American* when the hero Fowler turned memories over at random: 'a fox … seen by the light of an enemy flare ... the body of a bayoneted Malay ... my wife's face at a window when I came home to say good-bye for the last time'.

Stunned by her husband's departure, Vivien wrote to Greene's mother, who replied in distress: 'I am ashamed of my son. It absolutely makes my heart bleed. I could never have believed it of Graham. What about his religion – surely one cannot get absolution if he confesses such sin. Like you, I am appalled at K. – too terrible.'[8]

'K' was Catherine Walston, whose influence upon Greene would be paramount for over a decade. According to Greene's biographer, Norman Sherry, she was 'the source of his creativity' during this period, 'for *The Heart of the Matter* would not have been completed without her and *The End of the Affair* would not have been started'.[9]

Catherine Walston was described charitably by Kitty Muggeridge as 'a sort of belle dame', and acerbically by Malcolm Muggeridge as 'sans merci but so belle'. It was, however, the description of her by Father Vincent Turner, the Jesuit who had received her into the Catholic Church, which struck home most accurately: 'She was determined not to be chaste and yet she was deeply religious.'[10] The description was equally applicable to Greene who, perversely, had acted as Walston's godfather at her reception into the Church.

Bearing in mind Sherry's assertion that Greene's affair with Walston was 'the source of his creativity' and that '*The Heart of the Matter* would not have been completed without her', the controversy which surrounded the publication of this novel in 1948 was scarcely surprising. Father C. C. Martindale, the recipient of Greene's kindness during the war,[11] had nothing but praise for the book:

> this is a magnificent book, both theologically accurate and by a layman who 'knows as much as any man can know about human nature.'
>
> I know one, a hard-headed man to whom this book has given the last necessary stimulus to becoming a Catholic, and many who, like me, will continue to draw from re-reading it a deeper love of suffering distraught humanity and of God.[12]

This view was corroborated in a letter from M. M. Farr: 'I should like to put on record the fact that one great sinner was so moved by Mr Greene's last book that he has completely changed his way of life and returned to the practice of the Faith.'[13]

Others were less sympathetic, or were avowedly hostile. Many reacted angrily to the suggestion made by some writers, including Evelyn Waugh, Edward Sackville-West and Raymond Mortimer, that Scobie, the novel's hero, was a saint. 'Scobie commits adultery, sacrilege, murder (indirectly), suicide in quick succession,' one correspondent wrote. 'In three of these cases he is well aware of what he is doing ... he takes communion in mortal sin because he can't bear to hurt his wife's feelings. This isn't the way a saint behaves.'[14]

The same point was put with more subtlety in an unfavourable review by Father John Murphy:

> Scobie is a Catholic with a conscience of the highest sensitivity and insight whose weak will ultimately leads him to adultery, sacrilegious Holy Communions, responsibility for a murder ... and for full measure, to a suicide ... To be precise, he fears woman more than he fears God ... How can you account for the fact that a man commits suicide in order, among other things, to avoid making any more bad Communions? But the answer is obvious: Because he despaired where he should have repented.[15]

Whether Scobie feared women more than he feared God, it was clear that Scobie's creator now seemed to desire women more than he desired God, a fact which would shape the rest of his life. One wonders, for instance, what Greene's response was to Bishop Brown's attack in the *Universe* on his portrayal of adultery in *The Heart of the Matter*: 'Adultery is adultery whatever attempts may be made to disguise it by not using the hard word.'[16]

Perhaps the most poignant contribution to the debate was provided by a certain Ronald Brownrigg, who asked: 'I wonder if your correspondents can conceive, as I most certainly can, of mentalities that will be muddled by *The Heart of the Matter* into thinking that what Christ said was "If you love me, break my commandments"?'[17]

This view appeared to be vindicated by pencilled notes discovered by the present author in the margins of *Graham Greene and the heart of the matter: An essay by Marie-Beatrice Mesnet* (Greenwood Press, Westport, Connecticut, 1972) in the course of his research at the University of East Anglia library. The notes, no doubt scribbled by an enthusiastic though naïve student, read: 'God responsible for our sins – Sinner nearer to God'.

One prominent non-Catholic writer who found Scobie's actions irreconcilable with the beliefs he espoused was George Orwell. If Scobie 'really felt that adultery is mortal sin,' wrote Orwell, 'he would stop committing it ... If he believed in Hell, he would not risk going there merely to spare the feelings of a couple of neurotic women.'[18] The logical conclusion of Orwell's clinical approach was that Scobie's slapdash attitude to the moral teaching of the Church illustrated a lack of faith; that Scobie, and by implication Greene, did not really believe in the existence of Hell and consequently was prepared to take the risk of going there. Greene's faith was a little like the Emperor's new clothes, nothing more than a figment of his fertile and fetid imagination. Orwell's view gained credence with the publication of Greene's novel *A Burnt Out Case* in 1961 which many took to indicate the author's loss of faith.

Yet Greene's own explanation of Scobie's actions, given candidly in a letter to Evelyn Waugh, illustrates that his intentions were very orthodox: 'I did not regard Scobie as a saint, & his offering his damnation up was intended to show how muddled a mind full of good will could become when once "off the rails".'[19]

The words were prophetically autobiographical. The longer Greene remained 'off the rails' the more muddled became his approach to Catholicism. As the years passed, he became more subjectively selective in his acceptance or rejection of the tenets of faith and, although he always called himself a Catholic, he slowly constructed a custom-made religion, keeping only those parts of the faith which he found palatable or convenient. In short, during the last four decades of his life Greene set about making God in his own image. 'In his last interview with *The Tablet*,' remembered his wife, 'he said that he didn't believe in angels. I wrote to him quoting scripture, particularly the Acts of the Apostles. Graham was rather inclined to pick and choose.'[20]

While the controversy surrounding *The Heart of the Matter* was still raging, Greene found himself affected profoundly by his attendance at a Mass celebrated by Padre Pio in the south of Italy. Almost forty years afterwards, in a discussion with Norman Sherry, he still recalled in some awe the impact which the renowned holy man had on him:

> the curious thing was that I'd been told that it was a very long Mass. He spoke it clearly ... and I thought it wouldn't take more than 55 minutes, and then finally we came out and found that it had taken two hours. I couldn't see where I had lost the sense of time.
>
> I can recall the stigmata, the dried blood sticking out. It would dry and then it would bleed again and then dry again. He also had to have his feet padded because they also bled. So the blood dried and then it starts again and then there will be a period when it gets rather old. I was as near to him as I am now to you and those hands looked terrible, sort of circular pieces of dried blood.[21]

On 19 January 1950 Greene mentioned this experience to Malcolm Muggeridge who recorded in his diary that Greene had described Padre Pio's stigmata to him 'in his usual lurid way'.[22] Yet Greene's encounter with Padre Pio was not destined to have the same impact that Muggeridge's encounter with Mother Teresa would have twenty years later. Greene told Sherry that he had been invited to meet Padre Pio but refused. 'No, I don't want to,' he had replied when the invitation had been extended. 'I don't want to change my life by meeting a saint.'[23]

Greene mentioned the same incident in a conversation with Marie-Françoise Allain in 1979: 'I was so convinced of his powers of goodness that I refused to approach him and speak with him. I explained to the friends who had brought me along that I was too afraid that it might upset my entire life.'[24] One of the 'friends' with whom Greene had attended the Mass was Catherine Walston.

In the end it was Catherine Walston herself who upset the apple-cart by allowing her conscience to trouble her. 'I know that you are worried and unhappy,' Greene wrote, 'at the conflict which you feel between your relation with me and Catholicism. That means that I *know* – and it's always a grim thought – that *in that way* you'd be happier if I left you. And that for a lover is a horrid thought.'[25] On their last holiday together in Rome, she had insisted on twin beds. It was the beginning of the end – at least it was the beginning of the end of the affair with Catherine Walston. Another affair followed and Greene would still have a mistress when he died at the age of eighty-six.

If Greene's practice of his faith was somewhat eccentric, his theological interpretation of it was equally so. In fact, his increasingly bizarre treatment of religious issues was beginning to try the patience of his more orthodox Catholic friends. Waugh wrote plaintively to his wife on 6 February 1958 of Greene's play *The Potting Shed* that it was 'great nonsense theologically and will puzzle people needlessly'.[26] Four days later Waugh repeated his annoyance with the play in a letter to Ann Fleming: 'The theme is great balls theologically. The reviews next day all said: "only Roman Catholics will understand it". We are just the people who don't.'[27]

Three years later Waugh's exasperation reached new heights, or depths, with the publication of Greene's *A Burnt Out Case*. 'It is the first time Graham has come out as specifically faithless,' Waugh wrote in his diary, 'pray God it is a mood, but it strikes deeper and colder. What is more – no, less – Graham's skill is fading … His early books are full of self pity at poverty and obscurity; now self pity at his success … He complained of the heat of his sexual passions, now at their coldness.'[28]

Waugh wrote to Greene about *A Burnt Out Case* on 3 January 1961 giving his reasons for not reviewing the book. Greene replied the following day, stating that he had 'always found our points of disagreement … refreshing or enlightening and miles away from the suburbia of the *Catholic Herald* or *The Universe*'.

His intention in the novel, he explained, had been 'to give expression to various states or moods of belief or unbelief'. The characterization of the doctor in his novel represented 'a settled and easy atheism'.[29]

Waugh replied on 5 January:

> I don't think you can blame people who read the book as a recantation of faith. To my mind the expression 'settled and easy atheism' is meaningless, for an atheist denies his whole purpose as a man – to love and serve God. Only in the most superficial way can atheists appear 'settled and easy'. Their waste land is much more foreign to me than 'the suburbia of *The Universe*'.[30]

A few days after this letter was written, Greene's psychoanalyst, Dr Eric Strauss, died. Dr Strauss, head of the psychiatric department at St Bartholomew's hospital, was a Catholic as well as a psychoanalyst which gave him a unique insight into Greene's difficulties. In fact, as Greene became increasingly alienated from the sacraments, Strauss became his surrogate confessor, which enabled him to pry into the secrets of Greene's soul more deeply than anyone. In January 1961, he took those secrets to the grave. Commenting on Dr Strauss's death in a letter to Lady Diana Cooper on 21 January, Waugh wrote that Greene had 'no one to keep an eye on him now'.

Later the same year, Greene reached a whole new audience when an American television version of *The Power and the Glory* was broadcast on the CBS network on 29 October. Sir Laurence Olivier played the priest and George C. Scott the lieutenant in a very strong cast. The broadcast shocked many viewers who were outraged at the presentation of a Catholic priest as both a drunkard and the father of an illegitimate child. Greene's main concern, however, was the way the televised version completely ignored the arrival of the new priest which was so important to the novel. 'Without the appearance of the new priest,' Greene complained, 'the theme of the Church's permanency is entirely missing from the television version.'[31]

The positive effects of the religious dimension in Greene's work were stressed by the actor Paul Scofield who had played the priest in the 1959 stage dramatization of *The Power and the Glory*:

> it changed my whole attitude to my work as an actor, making me feel (if this is not too large or presumptuous a claim) that there is or should be a spiritual element in the relationship between actor and audience, and that the actor can if he wishes, and is provided with the right material

by the author, heighten and bring into focus an awareness of an existence larger than our own.[32]

The negative effects were due principally to Greene's obsession with the darker side of his own character and his insistence on transposing this darker side onto all his fictional characters, so that even their goodness is warped. He saw human nature as 'not black and white' but 'black and grey'[33] and he referred to his need to write as 'a neurosis ... an irresistible urge to pinch the abscess which grows periodically in order to squeeze out all the pus'.[34] Neither was this tendency to paint characters black – or more accurately Greene – confined to the products of his fiction. When Greene was awarded the Shakespeare Prize by the University of Hamburg in the mid-sixties, he compared Shakespeare unfavourably with St Robert Southwell, his contemporary, who was hanged, drawn and quartered for being a Jesuit priest in Elizabethan England. Greene remarked that 'if only Shakespeare had shared Southwell's disloyalty we could have loved him better as a man'.[35] This is a perfect example of Greene's insistence on seeing through real human motives to an often non-existent darker motive beyond. Southwell was certainly charged with 'disloyalty' by the secular power in Elizabethan England, but he was motivated by a romantic and resolute loyalty to the 'old faith' which was itself inspired by a love for God so deep that he was prepared to suffer a hideously slow and painful death. In Greene's eyes, Shakespeare would be more lovable as a man not if he shared the depth of Southwell's love for God but if he shared what is perceived as Southwell's disloyalty. Such a tortured outlook may have inspired sordidly entertaining novels but would not and could not produce any true sense of reality. Greene's novels were Frankenstein monsters that were not so much in need of Freudian analysis as the products of it.

The inner darkness at the heart of Greene's work was a consistent and persistent presence. In his first novel *The Man Within*, published in 1929, he had used the words of Sir Thomas Browne as an epigraph: 'There's another man within me that's angry with me.' Half a century later, during an interview with Marie-Françoise Allain in 1979, it seemed that nothing had changed. When asked if he didn't like himself, he replied: 'No, but then how many people do like themselves, if they stop to think of it? I am not at ease with myself, it's true – but I don't regard this as a fault. Besides, how can one be at ease with oneself?'[36]

During the same interview Greene admitted that 'I've betrayed a great number of things and people in the course of my life, which probably explains this uncomfortable feeling I have about myself, this sense of having been cruel, unjust. It still torments me often enough before I go to sleep.'[37]

Faced with these failures Greene was asked whether he was afraid of Hell, to which he replied that he didn't believe in Hell. One hears echoes of Orwell's intuition thirty years earlier that 'if he believed in Hell, he would not risk going there merely to spare the feelings of a couple of neurotic women'. One is also tempted to turn Orwell's intuition on its head. Instead of assuming that Greene continued to sin because he didn't really believe in Hell, it was equally possible that he stopped believing in Hell because he continued to sin. In other words, Greene's stubborn unwillingness to amend his life led him to the unpleasant conclusion that if Hell existed it was possible that he was at risk of going there. It was therefore easier to try not to believe in it. Since Hell was an uncomfortable and inconvenient concept (and, if it exists, an uncomfortable and inconvenient place) it would be easier merely to abolish it.

In similar vein, Greene confessed in the same interview that he didn't like the term 'sin': 'it's redolent of a child's catechism. The term has always stuck in my throat.'[38] Perhaps the same psychological 'way of escape' had been used with the concept of sin as had been used with the concept of Hell. If one is determined to continue sinning, it is far easier to scoff at the concept of sin than to admit that one is a sinner. At this point one hears echoes of Greene's own words to Evelyn Waugh concerning 'how muddled a mind full of good will could become when once "off the rails".'

Throughout this interview, which serves as an invaluable record of Greene's religious position as he reached old age, he continued to indulge his tendency 'to pick and choose'. He criticized the new Pope, John Paul II, for raising 'the tired old question of contraception' during his recent visit to the United States yet supported the Pope's insistence on priestly celibacy:

> I think that for many people, especially the young, the priesthood must have the attraction of a crack unit. It's an organisation which has to train for combat, one which demands self-sacrifice ... I'm convinced that the drop in vocations has to do with the fact that we don't put across clearly enough the attraction to be found in a difficult and dangerous calling.[39]

Surprisingly perhaps, considering his own unorthodox views on Hell and sin, he came out against liberal theologians such as Hans Küng and Edward Schillebeeckx. 'I would defend them as Christian theologians,' he explained, 'but not as Catholic theologians.' Amazingly, Greene then delivered a very orthodox defence of orthodoxy:

I'm not in opposition to Rome. I know that in my books I've introduced characters – especially priests – who verged on heresy ... But I've
too often seen the absurdity, exemplified in the Anglican Church, of a
bishop remaining a bishop even though he doesn't believe in the Resurrection, nor even in the historical existence of Christ ... I believe in the
necessity of a minimum of dogmas, and I certainly believe in heresy, for
it's heresy that creates dogmas. In this sense heresy has great value.[40]

Greene criticized Schillebeeckx for daring to question the nature of the
Crucifixion:

as a barely practising Catholic, I find it very disagreeable when a historical event like the Crucifixion is turned into some woolly sort of symbol. The twentieth chapter of St John's gospel can stand with the best of
eyewitness reports, and I don't see why Father Schillebeeckx has to
turn it into a symbolic sequence. If one considers oneself a Catholic,
there is a certain number of facts which have to be accepted.[41]

This was followed by a leap of fatuity which seemed to contradict all that he had
just said. Although Schillebeeckx was wrong to question the Crucifixion, Greene
considered that the Church's dogmatic assertions about the Virgin Mary and the
nature of the Trinity were 'of no importance'.[42] It seemed that all the teachings of
the Church were sacrosanct except where they contradicted the Gospel according to Graham Greene.

Later in the interview Greene explained why he no longer went to communion: 'In my private life, my situation is not regular. If I went to Communion, I
would have to confess and make promises. I prefer to excommunicate myself.'[43]

'I still often go to Sunday Mass, but I no longer feel at home, for reasons of
my own – besides, the Mass has changed considerably. It's no longer said in
Latin ... Since the change to the vernacular, when I travel, I can't follow the
Catholic services; they're in a different tongue each time.'[44]

'My faith remains in the background,' Greene insisted, 'but it remains.'[45]

Ironically it was the modernist speculations of Küng and Schillebeeckx, or
rather a reaction against them, which had helped Greene's ailing faith:

I think that, all in all, this controversy has enabled me to discover an
amusing paradox, almost a Chestertonian one: while Father Schillebeeckx's declarations were intended to make the unbelievable credible,
they have had the opposite effect on me – they have suddenly revived

in me a deep faith in the inexplicable, in the mystery of Christ's resurrection. And I don't think I'm alone in having reacted this way. Don't
you think there's something like a small miracle of grace there for we
who are semi-lapsed?'[46]

The reference to Chesterton was an illustration of Greene's enduring admiration
for a writer who was, in many respects, his opposite. His love for Chesterton
was very much an attraction of opposites as was clear from Greene's allusion to
Chesterton's colourful approach to life and literature compared with his own
more sombre and monochromatic view: 'Take G. K. Chesterton: he describes
nature very flamboyantly. In his pages a sunset is practically like a chromo. Inci-
dentally, he wanted to be a painter – that's something I lack. I think I see the
world in black and white, with an occasional touch of colour.'[47]

There was also, perhaps, a deeper psychological reason for Greene's attraction to Chesterton which was brought out in an interview published in the
Observer on 12 March 1978. Describing Chesterton as 'another underestimated
poet', Greene compared him to Eliot: 'Put *The Ballad of the White Horse* against
The Waste Land. If I had to lose one of them, I'm not sure that ... well, anyhow,
let's just say I re-read *The Ballad* more often!' One can scarcely imagine a work
of literature which contrasts more dramatically with the works of Greene than
the joyful and innocent rumbustiousness of Chesterton's *The Ballad of the
White Horse*. Consequently, one feels that Greene re-read it regularly as an antidote, a pick-me-up, offering a means of escape from his own gloom-laden waste
lands. Even if the 'man within' prevented him from seeing reality in anything but
the dark glasses of his own psyche, it helped to be able to look through the eyes
of someone who saw it in much brighter colours.

Such a view would appear to be shared by Greene's wife: 'Many of the later
Catholic writers had a dark view, whereas Chesterton had high spirits. The later
writers seemed depressed in comparison. Perhaps it had something to do with
what was happening to the world.'[48]

Throughout the 1980s it was Greene's politics rather than his religion which
was the cause of most controversy. Going against the grain he opposed American
influence around the world and even intimated that the Soviet Union was the
better of two evils in the Cold War. He was bitterly opposed to the American
invasion of Panama in 1989.

He was one of the most vocal critics of the Israeli government following the
abduction of Mordechai Vanunu from Italy by Israeli agents in 1987. According
to Meir Vanunu, the abducted man's brother, 'very few bothered or dared to
protest against this violation of international law'. Consequently, a letter in *The*

Times, signed by Greene and others, on 14 July 'proved to be of great moral significance and encouragement'. In September 1988, Greene referred to the kidnapping and trial as 'a disgrace to the government of Israel'. Meir Vanunu remained grateful to Greene, writing after his death that he had seen through 'the moral and political implications of Mordechai's exposé of Israel's nuclear arsenal'. Greene's death was, he added, 'a great loss to the cause of justice'.[49]

Greene's last novel, *The Captain and the Enemy*, published in 1988, was similar to so many of his previous works of fiction. Superficially an adventure, it was a reworking of the familiar themes of innocent naïveté, bitter experience and worldly disillusionment.

He also returned to familiar themes when, in September 1989, he was interviewed by John Cornwell for the *Tablet*. The interview, published on 23 September under the heading 'Why I am still a Catholic', displayed the same singular approach to faith that was evident in the interview ten years earlier with Marie-Françoise Allain. As ever, he seemed more certain of the things he did not believe in than those he did. There were, he maintained, no demons, no angels, no Satan and no Hell. Yet, aside from the familiar doubts, there were other insights into Greene's situation as he approached his eighty-fifth birthday.

'I go to Mass usually on a Sunday,' he revealed.

> I've got a great friend, a priest from Spain, Father Leopold Duran, who has permission from his bishop to say the Mass in Latin and say it anywhere, so if he comes here he says it at that table. And if I'm travelling with him, he'll say Mass in the hotel room ... although only on a Sunday. And to please Father Duran I make a confession now – of about two minutes; although I've nothing much to confess at the age of 85; and I take the host then, because that pleases him. There's plenty in my past to confess, which would take a long time, but there's nothing in my present because of age. And lack of belief is not something to confess. One's sorry, but one wishes one could believe. And I pray at night ... that a miracle should be done and that I *should* believe.

Curiously, it seemed that his encounter with Padre Pio forty years earlier continued to exert a benign influence on him. Almost shyly, he confessed that he carried a photograph of Padre Pio in his wallet. 'Greene took a well-worn wallet from his trouser pocket,' Cornwell reported, 'and fished out two small photographs. They were slightly dog-eared; sepia. As he handed them to me I detected a faint air of self-consciousness; as if, English gentleman that he was, he had been caught out in a gesture of Romish extravagance.'

Cornwell asked Greene whether he thought he may have lost his faith if he hadn't had the 'mysterious experience' with Padre Pio. 'I don't think my belief is very strong,' Greene replied, 'but, yes, perhaps I would have lost it altogether'.

During the course of the interview Greene reiterated his oft-repeated disclaimer that he was 'not a Catholic writer' but 'a writer who happens to be a Catholic'. Yet, almost immediately afterwards he eloquently expressed the importance of his faith on his writing:

> I think I was in revolt against the Bloomsbury School, E. M. Forster, Virginia Woolf, and I thought that one of the things that gave reality to characters was the importance of human beings with a future world: it made the characters far more important ... I found a certain flatness in the Bloomsbury circle of writers. There was something missing.

The 'something missing' was the existence of an omniscient and omnipotent God who gave an eternal significance to human actions and therefore an added depth to human characters unattainable in the novels of non-believers. This belief was central to Greene's whole approach to fiction. He was a Catholic writer even though he evidently resented the fact; and what was true of his art was also true of the man himself. Like it or not, and as often as not he didn't like it, Greene remained a Catholic until the end of his days. The quintessential rebel, he belonged heart and soul to a system he resented but from which he was unable to extricate himself.

Greene's last interview with the *Tablet* had been conducted from his home in Antibes on the French Riviera where he had lived for the previous thirty-five years. During the following year he was forced to move to Vevey on Lake Geneva in Switzerland to receive treatment for a blood disease. It was here that he died on 3 April 1991 at the age of eighty-six. In the following morning's edition of *The Times*, Philip Howard, the paper's literary editor, drew an allusive parallel between Greene and T. S. Eliot:

> He said that he saw himself as one of his characters, but with characteristic ambiguity refused to say which of his flawed failures, his hollow men unable to find, or even to seek, the void left by the disappearance of God. The difference was that, at least as a novelist, he was a prodigious success, with a unique and melancholy vision of late 20th-century man.

Howard also wrote that it was 'a blot on the judges rather than on Greene that he was never given the Nobel Prize for literature'. The next day, ironically considering Greene's continued denial that he was a Catholic writer, the alleged reason for his failure to receive the Nobel Prize emerged. Greene's candidature for the Prize had been turned down consistently for more than twenty-five years, largely due to the opposition of one of the judges, Dr Artur Lundkvist. When Dr Lundkvist was asked what had motivated his objections over the years to Greene being awarded the prize, he had replied: 'Because he is a Catholic.'[50]

The novelist P. D. James added to the controversy by stating that 'it has always seemed reprehensible' that Greene had been overlooked. None the less, his faith had proved no obstacle to his receiving other awards during the final decades of his life. In 1966 he was made a Companion of Honour and in 1969 a Chevalier of the Legion of Honour. In 1986 he was appointed a member of the Order of Merit. His publisher, Max Reinhardt, said that he had been 'immensely proud to have been awarded the Order of Merit in 1986, even if it was seen as some sort of consolation prize' for his failure to be honoured with the Nobel Prize.[51]

There was certainly no failure to honour Greene among the ranks of his literary peers when news of his death was announced. 'Until today,' said Sir Kingsley Amis, 'he was our greatest living novelist.' Sir Alec Guinness, who had starred in the 1960 film dramatization of Greene's novel *Our Man in Havana*, said: 'He was a great writer who spoke brilliantly to a whole generation. He was almost prophet-like, with a surprising humility.' Perhaps more perceptively, Auberon Waugh, novelist and editor of *The Literary Review*, remarked that he was 'a good man and a confused man who did not always follow logic'.[52]

Greene's funeral service was held at the small Catholic church of St Jean in Corseaux, a hamlet on the slopes of Mount Pèlerin, overlooking Lake Geneva, on 8 April. Both his wife and Yvonne Cloette, his mistress of three decades, were in attendance. Father Leopold Duran, his friend who had travelled with him through Spain and who was the inspiration for *Monsignor Quixote*, described him as the last classic writer of the twentieth century, whose 'work is his legacy to history'.[53]

The Times on 7 June 1991 reported that the memorial service for Greene at Westminster Cathedral was a 'requiem Mass in the traditional Latin that Greene so loved'. The homily was preached by Dr Roderick Strange, former Catholic chaplain to Oxford University, who alluded to the aptness of Greene's choice of St Thomas the Doubter as his patron saint. Greene, like St Thomas, had wrestled with faith and doubt: 'It was Graham's extraordinary grace to see the power, strength and virtue in failure. He was faithful to that vision, that sense of virtue within failure.'

Greene's estranged wife and his long-term mistress were both present at the requiem Mass, a fact reported eagerly by the press. It appeared as though his private life continued to raise eyebrows after his death as it had so often done during his life – and Greene still had one further surprise up his sleeve. When his will was published five months later many were astonished to find that he had named his widow from whom he had parted in the 1940s but not his mistress who had been a constant companion for more than three decades. It was difficult to see anything in Greene's decision other than the offering of conscience money to his wife, a posthumous peace offering representing a desire to right the wrong he had done her so many years earlier. It was the apology he was never able to make during his lifetime. Yet if this was the explanation for his generosity towards his wife it does not explain why his mistress was completely ignored. The decision is very curious and one is tempted to interpret an element of fear in Yvonne Cloetta's absence from his will. Perhaps Greene had enough faith in God, or at least enough fear of the possibility of God's existence, to avoid breaking the rules in death which he had so brazenly broken in life. It certainly implies a sense of guilt, even if not a sense of contrition. Greene left as many unanswered questions in his death as he had during his life.

Malcolm Muggeridge, who died only five months before Greene and knew him better than most, offered a few clues to his friend's enigmatic character. According to Muggeridge, Greene was 'a curious man in the sense that there is no one who has any ultimate intimacy with him ... The characteristic of Greene is that he has shunned intimacy, even with his brother Hugh, his closest friend.'[54] Added to Greene's alienation from the world outside, Muggeridge believed that he was also alienated from the world inside himself:

> Greene ... is a Jekyll and Hyde character, who has not succeeded in fus-
> ing the two sides of himself into any kind of harmony. There is a con-
> flict within him, and therefore he is liable to pursue conflict without. I
> remember him saying to me once that he had to have a row with some-
> one or other because rows were almost a physical necessity to him.[55]

Seen in this light, it is clear that Greene's doubts about the Catholic faith say more about himself than about the objective truth of his beliefs. He never felt comfortable with Catholicism but nor was he ever comfortable with anything else. Above all, Greene was a doubter. He doubted others, he doubted himself and he doubted God. The profundity of his novels lies not in doubt itself but in an ultimate doubt about the doubt. It was this doubt about doubt that kept Greene clinging desperately to the Catholic faith.

'As for Greene,' writes Norman Sherry, his biographer, 'despite his remarks, I do think he remained a strong Catholic until his death.'[56] Yet perhaps it was

Greene's weakness, rather than his strength, which kept him within the Church. He always felt that Catholicism, for all its perceived weaknesses, was stronger than he was. Painfully aware of his own failings, he never possessed the strength of will to make the break. Either way, whether a strong Catholic or a weak one, he remained a member of the Church. Although he continued to doubt, he gave God the benefit of the doubt, believing that to be anything other than a Catholic would be to become something less than a Catholic. Begrudgingly, and ironically considering his continued attacks on the Papacy, he found himself repeating the words of St Peter with, of course, the enigmatic reservations: 'Lord, where else is there to go? You have the message of eternal life ... or, then again, perhaps you don't.'

NOTES

1. Gregory Wolfe, *Malcolm Muggeridge: A Biography*, p. 409.
2. Malcolm Muggeridge, *The Infernal Grove*, London, 1973, p. 105.
3. Norman Sherry, *The Life of Graham Greene: Volume One 1904–1939*, London, 1988, p. 660.
4. ibid., pp. 660–1.
5. ibid., p. 664.
6. Leslie von Goetz, letter to the author, 16 August 1996.
7. Norman Sherry, *The Life of Graham Greene: Volume Two*, London, 1992, p. 276.
8. ibid., p. 276.
9. ibid., p. 219.
10. ibid., p. 219.
11. Mrs Graham Greene, interview with the author, Oxford, 20 August 1996.
12. Norman Sherry, *The Life of Graham Greene: Volume Two*, pp. 298–9.
13. ibid., p. 299.
14. ibid., p. 297.
15. ibid., pp. 297–8.
16. ibid., p. 297.
17. ibid., p. 297.
18. ibid., p. 299.
19. ibid., p. 299.
20. Mrs Graham Greene, interview with the author.
21. Norman Sherry, *The Life of Graham Greene: Volume One*, p. xx.
22. John Bright-Holmes (ed.), *Like It Was: The Diaries of Malcolm Muggeridge*, p. 374.
23. Norman Sherry, *The Life of Graham Greene: Volume One*, p. xx.
24. Marie-Françoise Allain, *The Other Man: Conversations with Graham Greene*, London, 1983, pp. 156–7.
25. Norman Sherry, *The Life of Graham Greene: Volume Two*, p. 502.
26. Mark Amory (ed.), *The Letters of Evelyn Waugh*, p. 502.
27. ibid., p. 504.
28. Michael Davie (ed.), *The Diaries of Evelyn Waugh*, p. 779.
29. Mark Amory (ed.), *The Letters of Evelyn Waugh*, p. 557.
30. ibid., pp. 559–60.
31. Gene D. Phillips, SJ, *Graham Greene: The Films of His Fiction*, Columbia University, USA, 1974, p. 112.
32. ibid., p. 113.
33. Marie-Françoise Allain, *The Other Man: Conversations with Graham Greene*, p. 134.
34. ibid., p. 149.

35. Norman Sherry, *The Life of Graham Greene: Volume One*, p. 316.
36. Marie-Françoise Allain, *The Other Man: Conversations with Graham Greene*, p. 14.
37. ibid., p. 20.
38. ibid., p. 158.
39. ibid., pp. 167–8.
40. ibid., p. 168.
41. ibid., p. 169.
42. ibid., p. 169.
43. ibid., p. 173.
44. ibid., p. 172.
45. ibid., p. 173.
46. ibid., p. 170.
47. ibid., pp. 133–4.
48. Mrs Graham Greene, interview with the author.
49. *The Times*, 13 April 1991.
50. ibid., 5 April 1991.
51. ibid., 4 April 1991.
52. ibid.
53. ibid., 9 April 1991.
54. Norman Sherry, *The Life of Graham Greene: Volume Two*, p. 23.
55. ibid., p. 68.
56. Professor Norman Sherry, letter to the author, 26 September 1996.

CHAPTER THIRTY TWO

CELTIC TWILIGHT

It was partly under the influence of Graham Greene's novels that the Scottish poet George Mackay Brown became attracted to Catholicism. 'Graham Greene's *The Power and the Glory* impressed me deeply,' Brown wrote in his autobiography, 'for here was a hunted and driven priest, and in many ways a worthless one, who nevertheless kept faith to the end, as better martyrs had done in other places.'[1] Ironically, Brown was received into the Church in 1961, the year that Greene's *A Burnt Out Case* signalled to many people that Greene was losing his own faith.

George Mackay Brown was born in Stromness, Orkney, on 17 October 1921, the son of the local postman who also doubled as a part-time tailor. His childhood and youth were spent in Orkney and the life and landscape of the islands were destined to affect profoundly his whole outlook on life. His parents were lukewarm Presbyterians and Brown remembered as a child going through the motions of religion 'with some distaste for the drab Presbyterian services': 'My parents were not deeply religious though they brought the whole family to church every Sunday. (My father could be very satirical about some ministers and elders.) There we sat and ate sweets during the long boring sermons. My father sang the hymns and psalms with gusto: he had a good light tenor voice.'[2]

The shadow of his Presbyterian upbringing, and the 'anti-papist' bigotry that accompanied it, was cast evocatively in his short story 'The Tarn and the Rosary', published in *Hawkfall and Other Stories* in 1974:

'It's very hard to credit,' said Mr Smith, 'that people could ever be taken in by such darkness.'

'We were all Roman Catholics once,' said Corporal Hourston. 'All our forefathers here in Orkney were Roman Catholics.'

'That was a long time ago,' said Timothy Sinclair. 'People were very ignorant in those days. There was no education. They couldn't read the

Bible. They knew no better. They had to believe whatever the priests told them to believe.'

'The Pope, though, he still rules a great part of the world,' said Andrew Custer. 'France, Italy, Spain, South America.'

'And Ireland too,' said Corporal Hourston.

'The Irish people are very poor,' said Mr Smith. 'Very poor and very oppressed. You'll find, if you study the matter, that all Roman Catholic countries are very backward.'[3]

The effect of this conversation on the young developing mind of Colm Sinclair, a character in the story, is chilling: 'The Virgin Mary. Priests in black, accepting money from sinners. Rosary beads. Colm shivered with supernatural dread. The dark pool of the human mind. He moved closer in to the fading warmth of the forge.'[4]

There were strong autobiographical elements in this story and Brown would have to overcome his own 'supernatural dread' of Catholicism before he began to feel its attraction. He remembered as a child that 'there was something sinister in the very word Catholic; all the words that clustered about it – rosary, pope, confession, relics, purgatory, monks, penance – had the same sinister connotations'.[5] His eventual rejection of 'no popery' rhetoric paralleled the experience of George Scott-Moncrieff, another Scottish convert who had been received into the Church at Easter 1940. In 1960, a year before Brown's conversion, Scott-Moncrieff recalled his first-hand experience of an anti-Catholic riot in Edinburgh in his book, *The Mirror and the Cross: Scotland and the Catholic Faith*:

> I remember bitterly the horror of seeing human beings, largely adolescents and women of a disappointed mien, possessed beyond the reach of reason, screaming and rushing, ready for murder, upon the car in which Archbishop Andrew Joseph MacDonald drove up to the City Chambers ... This was 'protest' and as such it was of the genesis of Protestantism. Whatsoever Protestantism had retained of Christianity ... it seemed to me then to exist in distinction only as a negation, a protest against something that it did not appear even to wish to understand ...
>
> ... I was not the only Protestant witness of those ugly scenes in the summer of 1935 who within a few years found himself no longer protestant, having progressively discovered how much of the stock picture of my country's history was mere myth.[6]

George Scott-Moncrieff was a young man of twenty-five when he witnessed these riots in Edinburgh. He was born in 1910, the second son of the Reverend C. W. Scott-Moncrieff, a minister of the Church of Scotland. His grandparents were Presbyterians and his ancestors Covenanters, although his uncle Charles Scott-Moncrieff, the translator of Proust, Pirandello and Stendhal, had broken with family tradition by becoming a convert to Catholicism when his nephew was still a child.

In 1934 George Scott-Moncrieff married Ann Shearer who, like George Mackay Brown, was a native of Orkney, having been born in Kirkwall in 1914. In 1931, while Brown was a schoolboy at Stromness Academy, Ann Shearer, as a mere seventeen-year-old, was working on the local paper, *The Orcadian*. She moved to London to pursue her literary career and it was there that she met her future husband who was also working as a journalist. They returned to Scotland before their marriage and were received into the Catholic Church together six years later. Both continued to pursue their literary careers. George Scott-Moncrieff wrote novels such as *Café Bar* and *Tinkers' Wind*, a volume of verse entitled *A Book of Uncommon Prayer* and a one-act play entitled *The Wind in the East*. He also wrote *The Lowlands of Scotland*, *Scottish Country*, *The Stones of Scotland* and was co-editor from 1939 till 1941 of *The New Alliance*, a Scottish cultural magazine which championed the Scottish nationalist cause. His wife also wrote for *The New Alliance* and became a successful author of children's stories. Her book *Auntie Robbo* was rejected by London publishers as 'too Scottish' but was accepted and successfully published in New York. Tragically, she died in 1943 at the age of twenty-nine. Following her death a friend remarked: 'During all my long friendship with Ann, she seemed to be fighting for an inner peace and purity of spirit – sometimes the goal was lost sight of but never for very long. I believe she achieved it when she entered the Catholic Church.'[7] The Scottish poet and critic Edwin Muir wrote in *The Scotsman* at the time of her death that 'she had great gifts, and if she had lived might have been one of the best Scottish writers of her time'.[8]

Within a decade Edwin Muir would be lauding George Mackay Brown in similar fashion, his encouragement instrumental in launching the young writer's literary career. Muir was also a native of Orkney, being born on the islands in 1887, the son of crofter folk. When he was fourteen his parents migrated to Glasgow. The culture shock which this entailed and the drab existence Muir endured in the city following the earlier halcyon days in Orkney formed the basis of his book, *The Story and the Fable*, published in 1940. This was read by the young Brown and left a deep and lasting impression, moulding his thought and the future direction of his writing.

Brown had first been introduced to Muir and his wife when they had visited Orkney during the summer of 1951. They had tea together at the Stromness Hotel and Muir invited him to Newbattle Abbey, a residential adult education college in Dalkeith, near Edinburgh, at which Muir was the warden. He jumped at the opportunity and went to Newbattle that October for 'probably the happiest year of my life'.[9]

Brown was already somewhat in awe of Edwin Muir, whose work had influenced him so much, but it soon became clear that Muir was himself greatly impressed by Brown's work, none of which had been published. Muir recommended one of Brown's poems, 'The Exile', to the *New Statesman* and it was duly published on 5 April 1952. Two years later, when a book of Brown's poems, *The Storm*, was published by the Orkney Press, Muir contributed a glowing introduction: 'I am a great admirer of George Brown's poetry ... He has the gift of imagination and the gift of words: the poet's endowment'.

Muir, of course, possessed exactly the same gifts. He had enjoyed a highly successful literary career and was preparing to sign off even as he was helping to launch the career of his young protégé. In 1954 *The Story and the Fable* was revised and published as *An Autobiography*. Its concluding paragraphs are of interest as an incisive and succinct self-appraisal by Muir of his own life, written five years before its end, but also as an intriguing insight into the thought which was so crucial to Brown's journey towards the Church:

> In my middle thirties I became aware of immortality, and realized that it gave me a truer knowledge of myself and my neighbours. Years later in St Andrews I discovered that I had been a Christian without knowing it ...
>
> ... I think that if any of us examines his life, he will find that most good has come to him from a few loyalties, and a few discoveries made many generations before he was born, which must always be made anew. These too may sometimes appear to come by chance, but in the infinite web of things and events chance must be something different from what we think it to be. To comprehend that is not given to us, and to think of it is to recognize a mystery, and to acknowledge the necessity of faith. As I look back on the part of the mystery which is my own life, my own fable, what I am most aware of is that we receive more than we can ever give; we receive it from the past, on which we draw with every breath, but also – and this is a point of faith – from the Source of the mystery itself, by the means which religious people call Grace.[10]

Muir bequeathed this belief in the transcendent mystery at the heart and the root of life to his disciple. (Muir's autobiography was published at the same time as J. R. R. Tolkien's epic *The Lord of the Rings*, the potency of which rested securely in an identical view: that truth was a reality beyond finite facts and, as such, was best expressed in the mystical language of myth and fable.) The extent to which Brown was under Muir's influence during the fifties was exemplified by his description of Scotland in the prologue to *The Storm* as 'the Knox-ruined nation', referring to the effects of John Knox's religious fanaticism at the time of the Reformation. This was an echo of Edwin Muir's view in his controversial study, *John Knox: Portrait of a Calvinist*: 'What Knox really did was to rob Scotland of all the benefits of the Renaissance.'[11]

Although Muir left Newbattle in the summer of 1955 to become Charles Eliot Norton Professor at Harvard, his benign influence on Brown continued. He wrote to him on 9 April 1956 from his hotel in Cambridge, Massachusetts: 'I admire these poems of yours more and more the more I read them: you have a feeling for words which I sincerely envy! ... The genius is there, my dear George, and I wish you all that it offers you.'[12] These were indeed magnanimous words considering that Muir's *Collected Poems*, published four years earlier, had established him as one of the most respected living poets in the English language. On 6 March 1958 Muir sent a collection of Brown's poems to the Hogarth Press, recommending them and suggesting they be considered for publication. 'I was surprised,' Brown recalled, 'one day in 1958 ... to get a letter from Hogarth Press saying they'd like to publish a book of my poems. A typescript had been sent to them by Edwin Muir ... Myself, I'm quite sure I'd have done little or nothing in the way of getting them published.'[13] The book was published as *Loaves and Fishes* in 1959, the year of Muir's death.

The following year Brown graduated from Edinburgh University with a second-class honours degree in English literature. Two years later he returned to do postgraduate work on the Jesuit poet Gerard Manley Hopkins, having been received into the Catholic Church in the interim. Completing his studies on Hopkins, he returned to Orkney in 1964 and remained on the islands for the rest of his life.

Back on his native ground he began to produce his best work. *The Year of the Whale* in 1965 consolidated his reputation as a poet and the appearance of *A Calendar of Love* in 1967 heralded his arrival as an eminent writer of short stories. Imbued with a deep love for the Orcadian way of life, past and present – the lives of crofters and fishermen, monks and Vikings – his work was overlaid and underpinned by a deeply religious comprehension of eternal verities – a passion for the ancient, the traditional and the spiritual. His stories and verse abound with legend and myth, image and symbol, the language of mystereality.

Brown observed and understood the lives of the crofters and fishermen among whom he lived which, in the words of the critic Alan Bold, made him aware of 'the elemental relationship these folk have with, respectively, the soil and the sea':

> One of Brown's great images concerns the circle of life, a sunwards ritual dance of seedtime, birth, harvest, death, a 'potent mysterious wheel of being' ... The crofter in his field, the fisherman in his boat: they are taken up in the rhythms of this great dance and its movement gives dignity to their otherwise hard lives ...
>
> Brown's renewal of the folk consciousness is no cerebral exercise, no erudite essay in nostalgia. He has spent a lifetime watching the corn rise and die then reappear as bread and ale; he has felt the rhythms of the waves as they smash against the Orkney coastline. The miracle of the loaves and fishes is something he perceives in the way crofters and fishermen wrench a living from the obdurate soil and the vindictive sea. His religious attitude to life derives from such personal observation and naturally a religious faith pervades everything Brown writes so that the corn always rises like a symbol of resurrection ...[14]

Brown stressed the importance of Christ's parable of the sower and the seed to his basic vision of reality:

> That image seemed to illustrate the whole of life for me. It made everything simple and marvellous. It included within itself everything from the most primitive breaking of the soil to Christ himself with his parables of agriculture and the majestic symbolism of his passion, and death, and resurrection. 'I am the bread of life.' 'This is my body that is broken for you.'[15]

The passionate belief in the rituals of nature, played out in an eternal dance of life, is interwoven here with a love for the sacrifice of the Mass so that all are seen as inextricable, a seamless garment. The seasonal cycle of life and the ceremonies and rituals of the Church are seen as one, a holy and holistic expression of God's will on earth.

Brown returned to this theme in his semi-autobiographical story 'The Tarn and the Rosary'. Colm Sinclair, the youth who had heard the 'anti-papist' conversation of his elders in Orkney, converts to Catholicism while away in

Edinburgh. Writing home, he attempts to explain his reasons for taking such a dramatic step:

'It is ceremony that makes bearable for us the terrors and ecstasies that lie deep in the earth and in our earth-nourished human nature. Only the saints can encounter those "realities". What saves us is ceremony. By means of ceremony we keep our foothold in the estate of man, and remain good citizens of the kingdom of the ear of corn. Ceremony makes everything bearable and beautiful for us. Transfigured by ceremony, the truths we could not otherwise endure come to us. We invite them to enter. We set them down at our tables. These angels bring gifts for the house of the soul ...

'It is this saving ceremony that you call "idolatry" and "mumbo-jumbo".'[16]

Completing this letter, Colm walks the quarter of a mile from his lodgings to hear Mass at a small Catholic church:

The celebrant entered. Colm had not seen this particular priest before – he looked like an Indo-Chinese. Once again, for the thousandth time, Colm watched the ancient endless beautiful ceremony, the exchange of gifts between earth and heaven, dust and spirit, man and God. The transfigured Bread shone momentarily in the saffron fingers of the celebrant. Colm did not take communion. He had a dread of receiving the Sacrament unworthily, and he considered that the envy and self-pity he had indulged in these last few sun-smitten days were blemishes he would have to be purged of.[17]

Against the discovered beauty of the Mass lurked the stifling shadow of the cold Presbyterianism Brown had rejected. According to Alan Bold, 'the Reformers stalk like servants of the devil in his poems and stories'.[18] In 'Master Halcrow, Priest', one of the stories in *A Calendar of Love*, the religious images are callously and iconoclastically destroyed by the Reformers. In his play, *A Spell for Green Corn*, published in 1970, the Reformation is blamed for eliminating the old faith of the island folk in the name of a rootless 'Progress'. Furthermore, the puritanism of the Reformation had removed the joy from religion, replacing the beauty and miracle of the Mass with a coldness that forced people to express the joy of God in other ways: 'The Word was imprisoned between black boards, and chained and padlocked, in the pulpit of the kirk – impossible for it to get free among the ploughs and the nets, that season of famine. Therefore the lesser word, the fiddle, the poem, the rune, must work the miracle of bread.'[19]

Against the rootless 'Progress' heralded by the Reformation, the Catholic Church stood for Tradition. It was this aspect of Catholicism which had first impressed Brown when he was still in his mid-teens. He was 'intrigued by the majesty and mystery' of Catholicism, by 'the long history of the Church from that stark beginning, that incredibly endured through the changing centuries, always adapting itself; enriched by all that poetry and music, art and architecture, could give; and still apparently as strong as ever in our gray twentieth century'.[20]

This respect for tradition stayed with Brown throughout his life and was one of the factors behind his conversion. Catholicism was the Old Religion, the champion and defender of tradition and its last bastion and refuge. The new religion of 'our gray twentieth century' was Progress:

> There is a new religion, Progress, in which we all devoutly believe, and it is concerned only with material things in the present and in a vague golden-handed future. It is a rootless utilitarian faith, without beauty or mystery ... The notion of progress is a cancer that makes an elemental community look better, and induces a false euphoria, while it drains the life out of it remorselessly.[21]

These sentiments, expressed in *An Orkney Tapestry*, Brown's eulogy to the islands of his birth, were also put into the mouth of one of the characters in 'The Tarn and the Rosary':

> 'Progress, that's the modern curse. This island is enchanted with the idea of Progress ... This worship of Progress, it will drain the life out of every island and lonely place. In three generations Norday will be empty. For, says Progress, life in a city must be superior to life in an island ... Will there be a few folk left in the world, when Progress is choked at last in its own too much? Yes, there will be. A few folk will return by stealth to the wind and the mist and the silences. I know it ...'[22]

One is struck by the similarities between Brown's Norse-Celtic vision of the 'modern curse' and David Jones's Cockney-Celtic view of the decline of the West. Jones spent his last days in the conurbation of Greater London whereas Brown remained as far from the modern metropolis as possible and avoided it like the plague. Yet both shared a truly mystical understanding of the Mass, a love for tradition and culture, and a passionate desire to preserve the Celtic way of life from the encroachments of cosmopolitan modernity. In Jones this desire found expression in his love for the Welsh language and his concern for its survival, while in Brown it was rooted in a longing to see the Orcadian way of life preserved. It was not coincidental that both greatly admired the poetry of Gerard Manley Hopkins. Jones, in particular, gained solace that Hopkins had developed a love for the Welsh language and landscape.

The similarities between Jones and Brown were encapsulated in the comments of Jeremy Hooker, lecturer in English at the University College of Wales in Aberystwyth, in the December 1972 issue of *Poetry Wales*. Although Hooker was writing specifically about Jones, his comments are as valid for Brown:

> For a Christian poet I suppose it can be said that a tragic view of history is, ultimately, impossible: the 'Sleeping Lord' is always there, and can never die. On the other hand there can be a tragic tension in his work between faith in the redemption and the knowledge that the culture which is the fruit of Christianity is being destroyed. This tension is also, ironically, creative and it is, I think, the mainspring of David Jones's work.

Jones read this appraisal of his work and agreed that it was 'perceptive and hits some crucial nails on the head'.[23]

The issue of *Poetry Wales* containing Jeremy Hooker's essay on Jones was a special 'David Jones Number' that also included a whole range of essays on his work by prominent Welsh writers and academics. It was a fitting tribute to one of the most original literary figures of the century as he approached the end of his life. He died on 28 October 1974 at the age of seventy-nine. The same year saw the death of Dunstan Pruden who, like Jones, had been a follower of Eric Gill and a member of the Ditchling community, converting to Catholicism as a young man. Arnold Lunn and Ernest Milton also died in 1974, J. R. R. Tolkien the previous year.

Another two literary champions of both Celtic nationalism and Catholicism who were to die in the early seventies were Shane Leslie and Compton Mackenzie.

Leslie died on 13 August 1971, aged eighty-five. Described in his obituary in *The Times* as 'author, poet, and notable Anglo-Irish personality', Leslie's rebellion in his youth against his Unionist upbringing, and his adoption of Irish Nationalism, had given him a lifelong cause. In 1946 his book *The Irish Tangle* addressed the perennial problems of Ireland but was marred, like so many books on the subject, by historical inaccuracies and sweeping generalizations. He also wrote a host of other books, most notably a *Life of Cardinal Manning*, which was intended to counter the effect of Lytton Strachey's essay, and a study of the Oxford Movement from a conspicuously Catholic viewpoint.

Compton Mackenzie died in the early hours of 30 November 1972, seven weeks short of his ninetieth birthday. He was suffering from cancer of the prostate and had collapsed following a television interview the previous day. Although he was born at West Hartlepool in England, he felt from an early age a passionate attraction to the land of his forefathers, a passion inspired by a gift of Scott's *Tales of a Grandfather* on his seventh birthday. His reception into the Catholic Church in April 1914 had further inflamed his Jacobite tendencies. In the 1930s, having secured property in Scotland, he began to learn Gaelic and became a vociferous Scottish Nationalist. Between 1932 and 1936 he wrote several Jacobite books, including *Prince Charlie*, *The Lost Cause* and *Catholicism and Scotland*. However, he was a man of many parts, both in the literature he wrote and the life he lived, and he will probably be remembered principally for his early novels, such as *Sinister Street*, and his comedies of Capri and the Western Isles of Scotland. The most notable of these was *Whisky Galore*, published in 1947, which was set on the isle of Barra, forty miles west of Skye, where Mackenzie had lived since May 1933. The novel was made into a highly successful film, for which Mackenzie had not only written the script but in which he acted.

Appropriately, there was a quixotically comic postscript to Mackenzie's life which would not have been out of place in one of his comedies. When the plane carrying his body to Barra for burial landed on the cockle beach of Traigh Mhor, eighty-two-year-old Calum Johnston, a friend from before the war, was waiting to pipe the body home to its resting place. Cold rain was driving in on a bitter south-west wind but, undeterred, the octogenarian played a lament as the coffin was carried from the plane. Accompanied by a large crowd of mourners he followed it up the steep slope to the cemetery at Eoligarry. He stood to attention while Father Aeneas MacQueen of Castlebay conducted the brief burial service. As the rites were ending, the aged piper began to sway before collapsing and dying on the wet turf beside the grave.

'There was a dramatic quality in that graveside death which those familiar with Monty's life immediately recognised,' wrote Andro Linklater, Mackenzie's biographer. 'It belonged to a more romantic age when a knight might share his sovereign's fate or a harper fall by his chieftain's side.'[24]

Whereas Compton Mackenzie courted publicity and wrote ten volumes of autobiography between 1963 and 1971, the reclusive George Mackay Brown was notoriously shy and seldom ventured onto the mainland from the womblike safety of his island. Yet in April 1984 he was a little more candid than usual during the course of an interview with Isobel Murray, with whom he had been an undergraduate in Edinburgh. The interview was conducted in Brown's home, a little council flat in the heart of the port of Stromness. Murray remembered that 'he was uncomfortable, and at times rocked away in his old rocking chair, as if trying to get further away from the microphone. He hates talking about himself, and is allergic to modern technology, but he persevered with good temper.'[25]

Predictably enough the interview commenced with childhood reminiscences. His mother was a Gaelic speaker, his father was a tailor by trade but had to work as a postman to supplement the family income. He went unbaptized because his father 'didn't believe in christening or anything like that', and he still nurtured uncomfortable memories of church attendance every Sunday. He recalled sitting through 'dreadful sermons on a Sunday afternoon – oh God! it was awful! Because the sermons then were much longer than they are now – they were about twenty-five minutes or half an hour ... it seemed endless, eternity'.[26]

Ironically, Brown's early interest in Catholicism was sparked off by his reading of Lytton Strachey's hostile portrait of Cardinal Manning in *Eminent Victorians*, the same biased account which had prompted Shane Leslie to write his life of Manning. Yet Strachey's scathing attacks on Manning and the Catholic Church failed to deter the young Brown from wishing to know more about Catholicism. He found Strachey's discussion of the dogmas of successive Popes over the centuries 'absolutely fascinating'. Inadvertently, Strachey had planted a seed of curiosity in Brown's fertile imagination which would come to fruition a quarter of a century later in his reception into the Church.

Concerning his conversion at the age of forty, he said:

> I was convinced more or less for a long time, and then I went to see the priest in Kirkwall, who was a very good man, a Jesuit, too, Father Cairns. We always had Jesuits in Kirkwall, and in Shetland and in the Hebrides, they send them to these desolate outposts ... But there's something about them, Jesuits, I like them very much.[27]

He went on to confess specific debts to two famous Jesuits – Gerard Manley Hopkins and F. C. Copleston. His debt to Copleston dated back to his days as an undergraduate, shortly before his conversion, when he had been struggling with the philosophy of Kant. He 'came by luck' across an essay on Kant by Copleston which helped him immensely: 'he was so lucid ... he was far more lucid of course than old Kant, and he took it to pieces and explained it so wonderfully, so I just read this Copleston and got through all right.'[28]

Brown's usual reticence was completely absent when he was asked whether he had welcomed the changes heralded by the Second Vatican Council. 'No, I didn't welcome it at all,' he replied. The vernacular had robbed the Mass of its 'majesty and mystery': 'it's wiped so many things away. Well, I suppose the heart of the thing is still there, but, I don't know, so much of its glory has been sort of shed – all of a sudden too. There was something very mysterious about the same language being used all over the world'.[29]

In his vociferous and heartfelt opposition to many of the changes wrought by Vatican Two, Brown was lining up beside the likes of David Jones and Evelyn Waugh, and later in the interview he named Waugh as a writer whose work he enjoyed. Waugh and Brown, so different in many respects, were so strikingly alike in their reclusive stance *contra mundum*. Both wrote evocatively of traditional ways of life becoming extinct in the torrent of change in the twentieth century; both shared an *après moi, le deluge* pessimism tempered by religious faith; and both had a culturally conservative love for tradition which made the cult of 'progress' anathema.

Inevitably, he was asked about the 'tremendous antipathy to progress' which had become 'one of the central *planks* of the Mackay Brown legend'. He answered lightheartedly, stating that if not for medical progress he would probably have died twenty years earlier of tuberculosis. Yet, true to form, he condemned the vacuity and vulgarity of modern mass culture: 'People are worshipping all these false Gods nowadays, progress and money and mammon ... even in Orkney. These television advertisements ... you must get a better car, and a better washing machine ... terrible!'[30]

Considering his hostile attitude to television, Murray expressed surprise that he possessed a black and white set. Wasn't his ownership of a television a 'hypocritical compromise'?

> I suppose it is ... I'm not against progress, or I wouldn't have a coal fire – I suppose I'd have peats, and I'd be living in a little croft on the edge of the moor with a few hens around the door, so no. But it's just that you've got to take up a certain position I think, and keep people in touch with their roots and sources.

Murray then questioned whether some people had roots to be kept in touch with. 'Most of the Orcadians have you know,' Brown replied, 'some of them have been on the same farm for nine hundred years ... direct descent.'

As far as Murray was concerned, Orkney was the exception that proved the rule: what of the millions living in cities who felt they had no roots? Brown replied that 'if you keep reminding them of the first essential things and the four elements ... you can't go very far wrong and you *may* do them a bit of good'.[31]

Brown's 'tremendous antipathy to progress' would have struck a resonant chord with John Seymour, the English writer, broadcaster and self-sufficient farmer, who had written of 'progress' in his book *Bring Me My Bow*, published in 1977:

> ... if progress towards a better life for more people were inevitable, and happening, then there would be no point in me writing this book. Even though the world is not absolutely perfect right now, all we would have to do is to sit back and wait for it to become perfect as the Victorians did. But if we have a feeling that the current progress is progress in the wrong direction then it is very important that we should work to see that we cease progressing in that direction and progress, instead, in another.[32]

Unlike George Mackay Brown, however, Seymour had spurned the trappings of 'progress' altogether and, to employ Brown's apt description, had decided to live with 'a few hens around the door'. Like Malcolm Muggeridge, Seymour had decided to 'have his aerials removed' so that he could live without television. In short, he had gone the 'whole hog':

> I am a man who lives in the country, on a piece of land from which I try to produce my own food. Since I also write about this way of life, I am frequently told: 'You think you can solve all the ills of the world by persuading people to keep pigs!' As a matter of fact I do think some problems would be solved if more people kept these useful animals, but I have never tried to persuade anyone to keep a pig. I have merely tried to tell them how to do it if they want to.[33]

Seymour had first written about the benefits of living self-sufficiently in his book *The Fat of the Land*, published in 1961, in which he described how he and his family supported themselves on five Suffolk acres. In the early seventies, having moved from Suffolk to a small farm in Wales, Seymour shot to fame with the publication of several books on self-sufficiency. *The Complete Book of Self-Sufficiency* sold a quarter of a million copies in its German edition alone and was translated into eight languages. Seymour now ranked alongside E. F. Schumacher as a champion of the 'green' alternative to rampant consumerism. The two became acquainted and Schumacher's daughter recalled visiting Seymour with her father 'when he had suddenly become very famous': 'It was during his time in Wales and my father wrote the foreword for *The Complete Book of Self-Sufficiency* ... By that time Pop was president of the Soil Association.'[34]

Seymour also recalled his meetings with Schumacher:

> He came and stayed on my farm in Pembrokeshire once, intending to buy himself a little farm. Together we found just the place he wanted – very near to my home – but he eventually decided to delay buying it and went on a lecture tour in America instead. I believe if he had taken the farm and scrapped the lecture tour he would still be alive![35]

Whatever else Schumacher and Seymour discussed during the visit, religion appears not to have been mentioned. Seymour wrote: 'As for Fritz Schumacher – I knew him quite well – but until I went to his memorial service in Westminster Cathedral I did not know that he was a Christian!'[36] It was not until Seymour moved to County Wexford in Ireland in 1981 that he emulated the step Schumacher had taken ten years earlier by joining the Catholic Church:

> I was immediately, although a heathen, drawn into the community, and expected and required to take my part in it, and I could immediately see that it was the Church that held it all together, and kept it healthy and good ... at last I worked my way to the humility to admit that I do not know *everything* – and who am I to despise and reject the wisdom of Christendom during the last two thousand years? Have I anything better to offer? The answer is I have not. I have seen ... the beastly mess that modern atheism has led the world of humans into during our lifetimes: a mess that is steadily worsening, at an increasing speed, until it must inevitably lead to frightful disaster. Mankind has got itself into this state because men think they are so blooming clever. Well it is time they found a little humility before it is too late.[36]

There seems little to add to this exposition of the experiences which led to John Seymour's conversion, yet other influences also contributed to his slow progress towards the Catholic faith.

An early, negative influence was that of H. G. Wells: 'I tried to be, in my youth, a happy atheist, or agnostic, but never for a moment did it work for me no matter how hard I tried. I was actually a paid-up member of the H. G. Wells Society when I was a teenager, but long before Wells got to the end of his tether I had got to mine.'[38]

It was not until he had returned from thirteen years in Africa, India and Burma, after the war, that he 'managed to sort my own ideas out' and 'became open to the Chesterbellocs of this world'. In later life, Seymour has come to believe that Chesterton 'and the small group of people near to him – hold the antidote (if antidote there is) to the poison of cynicism and materialism that is at present suffocating what little there is left of European civilisation'.[39]

'I cannot read enough by, or about, G. K. C. I was entranced by the man's writings long before I felt any leaning towards Christianity – when I considered myself a merry pagan in fact. There seems to be a kind of rumbustious quality – even an outrageousness – that goes with perfect faith and lack of doubt.'[40]

As an outspoken practitioner of self-sufficiency in the early decades of the century, Eric Gill would appear to have much in common with Seymour yet Seymour confesses to having 'only occasionally come across his writing but whenever I have I have felt an immediate affinity'.[41]

Ultimately, however, Seymour returned to 'the benign and wholesome influence of living amongst Irish country people' as the main reason for his conversion.

In 1989, at the age of seventy-six, he described his life on the three-and-a-half-acre riverside smallholding in Ireland to a reporter from the *Sunday Times*:

> The people around here are mostly farmers or fishermen. Religion is part of the air you breathe. Their conversation is larded with references to God and the Virgin Mary ...
>
> I believe in Him and that we are His viceroys on earth. If we think we can kick the ladder of nature away from us and use other living things just for our own selfish purposes, well, we are doomed.

Seymour explained that he wrote in the mornings and then, after lunch, dug in his garden before going out to shoot rabbits, or down to the sea to fish for mackerel and herring. The evenings were spent reading:

> We don't have television. It stops you from doing anything useful – you watch other people live instead of living yourself. And it's extremely bad for children.
>
> Our son was about twelve when my wife and I parted. He was a marvellous little naturalist. He had the knack of finding fox earths and badger lairs and he'd observe them for hours. Then somebody gave them a television and instead of going out and looking at the things, he sat indoors watching them on a box. That sums television up for me.

By comparison the Irish children in the neighbourhood around his smallholding seemed much happier:

> Kids come and visit us from all around, helping in the garden or on the boat. This is a tight, family community. It's not rich but happy and stable. There's virtually no divorce. The children are secure, knowing that their mummy and daddy are not suddenly going to split up. There is no violence worse than the effect on children when that happens.

Seymour gave this interview at a time when 'the resurgence of the green issue' had given his books 'a vigorous revival'. He was about to embark on a two-month lecture tour of England sponsored by Friends of the Earth and his new book *Blueprint for a Green Planet*, co-written with Herbert Girardet, was selling well.

Eight years later, in the spring of 1997, as the century and his life drew to a close, John Seymour, at the age of eighty-four, still lived an active life, practising what he preached by living as self-sufficiently as possible: 'here, with three friends, I have managed to create a tiny microcosm of the sort of economy that I would dearly love to see on the planet. It is a lot of fun and it does us good. My publishers complain I don't have time to write any more: well it is more important to me to get my broad bean seed in at the right time.'[42]

However, if Seymour could find no time to write books for his publishers he was managing to write the odd verse purely for fun. 'The Scientist's Lament' may not have the subtlety and finesse of Mackay Brown's poems but it is full of the rumbustiousness which Seymour so admired in Chesterton:

> We scientists move in mysterious ways
> > Our wonders to perform
> With fission power and fusion power
> > To cheer us and keep us warm.
> And we have our wonderful flying machines
> > To take us away to the stars,
> To fly us about and sky us about
> > And take bits of machinery to Mars.
>
> We don't believe in a God any more
> > Any more than in fairies or elves,
> Roll ova Jehova we don' need a prime mova
> > We only believe in Ourselves.

For We are omniscient – omnipotent too
    And We really begin to suspect
That creation created itself for Ourselves
    And left it to Us to perfect.

But We're fed up with Earth for its lacking in mirth
    If you really consider it well,
The air is polluted the water is putrid
    And our cities are getting like hell.
Our crime rate is soaring – our lives they are boring
    The government's cutting our pay
The system's corroding the soil's all eroding
    And we're thinking of going away.

Yes somewhere up there boys – high in the sky
    Yes somewhere up over the Plough
We know we'll discover some pie in the sky
    So much better than what we got now.
For this world has been ruined by people like Us
    We've made it a premature Hell
So we'll look for another one high in the sky
    And make a bollocks of that one as well.[43]

Seymour's irreverent verse, with no holds barred and no punches pulled, could scarcely be further from the poetry of George Mackay Brown. Yet together with the Welsh poet R. S. Thomas they formed a holy trinity of plaintive voices crying in the Celtic wilderness.

Thomas was born in 1913, a year before Seymour and eight before Brown. Like them, he produced much of his most important work when he was already well advanced in years. His autobiography, *Neb*, written in Welsh, was published in 1985. *Counterpoint*, a collection of verse published in 1990, reinforced the view of many, expressed by Bernard O'Donoghue in the *Times Literary Supplement*, that he was 'the most resolute religious poet in English this century ... opposed to the materialistic ethic of our present age, he remains a mystical, uncompromising seeker after unpalatable verities'.[44] *Mass for Hard Times*, another collection of verse, was published in 1992, and his *Collected Poems 1945–1990* in 1993 to commemorate his eightieth birthday. The recurring themes of Thomas's poetry, so similar to those of Brown, related to the 'progressive' regression of values in the late twentieth century. His verse evokes a deep love for the wild landscape of the remote part of Wales in which he lives and deep concern over the harmful effects of technology on nature and rural life. Interwoven as a counterpoint is the search for self and for meaning in this automated wasteland and the quest for, and the questioning of, God.

George Mackay Brown also found himself coming of age as he reached his seventies. In 1994 he was shortlisted for the Booker Prize, but shunned the literary establishment by refusing to travel to London for the prize-giving. He stayed in his beloved Orkney, promising to watch the glittering event on television. The shortlisting created renewed interest in his work and John Murray published his *Selected Poems* in 1996. In his short introduction to this collection, Brown wrote:

> More poetry has come out of Orkney than perhaps from any community of comparative size in the world.
>
> The minglings of sea and earth – creel and plough – fish and cornstalk – shore people and shepherds – are the warp and weft that go to make the very stuff of poetry: 'the embroidered cloths' that Yeats wrote about.
>
> More than in cities, the stars in their courses rule our comings and goings. The moon gathers the shoals, the sun sets the well-crusted bread on the tables.

George Mackay Brown was signing off. Two months after these words were written he died as he would have wished – at home in Orkney.

By the time of his death at the age of seventy-four Brown had become one of the Grand Old Men of Scottish literature and generations of schoolchildren had studied his works as part of their Highers syllabus. At his funeral farmers and fishermen rubbed shoulders with London publishers and television cameramen. In the great red Viking cathedral of St Magnus in Kirkwall, a requiem Mass was celebrated for the first time since the Reformation, religious differences swept aside as the island paid its respects.

An obvious question is prompted by the way that George Mackay Brown was lauded in death by those at the very heart of the consumerist society he despised. Why was his work so popular when he was so defiantly out of step with popular culture? The answers are difficult to come by. Perhaps he was only enjoyed as an object of curiosity, a peculiar anti-technological Luddite about to be washed away by the merciless tidal wave of progress. Perhaps he was loved as a member of an endangered species, precious because he was rare. Perhaps he was already extinct and soon to be forgotten except for the fossilized remains of his work.

There were also broader questions. Was Catholicism, at the end of the twenti-eth century, about to be exiled to the fringes of society, where so many of her lat-ter-day converts had sought refuge from an increasingly irreligious world? Admittedly, there were new generations of converts at the very heart of modern society, in politics and in journalism, even in the royal family and the aristocracy, but were they the first of a new wave or the last of a dying breed?

As the century which spawned so many literary converts comes to an end it seems there are very few answers. There are, however, a few clues. In January 1997 it was announced that Tolkien's *The Lord of the Rings* had been voted the 'greatest' book of the twentieth century in a national poll carried out jointly by Waterstone's booksellers and Channel Four television. Tolkien's novel, an Arca-dian epic with the same Catholic and Norse roots that inspired Brown's Orca-dian vision, polled far more votes than its nearest rivals. Furthermore, George Orwell's cautionary tales about the horrors and dangers of twentieth-century life, *Nineteen Eighty-Four* and *Animal Farm*, were voted second and third 'greatest' book respectively. Since Orwell was as alienated by modern con-sumerism as any of his Catholic contemporaries it appears that Brown's plaintive cries from the Celtic wilderness were not so out of touch with popular sentiment as many believed.

In tune with the melancholy at the heart of his work, George Mackay Brown's death can be envisaged as the heralding of a Celtic twilight. The sun was setting on a remarkable century in which countless converts, literary and other-wise, had returned to the faith of their fathers, succumbing to an eternal attrac-tion. Whether this remarkable phenomenon will continue in the new millennium or whether it was merely a century-long aberration, a mere blip on humanity's long march of 'progress', only time or eternity will tell.

Ten days before his death George Mackay Brown wrote the last of his weekly columns for *The Orcadian*. It was April. He had come through another winter 'a little bruised, maybe, but unbowed'. Spring had begun to wash over Orkney. Seeds planted in death were about to burst forth in nature's perennial resurrec-tion. Brown urged his fellow Orcadians to 'relish each one of the days of April, the month that tastes of childhood'.[45]

NOTES

1. George Mackay Brown, *For the Islands I Sing*, London, 1997, pp. 54–5.
2. Alan Bold, *George Mackay Brown*, Edinburgh, 1978, p. 11.
3. George Mackay Brown, *Hawkfall and Other Stories*, London, 1974, p. 190.
4. ibid., p. 191.
5. George Mackay Brown, *For the Islands I Sing*, p. 49.

6. George Scott-Moncrieff, *The Mirror and the Cross: Scotland and the Catholic Faith*, London, 1960, pp. 153–4.
7. Matthew Hoehn, OSB (ed.), *Catholic Authors: Contemporary Biographical Sketches 1930–1947*, Newark, NJ, USA, 1948, p. 680.
8. ibid., p. 680.
9. Alan Bold, *George Mackay Brown*, p. 4.
10. Edwin Muir, *An Autobiography*, London, 1954, pp. 280–1.
11. Edwin Muir, *John Knox: Portrait of a Calvinist*, London, 1929, p. 309.
12. Alan Bold, *George Mackay Brown*, p. 5.
13. ibid., p. 5.
14. ibid., p. 7.
15. ibid., p. 11.
16. George Mackay Brown, *Hawkfall and Other Stories*, p. 198.
17. ibid., p. 199.
18. Alan Bold, *George Mackay Brown*, p. 11.
19. George Mackay Brown, *A Spell for Green Corn*, London, 1970, pp. 90–1.
20. Alan Bold, *George Mackay Brown*, p. 11.
21. George Mackay Brown, *An Orkney Tapestry*, London, 1969, p. 20 and pp. 50–1.
22. George Mackay Brown, *Hawkfall and Other Stories*, p. 187.
23. William Blisset, *The Long Conversation: A Memoir of David Jones*, p. 114.
24. Andro Linklater, *Compton Mackenzie: A Life*, London, 1992, p. 324.
25. Isobel Murray (ed.), *Scottish Writers Talking*, Tuckwell Press, East Lothian, 1996, p. 1.
26. ibid., pp. 12–13.
27. ibid., p. 19.
28. ibid., p. 16.
29. ibid., p. 20.
30. ibid., p. 42.
31. ibid., pp. 42–3.
32. John Seymour, *Bring Me My Bow*, London, 1977, p. 16.
33. ibid., p. 7.
34. Barbara Wood, interview with the author, Kew, 3 January 1997.
35. John Seymour, letter to the author, undated (Spring 1997).
36. ibid.
37. ibid.
38. ibid.
39. ibid.
40. ibid.
41. ibid.
42. ibid.
43. John Seymour, poem sent to the author, Spring 1997.
44. R. S. Thomas, *Mass for Hard Times*, Newcastle-upon-Tyne, 1992, p. 90.
45. *Telegraph Magazine*, 5 April 1997.

INDEX